PHILIP'S

MODERN SCHOOL ATLAS

97TH EDITION

IN ASSOCIATION WITH
THE ROYAL GEOGRAPHICAL SOCIETY
WITH THE INSTITUTE OF BRITISH GEOGRAPHERS

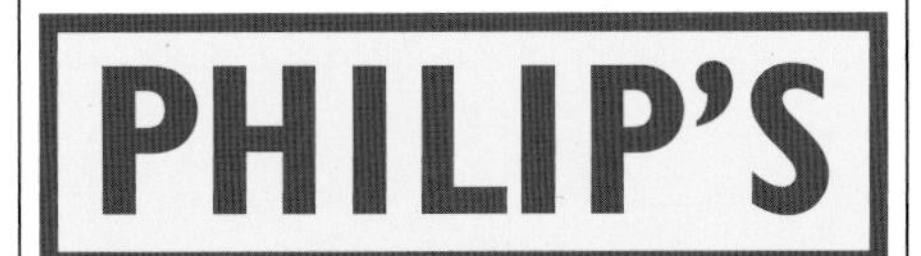

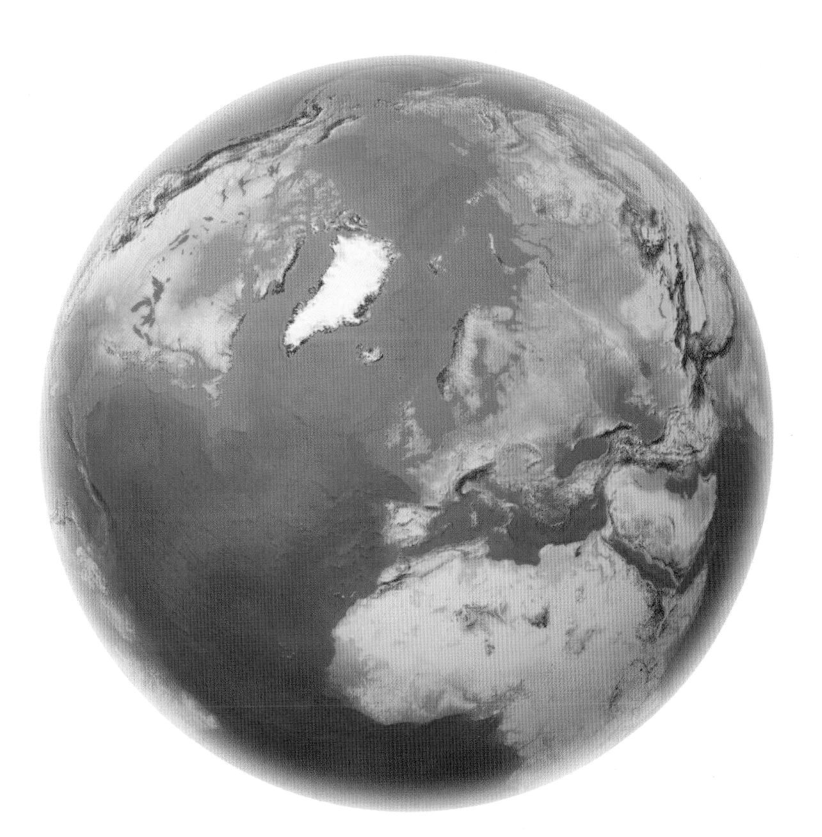

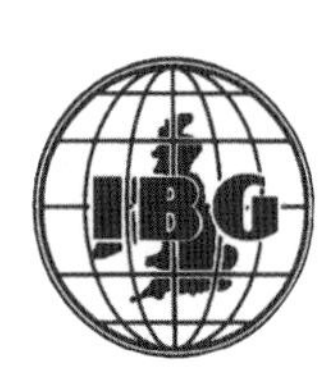

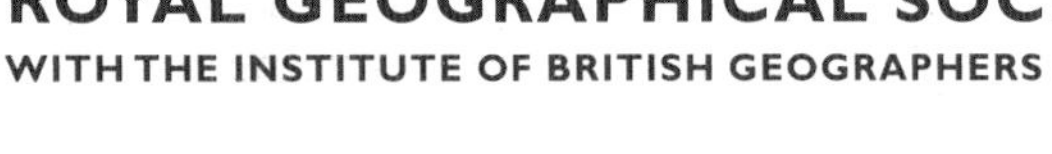

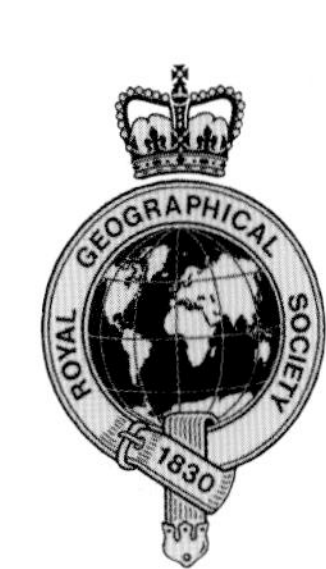

MAP SYMBOLS

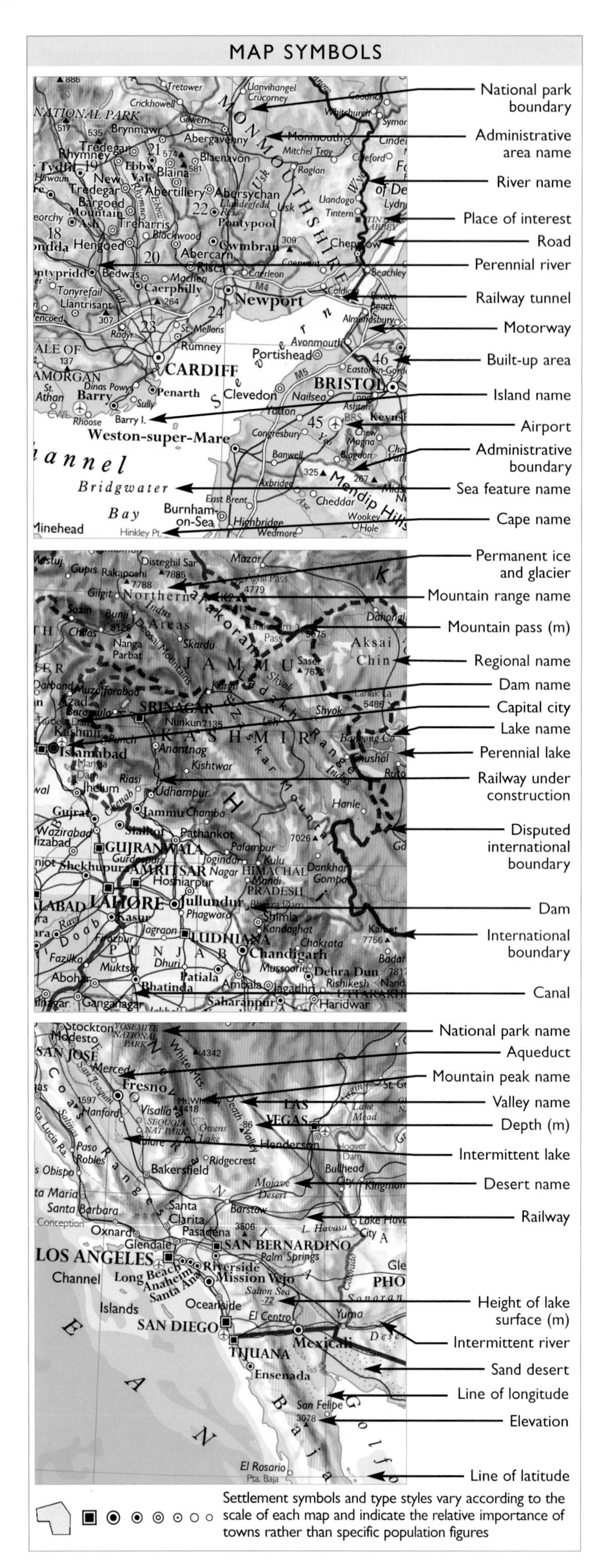

National park boundary

Administrative area name

River name

Place of interest

Road

Perennial river

Railway tunnel

Motorway

Built-up area

Island name

Airport

Administrative boundary

Sea feature name

Cape name

Permanent ice and glacier

Mountain range name

Mountain pass (m)

Regional name

Dam name

Capital city

Lake name

Perennial lake

Railway under construction

Disputed international boundary

Dam

International boundary

Canal

National park name

Aqueduct

Mountain peak name

Valley name

Depth (m)

Intermittent lake

Desert name

Railway

Height of lake surface (m)

Intermittent river

Sand desert

Line of longitude

Elevation

Line of latitude

Settlement symbols and type styles vary according to the scale of each map and indicate the relative importance of towns rather than specific population figures

SUBJECT LIST

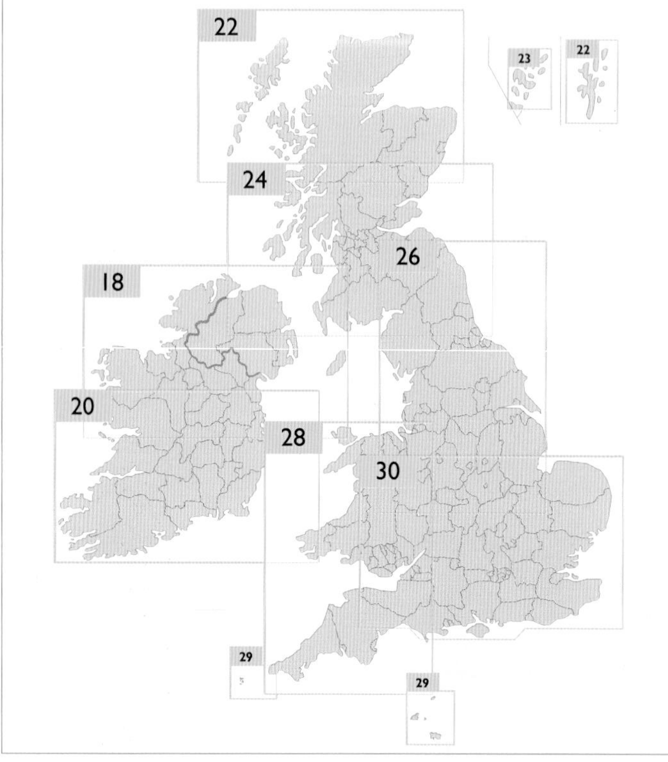

CONTENTS

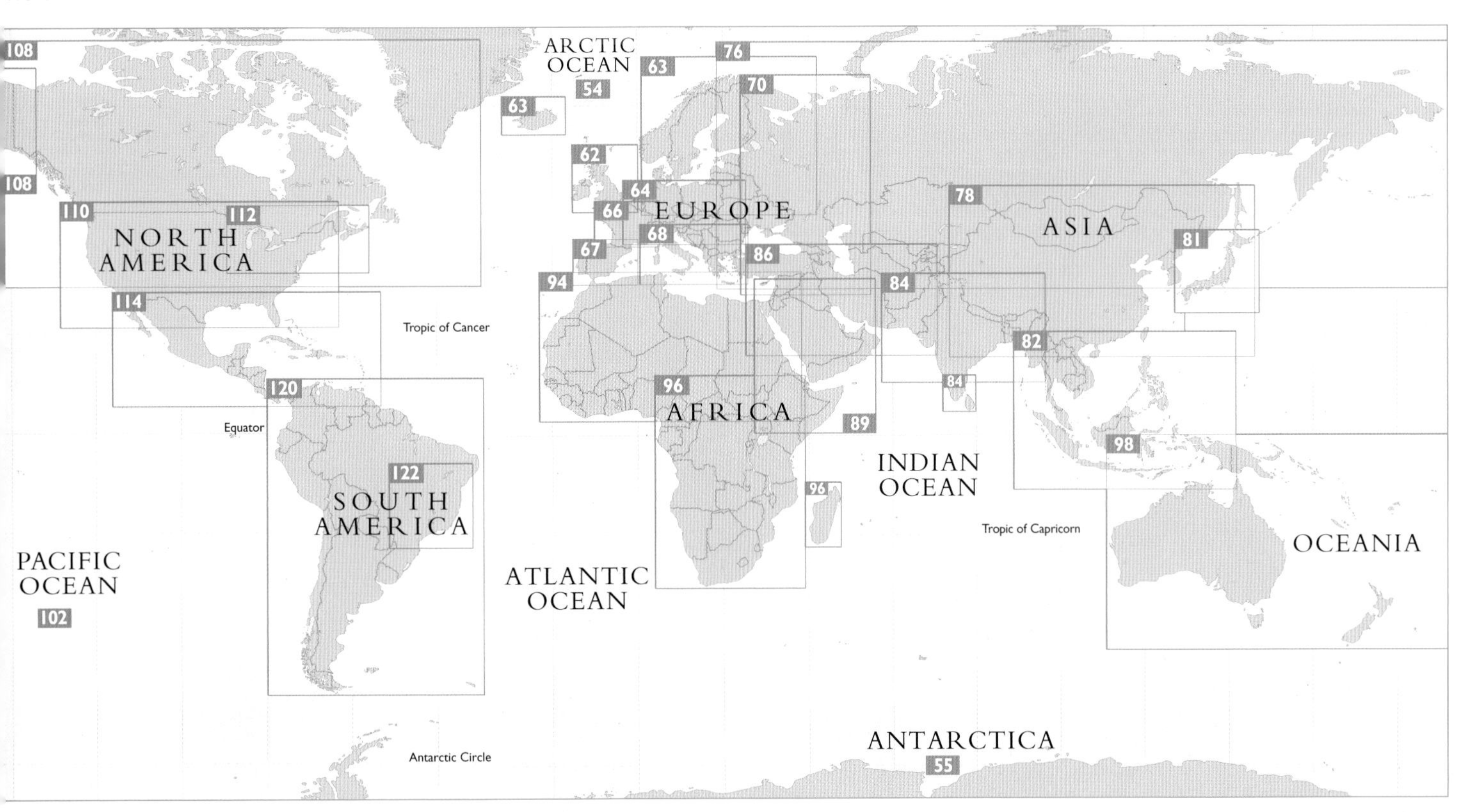

ARCTIC OCEAN
54
108
63
76
70
62
64
66
EUROPE
68
67
86
94
84
78
ASIA
81
110
112
NORTH AMERICA
114
Tropic of Cancer
120
Equator
96
AFRICA
89
82
84
98
INDIAN OCEAN
122
SOUTH AMERICA
96
Tropic of Capricorn
OCEANIA
PACIFIC OCEAN
102
ATLANTIC OCEAN
ANTARCTICA
55
Antarctic Circle

SCALE

The scale of a map is the relationship of the distance between two points shown on the map and the distance between the same two points on the Earth's surface. For instance, 1 inch on the map represents 1 mile on the ground, or 10 kilometres on the ground is represented by 1 centimetre on the map.

Instead of saying 1 centimetre represents 10 kilometres, we could say that 1 centimetre represents 1 000 000 centimetres on the map. If the scale is stated so that the same unit of measurement is used on both the map and the ground, then the proportion will hold for any unit of measurement. Therefore, the scale is usually written 1:1 000 000. This is called a 'representative fraction' and usually appears at the top of the map page, above the scale bar.

Calculations can easily be made in centimetres and kilometres by dividing the second figure in the representative fraction by 100 000 (i.e. by deleting the last five zeros). Thus at a scale of 1:5 000 000, 1 cm on the map represents 50 km on the ground. This is called a 'scale statement'. The calculation for inches and miles is more laborious, but 1 000 000 divided by 63 360 (the number of inches in a mile) shows that 1:1 000 000 can be stated as 1 inch on the map represents approximately 16 miles on the ground.

Many of the maps in this atlas feature a scale bar. This is a bar divided into the units of the map – miles and kilometres – so that a map distance can be measured with a ruler, dividers or a piece of paper, then placed along the scale bar, and the distance read off. To the left of the zero on the scale bar there are usually more divisions. By placing the ruler or dividers on the nearest rounded figure to the right of the zero, the smaller units can be counted off to the left.

The map extracts below show Los Angeles and its surrounding area at six different scales. The representative fraction, scale statement and scale bar are positioned above each map. Map 1 is at 1:27 000 and is the largest scale extract shown. Many of the individual buildings are identified and most of the streets are named, but at this scale only part of central Los Angeles can be shown within the given area. Map 2 is much smaller in scale at 1:250 000. Only a few important buildings and streets can be named, but the whole of central Los Angeles is shown. Maps 3, 4 and 5 show how greater areas can be depicted as the map scale decreases, down to Map 6 at 1:35 000 000. At this small scale, the entire Los Angeles conurbation is depicted by a single town symbol and a large part of the south-western USA and part of Mexico is shown.

The scales of maps must be used with care since large distances on small-scale maps can be represented by one or two centimetres. On certain projections scale is only correct along certain lines, parallels or meridians. As a general rule, the larger the map scale, the more accurate and reliable will be the distance measured.

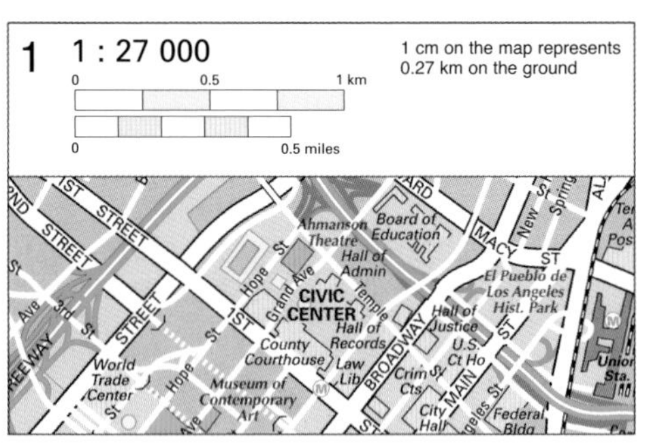

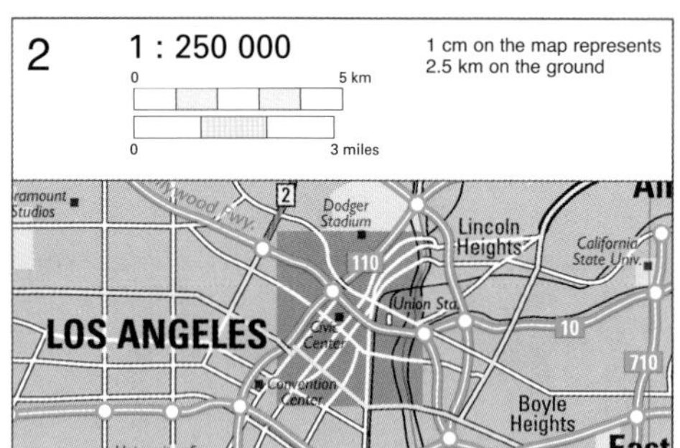

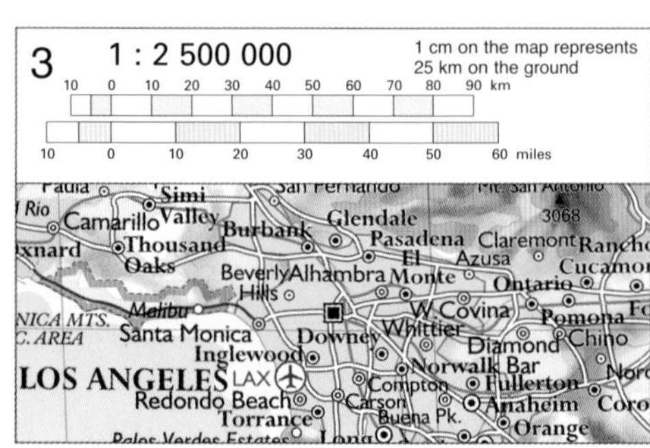

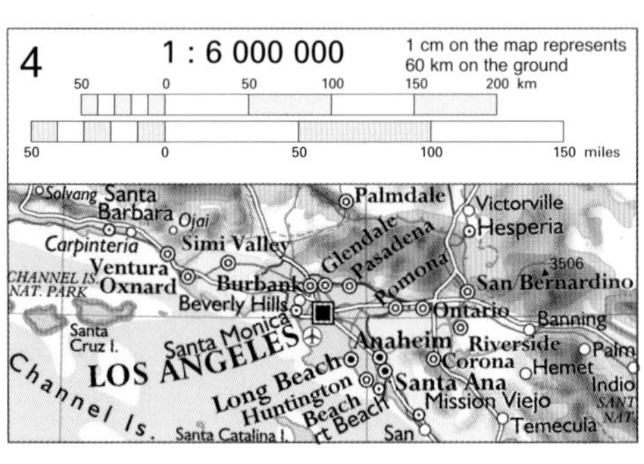

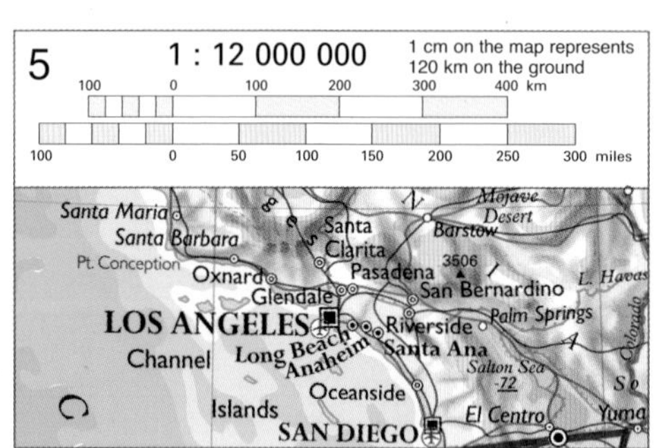

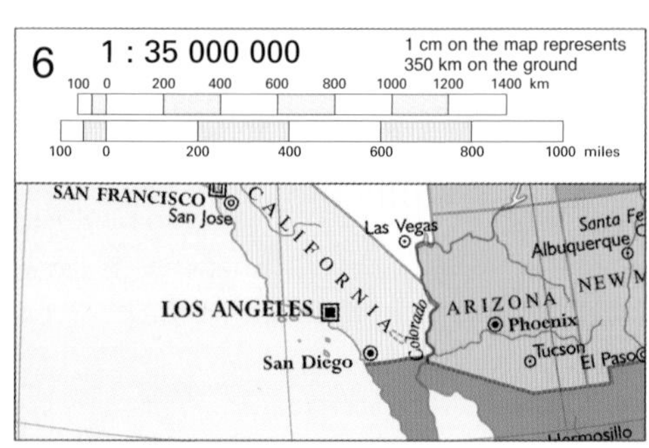

LATITUDE AND LONGITUDE

Accurate positioning of individual points on the Earth's surface is made possible by reference to the geometric system of latitude and longitude.

Latitude is the distance of a point north or south of the Equator measured at an angle with the centre of the Earth, whereby the Equator is latitude 0 degrees, the North Pole is 90 degrees north and the South Pole 90 degrees south. Latitude parallels are drawn west–east around the Earth, parallel to the Equator, decreasing in diameter from the Equator until they become a point at the poles. On the maps in this atlas the lines of latitude are represented by blue lines running across the map in smooth curves, with the degree figures in blue at the sides of the maps. The degree interval depends on the scale of the map.

Lines of longitude are meridians drawn north–south, cutting the lines of latitude at right angles on the Earth's surface and intersecting with one another at the poles. Longitude is measured by an angle at the centre of the Earth from the prime meridian (0 degrees), which passes through Greenwich in London. It is given as a measurement east or west of the Greenwich Meridian from 0 to 180 degrees. The meridians are normally drawn north–south vertically down the map, with the degree figures in blue in the top and bottom margins of the map.

In the index each place name is followed by its map page number, its letter-figure grid reference, and then its latitude and longitude. The unit of measurement is the degree, which is subdivided into 60 minutes. An index entry states the position of a place in degrees and minutes. The latitude is followed by N(orth) or S(outh) and the longitude E(ast) or W(est).

For example:
Helston, U.K.   29 G3   50 7N   5 17W
Helston is on map page 29, in grid square G3, and is 50 degrees 7 minutes north of the Equator and 5 degrees 17 minutes west of Greenwich.

McKinley, Mt., U.S.A.   108 C4   63 4N   151 0W
Mount McKinley is on map page 108, in grid square C4, and is 63 degrees 4 minutes north of the Equator and 151 degrees west of Greenwich.

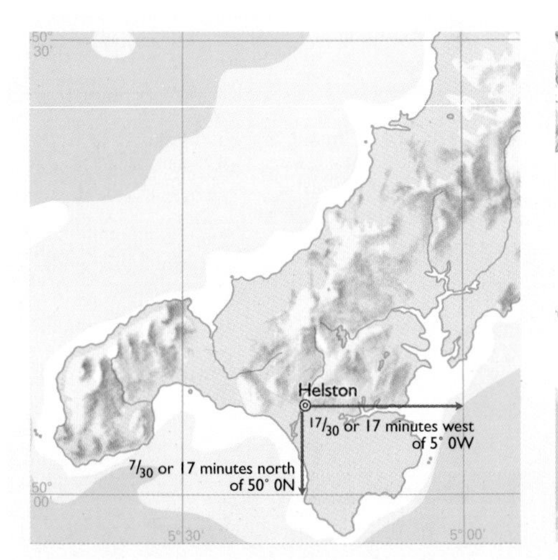

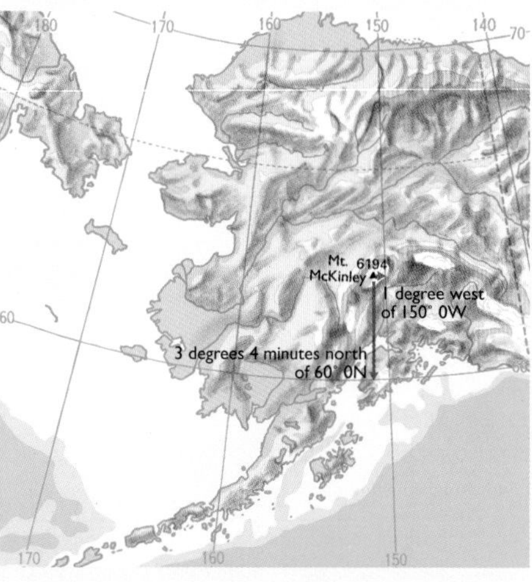

HOW TO LOCATE A PLACE OR FEATURE

The two diagrams (left) show how to estimate the required distance from the nearest line of latitude or longitude on the map page, in order to locate a place or feature listed in the index (such as Helston in the UK and Mount McKinley in the USA, as detailed in the above example).

In the left-hand diagram there are 30 minutes between the lines and so to find the position of Helston an estimate has to be made: 7 parts of the 30 minutes north of the 50 0N latitude line, and 17 parts of the 30 minutes west of the 5 0W longitude line.

In the right-hand diagram it is more difficult to estimate because there is an interval of 10 degrees between the lines. In the example of Mount McKinley, the reader has to estimate 3 degrees 4 minutes north of 60 0N and 1 degree west of 150 0W.

MAP PROJECTIONS

A map projection is the systematic depiction of the imaginary grid of lines of latitude and longitude from a globe on to a flat surface. The grid of lines is called the 'graticule' and it can be constructed either by graphical means or by mathematical formulae to form the basis of a map. As a globe is three dimensional, it is not possible to depict its surface on a flat map without some form of distortion. Preservation of one of the basic properties listed below can only be secured at the expense of the others and thus the choice of projection is often a compromise solution.

Correct area

In these projections the areas from the globe are to scale on the map. This is particularly useful in the mapping of densities and distributions. Projections with this property are termed 'equal area', 'equivalent' or 'homolographic'.

Correct distance

In these projections the scale is correct along the meridians, or, in the case of the 'azimuthal equidistant', scale is true along any line drawn from the centre of the projection. They are called 'equidistant'.

Correct shape

This property can only be true within small areas as it is achieved only by having a uniform scale distortion along both the 'x' and 'y' axes of the projection. The projections are called 'conformal' or 'orthomorphic'.

Map projections can be divided into three broad categories – **'azimuthal'**, **'conic'** and **'cylindrical'**. Cartographers use different projections from these categories depending on the map scale, the size of the area to be mapped, and what they want the map to show.

AZIMUTHAL OR ZENITHAL PROJECTIONS

These are constructed by the projection of part of the graticule from the globe on to a plane tangential to any single point on it. This plane may be tangential to the equator (equatorial case), the poles (polar case) or any other point (oblique case). Any straight line drawn from the point at which the plane touches the globe is the shortest distance from that point and is known as a 'great circle'. In its 'gnomonic' construction any straight line on the map is a great circle, but there is great exaggeration towards the edges and this reduces its general uses. There are five different ways of transferring the graticule to the plane and these are shown below. The diagrams below also show how the graticules vary, using the polar case as the example.

Equidistant   Equal Area   Orthographic   Gnomonic   Stereographic (conformal)

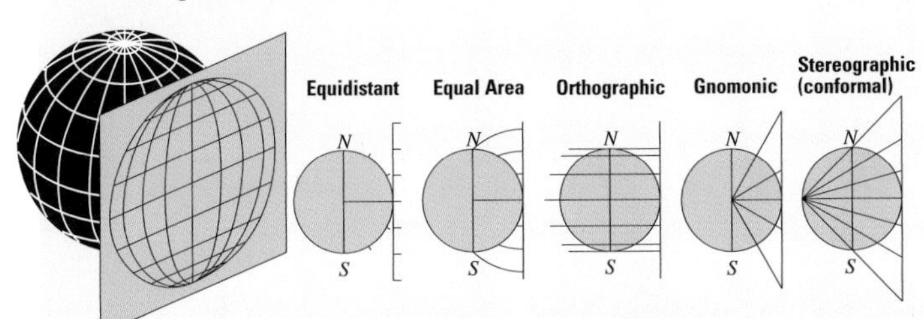

Polar case

The polar case is the simplest to construct and the diagram on the right shows the differing effects of all five methods of construction, comparing their coverage, distortion, etc, using North America as the example.

Equidistant   Equal Area   Stereographic   Gnomonic   Orthographic

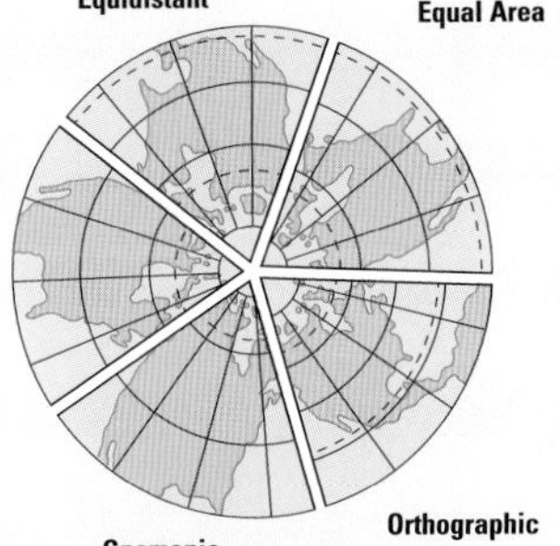

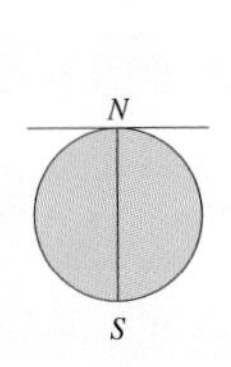

Oblique case

The plane touches the globe at any point between the Equator and poles. The oblique orthographic uses the distortion in azimuthal projections away from the centre to give a graphic depiction of the Earth as seen from any desired point in space.

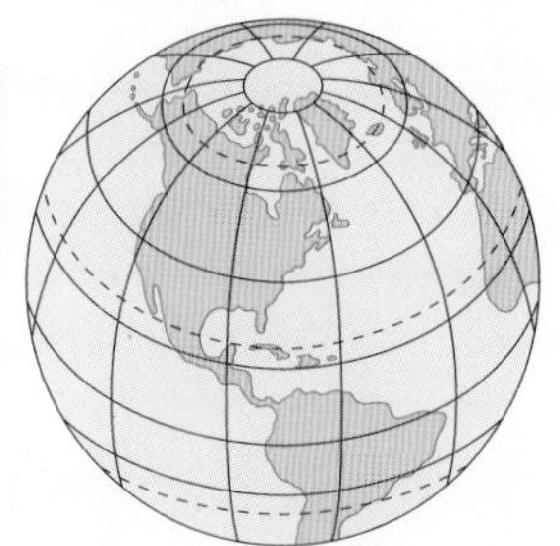

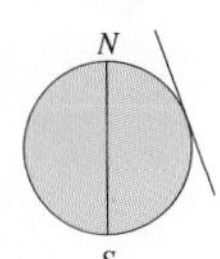

Equatorial case

The example shown here is Lambert's Equivalent Azimuthal. It is the only projection which is both equal area and where bearing is true from the centre.

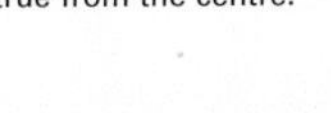

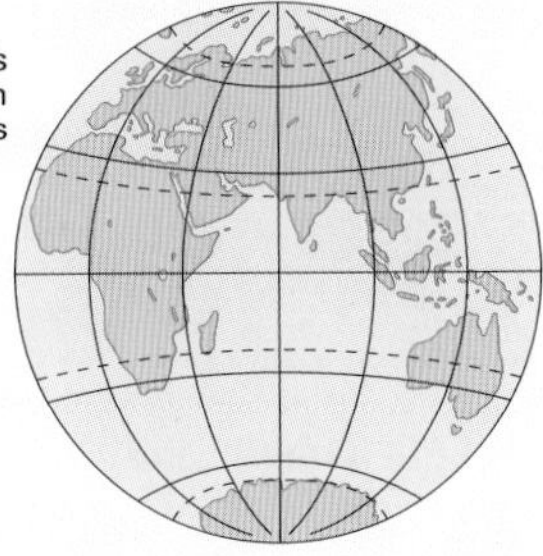

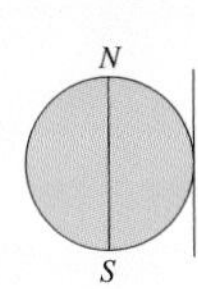

CONICAL PROJECTIONS

These use the projection of the graticule from the globe on to a cone which is tangential to a line of latitude (termed the 'standard parallel'). This line is always an arc and scale is always true along it. Because of its method of construction, it is used mainly for depicting the temperate latitudes around the standard parallel, i.e. where there is least distortion. To reduce the distortion and include a larger range of latitudes, the projection may be constructed with the cone bisecting the surface of the globe so that there are two standard parallels, each of which is true to scale. The distortion is thus spread more evenly between the two chosen parallels.

Simple Conical with one standard parallel

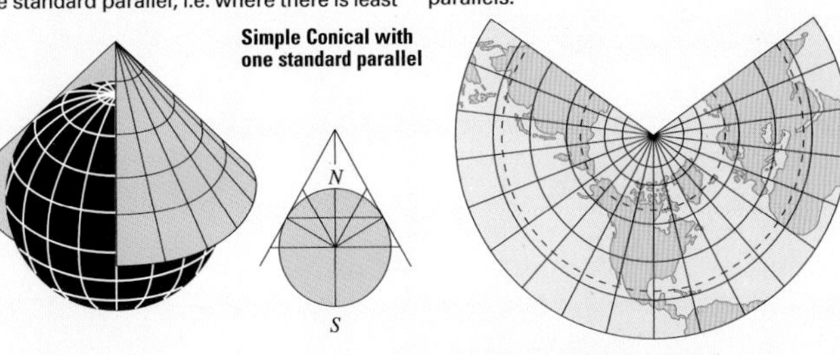

Bonne

This is a modification of the simple conic, whereby the true scale along the meridians is sacrificed to enable the accurate representation of areas. However, scale is true along each parallel but shapes are distorted at the edges.

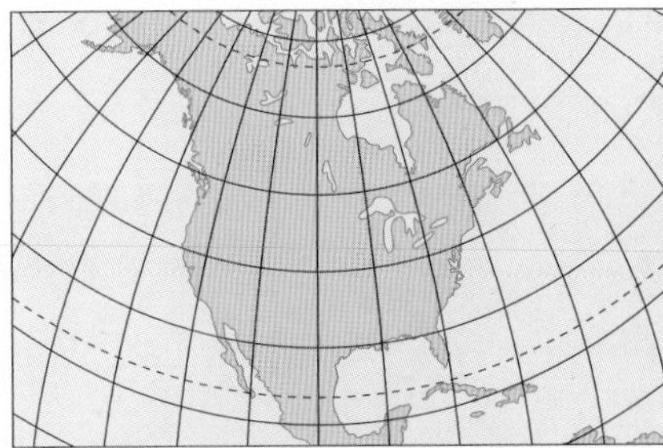

Albers Conical Equal Area

This projection uses two standard parallels. The selection of these relative to the land area to be mapped is very important. It is equal area and is especially useful for large land masses oriented east–west, such as the USA.

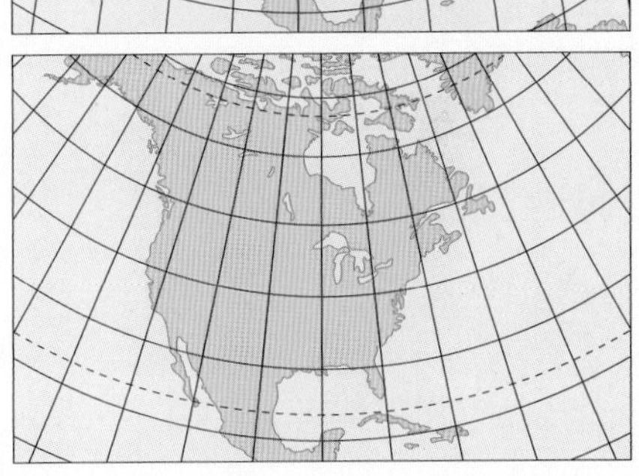

CYLINDRICAL AND OTHER WORLD PROJECTIONS

This group of projections are those which permit the whole of the Earth's surface to be depicted on one map. They are a very large group of projections and the following are only a few of them. Cylindrical projections are constructed by the projection of the graticule from the globe on to a cylinder tangential to the globe. Although cylindrical projections can depict all the main land masses, there is considerable distortion of shape and area towards the poles. One cylindrical projection, Mercator, overcomes this shortcoming by possessing the unique navigational property that any straight line drawn on it is a line of constant bearing ('loxodrome'). It is used for maps and charts between 15° either side of the Equator. Beyond this, enlargement of area is a serious drawback, although it is used for navigational charts at all latitudes.

Mercator

Eckert IV (pseudo-cylindrical equal area)

Simple Cylindrical

Cylindrical with two standard parallels

Hammer (polyconic equal area)

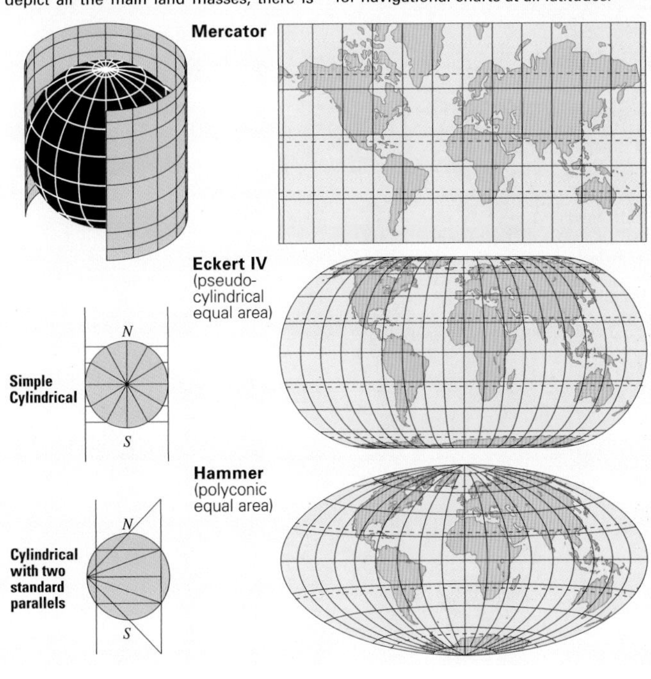

The first satellite to monitor our environment systematically was launched as long ago as April 1961. It was called TIROS-1 and was designed specifically to record atmospheric change. The first of the generation of Earth resources satellites was Landsat-1, launched in July 1972.

The succeeding decades have seen a revolution in our ability to survey and map our global environment. Digital sensors mounted on satellites now scan vast areas of the Earth's surface day and night. They collect and relay back to Earth huge volumes of geographical data which is processed and stored by computers.

Satellite imagery and remote sensing

Continuous development and refinement, and freedom from national access restrictions, have meant that sensors on these satellite platforms are increasingly replacing surface and airborne data-gathering techniques. Twenty-four hours a day, satellites are scanning and measuring the Earth's surface and atmosphere, adding to an ever-expanding range of geographic and geophysical data available to help us identify and manage the problems of our human and physical environments. Remote sensing is the science of extracting information from such images.

Satellite orbits

Most Earth-observation satellites (such as the Landsat, SPOT and IRS series) are in a near-polar, Sun-synchronous orbit (*see diagram opposite*). At altitudes of around 700–900 km the satellites revolve around the Earth approximately every 100 minutes and on each orbit cross a particular line of latitude at the same local (solar) time. This ensures that the satellite can obtain coverage of most of the globe, replicating the coverage typically within 2–3 weeks. In more recent satellites, sensors can be pointed sideways from the orbital path, and 'revisit' times with high-resolution frames can thus be reduced to a few days.

Exceptions to these Sun-synchronous orbits include the geostationary meteorological satellites, such as Meteosat. These have a 36,000 km high orbit and rotate around the Earth every 24 hours, thus remaining above the same point on the Equator.

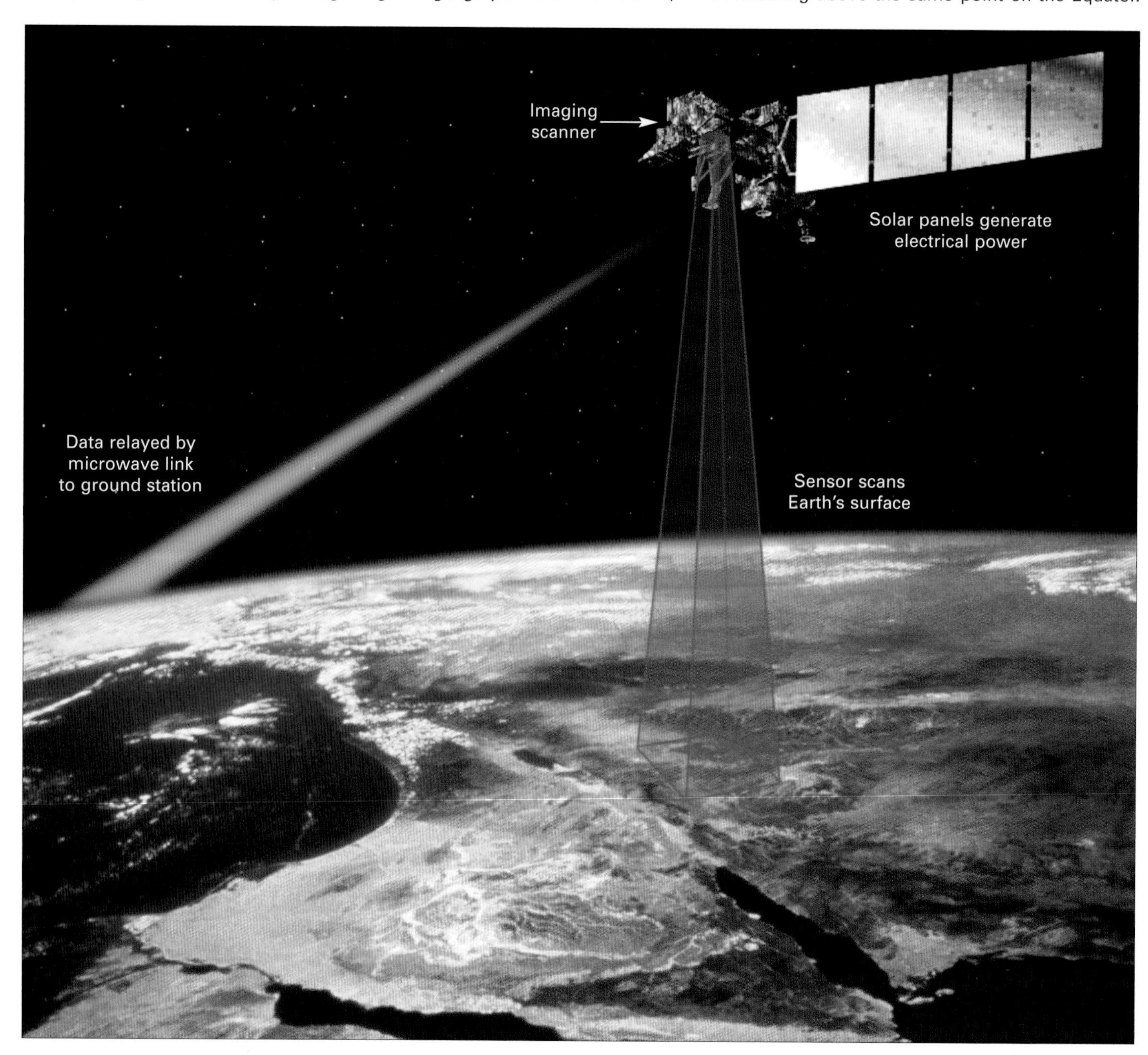

Imaging scanner

Solar panels generate electrical power

Data relayed by microwave link to ground station

Sensor scans Earth's surface

Landsat-7

This is the latest addition to the Landsat Earth-observation satellite programme, orbiting at 705 km above the Earth. With onboard recorders, the satellite can store data until it passes within range of a ground station. Basic geometric and radiometric corrections are then applied before distribution of the imagery to users.

These satellites acquire frequent images showing cloud and atmospheric moisture movements for almost a full hemisphere.

In addition, there is the Global Positioning System (GPS) satellite 'constellation', which orbits at a height of 20,200 km, consisting of 24 satellites. These circle the Earth in six different orbital planes, enabling us to fix our position on the Earth's surface to an accuracy of a few centimetres. Although developed for military use, this system is now available to individuals through hand-held receivers and in-car navigation systems. The other principal commercial uses are for surveying and air and sea navigation.

Digital sensors

Early satellite designs involved images being exposed to photographic film and returned to Earth by capsule for processing, a technique still sometimes used today. However, even the first commercial satellite imagery, from Landsat-1, used digital imaging sensors and transmitted the data back to ground stations (*see diagram opposite*).

Passive, or optical, sensors record the radiation reflected from the Earth for specific wavebands. Active sensors transmit their own microwave radiation, which is reflected from the Earth's surface back to the satellite and recorded. The SAR (Synthetic Aperture Radar) images on page 15 are examples of the latter.

Whichever scanning method is used, each satellite records image data of constant width but potentially several thousand kilometres in length. Once the data has been received on Earth, it is usually split into approximately square sections or 'scenes' for distribution.

Spectral resolution, wavebands and false-colour composites

Satellites can record data from many sections of the electro-magnetic spectrum (wavebands) simultaneously. Since we can only see images made from the three primary colours (red, green and blue), a selection of any three wavebands needs to be made in order to form a picture that will enable visual interpretation of the scene to be made. When any combination other than the visible bands are used, such as near or middle infrared, the resulting image is termed a 'false-colour composite'. An example of this is shown on page 8.

The selection of these wavebands depends on the purpose of the final image – geology, hydrology, agronomy and environmental requirements each have their own optimum waveband combinations.

GEOGRAPHIC INFORMATION SYSTEMS

A Geographic Information System (GIS) enables any available geospatial data to be compiled, presented and analysed using specialized computer software.

Many aspects of our lives now benefit from the use of GIS – from the management and maintenance of the networks of pipelines and cables that supply our homes, to the exploitation or protection of the natural resources that we use. Much of this is at a regional or national scale and the data collected from satellites form an important part of our interpretation and understanding of the world around us.

GIS systems are used for many aspects of central planning and modern life, such as defence, land use, reclamation, telecommunications and the deployment of emergency services. Commercial companies can use demographic and infrastructure data within a GIS to plan marketing strategies, identifying where their services would be most needed, and thus decide where best to locate their businesses. Insurance companies use GIS to determine premiums based on population distribution, crime figures and the likelihood of natural disasters, such as flooding or subsidence.

Whatever the application, all the relevant data can be prepared in a GIS so that a user can extract and display the information of particular interest on a map, or compare it with other material in order to help analyse and resolve a specific problem. From analysis of the data that has been acquired it is often possible to use a GIS to create a computer 'model' of possible future situations and see what impact various actions may have. A GIS can also monitor change over time, aiding the interpretation of long-term trends.

A GIS may also use satellite data to extract useful information and map large areas, which would otherwise take many man-years using other methods. For applications such as hydrocarbon and mineral exploration, forestry, agriculture, environmental monitoring and urban development, these developments have made it possible to undertake projects on a global scale unheard of before.

To find out more about how GIS works and how it affects our lives, why not go the Ordnance Survey's Mapzone website at: http://mapzone.ordnancesurvey.co.uk/mapzone/giszone.html

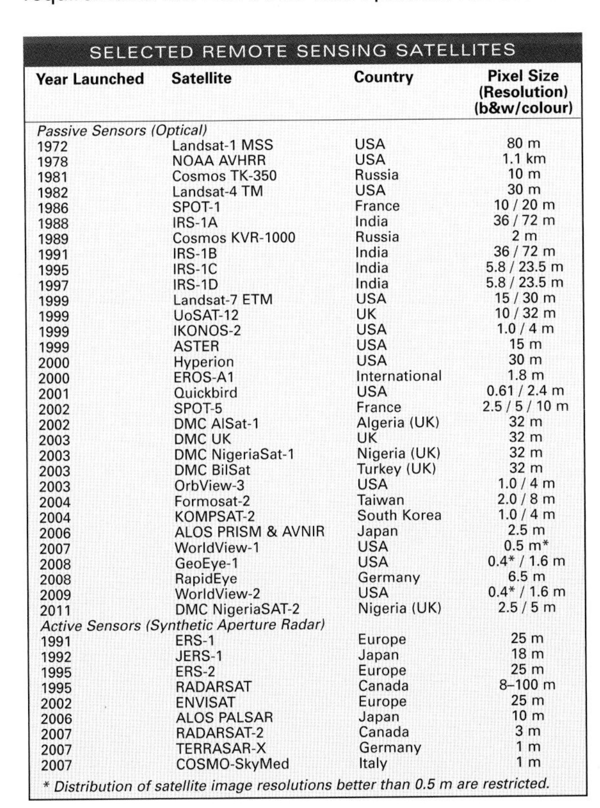

SELECTED REMOTE SENSING SATELLITES			
Year Launched	Satellite	Country	Pixel Size (Resolution) (b&w/colour)
Passive Sensors (Optical)			
1972	Landsat-1 MSS	USA	80 m
1978	NOAA AVHRR	USA	1.1 km
1981	Cosmos TK-350	Russia	10 m
1982	Landsat-4 TM	USA	30 m
1986	SPOT-1	France	10 / 20 m
1988	IRS-1A	India	36 / 72 m
1989	Cosmos KVR-1000	Russia	2 m
1991	IRS-1B	India	36 / 72 m
1995	IRS-1C	India	5.8 / 23.5 m
1997	IRS-1D	India	5.8 / 23.5 m
1999	Landsat-7 ETM	USA	15 / 30 m
1999	UoSAT-12	UK	10 / 32 m
1999	IKONOS-2	USA	1.0 / 4 m
1999	ASTER	USA	15 m
2000	Hyperion	USA	30 m
2000	EROS-A1	International	1.8 m
2001	Quickbird	USA	0.61 / 2.4 m
2002	SPOT-5	France	2.5 / 5 / 10 m
2002	DMC AlSat-1	Algeria (UK)	32 m
2003	DMC UK	UK	32 m
2003	DMC NigeriaSat-1	Nigeria (UK)	32 m
2003	DMC BilSat	Turkey (UK)	32 m
2003	OrbView-3	USA	1.0 / 4 m
2004	Formosat-2	Taiwan	2.0 / 8 m
2004	KOMPSAT-2	South Korea	1.0 / 4 m
2006	ALOS PRISM & AVNIR	Japan	2.5 m
2007	WorldView-1	USA	0.5 m*
2008	GeoEye-1	USA	0.4* / 1.6 m
2008	RapidEye	Germany	6.5 m
2009	WorldView-2	USA	0.4* / 1.6 m
2011	DMC NigeriaSAT-2	Nigeria (UK)	2.5 / 5 m
Active Sensors (Synthetic Aperture Radar)			
1991	ERS-1	Europe	25 m
1992	JERS-1	Japan	18 m
1995	ERS-2	Europe	25 m
1995	RADARSAT	Canada	8–100 m
2002	ENVISAT	Europe	25 m
2006	ALOS PALSAR	Japan	10 m
2007	RADARSAT-2	Canada	3 m
2007	TERRASAR-X	Germany	1 m
2007	COSMO-SkyMed	Italy	1 m

* Distribution of satellite image resolutions better than 0.5 m are restricted.

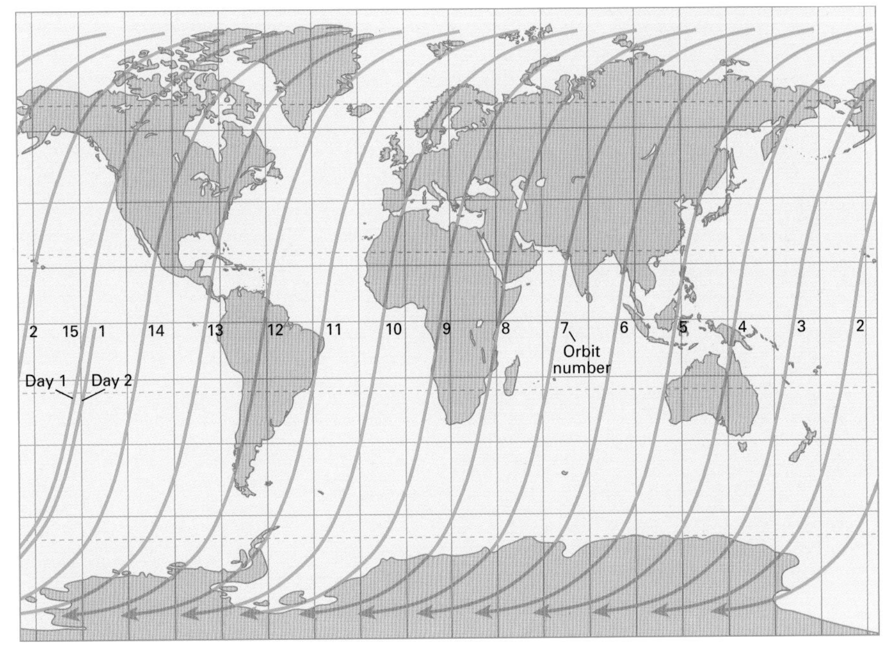

Satellite orbits
Landsat-7 makes over 14 orbits per day in its Sun-synchronous orbit. During the full 16 days of a repeat cycle, coverage of the areas between those shown is achieved.

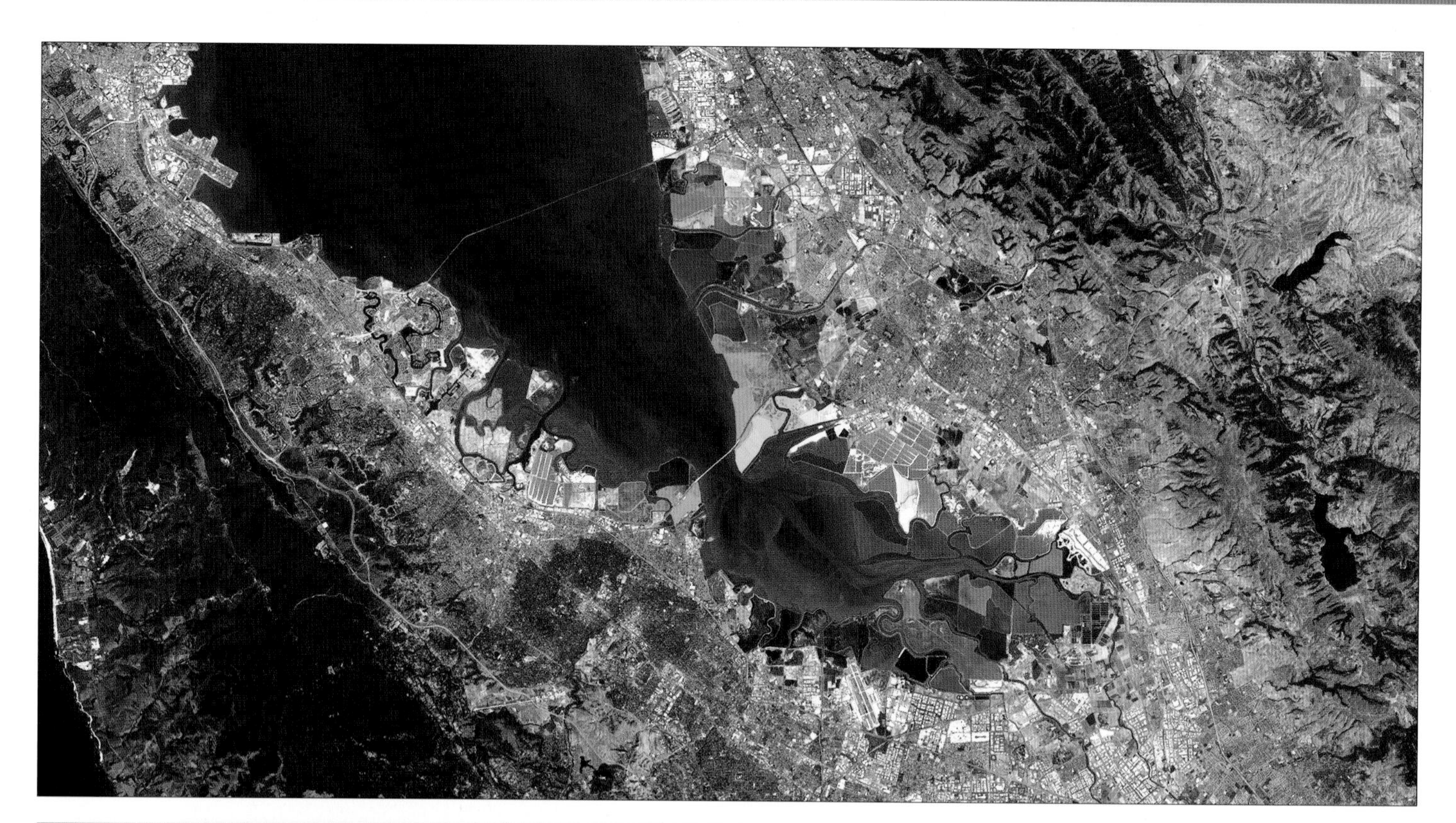

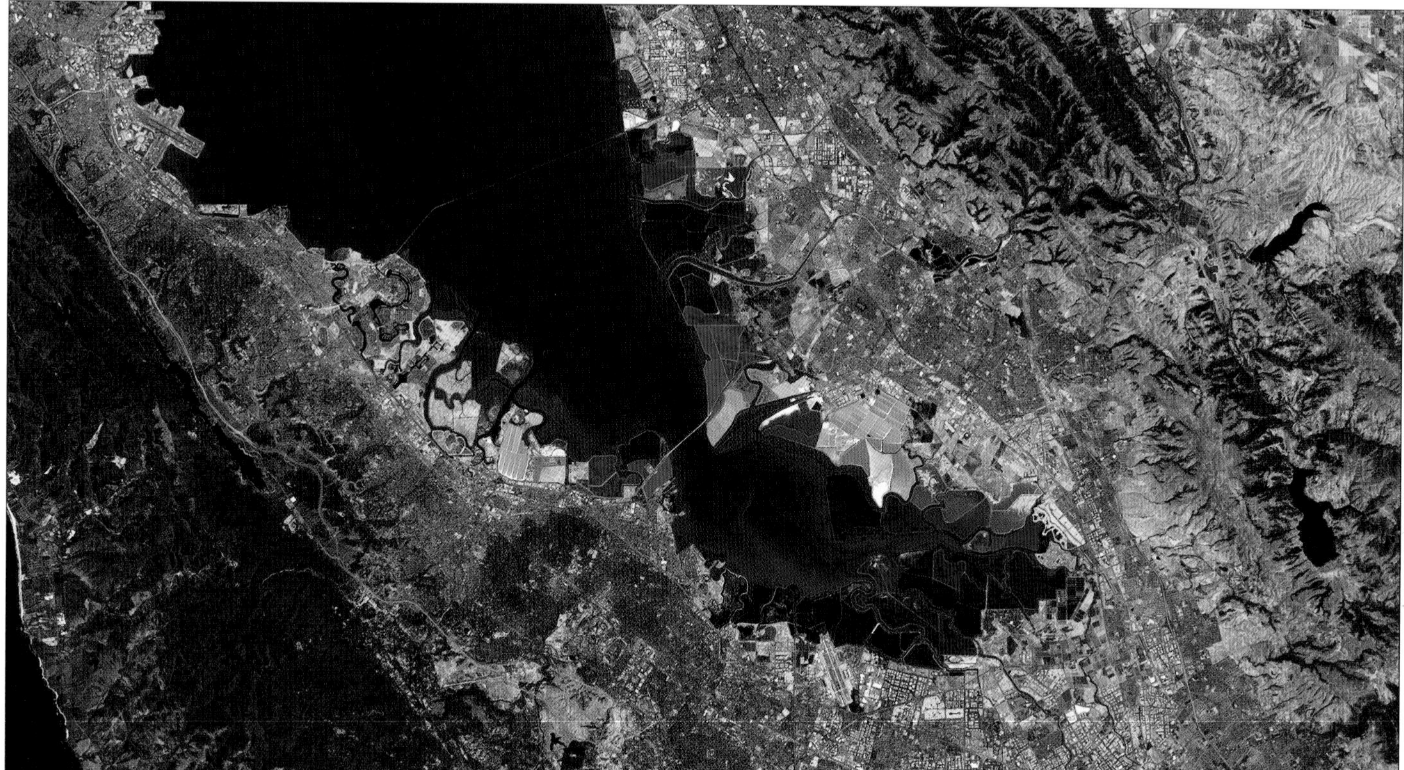

Natural-colour and false-colour composites

These images show the salt ponds at the southern end of San Francisco Bay, which now form the San Francisco Bay National Wildlife Refuge. They demonstrate the difference between 'natural colour' (*top*) and 'false colour' (*bottom*) composites.

The top image is made from visible red, green and blue wavelengths. The colours correspond closely to those one would observe from an aircraft. The salt ponds appear green or orange-red due to the colour of the sediments they contain. The urban areas appear grey and vegetation is either dark green (trees) or light brown (dry grass).

The bottom image is made up of near-infrared, visible red and visible green wavelengths. These wavebands are represented here in red, green and blue, respectively. Since chlorophyll in healthy vegetation strongly reflects near-infrared light, this is clearly visible as red in the image.

False-colour composite imagery is therefore very sensitive to the presence of healthy vegetation. The bottom image thus shows better discrimination between the 'leafy' residential urban areas, such as Palo Alto (south-west of the Bay), and other urban areas by the 'redness' of the trees. The high chlorophyll content of watered urban grass areas shows as bright red, contrasting with the dark red of trees and the brown of natural, dry grass. *(EROS)*

Western Grand Canyon, Arizona, USA
This false-colour image shows in bright red the sparse vegetation on the limestone plateau, including sage, mesquite and grasses. Such imagery is used to monitor this and similar fragile environments. The sediment-laden river, shown as blue-green, can be seen dispersing into Lake Mead to the north-west. Side canyons cross the main canyon in straight lines, showing where erosion along weakened fault lines has occurred. *(EROS)*

Har Nuur, Mongolia
'Har Nuur' means 'Black Lake'. It is situated in a remote inland basin in the west of Mongolia. The yellow areas are sand-desert dune fields, which are being blown eastwards on the prevailing westerly winds. This image, from the International Space Station, shows a spur of sand pushing across the south-west shore of the lake. *(NASA EO-1 team)*

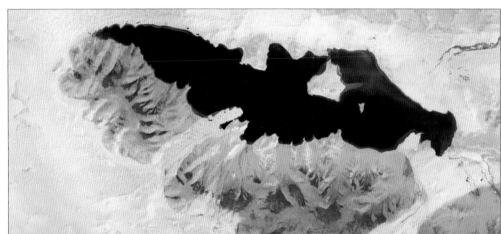

Washington State, USA
The chequerboard pattern shows the square or rectangular land parcels used for commercial forestry. Brown or orange indicates bare earth, light green represents grassland or young trees, and dark green shows mature woodland. Used over time, images such as this allow scientists to monitor deforestation and new planting, and their consequent effects on the carbon cycle. *(EROS)*

Niger Delta, West Africa
The River Niger is the third longest river in Africa after the Nile and Congo, and this false-colour image shows the different vegetation types. Deltas are by nature constantly evolving sedimentary features and often contain many ecosystems within them. In the case of the Niger Delta, there are also vast hydro-carbon reserves beneath it with associated wells and pipelines. Satellite imagery helps to plan activity and monitor this fragile and changing environment. *(EROS)*

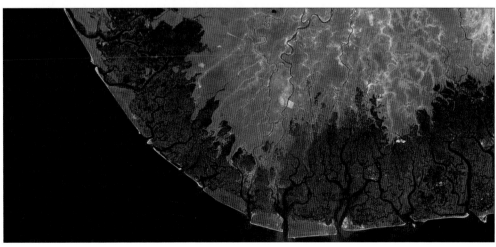

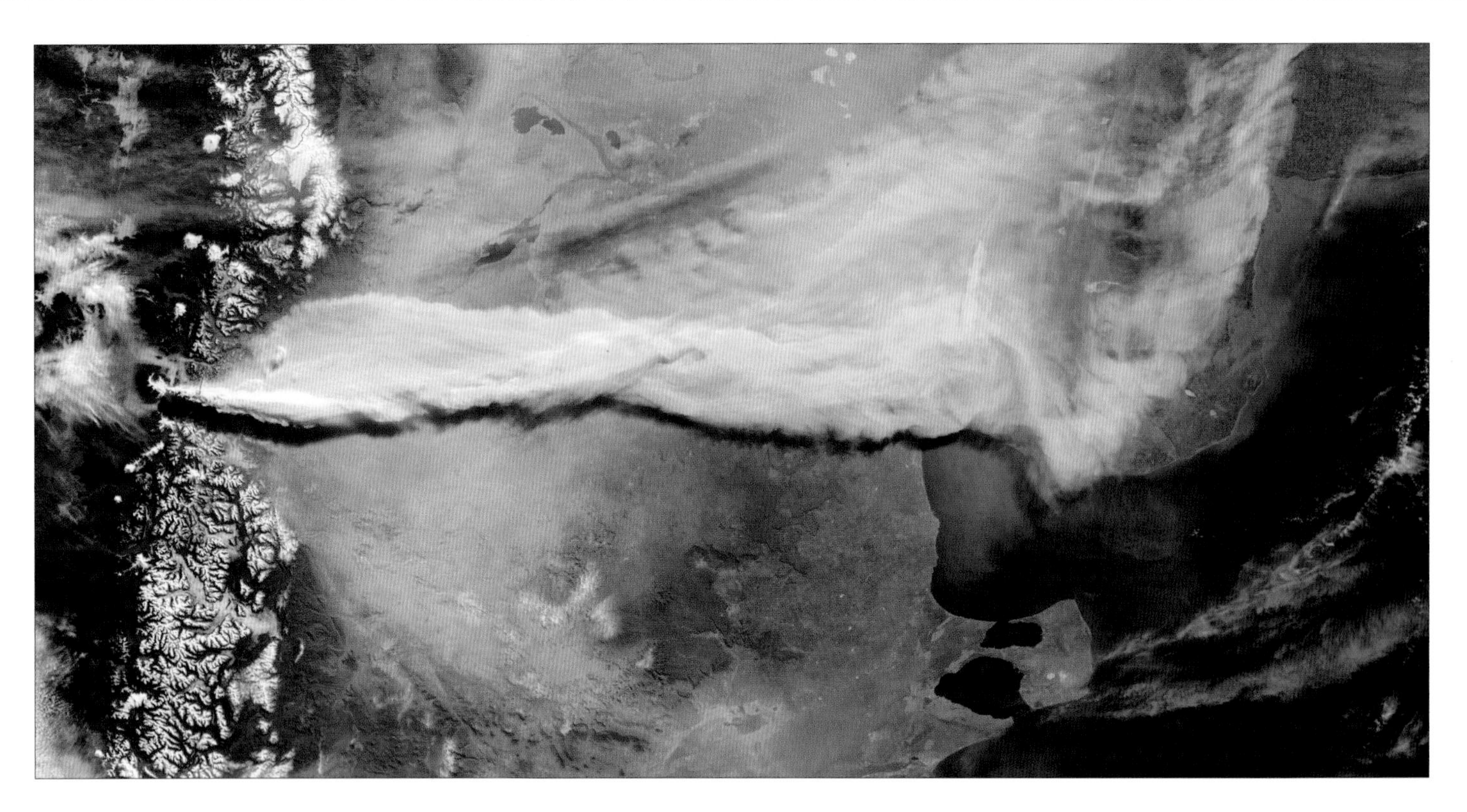

Puyehue-Cordón Volcano, Chile
Part of the ash plume from the June 2011 major eruption from this strato-volcano in the Andes can be seen drifting eastwards at high altitude across the coast of Argentina, to the north of the distinctive shape of the Valdés Peninsula. The ash eventually travelled in the upper atmosphere as far as Australia and New Zealand, causing disruption to commercial flights. *(Jeff Schmaltz, MODIS Rapid Response Team at NASA GSFC)*

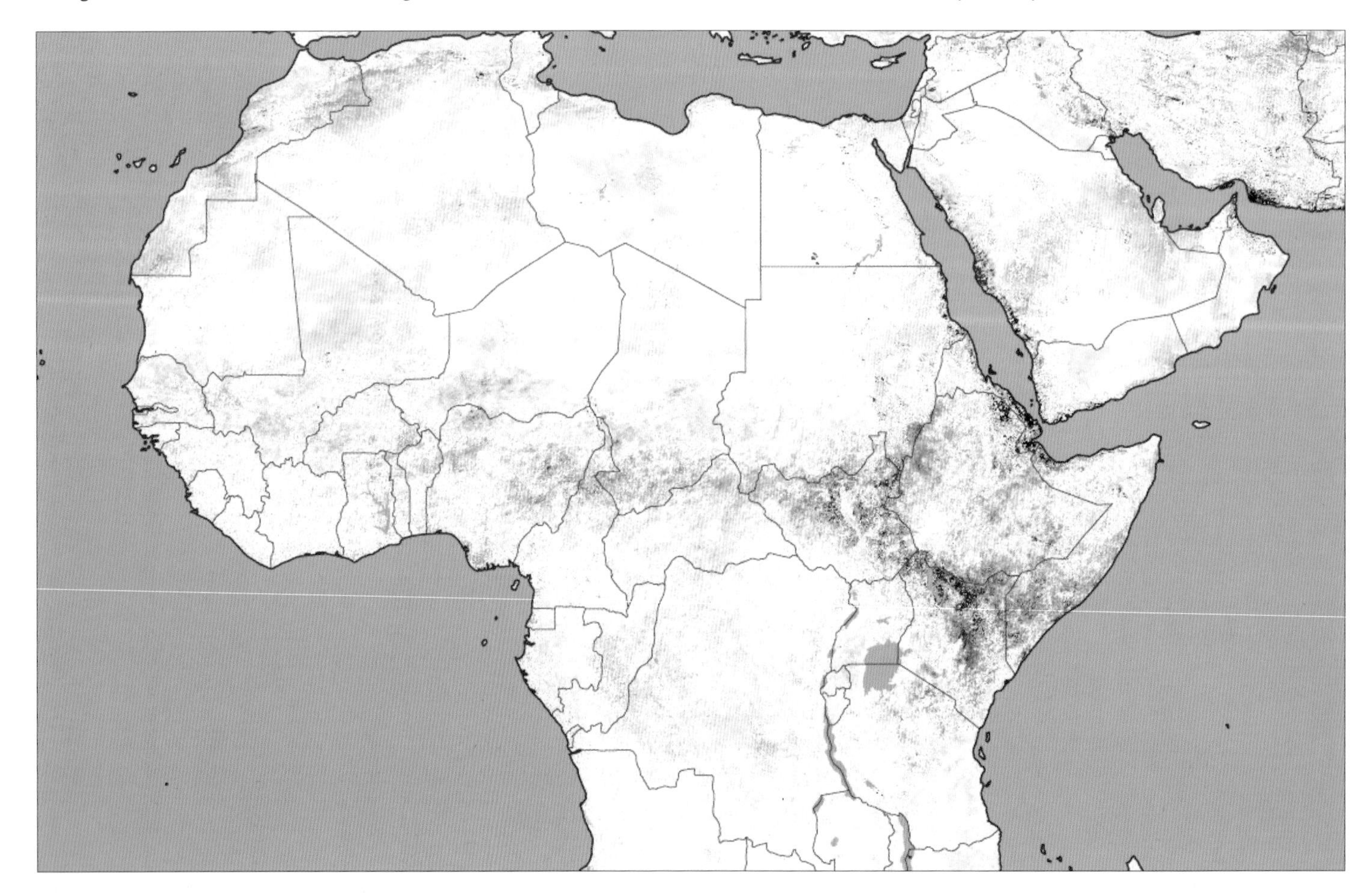

East African drought
The colours on the image represent the 'vegetation anomaly', i.e. the deviation from what would be considered normal growth, between April and June 2011. Brown indicates poor plant growth and highlights the severe drought in Somalia, South Sudan and northern Kenya. *(NASA GIMMS Group at GSFC)*

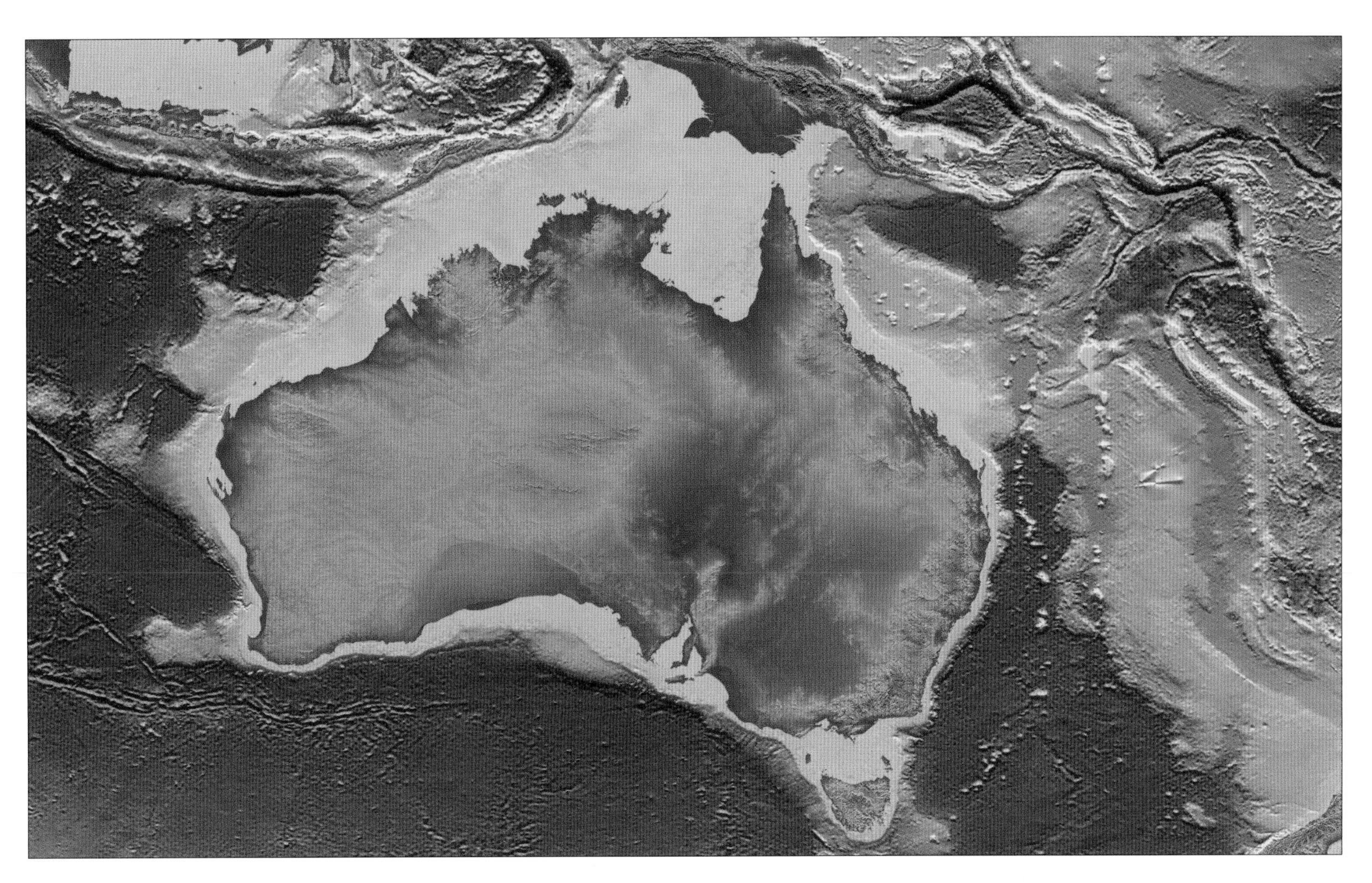

Mapping the ocean floors
The accurate global mapping of whole ocean floors has only been possible since the advent of satellite radar altimetry. From a precisely known orbit, microwave pulses measure the ocean surface. The effects of tides, waves and currents can mathematically be removed from these measurements and the resultant ocean-surface shape reflects that of the ocean floor beneath, due to the gravitational effects of the water over the sea-floor topography. However, for large-scale navigational charts, shipboard echo soundings are still used. *(Fugro NPA Ltd)*

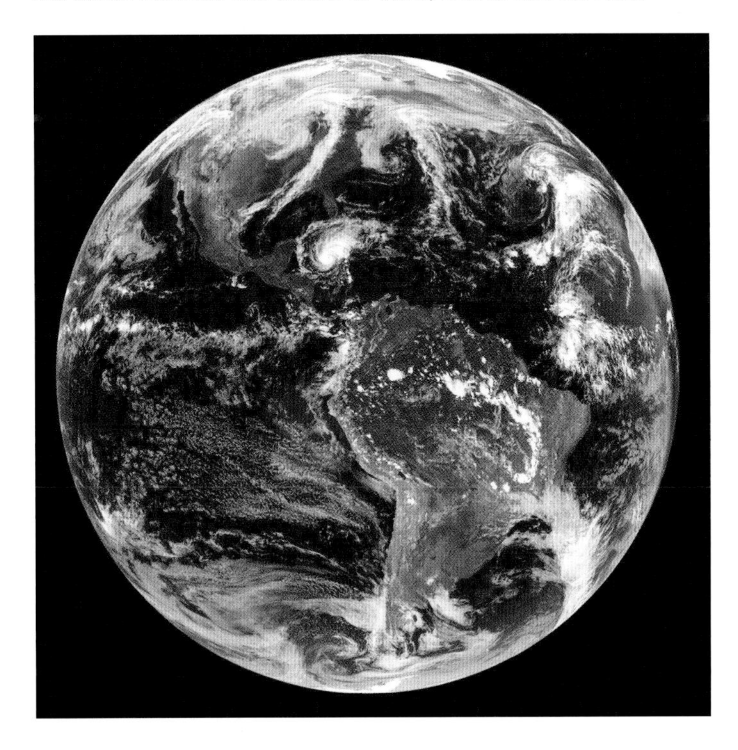

Weather monitoring
Geostationary and polar orbiting satellites monitor the Earth's atmospheric movements, giving us an insight into the global workings of the atmosphere and permitting us to predict weather change. *(NASA image courtesy GOES Project Science Office)*

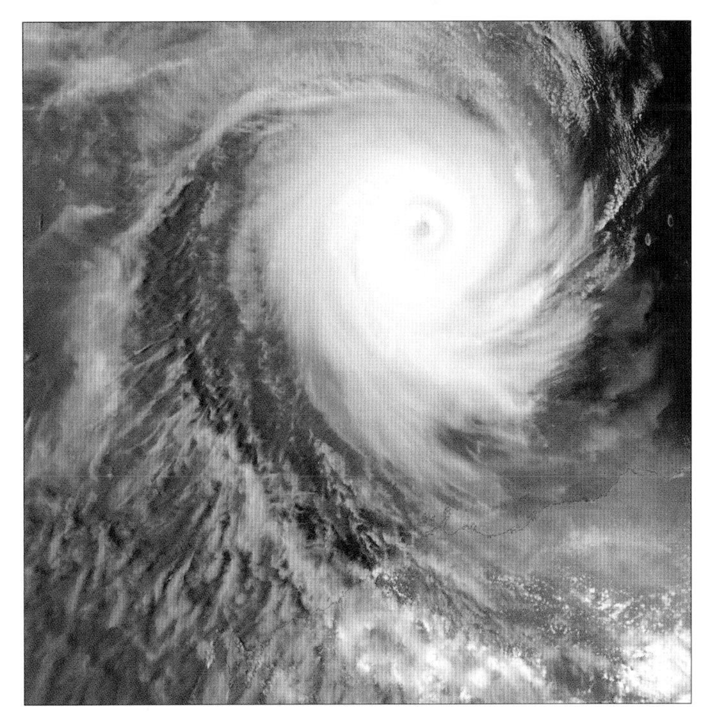

Tropical Cyclone 'Billy'
On Christmas Day 2008 the storm approaches Western Australia from the Indian Ocean. Such images aid in monitoring the development and track of weather systems. *(Jeff Schmaltz, MODIS Rapid Response Team at NASA GSFC)*

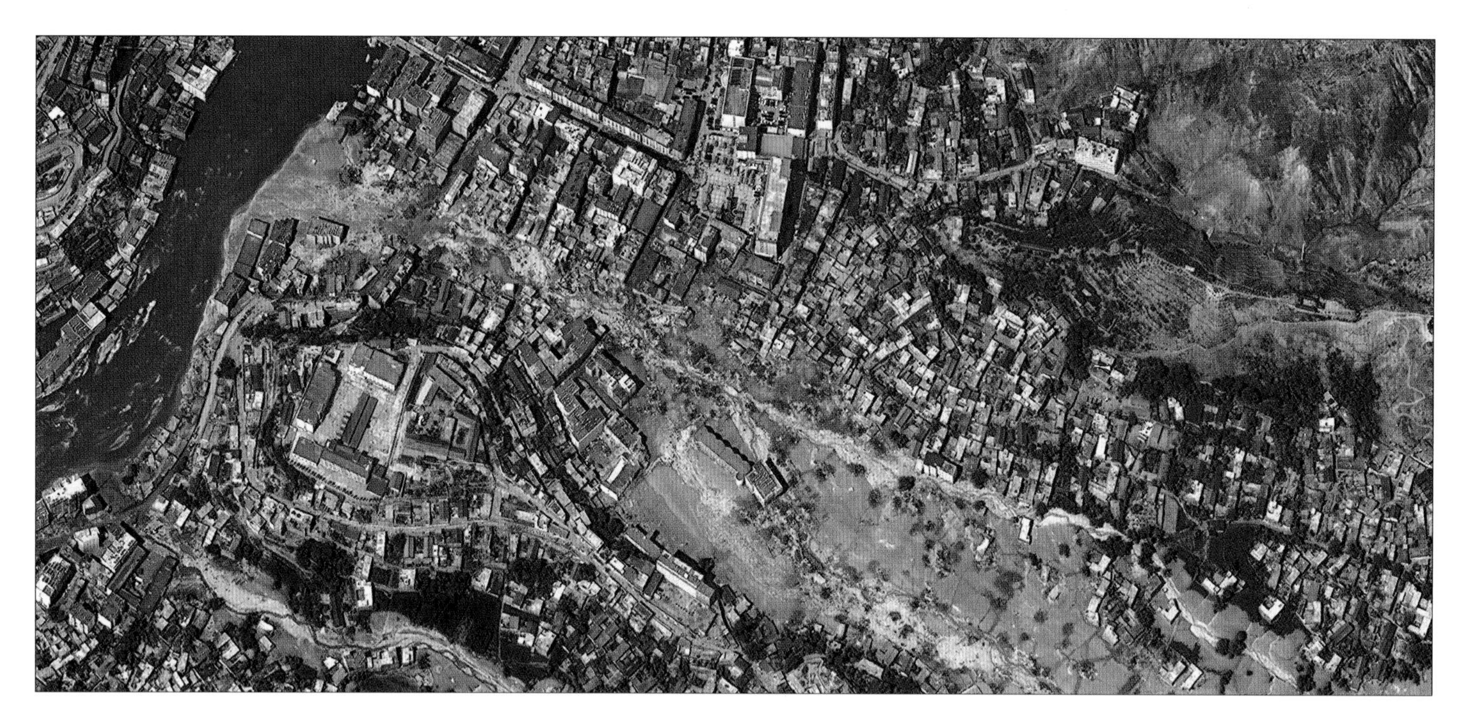

Zhugpu, China
On 10 August 2010, after intense monsoon rains, this remote region suffered disastrous flooding, followed by a series of landslides, which together claimed over 1,500 lives. Access to the area was very difficult and satellite imagery helped focus and direct rescue efforts, using scarce resources. *(WorldView-2 courtesy DigitalGlobe)*

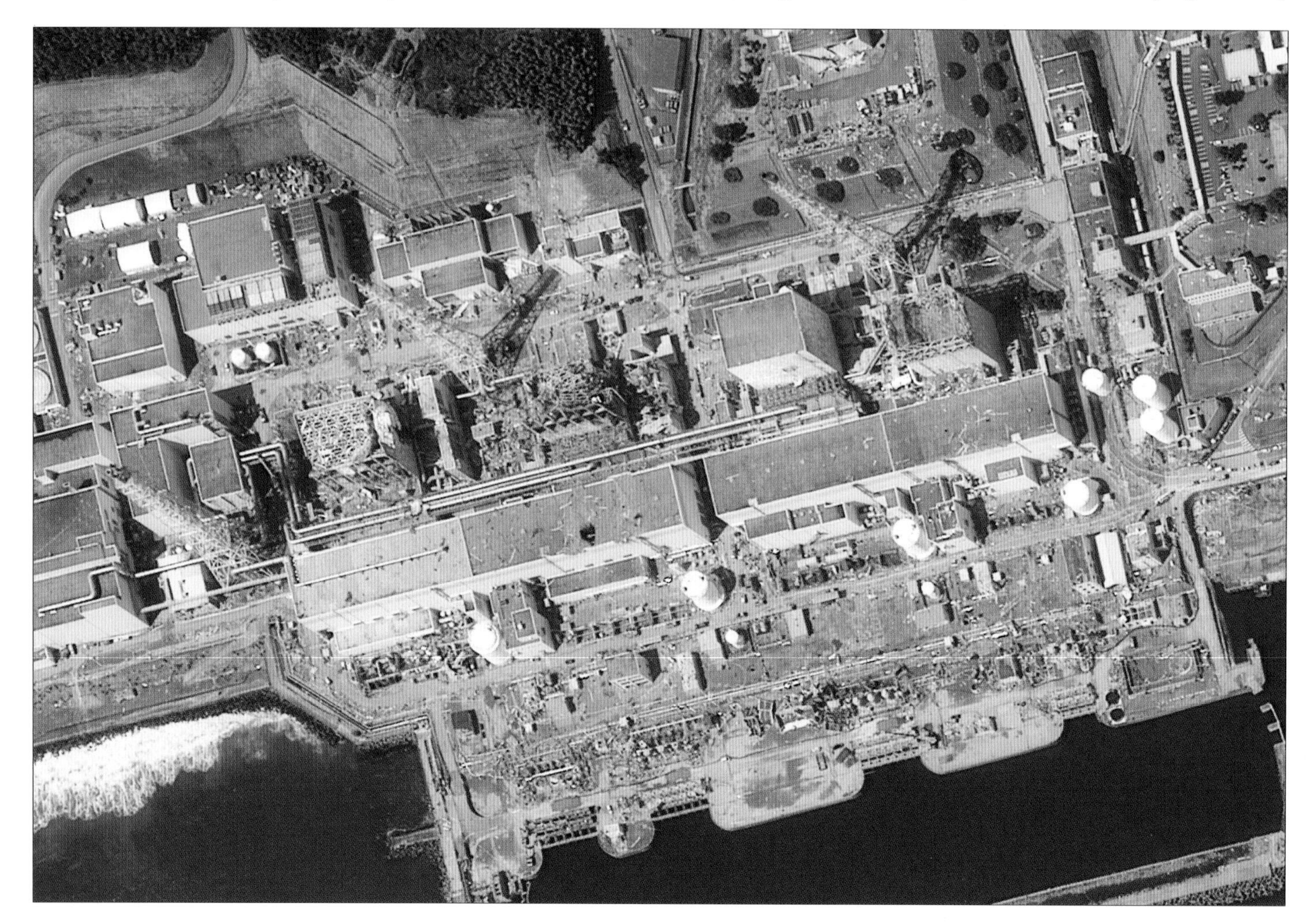

Fukushima Nuclear Power Station, Japan
This image was captured by the GeoEye-1 satellite, travelling at 6 km/sec and 680 km above the Earth. In front of the pylons, in the centre of the image, the damaged reactors in the heart of the irradiated area can be seen, following the March 2011 Japanese earthquake and tsunami. It allowed initial assessment of a very dangerous area to take place with minimum risk to human life. *(Image courtesy GeoEye)*

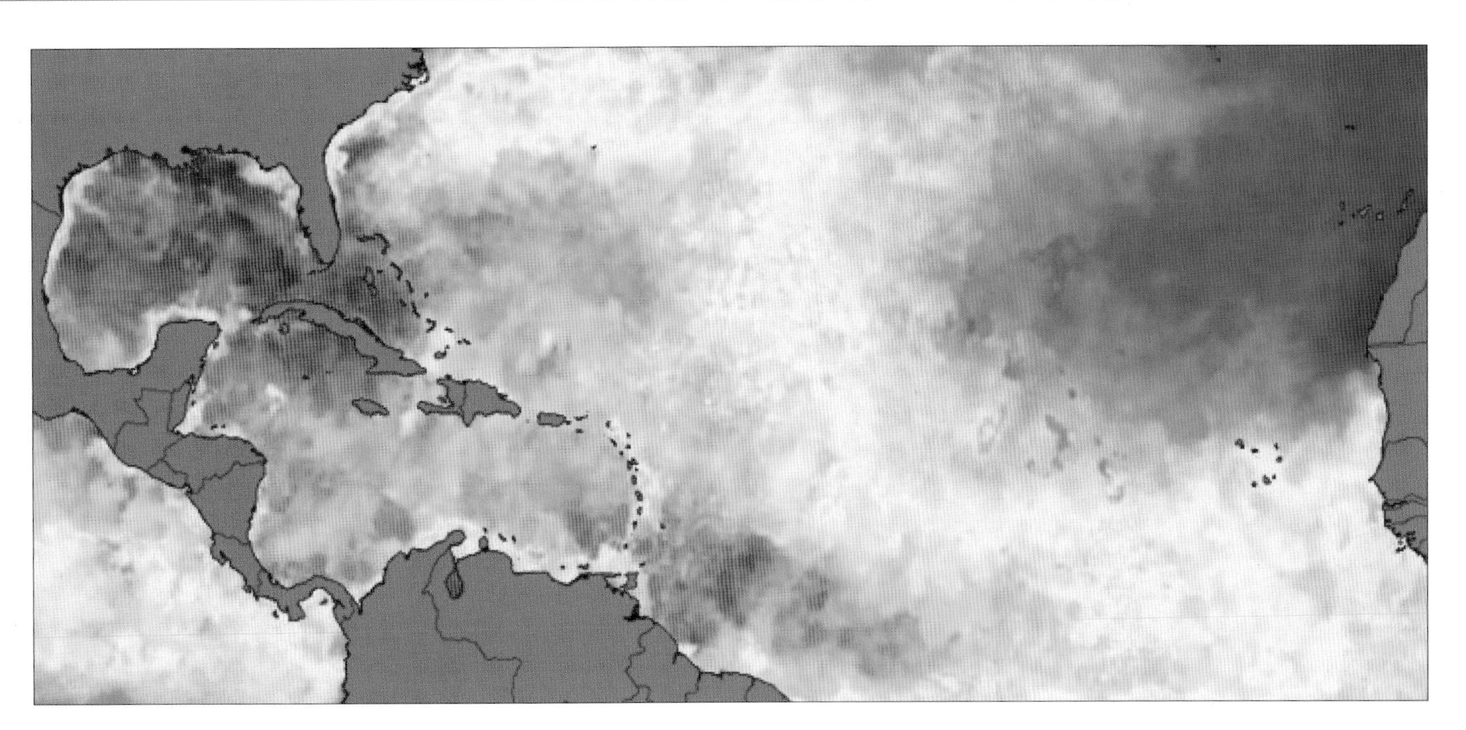

Ocean temperature monitoring

Part of a global dataset, the central Atlantic Ocean from West Africa across to Central America is shown during the hurricane season in Central and North America, in August 2011. The yellow and orange colours indicate surface water temperatures over 27.8°C, the critical temperature above which tropical storms are fuelled and intensified. The powerful Hurricane Irene hit the eastern United States later in the month. *(NASA image created by Jesse Allen, using merged AMSR-E/MODIS data)*

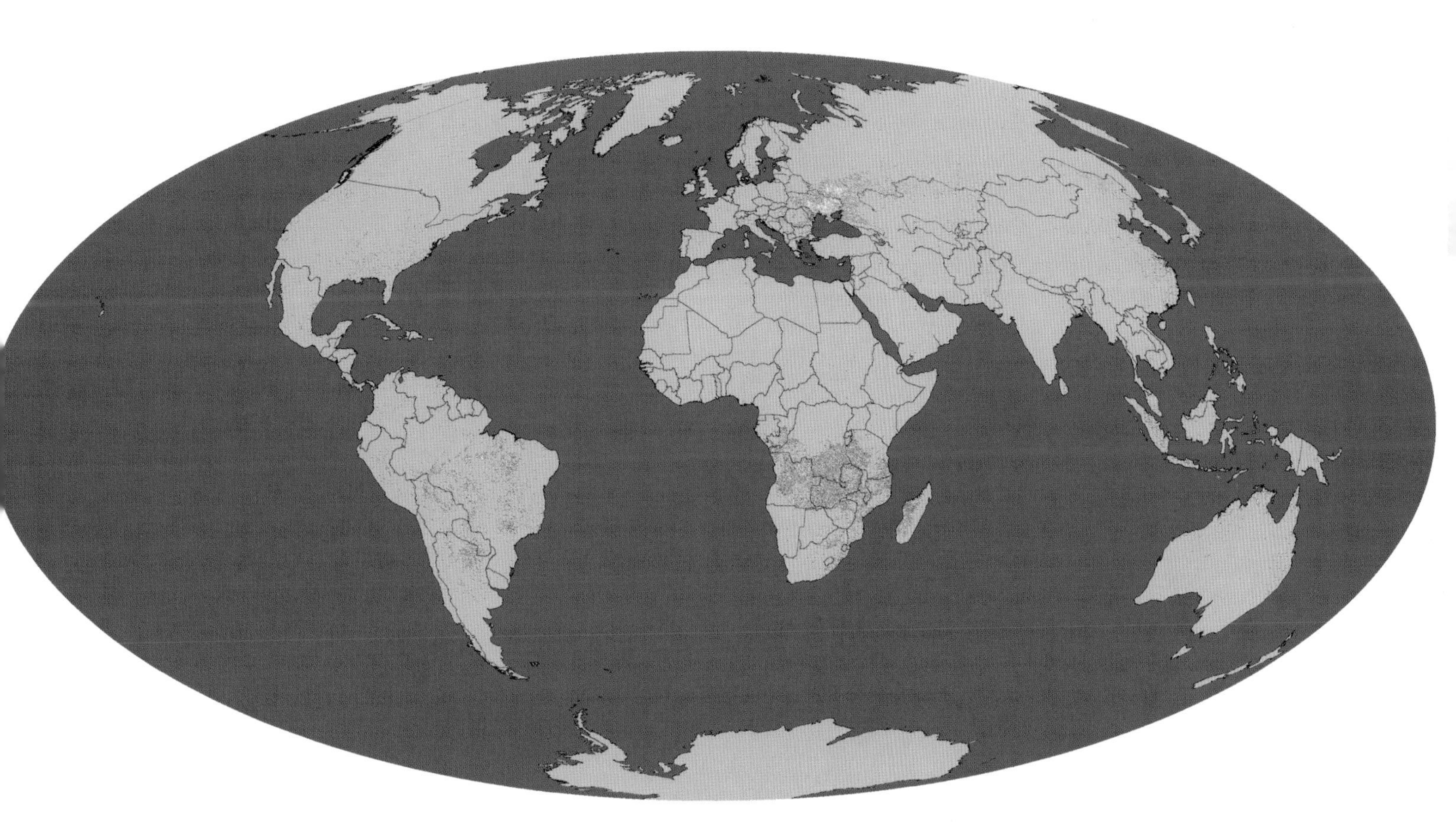

World fires

This image shows all the fires worldwide that were burning during August 2008, whether they were man-made to clear ground for crops, for example, or occurred naturally from, say, lightning strikes. The orange tint indicates where fires are at their fiercest. Over any given year the areas affected by the fires move with the seasons, February being the month with most fires in the tropics. Acquiring this data from satellites allows efficient management of scarce resources in remote and environmentally threatened areas. *(NASA image by Reto Stockli and Jesse Allen using data courtesy of the MODIS Land Science Team at NASA GSFC)*

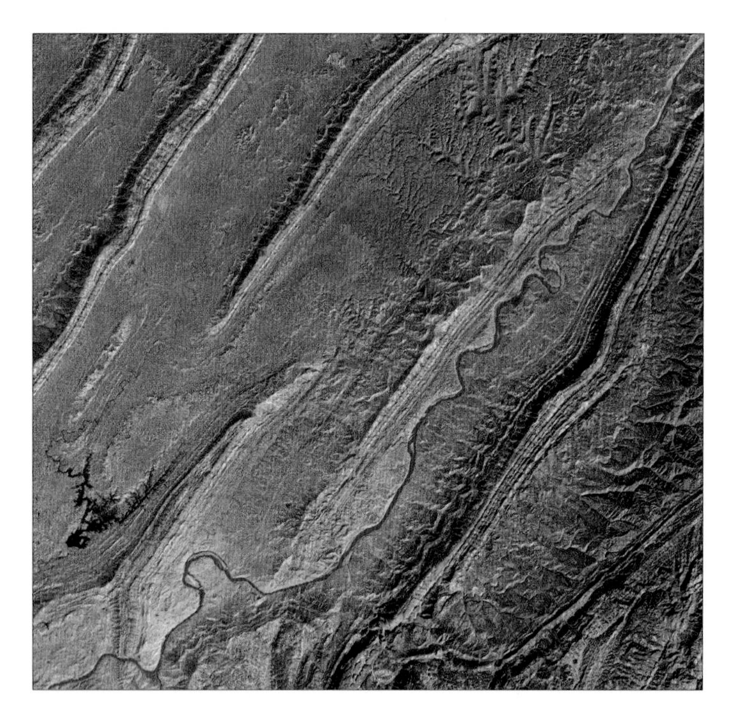

Sichuan Basin, China
The north-east/south-west trending ridges in this image are anticlinal folds developed in the Earth's crust as a result of plate collision and compression. Geologists map these folds and the lowlands between them formed by synclinal folds, as they are often the areas where oil or gas are found in commercial quantities. The river shown in this image is the Yangtse, near Chongqing. *(China RSGS)*

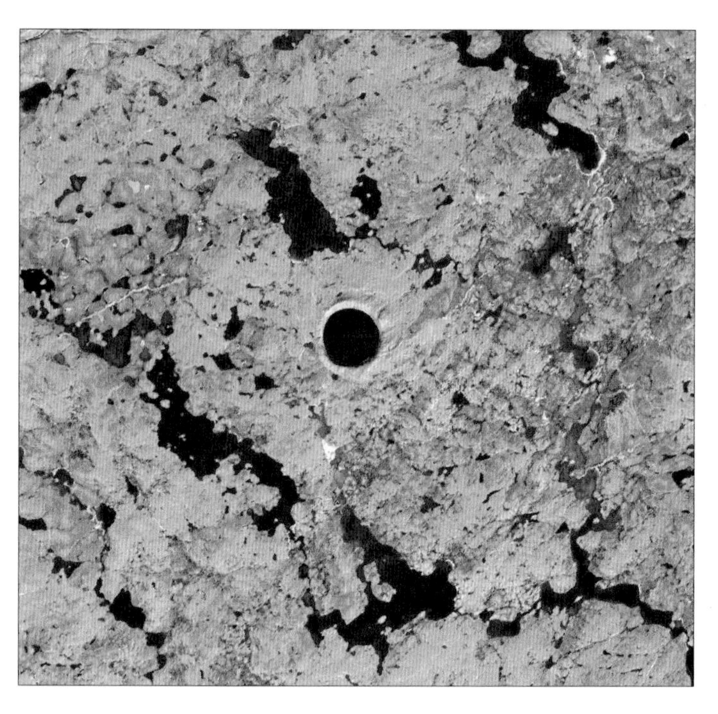

Pingualuit Crater, Canada
The circular feature is a meteorite crater in the Ungava Peninsula, Québec, formed by an impact over 1.4 million years ago. It is 3.4 km wide and the lake within is 264 m deep. The lake has no link to any water sources and has been formed only by rain and snow. Thus the water is very pure and among the world's clearest and least saline. Sediments at the bottom have been unaffected by ice sheets and are important for scientific research. *(Fugro NPA Ltd)*

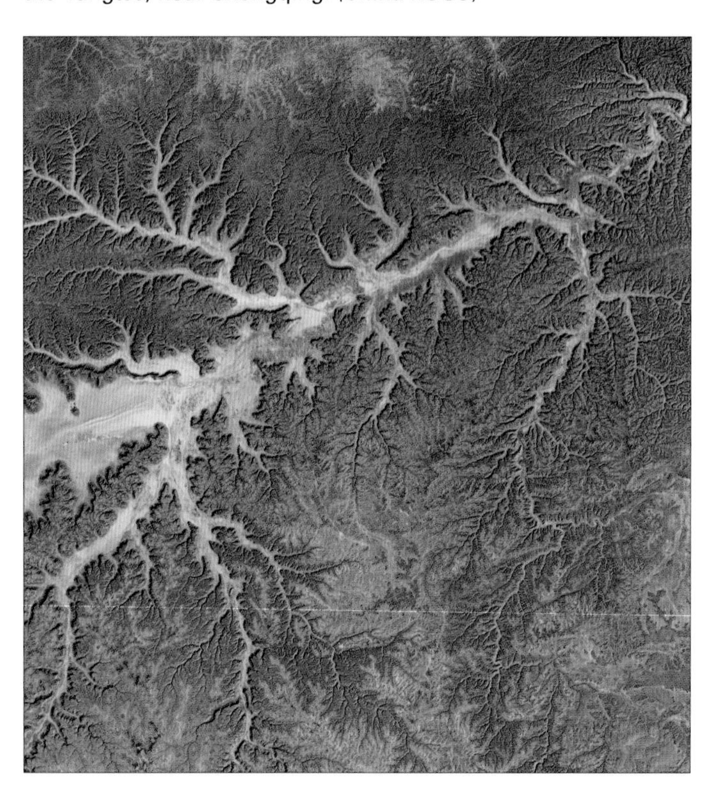

Wadi Hadramaut, Yemen
Yemen is extremely arid – however, in the past it was more humid and wet, enabling large river systems to carve out the deep and spectacular gorges and dried-out river beds (*wadis*) seen in this image. The erosion has revealed many contrasting rock types. The image has been processed to exaggerate this effect, producing many shades of red, pink and purple, which make geological mapping easier and more cost-effective. *(EROS)*

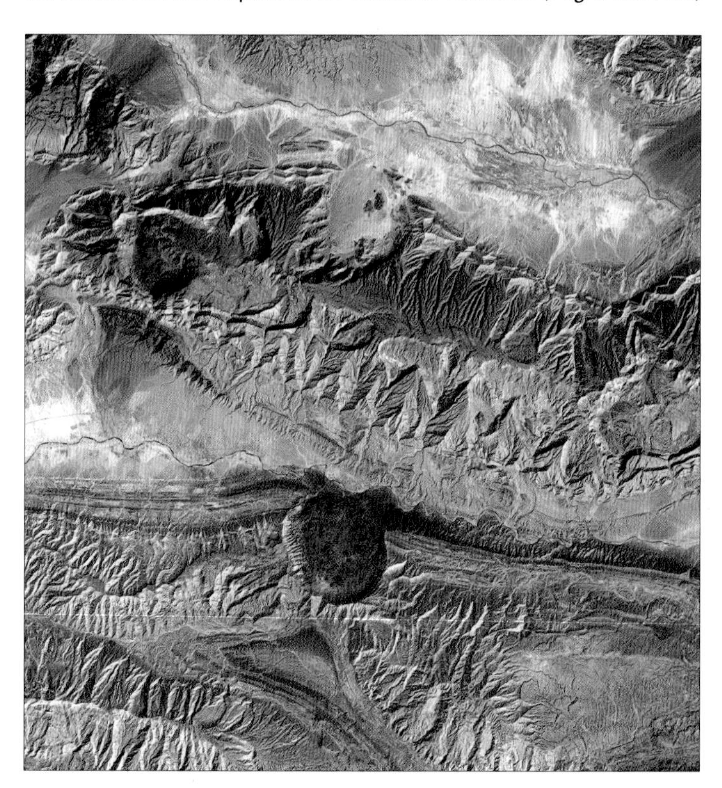

Zagros Mountains, Iran
These mountains were formed as Arabia collided with Southern Eurasia. The upper half of this colour-enhanced image shows an anticline that runs east–west. The dark grey features are called *diapirs*, which are bodies of viscous rock salt that are very buoyant and sometimes rise to the surface, spilling and spreading out like a glacier. The presence of salt in the region is important as it stops oil escaping to the surface. *(EROS)*

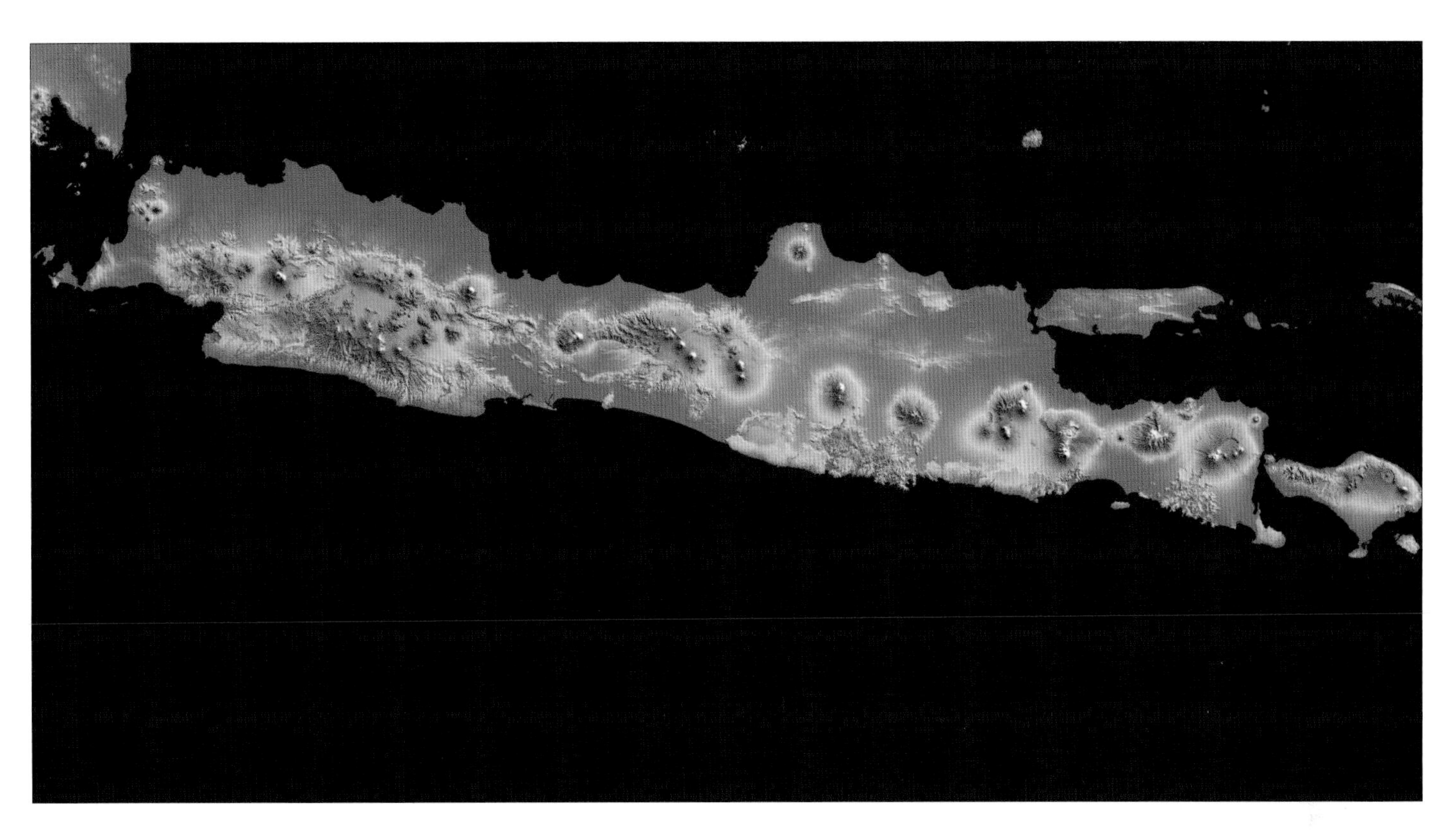

Topographic surveys

In February 2000 the Shuttle Radar Topography Mission (SRTM) was launched. Over 11 days, using specially developed radar equipment, it captured the topography of 80% of the Earth's land area at high resolution. This was the first time that this had been done on a consistent basis globally and for many inaccessible areas was the first survey. The image above shows the volcanic cones of the Indonesian islands of Java and Bali. *(Fugro NPA Ltd)*

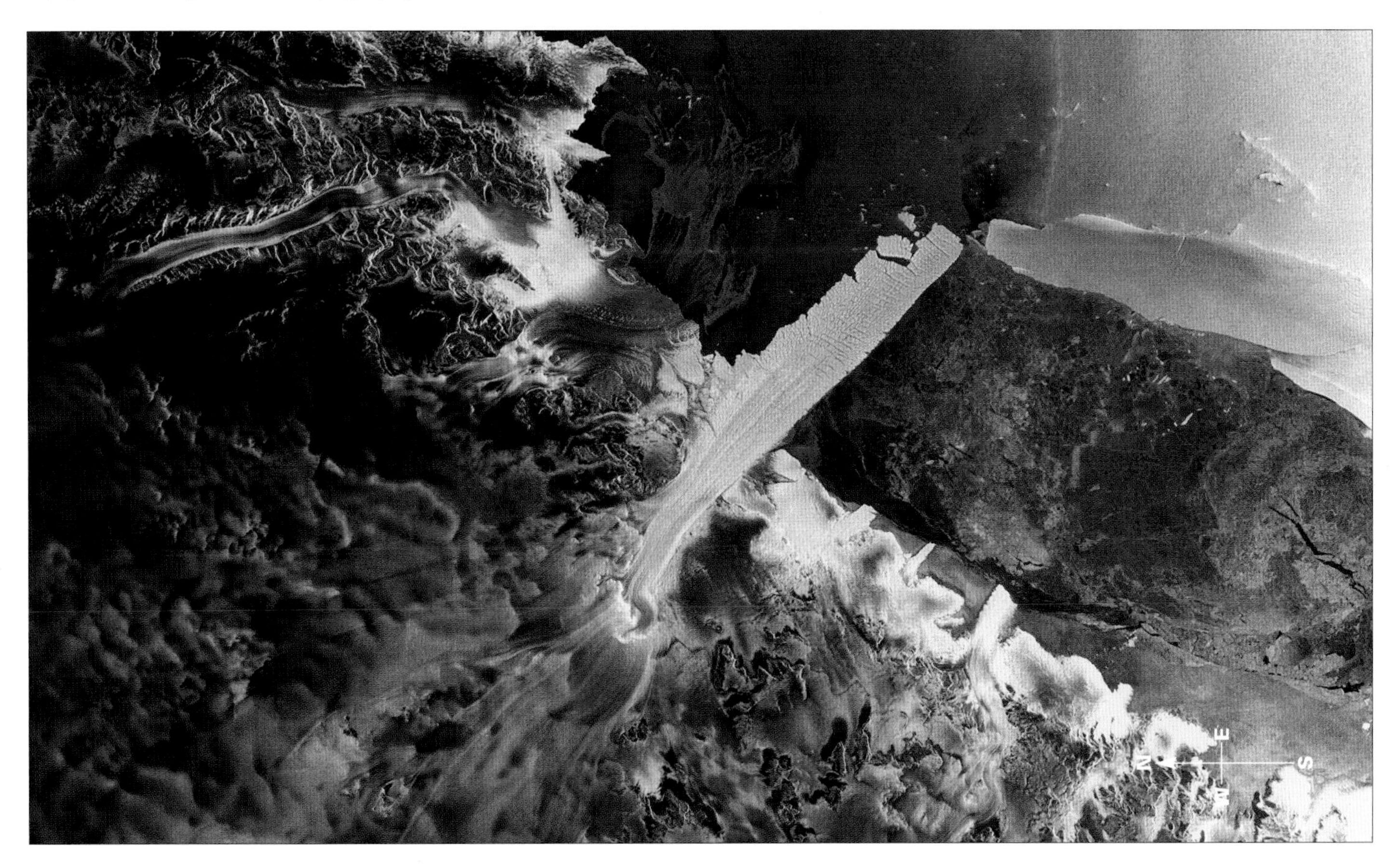

Environmental monitoring

Synthetic Aperture Radar (SAR) uses microwaves to penetrate cloud and needs no solar illumination, so is ideal for monitoring remote and difficult areas. In the middle of this image the David Glacier in Antarctica is seen flowing to the sea. Here it floats onwards and is known as the Drygalski Ice Tongue. At its end, a tabular iceberg is breaking off, or 'calving', whilst to the right is part of a 120 km long iceberg that almost collided with it. *(ESA)*

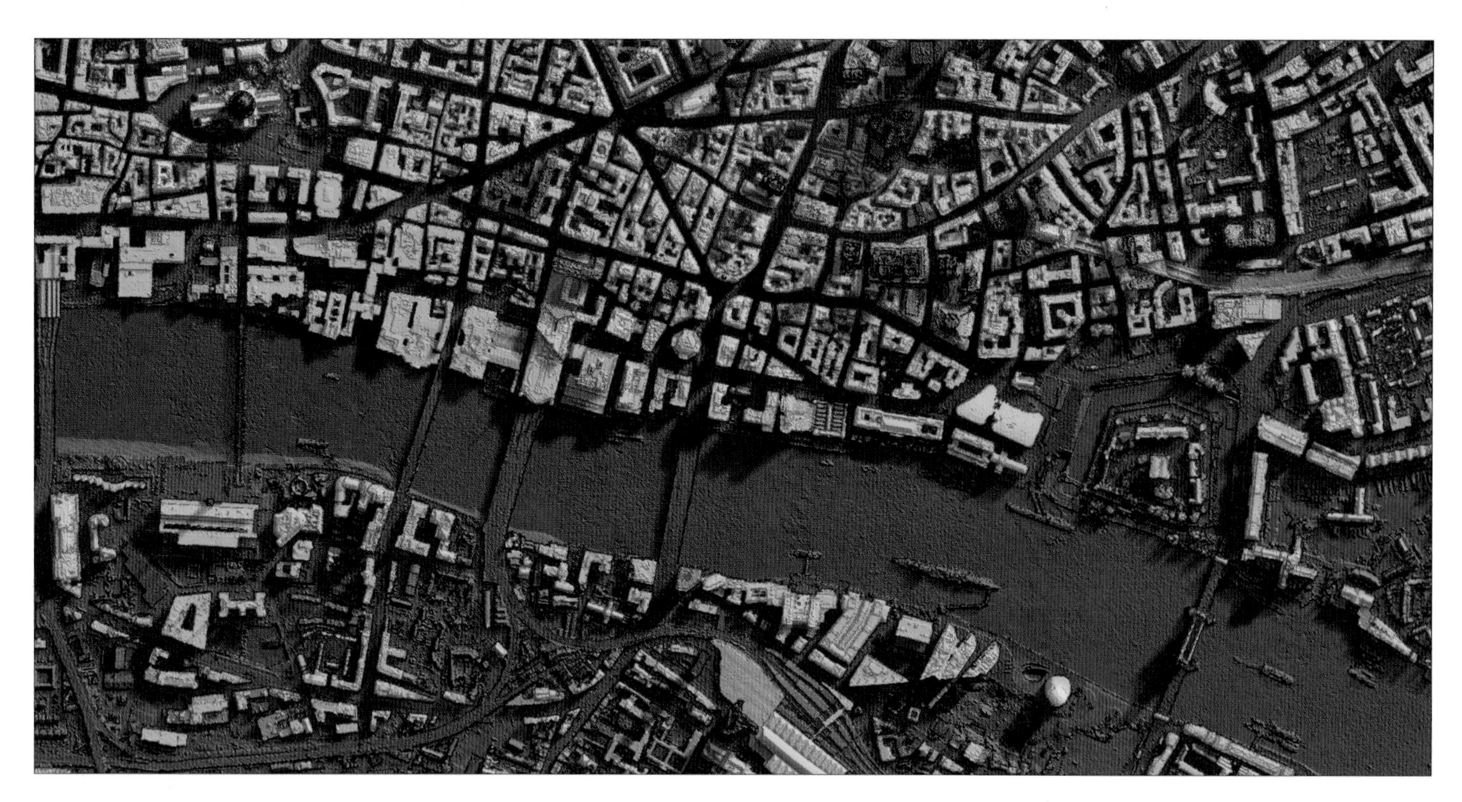

Lidar surveying

Lasers based on aircraft or satellites can be used to scan surface elevations to an accuracy of a few centimetres. This extract from a survey of the whole of London shows the City of London from St Paul's Cathederal in the north-west to the Tower of London and Tower Bridge in the south-east. The very narrow and deep urban canyons and atriums in this area clearly demonstrate the advantages of airborne laser scanning (Lidar), which only requires a single line-of-sight to obtain precise measurements. A basic variant of this technology has been used for several years from satellites to acquire elevation profiles of the surface of Mars. Sensors capable of more detailed scanning are currently under development for Earth-orbiting satellites. *(Precision Terrain Surveys Ltd – www.precisionterrain.com)*

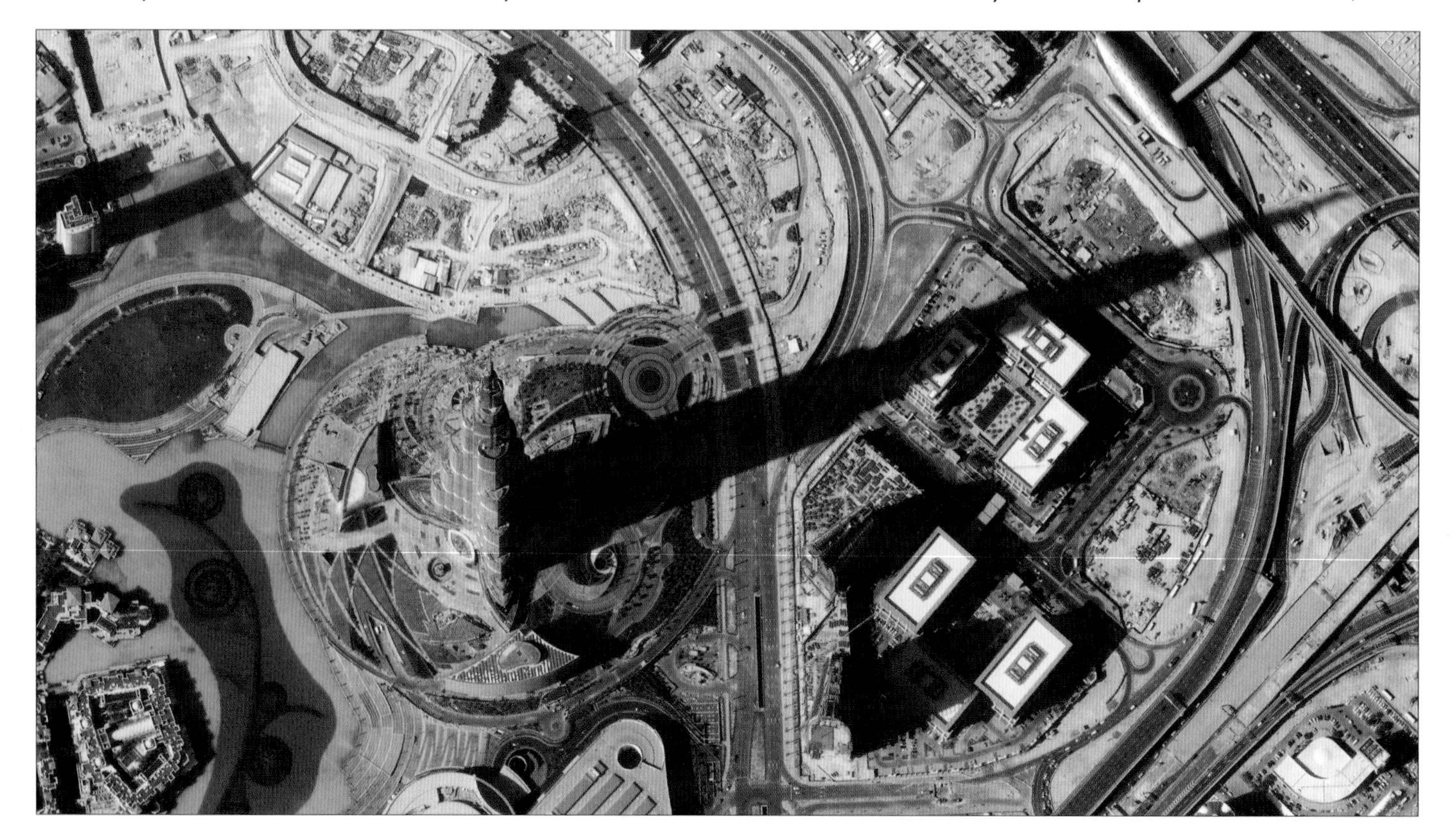

Dubai, United Arab Emirates

The long shadow of the the Burj Khalifa, currently the world's tallest free-standing structure at 848 metres, falls across this image. Completed in September 2009, it has 160 floors and the world's fastest elevators, which travel at 64 km/h. Dubai has expanded from a small fishing settlement to a modern city of over 1.5 million people in less than 50 years. *(Image courtesy GeoEye)*

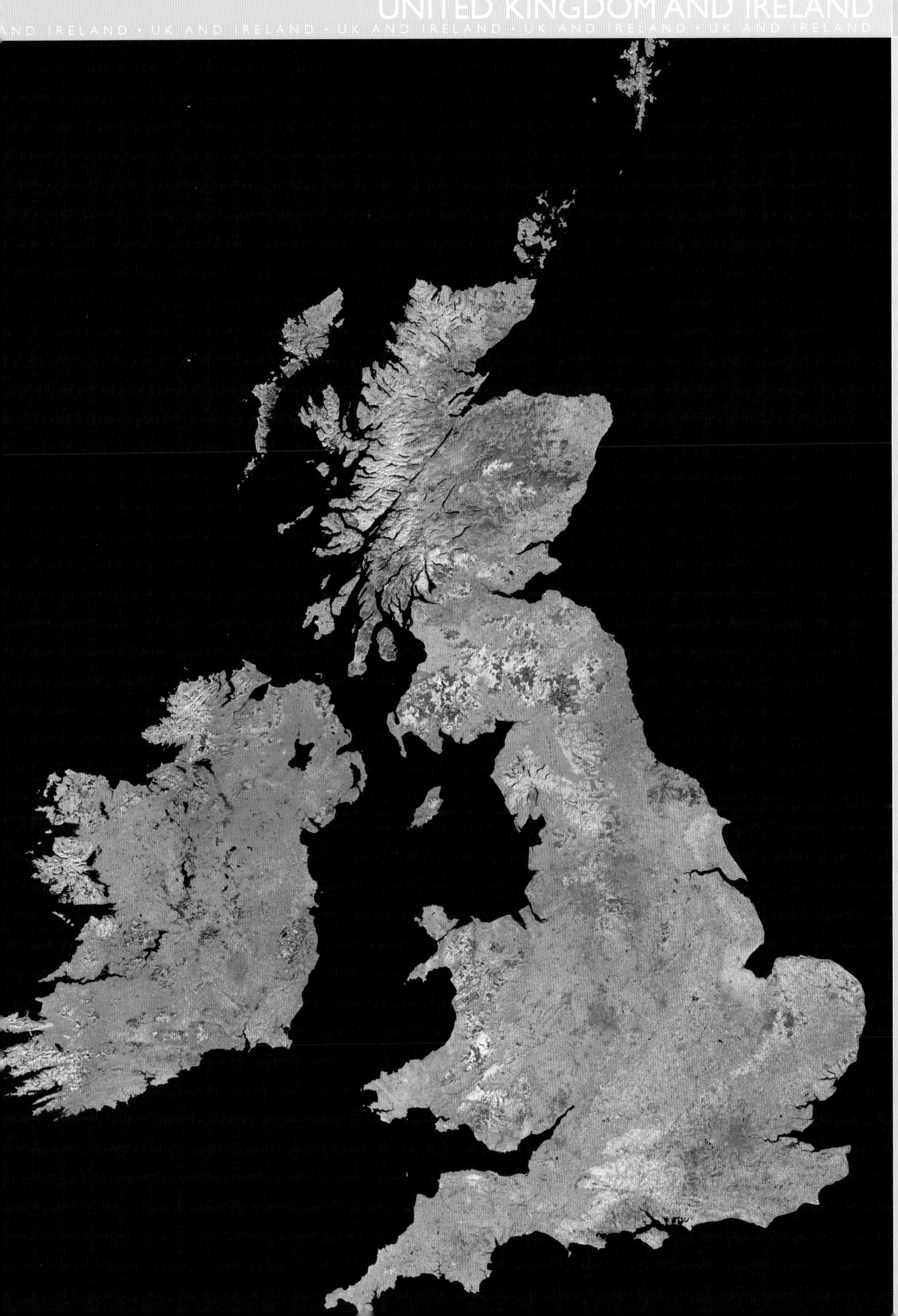

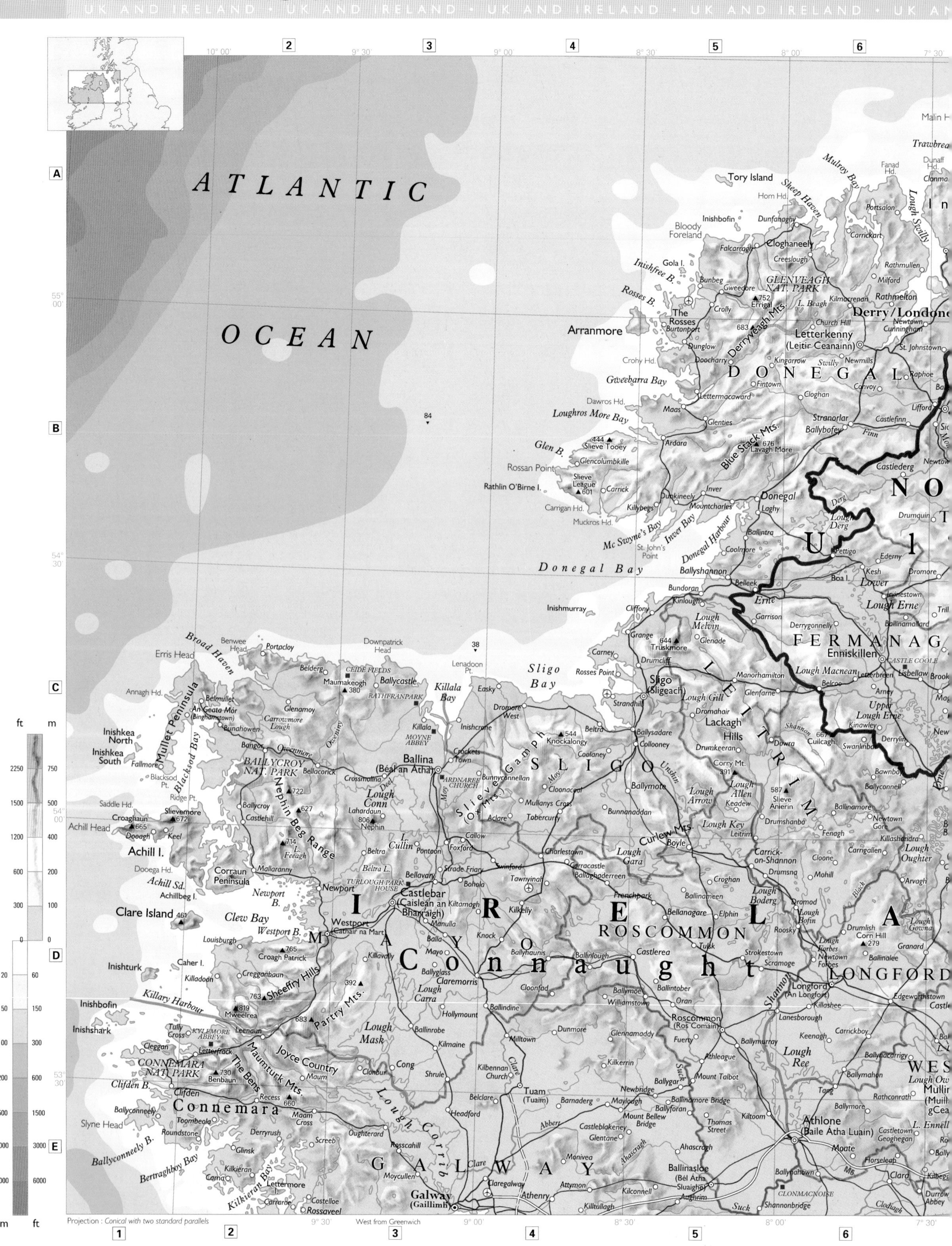
ATLANTIC
OCEAN
Tory Island
Horn Hd.
Sheep Haven
Mulroy Bay
Fanad Hd.
Dunaff Hd.
Malin H
Trawbrea
Clonma
Lough Swilly
Portsalon
Carrickart
Bloody Foreland
Inishbofin
Dunfanaghy
Falcarragh
Cloghaneely
Creeslough
Rathmullen
Milford
Gola I.
Inishfree B.
Bunbeg
Gweedore
GLENVEAGH NAT. PARK
Rosses B.
Crolly
752 Errigal
Kilmacrenan
Rathmelton
L. Beagh
Church Hill
Derry / Londonderry
Newtown Cunningham
The Rosses
Burtonport
683
Derryveagh Mts.
Letterkenny
(Leitir Ceanainn)
St. Johnstown
Arranmore
Dunglow
Doocharry
Kingarrow
Swilly
Newmills
Crohy Hd.
Gweebarra Bay
DONEGAL
Raphoe
Fintown
Convoy
Lettermacaward
Cloghan
Dawros Hd.
Loughros More Bay
Maas
Lifford
84
Glenties
Stranorlar
Ballybofey
Castlefinn
Finn
Glen B.
444 Slieve Tooey
Ardara
Blue Stack Mts.
676 Lavagh More
Glencolumbkille
Rossan Point
Castlederg
Newtown
Slieve League 601
Carrick
Rathlin O'Birne I.
Carrigan Hd.
Dunkineely
Inver
Donegal
Killybegs
Mountcharles
Laghy
Muckros Hd.
Mc Swyne's Bay
Inver Bay
Donegal Harbour
Ballintra
Derg
Lough Derg
Drumquin
St. John's Point
Coolmore
Pettigo
Ederny
Donegal Bay
Ballyshannon
Belleek
Kesh
Dromore
Boa I.
Lower
Bundoran
Erne
Irvinestown
Lough Erne
Kinlough
Inishmurray
Cliffony
Lough Melvin
Garrison
Derrygonnelly
Ballinamallard
Broad Haven
Benwee Head
Portacloy
Downpatrick Head
38
Grange
644 Truskmore
Glenade
FERMANAGH
Enniskillen
Erris Head
Carney
CASTLE COOLE
Belderg
CEIDE FIELDS
Lenadoon Pt.
Sligo Bay
Rosses Point
Drumcliff
Lough Macnean
Letterbreen
Lisbellaw
Brook
Maumakeogh 380
Ballycastle
Killala Bay
Easky
Manorhamilton
RATHFRANPARK
Sligo
(Sligeach)
Belcoo
Annagh Hd.
Mullet Peninsula
Belmullet
An Geata Mór
(Binghamstown)
Glenamoy
Carrowmore Lough
Dromore West
Strandhill
Lough Gill
Glenfarne
Arney
Upper Lough Erne
Inishkea North
Inishkea South
Bunahowen
Killala
MOYNE ABBEY
Inishcrone
544 Knockalongy
Beltra
Ballysadare
Collooney
Dromahair
Lackagh Hills
Shannon
667 Cuilcagh
Dowra
Kinawley
Derrylin
Swanlinbar
Blacksod Bay
Fallmore
Bangor
Owenmore
Ballina
(Béal an Átha)
Crossmolina
Crockets Town
ARDNAREE CHURCH
Bunnyconnellan
SLIGO
Coolaney
Drumkeeran
Corry Mt. 391
LEITRIM
Bawnboy
Ballyconnell
Blacksod Pt.
BALLYCROY NAT. PARK
Bellacorick
Nephin Beg Range
722
Lough Conn
Deel
Moy
Slieve Gamph (Ox Mts.)
Cloonacool
Ballymote
Lough Arrow
Lough Allen
587 Slieve Anierin
Keadew
Ballinamore
Saddle Hd.
Ridge Pt.
Slievemore 672
Croaghaun 665
Achill Head
Dooagh
Keel
Ballycroy
Castlehill
627
Lahardaun
806 Nephin
Aclare
Mullanys Cross
Tobercurry
Bunnanaddan
Unshin
Lough Key
Leitrim
Drumshanbo
Newtown Gore
Killashandra
Achill I.
714 L. Feeagh
L. Cullin
Pontoon
Foxford
Callow
Curlew Mts.
Boyle
Fenagh
Carrigallen
Lough Oughter
Dooega Hd.
Achill Sd.
Achillbeg I.
Corraun Peninsula
Mallaranny
Beltra
Beltra L.
Bellavary
Strade Friary
Swinford
Charlestown
Carracastle
Ballaghaderreen
Lough Gara
Carrick-on-Shannon
Drumsna
Cloone
Mohill
Arvagh
Newport B.
Newport
TURLOUGH PARK HOUSE
Castlebar
(Caisleán an Bharraigh)
Kiltamagh
Bohola
Tawnyinah
Frenchpark
Croghan
Ballinameen
Lough Boderg
Dromod
Black
Clare Island 461
Clew Bay
Westport
(Cathair na Mart)
Westport B.
Manulla
IRELAND
Kilkelly
Bellanagare
Elphin
Roosky
Lough Bofin
Drumlish
Corn Hill 279
Lough Gowna
Granard
Louisburgh
765 Croagh Patrick
MAYO
Balla
Mayo
Knock
Ballyhaunis
Ballinlough
ROSCOMMON
Castlerea
Tulsk
Lough Forbes
Newtown Forbes
Strokestown
Scramoge
Ballinalee
LONGFORD
Inishturk
Caher I.
Killadoon
Cregganbaun
Sheeffry Hills
Killavally
Ballyglass
Claremorris
Connaught
392
Partry Mts.
Lough Carra
Cloonfad
Ballymoe
Williamstown
Ballintober
Oran
Longford (An Longfort)
Killashee
Edgeworthstown
Castle
Inishbofin
Killary Harbour
819 Mweelrea
763
683
Hollymount
Ballindine
Roscommon
(Ros Comáin)
Lanesborough
Inishshark
Tully Cross
KYLEMORE ABBEY
Leenaun
Lough Mask
Ballinrobe
Milltown
Dunmore
Glennamaddy
Fuerty
Ballymurray
Keenagh
Carrickboy
Cleggan
Letterfrack
Joyce Country
Kilmaine
Lough Ree
Ballycarrigy
CONNEMARA NAT. PARK
730 Benbaun
The Bens
Maumturk Mts.
Clonbur
Cong
Maum
Shrule
Kilbennan Church
Clare
Kilkerrin
Athleague
Suck
Mount Talbot
Ballymahon
WES
Lough Owel
Mullingar
Clifden B.
Clifden
Recess
660
Tuam (Tuaim)
Newbridge
Ballygar
Tang
Belclare
Barnaderg
Mayloagh
Ballinamore Bridge
Rathconrath
Ballyconneely
Connemara
Toombeola
Maam Cross
Lough Corrib
Headford
Ballyforan
Kiltoom
Ballymore
Slyne Head
Roundstone
Derryrush
Abbey
Mount Bellew Bridge
Thomas Street
Athlone (Baile Átha Luain)
Castletown Geoghegan
L. Ennell
Ballyconneely B.
Oughterard
Screeb
Castleblakeney
Glentane
Ahascragh
Moate
Glinsk
Rosscahill
GALWAY
Horseleap
Bertraghboy Bay
Kilkieran
Carna
Kilkieran Bay
Lettermore
Carraroe
Moycullen
Claregalway
Monivea
Attymon
Ballinasloe
(Béal Átha Sluaighe)
Aughrim
Ballynahown
Clara
Kilbeggan
Costelloe
Rossaveel
Galway (Gaillimh)
Athenry
Kilconnell
Killtullagh
Suck
CLONMACNOISE
Shannonbridge
Clodiagh
Durrow Abbey
Projection : Conical with two standard parallels
West from Greenwich
10° 00'
9° 30'
9° 00'
8° 30'
8° 00'
7° 30'
55° 00'
54° 30'
54° 00'
53° 30'
A
B
C
D
E
1
2
3
4
5
6
ft
m
2250
1500
1200
600
300
750
500
400
200
100
0
20
50
100
200
500
1000
2000
60
150
300
600
1500
3000
6000

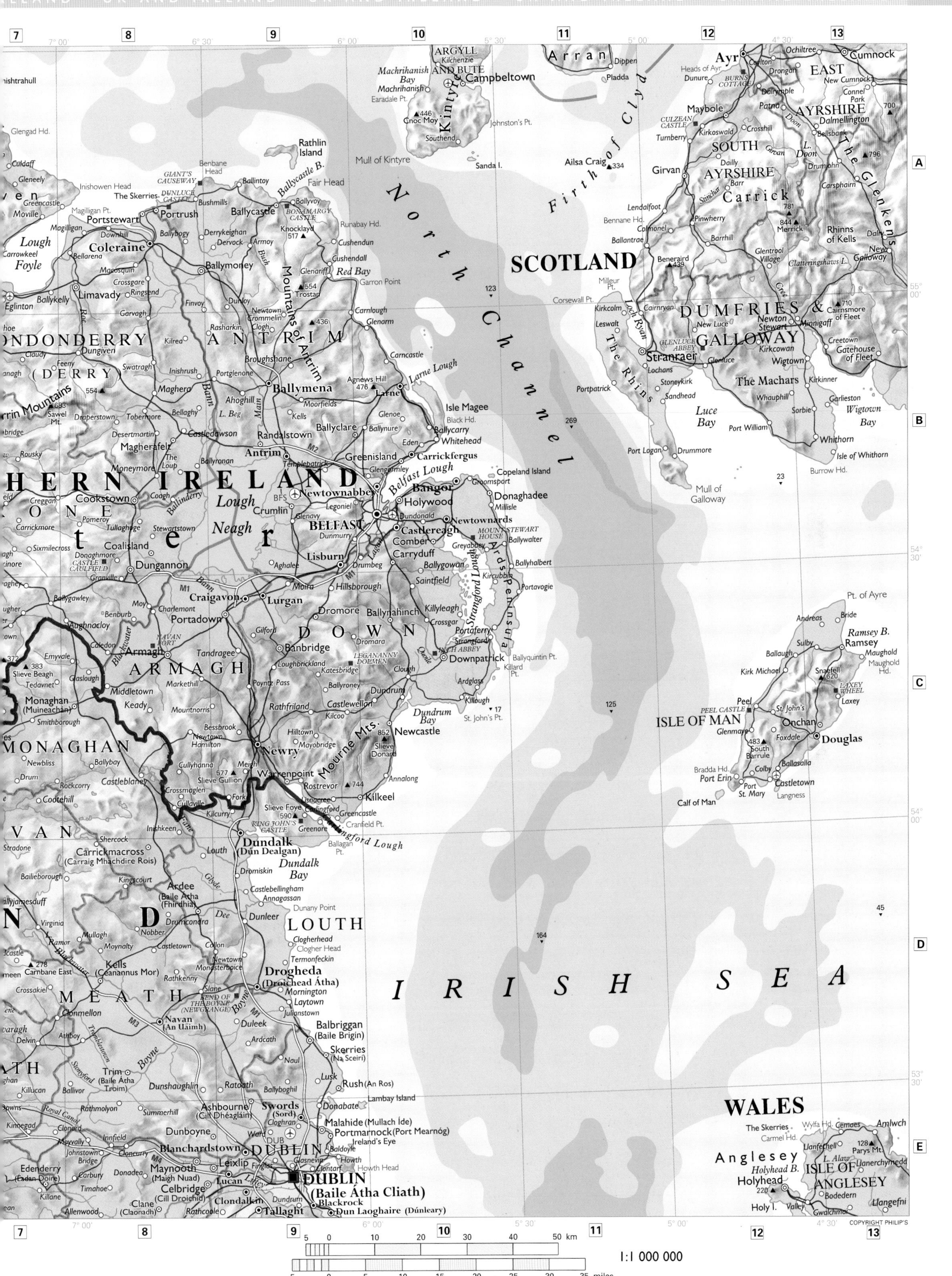
7 8 9 10 11 12 13
7° 00' 6° 30' 6° 00' 5° 30' 5° 00' 4° 30'
A B C D E
55° 00'
54° 30'
54° 00'
53° 30'
North Channel
Firth of Clyde
IRISH SEA
SCOTLAND
WALES
NORTHERN IRELAND
ISLE OF MAN
Arran
Dippen
Pladda
ARGYLL AND BUTE
Kilchenzie
Machrihanish Bay
Machrihanish
Campbeltown
Earadale Pt.
Kintyre
Cnoc Moy
Southend
Johnston's Pt.
Sanda I.
Mull of Kintyre
Ailsa Craig 334
Ayr
Carlton
Drongan
Ochiltree
Cumnock
EAST AYRSHIRE
Heads of Ayr
Dunure
BURNS' COTTAGE
Dalrymple
New Cumnock
Connel Park
Patna
Doon
Maybole
Dalmellington
CULZEAN CASTLE
Kirkoswald
Crosshill
Bellsbank
Turnberry
SOUTH AYRSHIRE
Girvan
L. Doon
Dailly
Drumjohn
Barr
Carsphairn
The Glenkens
Girvan
Carrick
Lendalfoot
Bennane Hd.
Colmonel
Pinwherry
Barrhill
Merrick
Rhinns of Kells
Dalry
Ballantrae
Glentrool Village
New Galloway
Clatteringshaws L.
Benerard 439
Millfeur Pt.
Corsewall Pt.
Kirkcolm
Cairnryan
Loch Ryan
DUMFRIES & GALLOWAY
Cairnsmore of Fleet
Leswalt
New Luce
Newton Stewart
Minnigaff
Creetown
GLENLUCE ABBEY
Stranraer
Glenluce
Kirkcowan
Gatehouse of Fleet
Wigtown
The Rhins
Lochans
Stoneykirk
Sandhead
The Machars
Kirkinner
Portpatrick
Luce Bay
Whauphill
Garlieston
Wigtown Bay
Port William
Sorbie
Whithorn
Port Logan
Drummore
Isle of Whithorn
Burrow Hd.
Mull of Galloway
Glengad Hd.
Inishtrahull
Rathlin Island
Benbane Head
GIANT'S CAUSEWAY
Ballintoy
Ballycastle B.
Fair Head
Culdaff
Gleneely
Inishowen Head
The Skerries
DUNLUCE CASTLE
Bushmills
Ballycastle
Ballyvoy
BONAMARGY CASTLE
Runabay Hd.
Greencastle
Magilligan Pt.
Moville
Portstewart
Portrush
Knocklayd 517
Magilligan
Lough Foyle
Downhill
Ballybogy
Derrykeighan
Dervock
Armoy
Cushendun
Coleraine
Carrowkeel
Bellarena
Cushendall
Ballymoney
Glenariff
Red Bay
Garron Point
Macosquin
Crossgare
Ringsend
Trostan 554
Limavady
Eglinton
Ballykelly
Garvagh
Finvoy
Dunloy
Newtown Crommelin
Carnlough
Glenarm
Clogh
Rasharkin
ANTRIM
Mountains of Antrim
LONDONDERRY (DERRY)
Dungiven
Kilrea
Claudy
Feeny
Broughshane
Carncastle
Swatragh
Inishrush
Portglenone
Larne Lough
Agnews Hill 476
Larne
Sperrin Mountains
Sawel Mt. 683
Maghera
Ahoghill
Ballymena
Bann
Bellaghy
L. Beg
Moorfields
Isle Magee
Draperstown
Tobermore
Kells
Glenoe
Black Hd.
Ballyclare
Ballynure
Ballycarry
Whitehead
Desertmartin
Castledawson
Randalstown
Eden
Magherafelt
Ballyronan
Antrim
Templepatrick
Greenisland
Carrickfergus
Rousky
The Loup
Moneymore
Glengormley
Belfast Lough
Copeland Island
Creggan
Cookstown
BFS
Newtownabbey
Bangor
Groomsport
Donaghadee
Millisle
Lough Neagh
Crumlin
Holywood
Pomeroy
Leganiel
Glenavy
Dundonald
Carrickmore
Tullaghoge
Stewartstown
BELFAST
Newtownards
Castlereagh
MOUNT STEWART HOUSE
Ballywalter
Dunmurry
Comber
Greyabbey
Sixmilecross
Coalisland
Ulster
Lisburn
Carryduff
Ards Peninsula
Donaghmore
CASTLE CAULFIELD
Dungannon
Aghalee
Lagan
Ballygowan
Ballyhalbert
Drumbeg
Kircubbin
Granville
Bann
Moira
Hillsborough
Saintfield
Strangford Lough
Portavogie
M1
Craigavon
Lurgan
Ballygawley
Moy
Charlemont
Dromore
Ballynahinch
Killyleagh
Benburb
Portadown
Crossgar
Aughnacloy
NAVAN FORT
DOWN
Portaferry
Strangford
Blackwater
Caledon
Armagh
Gilford
Banbridge
Dromara
INCH ABBEY
Downpatrick
Ballyquintin Pt.
Emyvale
Tandragee
LEGANANNY DOLMEN
Killard Pt.
ARMAGH
Loughbrickland
Katesbridge
Slieve Beagh 383
Glaslough
Clough
Quoile
Tedavnet
Middletown
Markethill
Poyntz Pass
Ballyroney
Ardglass
Keady
Dundrum
Monaghan (Muineachán)
Mountnorris
Rathfriland
Castlewellan
Killough
Smithborough
Kilcoo
Dundrum Bay
St. John's Pt.
Bessbrook
Hilltown
Newcastle
MONAGHAN
Newtown Hamilton
Mayobridge
Mourne Mts.
Slieve Donard 852
Newbliss
Ballybay
Newry
Cullyhanna
Meigh
Slieve Gullion 577
Drum
Castleblaney
Warrenpoint
Annalong
Rockcorry
Crossmaglen
Forkhill
Rostrevor
744
Kilkeel
Cootehill
Cullaville
Kilcurry
Slieve Foye 590
Carlingford
Greencastle
KING JOHN'S CASTLE
Greenore
Cranfield Pt.
Carlingford Lough
CAVAN
Inishkeen
Shercock
Dundalk (Dún Dealgan)
Ballagan Pt.
Stradone
Carrickmacross (Carraig Mhachdire Rois)
Louth
Dundalk Bay
Dromiskin
Bailieborough
Kingscourt
Ardee (Baile Átha Fhirdhia)
Glyde
Castlebellingham
Annagassan
Ballyjamesduff
Dunany Point
Dee
Dunleer
LOUTH
Virginia
Drumconrath
Nobber
Clogherhead
Clogher Head
Mullagh
Moynalty
Castletown
Collon
Termonfeckin
Carnbane East 278
Kells (Ceanannus Mor)
Newtown Monasterboice
Drogheda (Droichead Átha)
Rathkenny
Slane
BEND OF THE BOYNE (NEWGRANGE)
Mornington
Laytown
Crossakiel
MEATH
Boyne
Julianstown
Clonmellon
Navan (An Uaimh)
M3
M1
Duleek
Balbriggan (Baile Brigín)
Delvin
Athboy
Ardcath
Skerries (Na Sceirí)
Trimblestown
Naul
Trim (Baile Átha Troim)
Boyne
Killucan
Ballivor
Dunshaughlin
Ratoath
Ballyboghil
Lusk
Rush (An Ros)
Lambay Island
Royal Canal
Rathmolyon
Summerhill
Ashbourne (Cill Dhéagláin)
Swords (Sord)
Cloghran
Donabate
Kinnegad
Clonard
Dunboyne
Ward
Malahide (Mullach Íde)
Portmarnock (Port Mearnóg)
Moyvally
Innfield
Johnstown Bridge
Clonee
Blanchardstown
DUB
DUBLIN
Ireland's Eye
Baldoyle
Howth
Howth Head
Edenderry (Éadan Doire)
Carbury
Donadea
Maynooth (Maigh Nuad)
Leixlip
Finglas
Glasnevin
Clontarf
M4
Lucan
Liffey
DUBLIN (Baile Átha Cliath)
Timahoe
Celbridge
Clane (Claonadh)
(Cill Droichid)
Clondalkin
Dundrum
Blackrock
Killane
Allenwood
Rathcoole
Tallaght
Dun Laoghaire (Dúnleary)
Pt. of Ayre
Andreas
Bride
Ramsey B.
Ramsey
Sulby
Ballaugh
Maughold
Maughold Hd.
Kirk Michael
Snaefell 620
LAXEY WHEEL
Laxey
Peel
PEEL CASTLE
St. John's
Onchan
Glenmaye
Foxdale
Douglas
South Barrule 483
Ballasalla
Bradda Hd.
Port Erin
Colby
Castletown
Port St. Mary
Langness
Calf of Man
The Skerries
Wylfa Hd.
Cemaes
Amlwch
Carmel Hd.
Llanfechell
Parys Mt. 128
Anglesey
L. Alaw
Llanerchymedd
Holyhead B.
ISLE OF ANGLESEY
Holyhead
220
Bodedern
Holy I.
Valley
Gwalchmai
Llangefni
123
269
23
125
17
164
45
700
796
781
844
710
COPYRIGHT PHILIP'S
5 0 10 20 30 40 50 km
5 0 5 10 15 20 25 30 35 miles
1:1 000 000

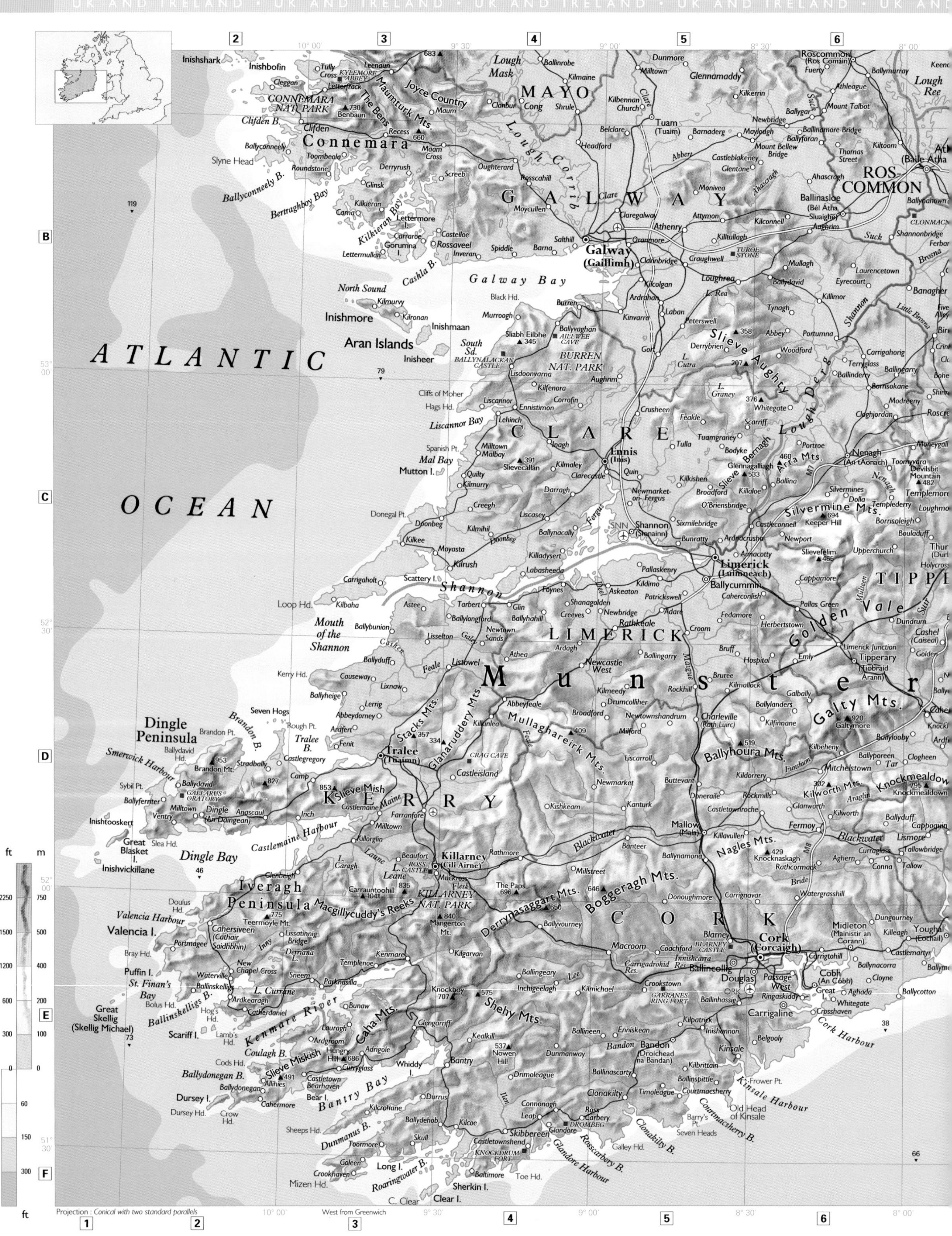
ATLANTIC OCEAN
MAYO
GALWAY
ROSCOMMON
CLARE
LIMERICK
KERRY
CORK
TIPPERARY
Munster
Connemara
Galway Bay
Aran Islands
Inishmore
Inishmaan
Inisheer
Dingle Peninsula
Dingle Bay
Iveragh Peninsula
Macgillycuddy's Reeks
Bantry Bay
Kenmare River
Shannon
Mouth of the Shannon
Lough Corrib
Lough Mask
Lough Derg
Lough Ree
Galway (Gaillimh)
Limerick (Luimneach)
Cork (Corcaigh)
Killarney (Cill Airne)
Tralee (Trá Lí)
Ennis (Inis)
Tipperary (Tiobraid Árann)
Galty Mts.
Slieve Aughty
Silvermine Mts.
Boggeragh Mts.
Nagles Mts.
Ballyhoura Mts.
Caha Mts.
Shehy Mts.
Cork Harbour
Kinsale Harbour
Projection : Conical with two standard parallels
West from Greenwich
ft
m

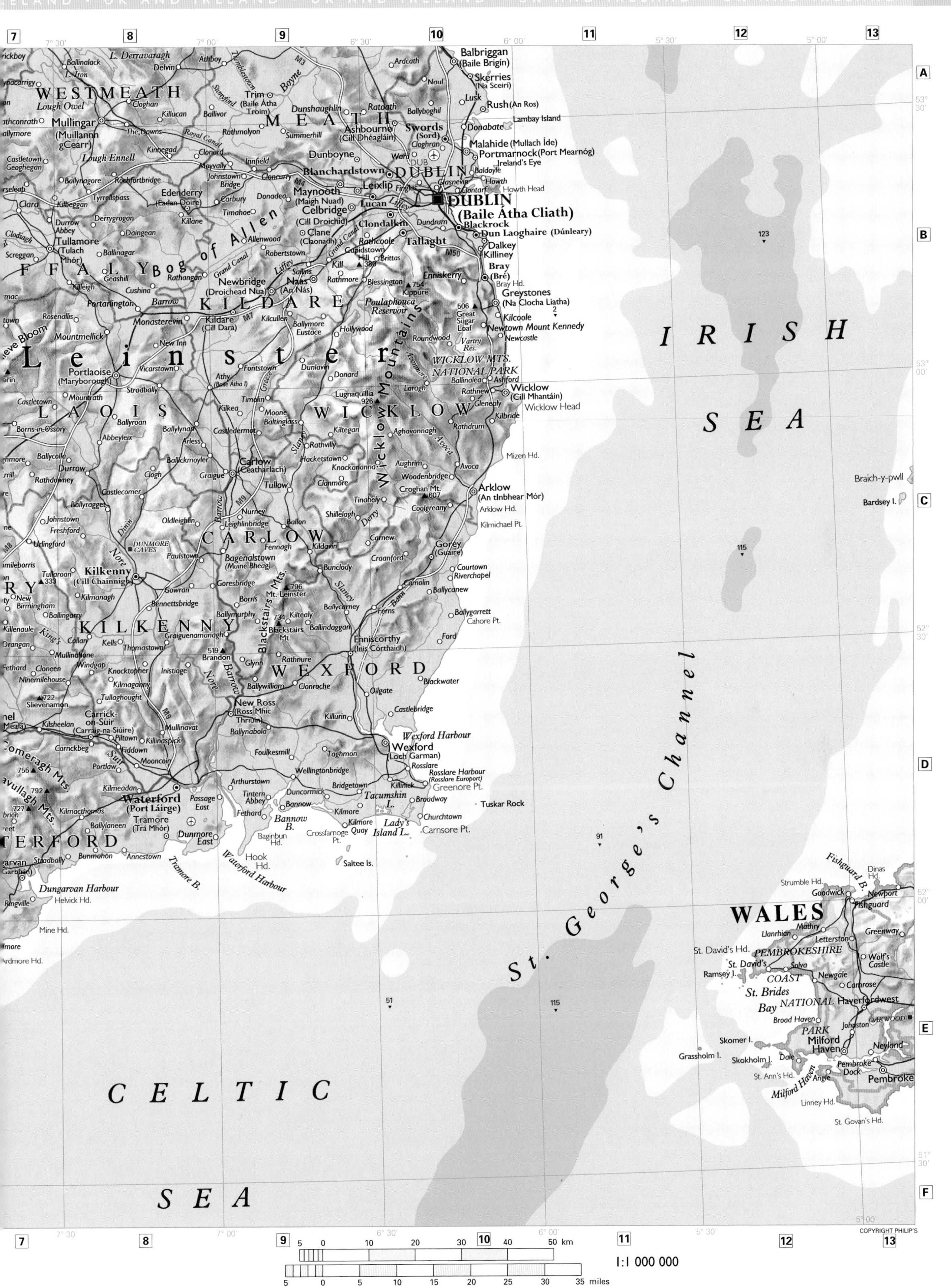

WESTMEATH

L. Derravaragh
Ballinalack
Delvin
ickboy
Athboy
L. Iron
Ardcath
Balbriggan
(Baile Brigín)
Skerries
(Na Sceirí)

rracarrigg
Mullingar
(Muilleann
gCearr)
The Downs
Lough Ennell
Killucan
Ballivor
Trim
(Baile Átha
Troim)
Dunshaughlin
Ratoath
Ballyboghil
Naul
Lusk
Rush (An Ros)
Donabate
Lambay Island

MEATH

Ashbourne
(Cill Dhéagláin)
Swords
(Sord)
Malahide (Mullach Íde)
Portmarnock (Port Mearnóg)
Ireland's Eye

Castletown
Geoghegan
Ballynagore
Rochfortbridge
Summerhill
Rathmolyon
Dunboyne
Cloghran
DUB

Clara
Kilbeggan
Tyrrellspass
Johnstown
Bridge
Moyvally
Cloncurry
Blanchardstown
Maynooth
(Maigh Nuad)
Leixlip
Fingles
Howth
Howth Head

rseleap
Durrow
Abbey
Derrygrogan
Daingean
Edenderry
(Éadan Doire)
Carbury
Timahoe
Donadea
Lucan
Liffey
DUBLIN
(Baile Átha Cliath)
Clontarf

mac
Tullamore
(Tulach
Mhór)
Ballinagar
Geashill
Cushina
Allenwood
Celbridge
(Cill Droichid)
Clane
(Claonadh)
Clondalkin
Dundrum
Blackrock

FFALY
Bog of Allen
Killeigh
Portarlington
Rathangan
Newbridge
(Droichead Nua)
Naas
(An Nás)
Rathcoole
Saggart
Tallaght
Dún Laoghaire (Dúnleary)
Dalkey
Killiney

own
Rosenallis
Portlaoise
(Maryborough)
Monasterevin
Kildare
(Cill Dara)
Kilcullen
Ballymore
Eustace
Cupidstown
Hill
390
Brittas
Blessington
Kippure
Bray
(Bré)
Bray Hd.

Slieve
Bloom
Mountmellick
KILDARE
New Inn
Vicarstown
Hollywood
Poulaphouca
Reservoir
506
Great
Sugar
Loaf
Enniskerry
Greystones
(Na Clocha Liatha)

arin
Mountrath
Stradbally
Athy
(Baile Átha I)
Fontstown
Dunlavin
Roundwood
Vartry
Res.
Newcastle
Kilcoole
Newtown Mount Kennedy
2

L e i n s t e r

LAOIS
Castletown
Borris-in-Ossory
Abbeyleix
Ballyroan
Timolin
Moone
Donard
Laragh
**WICKLOW MTS.
NATIONAL PARK**
Ballinalea
Ashford

more
Ballycolla
Durrow
Rathdowney
Clogh
Ballylynan
Arless
Castledermot
Baltinglass
Wicklow Mountains
Lugnaquillia
926
Aghavannagh
Rathnew
Glenealy
Wicklow
(Cill Mhantáin)
Wicklow Head

rill
Ballyragget
Castlecomer
Ballacolly
Rathvilly
Kiltegan
Hacketstown
Rathdrum
Kilbride

I R I S H

Johnstown
Freshford
Urlingford
Graigue
Carlow
(Ceatharlach)
Tullow
Knockananna
Aughrim
Woodenbridge
Avoca
Mizen Hd.

ny
New
Birmingham
Ballinagarry
Kilmanagh
CARLOW
Leighlinbridge
Nurney
Clonmore
Croghan Mt.
607
Arklow
(An tInbhear Mór)
Arklow Hd.

Tullaroan
333
Kilkenny
(Cill Chainnigh)
Gowran
Bennettsbridge
Bagenalstown
(Muine Bheag)
Shillelagh
Darry
Tinahely
Coolgreany
Kilmichael Pt.

S E A

Kilmanagh
Kells
Thomastown
Goresbridge
Borris
796
Mt. Leinster
Carnew
Craanford
Gorey
(Guaire)
Courtown
Riverchapel

Callan
Ballymurphy
734
Kiltealy
Ballycarney
Ferns
Camolin
Ballycanew

Cloneen
Ninemilehouse
Windgap
Knocktopher
Inistioge
519
Brandon
Glynn
Ballyduff
Slaney
Enniscorthy
(Inis Córthaidh)
Ballygarrett
Cahore Pt.

KILKENNY
Mullinahone
722
Slievenamon
Tullaghought
Kilmaganny
Graiguenamanagh
Rathnure
Clonroche
Ford
Blackwater

el
Meala
Carrick-on-Suir
(Carraig-na-Siúire)
Piltown
Fiddown
Mullinavat
Ballywilliam
Oilgate
Castlebridge

omeragh Mts.
755
Kilsheelan
Carrickbeg
Killinaspick
Mooncoin
Ballynabola
Foulkesmill
Taghmon
Wexford
(Loch Garman)
Wexford Harbour

avullagh Mts.
792
Portlaw
WEXFORD
Wellingtonbridge
Rosslare
Rosslare Harbour
(Rosslare Europort)
Greenore Pt.

brien
727
Kilmeaden
Arthurstown
Duncormick
Bridgetown
Killinick
Rosslare

arvan
Garbhán)
Kilmacthomas
Waterford
(Port Láirge)
Tintern
Abbey
Bannow
Kilmore
Tacumshin
L.
Broadway
Churchtown
Tuskar Rock

ingville
Ballylaneen
Tramore
(Trá Mhór)
Passage
East
Fethard
Bannow
B.
Kilmore
Quay
Lady's
Island L.
Carnsore Pt.

RFORD
Stradbally
Bunmahon
Annestown
Dunmore
East
Baginbun
Hd.
Crossfarnoge
Pt.
Saltee Is.

more
Mine Hd.
Dungarvan Harbour
Helvick Hd.
Hook
Hd.
Waterford Harbour

ardmore Hd.

C E L T I C

S E A

IRISH

SEA

123

Braich-y-pwll
Bardsey I.

115

St. George's Channel

91

115

51

WALES

Fishguard B.
Dinas
Hd.
Strumble Hd.
Goodwick
Newport
Fishguard

Llanrhian
Mathry
Letterston
Greenway

St. David's Hd.
PEMBROKESHIRE
St. David's
Solva
Newgale
Wolf's
Castle
Ramsey I.
COAST
Simpson Cross

St. Brides
Bay
NATIONAL
Haverfordwest
Broad Haven
Johnston
OAKWOOD

Skomer I.
PARK
Milford
Haven
Pembroke
Dock
Neyland

Grassholm I.
Skokholm I.
Dale
St. Ann's Hd.
Angle
Pembroke

Milford Haven
Linney Hd.
St. Govan's Hd.

1:1 000 000

5 10 20 30 40 50 km

5 0 5 10 15 20 25 30 35 miles

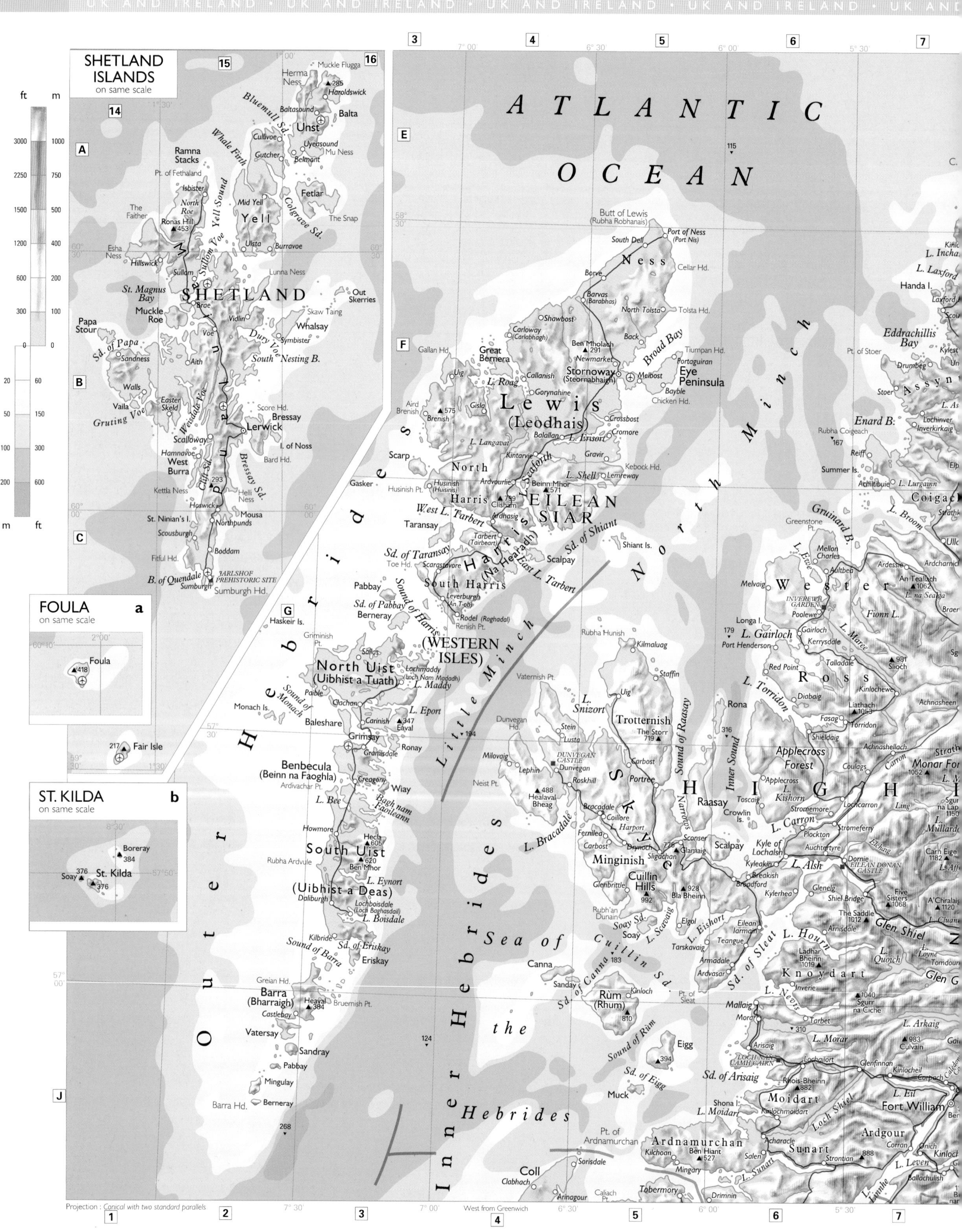

SHETLAND ISLANDS
on same scale

FOULA
on same scale

ST. KILDA
on same scale

ATLANTIC OCEAN

SHETLAND

Yell

Unst

Fetlar

Lerwick

Bressay

SHETLAND

Foula

Fair Isle

Boreray
St. Kilda
Soay

Butt of Lewis
(Rubha Robhanais)

Ness

Lewis
(Leodhais)

Stornoway
(Steornabhaigh)

Broad Bay
Eye Peninsula

North Minch

Harris

EILEAN SIAR

North Uist
(Uibhist a Tuath)

WESTERN ISLES

Benbecula
(Beinn na Faoghla)

South Uist
(Uibhist a Deas)

Outer Hebrides

Sea of the Hebrides

Inner Hebrides

Barra
(Bharraigh)

Little Minch

Skye

Trotternish

Raasay

Cuillin Hills

Minginish

Rùm
(Rhum)

Eigg

Muck

Coll

Wester Ross

HIGHLAND

Applecross Forest

Knoydart

Moidart

Ardgour

Fort William

Ardnamurchan

Sunart

Projection : Conical with two standard parallels

West from Greenwich

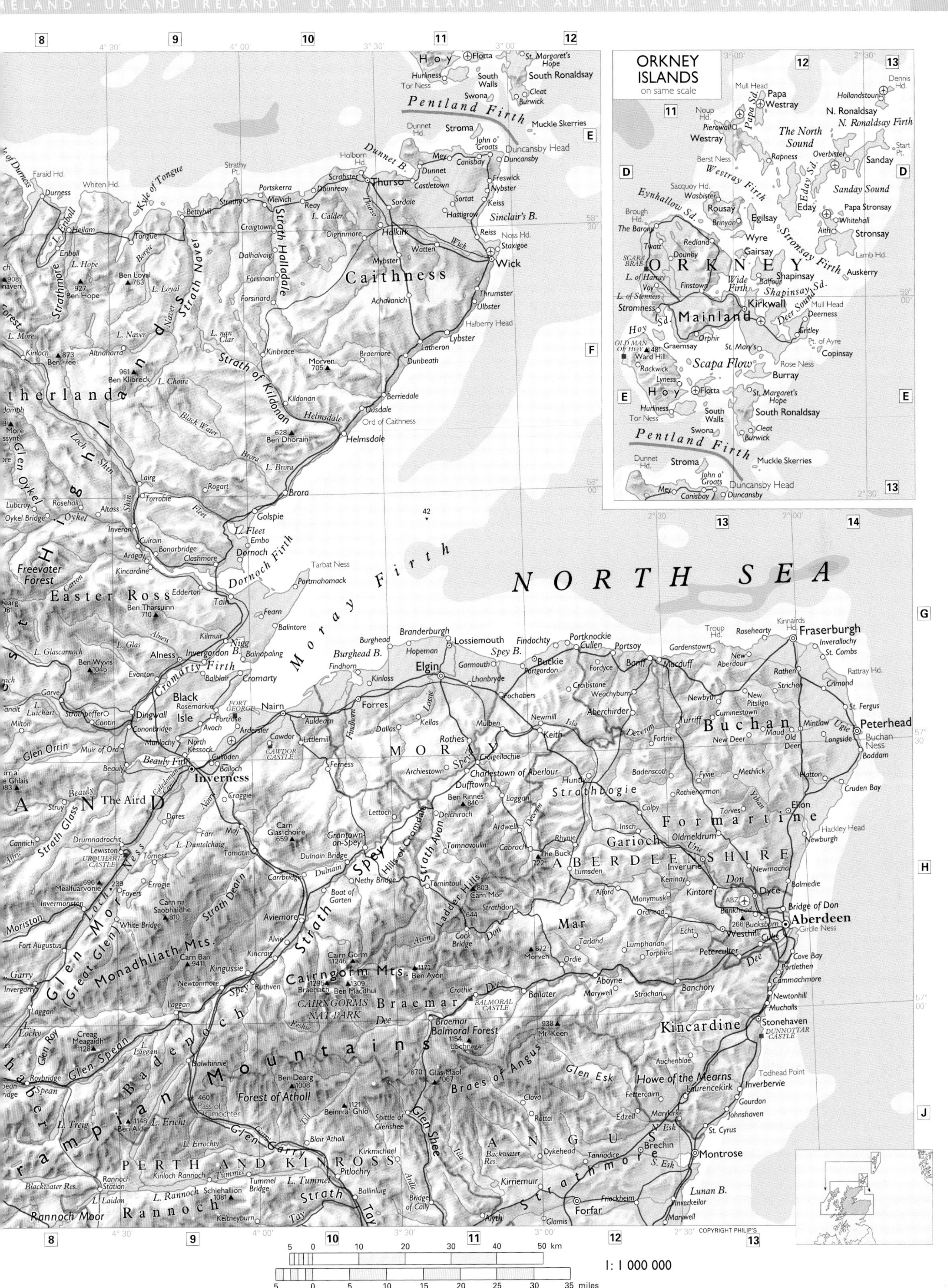

ORKNEY ISLANDS
on same scale

NORTH SEA

Caithness

Pentland Firth

Moray Firth

Easter Ross

Black Isle

Inverness

MORAY

BUCHAN

ABERDEENSHIRE

Aberdeen

Cairngorm Mts.

CAIRNGORMS NAT. PARK

Braemar

Grampian Mountains

Kincardine

PERTH AND KINROSS

ANGUS

1 : 1 000 000

COPYRIGHT PHILIP'S

5 0 10 20 30 40 50 km

5 0 5 10 15 20 25 30 35 miles

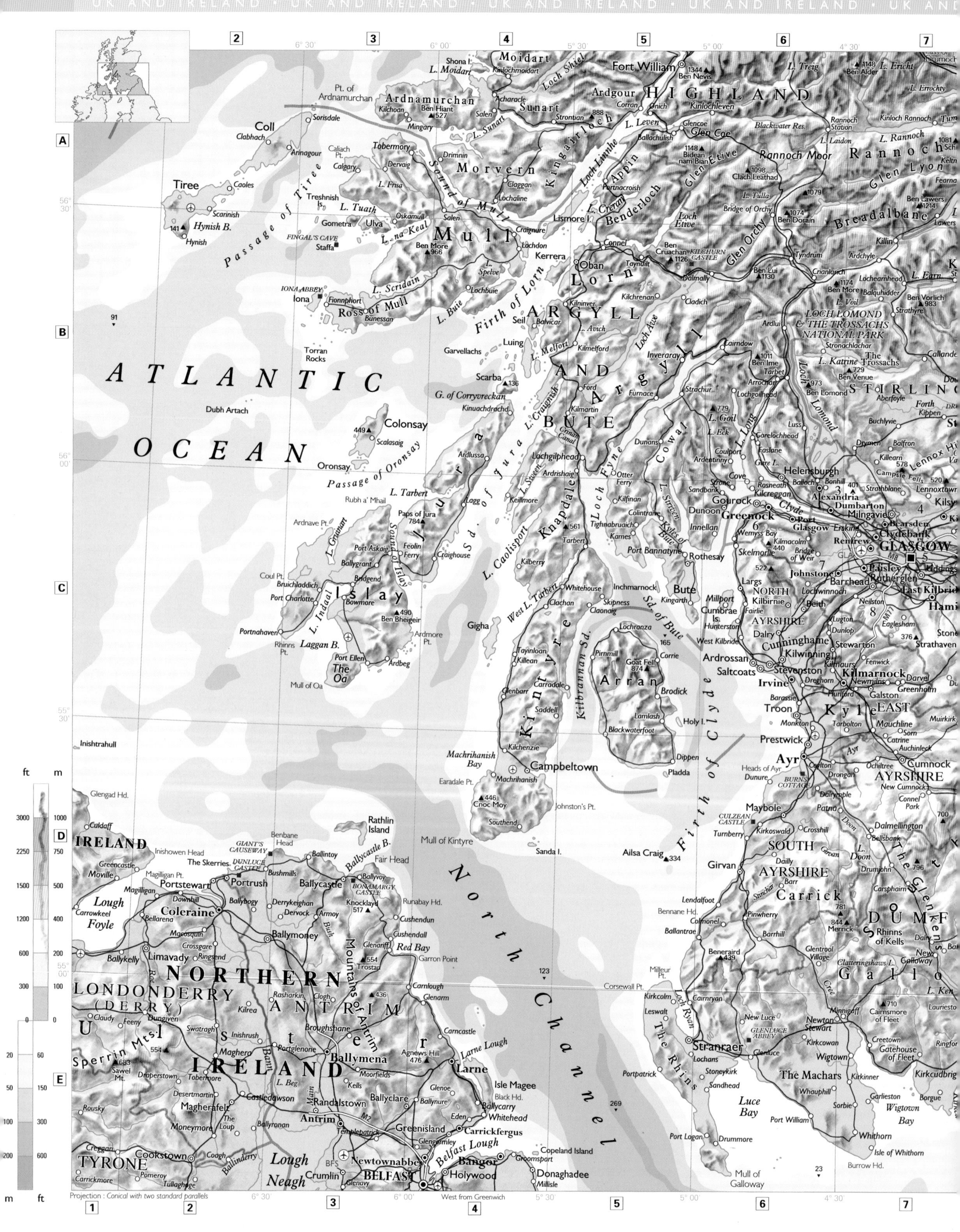
ATLANTIC OCEAN
HIGHLAND
ARGYLL AND BUTE
STIRLING
NORTH AYRSHIRE
EAST AYRSHIRE
SOUTH AYRSHIRE
NORTHERN IRELAND
LONDONDERRY (DERRY)
ANTRIM
TYRONE
IRELAND
North Channel
Firth of Clyde
Firth of Lorn
Sound of Mull
Passage of Tiree
Passage of Oronsay
Sound of Jura
Sound of Islay
Kilbrannan Sd.
Sd. of Bute
Loch Linnhe
Loch Fyne
Loch Lomond
Loch Ryan
Luce Bay
Wigtown Bay
Lough Neagh
Lough Foyle
Belfast Lough
Larne Lough
Coll
Tiree
Mull
Iona
Staffa
Ulva
Colonsay
Oronsay
Jura
Islay
Gigha
Arran
Bute
Kerrera
Lismore I.
Scarba
Luing
Seil
Rathlin Island
Ailsa Craig
Sanda I.
Holy I.
Pladda
Isle Magee
Copeland Island
Inishtrahull
Dubh Artach
Torran Rocks
Moidart
Ardnamurchan
Pt. of Ardnamurchan
Morvern
Sunart
Ardgour
Appin
Benderloch
Lorn
Knapdale
Kintyre
Cowal
Cunninghame
Kyle
Carrick
The Machars
The Rhins
Mull of Kintyre
Mull of Galloway
Mull of Oa
The Oa
Fort William
Ben Nevis
Glen Coe
Rannoch Moor
Breadalbane
Glen Lyon
Glen Etive
Glen Orchy
Ben More
Ben Lomond
Ben Lui
Ben Cruachan
Ben Hiant
LOCH LOMOND & THE TROSSACHS NATIONAL PARK
The Trossachs
Oban
Tobermory
Inveraray
Lochgilphead
Campbeltown
Tarbert
Dunoon
Rothesay
Gourock
Greenock
Helensburgh
Dumbarton
Alexandria
Clydebank
GLASGOW
Paisley
Renfrew
Johnstone
Barrhead
Rutherglen
East Kilbride
Kilmarnock
Irvine
Kilwinning
Stevenston
Saltcoats
Ardrossan
Largs
Troon
Prestwick
Ayr
Maybole
Girvan
Cumnock
Stranraer
Portpatrick
Newton Stewart
Wigtown
Whithorn
Isle of Whithorn
Kirkcudbright
Gatehouse of Fleet
Brodick
Lamlash
Port Ellen
Bowmore
Port Askaig
Port Charlotte
Portnahaven
Machrihanish
Southend
Coleraine
Portrush
Portstewart
Ballycastle
Ballymoney
Limavady
Ballymena
Larne
Carrickfergus
Whitehead
Antrim
Randalstown
Magherafelt
Cookstown
Newtownabbey
BELFAST
Holywood
Bangor
Donaghadee
Moville
Greencastle
Giant's Causeway
Bushmills
Fair Head
Red Bay
Cushendall
Cushendun
Sperrin Mts.
Sawel Mt.
Mountains of Antrim
Projection : Conical with two standard parallels
West from Greenwich
ft
m
3000
2250
1500
1200
600
300
1000
750
500
400
200
100
0
20
50
100
200
60
150
300
600

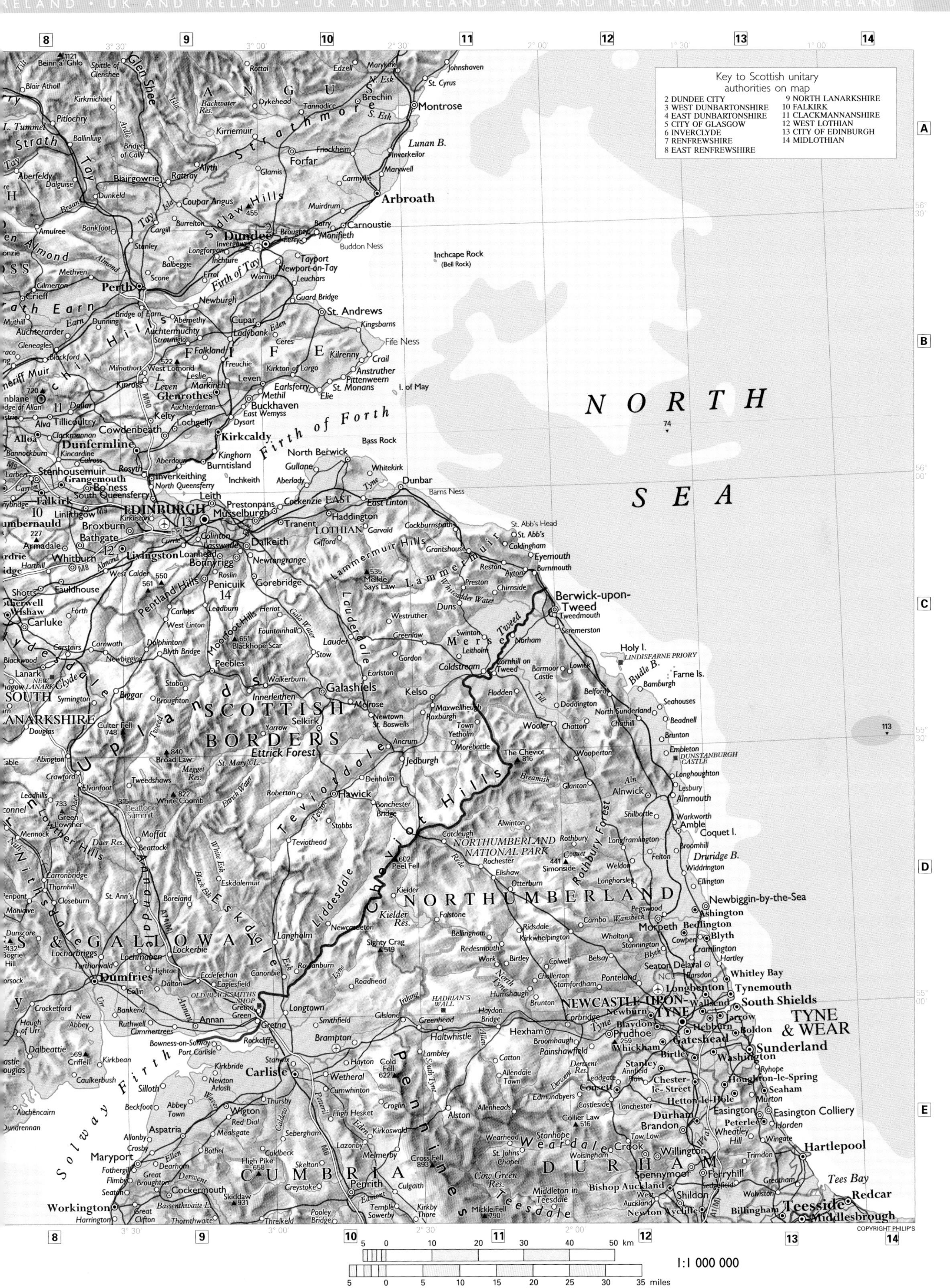

Key to Scottish unitary authorities on map
2 DUNDEE CITY
3 WEST DUNBARTONSHIRE
4 EAST DUNBARTONSHIRE
5 CITY OF GLASGOW
6 INVERCLYDE
7 RENFREWSHIRE
8 EAST RENFREWSHIRE
9 NORTH LANARKSHIRE
10 FALKIRK
11 CLACKMANNANSHIRE
12 WEST LOTHIAN
13 CITY OF EDINBURGH
14 MIDLOTHIAN

NORTH

SEA

Firth of Tay

Firth of Forth

ANGUS

Montrose

Arbroath

Dundee

Perth

St. Andrews

FIFE

EDINBURGH

LOTHIAN

SCOTTISH
BORDERS

Berwick-upon-Tweed

NORTHUMBERLAND

NORTHUMBERLAND
NATIONAL PARK

Cheviot Hills

Teviotdale

& GALLOWAY

Dumfries

Carlisle

CUMBRIA

Pennines

NEWCASTLE-UPON-TYNE

TYNE
& WEAR

Sunderland

DURHAM

Teesdale

Weardale

Hartlepool

Tees Bay

Teesside
Middlesbrough

Redcar

1:1 000 000

COPYRIGHT PHILIP'S

5 0   10   20   30   40   50 km

5 0   5   10   15   20   25   30   35 miles

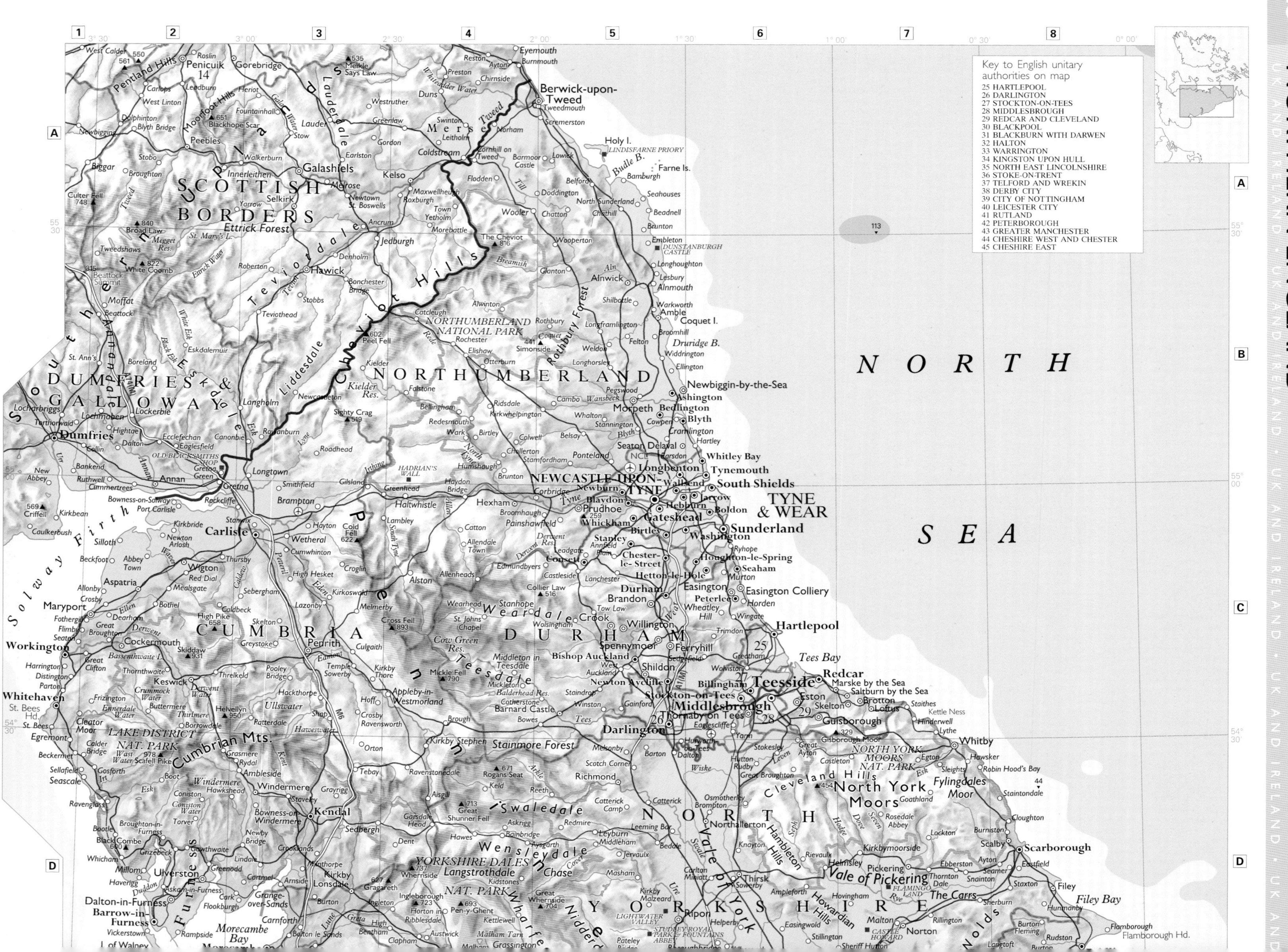

Key to English unitary
authorities on map
25 HARTLEPOOL
26 DARLINGTON
27 STOCKTON-ON-TEES
28 MIDDLESBROUGH
29 REDCAR AND CLEVELAND
30 BLACKPOOL
31 BLACKBURN WITH DARWEN
32 HALTON
33 WARRINGTON
34 KINGSTON UPON HULL
35 NORTH EAST LINCOLNSHIRE
36 STOKE-ON-TRENT
37 TELFORD AND WREKIN
38 DERBY CITY
39 CITY OF NOTTINGHAM
40 LEICESTER CITY
41 RUTLAND
42 PETERBOROUGH
43 GREATER MANCHESTER
44 CHESHIRE WEST AND CHESTER
45 CHESHIRE EAST

NORTH SEA

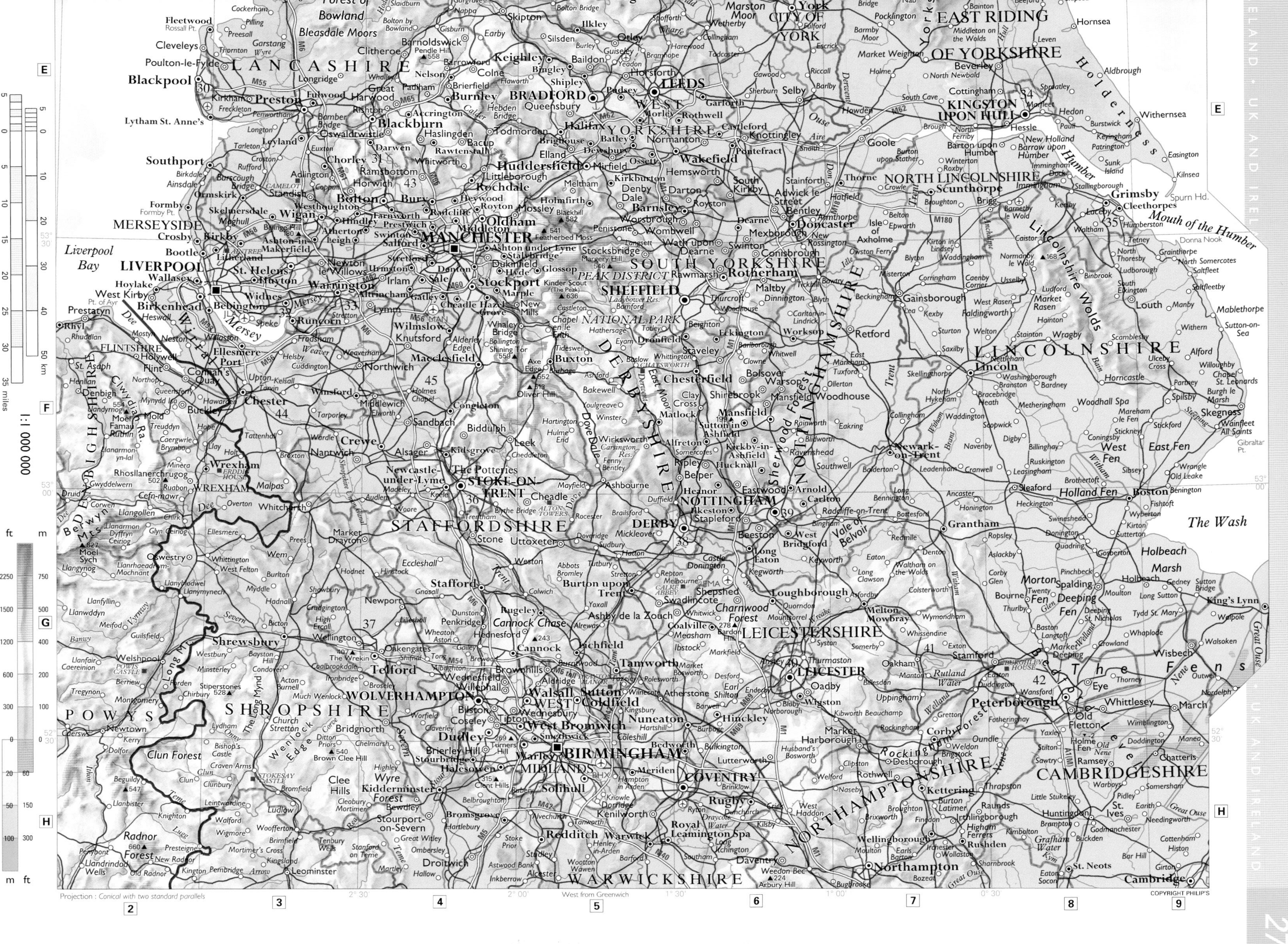
LANCASHIRE
WEST YORKSHIRE
SOUTH YORKSHIRE
EAST RIDING OF YORKSHIRE
CITY OF YORK
KINGSTON UPON HULL
NORTH LINCOLNSHIRE
LINCOLNSHIRE
NOTTINGHAMSHIRE
DERBYSHIRE
STAFFORDSHIRE
SHROPSHIRE
LEICESTERSHIRE
NORTHAMPTONSHIRE
WARWICKSHIRE
CAMBRIDGESHIRE
WEST MIDLANDS
MERSEYSIDE
FLINTSHIRE
DENBIGHSHIRE
WREXHAM
POWYS
PEAK DISTRICT NATIONAL PARK
Forest of Bowland
Bleasdale Moors
Holderness
Lincolnshire Wolds
Mouth of the Humber
The Wash
The Fens
Sherwood Forest
Cannock Chase
Charnwood Forest
Rockingham Forest
Clun Forest
Radnor Forest
Clwydian Ra.
Berwyn Mts.
Wirral
Liverpool Bay
Vale of Belvoir
LEEDS
BRADFORD
MANCHESTER
LIVERPOOL
SHEFFIELD
NOTTINGHAM
DERBY
LEICESTER
BIRMINGHAM
COVENTRY
WOLVERHAMPTON
STOKE-ON-TRENT
Blackpool
Preston
Blackburn
Chester
Shrewsbury
Lincoln
Grimsby
Scunthorpe
Doncaster
Peterborough
Northampton
Cambridge
1:1 000 000
km
miles
ft
m
Projection : Conical with two standard parallels
West from Greenwich
COPYRIGHT PHILIP'S

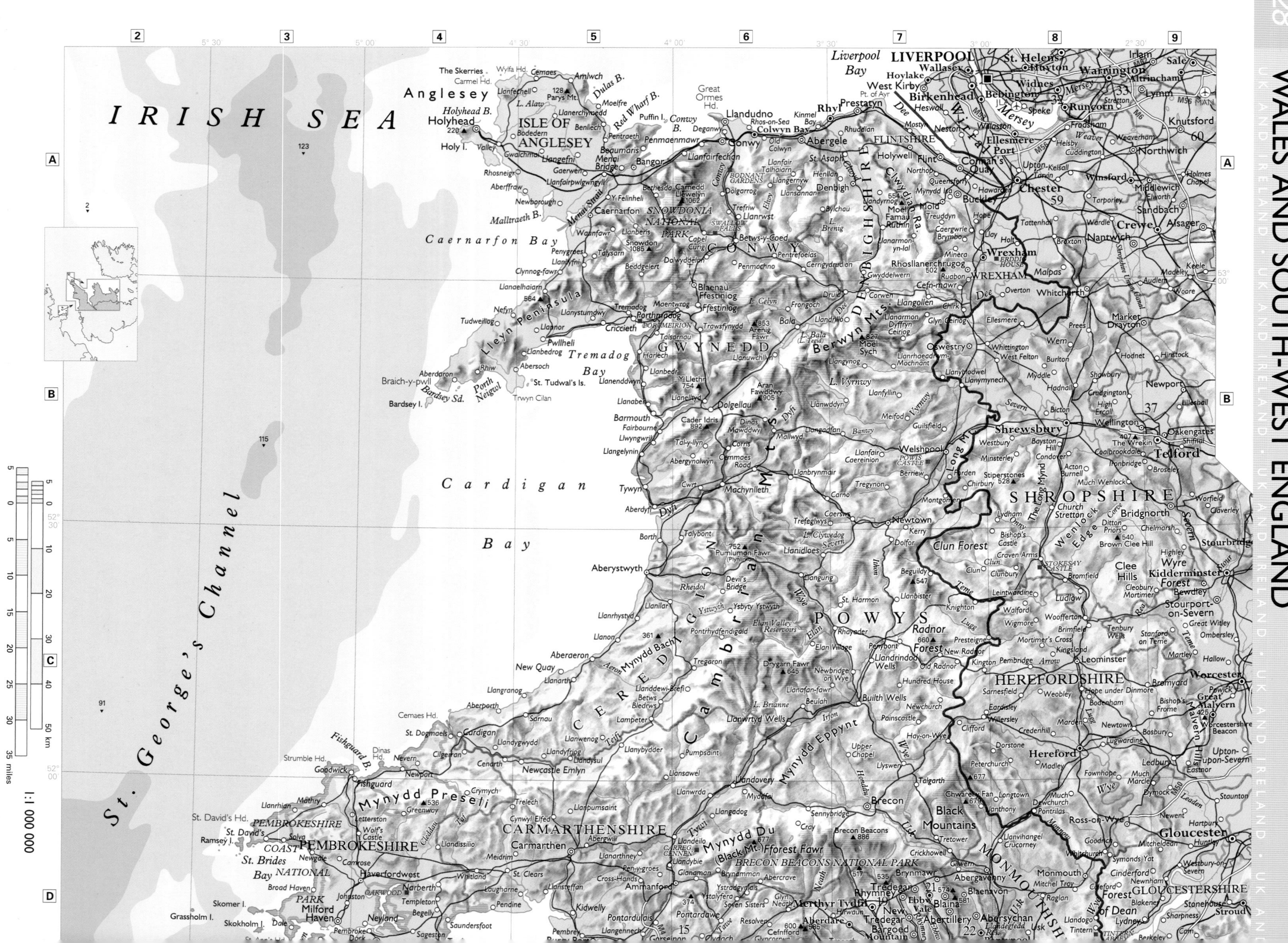
IRISH SEA
St. George's Channel
Cardigan Bay
Caernarfon Bay
Tremadog Bay
Liverpool Bay
Anglesey
ISLE OF ANGLESEY
GWYNEDD
CONWY
DENBIGHSHIRE
FLINTSHIRE
WREXHAM
POWYS
CEREDIGION
CARMARTHENSHIRE
PEMBROKESHIRE
MONMOUTHSHIRE
HEREFORDSHIRE
SHROPSHIRE
GLOUCESTERSHIRE
SNOWDONIA NATIONAL PARK
BRECON BEACONS NATIONAL PARK
PEMBROKESHIRE COAST NATIONAL PARK
Cambrian Mts.
Berwyn Mts.
Black Mountains
Mynydd Preseli
Clwydian Ra.
Lleyn Peninsula
Wirral
LIVERPOOL
Chester
Wrexham
Shrewsbury
Telford
Hereford
Worcester
Gloucester
Aberystwyth
Bangor
Holyhead
Carmarthen
Brecon
Newtown
Welshpool
Llandudno
Rhyl
Fishguard
Milford Haven
Cardigan
Caernarfon
Dolgellau
Machynlleth
Kidderminster
Leominster
Ludlow
Monmouth
Bardsey I.
Skomer I.
Ramsey I.
Grassholm I.
A
B
C
D
2
3
4
5
6
7
8
9
1:1 000 000
5 0 10 20 30 40 50 km
5 0 5 10 15 20 25 30 35 miles

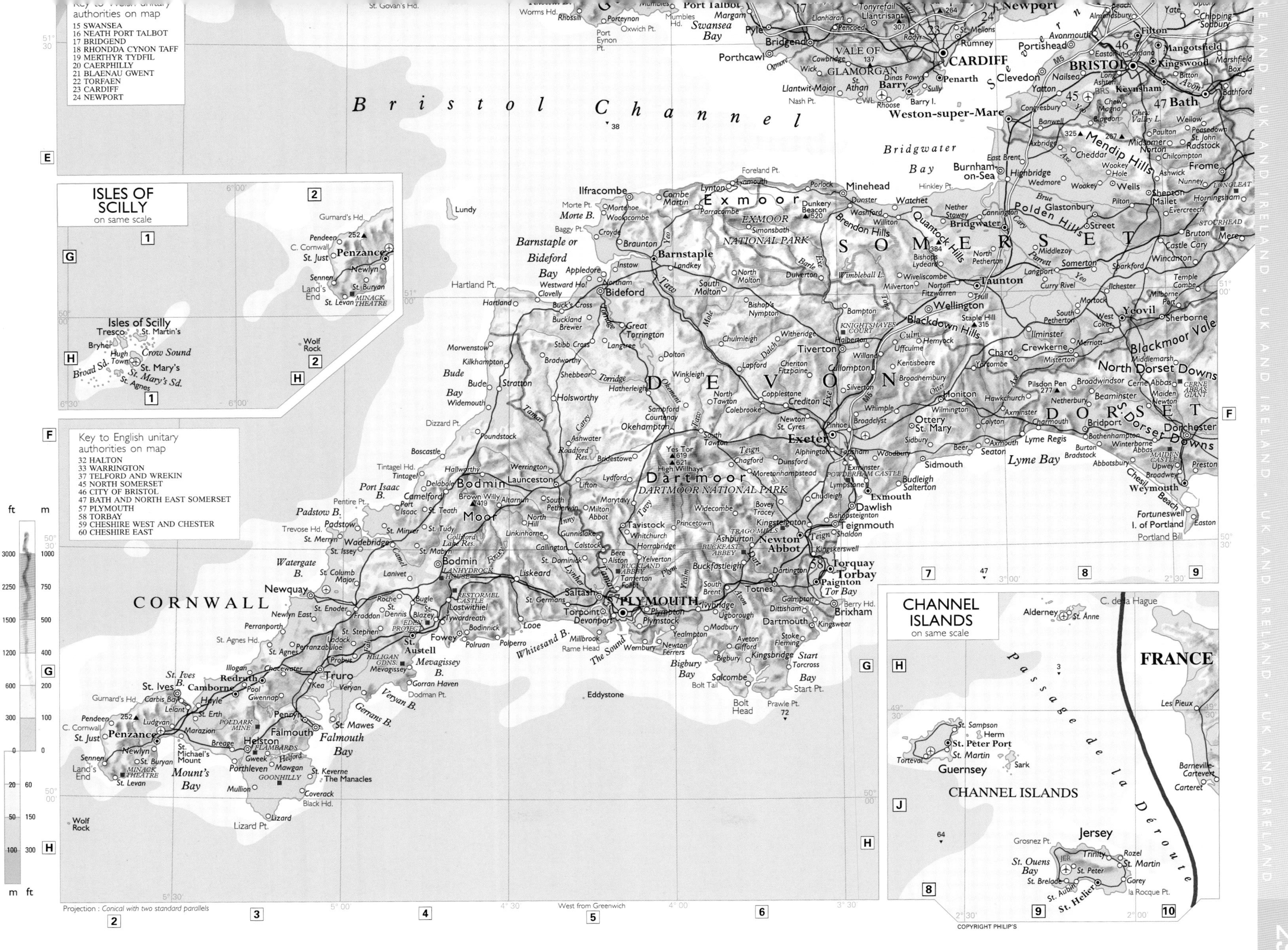

FRANCE

C. de la Hague

Passage de la Déroute

Jersey

CHANNEL ISLANDS
on same scale

CHANNEL ISLANDS

Alderney

Guernsey

St. Peter Port

Sark

Herm

COPYRIGHT PHILIP'S

Bristol Channel

Bridgwater Bay

Barnstaple or Bideford Bay

SOMERSET

DORSET

DEVON

Exmoor National Park

Dartmoor National Park

CORNWALL

Lyme Bay

ISLES OF SCILLY
on same scale

Isles of Scilly

Tresco
St. Martin's
Hugh Town
St. Mary's
St. Agnes

Crow Sound
St. Mary's Sd.
Broad Sd.

Bryher

Key to English unitary
authorities on map

32 HALTON
33 WARRINGTON
37 TELFORD AND WREKIN
45 NORTH SOMERSET
46 CITY OF BRISTOL
47 BATH AND NORTH EAST SOMERSET
57 PLYMOUTH
58 TORBAY
59 CHESHIRE WEST AND CHESTER
60 CHESHIRE EAST

authorities on map

15 SWANSEA
16 NEATH PORT TALBOT
17 BRIDGEND
18 RHONDDA CYNON TAFF
19 MERTHYR TYDFIL
20 CAERPHILLY
21 BLAENAU GWENT
22 TORFAEN
23 CARDIFF
24 NEWPORT

Projection: Conical with two standard parallels

m
1000
750
500
400
300
200
100
0

ft
3000
2250
1500
1200
600
300
0

ft
200
150
100
50
0

m
60
150
300

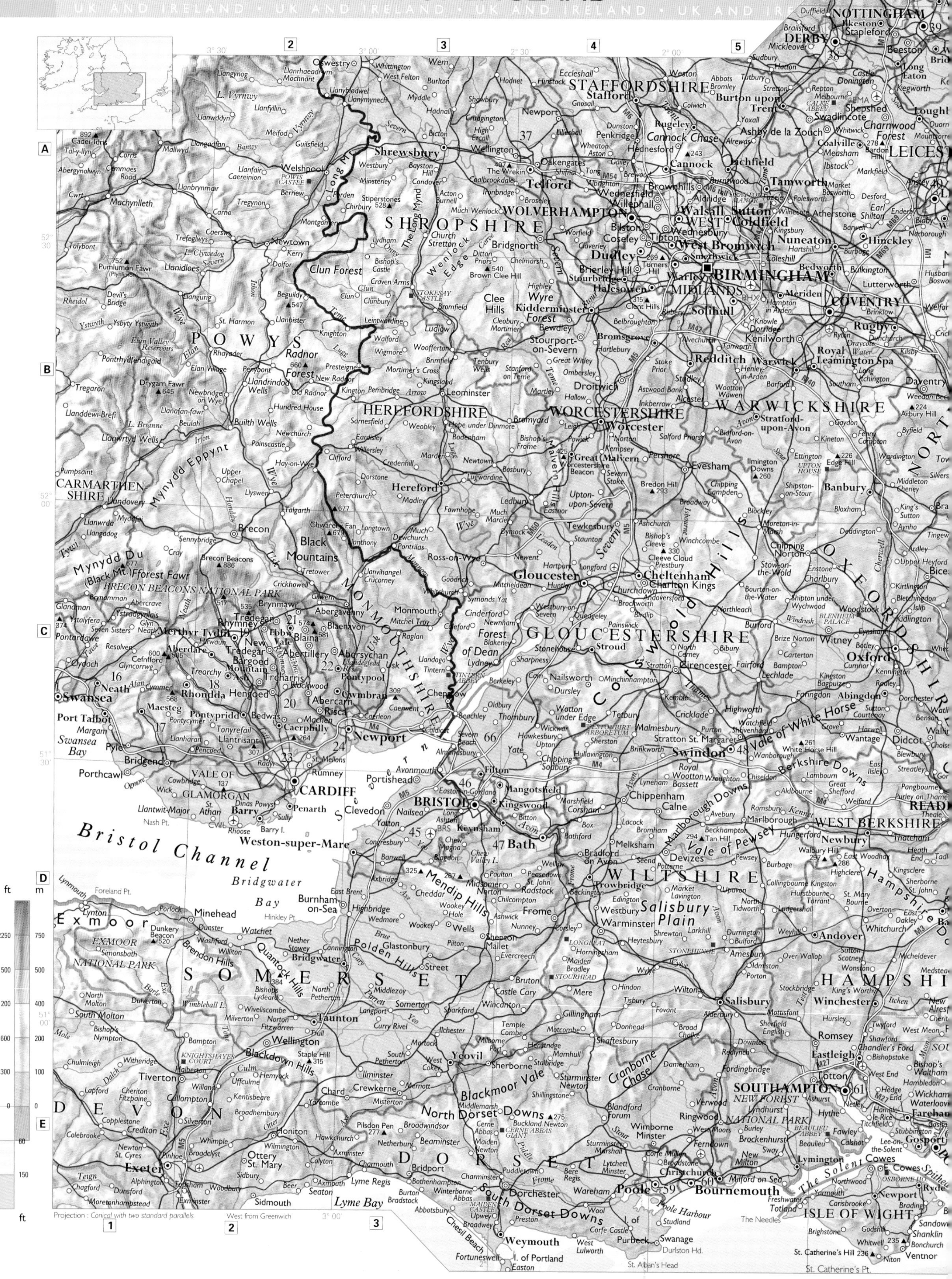
SHROPSHIRE
STAFFORDSHIRE
POWYS
HEREFORDSHIRE
WORCESTERSHIRE
WARWICKSHIRE
GLOUCESTERSHIRE
MONMOUTHSHIRE
OXFORDSHIRE
WILTSHIRE
SOMERSET
DORSET
DEVON
HAMPSHIRE
WEST BERKSHIRE
CARMARTHENSHIRE
VALE OF GLAMORGAN
WEST MIDLANDS
ISLE OF WIGHT
BIRMINGHAM
WOLVERHAMPTON
COVENTRY
NOTTINGHAM
DERBY
LEICESTER
CARDIFF
BRISTOL
SOUTHAMPTON
Shrewsbury
Telford
Stafford
Walsall
Dudley
Worcester
Hereford
Gloucester
Cheltenham
Oxford
Swindon
Bath
Newport
Swansea
Salisbury
Winchester
Bournemouth
Poole
Exeter
Taunton
Yeovil
Weymouth
Bristol Channel
Severn
Cotswold Hills
Mendip Hills
Quantock Hills
Blackdown Hills
Exmoor
EXMOOR NATIONAL PARK
BRECON BEACONS NATIONAL PARK
NEW FOREST NATIONAL PARK
Black Mountains
Forest of Dean
Salisbury Plain
Vale of White Horse
Vale of Pewsey
Marlborough Downs
Berkshire Downs
Cranborne Chase
Blackmoor Vale
North Dorset Downs
South Dorset Downs
The Solent
Lyme Bay
Bridgwater Bay
Swansea Bay
Clun Forest
Radnor Forest
Wyre Forest
Cannock Chase
Mynydd Eppynt
Mynydd Du (Black Mt.)
Fforest Fawr
Long Mynd
Wenlock Edge
Clee Hills
Malvern Hills
Polden Hills
Brendon Hills
Projection : Conical with two standard parallels
West from Greenwich
ft
m
2250
750
1500
500
1200
400
600
200
300
100
0
0
20
60
50
150
m
ft

Key to English unitary authorities on map
37 TELFORD AND WREKIN
38 DERBY CITY
39 CITY OF NOTTINGHAM
40 LEICESTER CITY
41 RUTLAND
42 PETERBOROUGH
43 MILTON KEYNES
44 LUTON
45 NORTH SOMERSET
46 CITY OF BRISTOL
47 BATH AND NORTH EAST SOMERSET
48 SWINDON
49 READING
50 WOKINGHAM
51 WINDSOR AND MAIDENHEAD
52 SLOUGH
53 BRACKNELL FOREST
54 THURROCK
55 SOUTHEND-ON-SEA
56 MEDWAY
59 POOLE
60 BOURNEMOUTH
61 SOUTHAMPTON
62 PORTSMOUTH
63 BRIGHTON AND HOVE
64 BEDFORD
65 CENTRAL BEDFORDSHIRE
66 SOUTH GLOUCESTERSHIRE

Key to Welsh unitary authorities on map
16 NEATH PORT TALBOT
17 BRIDGEND
18 RHONDDA CYNON TAFF
19 MERTHYR TYDFIL
20 CAERPHILLY
21 BLAENAU GWENT
22 TORFAEN
23 CARDIFF
24 NEWPORT

1:1 000 000

COPYRIGHT PHILIP'S

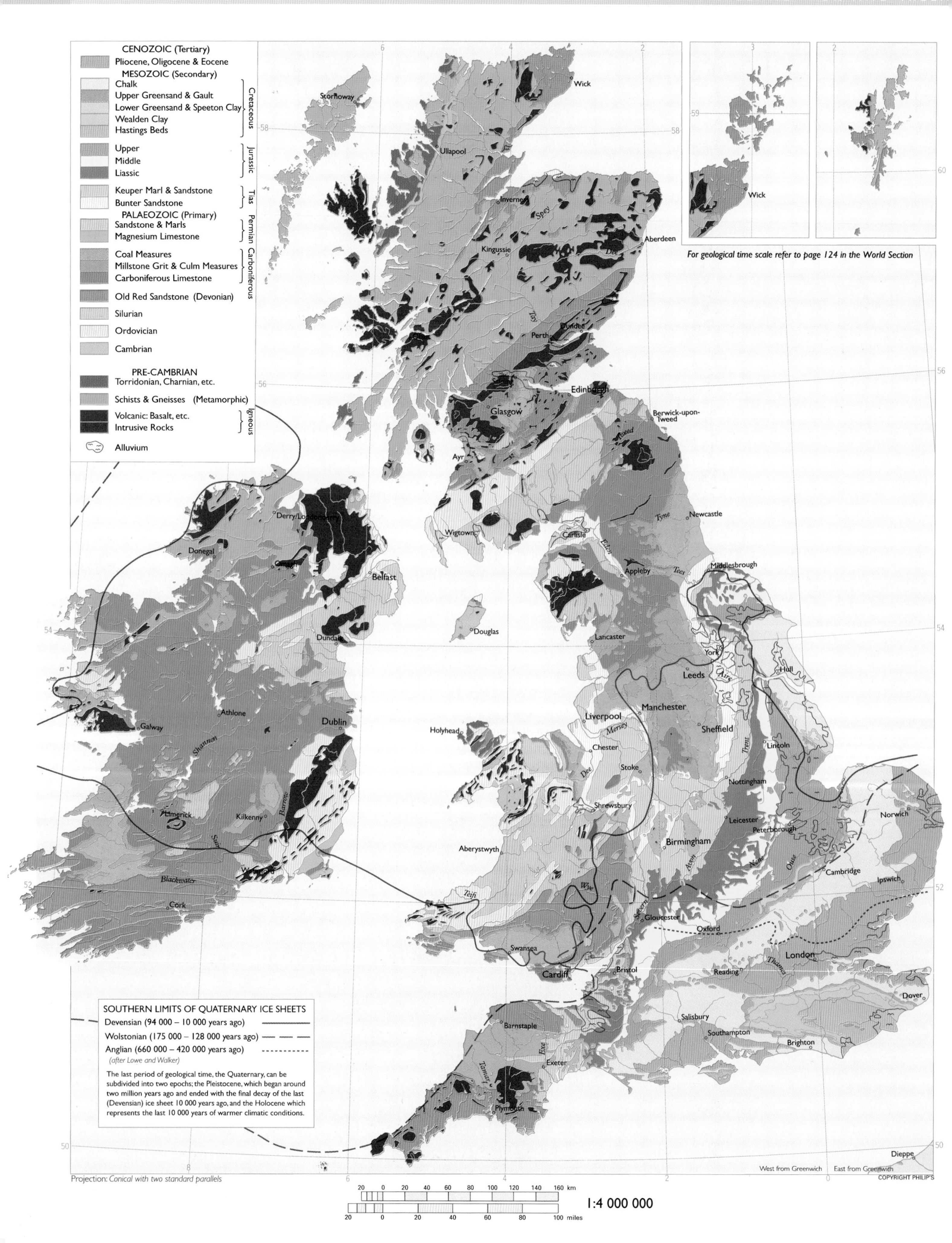

CENOZOIC (Tertiary)
Pliocene, Oligocene & Eocene
MESOZOIC (Secondary)
Chalk
Upper Greensand & Gault
Lower Greensand & Speeton Clay
Wealden Clay
Hastings Beds
Cretaceous

Upper
Middle
Liassic
Jurassic

Keuper Marl & Sandstone
Bunter Sandstone
Trias

PALAEOZOIC (Primary)
Sandstone & Marls
Magnesium Limestone
Permian

Coal Measures
Millstone Grit & Culm Measures
Carboniferous Limestone
Carboniferous

Old Red Sandstone (Devonian)

Silurian

Ordovician

Cambrian

PRE-CAMBRIAN
Torridonian, Charnian, etc.

Schists & Gneisses (Metamorphic)

Volcanic: Basalt, etc.
Intrusive Rocks
Igneous

Alluvium

For geological time scale refer to page 124 in the World Section

SOUTHERN LIMITS OF QUATERNARY ICE SHEETS
Devensian (94 000 – 10 000 years ago) ————
Wolstonian (175 000 – 128 000 years ago) – – – –
Anglian (660 000 – 420 000 years ago) ··········
(after Lowe and Walker)

The last period of geological time, the Quaternary, can be subdivided into two epochs; the Pleistocene, which began around two million years ago and ended with the final decay of the last (Devensian) ice sheet 10 000 years ago, and the Holocene which represents the last 10 000 years of warmer climatic conditions.

Projection: Conical with two standard parallels

West from Greenwich   East from Greenwich
COPYRIGHT PHILIP'S

20 0 20 40 60 80 100 120 140 160 km
20 0   20   40   60   80   100 miles

1:4 000 000

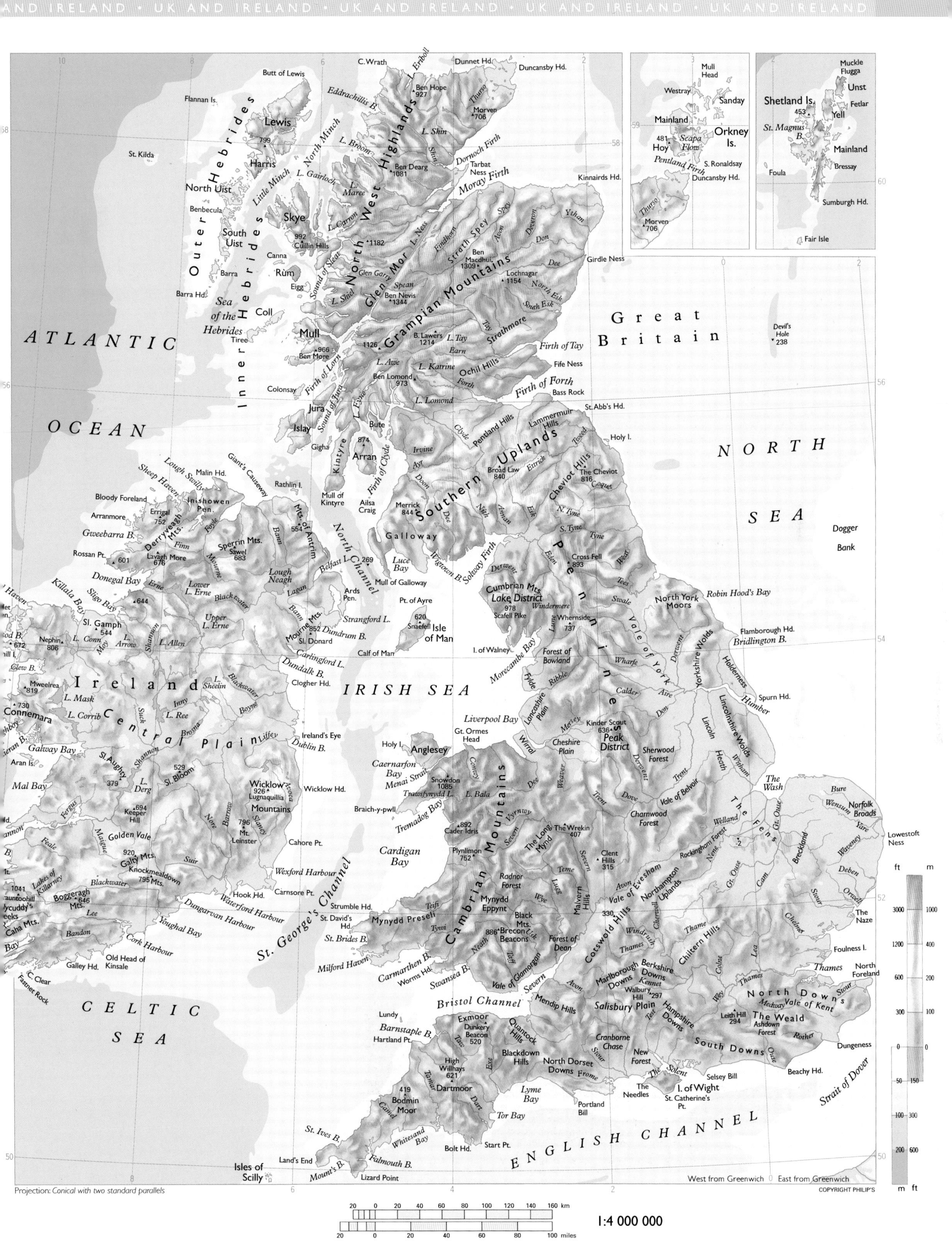

Projection: Conical with two standard parallels

West from Greenwich   East from Greenwich

COPYRIGHT PHILIP'S

1:4 000 000

20 0 20 40 60 80 100 120 140 160 km

20 0 20 40 60 80 100 miles

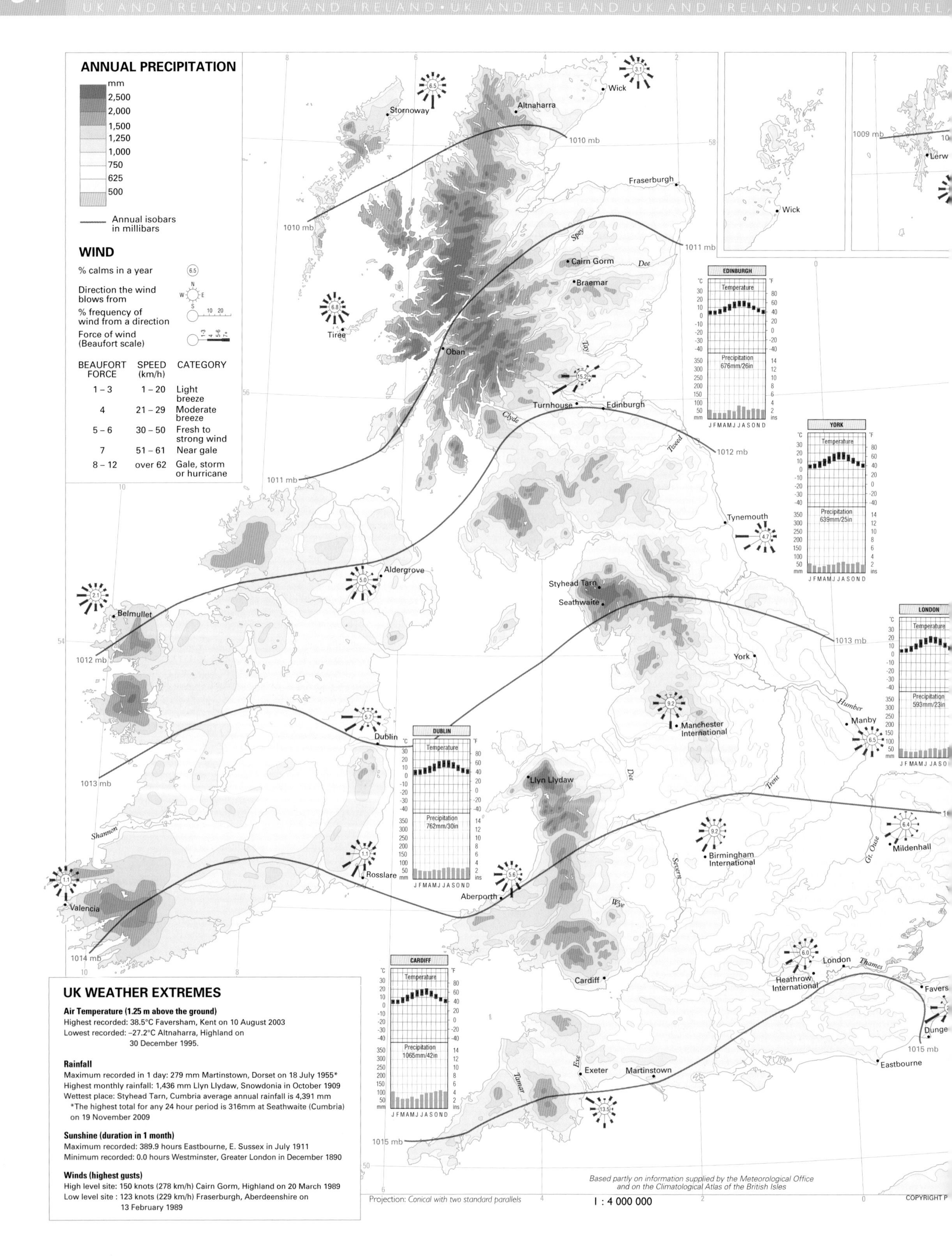

ANNUAL PRECIPITATION

mm
2,500
2,000
1,500
1,250
1,000
750
625
500

— Annual isobars
in millibars

WIND

% calms in a year   (6.5)

Direction the wind
blows from

% frequency of
wind from a direction   10 20

Force of wind
(Beaufort scale)   1-3 / 4 / 5-6 / 7+

BEAUFORT FORCE	SPEED (km/h)	CATEGORY
1 – 3	1 – 20	Light breeze
4	21 – 29	Moderate breeze
5 – 6	30 – 50	Fresh to strong wind
7	51 – 61	Near gale
8 – 12	over 62	Gale, storm or hurricane

UK WEATHER EXTREMES

Air Temperature (1.25 m above the ground)
Highest recorded: 38.5°C Faversham, Kent on 10 August 2003
Lowest recorded: –27.2°C Altnaharra, Highland on
30 December 1995.

Rainfall
Maximum recorded in 1 day: 279 mm Martinstown, Dorset on 18 July 1955*
Highest monthly rainfall: 1,436 mm Llyn Llydaw, Snowdonia in October 1909
Wettest place: Styhead Tarn, Cumbria average annual rainfall is 4,391 mm
  *The highest total for any 24 hour period is 316mm at Seathwaite (Cumbria)
  on 19 November 2009

Sunshine (duration in 1 month)
Maximum recorded: 389.9 hours Eastbourne, E. Sussex in July 1911
Minimum recorded: 0.0 hours Westminster, Greater London in December 1890

Winds (highest gusts)
High level site: 150 knots (278 km/h) Cairn Gorm, Highland on 20 March 1989
Low level site : 123 knots (229 km/h) Fraserburgh, Aberdeenshire on
13 February 1989

Projection: Conical with two standard parallels

Based partly on information supplied by the Meteorological Office
and on the Climatological Atlas of the British Isles

1 : 4 000 000

COPYRIGHT P

JANUARY TEMPERATURE

Actual surface temperature

°C
7
6
5
4
3
2
1
0

Sunshine

453 Average duration
of bright sunshine
in hours
November–April

January isotherms
reduced to sea-level
° Celsius

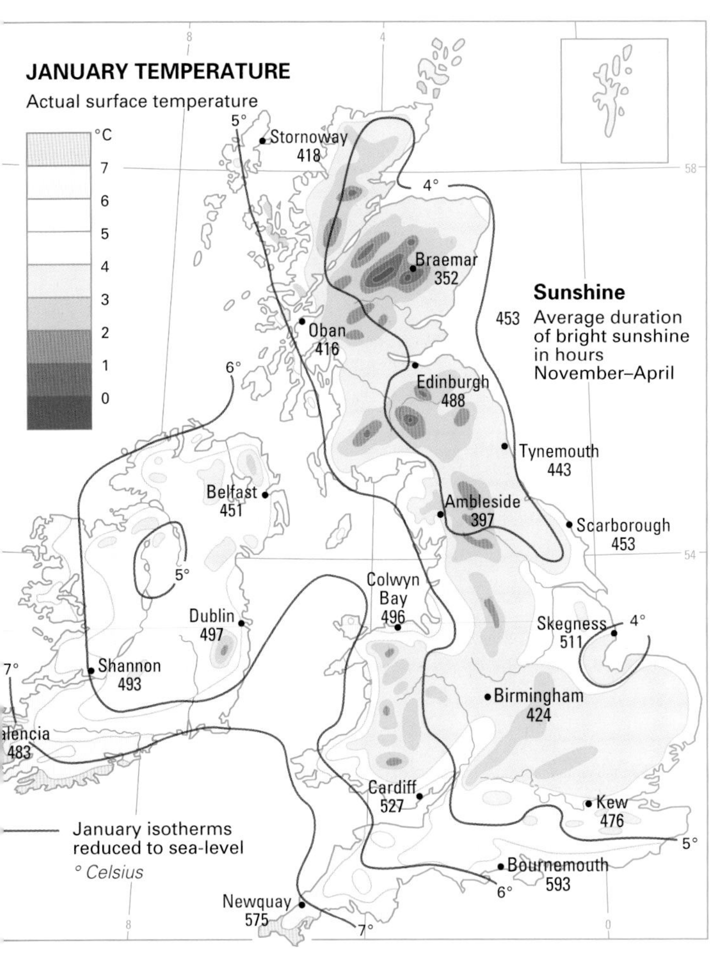

Stornoway 418
Braemar 352
Oban 416
Edinburgh 488
Tynemouth 443
Belfast 451
Ambleside 397
Scarborough 453
Colwyn Bay 496
Skegness 511
Dublin 497
Shannon 493
Birmingham 424
alencia 483
Cardiff 527
Kew 476
Newquay 575
Bournemouth 593

CHANGES IN UK RAINFALL PATTERNS

Annual percentage change
in precipitation, 1914-2007

Over 10% increase
0 – 10% increase
0 – 2.5% decrease
2.5 – 5% decrease
Over 5% decrease

Seasonal percentage change
in precipitation, 1914-2007
region

increase

decrease

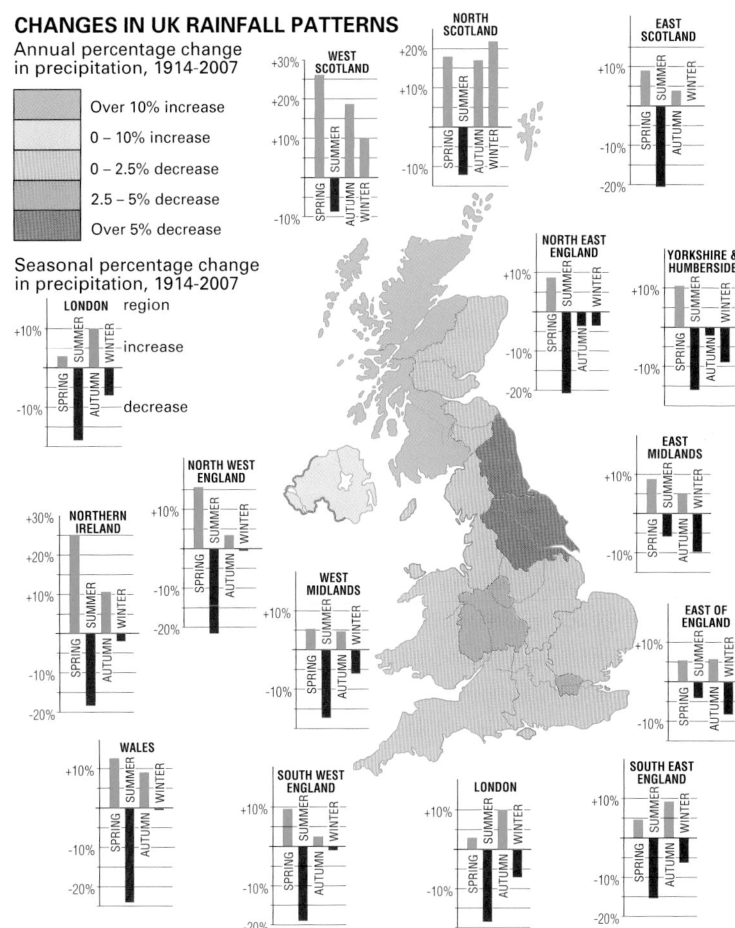

NORTH SCOTLAND
WEST SCOTLAND
EAST SCOTLAND
NORTH EAST ENGLAND
YORKSHIRE & HUMBERSIDE
NORTHERN IRELAND
NORTH WEST ENGLAND
EAST MIDLANDS
WEST MIDLANDS
EAST OF ENGLAND
WALES
SOUTH WEST ENGLAND
LONDON
SOUTH EAST ENGLAND

JULY TEMPERATURE

Actual surface temperature

°C
17
16
15
14
13
12
11
10

Sunshine

944 Average duration
of bright sunshine
in hours
May–October

July isotherms
reduced to sea-level
° Celsius

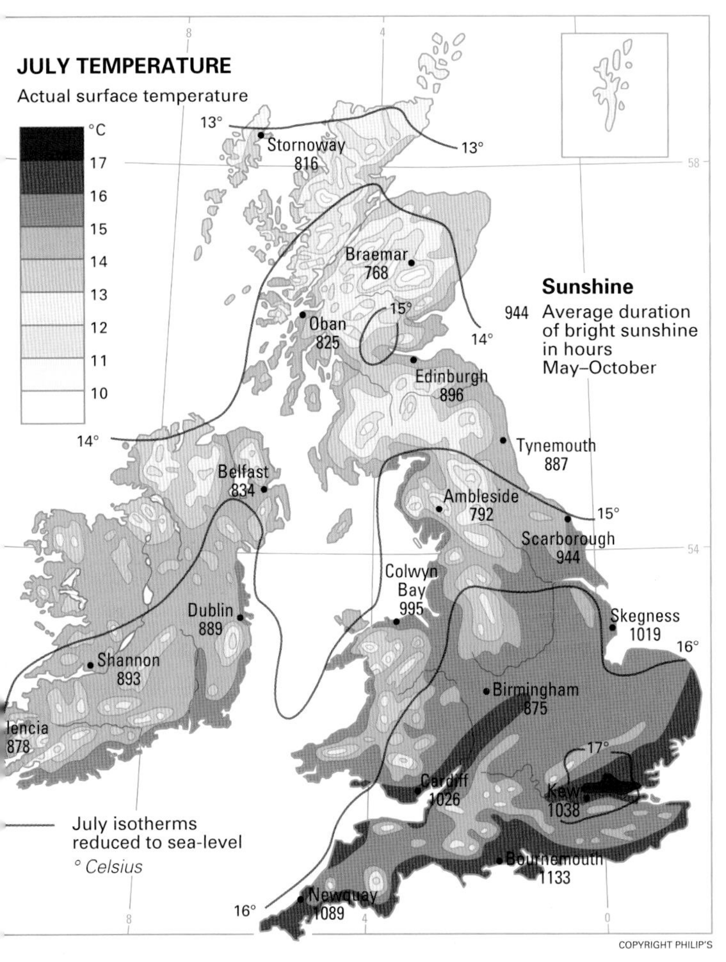

Stornoway 816
Braemar 768
Oban 825
Edinburgh 896
Tynemouth 887
Belfast 834
Ambleside 792
Scarborough 944
Colwyn Bay 995
Skegness 1019
Dublin 889
Shannon 893
Birmingham 875
lencia 878
Cardiff 1026
Kew 1038
Bournemouth 1133
Newquay 1089

COPYRIGHT PHILIP'S

CHANGES IN SUMMER AND WINTER RAINFALL 1870–2010

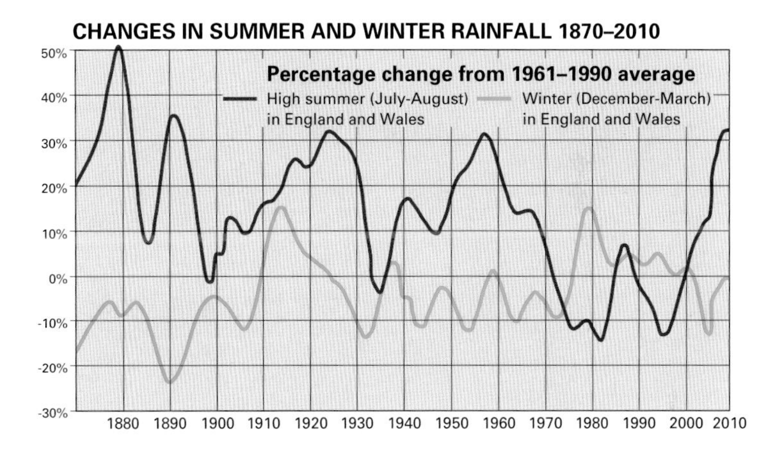

Percentage change from 1961–1990 average

High summer (July-August) in England and Wales
Winter (December-March) in England and Wales

CHANGES IN AVERAGE SURFACE TEMPERATURE 1850–2010

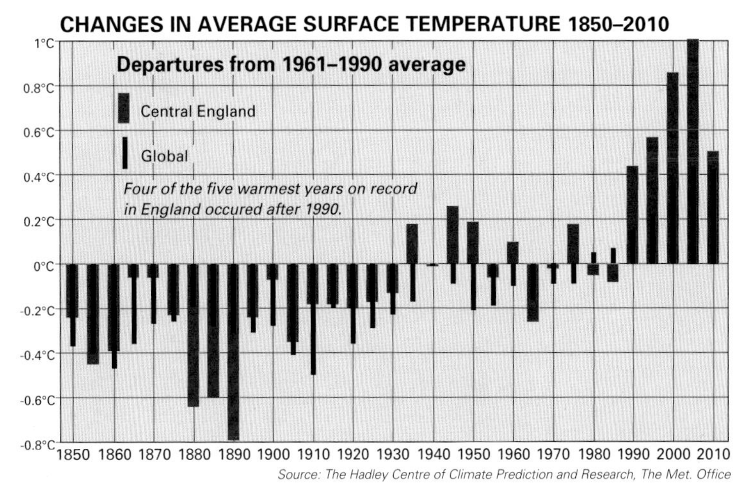

Departures from 1961–1990 average

Central England

Global

*Four of the five warmest years on record
in England occured after 1990.*

Source: The Hadley Centre of Climate Prediction and Research, The Met. Office

WATER SUPPLY

Regions of reliably high rainfall (more than 1,250 mm in at least 70% of the years)

③ Major reservoirs (capacity over 20 million cubic metres, see list opposite for details)

→ Existing inter-regional transfers of water (by pipeline and river)

→ Proposed inter-regional transfers of water (by pipeline and river)

□ Proposed estuary storage site

▽ Proposed groundwater storage site

Principal sources of groundwater (porous and jointed aquifers)

THAMES WATER Water supply and sewerage companies in the UK

There are no water authorities in Ireland, each county and urban borough is responsible for its own water supply

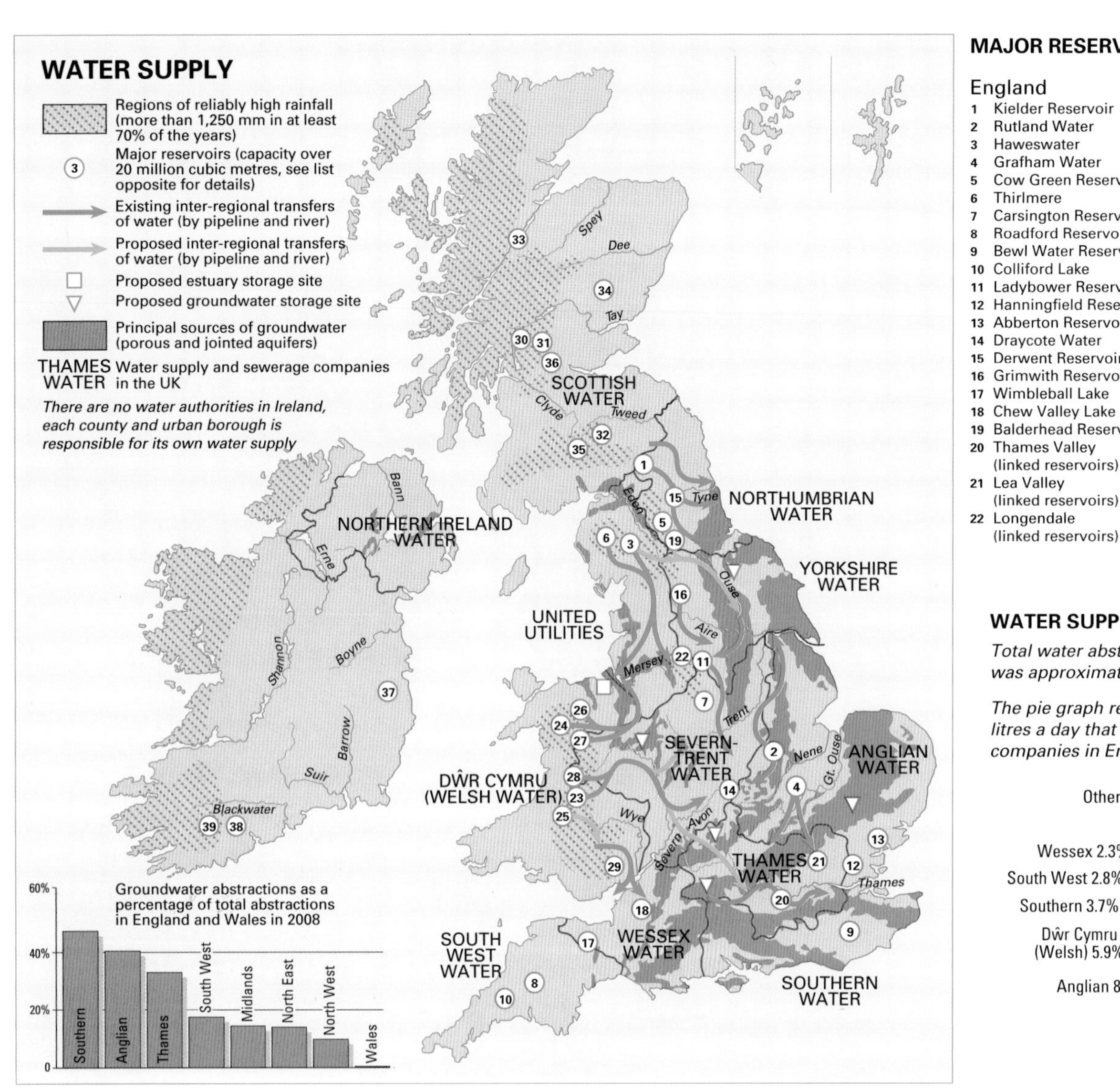
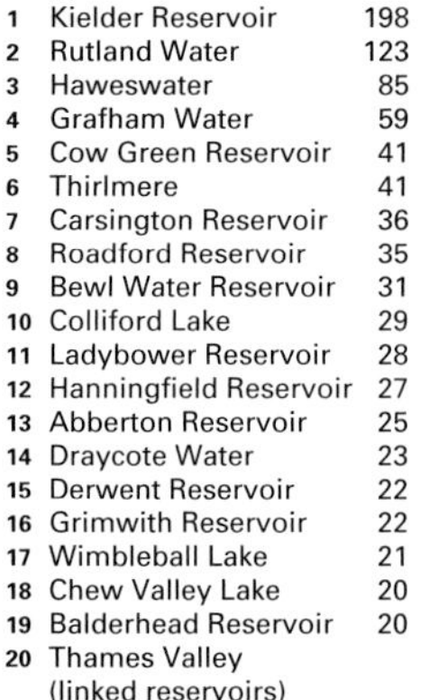

Groundwater abstractions as a percentage of total abstractions in England and Wales in 2008

MAJOR RESERVOIRS (with capacity in million

England

1	Kielder Reservoir	198
2	Rutland Water	123
3	Haweswater	85
4	Grafham Water	59
5	Cow Green Reservoir	41
6	Thirlmere	41
7	Carsington Reservoir	36
8	Roadford Reservoir	35
9	Bewl Water Reservoir	31
10	Colliford Lake	29
11	Ladybower Reservoir	28
12	Hanningfield Reservoir	27
13	Abberton Reservoir	25
14	Draycote Water	23
15	Derwent Reservoir	22
16	Grimwith Reservoir	22
17	Wimbleball Lake	21
18	Chew Valley Lake	20
19	Balderhead Reservoir	20
20	Thames Valley (linked reservoirs)	
21	Lea Valley (linked reservoirs)	
22	Longendale (linked reservoirs)	

Wales

23	Elan Valley
24	Llyn Celyn
25	Llyn Brianne
26	Llyn Brenig
27	Llyn Vyrnwy
28	Llyn Clywedog
29	Llandegfedd Reservoir

Scotland

30	Loch Lomond
31	Loch Katrine
32	Megget Reservoir
33	Loch Ness
34	Blackwater Reservoir
35	Daer Reservoir
36	Carron Valley Reservoir

Ireland

37	Poulaphouca Reservoir
38	Inishcarra Reservoir
39	Carrigadrohid Reservoir

WATER SUPPLY IN ENGLAND AND WALES

Total water abstraction in England and Wales in 20 was approximately 55,000 million litres a day.

The pie graph represents the almost 15,000 million litres a day that were supplied by the water supply companies in England and Wales in 2008.

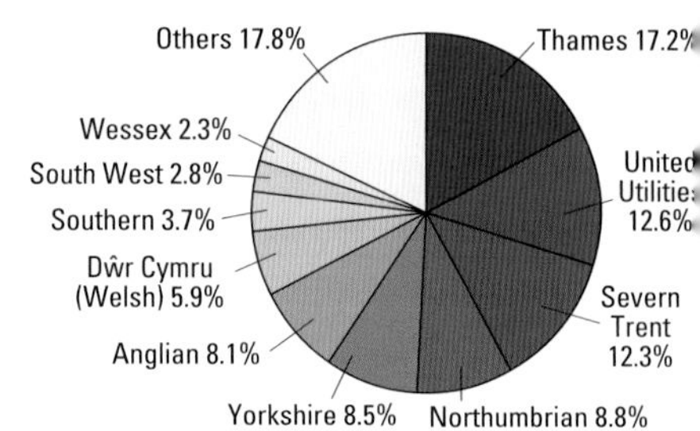

Others 17.8%
Wessex 2.3%
South West 2.8%
Southern 3.7%
Dŵr Cymru (Welsh) 5.9%
Anglian 8.1%
Yorkshire 8.5%
Northumbrian 8.8%
Severn Trent 12.3%
United Utilities 12.6%
Thames 17.2%

WASTE RECYCLING

The percentage of total household waste recycled in 2010

Over 45%
40 – 45%
35 – 40%
Under 35%

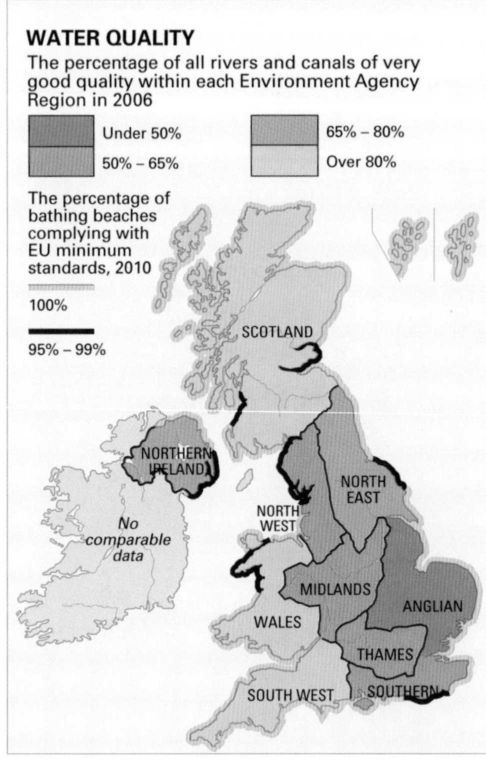

WATER QUALITY

The percentage of all rivers and canals of very good quality within each Environment Agency Region in 2006

Under 50%
50% – 65%
65% – 80%
Over 80%

The percentage of bathing beaches complying with EU minimum standards, 2010

100%
95% – 99%

FLOOD RISK IN ENGLAND AND WALES

Areas at greatest risk from flooding (as designated by the Environment Agency

Counties worst affected by flooding in summer 2007

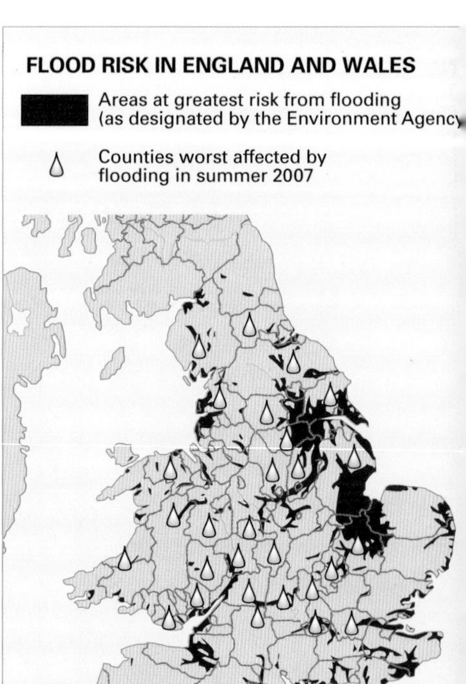

U AIR QUALITY
Greenhouse gas emissions for elected EU countries 1998-2009

	million tonnes of CO$_2$ equivalent			Share of total EU 27 emissions (2009)
	1998	2003	2009	
U 27	5,192.5	5,177.4	4,614.5	100%
elgium	151.0	145.9	124.4	2.7%
enmark	75.2	73.6	61.0	1.3%
rance	585.6	565.7	517.2	11.2%
ermany	1,077.6	1,030.6	919.7	19.9%
reece	122.4	130.9	122.5	2.7%
eland	64.8	67.8	62.4	1.4%
aly	540.8	573.5	491.1	10.6%
etherlands	225.5	215.4	198.9	4.3%
oland	413.1	384.6	376.7	8.2%
ortugal	74.9	81.7	74.6	1.6%
pain	337.9	403.7	367.5	8.0%
weden	73.8	70.9	60.0	1.3%
nited Kingdom	700.2	657.6	566.2	12.3%

SOILS

- Calcareous brown earth
- Brown earth
- Acid brown earth
- Podsol
- Peaty podsol
- Grey-brown podsol
- Gley
- Basin peat and alluvial gleys
- Peaty gley and blanket peat

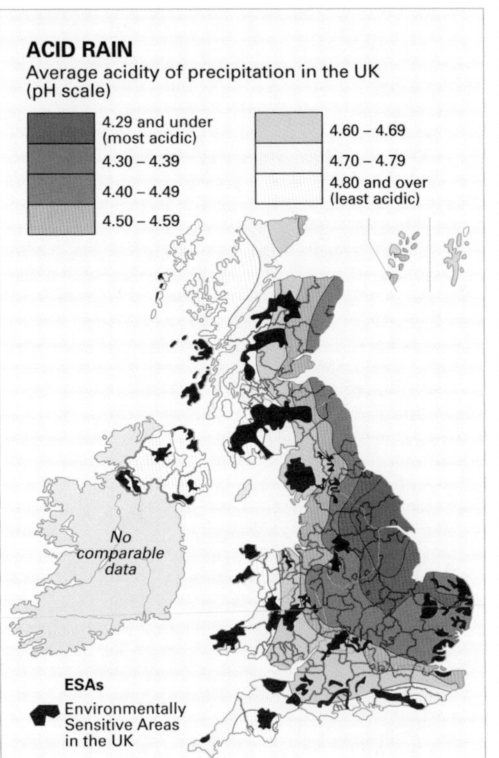

NATURAL VEGETATION
The plant cover associated with a particular environment if it was unaffected by human activity

- Oak
- Beech and oak
- Ash and oak
- Birch and oakwood
- Scots pine
- Heath, moorland, water meadows, fen, bog and marsh

ACID RAIN
Average acidity of precipitation in the UK (pH scale)

- 4.29 and under (most acidic)
- 4.30 – 4.39
- 4.40 – 4.49
- 4.50 – 4.59
- 4.60 – 4.69
- 4.70 – 4.79
- 4.80 and over (least acidic)

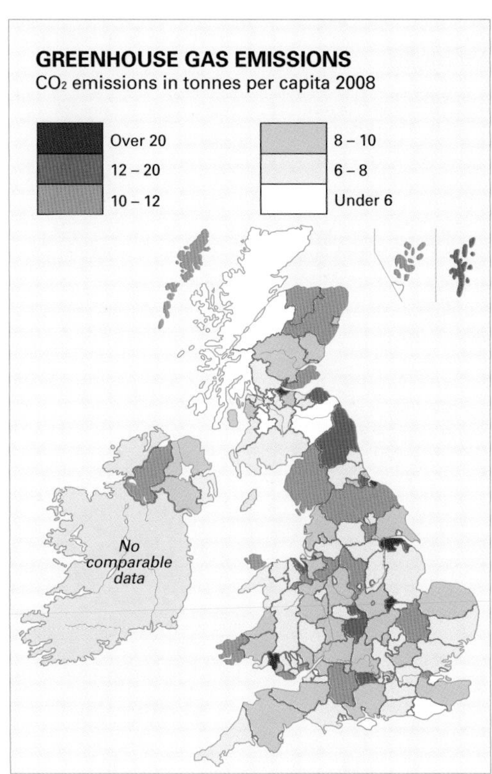

No comparable data

ESAs
Environmentally Sensitive Areas in the UK

GREENHOUSE GAS EMISSIONS
CO$_2$ emissions in tonnes per capita 2008

- Over 20
- 12 – 20
- 10 – 12
- 8 – 10
- 6 – 8
- Under 6

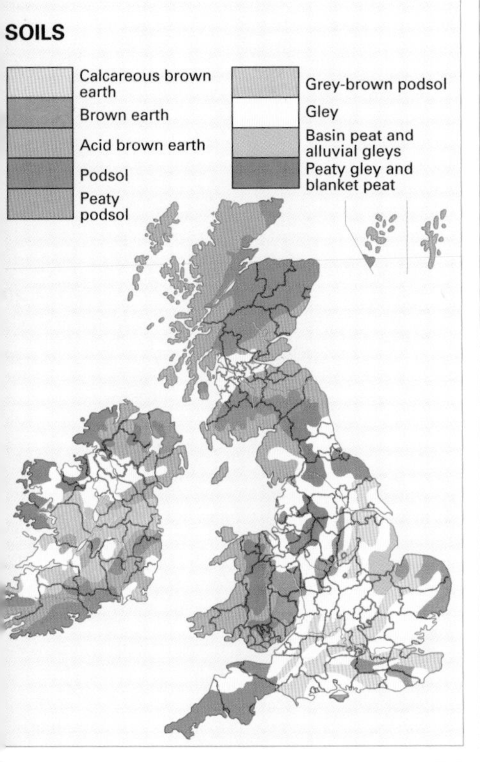

No comparable data

CONSERVATION

- National Parks
- Areas of Outstanding Natural Beauty (AONBs)
- National Scenic Areas (NSAs)
- Forest Parks, Regional Parks in Scotland and Special Protection Areas (SPAs)
- Green Belts (and the urban areas they surround)
- Heritage Coast (England and Wales)

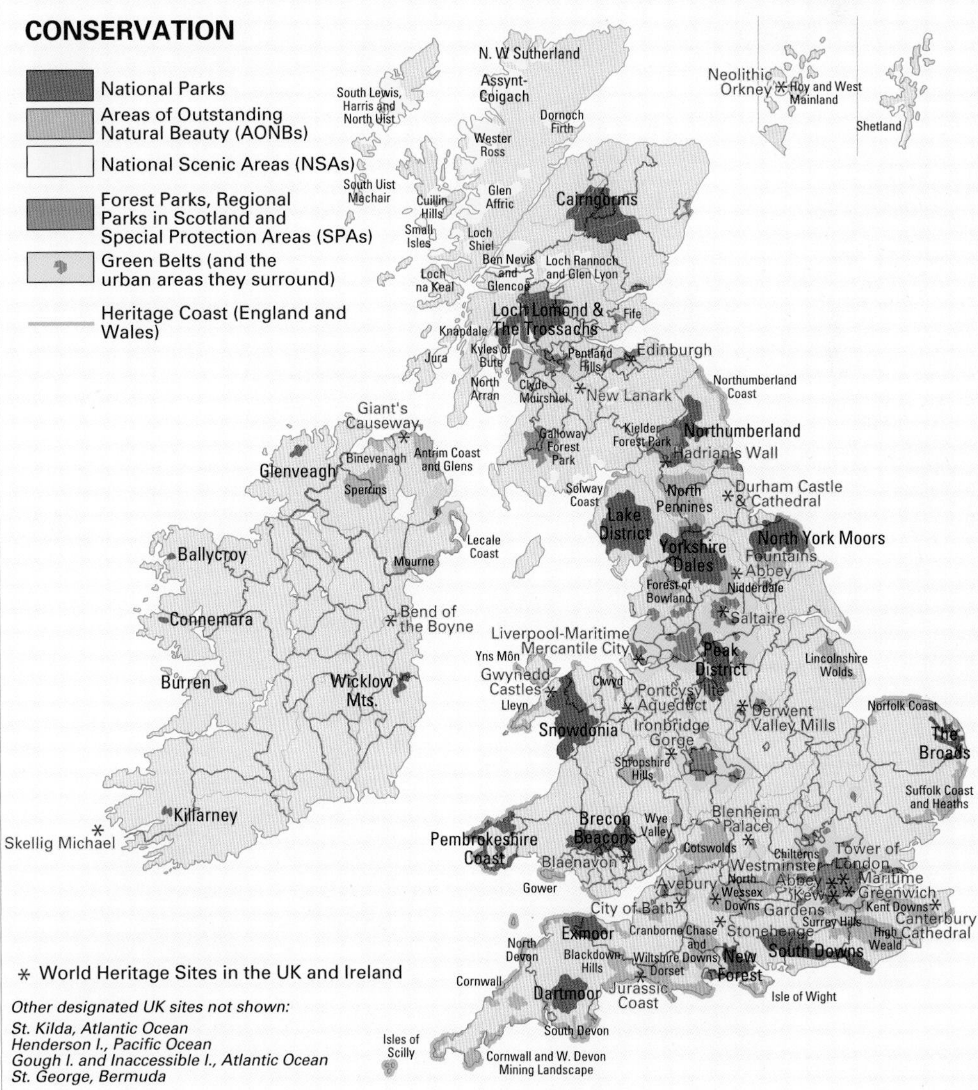

✳ World Heritage Sites in the UK and Ireland

Other designated UK sites not shown:
St. Kilda, Atlantic Ocean
Henderson I., Pacific Ocean
Gough I. and Inaccessible I., Atlantic Ocean
St. George, Bermuda

TYPES OF FARM

- Dairy cattle
- Beef cattle
- Sheep
- ● Pigs and/or poultry
- Mixed farming
- Market gardening (fruit and vegetables)
- Cereals
- Other crops (mainly potatoes, sugar beet)
- — Northern limit of 9 month growing season
- Forests
- Built-up areas
- Areas with over 1,000 mm rainfall per year

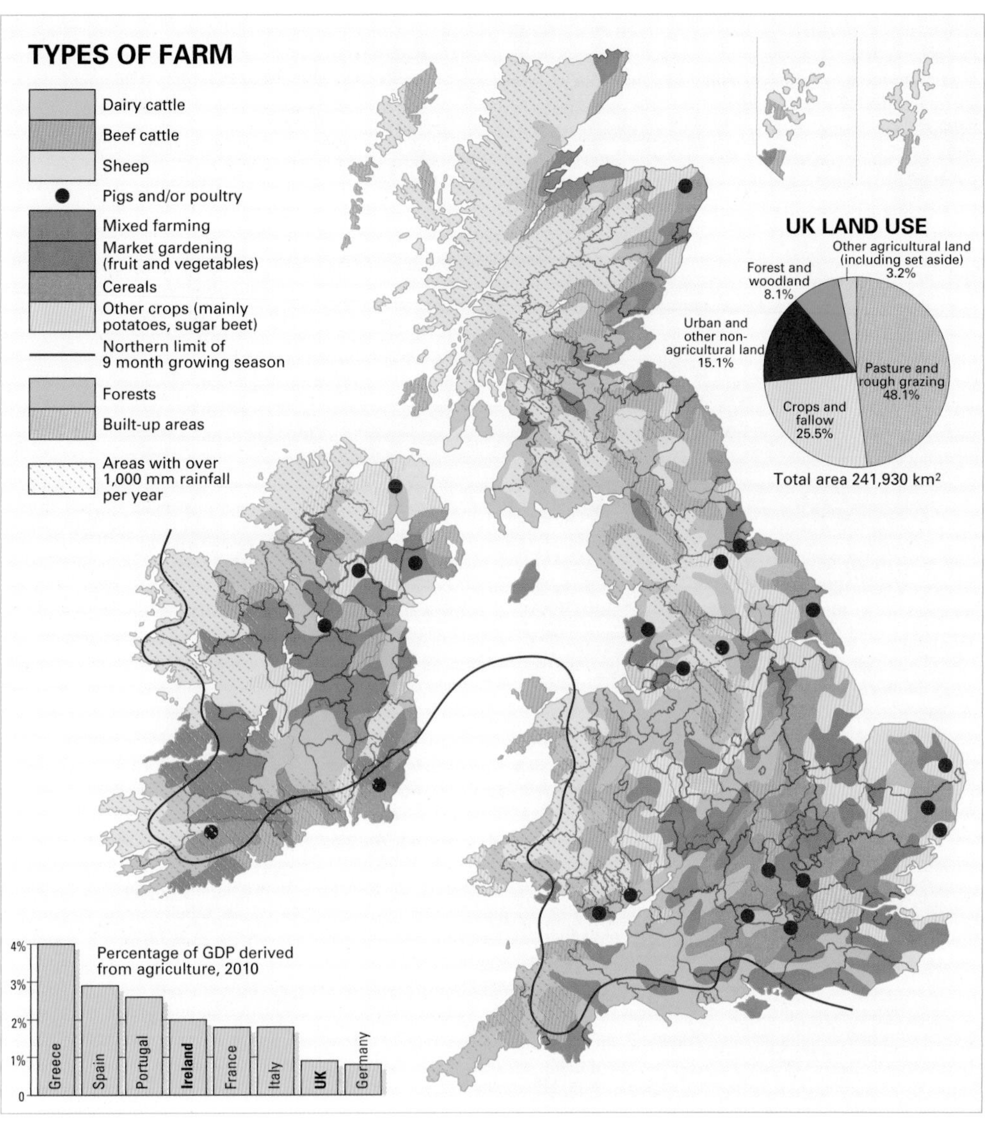

UK LAND USE

- Other agricultural land (including set aside) 3.2%
- Forest and woodland 8.1%
- Urban and other non-agricultural land 15.1%
- Pasture and rough grazing 48.1%
- Crops and fallow 25.5%

Total area 241,930 km²

Percentage of GDP derived from agriculture, 2010

(bar chart, y-axis 0–4%)
Greece, Spain, Portugal, Ireland, France, Italy, UK, Germany

CEREAL FARMING

The percentage of the total farmland used for growing cereals in 2009

- Over 40
- 25 – 40
- 10 – 25
- 5 – 10
- 0 – 5

Cereal production 2009
UK 22.0 million tonnes
Ireland 1.9 million tonnes

DAIRY FARMING

The number of dairy cows per 100 hectares of farmland in 2009

- Over 40
- 30 – 40
- 20 – 30
- 10 – 20
- 0 – 10

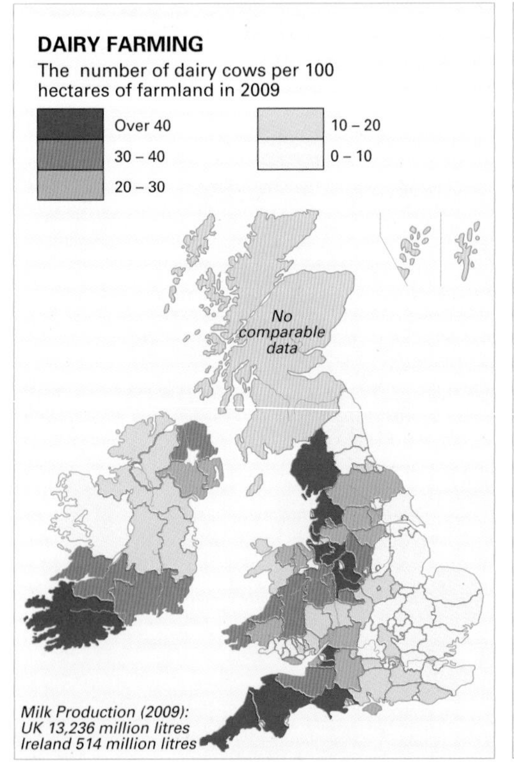

No comparable data

Milk Production (2009):
UK 13,236 million litres
Ireland 514 million litres

LIVESTOCK FARMING

The number of beef cattle, sheep and pigs per 100 hectares of farmland in 2009

- Over 400
- 300 – 400
- 200 – 300
- 100 – 200
- Under 100

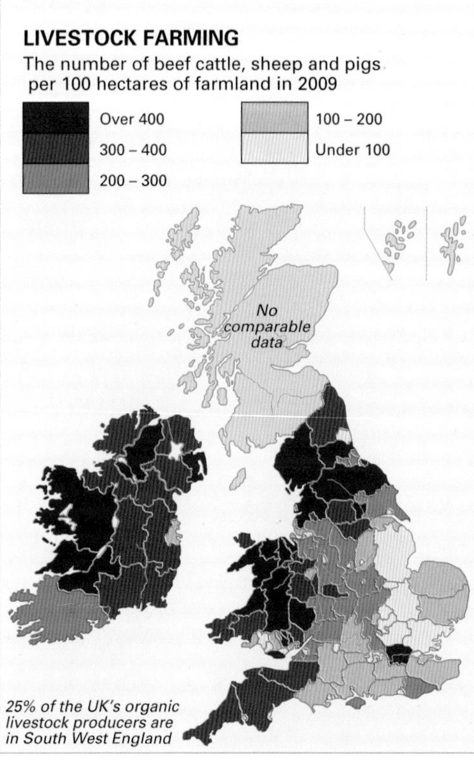

No comparable data

25% of the UK's organic livestock producers are in South West England

FISHING

(fishing region map)

Scalloway — Lerwick
Scrabster
Kinlochbervie
Ullapool
Mallaig
West Coast of Scotland 366,569 tonnes
Fraserburgh
Peterhead
North Sea 295,367 tonnes

Killybegs
Kirkcudbright
Portavogie
Kilkeel — Ardglass
Rossaveel
Howth
Holyhead
Penrhyn
Dunmore East
Castletown Bearhaven
Milford Haven
Bristol Channel and Celtic Sea 25,384 tonnes
Shoreham
Brixham
Newhaven
Plymouth
Newlyn
West Ireland and Sole Bank 34,378 tonnes
English Channel 49,507 tonnes

Major fishing ports by size of catch landed

- ▽ Demersal e.g. cod (Deep sea fish)
- ▼ Pelagic e.g. mackerel (Shallow sea fish)
- ▽ Shellfish e.g. lobster

The most important inshore fishing grounds

North Sea 295,367 tonnes
Total amount caught in each fishing region 2010

1000 500 200 100 50 m
Depth of sea in metres

MPLOYMENT IN SERVICES

e percentage of the workforce employed
the service industry in 2010

Over 85%   70 – 75%
80 – 85%   Under 70%
75 – 80%

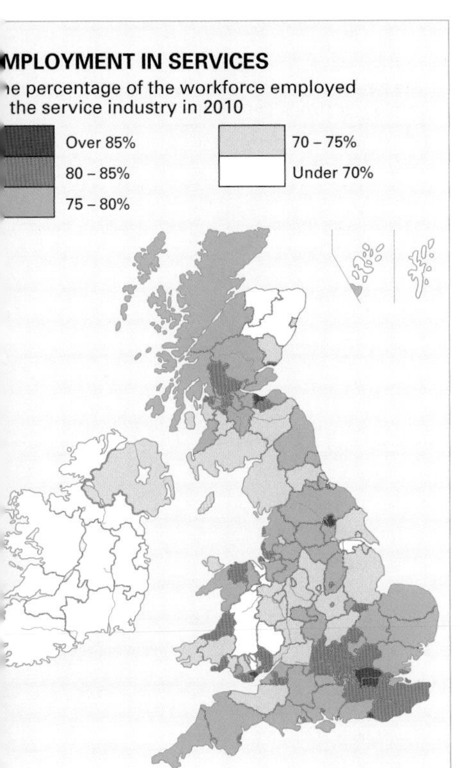

EMPLOYMENT IN MANUFACTURING

The percentage of the workforce employed
in the manufacturing in 2010

Over 15%   7.5 – 10%
12.5 – 15%   5 – 7.5%
10 – 12.5%   Under 5%

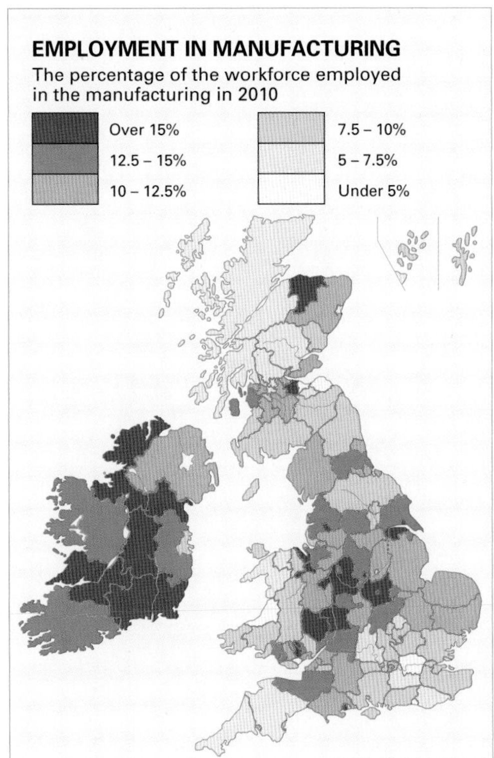

MOTOR MANUFACTURING
IN ENGLAND AND WALES

■ Car manufacturing sites
■ Commercial vehicle manufacturing sites
□ Selected engine manufacturing sites
Source: SMMT 2011

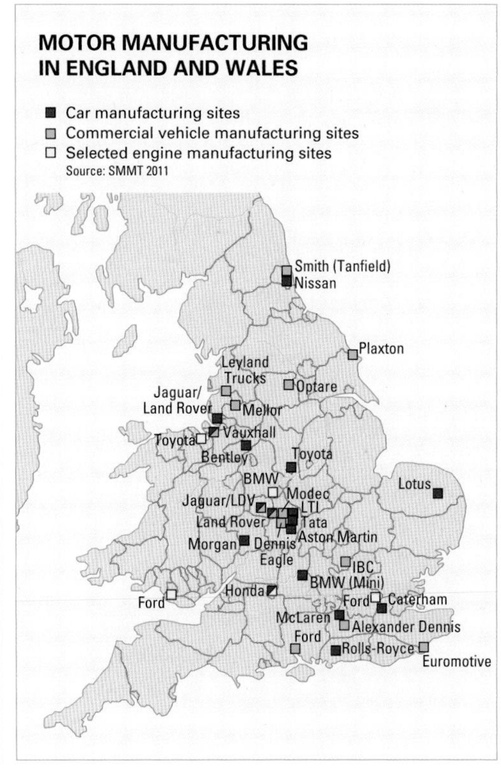

CHANGES IN EMPLOYMENT
IN THE UK

Employment by industry

Services

Transport

Manufacturing

Mining & energy supply

Agriculture, forestry & fishing

1931 1941 1951 1961 1971 1981 1991 2001 2010

MANUFACTURING OUTPUT IN THE UK

Other manufacturing 4.6%
Fuels 1.7%
Wood products 1.8%
Textiles & leather 2.9%
Non-metal mineral products 3.4%
Rubber & plastics 4.7%

Machinery 8.5%

Transport equipment 10.7%

Metals 11.0%

Electrical & optical equipment 11.1%

Chemicals 12.0%

Paper, publishing & printing 12.9%

Food, beverages & tobacco 14.7%

Total value 2010: £140.0 billion

UK FOREIGN TRADE

TOP TEN TRADING PARTNERS One container represents 1% of the total value of imports or 1% of the total value of exports in 2010

Imports to UK

From Germany $89.1b
From Norway $38.9b
From USA $62.8b
From Belgium $33.9b
From China $56.5b
From Italy $27.8b
From Netherlands $51.9b
From Ireland $25.4b
From France $43.4b
From Spain $19.8b

TRADE BY TYPE OF GOODS 2003 AND 2010

Imports   Exports
(2003 figures are in brackets)

Imports:
Food and live animals 2.0% (7.1%)
Drink and tobacco 7.1% (1.6%)
Mineral fuels 11.3% (4.6%)
Other raw materials 3.0% (2.4%)
Chemicals 12.1% (11.0%)
Manufactured goods 12.3% (12.9%)
Machinery and transport 31.3% (38%)
Other manufactures 15.3% (16.3%)
Miscellaneous goods 5.6% (6.1%)

Exports:
Food and live animals 3.6% (3.4%)
Drink and tobacco 2.5% (2.3%)
Mineral fuels 12.7% (8.2%)
Other raw materials 2.6% (1.5%)
Chemicals 17.9% (15.5%)
Manufactured goods 11.0% (12.1%)
Machinery and transport 31.6% (39.2%)
Other manufactures 11.9% (12.0%)
Miscellaneous goods 6.2% (5.8%)

Total value of imports 2010 $558.6 billion
(Total value of imports 2003 $393.5 billion)

Total value of exports 2010 $404.7 billion
(Total value of exports 2003 $307.7 billion)

Exports from UK

To USA $61.6b
To Belgium $21.2b
To Germany $46.6b
To Spain $15.8b
To Netherlands $33.6m
To Italy $14.3b
To France $33.0b
To China $11.8b
To Ireland $26.7b
To Sweden $8.8b

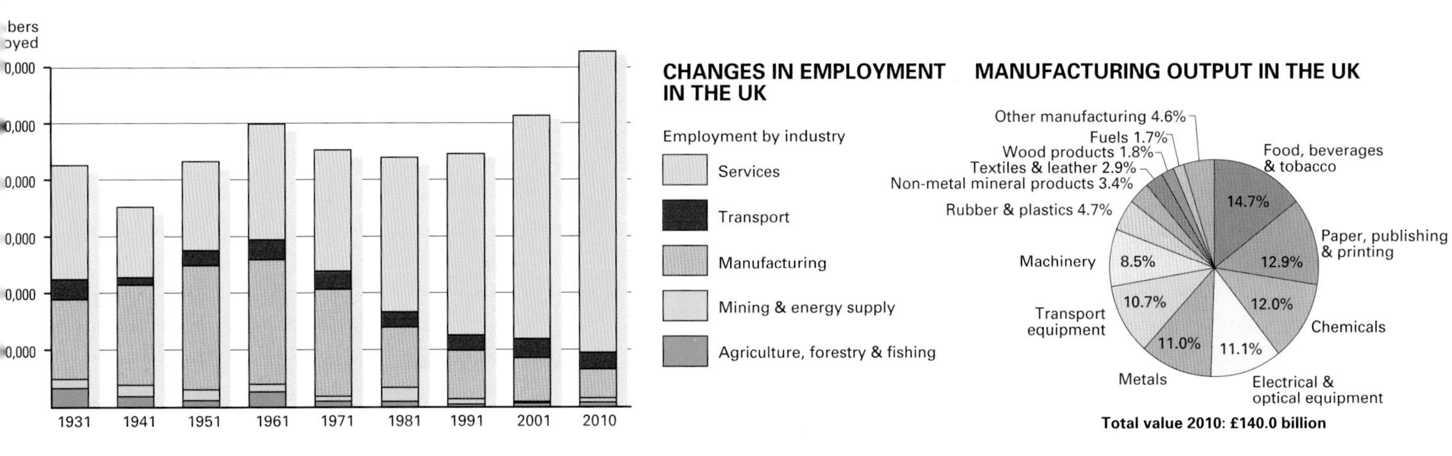
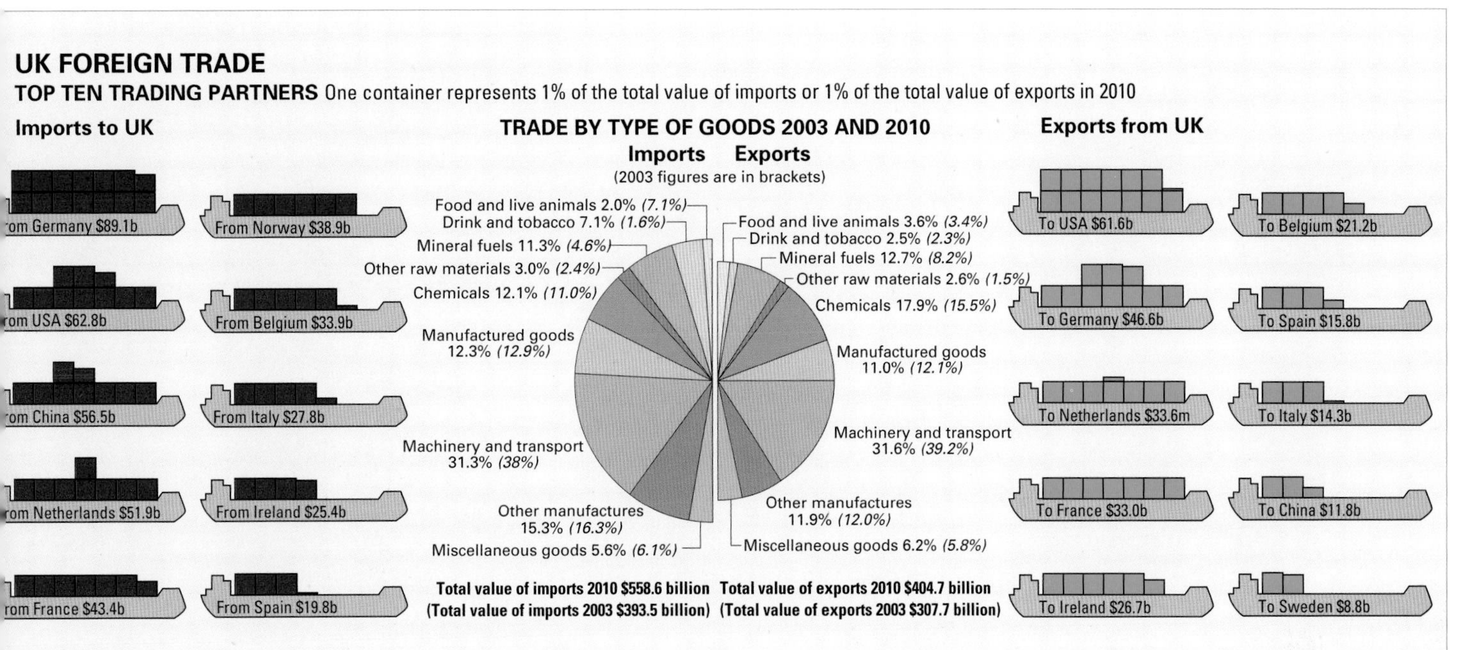

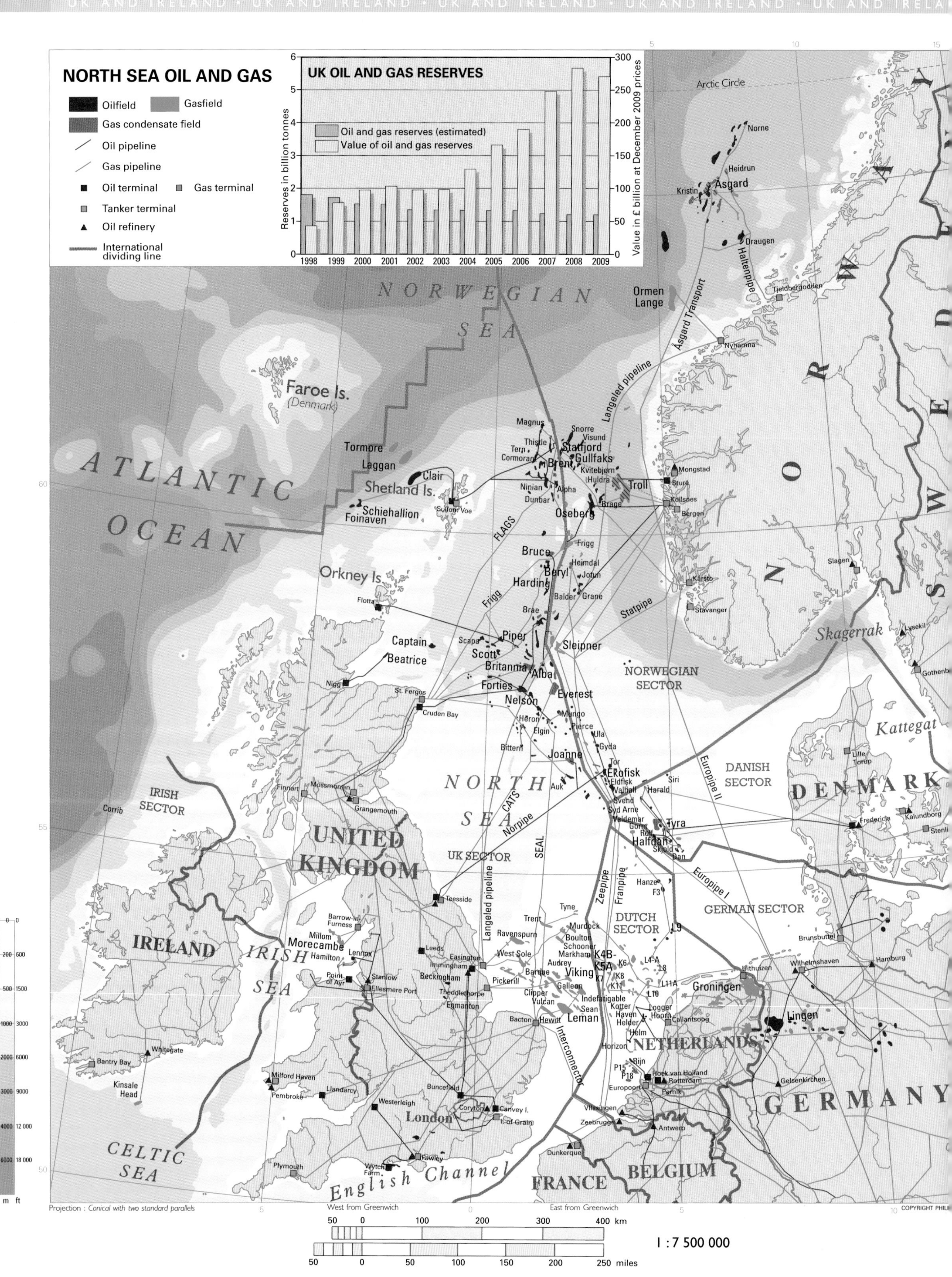

NORTH SEA OIL AND GAS

- Oilfield
- Gasfield
- Gas condensate field
- / Oil pipeline
- / Gas pipeline
- ■ Oil terminal
- ■ Gas terminal
- ■ Tanker terminal
- ▲ Oil refinery
- International dividing line

UK OIL AND GAS RESERVES

Reserves in billion tonnes

Value in £ billion at December 2009 prices

- Oil and gas reserves (estimated)
- Value of oil and gas reserves

1998 1999 2000 2001 2002 2003 2004 2005 2006 2007 2008 2009

Projection : Conical with two standard parallels

West from Greenwich   East from Greenwich

1 : 7 500 000

COPYRIGHT PHILI

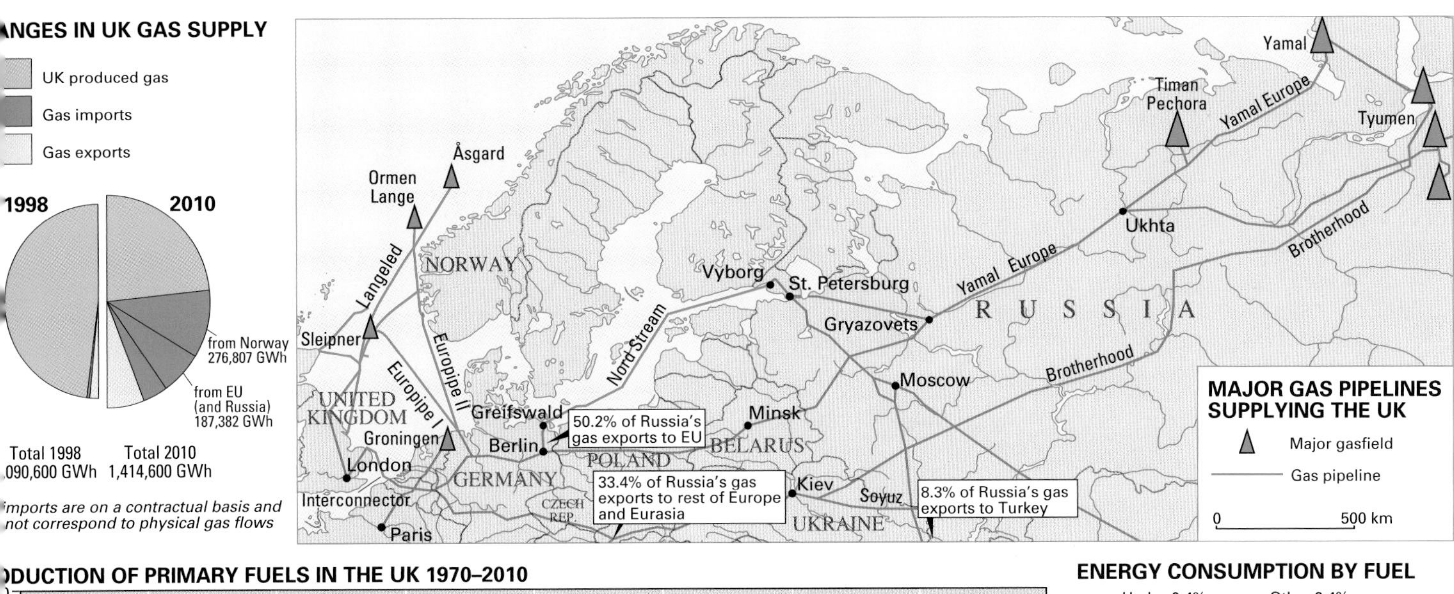

ANGES IN UK GAS SUPPLY

- UK produced gas
- Gas imports
- Gas exports

1998 **2010**

from Norway 276,807 GWh

from EU (and Russia) 187,382 GWh

Total 1998
090,600 GWh

Total 2010
1,414,600 GWh

imports are on a contractual basis and not correspond to physical gas flows

MAJOR GAS PIPELINES SUPPLYING THE UK

▲ Major gasfield

— Gas pipeline

0 — 500 km

50.2% of Russia's gas exports to EU

33.4% of Russia's gas exports to rest of Europe and Eurasia

8.3% of Russia's gas exports to Turkey

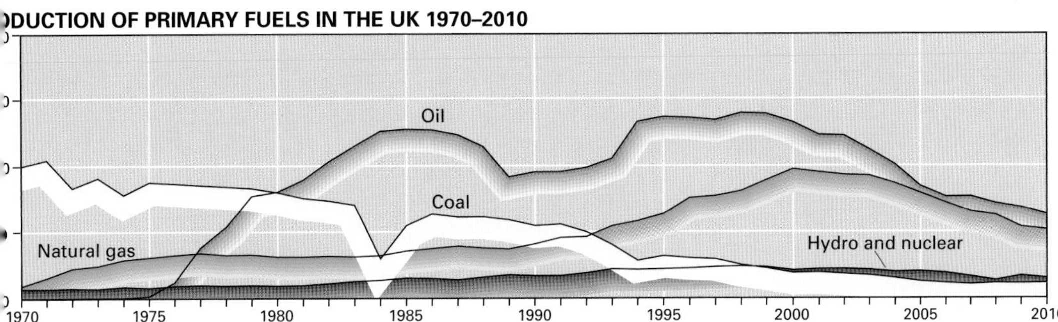

DUCTION OF PRIMARY FUELS IN THE UK 1970–2010

Oil

Coal

Natural gas

Hydro and nuclear

1970 1975 1980 1985 1990 1995 2000 2005 2010

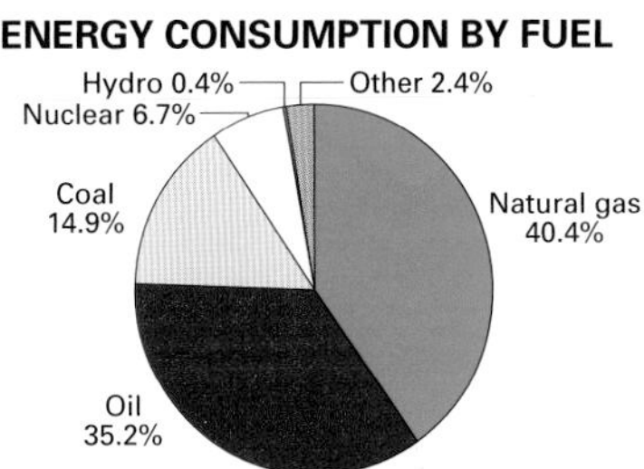

ENERGY CONSUMPTION BY FUEL

Hydro 0.4%
Nuclear 6.7%
Other 2.4%
Coal 14.9%
Natural gas 40.4%
Oil 35.2%

Total U.K. consumption in 2010:
209.1 million tonnes of oil equivalent

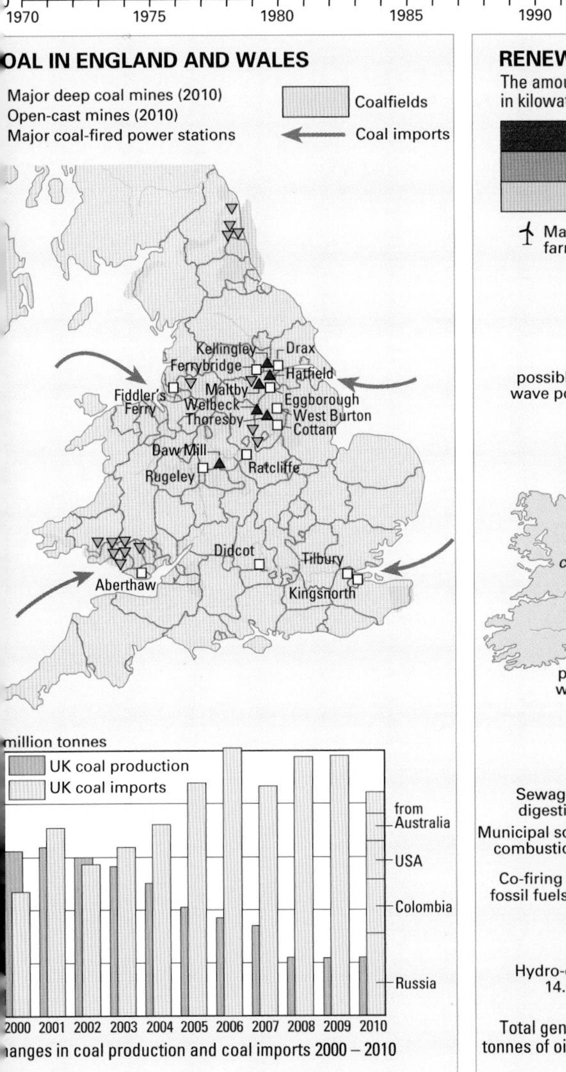

OAL IN ENGLAND AND WALES

- ▽ Major deep coal mines (2010)
- □ Open-cast mines (2010)
- ▲ Major coal-fired power stations
- Coalfields
- ← Coal imports

Kellingley Drax
Ferrybridge Hatfield
Fiddler's Maltby
Ferry Welbeck Eggborough
Thoresby West Burton
Cottam
Daw Mill Ratcliffe
Rugeley

Didcot Tilbury
Kingsnorth
Aberthaw

million tonnes
- UK coal production
- UK coal imports

from Australia
USA
Colombia
Russia

2000 2001 2002 2003 2004 2005 2006 2007 2008 2009 2010

anges in coal production and coal imports 2000 – 2010

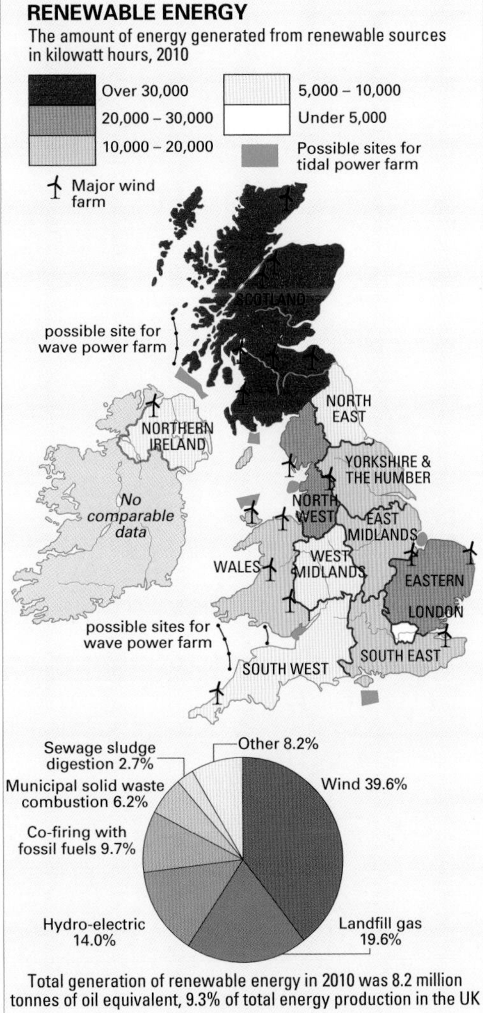

RENEWABLE ENERGY

The amount of energy generated from renewable sources in kilowatt hours, 2010

- Over 30,000
- 20,000 – 30,000
- 10,000 – 20,000
- 5,000 – 10,000
- Under 5,000
- Possible sites for tidal power farm

↟ Major wind farm

SCOTLAND

possible site for wave power farm

NORTHERN IRELAND

No comparable data

NORTH EAST

YORKSHIRE & THE HUMBER

NORTH WEST

EAST MIDLANDS

WALES

WEST MIDLANDS

EASTERN

LONDON

possible sites for wave power farm

SOUTH WEST

SOUTH EAST

Sewage sludge digestion 2.7%
Municipal solid waste combustion 6.2%
Co-firing with fossil fuels 9.7%
Hydro-electric 14.0%
Other 8.2%
Wind 39.6%
Landfill gas 19.6%

Total generation of renewable energy in 2010 was 8.2 million tonnes of oil equivalent, 9.3% of total energy production in the UK

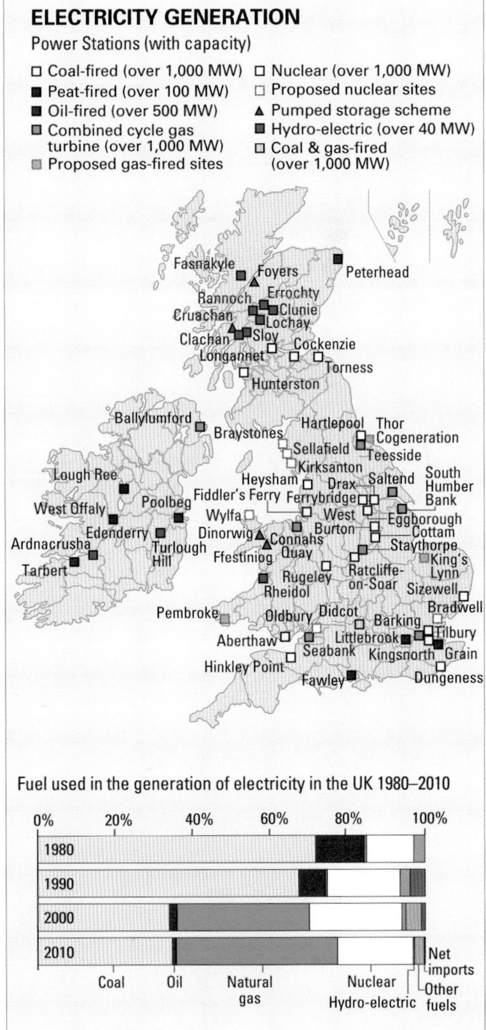

ELECTRICITY GENERATION

Power Stations (with capacity)
- □ Coal-fired (over 1,000 MW)
- ■ Peat-fired (over 100 MW)
- ■ Oil-fired (over 500 MW)
- ■ Combined cycle gas turbine (over 1,000 MW)
- ■ Proposed gas-fired sites
- □ Nuclear (over 1,000 MW)
- □ Proposed nuclear sites
- ▲ Pumped storage scheme
- ■ Hydro-electric (over 40 MW)
- □ Coal & gas-fired (over 1,000 MW)

Fasnakyle Foyers Peterhead
Rannoch Errochty
Cruachan Clunie
Clachan Sloy Lochay
Longannet Cockenzie
Torness
Hunterston

Ballylumford

Braystones
Hartlepool Thor Cogeneration
Sellafield Teesside
Kirksanton
Lough Ree Heysham Saltend
West Offaly Poolbeg Drax South Humber Bank
Fiddler's Ferry Ferrybridge
Wylfa West Eggborough
Ardnacrusha Edenderry Dinorwig Burton Cottam
Turlough Connahs Staythorpe
Tarbert Hill Quay King's Lynn
Ffestiniog Ratcliffe- Sizewell
Rugeley on-Soar
Rheidol
Pembroke Oldbury Didcot Bradwell
Barking Tilbury
Aberthaw Littlebrook Grain
Hinkley Point Seabank Kingsnorth
Fawley Dungeness

Fuel used in the generation of electricity in the UK 1980–2010

0% 20% 40% 60% 80% 100%

1980
1990
2000
2010

Coal Oil Natural gas Nuclear Hydro-electric Net imports Other fuels

ROADS AND FERRIES

M6 Motorways
Other main roads
Principal car ferry routes

56 Average 24 hour flow of vehicles for major sections of motorway network. Figures are given in thousands for 2010

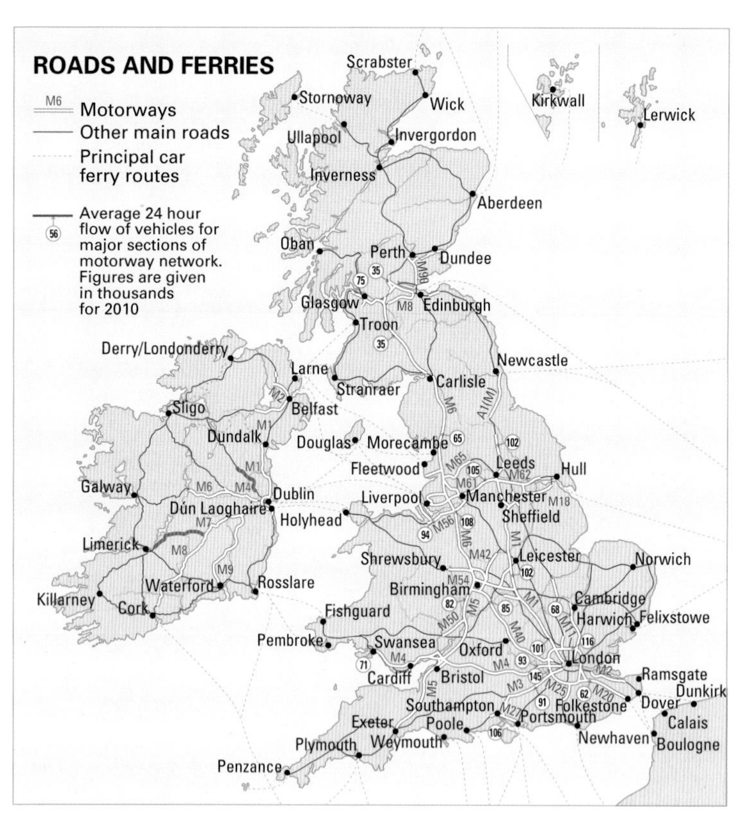

RAILWAYS

—— Electrified lines
—— Other main lines
—— High-speed rail link
- - - Planned high-speed rail link (HSR 2)

Furthest distances from London reached within a journey time of

	3 hours	6 hours
1950	○	○
2010	●	●

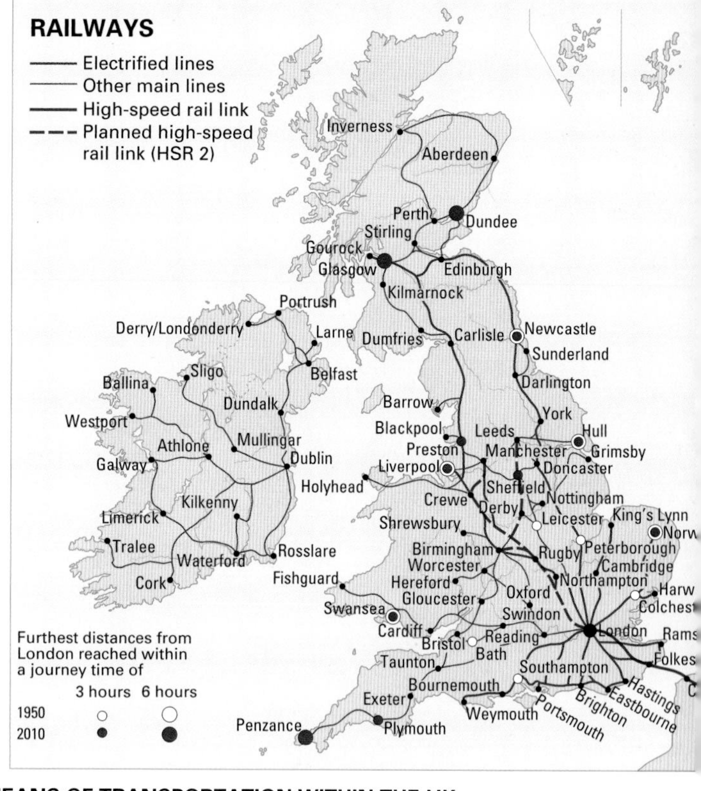

CHANNEL TUNNEL AND HIGH-SPEED RAIL LINKS IN EUROPE

Estimated journey times between London and other selected European cities

London–Berlin
London–Amsterdam
London–Paris
London–Brussels

5   10   15   20 hours

1990   Best time achievable before opening of Channel Tunnel

2002   Opening of Channel Tunnel in 1994 and completion of high-speed links in Europe

2010   Journey time on completion of high speed link from London St. Pancras to Folkestone

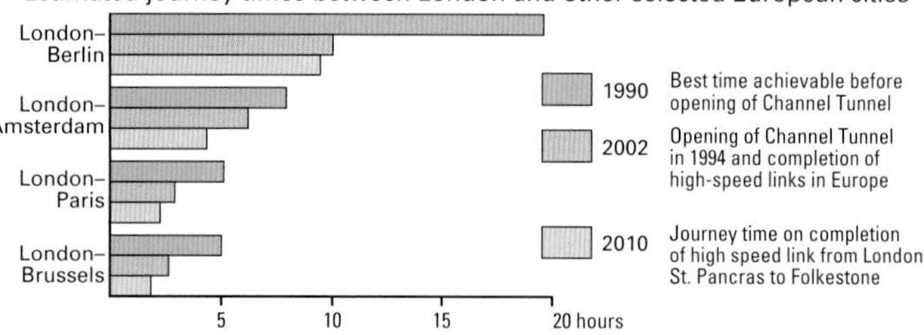

MEANS OF TRANSPORTATION WITHIN THE UK

250 225 200 175 150 125 100 75 50 25 0
billion tonne km

GOODS

0 100 200 300 400 500 600 700 8
billion passenger km

PASSENGER

| 1980 |
| 1990 |
| 2000 |
| 2009 |

Pipelines Rail Water Road

Private Transport (cars)   Public Transport (buses and coaches)

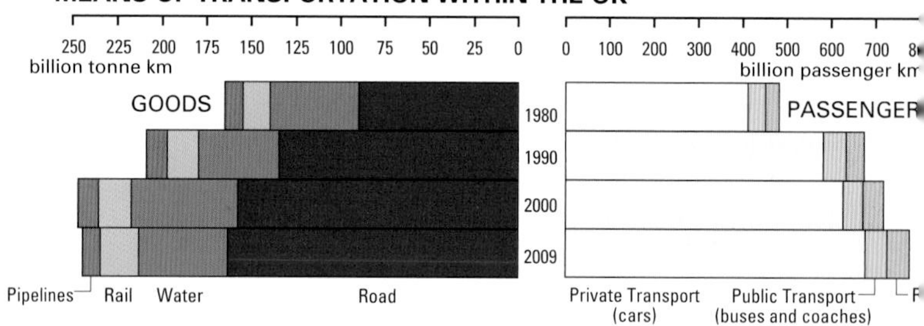

SEAPORTS

Goods traffic by port in thousand tonnes (2010)

50,000
25,000
10,000
5,000

Orkney
Sullom Voe
Cromarty Firth
Aberdeen
Glensanda
Forth
Clyde
Larne
Tyne
Belfast
Tees & Hartlepool
Heysham
Humber
Warrenpoint
Liverpool
Goole
Hull
Dublin
Holyhead
Manchester
Grimsby & Immingham
Dún Laoghaire
Shannon Foynes
Felixstowe
Waterford
Rosslare
Ipswich
Cork
London
Newport
Bristol
Harwich
Milford Haven
Port Talbot
Cardiff
Dover
Medway
Portsmouth
Plymouth
Southampton
All Irish Ports

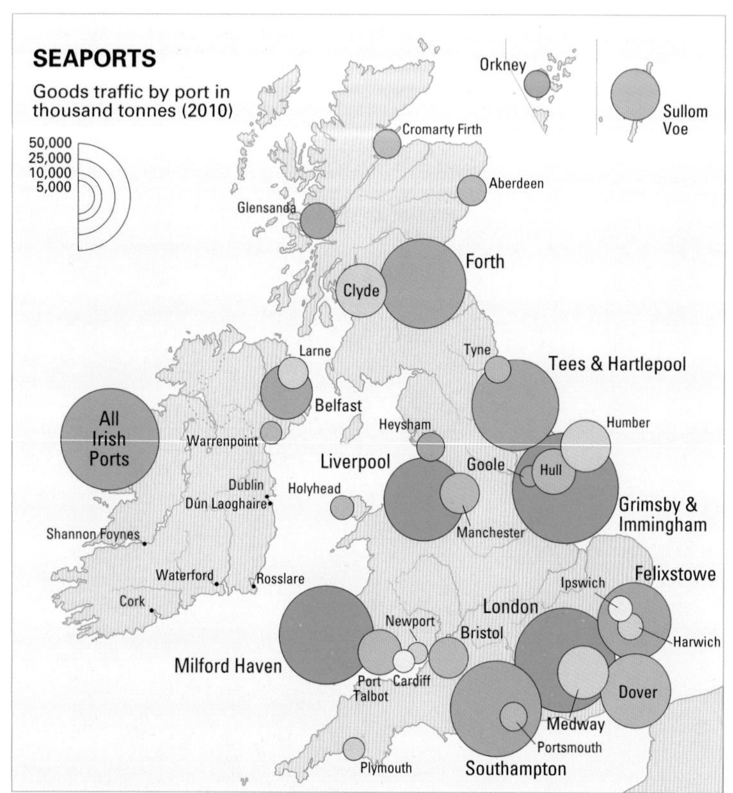

AIRPORTS

Passenger traffic in thousands (2010)

60,000
30,000
5,000
1,000

Stornoway
Kirkwall
Seats
Inverness
Sumb
Aberdeen (42.0%)
Glasgow International (47.2%)
Edinburgh (48.4%)
Glasgow Prestwick
Newcastle (71.2%)
City of Derry
Belfast International (40.4%)
George Best Belfast City
Durham Tees Valley
Leeds/Bradford International
Ireland West (Knock)
Isle of Man
Blackpool
Robin Hood Doncaster/Sheffield
Galway
Liverpool John Lennon (83.9%)
Humberside
Dublin (94.2%)
East Midlands (85.9%)
Manchester (87.3%)
Norwi Internat
Shannon
Birmingham (86.8%)
London Luton (89.3%)
Kerry
Bristol International (81.1%)
Cork
Waterford
Cardiff
Lonc Stans (90.7
Exeter International
London Heathrow (92.6%)
Lond (80.0%
Newquay
Bournemouth
Southampton
London Gatwick (88.8%)

(34.6%) International Passengers as a percentage of the total for busiest airports

Isles of Scilly

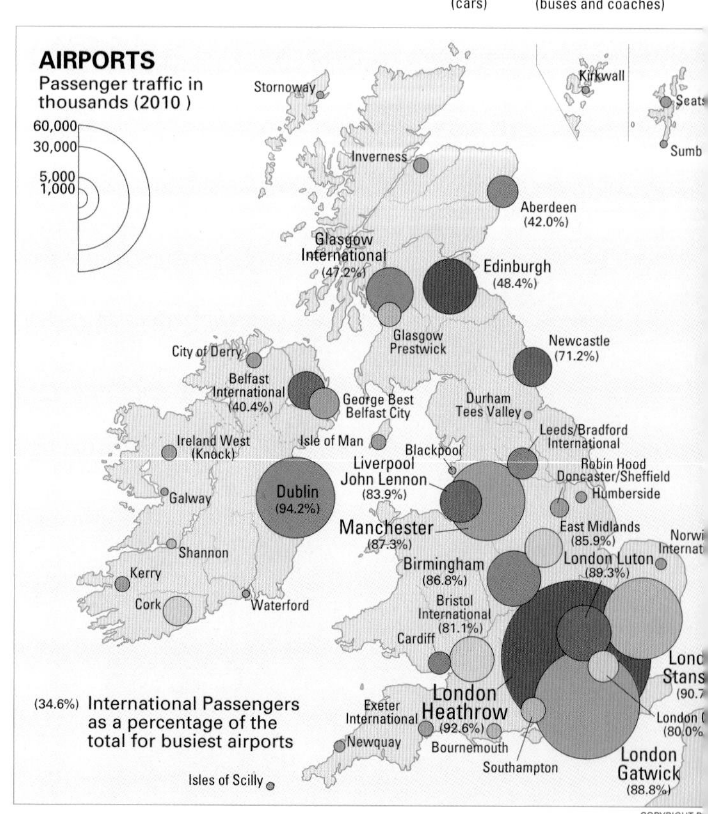

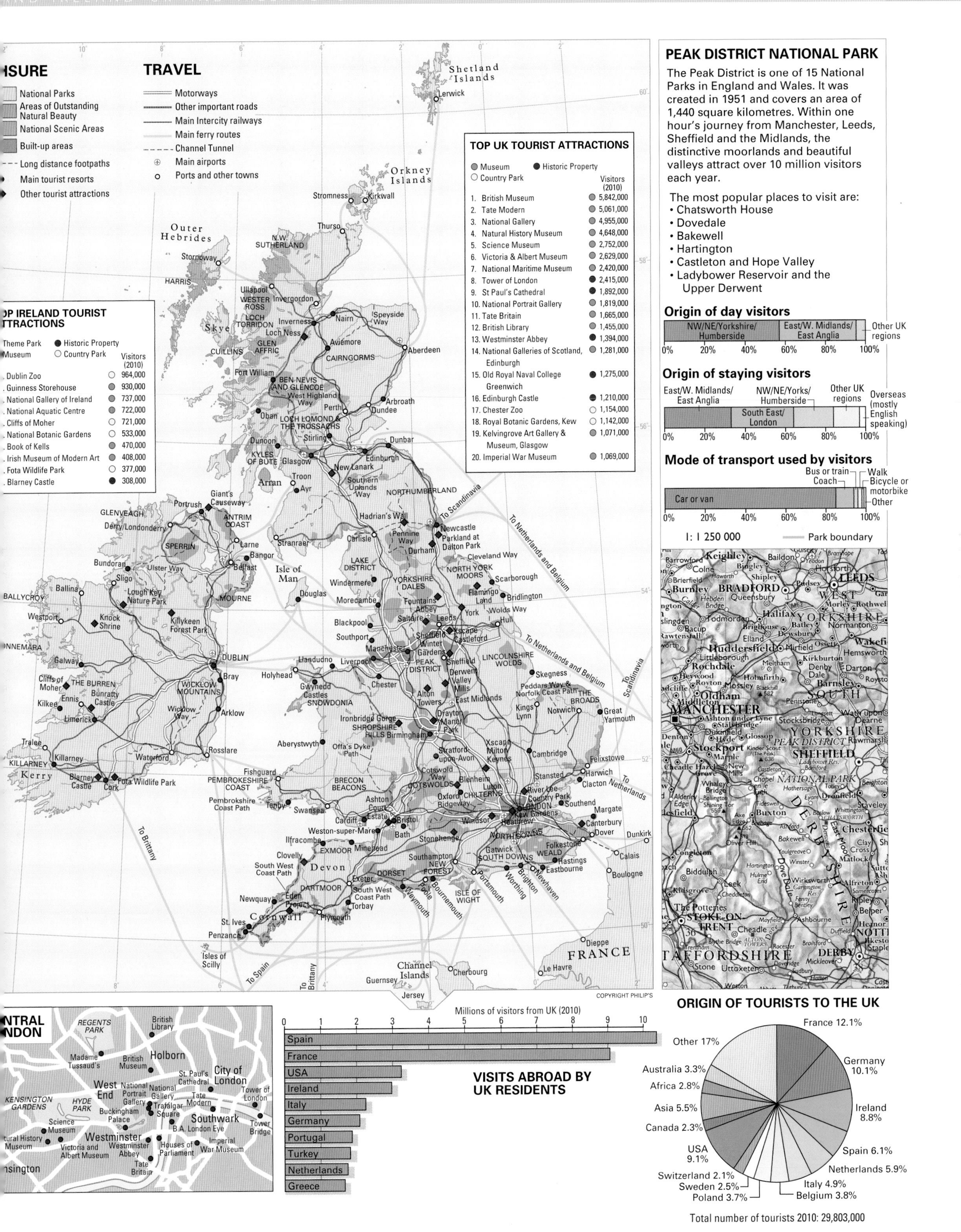

LEISURE

- National Parks
- Areas of Outstanding Natural Beauty
- National Scenic Areas
- Built-up areas
- - - Long distance footpaths
- ● Main tourist resorts
- ◆ Other tourist attractions

TRAVEL

- ══ Motorways
- ═══ Other important roads
- ── Main Intercity railways
- ── Main ferry routes
- - - Channel Tunnel
- ⊕ Main airports
- ○ Ports and other towns

TOP UK TOURIST ATTRACTIONS

● Museum ● Historic Property
○ Country Park

		Visitors (2010)
1.	British Museum	5,842,000
2.	Tate Modern	5,061,000
3.	National Gallery	4,955,000
4.	Natural History Museum	4,648,000
5.	Science Museum	2,752,000
6.	Victoria & Albert Museum	2,629,000
7.	National Maritime Museum	2,420,000
8.	Tower of London	2,415,000
9.	St Paul's Cathedral	1,892,000
10.	National Portrait Gallery	1,819,000
11.	Tate Britain	1,665,000
12.	British Library	1,455,000
13.	Westminster Abbey	1,394,000
14.	National Galleries of Scotland, Edinburgh	1,281,000
15.	Old Royal Naval College Greenwich	1,275,000
16.	Edinburgh Castle	1,210,000
17.	Chester Zoo	1,154,000
18.	Royal Botanic Gardens, Kew	1,142,000
19.	Kelvingrove Art Gallery & Museum, Glasgow	1,071,000
20.	Imperial War Museum	1,069,000

TOP IRELAND TOURIST ATTRACTIONS

■ Theme Park ● Historic Property
◆ Museum ○ Country Park

		Visitors (2010)
	Dublin Zoo	964,000
	Guinness Storehouse	930,000
	National Gallery of Ireland	737,000
	National Aquatic Centre	722,000
	Cliffs of Moher	721,000
	National Botanic Gardens	533,000
	Book of Kells	470,000
	Irish Museum of Modern Art	408,000
	Fota Wildlife Park	377,000
	Blarney Castle	308,000

PEAK DISTRICT NATIONAL PARK

The Peak District is one of 15 National Parks in England and Wales. It was created in 1951 and covers an area of 1,440 square kilometres. Within one hour's journey from Manchester, Leeds, Sheffield and the Midlands, the distinctive moorlands and beautiful valleys attract over 10 million visitors each year.

The most popular places to visit are:
- Chatsworth House
- Dovedale
- Bakewell
- Hartington
- Castleton and Hope Valley
- Ladybower Reservoir and the Upper Derwent

Origin of day visitors

NW/NE/Yorkshire/Humberside | East/W. Midlands/East Anglia | Other UK regions
0% 20% 40% 60% 80% 100%

Origin of staying visitors

East/W. Midlands/East Anglia | NW/NE/Yorks/Humberside | Other UK regions | Overseas (mostly English speaking)
South East/London
0% 20% 40% 60% 80% 100%

Mode of transport used by visitors

Car or van | Bus or train | Coach | Walk | Bicycle or motorbike | Other
0% 20% 40% 60% 80% 100%

1: 1 250 000 — Park boundary

VISITS ABROAD BY UK RESIDENTS

Millions of visitors from UK (2010)
0 1 2 3 4 5 6 7 8 9 10

- Spain
- France
- USA
- Ireland
- Italy
- Germany
- Portugal
- Turkey
- Netherlands
- Greece

ORIGIN OF TOURISTS TO THE UK

- France 12.1%
- Germany 10.1%
- Ireland 8.8%
- Spain 6.1%
- Netherlands 5.9%
- Italy 4.9%
- Belgium 3.8%
- Poland 3.7%
- Sweden 2.5%
- Switzerland 2.1%
- USA 9.1%
- Canada 2.3%
- Asia 5.5%
- Africa 2.8%
- Australia 3.3%
- Other 17%

Total number of tourists 2010: 29,803,000

COPYRIGHT PHILIP'S

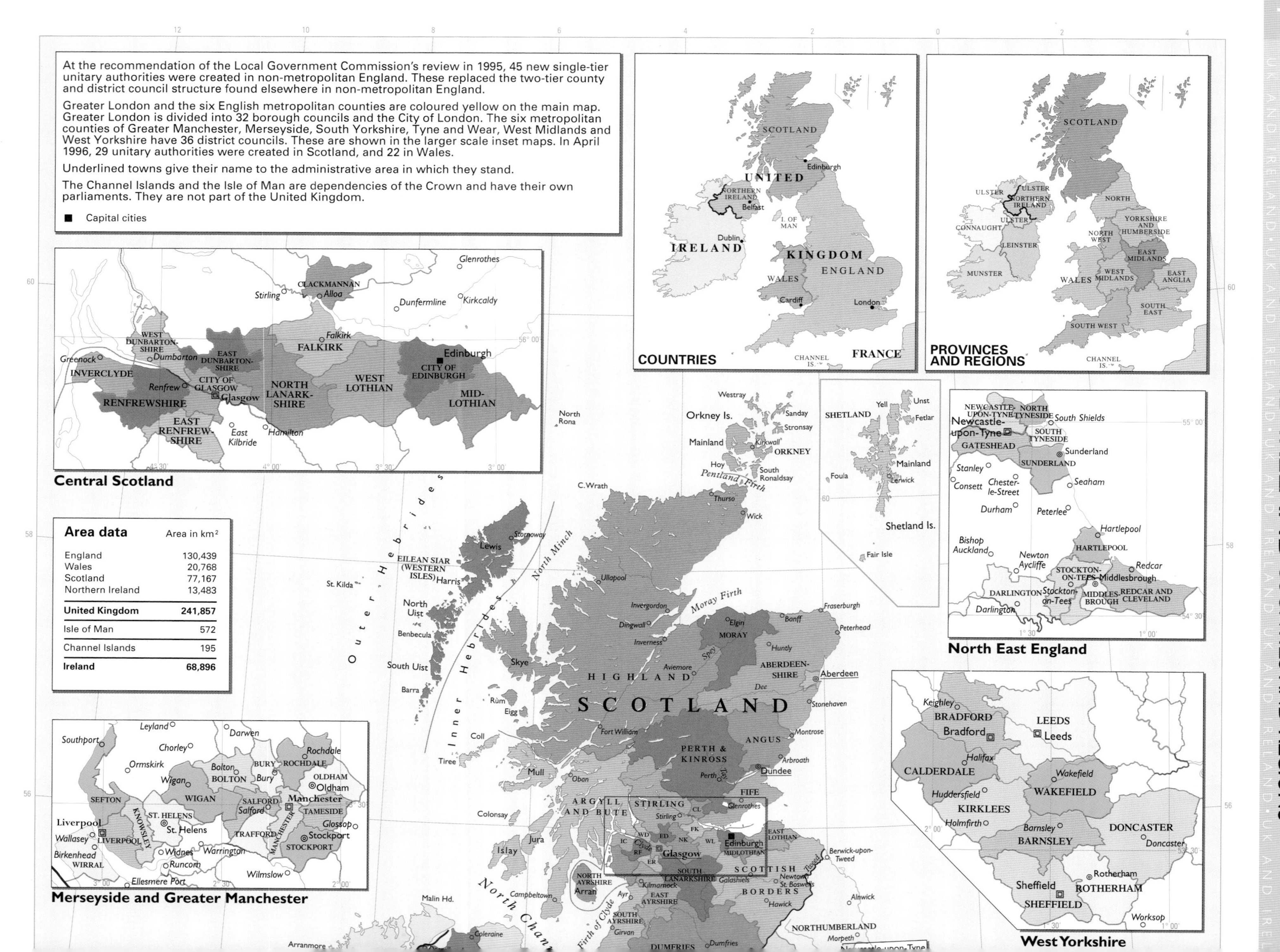

At the recommendation of the Local Government Commission's review in 1995, 45 new single-tier unitary authorities were created in non-metropolitan England. These replaced the two-tier county and district council structure found elsewhere in non-metropolitan England.

Greater London and the six English metropolitan counties are coloured yellow on the main map. Greater London is divided into 32 borough councils and the City of London. The six metropolitan counties of Greater Manchester, Merseyside, South Yorkshire, Tyne and Wear, West Midlands and West Yorkshire have 36 district councils. These are shown in the larger scale inset maps. In April 1996, 29 unitary authorities were created in Scotland, and 22 in Wales.

Underlined towns give their name to the administrative area in which they stand.

The Channel Islands and the Isle of Man are dependencies of the Crown and have their own parliaments. They are not part of the United Kingdom.

■ Capital cities

COUNTRIES

PROVINCES AND REGIONS

North East England

West Yorkshire

Central Scotland

Merseyside and Greater Manchester

Area data

	Area in km²
England	130,439
Wales	20,768
Scotland	77,167
Northern Ireland	13,483
United Kingdom	**241,857**
Isle of Man	572
Channel Islands	195
Ireland	**68,896**

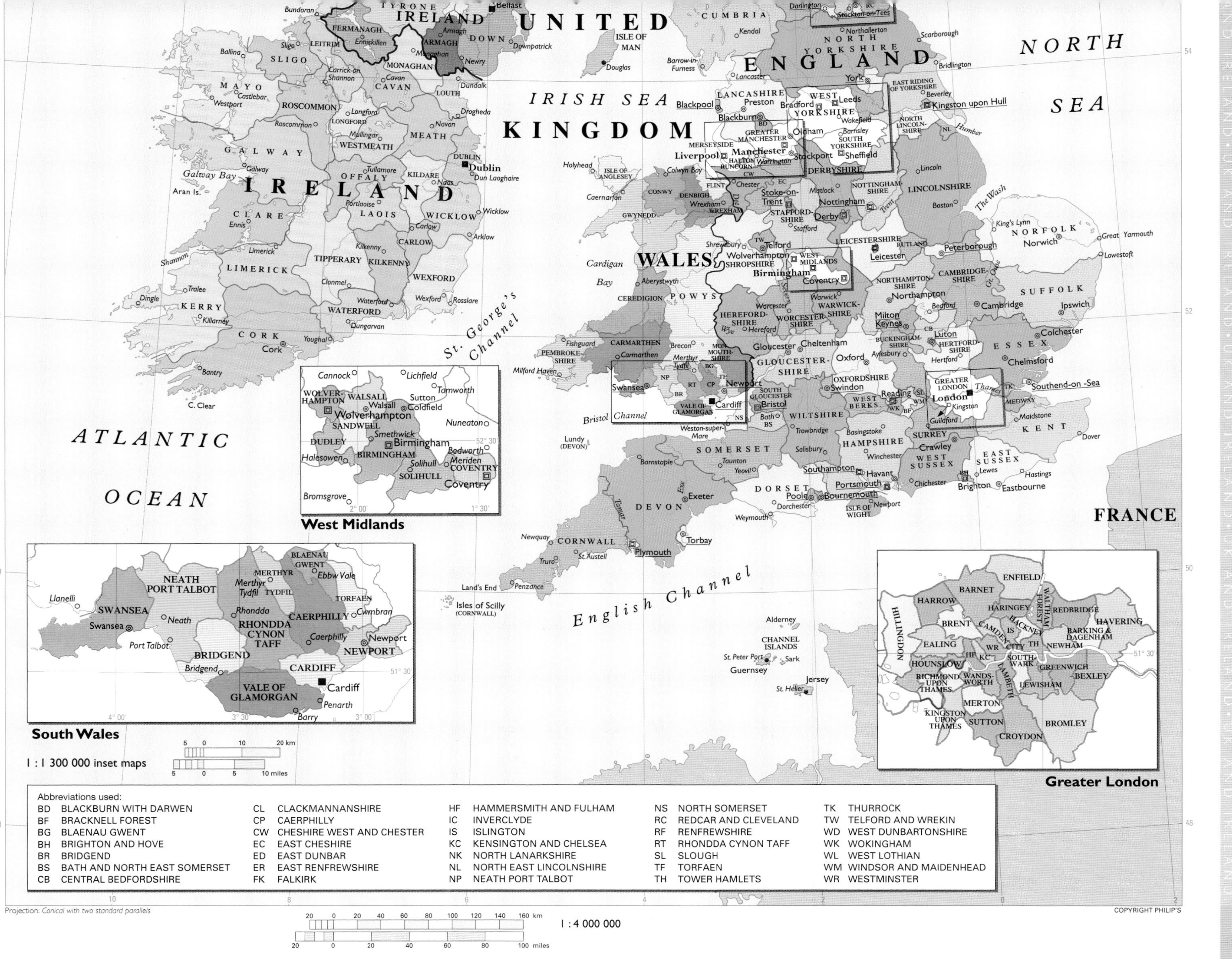
NORTH SEA
UNITED KINGDOM
ENGLAND
WALES
IRELAND
IRISH SEA
ATLANTIC OCEAN
St. George's Channel
Bristol Channel
English Channel
FRANCE
ISLE OF MAN
CHANNEL ISLANDS
West Midlands
South Wales
1 : 1 300 000 inset maps
Greater London
1 : 4 000 000
Projection: Conical with two standard parallels
COPYRIGHT PHILIP'S
Abbreviations used:
BD BLACKBURN WITH DARWEN
BF BRACKNELL FOREST
BG BLAENAU GWENT
BH BRIGHTON AND HOVE
BR BRIDGEND
BS BATH AND NORTH EAST SOMERSET
CB CENTRAL BEDFORDSHIRE
CL CLACKMANNANSHIRE
CP CAERPHILLY
CW CHESHIRE WEST AND CHESTER
EC EAST CHESHIRE
ED EAST DUNBAR
ER EAST RENFREWSHIRE
FK FALKIRK
HF HAMMERSMITH AND FULHAM
IC INVERCLYDE
IS ISLINGTON
KC KENSINGTON AND CHELSEA
NK NORTH LANARKSHIRE
NL NORTH EAST LINCOLNSHIRE
NP NEATH PORT TALBOT
NS NORTH SOMERSET
RC REDCAR AND CLEVELAND
RF RENFREWSHIRE
RT RHONDDA CYNON TAFF
SL SLOUGH
TF TORFAEN
TH TOWER HAMLETS
TK THURROCK
TW TELFORD AND WREKIN
WD WEST DUNBARTONSHIRE
WK WOKINGHAM
WL WEST LOTHIAN
WM WINDSOR AND MAIDENHEAD
WR WESTMINSTER

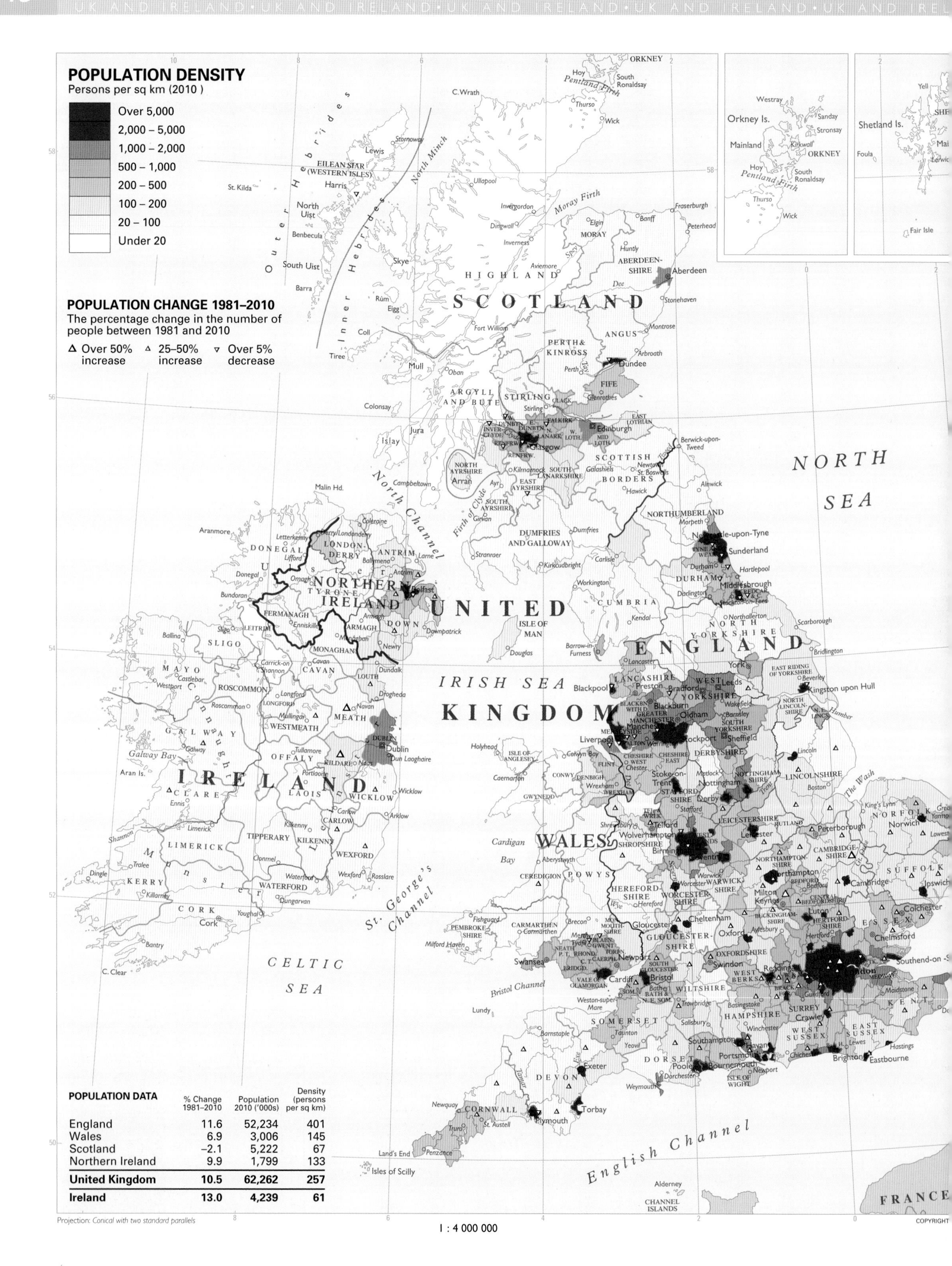

POPULATION DENSITY
Persons per sq km (2010)

- Over 5,000
- 2,000 – 5,000
- 1,000 – 2,000
- 500 – 1,000
- 200 – 500
- 100 – 200
- 20 – 100
- Under 20

POPULATION CHANGE 1981–2010
The percentage change in the number of people between 1981 and 2010

△ Over 50% increase △ 25–50% increase ▽ Over 5% decrease

POPULATION DATA	% Change 1981–2010	Population 2010 ('000s)	Density (persons per sq km)
England	11.6	52,234	401
Wales	6.9	3,006	145
Scotland	-2.1	5,222	67
Northern Ireland	9.9	1,799	133
United Kingdom	**10.5**	**62,262**	**257**
Ireland	**13.0**	**4,239**	**61**

Projection: Conical with two standard parallels

I : 4 000 000

COPYRIGHT

POPULATION DENSITY IN 1891

Persons per sq km

- Over 1,000
- 500 – 1,000
- 200 – 500
- 100 – 200
- 50 – 100
- 25 – 50
- Under 25

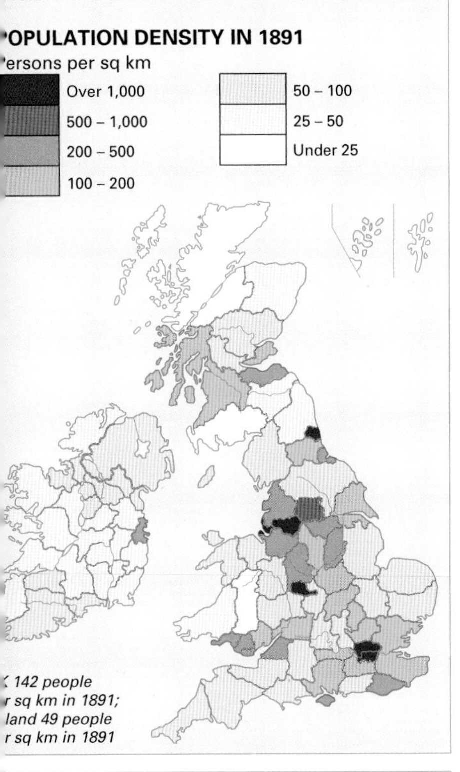

142 people
r sq km in 1891;
land 49 people
r sq km in 1891

ETHNIC GROUPS

Ethnic minorities as a percentage of total population in 2010

- Over 25%
- 10 – 25%
- 5 – 10%
- 0 – 5%

Ethnic minority groups

138 000 Total number of ethnic minority people in each region

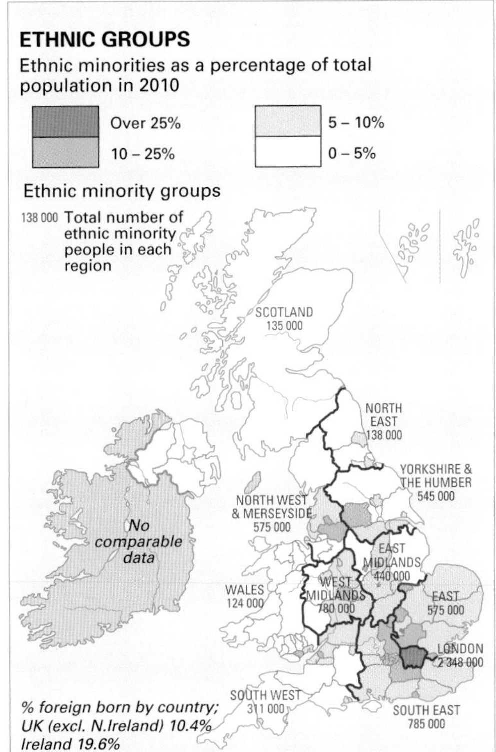

SCOTLAND 135 000
NORTH EAST 138 000
YORKSHIRE & THE HUMBER 545 000
NORTH WEST & MERSEYSIDE 575 000
No comparable data
EAST MIDLANDS 440 000
WALES 124 000
WEST MIDLANDS 780 000
EAST 575 000
LONDON 2 348 000
SOUTH WEST 311 000
SOUTH EAST 785 000

% foreign born by country;
UK (excl. N.Ireland) 10.4%
Ireland 19.6%

MIGRATION

The difference between the number moving in and the number moving away per 1,000 inhabitants 2010

- Over 10 moved in
- 1 – 10 moved in
- 0 – 1 moved in
- 0 – 1 moved away
- 1 – 10 moved away
- Over 10 moved away

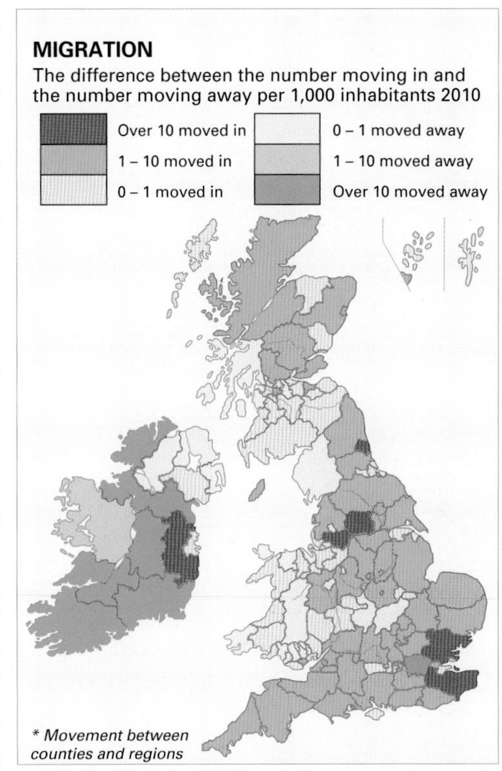

* Movement between counties and regions

NATURAL POPULATION CHANGE

The difference between the number of births and the number of deaths per thousand inhabitants in 2010

- Over 10 more births
- 5 – 10 more births
- 2.5 – 5 more births
- 1 – 2.5 more births
- 0 – 1 more births
- 0 – 1 more deaths

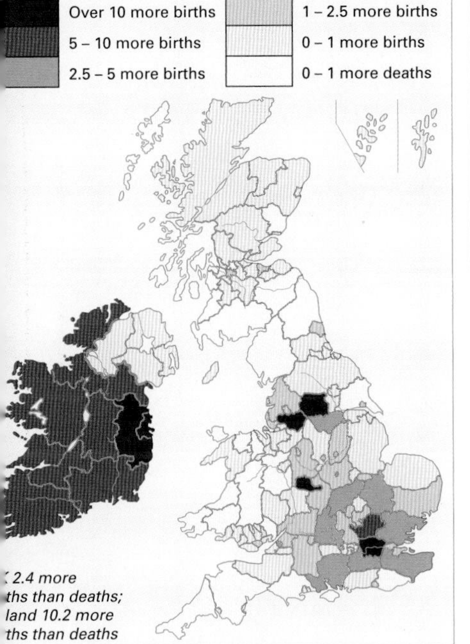

2.4 more
ths than deaths;
land 10.2 more
ths than deaths

YOUNG PEOPLE

The percentage of the population under 15 years old in 2010

- Over 22%
- 20 – 22%
- 18 – 20%
- 16 – 18%
- 14 – 16%

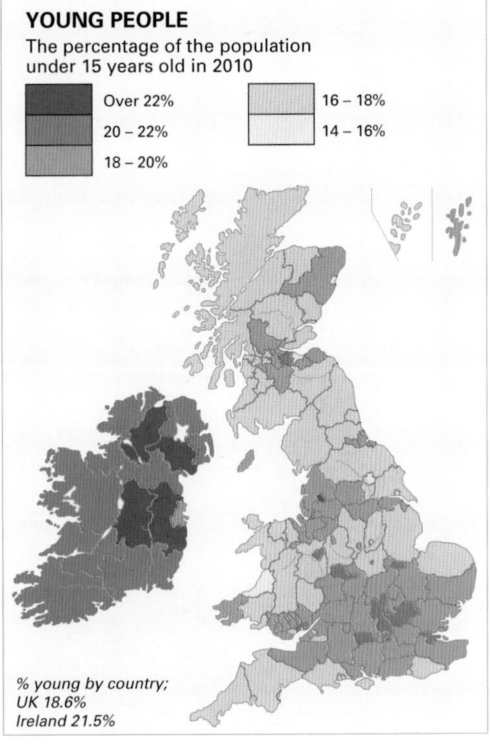

% young by country;
UK 18.6%
Ireland 21.5%

OLD PEOPLE

The percentage of the population aged 65 and over in 2010

- Over 22%
- 20 – 22%
- 18 – 20%
- 16 – 18%
- 14 – 16%
- Under 14%

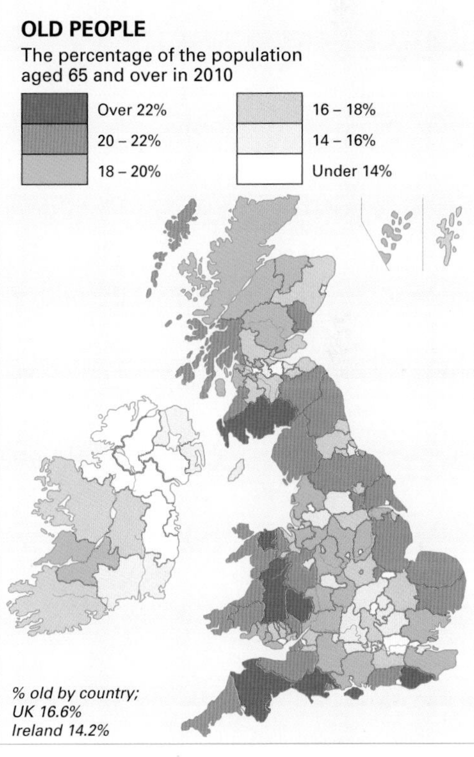

% old by country;
UK 16.6%
Ireland 14.2%

VITAL STATISTICS (1900–2010)

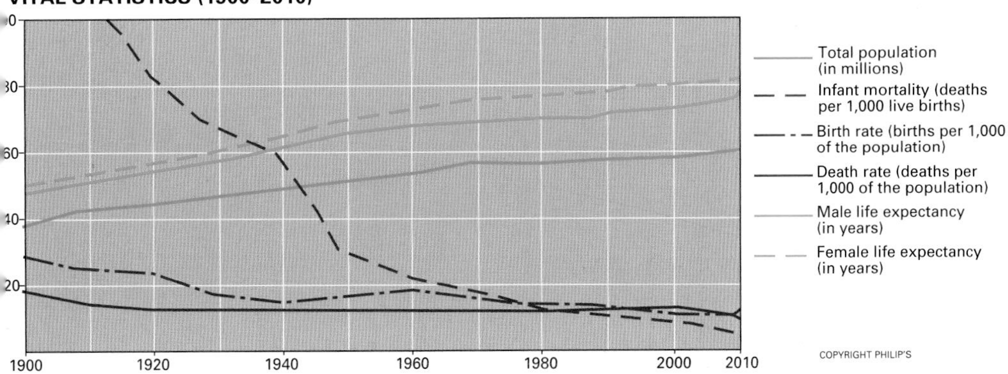

- —— Total population (in millions)
- – – – Infant mortality (deaths per 1,000 live births)
- – · – Birth rate (births per 1,000 of the population)
- —— Death rate (deaths per 1,000 of the population)
- —— Male life expectancy (in years)
- – – – Female life expectancy (in years)

COPYRIGHT PHILIP'S

AGE STRUCTURE OF THE UK

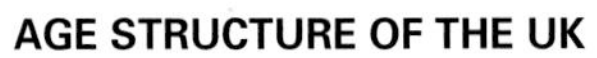
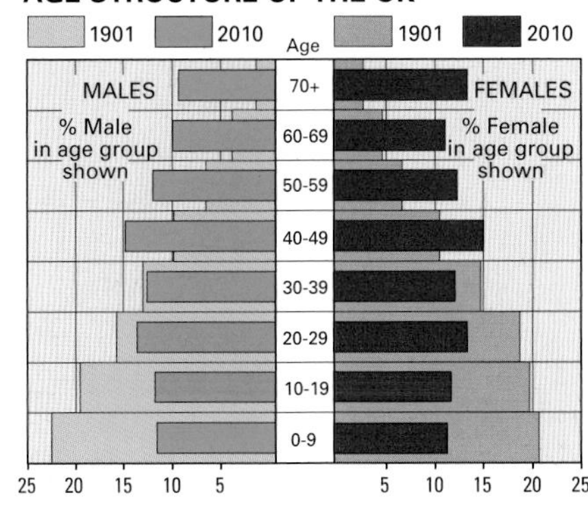

- 1901
- 2010
- 1901
- 2010

Age

MALES
% Male in age group shown

FEMALES
% Female in age group shown

70+
60-69
50-59
40-49
30-39
20-29
10-19
0-9

25 20 15 10 5   5 10 15 20 25

HOUSE PRICES
The average house price in 2011

Over £250,000	£100,000 – £150,000
£200,000 – £250,000	Under £100,000
£150,000 – £200,000	

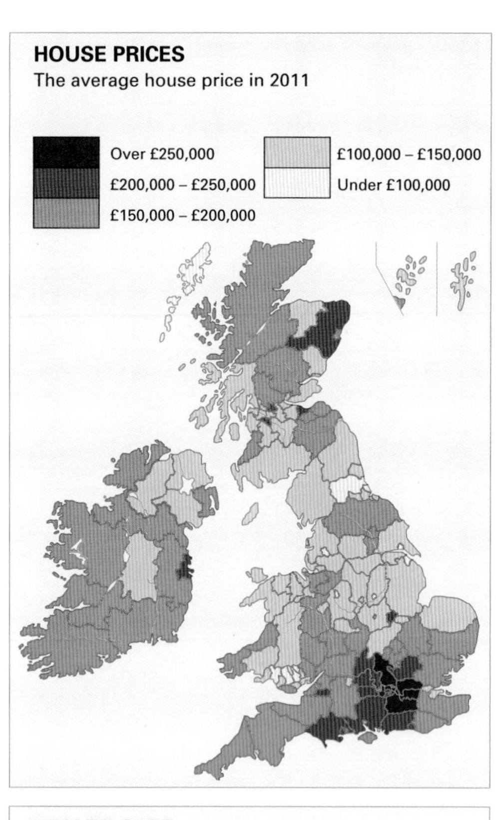

UNEMPLOYMENT
The percentage of the workforce unemployed in 2010

Over 12%	6 – 8%
10 – 12%	4 – 6%
8 – 10%	Under 4%

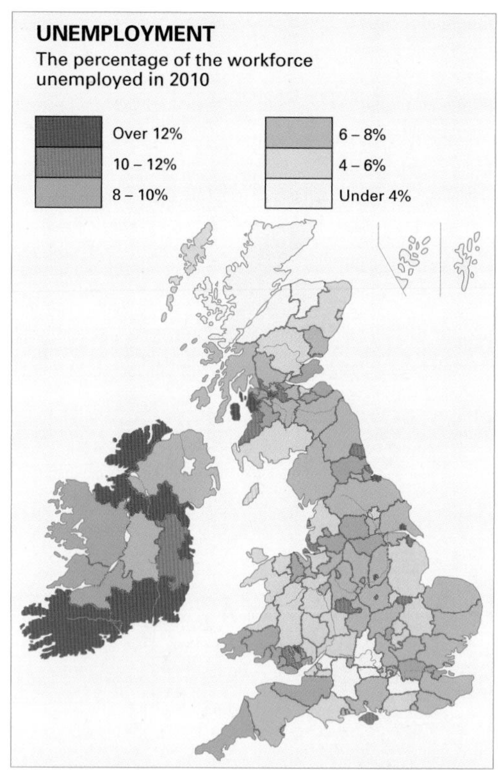

INCOME
The average gross weekly earnings of males and females in full employment in 2010

Over £600	£450 – £500
£550 – £600	£400 – £450
£500 – £550	Under £400

No comparable data

Average weekly; earnings (2010)
UK £499
Ireland €684

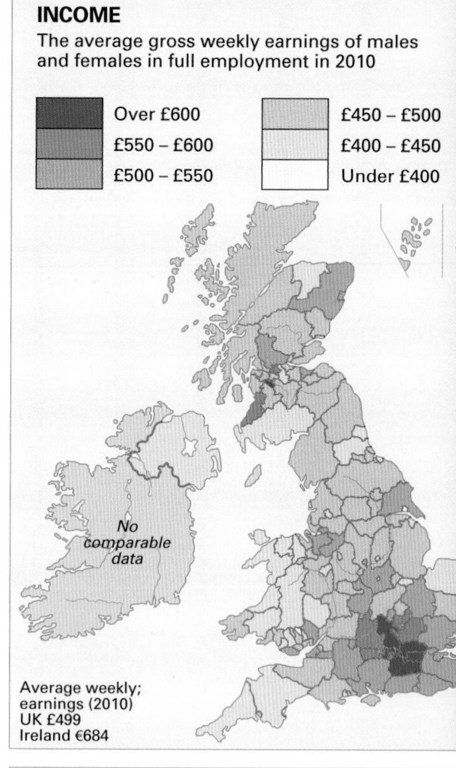

HEALTH CARE
The number of people per doctor (GP) by Strategic Health Authority in 2010

Over 1,500	Under 1,400
1,400 – 1,500	
1,300 – 1,400	

SCOTLAND

NORTHERN IRELAND

NORTH EAST

YORKSHIRE & THE HUMBER

NORTH WEST

EAST MIDLANDS

No comparable data

WALES

WEST MIDLANDS

EAST OF ENGLAND

SOUTH CENTRAL

LONDON

SOUTH WEST

SOUTH EAST COAST

—— NHS Strategic Health Authority boundaries

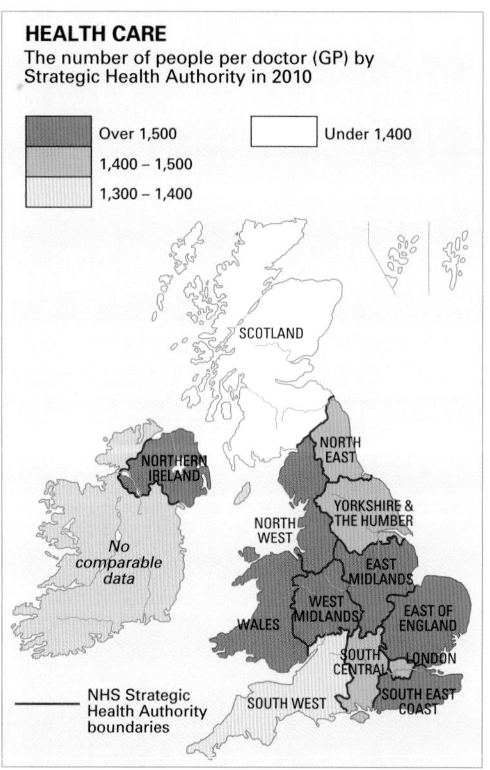

EDUCATION
The percentage of pupils achieving 5 grade A*– C at GCSE (or Standard Grades 1 – 3 in Scotland) in 2010

Over 80%	65 – 70%
75 – 80%	Under 65%
70 – 75%	

No comparable data

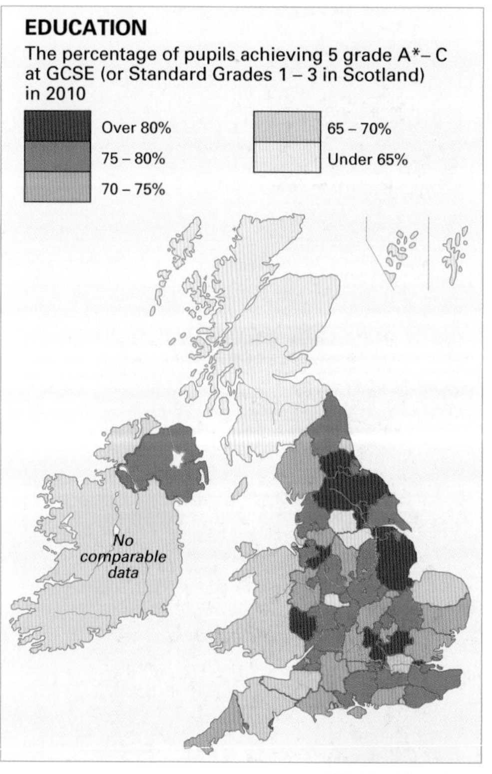

CRIME RATE
British Crime Survey recorded crimes per 1,000 people in 2010

Over 65	35 – 45
55 – 65	25 – 35
45 – 55	Under 25

No comparable data

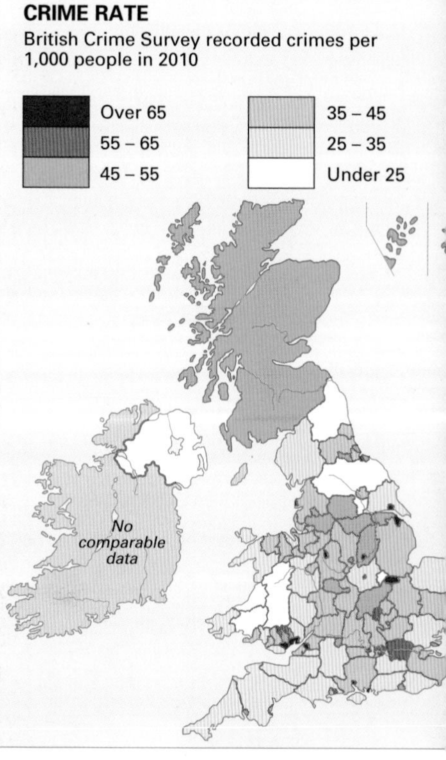

COMPARISON OF HOUSEHOLD EXPENDITURE IN THE UK, 2009

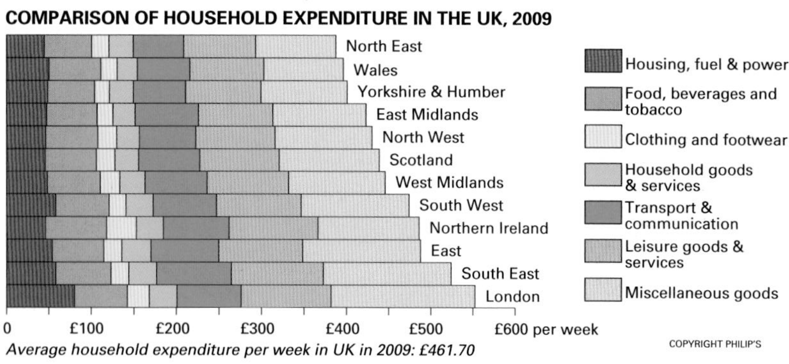

North East
Wales
Yorkshire & Humber
East Midlands
North West
Scotland
West Midlands
South West
Northern Ireland
East
South East
London

0   £100   £200   £300   £400   £500   £600 per week

Average household expenditure per week in UK in 2009: £461.70

▓	Housing, fuel & power
▓	Food, beverages and tobacco
░	Clothing and footwear
▒	Household goods & services
▓	Transport & communication
▒	Leisure goods & services
░	Miscellaneous goods

COPYRIGHT PHILIP'S

HOUSEHOLDS WITH INTERNET ACCESS, 2009

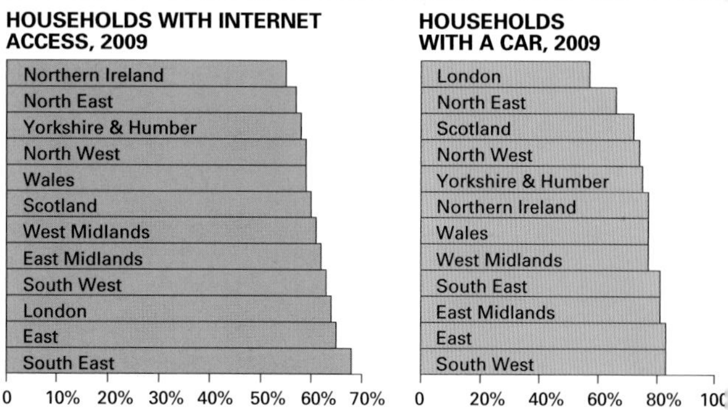

Northern Ireland
North East
Yorkshire & Humber
North West
Wales
Scotland
West Midlands
East Midlands
South West
London
East
South East

0   10%   20%   30%   40%   50%   60%   70%

HOUSEHOLDS WITH A CAR, 2009

London
North East
Scotland
North West
Yorkshire & Humber
Northern Ireland
Wales
West Midlands
South East
East Midlands
East
South West

0   20%   40%   60%   80%   100

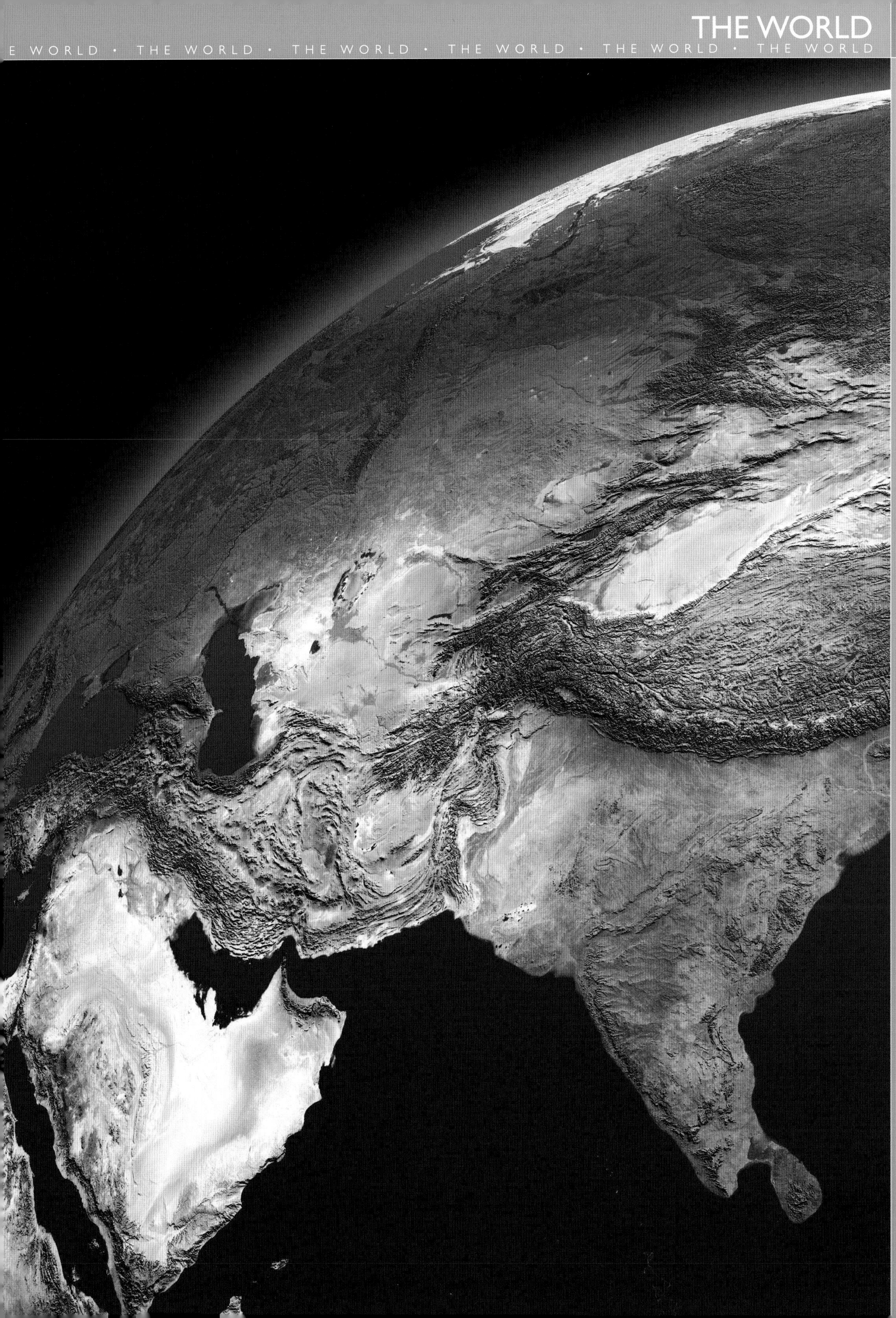

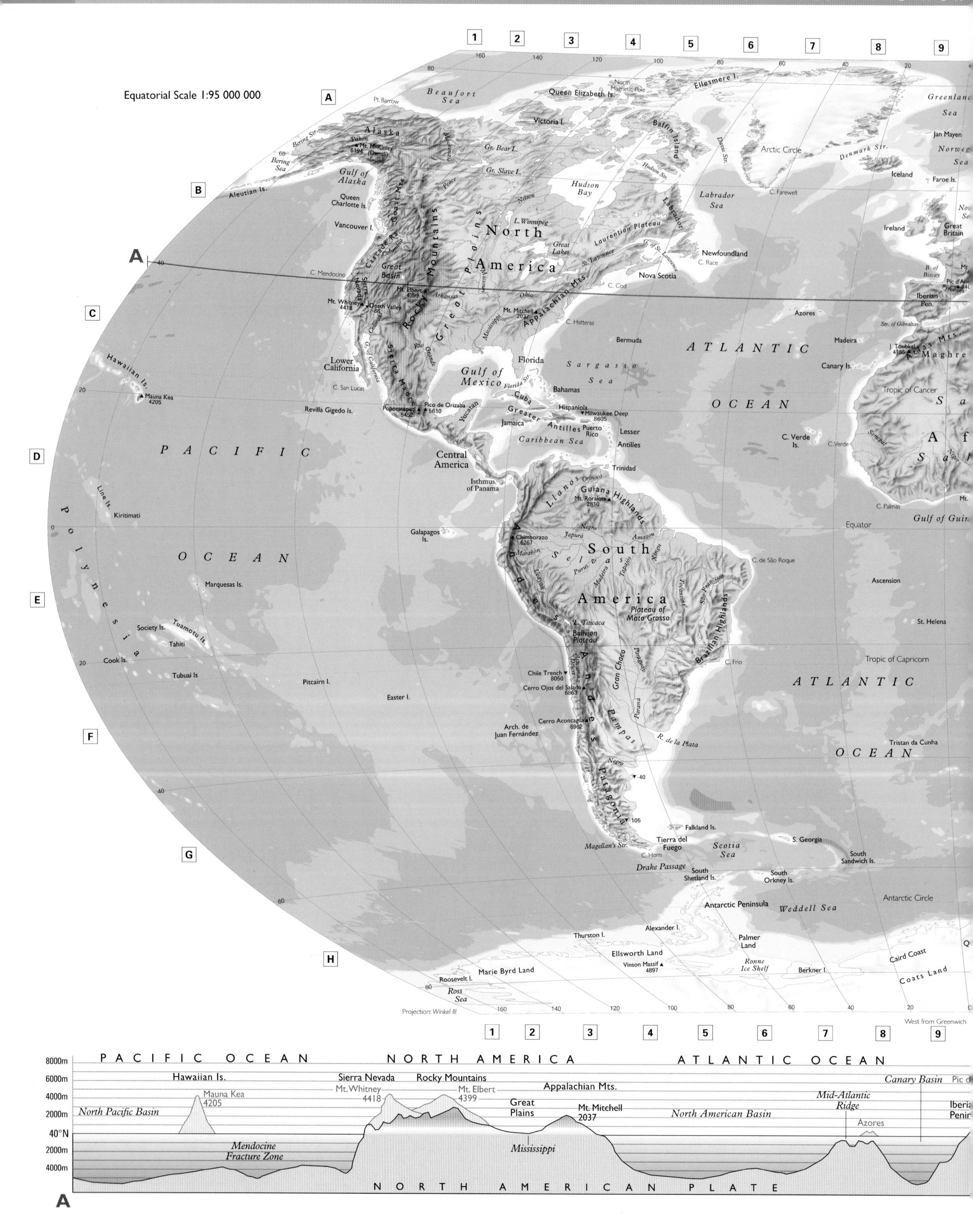

Equatorial Scale 1:95 000 000

Projection: Winkel III

West from Greenwich

PACIFIC OCEAN — *NORTH AMERICA* — *ATLANTIC OCEAN*

8000m		
6000m		

Hawaiian Is.
Mauna Kea 4205
North Pacific Basin

Sierra Nevada
Mt. Whitney 4418

Rocky Mountains
Mt. Elbert 4399
Great Plains

Appalachian Mts.
Mt. Mitchell 2037

North American Basin

Canary Basin   Pic d

Mid-Atlantic Ridge

Iberian Penir

Azores

40°N

Mendocine
Fracture Zone

Mississippi

NORTH AMERICAN PLATE

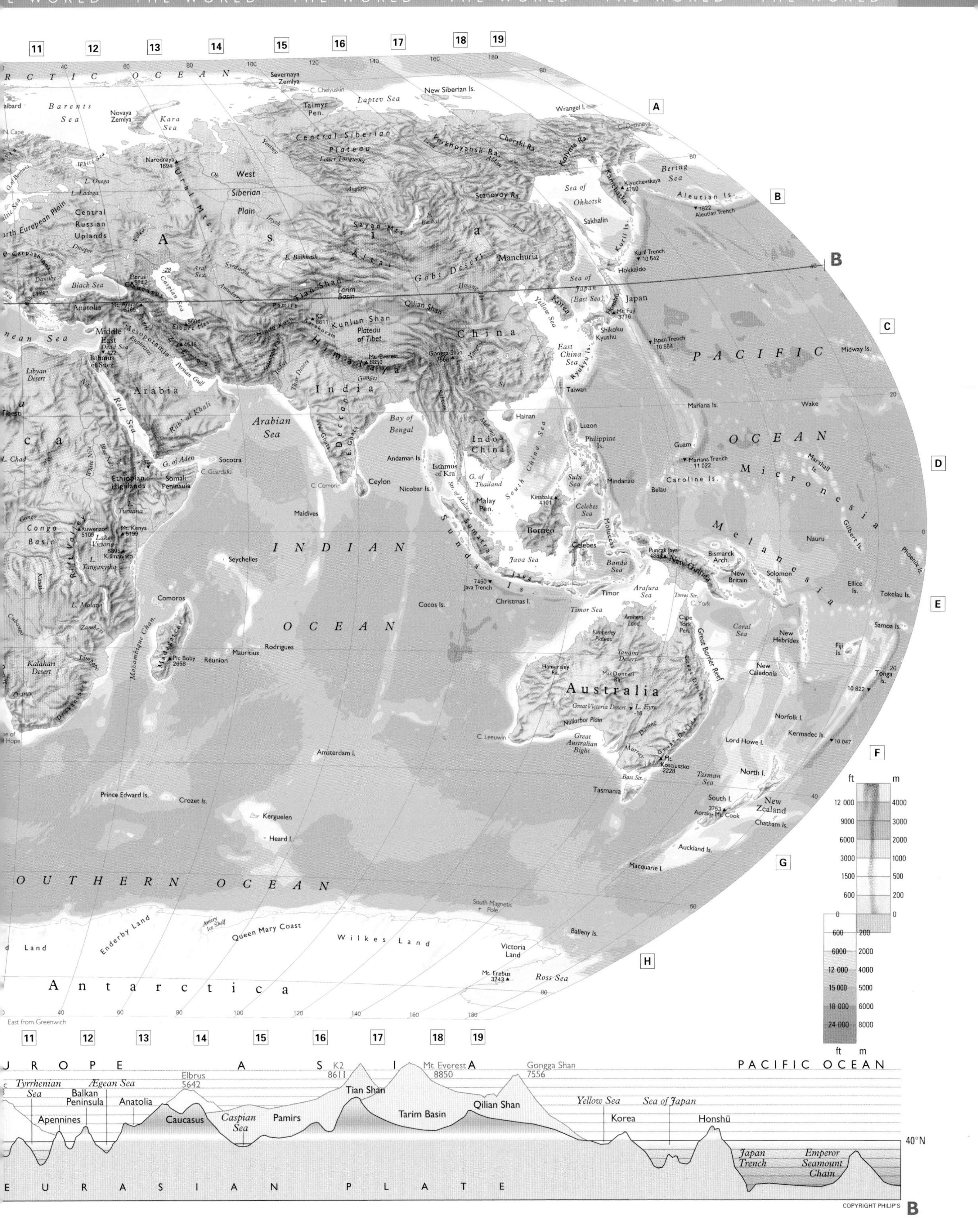
11
12
13
14
15
16
17
18
19
A
B
C
D
E
F
G
H
Barents Sea
Novaya Zemlya
Kara Sea
Severnaya Zemlya
C. Chelyuskin
Taimyr Pen.
Laptev Sea
New Siberian Is.
Wrangel I.
C. Dezhneva
Central Siberian Plateau
Lower Tunguska
Verkhoyansk Ra.
Cherski Ra.
Kolyma Ra.
Lena
Aldan
White Sea
L. Onega
L. Ladoga
Narodnaya 1894
Ural Mts.
Ob
West Siberian Plain
Yenisey
Angara
L. Baikal
Stanovoy Ra.
Sea of Okhotsk
Kamchatka
Klyuchevskaya 4750
Bering Sea
Aleutian Is.
7822 Aleutian Trench
Sakhalin
Amur
Kuril Is.
Kuril Trench 10 542
Hokkaido
Central Russian Uplands
North European Plain
Dnieper
Volga
Carpathians
Danube
Black Sea
A
s
i
a
Irtysh
Sayan Mts.
Altai
L. Balkhash
Gobi Desert
Manchuria
Aral Sea
Syrdarya
Amudarya
Caspian Sea
Elbrus 5642
Caucasus
Tian Shan
Tarim Basin
Pamirs
Hwang Ho
Sea of Japan (East Sea)
Korea
Japan
Honshu
Mt. Fuji 3776
Shikoku
Kyushu
Yellow Sea
Anatolia
Mt. Ararat 5165
Elburz Mts.
5604
K2 8611
Karakoram
Hindu Kush
Kunlun Shan
Qilian Shan
Plateau of Tibet
China
Middle East
Dead Sea
Mesopotamia
Euphrates
Zagros Mts.
4548
Isthmus of Suez
Persian Gulf
Indus
Sulaiman Ra.
Thar Desert
Himalaya
Mt. Everest 8850
Gongga Shan 7556
Yangtze
East China Sea
Ryukyu Is.
Japan Trench 10 554
PACIFIC
Midway Is.
Libyan Desert
Nile
Arabia
Red Sea
Rub' al Khali
India
Ganges
Bay of Bengal
Taiwan
Tibesti
Arabian Sea
W. Ghats
Deccan
E. Ghats
Salween
Mekong
Hainan
Luzon
Philippine Is.
Mariana Is.
Wake
L. Chad
White Nile
Blue Nile
G. of Aden
Socotra
C. Guardafui
Somali Peninsula
Ethiopian Highlands
Andaman Is.
Indo-China
South China Sea
Guam
Mariana Trench 11 022
OCEAN
Marshall Is.
Isthmus of Kra
G. of Thailand
Sulu Sea
Mindanao
Belau
Caroline Is.
Micronesia
C. Comorin
Ceylon
Nicobar Is.
Str. of Malacca
Malay Pen.
Kinabalu 4101
Celebes Sea
L. Turkana
Congo
Congo Basin
Ruwenzori 5109
Lake Victoria
Mt. Kenya 5199
Kilimanjaro 5895
Maldives
Sumatra
Borneo
Moluccas
Gilbert Is.
Melanesia
Nauru
Rift Valley
L. Tanganyika
Seychelles
INDIAN
Sunda Is.
Java Sea
Java
Celebes
Banda Sea
Puncak Jaya 4884
New Guinea
Bismarck Arch.
New Britain
Solomon Is.
Phoenix Is.
Kasai
L. Malawi
Zambezi
Comoros
7450 Java Trench
Christmas I.
Timor
Arafura Sea
Torres Str.
C. York
Ellice Is.
Tokelau Is.
Cubango
Mozambique Chan.
Madagascar
Pic Boby 2658
Cocos Is.
Timor Sea
Arnhem Land
Cape York Pen.
Coral Sea
Great Barrier Reef
Samoa Is.
Kalahari Desert
Limpopo
Mauritius
Réunion
Rodrigues
OCEAN
Kimberley Plateau
Tanami Desert
Hamersley Ra.
MacDonnell Ra.
New Hebrides
Fiji Is.
New Caledonia
Tonga Is.
10 822
Orange
Drakensberg
Australia
Great Victoria Desert
L. Eyre -16
Great Dividing Range
Nullarbor Plain
Darling
Norfolk I.
Kermadec Is.
10 047
C. Leeuwin
Great Australian Bight
Murray
Mt. Kosciuszko 2228
Lord Howe I.
Amsterdam I.
Tasman Sea
North I.
Bass Str.
Tasmania
New Zealand
South I.
3753 Aoraki Mt. Cook
Chatham Is.
Prince Edward Is.
Crozet Is.
Kerguelen
Heard I.
Auckland Is.
Macquarie I.
SOUTHERN OCEAN
South Magnetic Pole
Enderby Land
Amery Ice Shelf
Queen Mary Coast
Wilkes Land
Balleny Is.
Victoria Land
Mt. Erebus 3743
Ross Sea
Antarctica
East from Greenwich
ft
m
12 000
9000
6000
3000
1500
600
0
4000
3000
2000
1000
500
200
0
600
6000
12 000
15 000
18 000
24 000
200
2000
4000
5000
6000
8000
EUROPE
ASIA
PACIFIC OCEAN
Tyrrhenian Sea
Ægean Sea
Balkan Peninsula
Anatolia
Apennines
Elbrus 5642
Caucasus
Caspian Sea
Pamirs
K2 8611
Tian Shan
Mt. Everest 8850
Tarim Basin
Qilian Shan
Gongga Shan 7556
Yellow Sea
Sea of Japan
Korea
Honshū
40°N
Japan Trench
Emperor Seamount Chain
EURASIAN PLATE

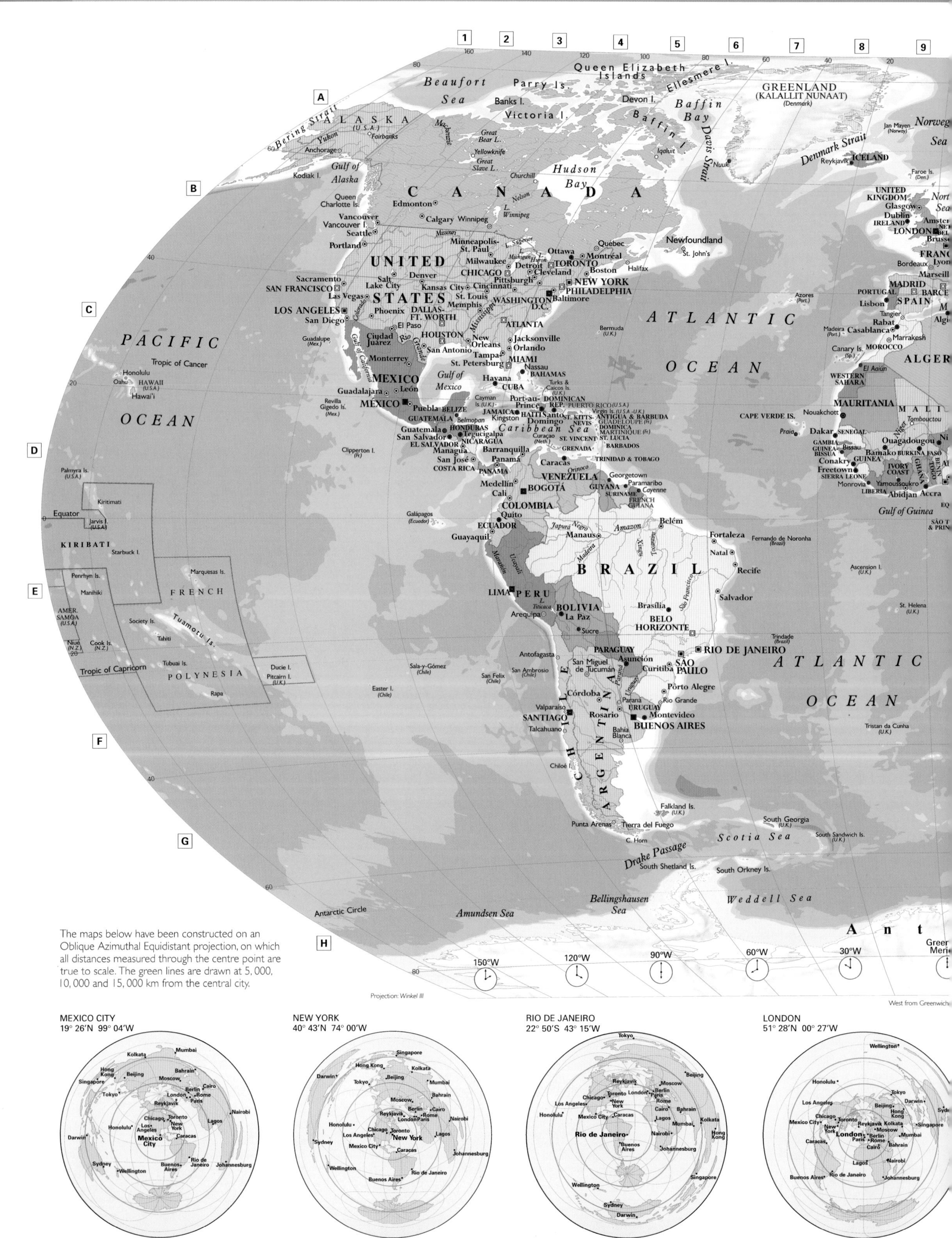

The maps below have been constructed on an Oblique Azimuthal Equidistant projection, on which all distances measured through the centre point are true to scale. The green lines are drawn at 5,000, 10,000 and 15,000 km from the central city.

Projection: Winkel III

West from Greenwich

MEXICO CITY
19° 26'N 99° 04'W

NEW YORK
40° 43'N 74° 00'W

RIO DE JANEIRO
22° 50'S 43° 15'W

LONDON
51° 28'N 00° 27'W

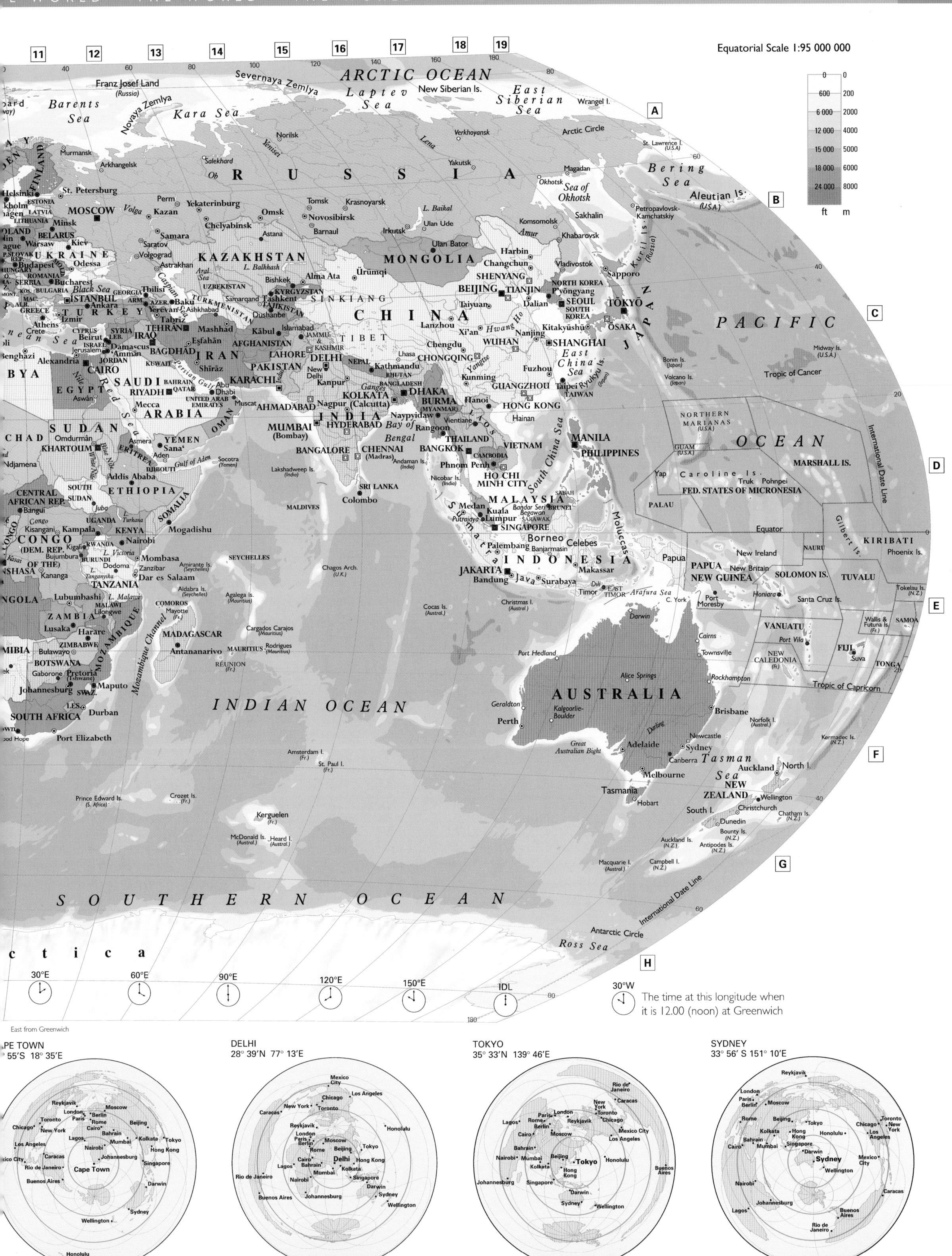

11 12 13 14 15 16 17 18 19

Equatorial Scale 1:95 000 000

ARCTIC OCEAN

Franz Josef Land
(Russia)

Severnaya Zemlya

Laptev Sea

New Siberian Is.

East Siberian Sea

Wrangel I.

Barents Sea

Novaya Zemlya

Kara Sea

Norilsk

Yenisey

Verkhoyansk

Arctic Circle

St. Lawrence I. (U.S.A.)

A

FINLAND

Murmansk

Arkhangelsk

Salekhard

Ob

R U S S I A

Lena

Yakutsk

Magadan

Bering Sea

Aleutian Is. (U.S.A.)

B

Helsinki

St. Petersburg

ESTONIA
LATVIA
LITHUANIA

Perm

Yekaterinburg

Tomsk

Krasnoyarsk

L. Baikal

Irkutsk

Ulan Ude

Komsomolsk

Sea of Okhotsk

Okhotsk

Sakhalin

Petropavlovsk-Kamchatskiy

MOSCOW

Volga

Kazan

Omsk

Novosibirsk

Barnaul

Amur

Khabarovsk

Kuril Is. (Russia)

BELARUS

Kiev

Samara

Saratov

Volgograd

Astrakhan

KAZAKHSTAN

Astana

Alma Ata

Ürümqi

MONGOLIA

Ulan Bator

Harbin

Changchun

Vladivostok

Sapporo

Warsaw

Minsk

Aral Sea

L. Balkhash

SHENYANG

NORTH KOREA

Pyongyang

40

Budapest

UKRAINE

Odessa

Black Sea

GEORGIA

Caspian Sea

UZBEKISTAN

Bishkek

KYRGYZSTAN

BEIJING TIANJIN

Dalian

SEOUL
SOUTH KOREA

TŌKYŌ

PACIFIC

C

ISTANBUL

Ankara

ARM.

AZER.

Baku

TURKMENISTAN

Samarqand

Tashkent

S I N K I A N G

Taiyuan

Kitakyūshū

ŌSAKA

Izmir

TURKEY

Yerevan

Tabriz

Ashkhabad

Dushanbe

C H I N A

Lanzhou

Xi'an

Hwang Ho

Nanjing

SHANGHAI

Bonin Is. (Japan)

Midway Is. (U.S.A.)

Athens

CYPRUS

Beirut

SYRIA LEB.

Mashhad

Kābul

AFGHANISTAN

Islamabad

JAMMU & KASHMIR

TIBET

Lhasa

Chengdu

WUHAN

CHONGQING

Yangtze

East China Sea

Volcano Is. (Japan)

Tropic of Cancer

Jerusalem

IRAQ

TEHRAN

Esfahān

LAHORE

DELHI

NEPAL

Kathmandu

BHUTAN

Kunming

Fuzhou

Taipei

Ryukyu Is. (Japan)

20

BAGHDAD

IRAN

Shīrāz

KUWAIT

PAKISTAN

New Delhi

Kanpur

BANGLADESH

Ganges

GUANGZHOU

HONG KONG

TAIWAN

CAIRO

Amman

JORDAN

BAHRAIN
QATAR

Abu Dhabi

KARACHI

AHMADABAD

Nagpur

KOLKATA
(Calcutta)

DHAKA

BURMA
(MYANMAR)

Naypyidaw

Hanoi

Hainan

EGYPT

Aswān

SAUDI

RIYADH

UNITED ARAB EMIRATES

Muscat

I N D I A

MUMBAI
(Bombay)

HYDERABAD

Bay of Bengal

Rangoon

THAILAND

VIETNAM

MANILA

NORTHERN MARIANAS (U.S.A.)

OCEAN

D

LIBYA

Alexandria

Red Sea

Mecca

A R A B I A

OMAN

Persian Gulf

Lakshadweep (India)

BANGALORE

CHENNAI
(Madras)

Andaman Is. (India)

BANGKOK

CAMBODIA

Phnom Penh

HO CHI MINH CITY

South China Sea

GUAM (U.S.A.)

MARSHALL IS.

Yap

Caroline Is.

Truk

Pohnpei

FED. STATES OF MICRONESIA

CHAD

KHARTOUM

Omdurman

SUDAN

Asmara

ERITREA

YEMEN

Sana'

Aden

Gulf of Aden

Socotra (Yemen)

SRI LANKA

Colombo

Nicobar Is. (India)

MALDIVES

MALAYSIA

SABAH

BRUNEI

Bandar Seri Begawan

PALAU

Ndjamena

Blue Nile

DJIBOUTI

Addis Ababa

CENTRAL AFRICAN REP.

Bangui

ETHIOPIA

Juba

SOUTH SUDAN

SOMALIA

Mogadishu

SEYCHELLES

Chagos Arch. (U.K.)

Medan

Kuala Lumpur

SARAWAK

Putrajaya

SINGAPORE

Borneo

Palembang

Banjarmasin

Celebes

Moluccas

Papua

PAPUA NEW GUINEA

New Ireland

New Britain

NAURU

SOLOMON IS.

KIRIBATI

Phoenix Is.

TUVALU

Equator

E

CONGO

Kisangani

Kampala

UGANDA

KENYA

Nairobi

Mombasa

L. Victoria

Kigali

RWANDA

BURUNDI

Bujumbura

Dodoma

Zanzibar

Amirante Is. (Seychelles)

Aldabra Is. (Seychelles)

JAKARTA

Bandung

Java

Surabaya

I N D O N E S I A

Makassar

Dili

EAST TIMOR

Arafura Sea

C. York

Honiara

Santa Cruz Is.

Tokelau (N.Z.)

CONGO
(DEM. REP. OF THE)

KINSHASA

Kananga

TANZANIA

Dar es Salaam

Tanganyika

Agalega Is. (Mauritius)

Cocos Is. (Austral.)

Christmas I. (Austral.)

Darwin

Port Moresby

Wallis & Futuna Is. (Fr.)

SAMOA

ANGOLA

Lubumbashi

L. Malawi

MALAWI

Lilongwe

COMOROS

Mayotte (Fr.)

MADAGASCAR

Antananarivo

MAURITIUS

Cargados Carajos (Mauritius)

Rodrigues (Mauritius)

Cairns

Townsville

VANUATU

Port Vila

NEW CALEDONIA (Fr.)

FIJI

Suva

TONGA

E

ZAMBIA

Lusaka

Harare

ZIMBABWE

MOZAMBIQUE

RÉUNION (Fr.)

Port Hedland

Alice Springs

Rockhampton

Tropic of Capricorn

NAMIBIA

Bulawayo

BOTSWANA

Gaborone

Pretoria (Tshwane)

Johannesburg

Maputo

SWAZ.

INDIAN OCEAN

Amsterdam I. (Fr.)

St. Paul I. (Fr.)

Port Hedland

AUSTRALIA

Geraldton

Kalgoorlie-Boulder

Great Australian Bight

Perth

Darling

Brisbane

Newcastle

Norfolk I. (N.Z.)

Kermadec Is. (N.Z.)

F

SOUTH AFRICA

Durban

Port Elizabeth

Good Hope

LES.

Prince Edward Is. (S. Africa)

Crozet Is. (Fr.)

Kerguelen (Fr.)

McDonald Is. (Austral.)

Heard I. (Austral.)

Adelaide

Canberra

Melbourne

Tasman Sea

Tasmania

Hobart

Sydney

Auckland

North I.

NEW ZEALAND

Wellington

South I.

Dunedin

Christchurch

Chatham Is. (N.Z.)

Bounty Is. (N.Z.)

40

Auckland Is. (N.Z.)

Antipodes Is. (N.Z.)

Macquarie I. (Austral.)

Campbell I. (N.Z.)

International Date Line

G

SOUTHERN OCEAN

ctica

Antarctic Circle

60

Ross Sea

H

Scale legend (top right):
0
600 / 200
6 000 / 2000
12 000 / 4000
15 000 / 5000
18 000 / 6000
24 000 / 8000
ft m

30°E 60°E 90°E 120°E 150°E IDL 30°W

The time at this longitude when it is 12.00 (noon) at Greenwich

East from Greenwich

CAPE TOWN
33° 55'S 18° 35'E

Reykjavik Moscow
Chicago Toronto London, Paris Berlin Rome Cairo Bahrain Beijing
New York Los Angeles Lagos Mumbai Kolkata Tokyo Hong Kong
Mexico City Caracas Nairobi Johannesburg Singapore
Rio de Janeiro Cape Town Darwin
Buenos Aires
Wellington
Honolulu
Sydney

DELHI
28° 39'N 77° 13'E

Mexico City
Los Angeles Chicago New York
Caracas Reykjavik London Paris Moscow
Lagos Cairo Bahrain Delhi Hong Kong
Nairobi Mumbai Kolkata Tokyo
Rio de Janeiro Singapore Honolulu
Buenos Aires Johannesburg Darwin Sydney
Wellington

TOKYO
35° 33'N 139° 46'E

Rio de Janeiro
New York Caracas
Paris Rome London Reykjavik Mexico City
Lagos Berlin Moscow Chicago Los Angeles
Cairo Bahrain Beijing Honolulu
Nairobi Mumbai Delhi TOKYO
Kolkata Hong Kong Buenos Aires
Johannesburg Singapore Darwin
Sydney Wellington

SYDNEY
33° 56'S 151° 10'E

Reykjavik
London Paris Berlin Moscow
Rome Beijing Tokyo Chicago Toronto
Cairo Bahrain Kolkata Hong Kong Honolulu New York Los Angeles
Nairobi Mumbai Singapore Darwin Mexico City
SYDNEY Wellington
Johannesburg Caracas
Lagos Buenos Aires
Rio de Janeiro

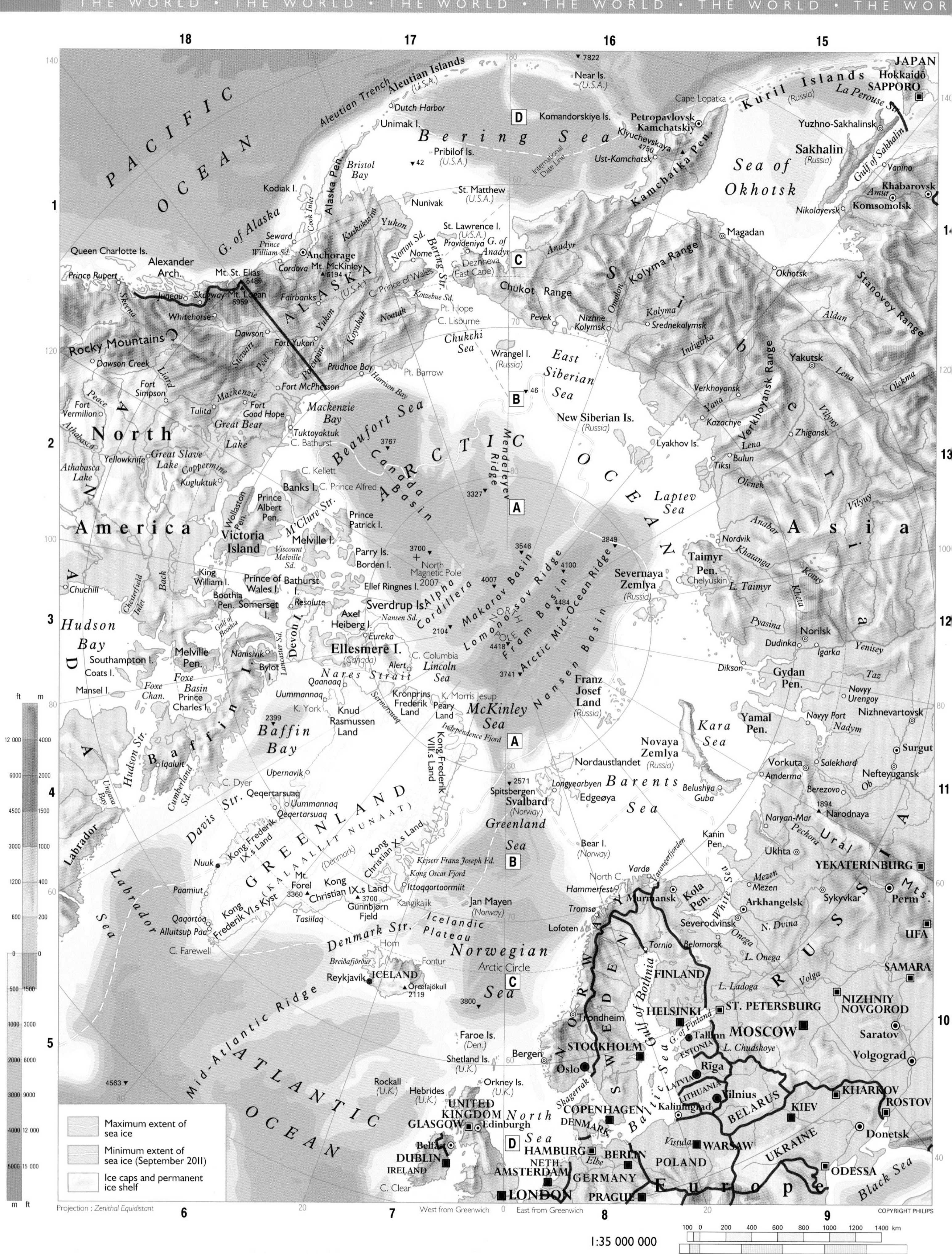
PACIFIC OCEAN
Aleutian Islands (U.S.A.)
Aleutian Trench
Dutch Harbor
Unimak I.
Near Is. (U.S.A.)
Komandorskiye Is.
Bering Sea
Pribilof Is. (U.S.A.)
Bristol Bay
Kodiak I.
St. Matthew (U.S.A.)
Nunivak
St. Lawrence I. (U.S.A.)
G. of Alaska
Alaska Pen.
Cook Inlet
Kuskokwim
Yukon
Seward
Prince William Sd.
Anchorage
Cordova
Mt. McKinley 6194
Norton Sd.
Nome
Bering Str.
Provideniya
G. of Anadyr
C. Dezhneva (East Cape)
Queen Charlotte Is.
Alexander Arch.
Prince Rupert
Mt. St. Elias 5489
Juneau
Skagway
Mt. Logan 5959
Fairbanks
ALASKA (U.S.A.)
C. Prince of Wales
Kotzebue Sd.
Pt. Hope
C. Lisburne
Noatak
Koyukuk
Whitehorse
Skeena
Rocky Mountains
Dawson
Fort Yukon
Porcupine
Stewart
Peel
Dawson Creek
Liard
Fort Simpson
Mackenzie
Fort McPherson
Prudhoe Bay
Harrison Bay
Pt. Barrow
Chukchi Sea
Wrangel I. (Russia)
East Siberian Sea
Fort Vermilion
Peace
Tulita
Fort Good Hope
Great Bear Lake
Mackenzie Bay
Beaufort Sea
Tuktoyaktuk
C. Bathurst
Athabasca
Yellowknife
Great Slave Lake
Athabasca Lake
Coppermine
Kugluktuk
C. Kellett
Banks I.
C. Prince Alfred
Canada Basin
Prince Albert Pen.
Wollaston Pen.
M'Clure Str.
Prince Patrick I.
Victoria Island
Melville I.
Viscount Melville Sd.
North America
Parry Is.
Borden I.
North Magnetic Pole 2007
Chuchill
Chesterfield Inlet
Back
King William I.
Boothia Pen.
Prince of Wales I.
Bathurst I.
Somerset I.
Resolute
Ellef Ringnes I.
Sverdrup Is.
Axel Heiberg I.
Nansen Sd.
Alpha Cordillera
Makarov Basin
Lomonosov Ridge
NORTH POLE
Fram Basin
Arctic Mid-Ocean Ridge
Nansen Basin
Mendeleyev Ridge
ARCTIC OCEAN
Hudson Bay
Gulf of Boothia
Lancaster Sd.
Devon I.
Eureka
Ellesmere I. (Canada)
C. Columbia
Alert
Lincoln Sea
Southampton I.
Coats I.
Mansel I.
Melville Pen.
Nanisivik
Bylot I.
Foxe Basin
Foxe Chan.
Prince Charles I.
Qaanaaq
Nares Strait
Uummannaq
K. York
Kronprins Frederik Land
K. Morris Jesup
Peary Land
McKinley Sea
Independence Fjord
Knud Rasmussen Land
Baffin Bay
Baffin I.
Hudson Str.
Iqaluit
Cumberland Sd.
Ungava Bay
Upernavik
C. Dyer
Davis Str.
Qeqertarsuaq
Labrador
Nuuk
Kong Frederik IX.s Land
GREENLAND (KALAALLIT NUNAAT) (Denmark)
Kong Christian X.s Land
Kejserr Franz Joseph Fd.
Kong Oscar Fjord
Ittoqqortoormiit
Mt. Forel 3360
Kong Christian IX.s Land
Gunnbjørn Fjeld 3700
Kangikajik
Paamiut
Kong Frederik VI.s Kyst
Qaqortoq
Alluitsup Paa
Tasiilaq
C. Farewell
Labrador Sea
Denmark Str.
Icelandic Plateau
Jan Mayen (Norway)
Horn
Breiðafjörður
Fontur
Reykjavík
ICELAND
Öræfajökull 2119
Norwegian Sea
Arctic Circle
Mid-Atlantic Ridge
ATLANTIC OCEAN
Faroe Is. (Den.)
Shetland Is. (U.K.)
Rockall (U.K.)
Hebrides (U.K.)
Orkney Is. (U.K.)
UNITED KINGDOM
GLASGOW
Edinburgh
Belfast
DUBLIN
IRELAND
C. Clear
North Sea
LONDON
AMSTERDAM
NETH.
HAMBURG
BERLIN
GERMANY
PRAGUE
POLAND
Vistula
WARSAW
Elbe
Europe
Kamchatka Pen.
Petropavlovsk Kamchatskiy
Klyuchevskaya 4750
International Date Line
Ust-Kamchatsk
Cape Lopatka
Kuril Islands (Russia)
JAPAN
Hokkaidō
SAPPORO
La Perouse Str.
Yuzhno-Sakhalinsk
Sakhalin (Russia)
Gulf of Sakhalin
Vanino
Sea of Okhotsk
Khabarovsk
Amur
Komsomolsk
Nikolayevsk
Magadan
Anadyr
Kolyma Range
Chukot Range
Pevek
Nizhne Kolymsk
Omolon
Kolyma
Srednekolymsk
Okhotsk
Stanovoy Range
Aldan
Indigirka
Siberia
Yakutsk
Lena
Olekma
Verkhoyansk
Verkhoyansk Range
Yana
New Siberian Is. (Russia)
Kazachye
Zhigansk
Vilyuy
Lyakhov Is.
Bulun
Tiksi
Olenek
Laptev Sea
Anabar
Khatanga
Nordvik
Asia
Taimyr Pen.
C. Chelyuskin
L. Taimyr
Kotuy
Kheta
Severnaya Zemlya (Russia)
Pyasina
Norilsk
Dudinka
Igarka
Yenisey
Dikson
Gydan Pen.
Taz
Novyy Urengoy
Franz Josef Land (Russia)
Kara Sea
Yamal Pen.
Novyy Port
Nadym
Nizhnevartovsk
Surgut
Novaya Zemlya (Russia)
Nordaustlandet
Vorkuta
Amderma
Salekhard
Nefteyugansk
Ob
Spitsbergen
Longyearbyen
Svalbard (Norway)
Edgeøya
Barents Sea
Belushya Guba
Berezovo
Narodnaya 1894
Naryan-Mar
Pechora
Ural Mts.
Greenland Sea
Bear I. (Norway)
Kanin Pen.
Ukhta
YEKATERINBURG
North C.
Vardø
Varangerfjorden
Hammerfest
Murmansk
Kola Pen.
White Sea
Mezen
Arkhangelsk
Syktyvkar
Perm
Tromsø
Severodvinsk
N. Dvina
Onega
UFA
Lofoten
Tornio
Belomorsk
L. Onega
NORWAY
SWEDEN
FINLAND
Gulf of Bothnia
L. Ladoga
Volga
SAMARA
RUSSIA
NIZHNIY NOVGOROD
Trondheim
HELSINKI
ST. PETERSBURG
G. of Finland
Tallinn
ESTONIA
MOSCOW
Saratov
L. Chudskoye
Bergen
Oslo
STOCKHOLM
Volgograd
Riga
LATVIA
Skagerrak
Baltic Sea
LITHUANIA
Vilnius
Kaliningrad
BELARUS
KHARKOV
ROSTOV
COPENHAGEN
DENMARK
KIEV
UKRAINE
Donetsk
ODESSA
Black Sea
Maximum extent of sea ice
Minimum extent of sea ice (September 2011)
Ice caps and permanent ice shelf
Projection : Zenithal Equidistant
West from Greenwich
East from Greenwich
COPYRIGHT PHILIPS
1:35 000 000
km
miles

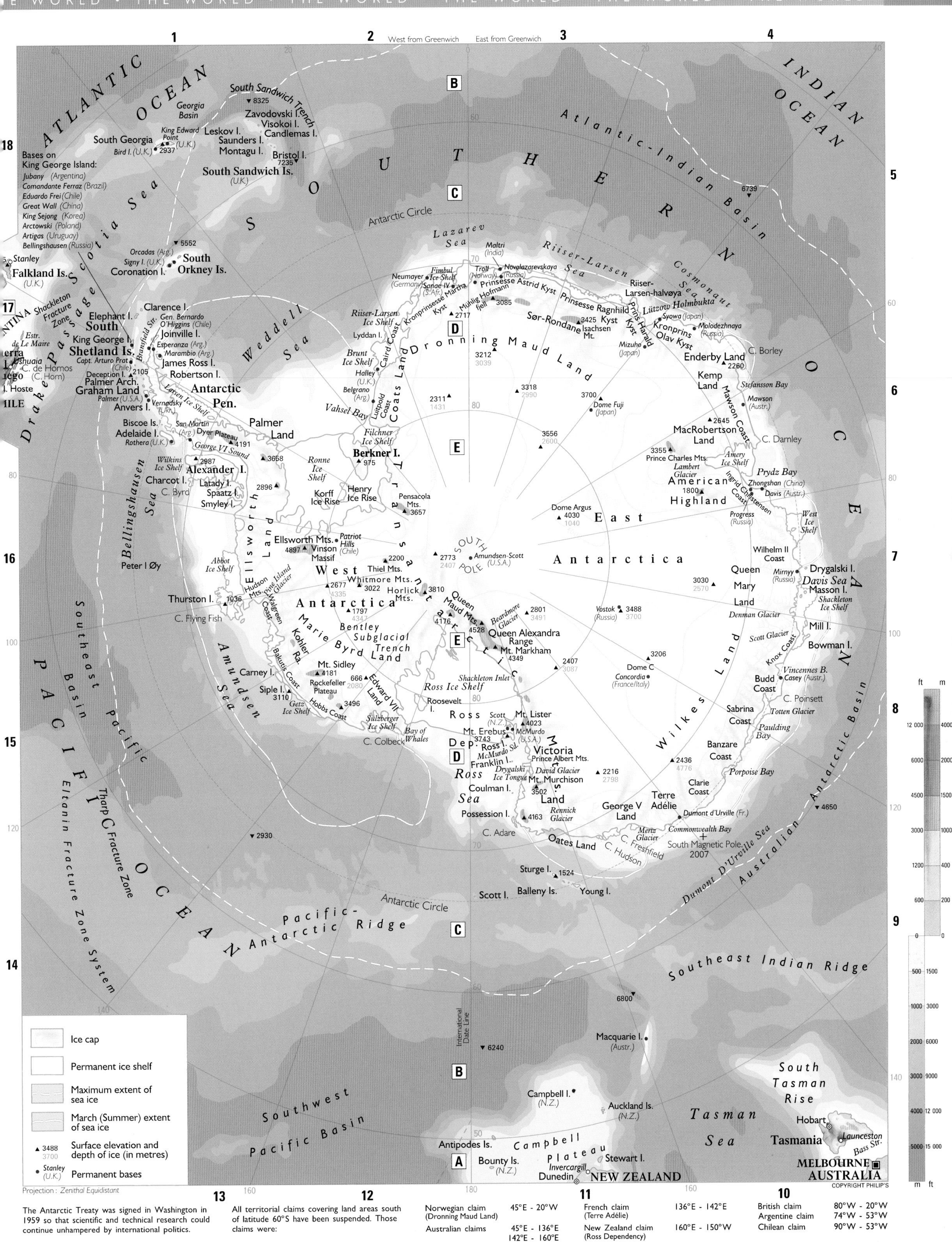

Projection : Zenithal Equidistant

Ice cap

Permanent ice shelf

Maximum extent of sea ice

March (Summer) extent of sea ice

▲3488 / 3700 Surface elevation and depth of ice (in metres)

• Stanley (U.K.) Permanent bases

The Antarctic Treaty was signed in Washington in 1959 so that scientific and technical research could continue unhampered by international politics.

All territorial claims covering land areas south of latitude 60°S have been suspended. Those claims were:

Norwegian claim (Dronning Maud Land)	45°E – 20°W	French claim (Terre Adélie)	136°E – 142°E
Australian claims	45°E – 136°E / 142°E – 160°E	New Zealand claim (Ross Dependency)	160°E – 150°W
		British claim	80°W – 20°W
		Argentine claim	74°W – 53°W
		Chilean claim	90°W – 53°W

COPYRIGHT PHILIP'S

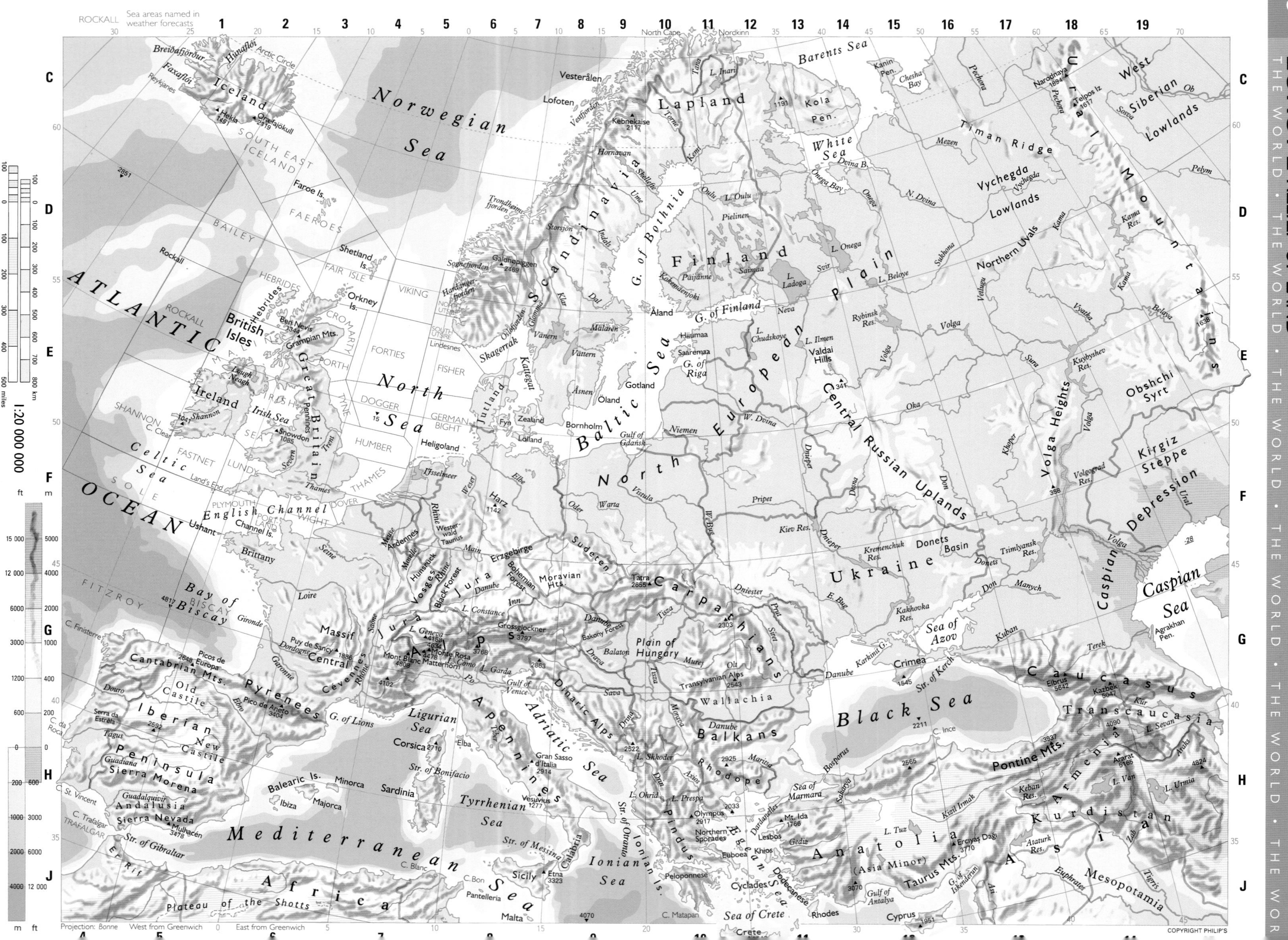

ROCKALL Sea areas named in weather forecasts
1:20 000 000
km
miles
Projection: Bonne
West from Greenwich
East from Greenwich
COPYRIGHT PHILIP'S
Norwegian Sea
North Sea
Baltic Sea
Barents Sea
White Sea
Black Sea
Caspian Sea
Sea of Azov
Mediterranean Sea
Adriatic Sea
Tyrrhenian Sea
Ionian Sea
Aegean Sea
Ligurian Sea
Celtic Sea
Irish Sea
Sea of Crete
Sea of Marmara
ATLANTIC OCEAN
Bay of Biscay
English Channel
G. of Bothnia
G. of Finland
G. of Riga
G. of Lions
Iceland
British Isles
Great Britain
Ireland
Scandinavia
Lapland
Finland
Kola Pen.
Ural Mountains
Timan Ridge
Vychegda Lowlands
Northern Uvals
West Siberian Lowlands
Caucasus
Transcaucasia
Carpathians
Alps
Pyrenees
Apennines
Balkans
Rhodope
Pindus
Dinaric Alps
Massif Central
Iberian Peninsula
Anatolia (Asia Minor)
Pontine Mts.
Taurus Mts.
Armenia
Kurdistan
Mesopotamia
Ukraine
Donets Basin
Central Russian Uplands
Volga Heights
Obshchi Syrt
Kirgiz Steppe
Caspian Depression
North European Plain
Plain of Hungary
Wallachia
Corsica
Sardinia
Sicily
Crete
Cyprus
Crimea
Africa
Plateau of the Shotts

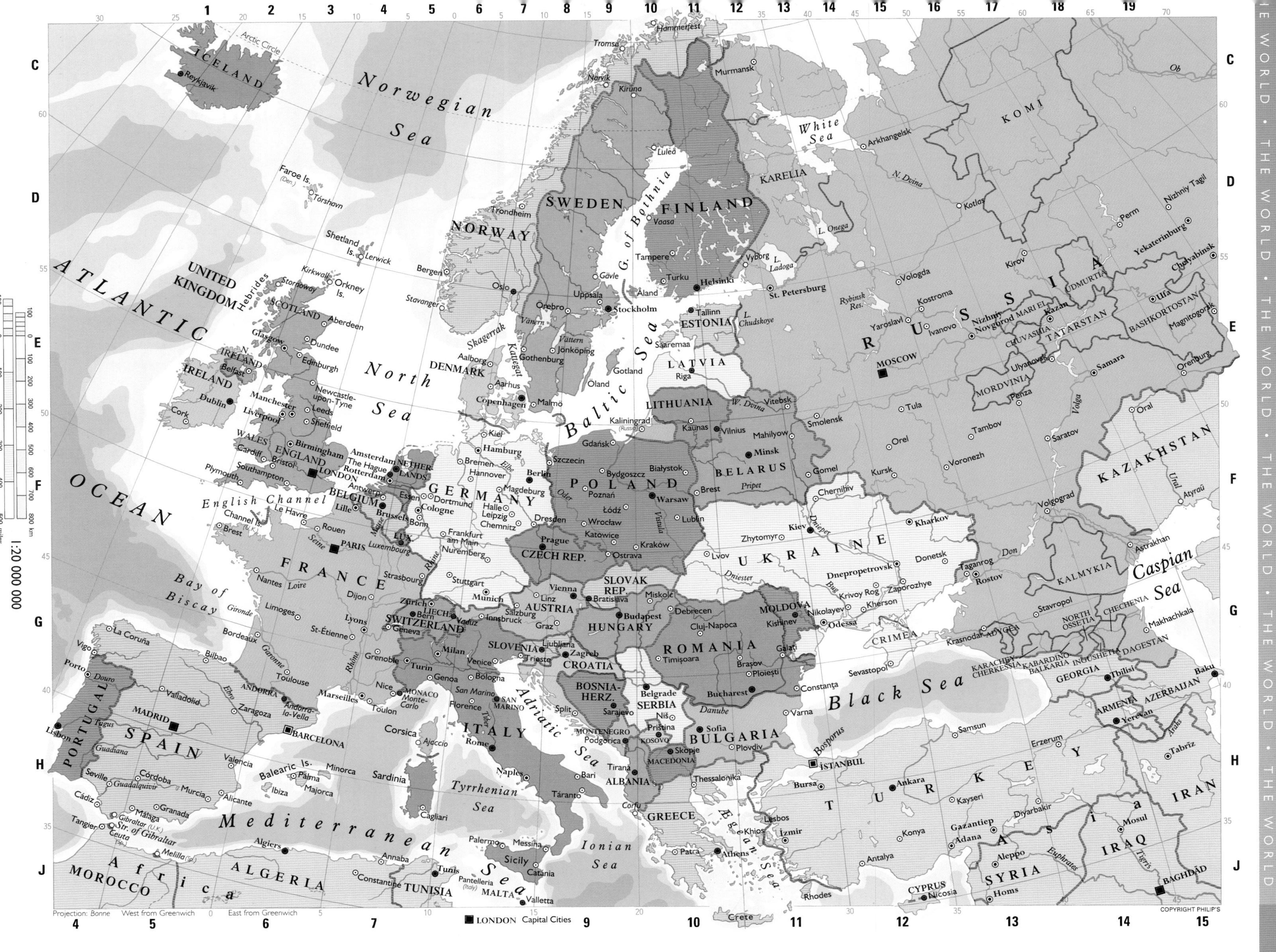
ICELAND
Reykjavík
Arctic Circle
Norwegian Sea
NORWAY
Oslo
Bergen
Stavanger
Trondheim
Narvik
Tromsø
Hammerfest
SWEDEN
Stockholm
Gothenburg
Malmö
Uppsala
Gävle
Örebro
Jönköping
Kiruna
Luleå
Vänern
Vättern
Gotland
Öland
FINLAND
Helsinki
Turku
Tampere
Vaasa
Åland
G. of Bothnia
Baltic Sea
Skagerrak
Kattegat
DENMARK
Copenhagen
Aalborg
Aarhus
UNITED KINGDOM
N. IRELAND
IRELAND
Dublin
Belfast
Cork
SCOTLAND
ENGLAND
WALES
LONDON
Edinburgh
Glasgow
Aberdeen
Dundee
Newcastle-upon-Tyne
Leeds
Sheffield
Manchester
Liverpool
Birmingham
Cardiff
Bristol
Plymouth
Southampton
Hebrides
Stornoway
Kirkwall
Orkney Is.
Shetland Is.
Lerwick
Faroe Is. (Den.)
Tórshavn
ATLANTIC
OCEAN
North Sea
English Channel
Channel Is. (U.K.)
Bay of Biscay
NETHERLANDS
Amsterdam
The Hague
Rotterdam
BELGIUM
Brussels
Antwerp
LUX.
Luxembourg
FRANCE
PARIS
Lille
Rouen
Le Havre
Brest
Nantes
Bordeaux
Limoges
Toulouse
Lyons
Dijon
Strasbourg
St-Étienne
Grenoble
Marseilles
Toulon
Nice
Seine
Loire
Garonne
Gironde
Rhône
MONACO
Monte-Carlo
Corsica
Ajaccio
GERMANY
Berlin
Hamburg
Bremen
Hannover
Kiel
Magdeburg
Halle
Leipzig
Dresden
Chemnitz
Essen
Dortmund
Cologne
Bonn
Frankfurt am Main
Nuremberg
Stuttgart
Munich
Elbe
Rhine
Meuse
SWITZERLAND
Bern
Zürich
Geneva
LIECH.
Vaduz
AUSTRIA
Vienna
Salzburg
Innsbruck
Linz
Graz
CZECH REP.
Prague
Ostrava
SLOVAK REP.
Bratislava
POLAND
Warsaw
Gdańsk
Szczecin
Poznań
Bydgoszcz
Łódź
Wrocław
Katowice
Kraków
Lublin
Białystok
Vistula
Oder
ESTONIA
Tallinn
Saaremaa
LATVIA
Riga
LITHUANIA
Vilnius
Kaunas
Kaliningrad (Russia)
BELARUS
Minsk
Brest
Gomel
Mahilyow
Vitebsk
W. Dvina
Pripet
HUNGARY
Budapest
Miskolc
Debrecen
SLOVENIA
Ljubljana
Trieste
CROATIA
Zagreb
Split
BOSNIA-HERZ.
Sarajevo
SERBIA
Belgrade
Niš
KOSOVO
Priština
MONTENEGRO
Podgorica
ALBANIA
Tirana
MACEDONIA
Skopje
ROMANIA
Bucharest
Cluj-Napoca
Timişoara
Braşov
Ploieşti
Galaţi
Constanţa
Danube
MOLDOVA
Kishinev
BULGARIA
Sofia
Plovdiv
Varna
GREECE
Athens
Thessaloniki
Patra
Corfu
Lesbos
Khios
Crete
Rhodes
Ægean Sea
Ionian Sea
ITALY
Rome
Milan
Turin
Genoa
Venice
Bologna
Florence
Naples
Bari
Taranto
Palermo
Messina
Catania
Cagliari
Sardinia
Sicily
SAN MARINO
San Marino
Tiber
Adriatic Sea
Tyrrhenian Sea
Pantelleria (Italy)
MALTA
Valletta
Mediterranean Sea
SPAIN
MADRID
BARCELONA
Valencia
Zaragoza
Bilbao
Valladolid
La Coruña
Vigo
Seville
Córdoba
Granada
Málaga
Murcia
Alicante
Cádiz
Ebro
Guadalquivir
Guadiana
Tagus
Douro
Balearic Is.
Majorca
Minorca
Ibiza
Palma
ANDORRA
Andorra-la-Vella
Gibraltar (U.K.)
Str. of Gibraltar
PORTUGAL
Lisbon
Porto
MOROCCO
Tangier
Ceuta (Sp.)
Melilla (Sp.)
ALGERIA
Algiers
Constantine
Annaba
TUNISIA
Tunis
Africa
UKRAINE
Kiev
Kharkov
Donetsk
Dnepropetrovsk
Zaporozhye
Krivoy Rog
Kherson
Nikolayev
Odessa
Sevastopol
Zhytomyr
Lvov
Chernihiv
CRIMEA
Dnieper
Dniester
Bug
Black Sea
Bosporus
RUSSIA
MOSCOW
St. Petersburg
Arkhangelsk
Murmansk
Vyborg
Vologda
Yaroslavl
Kostroma
Ivanovo
Nizhniy Novgorod
Kazan
Samara
Saratov
Volgograd
Astrakhan
Rostov
Taganrog
Krasnodar
Stavropol
Voronezh
Tula
Orel
Kursk
Smolensk
Tambov
Penza
Ulyanovsk
Perm
Kirov
Kotlas
Ufa
Orenburg
Yekaterinburg
Chelyabinsk
Magnitogorsk
Nizhniy Tagil
Makhachkala
KOMI
KARELIA
UDMURTIA
TATARSTAN
BASHKORTOSTAN
CHUVASHIA
MARI EL
MORDVINIA
KALMYKIA
DAGESTAN
CHECHENIA
INGUSHETIA
NORTH OSSETIA
KABARDINO-BALKARIA
KARACHAY-CHERKESSIA
ADYGEA
Volga
Don
Ural
Ob
N. Dvina
White Sea
L. Ladoga
L. Onega
L. Chudskoye
Rybinsk Res.
Caspian Sea
KAZAKHSTAN
Oral
Atyraū
GEORGIA
Tbilisi
ARMENIA
Yerevan
AZERBAIJAN
Baku
Aras
IRAN
Tabrīz
IRAQ
BAGHDĀD
Mosul
Tigris
Euphrates
SYRIA
Aleppo
Homs
TURKEY
Ankara
İSTANBUL
Bursa
İzmir
Antalya
Konya
Kayseri
Adana
Gaziantep
Diyarbakır
Erzurum
Samsun
CYPRUS
Nicosia
1:20 000 000
km
miles
LONDON Capital Cities
Projection: Bonne
West from Greenwich
East from Greenwich
COPYRIGHT PHILIP'S

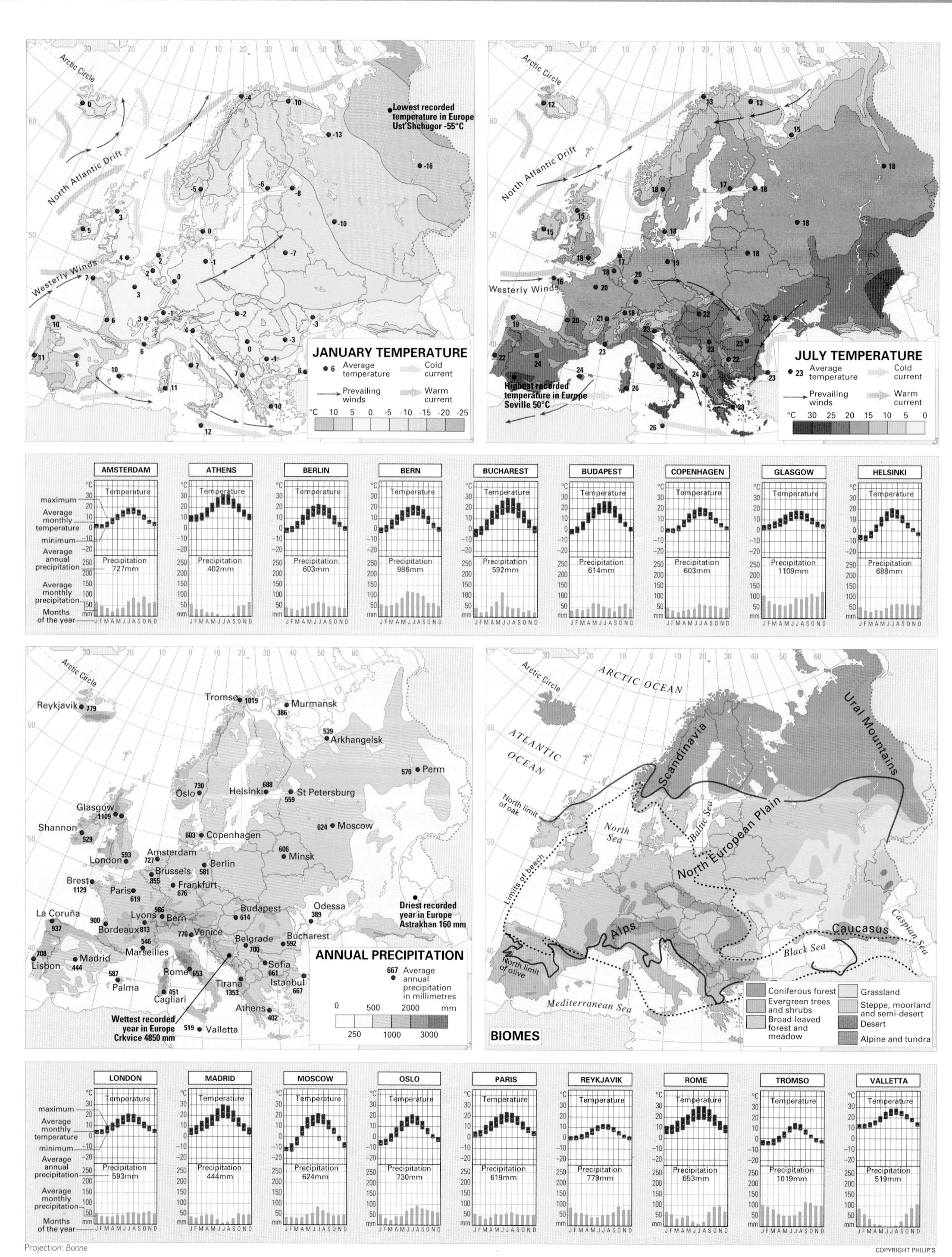

JANUARY TEMPERATURE
- 6 Average temperature
- Prevailing winds
- Cold current
- Warm current

Lowest recorded temperature in Europe Ust'Shchugor -55°C

°C 10 5 0 -5 -10 -15 -20 -25

JULY TEMPERATURE
- 23 Average temperature
- Prevailing winds
- Cold current
- Warm current

Highest recorded temperature in Europe Seville 50°C

°C 30 25 20 15 10 5 0

ANNUAL PRECIPITATION
- 667 Average annual precipitation in millimetres

0   500   2000   mm
   250 1000 3000

Wettest recorded year in Europe Crkvice 4850 mm

Driest recorded year in Europe Astrakhan 160 mm

BIOMES
- Coniferous forest
- Evergreen trees and shrubs
- Broad-leaved forest and meadow
- Grassland
- Steppe, moorland and semi-desert
- Desert
- Alpine and tundra

Climate graphs (top row): AMSTERDAM, ATHENS, BERLIN, BERN, BUCHAREST, BUDAPEST, COPENHAGEN, GLASGOW, HELSINKI
Precipitation: 727mm, 402mm, 603mm, 986mm, 592mm, 614mm, 603mm, 1109mm, 688mm

Climate graphs (bottom row): LONDON, MADRID, MOSCOW, OSLO, PARIS, REYKJAVIK, ROME, TROMSO, VALLETTA
Precipitation: 593mm, 444mm, 624mm, 730mm, 619mm, 779mm, 653mm, 1019mm, 519mm

Projection: Bonne

COPYRIGHT PHILIP'S

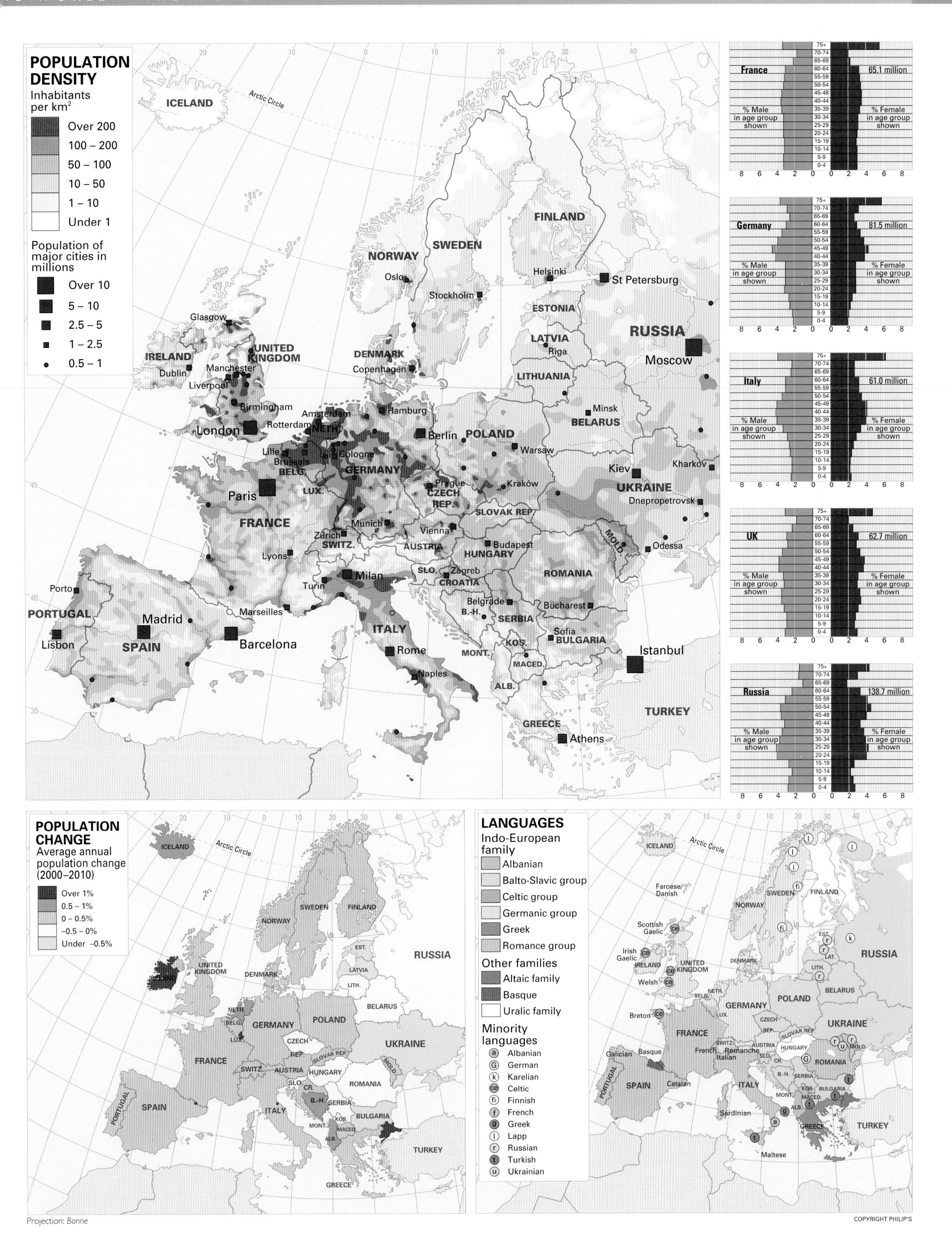

POPULATION DENSITY

Inhabitants per km²

- Over 200
- 100 – 200
- 50 – 100
- 10 – 50
- 1 – 10
- Under 1

Population of major cities in millions

- Over 10
- 5 – 10
- 2.5 – 5
- 1 – 2.5
- 0.5 – 1

France 65.1 million
% Male in age group shown / % Female in age group shown

Germany 81.5 million
% Male in age group shown / % Female in age group shown

Italy 61.0 million
% Male in age group shown / % Female in age group shown

UK 62.7 million
% Male in age group shown / % Female in age group shown

Russia 138.7 million
% Male in age group shown / % Female in age group shown

POPULATION CHANGE

Average annual population change (2000–2010)

- Over 1%
- 0.5 – 1%
- 0 – 0.5%
- –0.5 – 0%
- Under –0.5%

LANGUAGES

Indo-European family

- Albanian
- Balto-Slavic group
- Celtic group
- Germanic group
- Greek
- Romance group

Other families

- Altaic family
- Basque
- Uralic family

Minority languages

- a Albanian
- G German
- k Karelian
- ce Celtic
- fi Finnish
- f French
- g Greek
- l Lapp
- r Russian
- t Turkish
- u Ukrainian

Projection: Bonne

COPYRIGHT PHILIP'S

GROWTH OF THE EU

€ Euro-zone   o EU headquarters

- Founder members (Treaty of Rome 1957)
- Admission in 1973
- Admission in 1981
- Admission in 1986
- Admission in 1990 (German unification)
- Admission in 1995
- Admission in 2004
- Admission in 2007
- Admission in 2013

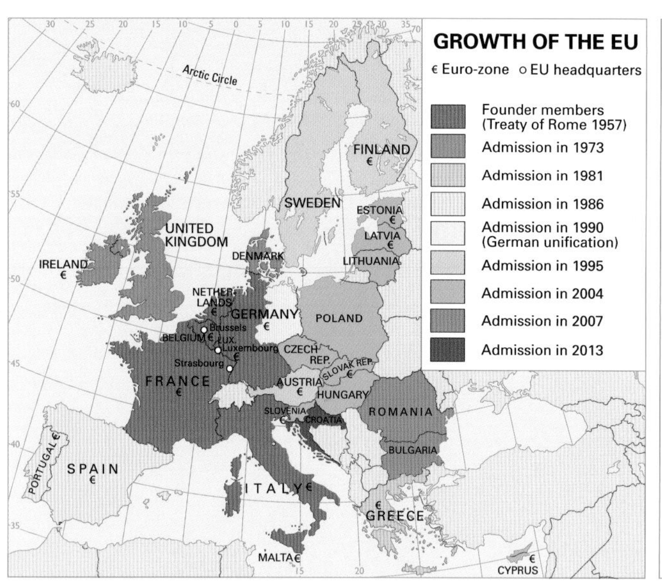

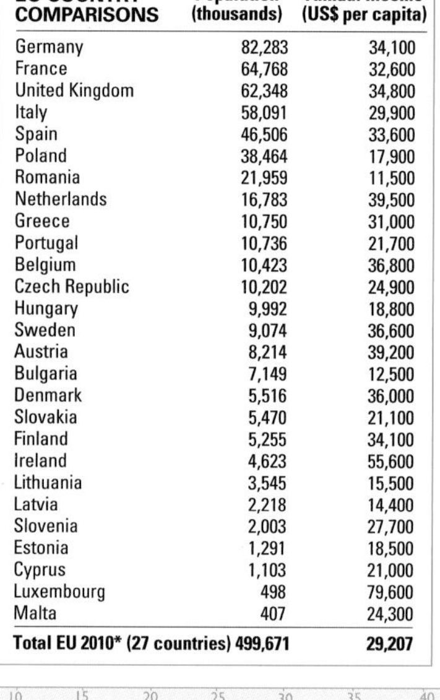

EU COUNTRY COMPARISONS	Population (thousands)	Annual Income (US$ per capita)
Germany	82,283	34,100
France	64,768	32,600
United Kingdom	62,348	34,800
Italy	58,091	29,900
Spain	46,506	33,600
Poland	38,464	17,900
Romania	21,959	11,500
Netherlands	16,783	39,500
Greece	10,750	31,000
Portugal	10,736	21,700
Belgium	10,423	36,800
Czech Republic	10,202	24,900
Hungary	9,992	18,800
Sweden	9,074	36,600
Austria	8,214	39,200
Bulgaria	7,149	12,500
Denmark	5,516	36,000
Slovakia	5,470	21,100
Finland	5,255	34,100
Ireland	4,623	55,600
Lithuania	3,545	15,500
Latvia	2,218	14,400
Slovenia	2,003	27,700
Estonia	1,291	18,500
Cyprus	1,103	21,000
Luxembourg	498	79,600
Malta	407	24,300
Total EU 2010* (27 countries)	**499,671**	**29,207**

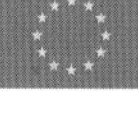

REGIONS OF THE EU*

Austria (States)
1 Niederösterreich   4 Kärnten   7 Tirol
2 Oberösterreich   5 Salzburg   8 Wien
3 Burgenland   6 Steiermark   9 Vorarlberg

Belgium (Regions)
1 Bruxelles   2 Vlaanderen   3 Wallonie

Bulgaria (Regions)
1 Severen tsentralen   3 Severozapaden   5 Yugozapaden
2 Severoiztochen   4 Yugoiztochrn   6 Yuzhen tsentralen

Cyprus (member state with no corresponding division)

Czech Republic (Kraj)
1 Jihovychod   4 Praha   7 Stredni Cechy
2 Jihozapad   5 Severovychod   8 Stredni Morava
3 Moravskoslezsko   6 Severozapad

Denmark (member state with no corresponding division)

Estonia (member state with no corresponding division)

Finland (Provinces)
1 Åland   3 Väli-Suomi   5 Uusimaa (Suuralue)
2 Itä-Suomi   4 Pohjois-Suomi   6 Etelä-Suomi

France (Regions)
1 Alsace   9 Franche-Comté   17 Normandie (Basse-)
2 Aquitaine   10 Ile-de-France   18 Normandie (Haute-)
3 Auvergne   11 Languedoc-Roussillon   19 Picardie
4 Bourgogne   12 Limousin   20 Poitou-Charentes
5 Bretagne   13 Loire (Pays de la)   21 Provence-Alpes-
6 Centre   14 Lorraine   Côte d'Azur
7 Champagne-Ardenne   15 Midi-Pyrénées   22 Rhône-Alpes
8 Corse   16 Nord-Pas-de-Calais

Germany (Länder)
1 Baden-Württemberg   7 Hamburg   11 Rheinland-Pfalz
2 Niedersachsen   8 Hessen   12 Saarland
3 Bayern   9 Mecklenburg-   13 Sachsen
4 Berlin   Vorpommern   14 Sachsen-Anhalt
5 Brandenburg   10 Nordrhein-   15 Schleswig-Holstein
6 Bremen   Westfalen   16 Thüringen

Greece (Regions)
1 Anatoliki Makedonia   5 Epiros   10 Dytiki Makedonia
  kai Thraki   6 Attiki   11 Kentriki Makedonia
2 Kriti   7 Sterea Ellas   12 Peloponnese
3 Voreio Aigaio   8 Dytiki Ellas   13 Thessaly
4 Notio Aigaio   9 Ionioi Nisoi

Hungary (Megyék)
1 Del-Alfold   4 Eszak-Magyarorszag   7 Nyugat-Dunantul
2 Del-Dunantul   5 Kozep-Dunantul
3 Eszak-Alfold   6 Kozep-Magyarorszag

Ireland (Regions)
1 Border, Midlands & Western
2 Southern & Eastern

Italy (Regions)
1 Abruzzo   8 Liguria   15 Sardegna
2 Basilicata   9 Lombardia   16 Sicilia
3 Calábria   10 Marche   17 Toscana
4 Campánia   11 Molise   18 Trentino-Alto Adige
5 Emilia-Romagna   12 Umbria   19 Valle d'Aosta
6 Friuli-Venézia Giulia   13 Piemonte   20 Véneto
7 Lazio   14 Puglia

Latvia (member state with no corresponding division)

Lithuania (member state with no corresponding division)

Luxembourg (member state with no corresponding division)

Malta (member state with no corresponding division)

Netherlands (Regions)
1 Noord-Nederland   3 West-Nederland
2 Oost-Nederland   4 Zuid-Nederland

Poland (Voivodships)
1 Dolnośląskie   7 Mazowieckie   13 Swietokrzyskie
2 Kujawsko-Pomorskie   8 Opolskie   14 Warmińsko-Mazurskie
3 Łódzkie   9 Podkarpackie   15 Wielkopolskie
4 Lubelskie   10 Podlaskie   16 Zachodniopomorskie
5 Lubuskie   11 Pomorskie
6 Małopolskie   12 Śląskie

Portugal (Autonomous regions)
1 Alentejo   3 Centro   5 Norte
2 Algarve   4 Lisboa-Vale do Tejo

Romania (Regions)
1 Bucureşti   4 Nord-Vest   7 Sud-Vest
2 Centru   5 Sud   8 Vest
3 Nord-Est   6 Sud-Est

Slovak Republic (Kraj)
1 Bratislavsky Kraj   3 Vychodne Slovensko
2 Stredne Slovensko   4 Zapadne Slovensko

Slovenia (member state with no corresponding division)

Spain (Autonomous communities)
1 Andalucía   7 Cantabria   13 Madrid
2 Aragon   8 Castilla y Léon   14 Murcia
3 Asturias   9 Castilla-La Mancha   15 Navarra
4 Islas Baleares   10 Cataluña   16 Rioja (La)
5 País Vasco   11 Extremadura   17 Valencia
6 Islas Canarias   12 Galicia

Sweden (Regions)
1 Stockholm   4 Västsverige   7 Övre Norrland
2 Östra Mellansverige   5 Norra Mellansverige   8 Småland med öarna
3 Sydsverige   6 Mellersta Norrland

United Kingdom (Regions)
1 North East   5 West Midlands   9 South West
2 North West   6 East   10 Wales
3 Yorkshire & The Humber   7 London   11 Scotland
4 East Midlands   8 South East   12 Northern Ireland

*Croatia joined the EU in July 2013.

Projection: Bonne

COPYRIGHT PH

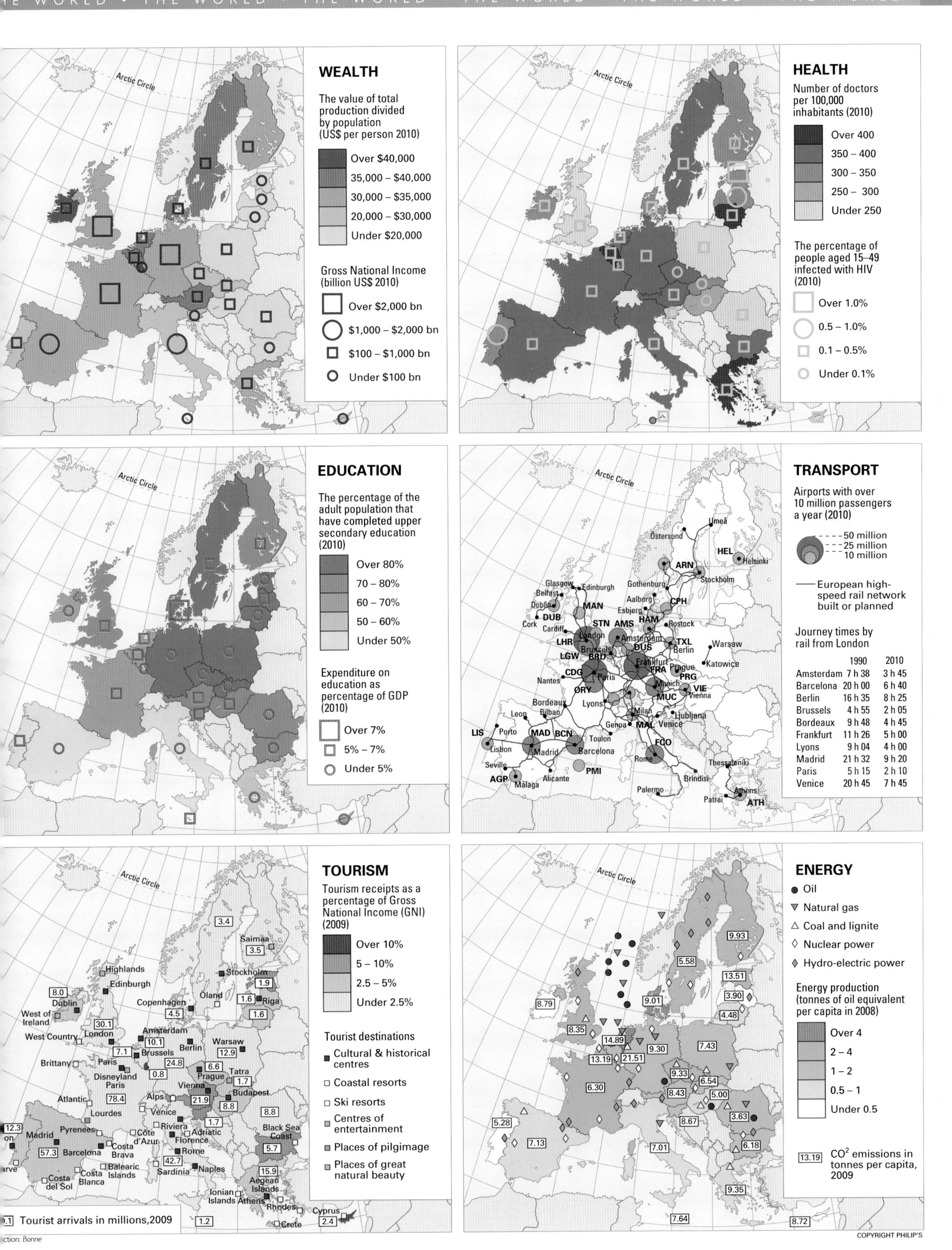

WEALTH

The value of total production divided by population (US$ per person 2010)

- Over $40,000
- 35,000 – $40,000
- 30,000 – $35,000
- 20,000 – $30,000
- Under $20,000

Gross National Income (billion US$ 2010)

- ☐ Over $2,000 bn
- ◯ $1,000 – $2,000 bn
- ☐ $100 – $1,000 bn
- ◯ Under $100 bn

HEALTH

Number of doctors per 100,000 inhabitants (2010)

- Over 400
- 350 – 400
- 300 – 350
- 250 – 300
- Under 250

The percentage of people aged 15–49 infected with HIV (2010)

- ☐ Over 1.0%
- ◯ 0.5 – 1.0%
- ☐ 0.1 – 0.5%
- ◯ Under 0.1%

EDUCATION

The percentage of the adult population that have completed upper secondary education (2010)

- Over 80%
- 70 – 80%
- 60 – 70%
- 50 – 60%
- Under 50%

Expenditure on education as percentage of GDP (2010)

- ☐ Over 7%
- ☐ 5% – 7%
- ◯ Under 5%

TRANSPORT

Airports with over 10 million passengers a year (2010)

- 50 million
- 25 million
- 10 million

— European high-speed rail network built or planned

Journey times by rail from London

	1990	2010
Amsterdam	7 h 38	3 h 45
Barcelona	20 h 00	6 h 40
Berlin	16 h 35	8 h 25
Brussels	4 h 55	2 h 05
Bordeaux	9 h 48	4 h 45
Frankfurt	11 h 26	5 h 00
Lyons	9 h 04	4 h 00
Madrid	21 h 32	9 h 20
Paris	5 h 15	2 h 10
Venice	20 h 45	7 h 45

Transport map labels: Umeå, Östersund, HEL, Helsinki, ARN, Stockholm, Gothenburg, Glasgow, Edinburgh, Aalborg, CPH, Belfast, Dublin, Esbjerg, DUB, Cork, Cardiff, STN, AMS, HAM, Rostock, London, Amsterdam, DUS, TXL, Berlin, Warsaw, LHR, Brussels, BRU, Frankfurt, Prague, Katowice, LGW, CDG, Paris, FRA, PRG, Nantes, Munich, VIE, ØRY, Lyons, MUC, Vienna, Bordeaux, Milan, Ljubljana, Leon, Bilbao, Genoa, MXP, Venice, LIS, Porto, MAD, BCN, Toulon, FCO, Lisbon, Madrid, Barcelona, Rome, Thessaloniki, Seville, Brindisi, AGP, Alicante, PMI, Palermo, Athens, Patrai, ATH, Málaga

TOURISM

Tourism receipts as a percentage of Gross National Income (GNI) (2009)

- Over 10%
- 5 – 10%
- 2.5 – 5%
- Under 2.5%

Tourist destinations

- ■ Cultural & historical centres
- ☐ Coastal resorts
- ☐ Ski resorts
- ■ Centres of entertainment
- ■ Places of pilgrimage
- ■ Places of great natural beauty

Tourism map labels and values: 3.4, Saimaa 3.5, Highlands, Stockholm 1.9, Edinburgh, Öland, Riga 1.6, 1.6, 8.0, Dublin, Copenhagen 4.5, West of Ireland 30.1, Amsterdam 10.1, Berlin, Warsaw 12.9, West Country, London 7.1, Brussels, Brittany, Paris 24.8, 0.8, Prague 6.6, Tatra 1.7, Disneyland Paris, Vienna 21.9, Budapest 8.8, Atlantic 78.4, Alps 8.8, Lourdes, Venice 1.7, 12.3, Madrid, Pyrenees, Riviera, Adriatic, Black Sea Coast, 57.3, Barcelona, Côte d'Azur, Florence, Rome, 5.7, Costa Brava, 42.7, Naples 15.9, Balearic Islands, Sardinia, Aegean Islands, Costa del Sol, Costa Blanca, Ionian Islands, Athens, Rhodes, Cyprus 2.4, Crete 1.2

Tourist arrivals in millions, 2009

Projection: Bonne

ENERGY

- ● Oil
- ▽ Natural gas
- △ Coal and lignite
- ◇ Nuclear power
- ◈ Hydro-electric power

Energy production (tonnes of oil equivalent per capita in 2008)

- Over 4
- 2 – 4
- 1 – 2
- 0.5 – 1
- Under 0.5

CO² emissions in tonnes per capita, 2009 (example value 13.19)

Energy map values: 9.93, 5.58, 13.51, 8.79, 9.01, 3.90, 4.48, 8.35, 14.89, 9.30, 7.43, 13.19, 21.51, 9.33, 6.54, 6.30, 8.43, 5.00, 3.63, 8.67, 5.28, 7.13, 7.01, 6.18, 9.35, 7.64, 8.72

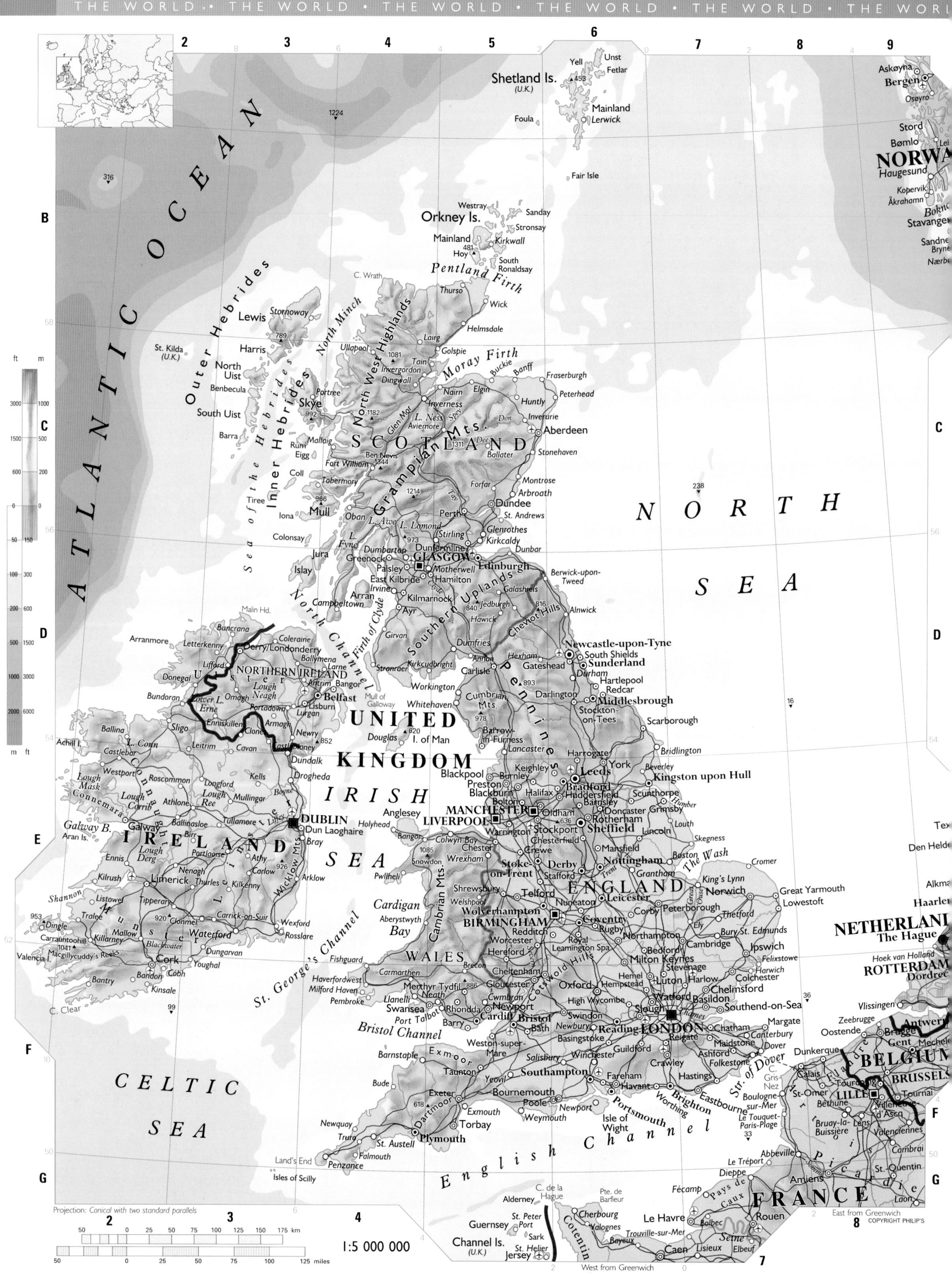

Projection: Conical with two standard parallels

1:5 000 000

East from Greenwich
COPYRIGHT PHILIP'S

West from Greenwich

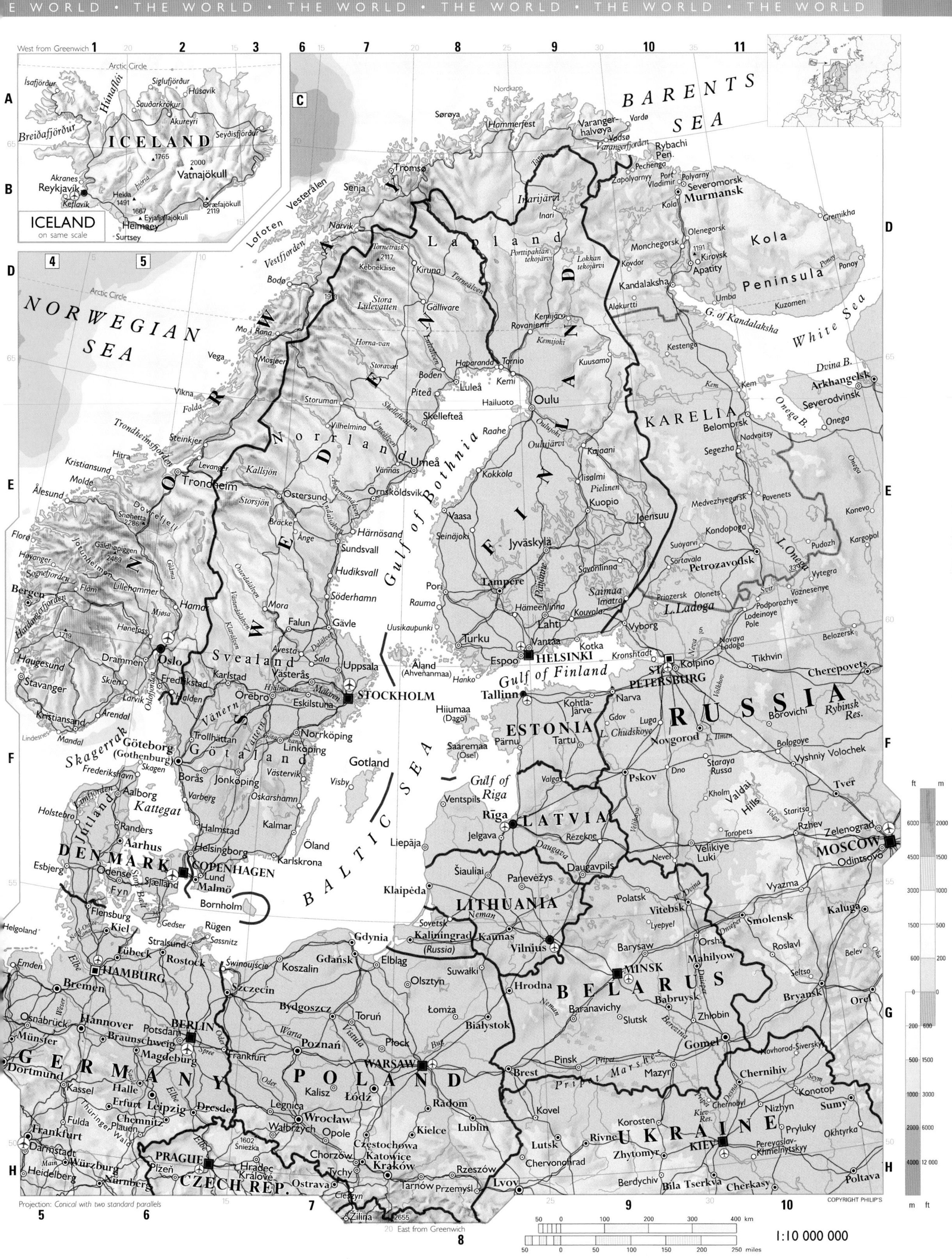
ICELAND
on same scale
Ísafjörður
Siglufjörður
Húsavík
Húnaflói
Sauðárkrókur
Akureyri
Breiðafjörður
Seyðisfjörður
ICELAND
Vatnajökull
Akranes
Reykjavík
Keflavík
Hekla
Eyjafjallajökull
Heimaey
Surtsey
Öræfajökull
Arctic Circle
NORWEGIAN SEA
BARENTS SEA
Nordkapp
Sørøya
Hammerfest
Varanger-halvøya
Vardø
Vadsø
Varangerfjorden
Rybachi Pen.
Pechenga
Zapolyarnyy
Polyarny
Severomorsk
Murmansk
Tromsø
Senja
Vesterålen
Lofoten
Narvik
Vestfjorden
Inarijärvi
Inari
Lapland
Torneträsk
Kebnekaise
Kiruna
Bodø
Stora Lulevatten
Gällivare
Mo i Rana
Vega
Mosjøen
Haparanda
Tornio
Kemi
Boden
Luleå
Piteå
Rovaniemi
Kemijärvi
Kemijoki
Monchegorsk
Olenegorsk
Kirovsk
Apatity
Kandalaksha
Kola
Peninsula
Umba
G. of Kandalaksha
White Sea
Kestenga
Kuusamo
Oulu
Hailuoto
Raahe
Oulujärvi
Kajaani
Skellefteå
Umeå
Vännäs
Storuman
Vilhelmina
Norrland
Gulf of Bothnia
Vikna
Folda
Steinkjer
Trondheimsfjorden
Trondheim
Levanger
Kristiansund
Molde
Ålesund
Hitra
Kallsjön
Östersund
Storsjön
Örnsköldsvik
Kokkola
Vaasa
Seinäjoki
Iisalmi
Pielinen
Kuopio
Joensuu
KARELIA
Belomorsk
Segezha
Kem
Arkhangelsk
Severodvinsk
Onega
Dvina B.
Onega B.
Medvezhyegorsk
Povenets
Kondopoga
Petrozavodsk
L. Onega
Pudozh
Kargopol
Konevo
Vytegra
Voznesenye
Sortavala
Suoyarvi
Olonets
Priozersk
L. Ladoga
Podporozhye
Lodeinoye Pole
Dovrefjell
Snøhetta
Galdhøpiggen
Jotunheimen
Florø
Høyanger
Sognefjorden
Bergen
Flåm
Lillehammer
Hamar
Mjøsa
Hardangerfjorden
Hønefoss
Drammen
Oslo
Haugesund
Stavanger
Skien
Larvik
Fredrikstad
Halden
Kristiansand
Arendal
Mandal
Lindesnes
Skagerrak
Bräcke
Ånge
Härnösand
Sundsvall
Hudiksvall
Söderhamn
Mora
Falun
Gävle
Avesta
Sala
Uppsala
Svealand
Karlstad
Västerås
Örebro
Hjälmaren
Mälaren
Eskilstuna
STOCKHOLM
Vänern
Vättern
Norrköping
Linköping
Trollhättan
Göteborg (Gothenburg)
Götaland
Västervik
Jönköping
Borås
Varberg
Oskarshamn
Halmstad
Kalmar
Öland
Helsingborg
COPENHAGEN
Lund
Malmö
Karlskrona
Bornholm
Jyväskylä
FINLAND
Tampere
Pori
Rauma
Päijänne
Savonlinna
Saimaa
Imatra
Hämeenlinna
Kouvola
Lahti
Turku
Uusikaupunki
Vantaa
Espoo
HELSINKI
Kotka
Vyborg
Åland (Ahvenanmaa)
Hanko
Gulf of Finland
Kronshtadt
Kolpino
ST. PETERSBURG
Tallinn
Narva
Kohtla-Järve
Hiiumaa (Dagö)
Saaremaa (Ösel)
ESTONIA
Pärnu
Tartu
Gdov
Luga
L. Chudskoye
Novgorod
L. Ilmen
RUSSIA
Tikhvin
Belozersk
Cherepovets
Rybinsk Res.
Borovichi
Bologoye
Vyshniy Volochek
Staraya Russa
Dno
Pskov
Valdai Hills
Kholm
Tver
Staritsa
Rzhev
Toropets
Zelenograd
MOSCOW
Odintsovo
Gotland
Visby
BALTIC SEA
Gulf of Riga
Ventspils
Riga
LATVIA
Jelgava
Rēzekne
Daugava
Daugavpils
Liepāja
Šiauliai
Panevėžys
Klaipėda
LITHUANIA
Sovetsk
Neman
Kaliningrad (Russia)
Kaunas
Vilnius
Nevel
Velikiye Luki
Polatsk
Vitebsk
Lyepyel
Smolensk
Vyazma
Kaluga
Orsha
Roslavl
Barysaw
MINSK
Mahilyow
BELARUS
Babruysk
Zhlobin
Baranavichy
Slutsk
Hrodna
Bryansk
Orel
Belev
Seltso
Gomel
Novhorod-Siverskyy
Pinsk
Pripet Marshes
Mazyr
Brest
Chernihiv
Konotop
Kovel
Korosten
Nizhyn
Sumy
Pryluky
Okhtyrka
UKRAINE
Rivne
Lutsk
Zhytomyr
KIEV
Kiev Res.
Pereyaslav-Khmelnytskyy
Chervonohrad
Berdychiv
Bila Tserkva
Cherkasy
Poltava
Lvov
Kattegat
Frederikshavn
Skagen
Aalborg
Limfjorden
Jutland
Holstebro
Randers
Aarhus
DENMARK
Esbjerg
Odense
Sjælland
Fyn
Store Bælt
Flensburg
Kiel
Helgoland
Gedser
Rügen
Sassnitz
Stralsund
Lübeck
Rostock
Emden
HAMBURG
Bremen
Świnoujście
Koszalin
Gdańsk
Gdynia
Elbląg
Olsztyn
Suwałki
Szczecin
Bydgoszcz
Toruń
Łomża
Białystok
Osnabrück
Hannover
Potsdam
BERLIN
Münster
Braunschweig
Magdeburg
Frankfurt
Poznań
Płock
WARSAW
POLAND
Dortmund
GERMANY
Kassel
Halle
Erfurt
Leipzig
Dresden
Kalisz
Łódź
Radom
Legnica
Wrocław
Wałbrzych
Opole
Kielce
Lublin
Fulda
Chemnitz
Plauen
Frankfurt
Darmstadt
Śnieżka
Częstochowa
Katowice
Kraków
Chorzów
Tychy
Rzeszów
Przemyśl
Tarnów
Main
Würzburg
Heidelberg
Nürnberg
PRAGUE
Plzeň
Hradec Králové
CZECH REP.
Ostrava
Cieszyn
Žilina
Projection: Conical with two standard parallels
West from Greenwich
East from Greenwich
COPYRIGHT PHILIP'S
1:10 000 000
km
miles
ft
m

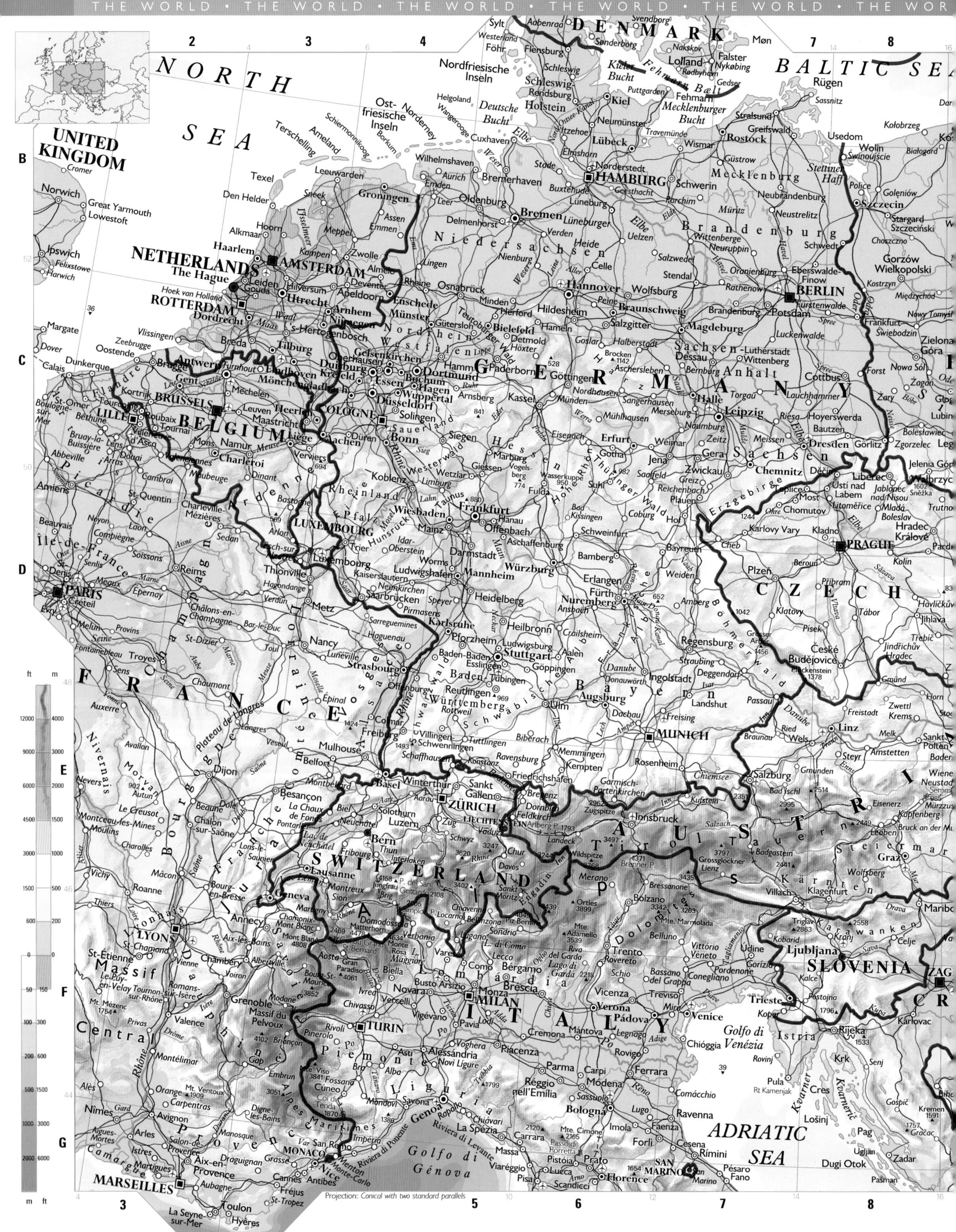
NORTH SEA
BALTIC SEA
UNITED KINGDOM
DENMARK
NETHERLANDS
AMSTERDAM
The Hague
ROTTERDAM
BELGIUM
BRUSSELS
LUXEMBOURG
FRANCE
PARIS
GERMANY
BERLIN
HAMBURG
MUNICH
COLOGNE
Frankfurt
Stuttgart
CZECH
PRAGUE
SWITZERLAND
ZÜRICH
Bern
Geneva
LIECHTENSTEIN
AUSTRIA
SLOVENIA
Ljubljana
ITALY
MILAN
TURIN
Genoa
Venice
MONACO
SAN MARINO
Golfo di Venézia
Golfo di Génova
ADRIATIC SEA
LYONS
MARSEILLES
Nordfriesische Inseln
Ostfriesische Inseln
Niedersachsen
Nordrhein-Westfalen
Hessen
Rheinland-Pfalz
Baden-Württemberg
Bayern
Sachsen
Sachsen-Anhalt
Brandenburg
Mecklenburg
Thüringer Wald
Schwarzwald
Böhmerwald
Erzgebirge
Tirol
Tauern
Kärnten
Steiermark
Lombárdia
Piemonte
Liguria
Dolomites
Alpes Maritimes
Massif Central
Provence
Dauphiné
Bourgogne
Champagne
Lorraine
Alsace
Picardie
Île-de-France
Jura
Plateau de Langres
Morvan
Nivernais
Camargue
Istria
Projection: Conical with two standard parallels

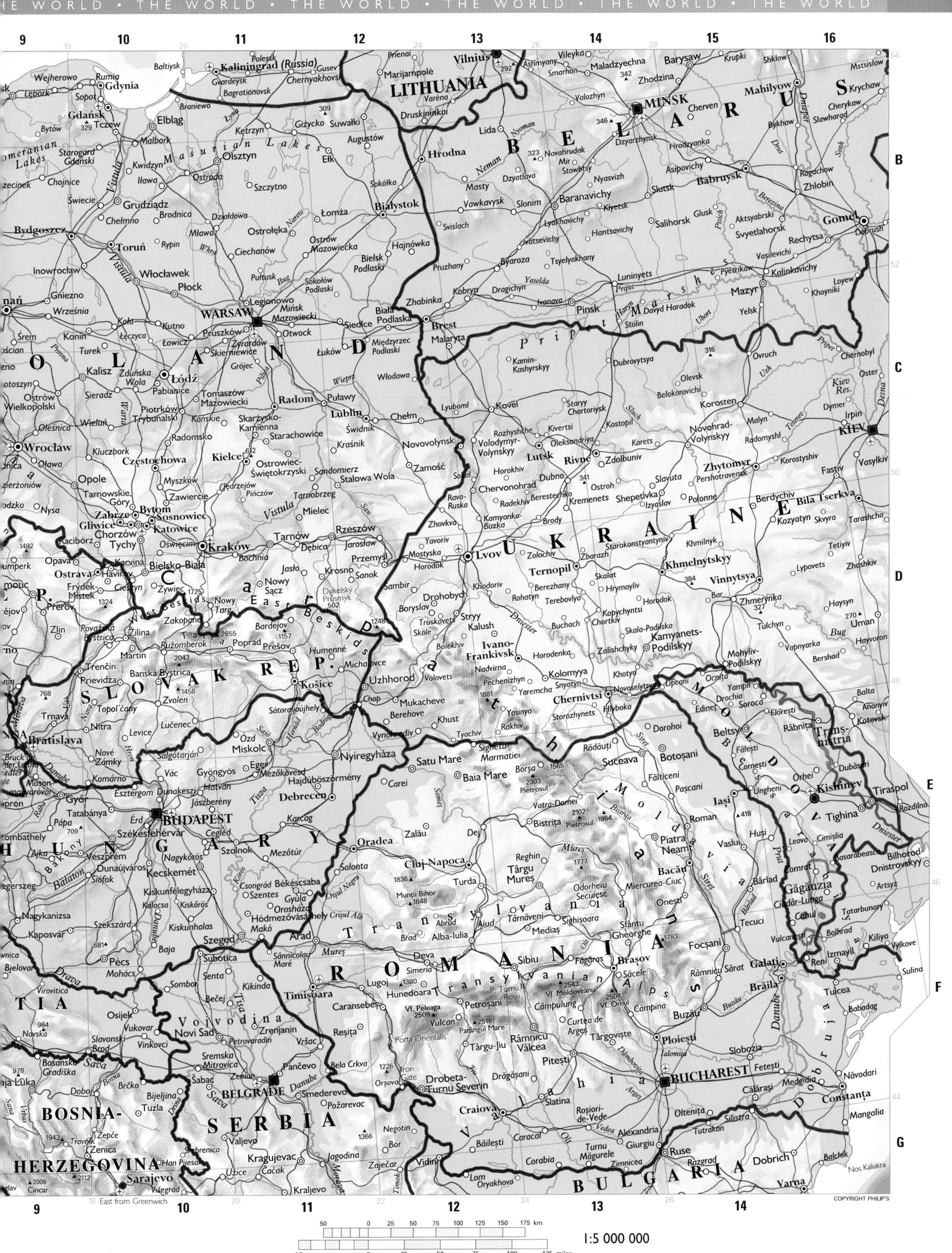

9 10 11 12 13 14 15 16

Wejherowo
Rumia
Gdynia
Lębork
Sopot
Gdańsk
Bytów
Tczew
Elbląg
Starogard Gdański
Chojnice
Świecie
Grudziądz
Brodnica
Toruń
Rypin
Włocławek
Gniezno
Wrzesień
Śrem
Konin
Koło
Kutno
Łowicz
WARSAW
Legionowo
Pruszków
Otwock
Siedlce
Kalisz
Zduńska Wola
Łódź
Pabianice
Tomaszów Mazowiecki
Radom
Puławy
Lublin
Świdnik
Chełm

POLAND
UKRAINE
BELARUS
LITHUANIA
SLOVAK REP.
HUNGARY
ROMANIA
SERBIA
BOSNIA-HERZEGOVINA
MOLDOVA
BULGARIA

Kaliningrad (Russia)
Vilnius
MINSK
KIEV
BUDAPEST
BRATISLAVA
BELGRADE
BUCHAREST
Kishinev
Gomel
Mahilyow
Babruysk

Scale 1:5 000 000

East from Greenwich

COPYRIGHT PHILIP'S

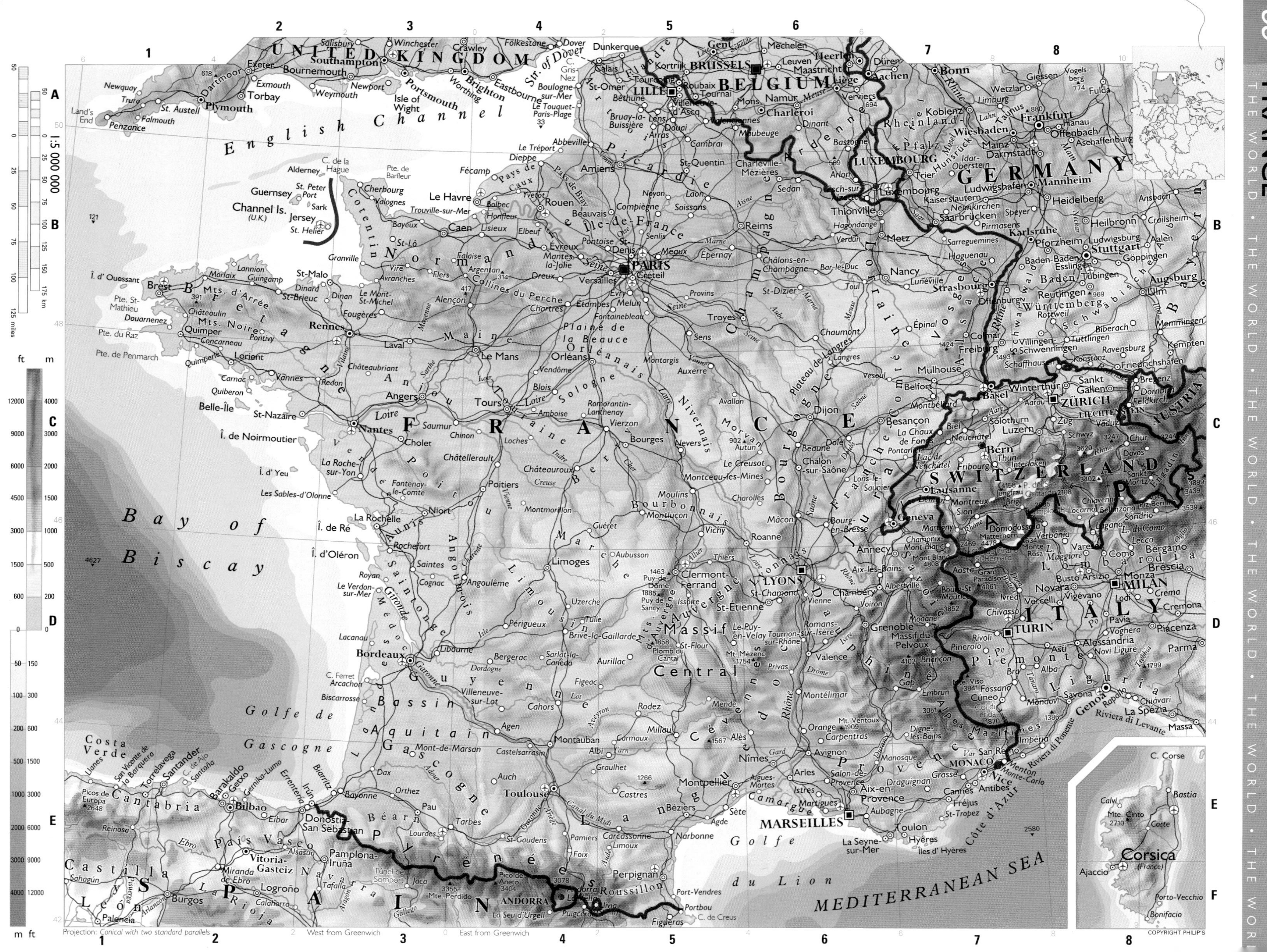
1:5 000 000
FRANCE
UNITED KINGDOM
BELGIUM
LUXEMBOURG
GERMANY
SWITZERLAND
AUSTRIA
ITALY
MONACO
ANDORRA
SPAIN
English Channel
Str. of Dover
Bay of Biscay
Golfe de Gascogne
MEDITERRANEAN SEA
Golfe du Lion
Côte d'Azur
Massif Central
Pyrénées
Channel Is. (U.K.)
Corsica (France)
PARIS
LYONS
MARSEILLES
BRUSSELS
LILLE
ZÜRICH
MILAN
TURIN
Bordeaux
Toulouse
Nantes
Rennes
Strasbourg
Projection: Conical with two standard parallels
West from Greenwich
East from Greenwich
COPYRIGHT PHILIP'S

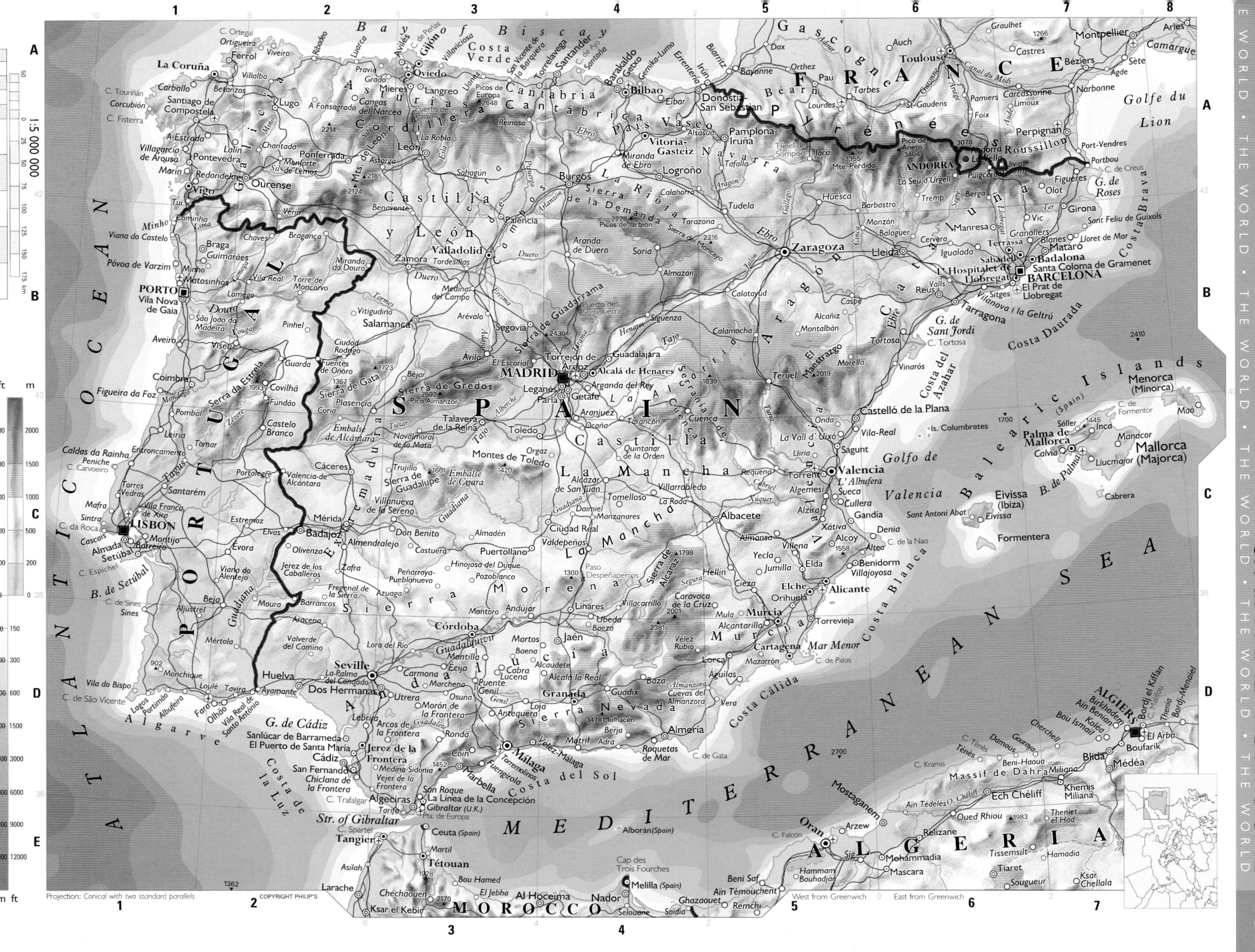
SPAIN
PORTUGAL
FRANCE
ALGERIA
MOROCCO
ANDORRA
ATLANTIC OCEAN
MEDITERRANEAN SEA
Bay of Biscay
Golfe du Lion
Balearic Islands
Mallorca (Majorca)
Menorca (Minorca)
Eivissa (Ibiza)
Formentera
Cabrera
Golfo de Valencia
G. de Cádiz
Str. of Gibraltar
Costa Verde
Costa Brava
Costa Daurada
Costa del Azahar
Costa Blanca
Costa Cálida
Costa del Sol
Costa de la Luz
Algarve
Pyrénées
Cordillera Cantábrica
Sierra de Gredos
Sierra de Guadarrama
Sierra Morena
Sierra Nevada
Castilla y León
Castilla-La Mancha
Aragón
Andalucía
Galicia
Asturias
Navarra
País Vasco
La Rioja
Extremadura
Murcia
Catalunya
MADRID
LISBON
PORTO
BARCELONA
Valencia
Seville
Zaragoza
Málaga
Bilbao
Granada
Córdoba
Valladolid
Alicante
Murcia
Palma de Mallorca
ALGIERS
Oran
Gibraltar (U.K.)
Ceuta (Spain)
Melilla (Spain)
Tangier
Ebro
Duero
Tajo
Guadiana
Guadalquivir
Júcar
1:5 000 000
50 0 25 50 75 100 125 150 175 km
50 0 25 50 75 100 125 miles
m 2000 1500 1000 500 200 0
ft 6000 4500 3000 1500 600 0
50 150 300 600 1500 3000 6000 9000 12000 ft
50 100 200 500 1000 2000 3000 4000 m
Projection: Conical with two standard parallels
COPYRIGHT PHILIP'S
West from Greenwich 0 East from Greenwich

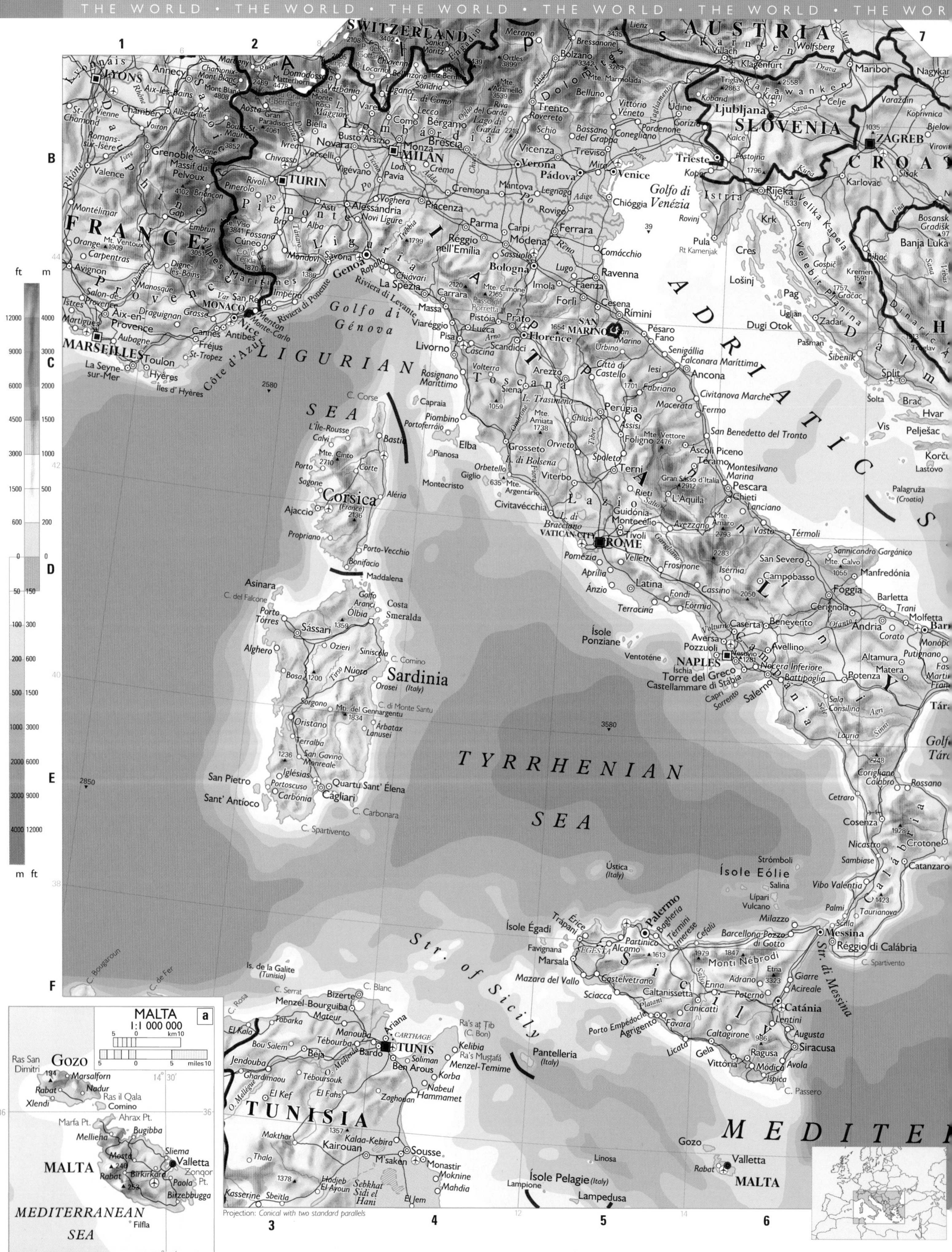
SWITZERLAND
AUSTRIA
SLOVENIA
CROAT
FRANCE
ITALY
TUNISIA
MALTA
LIGURIAN SEA
TYRRHENIAN SEA
ADRIATIC SEA
MEDITER
Golfo di Génova
Golfo di Venézia
Str. of Sicily
Str. di Messina
Corsica (France)
Sardinia (Italy)
Elba
Ústica (Italy)
Ísole Eólie
Ísole Égadi
Pantelleria (Italy)
Ísole Pelagie (Italy)
Lampedusa
Linosa
Lampione
Ísole Ponziane
Capri
Ischia
LYONS
Grenoble
Valence
Avignon
Aix-en-Provence
MARSEILLES
Toulon
Nice
MONACO
Cannes
Fréjus
Hyères
Îles d'Hyères
Côte d'Azur
Chambéry
Annecy
Mont Blanc 4808
Matterhorn 4478
TURIN
MILAN
Genoa
Bergamo
Brescia
Verona
Vicenza
Pádova
Venice
Trieste
Bolzano
Trento
Udine
Ljubljana
ZAGREB
Rijeka
Pula
Split
Zadar
Parma
Módena
Bologna
Ferrara
Ravenna
Rímini
SAN MARINO
Florence
Pisa
Livorno
Siena
Perúgia
Ancona
Pescara
L'Áquila
ROME
VATICAN CITY
Latina
Foggia
Bari
NAPLES
Salerno
Potenza
Taranto
Cosenza
Catanzaro
Réggio di Calábria
Messina
Palermo
Trápani
Marsala
Agrigento
Catánia
Siracusa
Etna 3323
Ajaccio
Bastia
Bonifacio
Sássari
Cágliari
Olbia
Oristano
Bizerte
TUNIS
CARTHAGE
Sousse
Kairouan
Valletta
Gozo
Comino
MALTA 1:1 000 000
MEDITERRANEAN SEA
Projection: Conical with two standard parallels

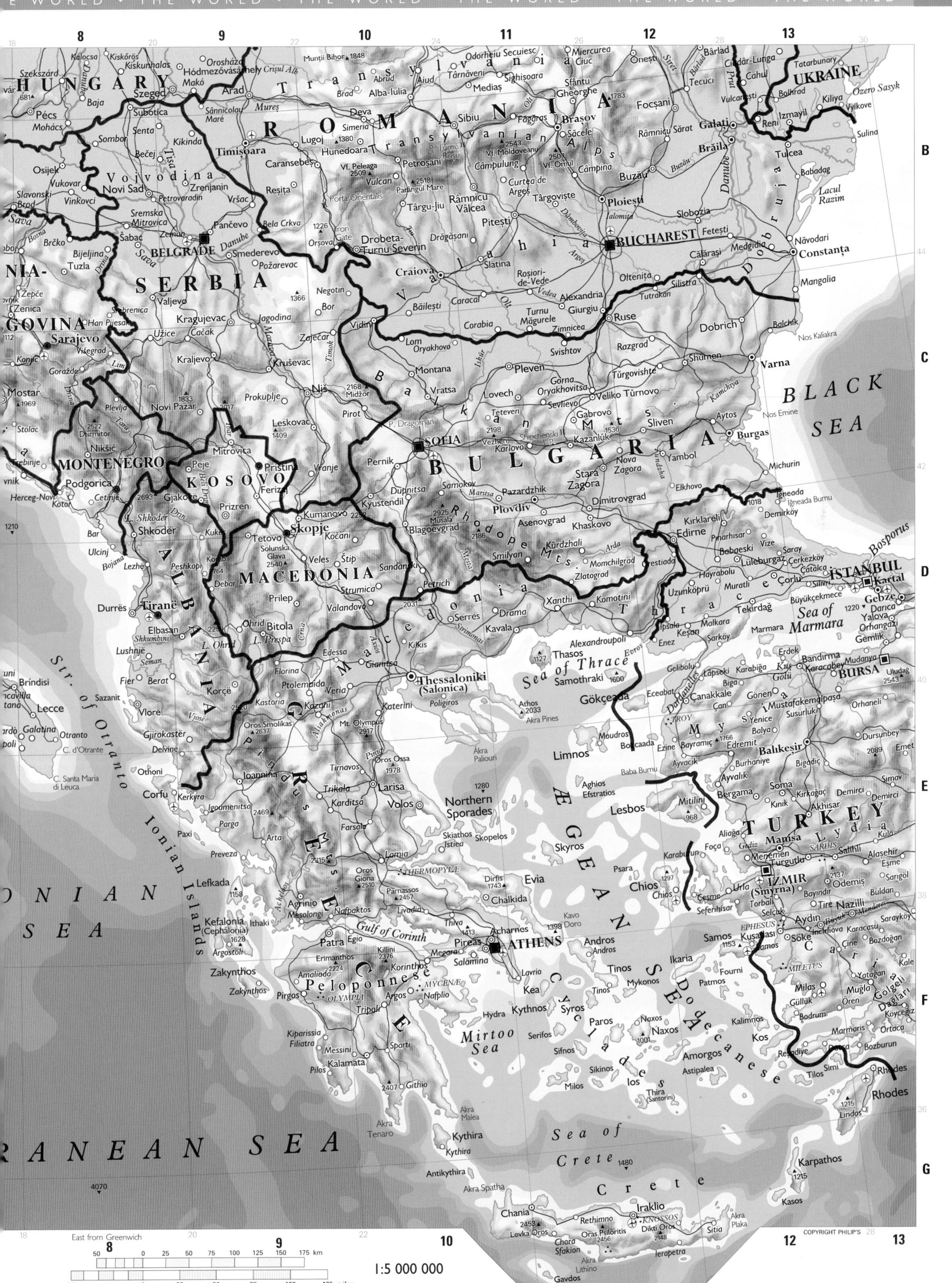

East from Greenwich

50   0   25 50 75 100 125 150 175 km

1:5 000 000

50   0   25   50   75   100 125 miles

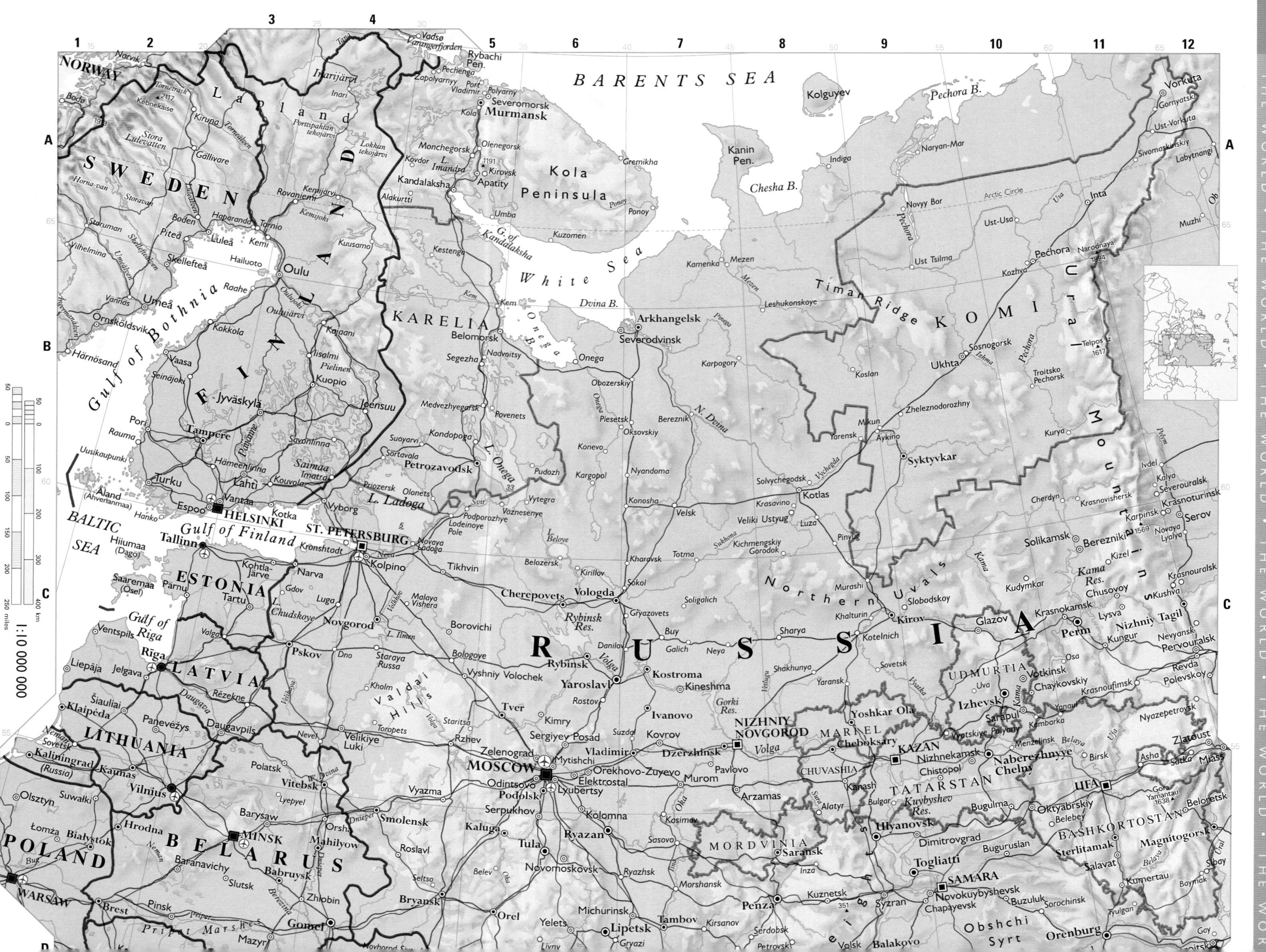
BARENTS SEA
White Sea
Kola Peninsula
KOMI
KARELIA
Ural Mountains
Timan Ridge
Northern Uvals
Valdai Hills
R U S S I A
FINLAND
SWEDEN
NORWAY
ESTONIA
LATVIA
LITHUANIA
BELARUS
POLAND
Gulf of Finland
Gulf of Bothnia
Gulf of Riga
BALTIC SEA
Lapland
MOSCOW
ST. PETERSBURG
HELSINKI
Tallinn
Riga
Vilnius
MINSK
WARSAW
NIZHNIY NOVGOROD
KAZAN
SAMARA
UFA
TATARSTAN
BASHKORTOSTAN
UDMURTIA
CHUVASHIA
MARI EL
MORDVINIA
Arkhangelsk
Murmansk
Perm
Kirov
Yaroslavl
Vologda
Kotlas
Syktyvkar
Ukhta
Pechora
Vorkuta
Inta
Izhevsk
Oulu
Tampere
Turku
L. Ladoga
L. Onega
Kolguyev
Kanin Pen.
Pechora B.
Chesha B.
Kaliningrad (Russia)
1:10 000 000
km
miles

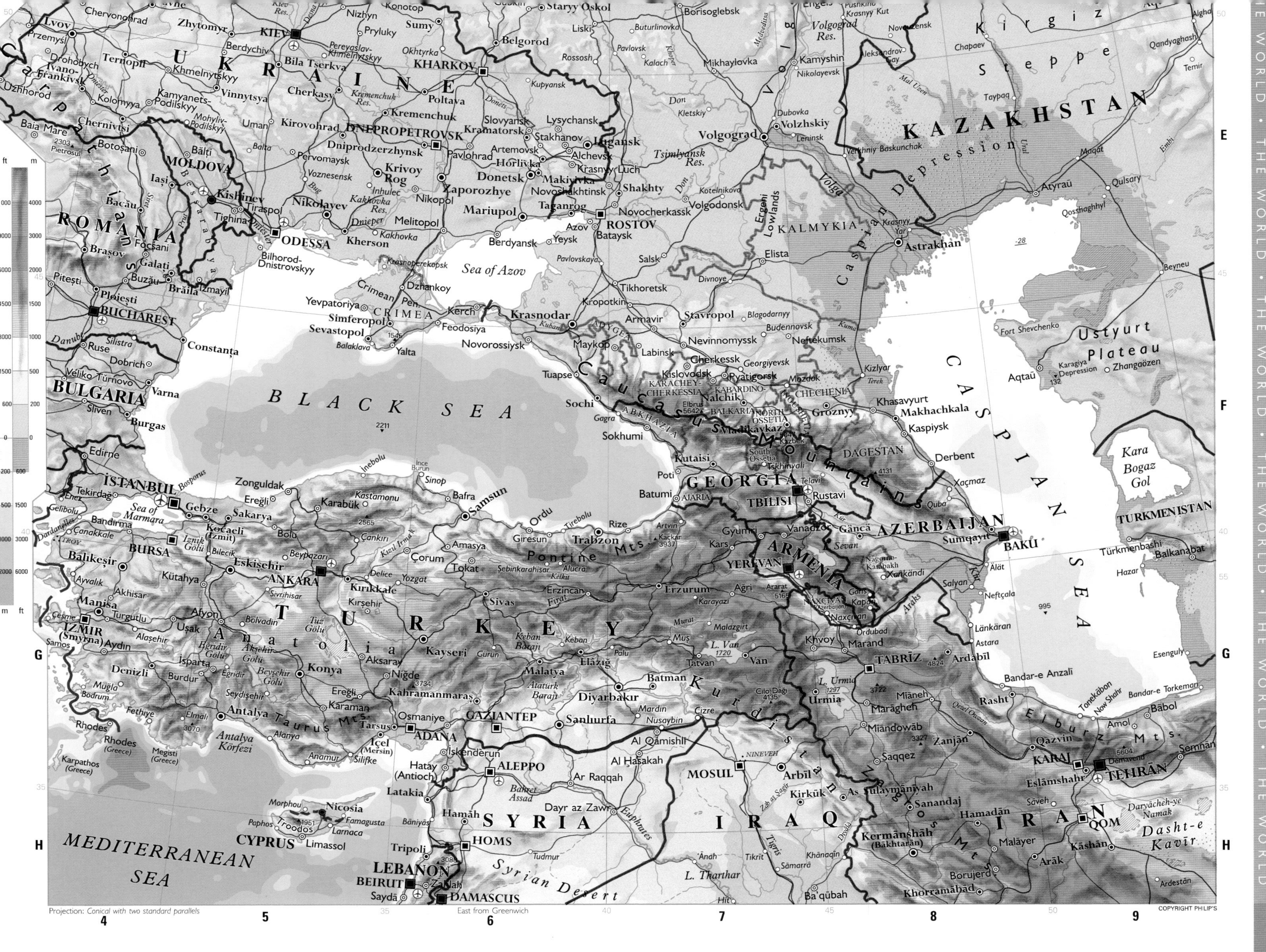
KAZAKHSTAN
UKRAINE
ROMANIA
BULGARIA
MOLDOVA
KALMYKIA
GEORGIA
ARMENIA
AZERBAIJAN
DAGESTAN
CHECHENIA
TURKMENISTAN
TURKEY
SYRIA
IRAQ
IRAN
LEBANON
CYPRUS
BLACK SEA
CASPIAN SEA
MEDITERRANEAN SEA
Sea of Azov
Sea of Marmara
CRIMEA
Caucasus Mountains
Pontine Mts.
Taurus Mts.
Elburz Mts.
Zagros Mts.
Anatolia
Kurdistan
Ustyurt Plateau
Caspian Depression
Kirgiz Steppe
Syrian Desert
Dasht-e Kavīr
Kara Bogaz Gol
Carpathians
KIEV
ODESSA
KHARKOV
DNIPROPETROVSK
ROSTOV
BUCHAREST
ISTANBUL
ANKARA
IZMIR (Smyrna)
BURSA
ADANA
GAZIANTEP
ALEPPO
HOMS
DAMASCUS
BEIRUT
MOSUL
TBILISI
YEREVAN
BAKU
TABRĪZ
TEHRĀN
KARAJ
QOM
Volgograd
Astrakhan
Krasnodar
Sochi
Trabzon
Erzurum
Kayseri
Konya
Antalya
Nicosia
Projection: Conical with two standard parallels
East from Greenwich
COPYRIGHT PHILIP'S

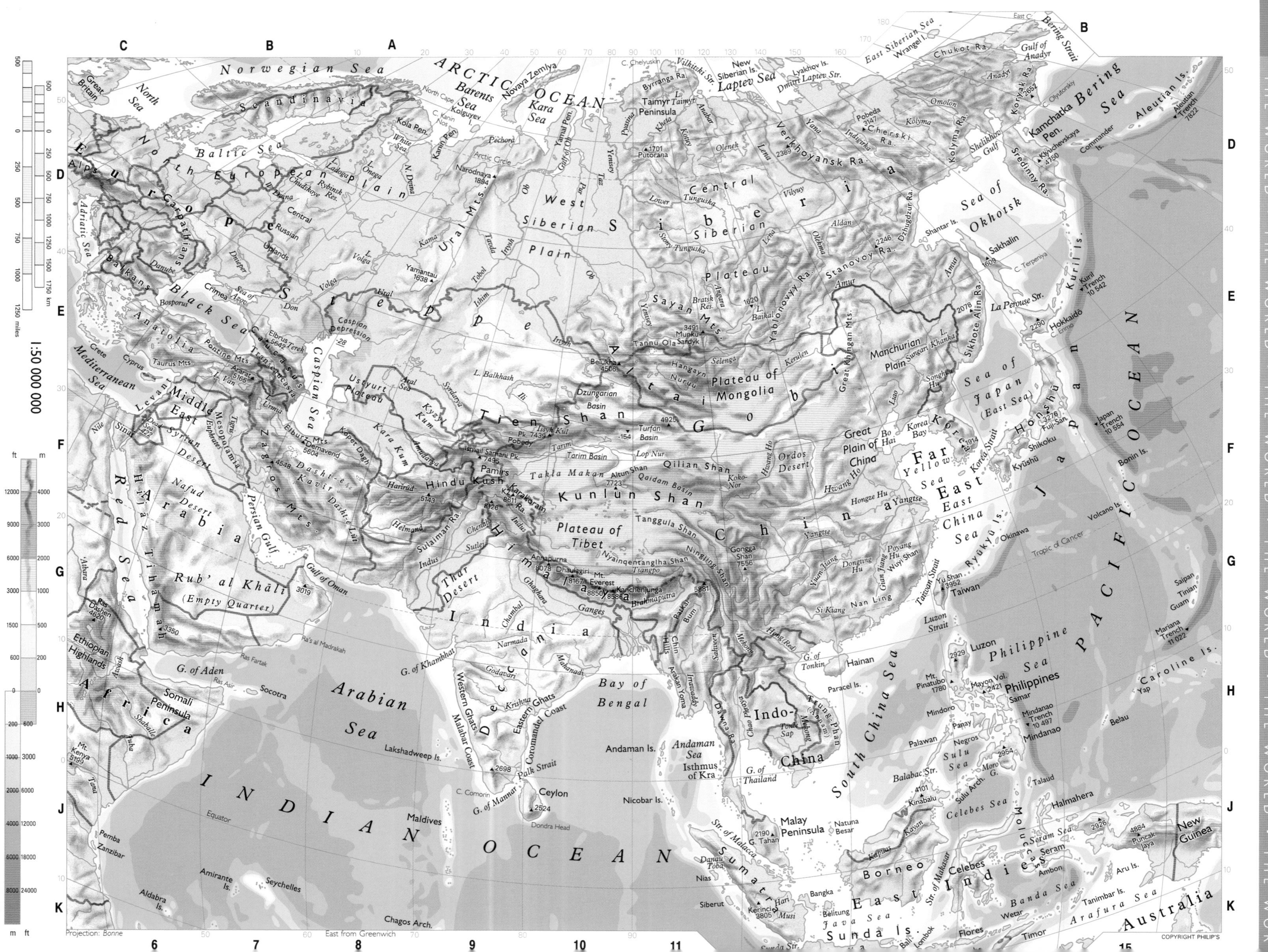
ARCTIC OCEAN
PACIFIC OCEAN
INDIAN OCEAN
Norwegian Sea
North Sea
Baltic Sea
Barents Sea
Kara Sea
Laptev Sea
East Siberian Sea
Bering Sea
Sea of Okhotsk
Sea of Japan (East Sea)
Yellow Sea
East China Sea
South China Sea
Philippine Sea
Sulu Sea
Celebes Sea
Banda Sea
Arafura Sea
Java Sea
Andaman Sea
Bay of Bengal
Arabian Sea
Red Sea
Persian Gulf
Gulf of Oman
G. of Aden
Caspian Sea
Black Sea
Mediterranean Sea
Adriatic Sea
Great Britain
Scandinavia
Kola Pen.
North European Plain
Central Russian Uplands
Ural Mts.
West Siberian Plain
Central Siberian Plateau
Verkhoyansk Ra.
Cherski Ra.
Kolyma Ra.
Chukot Ra.
Koryak Ra.
Kamchatka Pen.
Sredinny Ra.
Stanovoy Ra.
Yablonovyy Ra.
Sayan Mts.
Altai
Gobi
Plateau of Mongolia
Great Khingan Mts.
Manchurian Plain
Sikhote Alin Ra.
Tien Shan
Dzungarian Basin
Turfan Basin
Tarim Basin
Takla Makan
Qilian Shan
Qaidam Basin
Kunlun Shan
Plateau of Tibet
Tanggula Shan
Nyainqentanglha Shan
Himalaya
Mt. Everest 8850
Kanchenjunga 8586
Karakoram Ra.
Hindu Kush
Pamirs
Ismail Samani Pk. 7495
Pobedy Pk. 7439
Kara Kum
Kyzyl Kum
Ustyurt Plateau
Caspian Depression
Caucasus
Elbrus 5642
Anatolia
Pontine Mts.
Taurus Mts.
Zagros Mts.
Elburz Mts.
Demavend 5604
Dasht-e Kavir
Dasht-e Lut
Middle East
Mesopotamia
Syrian Desert
Nafud Desert
Arabia
Hijaz
Tihamah
Rub' al Khali (Empty Quarter)
Thar Desert
India
Deccan
Western Ghats
Eastern Ghats
Ceylon
Great Plain of China
Ordos Desert
China
Nan Ling
Indo-China
Malay Peninsula
Sumatra
Borneo
Celebes
East Indies
Sunda Is.
Philippines
Taiwan
Hainan
Japan
Honshu
Hokkaido
Korea
Sakhalin
Kuril Is.
Aleutian Is.
New Guinea
Australia
Africa
Ethiopian Highlands
Somali Peninsula
Maldives
Seychelles
Chagos Arch.
Equator
Tropic of Cancer
Arctic Circle
1:50 000 000
500 0 250 500 750 1000 1250 1500 1750 km
500 0 250 500 750 1000 1250 miles
Projection: Bonne
East from Greenwich
COPYRIGHT PHILIP'S

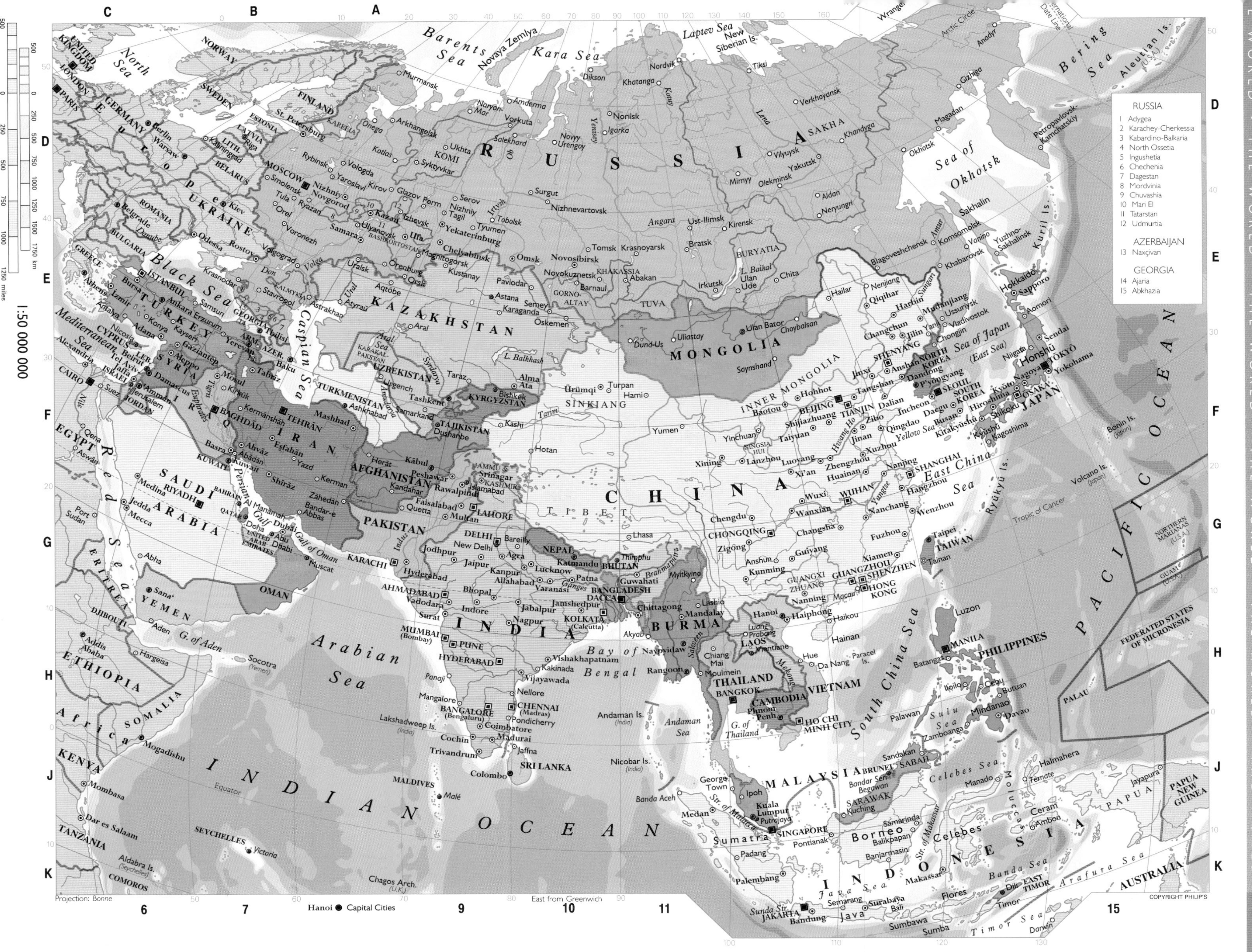
RUSSIA
1 Adygea
2 Karachey-Cherkessia
3 Kabardino-Balkaria
4 North Ossetia
5 Ingushetia
6 Chechenia
7 Dagestan
8 Mordvinia
9 Chuvashia
10 Mari El
11 Tatarstan
12 Udmurtia
AZERBAIJAN
13 Naxçivan
GEORGIA
14 Ajaria
15 Abkhazia
R U S S I A
C H I N A
MONGOLIA
K A Z A K H S T A N
I N D I A
PAKISTAN
AFGHANISTAN
I R A N
SAUDI ARABIA
TURKEY
JAPAN
PHILIPPINES
I N D O N E S I A
M A L A Y S I A
THAILAND
BURMA
VIETNAM
P A C I F I C O C E A N
I N D I A N O C E A N
Barents Sea
Kara Sea
Laptev Sea
Bering Sea
Sea of Okhotsk
Sea of Japan (East Sea)
East China Sea
South China Sea
Caspian Sea
Black Sea
Red Sea
Arabian Sea
Bay of Bengal
Andaman Sea
Hanoi ● Capital Cities
East from Greenwich
Projection: Bonne
COPYRIGHT PHILIP'S
1:50 000 000
500 0 250 500 750 1000 1250 1500 1750 km
500 0 250 500 750 1000 1250 miles

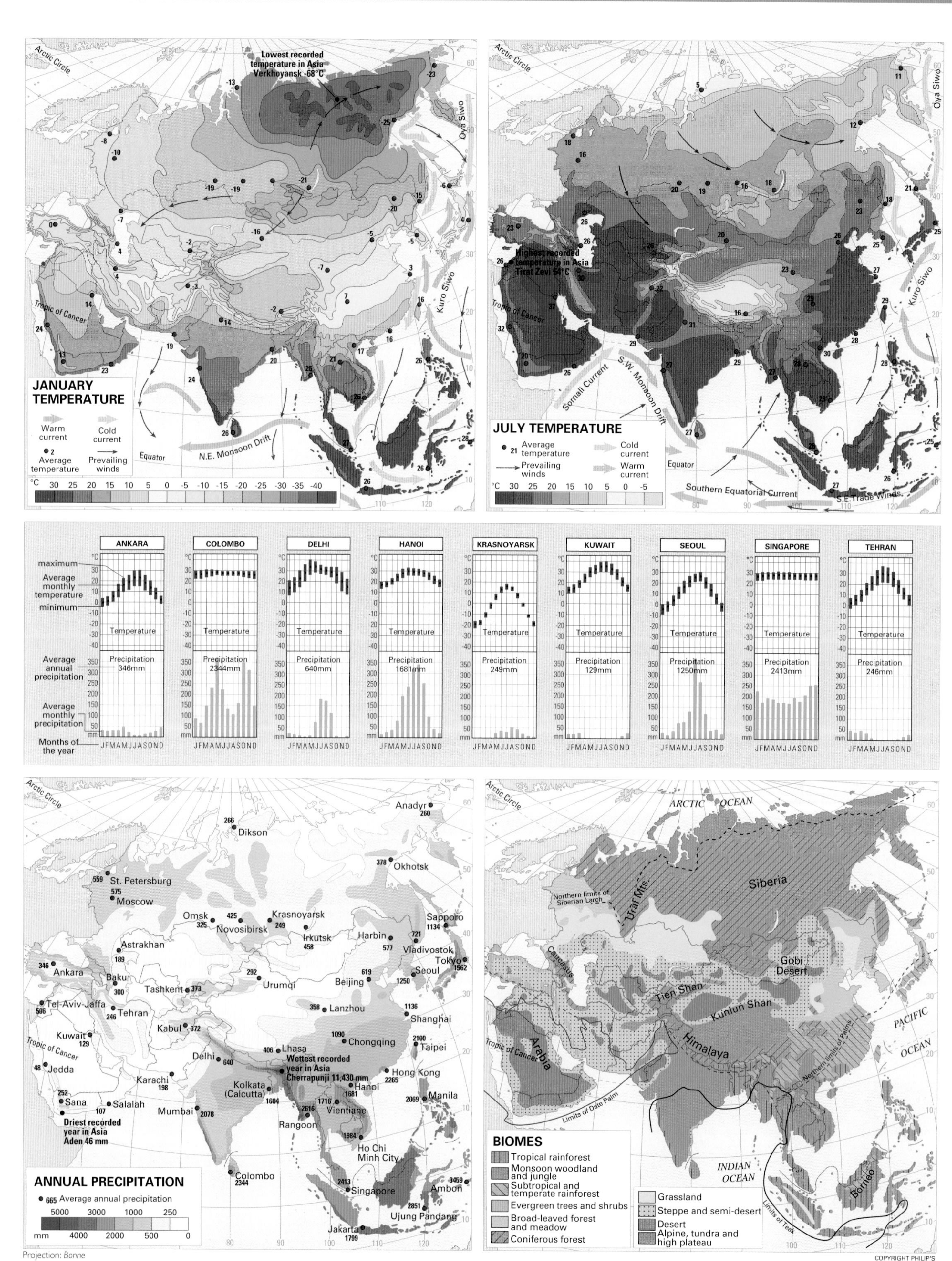

JANUARY TEMPERATURE

Lowest recorded temperature in Asia Verkhoyansk –68°C

Warm current
Cold current
●2 Average temperature
Prevailing winds

°C 30 25 20 15 10 5 0 -5 -10 -15 -20 -25 -30 -35 -40

JULY TEMPERATURE

Highest recorded temperature in Asia Tirat Zevi 54°C

●21 Average temperature
Cold current
Prevailing winds
Warm current

°C 30 25 20 15 10 5 0 -5

Climate graphs:

ANKARA — Temperature — Precipitation — Average annual precipitation 346mm
COLOMBO — Temperature — Precipitation 2344mm
DELHI — Temperature — Precipitation 640mm
HANOI — Temperature — Precipitation 1681mm
KRASNOYARSK — Temperature — Precipitation 249mm
KUWAIT — Temperature — Precipitation 129mm
SEOUL — Temperature — Precipitation 1250mm
SINGAPORE — Temperature — Precipitation 2413mm
TEHRAN — Temperature — Precipitation 246mm

maximum / Average monthly temperature / minimum
Average annual precipitation / Average monthly precipitation
Months of the year JFMAMJJASOND

ANNUAL PRECIPITATION

●665 Average annual precipitation

mm 5000 4000 3000 2000 1000 500 250 0

Wettest recorded year in Asia Cherrapunji 11,430 mm
Driest recorded year in Asia Aden 46 mm

BIOMES

Tropical rainforest
Monsoon woodland and jungle
Subtropical and temperate rainforest
Evergreen trees and shrubs
Broad-leaved forest and meadow
Coniferous forest
Grassland
Steppe and semi-desert
Desert
Alpine, tundra and high plateau

Northern limits of Siberian Larch
Northern limits of Palms
Limits of Date Palm
Limits of Teak

Projection: Bonne

COPYRIGHT PHILIP'S

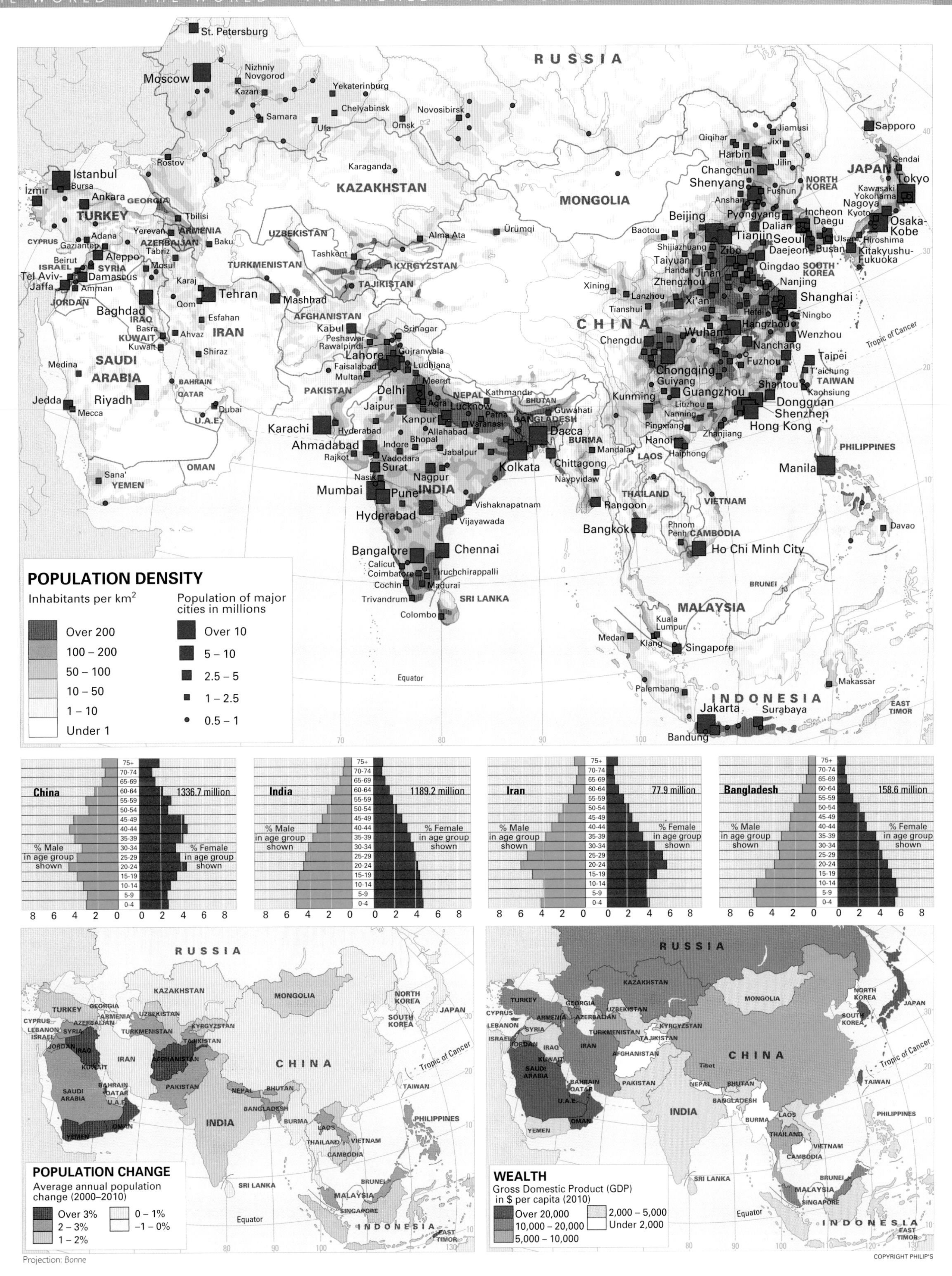

RUSSIA

St. Petersburg

Moscow
Nizhniy
Novgorod
Kazan
Yekaterinburg
Samara
Ufa
Chelyabinsk
Omsk
Novosibirsk
Rostov
Karaganda

KAZAKHSTAN

Ürümqi

MONGOLIA

Sapporo

Istanbul
İzmir
Bursa
Ankara
TURKEY
GEORGIA
Tbilisi
CYPRUS
Adana
Gaziantep
ARMENIA
Yerevan
AZERBAIJAN
Baku
Tabriz
Beirut
Aleppo
ISRAEL
SYRIA
Mosul
Tel Aviv-
Jaffa
Damascus
JORDAN
Amman
Baghdad
IRAQ
KUWAIT
Kuwait
Basra
Ahvaz
SAUDI
ARABIA
Medina
Jedda
Mecca
Riyadh
BAHRAIN
QATAR
Dubai
U.A.E.
OMAN
Sana'
YEMEN

UZBEKISTAN
TURKMENISTAN
Tashkent
KYRGYZSTAN
TAJIKISTAN
Karaj
Qom
Tehran
Esfahan
IRAN
Shiraz
Mashhad
Alma Ata

AFGHANISTAN
Kabul
Peshawar
Rawalpindi
PAKISTAN
Srinagar
Lahore
Gujranwala
Faisalabad
Ludhiana
Multan
Delhi
Meerut
Jaipur
Agra
Kanpur
Lucknow
NEPAL
Kathmandu
BHUTAN
Guwahati
BANGLADESH
Dacca
BURMA
Mandalay
Naypyidaw
Karachi
Hyderabad
Ahmadabad
Rajkot
Indore
Bhopal
Allahabad
Varanasi
Patna
Vadodara
Jabalpur
Surat
Nasik
Nagpur
Mumbai
Pune
INDIA
Hyderabad
Vishaknapatnam
Vijayawada
Bangalore
Calicut
Coimbatore
Cochin
Truchchirappalli
Madurai
Trivandrum
SRI LANKA
Colombo
Kolkata
Chennai
Chittagong

CHINA
Baotou
Shijiazhuang
Taiyuan
Handan
Xining
Lanzhou
Xi'an
Tianshui
Zhengzhou
Chengdu
Chongqing
Guiyang
Kunming
Liuzhou
Nanning
Pingxiang
Zhanjiang
Hanoi
Haiphong
LAOS
THAILAND
Bangkok
VIETNAM
Rangoon
Phnom
Penh
CAMBODIA
Ho Chi Minh City

Qiqihar
Jiamusi
Jixi
Harbin
Jilin
Changchun
Shenyang
Anshan
Fushun
Beijing
Tianjin
Dalian
Zibo
Jinan
Qingdao
Nanjing
Hefei
Wuhan
Nanchang
Fuzhou
Shantou
Guangzhou
Dongguan
Shenzhen
Hong Kong
Wenzhou
Ningbo
Shanghai
Hangzhou
NORTH
KOREA
Pyongyang
Incheon
Seoul
Daejeon
Daegu
Ulsan
Busan
SOUTH
KOREA
JAPAN
Sendai
Tokyo
Kawasaki
Yokohama
Nagoya
Kyoto
Osaka-
Kobe
Hiroshima
Kitakyushu-
Fukuoka
T'aichung
Taipei
Kaohsiung
TAIWAN
PHILIPPINES
Manila
Davao

MALAYSIA
Kuala
Lumpur
Medan
Klang
Singapore
BRUNEI
Palembang
Jakarta
Surabaya
Bandung
INDONESIA
EAST
TIMOR
Makassar

Tropic of Cancer
Equator

POPULATION DENSITY

Inhabitants per km²

	Over 200
	100 – 200
	50 – 100
	10 – 50
	1 – 10
	Under 1

Population of major cities in millions

■	Over 10
■	5 – 10
■	2.5 – 5
■	1 – 2.5
•	0.5 – 1

China — 1336.7 million

75+
70-74
65-69
60-64
55-59
50-54
45-49
40-44
35-39
30-34
25-29
20-24
15-19
10-14
5-9
0-4

% Male in age group shown   % Female in age group shown

8 6 4 2 0 0 2 4 6 8

India — 1189.2 million

% Male in age group shown   % Female in age group shown

8 6 4 2 0 0 2 4 6 8

Iran — 77.9 million

% Male in age group shown   % Female in age group shown

8 6 4 2 0 0 2 4 6 8

Bangladesh — 158.6 million

% Male in age group shown   % Female in age group shown

8 6 4 2 0 0 2 4 6 8

POPULATION CHANGE

RUSSIA
KAZAKHSTAN
MONGOLIA
NORTH KOREA
SOUTH KOREA
JAPAN
TURKEY
GEORGIA
CYPRUS
ARMENIA
AZERBAIJAN
UZBEKISTAN
KYRGYZSTAN
LEBANON
SYRIA
ISRAEL
JORDAN
IRAQ
KUWAIT
TURKMENISTAN
TAJIKISTAN
AFGHANISTAN
IRAN
CHINA
SAUDI
ARABIA
BAHRAIN
QATAR
U.A.E.
YEMEN
OMAN
PAKISTAN
NEPAL
BHUTAN
BANGLADESH
INDIA
BURMA
LAOS
THAILAND
VIETNAM
CAMBODIA
PHILIPPINES
SRI LANKA
BRUNEI
MALAYSIA
SINGAPORE
INDONESIA
EAST TIMOR
TAIWAN

Tropic of Cancer
Equator

Average annual population change (2000–2010)

	Over 3%		0 – 1%
	2 – 3%		–1 – 0%
	1 – 2%		

WEALTH

RUSSIA
KAZAKHSTAN
MONGOLIA
NORTH KOREA
SOUTH KOREA
JAPAN
TURKEY
GEORGIA
CYPRUS
LEBANON
ARMENIA
AZERBAIJAN
UZBEKISTAN
KYRGYZSTAN
SYRIA
ISRAEL
JORDAN
IRAQ
KUWAIT
TURKMENISTAN
TAJIKISTAN
AFGHANISTAN
IRAN
Tibet
CHINA
SAUDI
ARABIA
BAHRAIN
QATAR
U.A.E.
YEMEN
OMAN
PAKISTAN
NEPAL
BHUTAN
BANGLADESH
INDIA
BURMA
LAOS
THAILAND
VIETNAM
CAMBODIA
PHILIPPINES
SRI LANKA
BRUNEI
MALAYSIA
SINGAPORE
INDONESIA
EAST TIMOR
TAIWAN

Tropic of Cancer
Equator

Gross Domestic Product (GDP) in $ per capita (2010)

	Over 20,000		2,000 – 5,000
	10,000 – 20,000		Under 2,000
	5,000 – 10,000		

Projection: Bonne

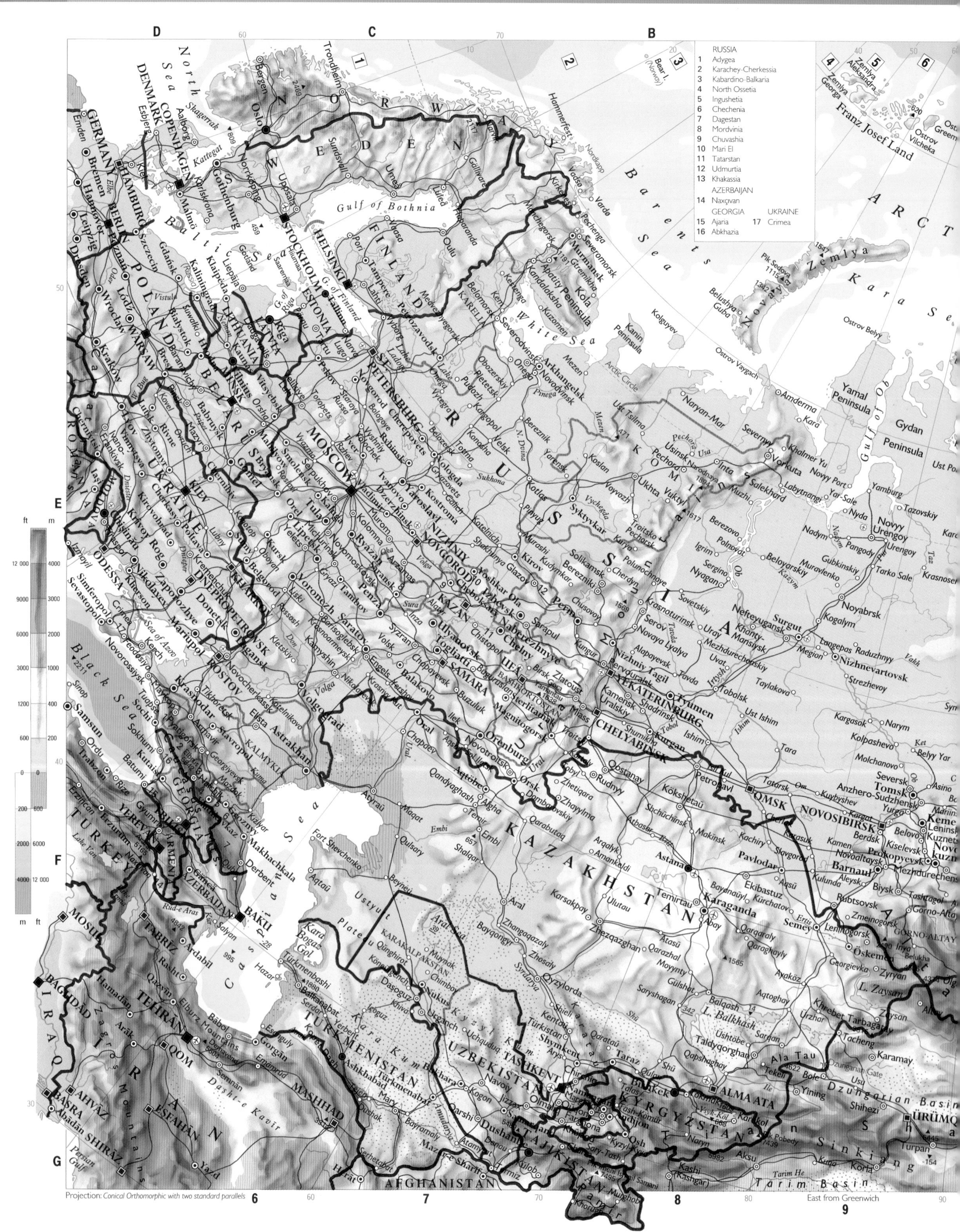

RUSSIA
1 Adygea
2 Karachey-Cherkessia
3 Kabardino-Balkaria
4 North Ossetia
5 Ingushetia
6 Chechenia
7 Dagestan
8 Mordvinia
9 Chuvashia
10 Mari El
11 Tatarstan
12 Udmurtia
13 Khakassia
AZERBAIJAN
14 Naxçivan
GEORGIA   UKRAINE
15 Ajaria   17 Crimea
16 Abkhazia

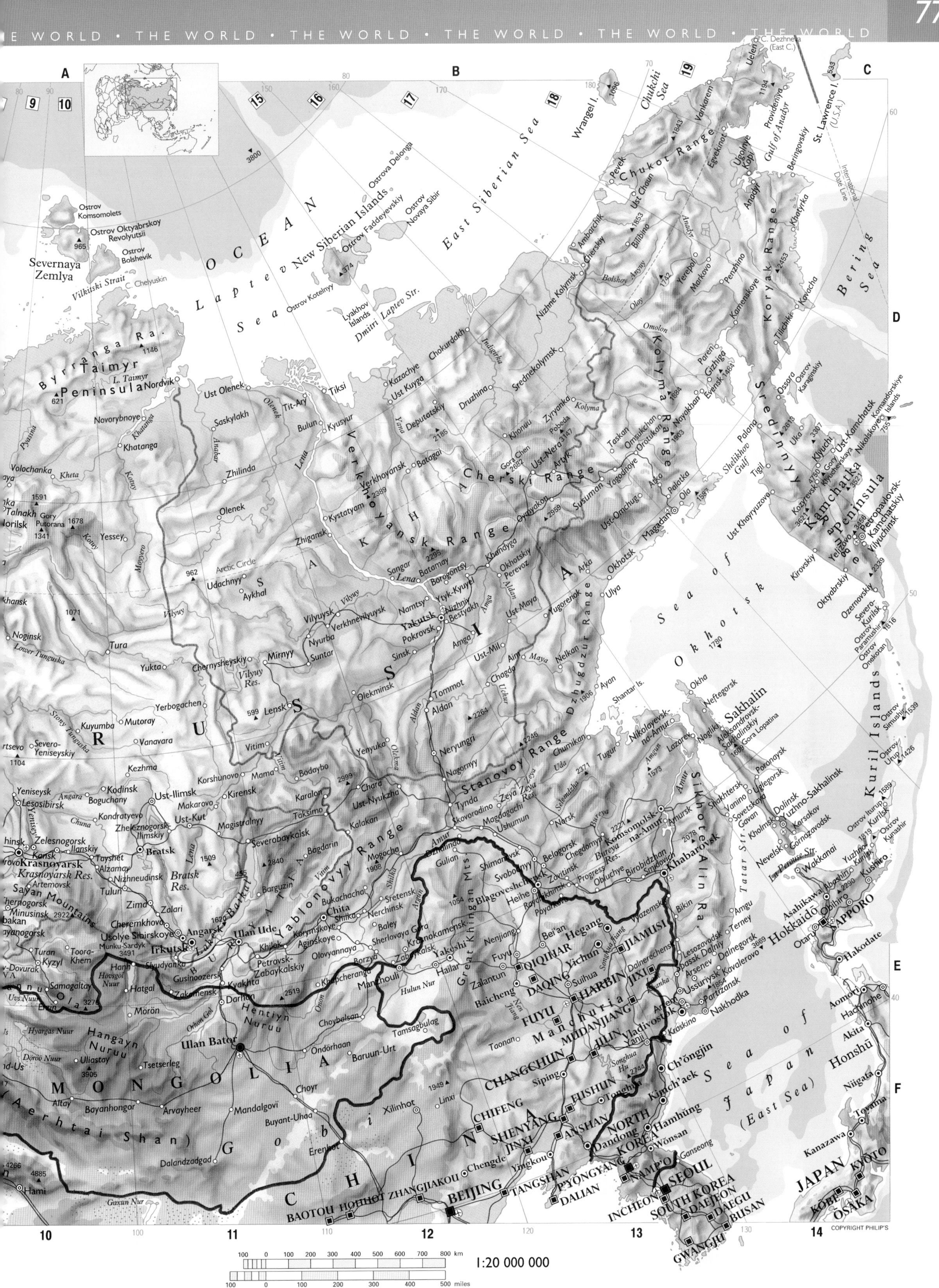
A
B
C
D
E
F
9
10
15
16
17
18
19
Severnaya Zemlya
Ostrov Komsomolets
Ostrov Oktyabrskoy Revolyutsii
Ostrov Bolshevik
Vilkitski Strait
C. Chelyuskin
Byrranga Ra.
Taimyr Peninsula
L. Taimyr
Nordvik
Laptev Sea
OCEAN
New Siberian Islands
Ostrova Delonga
Ostrov Faddeyevskiy
Ostrov Novaya Sibir
Ostrov Kotelnyy
Lyakhov Islands
Dmitri Laptev Str.
East Siberian Sea
Wrangel I.
Chukchi Sea
C. Dezhneva (East C.)
Uelen
St. Lawrence I. (U.S.A.)
Chukot Range
Pevek
Vankarem
Egvekinot
Provideniya
Gulf of Anadyr
Beringovskiy
Anadyr
International Date Line
Koryak Range
Bering Sea
Ambarchik
Cherskiy
Bilibino
Nizhne Kolymsk
Kolyma Range
Srednekolymsk
Chokurdakh
Indigirka
Kazachye
Ust Kuyga
Deputatskiy
Tiksi
Tit-Ary
Ust Olenek
Saskylakh
Bulun
Kyusyur
Verkhoyansk Range
Verkhoyansk
Batagai
Cherski Range
Zyryanka
Ust-Nera
Susuman
Magadan
Sredinnyy Range
Kamchatka Peninsula
Petropavlovsk-Kamchatskiy
Vilyuchinsk
Ust-Kamchatsk
Komandorskiye Islands
Sea of Okhotsk
Okhotsk
Ayan
Shantar Is.
Sakhalin
Okha
Nogliki
Yuzhno-Sakhalinsk
Kholmsk
Korsakov
Kuril Islands
Tatar Str.
La Perouse Str.
Wakkanai
Hokkaidō
SAPPORO
Hakodate
Khatanga
Novorybnoye
Volochanka
Norilsk
Talnakh
Gory Putorana
Zhilinda
Olenek
Zhigansk
Arctic Circle
Udachnyy
Aykhal
Vilyuysk
Verkhnevilyuysk
Yakutsk
Pokrovsk
Nyurba
Suntar
Mirnyy
Vilyuy Res.
Olekminsk
Lensk
Tommot
Aldan
Neryungri
Amga
Dzhugdzur Range
Stanovoy Range
Tynda
Skovorodino
Bodaybo
Chara
Vitim
Kirensk
Ust-Kut
Ust-Ilimsk
Bratsk
Bratsk Res.
Severobaykalsk
Lake Baikal
Irkutsk
Angarsk
Ulan Ude
Chita
Yablonovyy Range
Krasnoyarsk
Krasnoyarsk Res.
Sayan Mountains
Kyzyl
RUSSIA
Tura
Noginsk
Lower Tunguska
Stony Tunguska
Kuyumba
Vanavara
Blagoveshchensk
Khabarovsk
Komsomolsk-na-Amur
Sikhote Alin Ra.
Birobidzhan
Vladivostok
Nakhodka
Ussuriysk
Great Khingan Mts.
Hailar
Manchouli
Hulun Nur
QIQIHAR
DAQING
HARBIN
JIAMUSI
JIXI
MUDANJIANG
JILIN
CHANGCHUN
Manchuria
SHENYANG
FUSHUN
ANSHAN
CHIFENG
DALIAN
BEIJING
TANGSHAN
ZHANGJIAKOU
BAOTOU
HOHHOT
CHINA
MONGOLIA
Ulan Bator
Hangayn Nuruu
Hentiyn Nuruu
Choybalsan
Gobi
Altay
Hami
NORTH KOREA
PYONGYANG
NAMP'O
SOUTH KOREA
SEOUL
INCHEON
DAEJEON
DAEGU
BUSAN
GWANGJU
Sea of Japan (East Sea)
JAPAN
Honshū
Aomori
Akita
Niigata
Toyama
Kanazawa
KYOTO
KOBE
OSAKA
COPYRIGHT PHILIP'S
1:20 000 000
km
miles
10
11
12
13
14

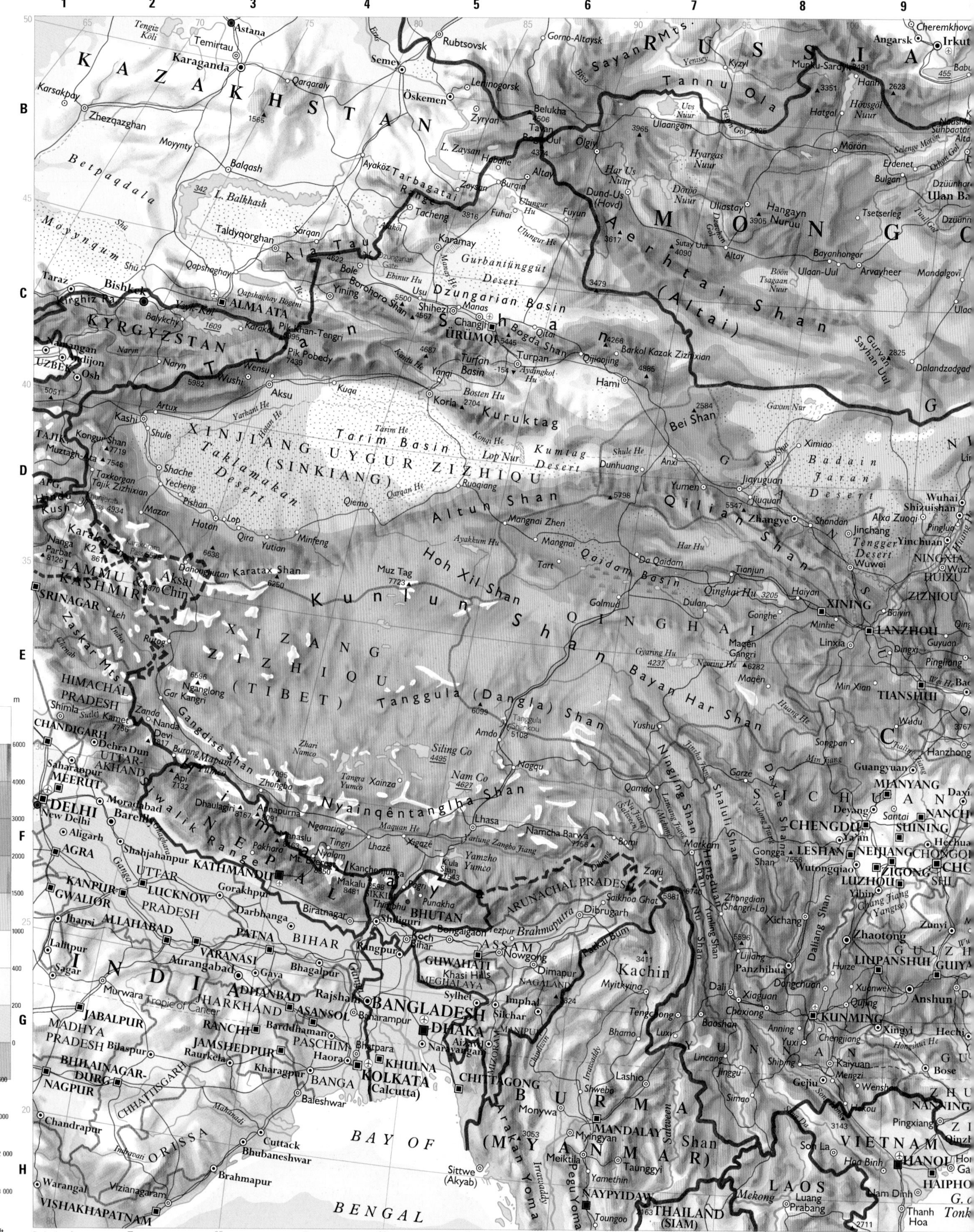
1
2
3
4
5
6
7
8
9
B
C
D
E
F
G
H
5
6
7
8
9
10
KAZAKHSTAN
Astana
Temirtau
Karaganda
Tengiz Köli
Karsakpay
Zhezqazghan
Qarqaraly
Semey
Rubtsovsk
Öskemen
Leninogorsk
Zyryan
Moyynty
Balqash
Betpaqdala
L. Balkhash
Moyynqum
Shū
Taldyqorghan
Sarqan
Qapshaghay
Taraz
Bishkek
Kirghiz Ra.
ALMA ATA
Qapshaghay Bögeni
Balykchy
Ysyk-Köl
KYRGYZSTAN
Naryn
Pik Khan-Tengri
Pik Pobedy
Osh
Andijon
UZBEK.
Ayaköz
Tarbagatai Range
Zaysan
L. Zaysan
Tacheng
Ala Tau
Dzungarian Gate
Ebinur Hu
Bole
Yining
Ili
Borohoro Shan
Karamay
Gurbantünggüt Desert
Dzungarian Basin
Usu
Shihezi
Manas
Changji
ÜRÜMQI
Bogda Shan
Qitai
Turpan
Turfan Basin
Aydingkol Hu
Tian Shan
Wensu
Wushi
Aksu
Kuqa
Yanqi
Bosten Hu
Korla
Kuruktag
Hami
Barkol Kazak Zizhixian
Qijiaojing
Bei Shan
Kashi
Artux
Shule
Kongur Shan
Muztagh Ata
Taxkorgan Tajik Zizhixian
TAJIK.
AFG.
Hindu Kush
Tarim Basin
Tarim He
XINJIANG UYGUR ZIZHIQU (SINKIANG)
Taklamakan Desert
Yarkant He
Hotan He
Shache
Yecheng
Pishan
Hotan
Lop
Qira
Yutian
Minfeng
Qiemo
Qarqan He
Ruoqiang
Lop Nur
Kumtag Desert
Dunhuang
Anxi
Shule He
Altun Shan
Mangnai Zhen
Mangnai
Ayakkum Hu
Karakoram
K2
Nanga Parbat
JAMMU & KASHMIR
Aksai Chin
SRINAGAR
Leh
Zaskar Mts.
Indus
Rutog
Karatax Shan
Muz Tag
Kunlun Shan
Hoh Xil Shan
Qaidam Basin
Da Qaidam
Golmud
Dulan
Qinghai Hu
QINGHAI
Gonghe
XINING
Tianjun
Haiyan
Minhe
LANZHOU
Linxia
XIZANG ZIZHIQU (TIBET)
Nganglong Kangri
Gar Kangri
Zanda
Gangdise Shan
Kamet
Nanda Devi
Burang
Mapam
Api
Zhari Namco
Tanggula (Dangla) Shan
Tanggula Shankou
Amdo
Siling Co
Nam Co
Nagqu
Tangra Yumco
Xainza
Zhongba
Nyainqêntanglha Shan
Lhasa
Yarlung Zangbo Jiang
Namcha Barwa
Xigazê
Lhazê
Tingri
Ngamring
Yamzho Yumco
Kula Shan
Maquan He
Gyaring Hu
Ngoring Hu
Bayan Har Shan
Maqên Gangri
Maqên
Yushu
Huang He
Qamdo
Nujiang
Lancang Jiang
Ningjing Shan
Shaluli Shan
Jinsha Jiang
Markam
Hengduan Shan
Daxue Shan
Garzê
Yalong Jiang
Gongga Shan
Songpan
Min Jiang
Min Xian
TIANSHUI
Wudu
Hanzhong
Guangyuan
MIANYANG
Deyang
CHENGDU
Ya'an
LESHAN
NEIJIANG
CHONGQING
Suining
Santai
ZIGONG
LUZHOU
Yibin
Chang Jiang (Yangtze)
Wutongqiao
Xichang
Daliang Shan
Zhaotong
Liupanshui
Huize
Qujing
Xuanwei
KUNMING
Anshun
Xingyi
Chengjiang
Yuxi
Kaiyuan
Mengzi
Gejiu
Wenshan
YUNNAN
Zhongdian (Shangri-La)
Yunling Shan
Lijiang
Panzhihua
Dali
Xiaguan
Baoshan
Chuxiong
Tengchong
Luxi
Lincang
Simao
Shiping
Anning
Dongchuan
HIMACHAL PRADESH
Shimla
Sutlej
CHANDIGARH
Dehra Dun
UTTARAKHAND
Saharanpur
MEERUT
DELHI
New Delhi
Moradabad
Bareilly
Aligarh
AGRA
Shahjahanpur
Siwalik Range
Dhaulagiri
Annapurna
Manaslu
Pokhara
Mt. Everest
Himalaya
Nyalam
Kanchenjunga
Makalu
KATHMANDU
NEPAL
Gorakhpur
UTTAR PRADESH
LUCKNOW
KANPUR
GWALIOR
Jhansi
ALLAHABAD
VARANASI
Lalitpur
Sagar
INDIA
Aurangabad
Gaya
PATNA
BIHAR
Darbhanga
Biratnagar
Bhagalpur
Ganga
SIKKIM
Thimphu
Punakha
BHUTAN
Siliguri
Koch Bihar
Rangpur
Bongaigaon
Tezpur
Brahmaputra
ARUNACHAL PRADESH
Dibrugarh
Saikhoa Ghat
Zayü
Bomi
ASSAM
GUWAHATI
Nowgong
Khasi Hills
MEGHALAYA
Dimapur
NAGALAND
Patkai Bum
Kachin
Myitkyina
Imphal
MANIPUR
Silchar
Sylhet
MIZORAM
Aizawl
Narayanganj
BANGLADESH
DHAKA
Rajshahi
Baharampur
KHULNA
Bhatpara
Haora
KOLKATA (Calcutta)
Kharagpur
PASCHIM BANGA
Baleshwar
JHARKHAND
DHANBAD
ASANSOL
RANCHI
Barddhaman
JAMSHEDPUR
Raurkela
Murwara
Tropic of Cancer
JABALPUR
MADHYA PRADESH
Bilaspur
BHILAINAGAR-DURG
NAGPUR
CHHATTISGARH
Mahanadi
ORISSA
Chandrapur
Cuttack
Bhubaneshwar
Brahmapur
Indravati
Warangal
Vizianagaram
VISHAKHAPATNAM
BAY OF BENGAL
CHITTAGONG
Sittwe (Akyab)
Arakan Yoma
Irrawaddy
Chindwin
Bhamo
Lashio
Shwebo
Monywa
MANDALAY
Myingyan
Meiktila
Taunggyi
Yamethin
BURMA (MYANMAR)
Shan
Salween
Pegu Yoma
NAYPYIDAW
Toungoo
THAILAND (SIAM)
LAOS
Mekong
Luang Prabang
VIETNAM
Son La
Hoa Binh
HANOI
Nam Dinh
Thanh Hoa
Pingxiang
NANNING
RUSSIA
Sayan Mts.
Gorno-Altaysk
Biya
Yenisey
Kyzyl
Tannu Ola
Belukha
Tavan Bogd Uul
Ölgiy
Uvs Nuur
Ulaangom
Munku-Sardyk
Hatgal
Hövsgöl Nuur
Irkutsk
Angarsk
Cheremkhovo
Mörön
Selenge Mörön
Erdenet
Bulgan
Orhon Gol
Sühbaatar
Dzüünharaa
Ulan Bator
Har Us Nuur
Hyargas Nuur
Dund-Us (Hovd)
Döröö Nuur
Uliastay
Hangayn Nuruu
Tsetserleg
Altay
Fuyun
Ulungur Hu
Ulungur He
Burqin
Fuhai
MONGOLIA
Aerhtai Shan (Altai)
Sutay Uul
Bayanhongor
Ulaan-Uul
Arvayheer
Mandalgovi
Böön Tsagaan Nuur
Gurvan Sayhan Uul
Dalandzadgad
Gaxun Nur
Ximiao
Badain Jaran Desert
Jiayuguan
Jiuquan
Yumen
Qilian Shan
Zhangye
Shandan
Jinchang
Tengger Desert
Wuwei
Alxa Zuoqi
Yinchuan
Shizuishan
Wuhai
NINGXIA HUIZU ZIZHIQU
Baiyin
Dingxi
Guyuan
Pingliang
Wei He
CHINA
Projection: Bonne
East from Greenwich

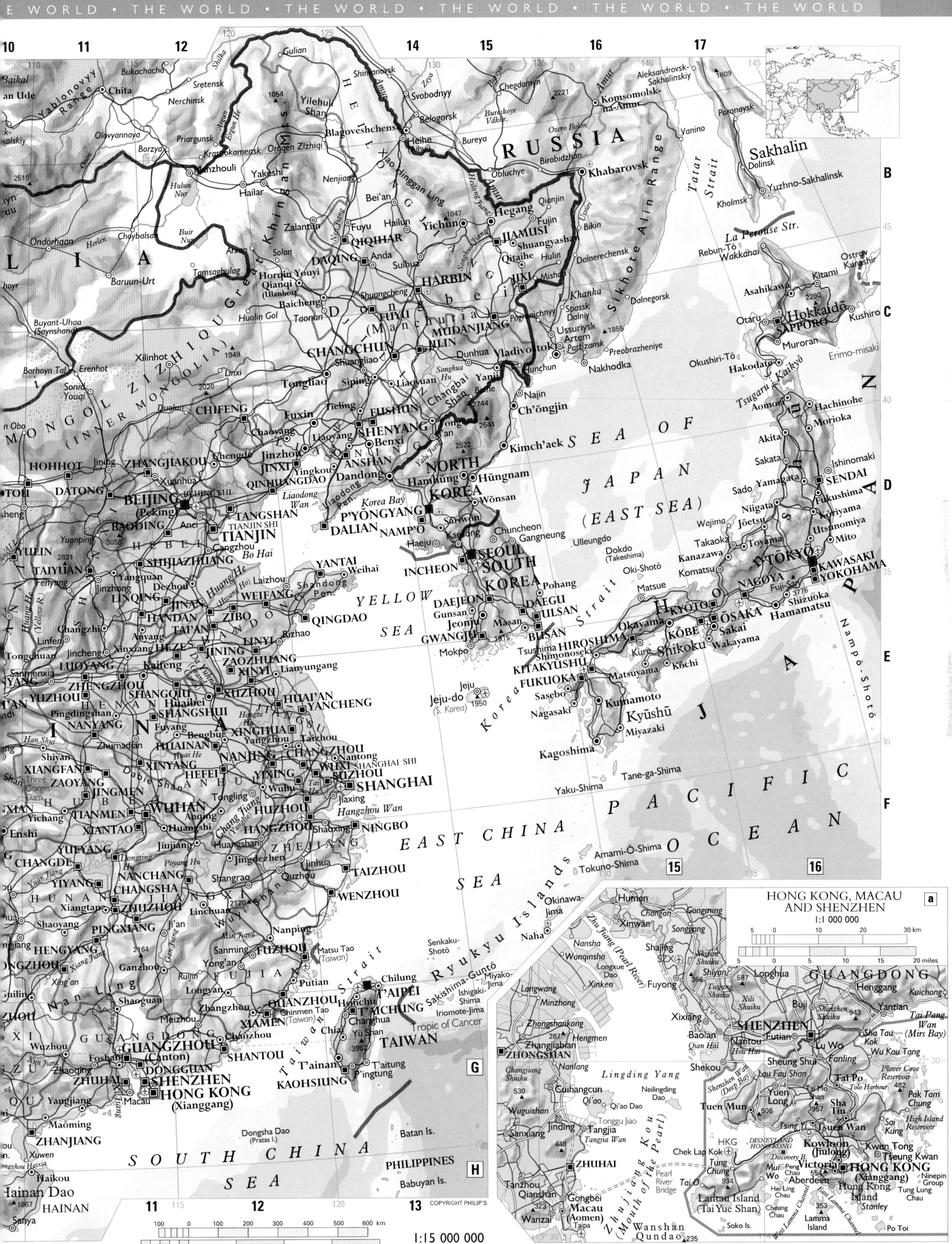
RUSSIA
Sakhalin
Tatar Strait
La Perouse Str.
Sikhote Alin Range
Khabarovsk
Komsomolsk-na-Amur
Aleksandrovsk-Sakhalinskiy
Yuzhno-Sakhalinsk
Vladivostok
Nakhodka
Ussuriysk
Blagoveshchensk
Heihe (Aihui)
Chita
Sretensk
Nerchinsk
Yablonovyy Range
Shilka
Amur
Zeya
Bureya
Birobidzhan
Obluchye
Svobodnyy
Belogorsk
Manzhouli
Hailar
Hulun Nur
Buir Nur
Choybalsan
Baruun-Urt
Erenhot
Xilinhot
Great Khingan Mts.
Da Hinggan Ling
Xiao Hinggan Ling
HEILONGJIANG
QIQIHAR
DAQING
HARBIN
JIAMUSI
Hegang
Yichun
Shuangyashan
JIXI
MUDANJIANG
JILIN
CHANGCHUN
Siping
Liaoyuan
Tongliao
Manchuria
Dongbei
NEI MONGOL ZIZHIQU (INNER MONGOLIA)
CHIFENG
FUSHUN
SHENYANG
ANSHAN
Benxi
Dandong
Fuxin
Jinzhou
Yingkou
DALIAN
Liaodong Pen.
Liaodong Wan
Korea Bay
Changbai Shan
NORTH KOREA
P'YŎNGYANG
Hamhŭng
Hŭngnam
Wŏnsan
Kimch'aek
Ch'ŏngjin
Najin
NAMP'O
Sariwŏn
Kaesŏng
Haeju
SEOUL
INCHEON
SOUTH KOREA
Chuncheon
Gangneung
DAEJEON
DAEGU
ULSAN
BUSAN
GWANGJU
Jeonju
Gunsan
Masan
Mokpo
Pohang
Jeju
Jeju-do (S. Korea)
Ulleungdo
Dokdo (Takeshima)
Korea Strait
SEA OF JAPAN (EAST SEA)
JAPAN
Hokkaidō
SAPPORO
Asahikawa
Kushiro
Otaru
Muroran
Hakodate
Tsugaru Kaikyō
Aomori
Hachinohe
Morioka
Akita
Sakata
SENDAI
Yamagata
Fukushima
Kōriyama
Niigata
Sado
Toyama
Kanazawa
TŌKYŌ
KAWASAKI
YOKOHAMA
Utsunomiya
Mito
NAGOYA
KYŌTO
ŌSAKA
KŌBE
Sakai
Wakayama
Okayama
HIROSHIMA
Shikoku
Matsuyama
Kōchi
KITAKYŪSHŪ
FUKUOKA
Kyūshū
Nagasaki
Kumamoto
Miyazaki
Kagoshima
Yaku-Shima
Tane-ga-Shima
Honshū
Shizuoka
Hamamatsu
Nampō-Shotō
Oki-Shotō
Matsue
Amami-Ō-Shima
Tokuno-Shima
Okinawa-Jima
Naha
Ryukyu Islands
PACIFIC OCEAN
EAST CHINA SEA
YELLOW SEA
Bo Hai
BEIJING (Peking)
TIANJIN
TANGSHAN
QINHUANGDAO
ZHANGJIAKOU
Chengde
DATONG
HOHHOT
BAODING
SHIJIAZHUANG
TAIYUAN
Yulin
HEBEI
SHANXI
SHANDONG
Shandong Pen.
YANTAI
Weihai
QINGDAO
WEIFANG
JINAN
ZIBO
TAI'AN
LINYI
Rizhao
JINING
ZAOZHUANG
Lianyungang
XUZHOU
HEZE
HANDAN
Anyang
Xinxiang
Kaifeng
ZHENGZHOU
LUOYANG
HENAN
Huang He (Yellow R.)
SHANGQIU
Huaibei
HUAI'AN
YANCHENG
JIANGSU
Bengbu
HUAINAN
NANJING
CHANGZHOU
WUXI
SUZHOU
SHANGHAI
Nantong
HEFEI
ANHUI
Wuhu
Tongling
Anqing
WUHAN
HUBEI
Yichang
Three Gorges Dam
XIANGFAN
Shiyan
HUZHOU
HANGZHOU
Hangzhou Wan
NINGBO
Shaoxing
ZHEJIANG
Jinhua
Quzhou
TAIZHOU
WENZHOU
Jingdezhen
NANCHANG
JIANGXI
Poyang Hu
Dongting Hu
CHANGSHA
HUNAN
ZHUZHOU
Xiangtan
YIYANG
CHANGDE
YUEYANG
HENGYANG
PINGXIANG
Chang Jiang (Yangtze)
FUJIAN
FUZHOU
Nanping
Sanming
Putian
QUANZHOU
XIAMEN
Zhangzhou
Longyan
Matsu Tao (Taiwan)
Chinmen Tao (Taiwan)
Taiwan Strait
TAIWAN
T'AIPEI
Chilung
T'AICHUNG
Changhua
Chiai
Yü Shan 3952
T'ainan
KAOHSIUNG
P'ingtung
T'aitung
Tropic of Cancer
Senkaku-Shotō
Sakishima-Guntō
Ishigaki-Shima
Iriomote-Jima
Miyako-Jima
GUANGDONG
GUANGZHOU (Canton)
DONGGUAN
SHENZHEN
HONG KONG (Xianggang)
ZHUHAI
Macau
Foshan
SHANTOU
Chaozhou
Meizhou
Shaoguan
Nan Ling
ZHANJIANG
Maoming
Yangjiang
Haikou
Hainan Dao
HAINAN
Sanya
SOUTH CHINA SEA
Dongsha Dao (Pratas I.)
Batan Is.
PHILIPPINES
Babuyan Is.
COPYRIGHT PHILIP'S
1:15 000 000
km
miles
HONG KONG, MACAU AND SHENZHEN
1:1 000 000
Humen
Zhu Jiang (Pearl River)
Lingding Yang
Zhujiang Kou (Mouth of the Pearl)
Shekou
Shenzhen Wan (Deep Bay)
Lantau Island (Tai Yue Shan)
Chek Lap Kok
Kowloon (Jiulong)
Victoria
Aberdeen
Hong Kong Island
Stanley
Lamma Island
Sha Tin
Tsuen Wan
Tai Po
Fanling
Sheung Shui
Yuen Long
Tuen Mun
Tai Pang Wan (Mirs Bay)
Macau (Aomen)
Taipa
Gongbei
ZHONGSHAN
Pearl River Bridge
Wanshan Qundao
Soko Is.
Po Toi

EMPLOYMENT IN INDUSTRY

Industrial population
by province in millions

20 10 4 2 1 0.5

GDP per capita
(US$ 2010)

Over $10,000
$5,000 – $10,000
$2,500 – $5,000
Under $2,500

CHINA'S SHARE OF WORLD MANUFACTURING
(for selected goods)

Textiles — China 24.3% | USA 19.2% | India 12.4% | Finland 3.5%
World total (2006): 23,300,000 tonnes

Paper — China 24.5% | USA 19.2% | Japan 6.2% | Germany 5.5% | Finland 3.3% | S. Korea 3.0%
World total (2010): 394,300,000 tonnes

Cement — China 48.9% | India 6.2% | USA 3.1% | Japan 2.2% | S. Korea 1.9%
World total (2010): 2,840,000,000 tonnes

Coal — China 48.3% | USA 14.8% | Australia 6.3% | India 5.8% | Indonesia 5.0%
World total (2010): 3,731,000,000 tOe

Hydroelectricity — China 21.0% | Canada 10.7% | Brazil 11.6% | USA 7.6% | Russia 4.9%
World total (2010): 775,600,000 tOe

Aluminium — China 34.6% | Russia 10.2% | Canada 8.1% | Australia 5.2% | USA 4.6%
World total (2010): 37,300,000 tonnes

Steel — China 44.2% | Japan 7.7% | USA 5.7% | Russia 4.7% | S. Korea 4.1%
World total (2010): 1,417,000,000 tonnes

TV and Radios — China 47.9% | Turkey 8.7% | Malaysia 6.5% | Portugal 5.5% | USA 5.5%
World total (2010): 164,272,000 units

Sulphuric Acid — China 43.8% | Russia 11.4% | Japan 8.5% | India 7.9% | Brazil 7.9%
World total (2006): 760,900,000 tonnes

tOe = tonnes of oil equivalent

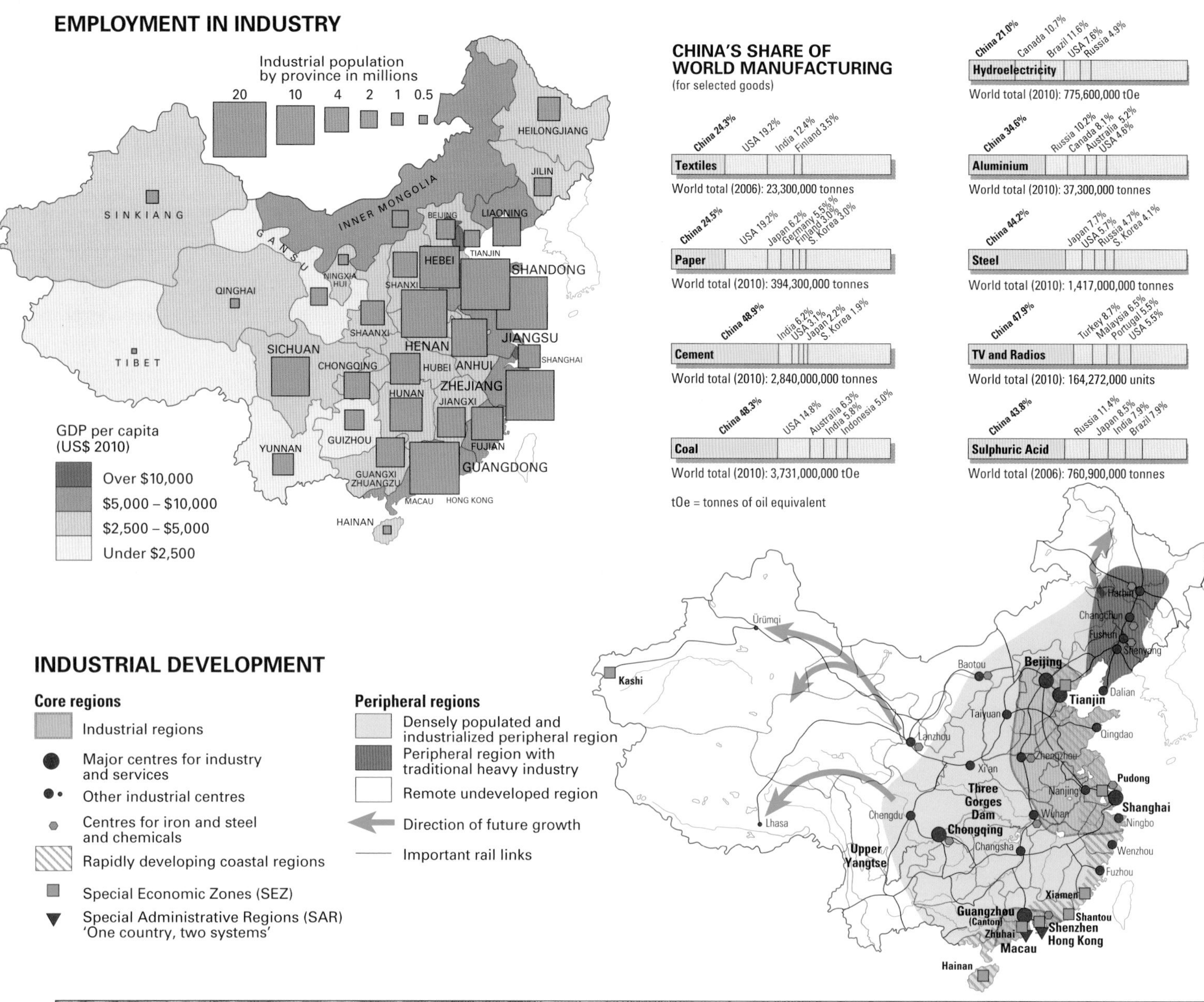

INDUSTRIAL DEVELOPMENT

Core regions

Industrial regions

⬤ Major centres for industry and services

•⬤• Other industrial centres

⬤ Centres for iron and steel and chemicals

▨ Rapidly developing coastal regions

▢ Special Economic Zones (SEZ)

▼ Special Administrative Regions (SAR) 'One country, two systems'

Peripheral regions

Densely populated and industrialized peripheral region

Peripheral region with traditional heavy industry

Remote undeveloped region

◀ Direction of future growth

— Important rail links

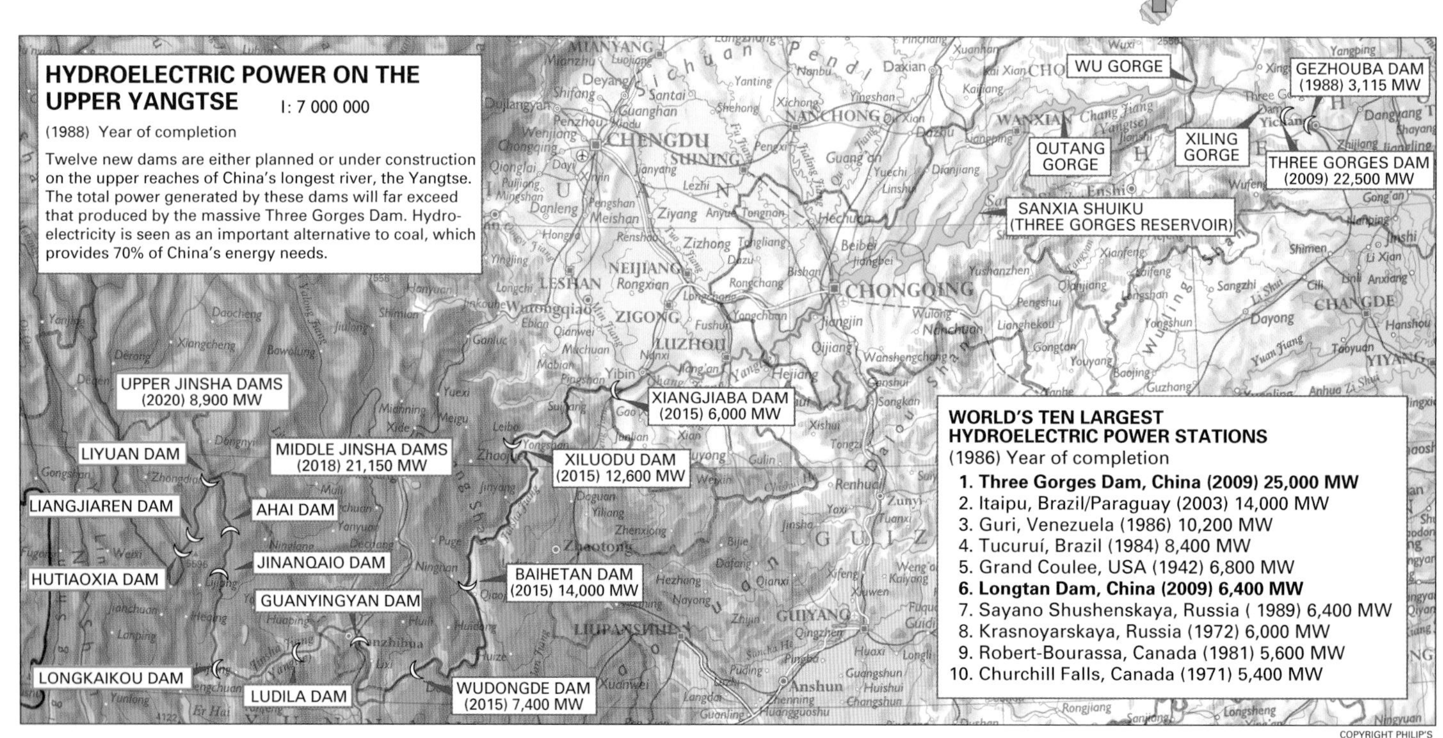

HYDROELECTRIC POWER ON THE UPPER YANGTSE
1: 7 000 000

(1988) Year of completion

Twelve new dams are either planned or under construction on the upper reaches of China's longest river, the Yangtse. The total power generated by these dams will far exceed that produced by the massive Three Gorges Dam. Hydro-electricity is seen as an important alternative to coal, which provides 70% of China's energy needs.

WU GORGE

GEZHOUBA DAM (1988) 3,115 MW

QUTANG GORGE

XILING GORGE

THREE GORGES DAM (2009) 22,500 MW

SANXIA SHUIKU (THREE GORGES RESERVOIR)

UPPER JINSHA DAMS (2020) 8,900 MW

LIYUAN DAM

MIDDLE JINSHA DAMS (2018) 21,150 MW

LIANGJIAREN DAM

AHAI DAM

XIANGJIABA DAM (2015) 6,000 MW

XILUODU DAM (2015) 12,600 MW

JINANQAIO DAM

HUTIAOXIA DAM

GUANYINGYAN DAM

BAIHETAN DAM (2015) 14,000 MW

LONGKAIKOU DAM

LUDILA DAM

WUDONGDE DAM (2015) 7,400 MW

WORLD'S TEN LARGEST HYDROELECTRIC POWER STATIONS
(1986) Year of completion

1. **Three Gorges Dam, China (2009) 25,000 MW**
2. Itaipu, Brazil/Paraguay (2003) 14,000 MW
3. Guri, Venezuela (1986) 10,200 MW
4. Tucuruí, Brazil (1984) 8,400 MW
5. Grand Coulee, USA (1942) 6,800 MW
6. **Longtan Dam, China (2009) 6,400 MW**
7. Sayano Shushenskaya, Russia (1989) 6,400 MW
8. Krasnoyarskaya, Russia (1972) 6,000 MW
9. Robert-Bourassa, Canada (1981) 5,600 MW
10. Churchill Falls, Canada (1971) 5,400 MW

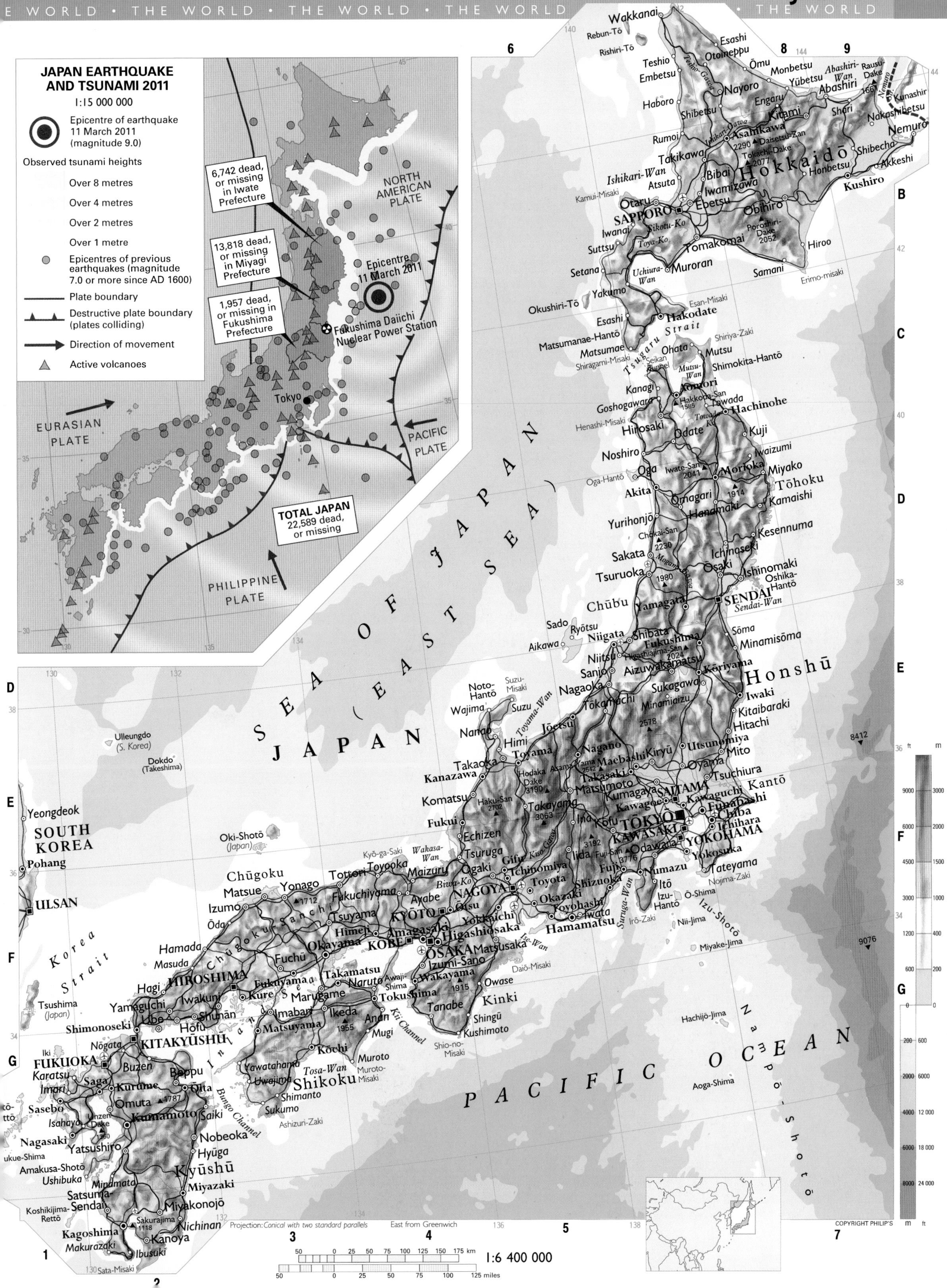

E WORLD • THE WORLD • THE WORLD • THE WORLD • THE WORLD

JAPAN EARTHQUAKE AND TSUNAMI 2011
1:15 000 000

Epicentre of earthquake
11 March 2011
(magnitude 9.0)

Observed tsunami heights

Over 8 metres
Over 4 metres
Over 2 metres
Over 1 metre

Epicentres of previous earthquakes (magnitude 7.0 or more since AD 1600)

Plate boundary

Destructive plate boundary (plates colliding)

Direction of movement

Active volcanoes

NORTH AMERICAN PLATE

6,742 dead, or missing in Iwate Prefecture

13,818 dead, or missing in Miyagi Prefecture

1,957 dead, or missing in Fukushima Prefecture

Epicentre 11 March 2011

Fukushima Daiichi Nuclear Power Station

Tokyo

EURASIAN PLATE

PACIFIC PLATE

PHILIPPINE PLATE

TOTAL JAPAN
22,589 dead, or missing

SEA OF JAPAN (EAST SEA)

JAPAN

SOUTH KOREA

Korea Strait

Tsushima (Japan)

Oki-Shotō (Japan)

Ulleungdo (S. Korea)

Dokdo (Takeshima)

Chūgoku

HIROSHIMA

KITAKYŪSHŪ

FUKUOKA

Kyūshū

Shikoku

Kinki

Chūbu

Honshū

Tōhoku

Hokkaidō

SAPPORO

SENDAI

TOKYO

YOKOHAMA

KAWASAKI

NAGOYA

KYŌTO

ŌSAKA

KŌBE

SAITAMA

Kantō

PACIFIC OCEAN

Projection: Conical with two standard parallels
East from Greenwich

1:6 400 000

COPYRIGHT PHILIP'S

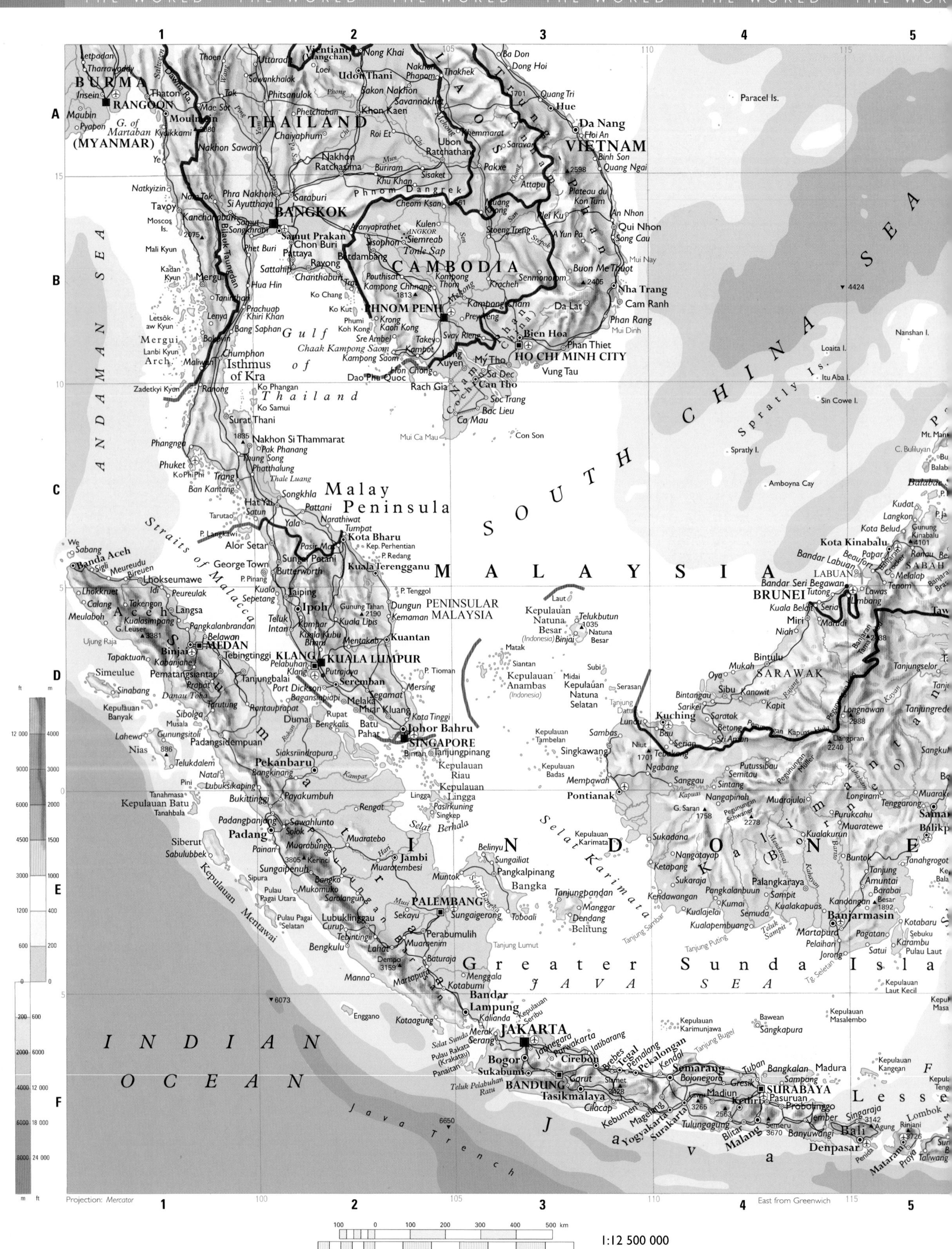
1
2
3
4
5
A
B
C
D
E
F
BURMA
(MYANMAR)
RANGOON
Insein
Maubin
Pyapon
Thaton
Moulmein
G. of
Martaban
Kyaikkami
Ye
Mae Sot
Thoen
Tak
Uttaradit
Sawankhalok
Phitsanulok
Phetchabun
THAILAND
Chaiyaphum
Nakhon Sawan
Loei
Vientiane
(Viangchan)
Nong Khai
Udon Thani
Nakhon Phanom
Thakhek
Sakon Nakhon
Savannakhet
Khon Kaen
Roi Et
Ubon Ratchathani
Khemmarat
Nakhon Ratchasima
Buriram
Sisaket
Khu Khan
Phnom Dangrek
LAOS
Saravan
Pakxe
Attapu
Ba Don
Dong Hoi
Quang Tri
Hue
Da Nang
Hoi An
VIETNAM
Binh Son
Quang Ngai
Paracel Is.
Natkyizin
Tavoy
Moscos Is.
Mali Kyun
Kadan Kyun
Mergui
Tanintharyi
Lenya
Letsôk-aw Kyun
Mergui Arch.
Lanbi Kyun
Bokpyin
Maliwan
Zadetkyi Kyun
Ranong
Nam Tok
Kanchanaburi
Bilauk Taungdan
Phra Nakhon Si Ayutthaya
Saraburi
BANGKOK
Samut Songkhram
Samut Prakan
Chon Buri
Pattaya
Phet Buri
Rayong
Sattahip
Chanthaburi
Hua Hin
Prachuap Khiri Khan
Bang Saphan
Chumphon
Isthmus of Kra
Ko Chang
Ko Kut
Aranyaprathet
Kulen
ANGKOR
Siemreab
Sisophon
Tonle Sap
Batdambang
CAMBODIA
Pouthisat
Kampong Chhnang
Kampong Thom
Kracheh
Stoeng Treng
Muang Khong
Senmonorom
PHNOM PENH
Kampong Cham
Prey Veng
Svay Rieng
Krong Kaoh Kong
Phumi Koh Kong
Sre Ambel
Takeo
Kampot
Chaak Kampong Saom
Kampong Saom
Gulf of Thailand
Hon Chong
Dao Phu Quoc
Long Xuyen
Rach Gia
My Tho
Sa Dec
Can Tho
Soc Trang
Bac Lieu
Ca Mau
Mui Ca Mau
Con Son
HO CHI MINH CITY
Bien Hoa
Vung Tau
Phan Thiet
Phan Rang
Mui Dinh
Da Lat
Cam Ranh
Nha Trang
Buon Me Thuot
Mui Nay
Song Cau
Qui Nhon
An Nhon
Pleiku
A Yun Pa
Plateau du Kon Tum
2598
2405
1813
4424
Nanshan I.
Loaita I.
Itu Aba I.
Sin Cowe I.
Spratly Is.
Spratly I.
Amboyna Cay
SOUTH CHINA SEA
Ko Phangan
Ko Samui
Surat Thani
Nakhon Si Thammarat
Pak Phanang
Thung Song
Phatthalung
Phangnga
Phuket
KoPhiPhi
Trang
Ban Kantang
Thale Luang
Songkhla
Hat Yai
Satun
Tarutao
Pattani
Yala
Narathiwat
Malay Peninsula
Tumpat
Kota Bharu
Kep. Perhentian
P. Redang
P. Langkawi
Alor Setar
Pasir Mas
Sungai Petani
George Town
P. Pinang
Butterworth
Kuala Terengganu
Taiping
Ipoh
Kuala
Sepetang
Teluk Intan
Kampar
Gunung Tahan
2190
Kuala Lipis
Dungun
Kemaman
PENINSULAR MALAYSIA
P. Tenggol
Kuantan
Kuala Kubu Bharu
Mentakab
KLANG
Pelabuhan Klang
KUALA LUMPUR
Putrajaya
Seremban
Port Dickson
P. Tioman
Mersing
Segamat
Melaka
Muar
Kluang
Kota Tinggi
Johor Bahru
SINGAPORE
Batu Pahat
Rupat
Dumai
Bengkalis
Bintan
Tanjungpinang
Kepulauan Riau
Kepulauan Lingga
Lingga
Pasirkuning
Singkep
Selat Berhala
MALAYSIA
ANDAMAN SEA
Straits of Malacca
We
Sabang
Banda Aceh
Sigli
Meureudu
Bireuen
Lhokseumawe
Idi
Lhokkruet
Calang
Meulaboh
Takengon
Peureulak
Langsa
Kualasimpang
Pangkalanbrandan
G. Leuser
3381
Ujung Raja
Belawan
MEDAN
Binjai
Tebingtinggi
Tapaktuan
Kabanjahe
Pematangsiantar
Simeulue
Sinabang
Danau Toba
Tanjungbalai
Prapat
Tarutung
Rantauprapat
Kepulauan Banyak
Sibolga
Musala
Lahewa
Gunungsitoli
Nias
886
Padangsidempuan
Telukdalem
Pekanbaru
Bangkinang
Siaksriindrapura
Kampar
Pini
Natal
Lubuksikaping
Tanahmasa
Kepulauan Batu
Tanahbala
Bukittinggi
Payakumbuh
Padangpanjang
Sawahlunto
Solok
Padang
Painan
Rengat
Siberut
Sabulubbek
Muarabungo
Kerinci
3805
Muaratebo
Jambi
Muaratembesi
Sungaipenuh
Bangko
Sipura
Pulau Pagai Utara
Pulau Pagai Selatan
Mukomuko
Sarolangun
Kepulauan Mentawai
Lubuklinggau
Curup
Tebingtinggi
Bengkulu
Lahat
Dempo
3159
Muaraenim
Perabumulih
PALEMBANG
Sekayu
Sungaigerong
Muntok
Belinyu
Sungailiat
Pangkalpinang
Bangka
Selat Bangka
Toboali
Baturaja
Martapura
Manna
Menggala
Kotabumi
Bandar Lampung
Kalianda
Kotaagung
Enggano
6073
Tanjung Lumut
Laut
Kepulauan Natuna Besar
(Indonesia)
Telukbutun
1035
Natuna Besar
Binjai
Matak
Siantan
Kepulauan Anambas
(Indonesia)
Subi
Midai
Kepulauan Natuna Selatan
Serasan
Tanjung Datu
Kepulauan Tambelan
Kepulauan Badas
Sambas
Singkawang
Mempawah
Pontianak
Selat Karimata
Kepulauan Karimata
Tanjungpandan
Manggar
Dendang
Belitung
Tanjung Sambar
Greater Sunda Islands
JAVA SEA
Kota Kinabalu
Kudat
Langkon
Kota Belud
Gunung Kinabalu
4101
Ranau
Bandar Labuan
LABUAN
Beaufort
SABAH
Melalap
Tenom
Papar
Bandar Seri Begawan
BRUNEI
Tutong
Lawas
Limbang
Kuala Belait
Seria
Miri
Marudi
Niah
Bintulu
Mukah
SARAWAK
Oya
Sibu
Kanowit
Kapit
Bintangor
Sarikei
Saratok
Betong
Kuching
Lundu
Bau
Serian
Sri Aman
Niut
1701
Tebedu
Ngabang
Putussibau
Semitau
Sanggau
Sintang
Nangapinoh
Kapuas
G. Saran
1758
Pegunungan Schwaner
2278
Muarajuloi
Puruk Cahu
Muaratewe
Kualakurun
Sukadana
Nangatayap
Ketapang
Sukaraja
Kendawangan
Kualajelai
Kualapembuang
Pangkalanbuun
Kumai
Sampit
Semuda
Teluk Sampit
Tanjung Puting
Palangkaraya
Kualakapuas
Kandangan
Besar
1892
Banjarmasin
Martapura
Pelaihari
Jorong
Tg. Selatan
Pagatan
Satui
Kotabaru
Sebuku
Karambu
Pulau Laut
Kepulauan Laut Kecil
Kalimantan (Borneo)
INDONESIA
Longnawan
Tanjungselor
Tanjungredeb
Dangpran
2240
2988
Longiram
Tenggarong
Tanah Grogot
Tanjung
Amuntai
Barabai
Buntok
Pegunungan Müller
Sangkulirang
Balikpapan
Samarinda
Kepulauan Seribu
JAKARTA
Merak
Serang
Selat Sunda
Pulau Rakata (Krakatau)
Panaitan
Bogor
Sukabumi
Teluk Pelabuhan Ratu
BANDUNG
Garut
Tasikmalaya
Cilacap
Jatinegara
Purwakarta
Jatibarang
Cirebon
Brebes
Tegal
Pemalang
Pekalongan
Kendal
Semarang
Slamet
3428
Kebumen
Magelang
Yogyakarta
Surakarta
Bojonegoro
Tuban
Gresik
SURABAYA
Bangkalan
Madura
Sampang
Pasuruan
Probolinggo
Madiun
Kediri
Lawu
3265
2563
Tulungagung
Blitar
Malang
Semeru
3670
Jember
Banyuwangi
Singaraja
3142
Agung
Bali
Denpasar
Penida
Lombok
Rinjani
3726
Mataram
Praya
Taliwang
Kepulauan Karimunjawa
Bawean
Sangkapura
Kepulauan Masalembo
Kepulauan Kangean
Tanjung Bugel
Lesser
Java
INDIAN OCEAN
Java Trench
6650
Projection: Mercator
East from Greenwich
100
105
110
115
15
10
5
0
ft
m
12 000
4000
9000
3000
6000
2000
4500
1500
3000
1000
1200
400
600
200
0
0
200
600
2000
6000
4000
12 000
6000
18 000
8000
24 000
m
ft
100
0
100
200
300
400
500 km
100
0
50
100
150
200
250
300
350 miles
1:12 500 000

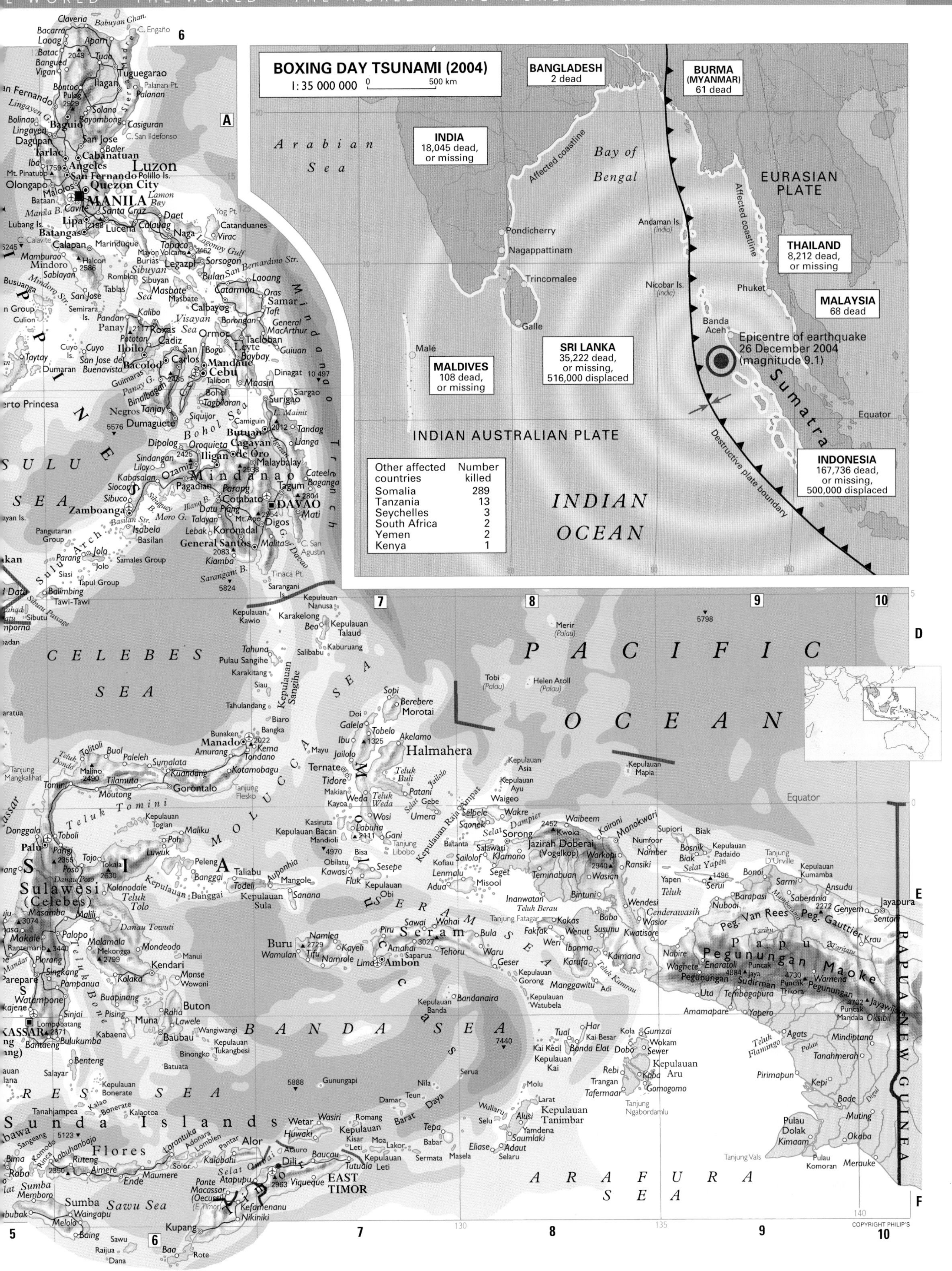
BOXING DAY TSUNAMI (2004)
1:35 000 000
0
500 km
BANGLADESH
2 dead
BURMA
(MYANMAR)
61 dead
INDIA
18,045 dead,
or missing
Arabian Sea
Affected coastline
Bay of Bengal
EURASIAN PLATE
Affected coastline
Pondicherry
Nagappattinam
Andaman Is.
(India)
THAILAND
8,212 dead,
or missing
Trincomalee
Nicobar Is.
(India)
Phuket
MALAYSIA
68 dead
Galle
Banda Aceh
Epicentre of earthquake
26 December 2004
(magnitude 9.1)
Malé
MALDIVES
108 dead,
or missing
SRI LANKA
35,222 dead,
or missing,
516,000 displaced
Sumatra
Equator
INDIAN AUSTRALIAN PLATE
Destructive plate boundary
INDONESIA
167,736 dead,
or missing,
500,000 displaced
Other affected countries | Number killed
Somalia | 289
Tanzania | 13
Seychelles | 3
South Africa | 2
Yemen | 2
Kenya | 1
INDIAN OCEAN
Luzon
MANILA
Quezon City
Mindoro
Samar
Panay
Negros
Cebu
Bohol
Mindanao
Zamboanga
DAVAO
General Santos
Mindanao Trench
SULU SEA
Sulu Arch.
CELEBES SEA
MOLUCCA SEA
PACIFIC OCEAN
Halmahera
Manado
Gorontalo
Teluk Tomini
Sulawesi
(Celebes)
Kendari
Buton
Seram
Ambon
Buru
BANDA SEA
Jazirah Doberai
(Vogelkop)
Teluk Cenderawasih
Biak
Pegunungan Maoke
Jayapura
PAPUA NEW GUINEA
Kepulauan Aru
Kepulauan Tanimbar
ARAFURA SEA
FLORES SEA
Sunda Islands
Flores
Sumba
Sawu Sea
Timor
EAST TIMOR
Dili
Equator
COPYRIGHT PHILIP'S

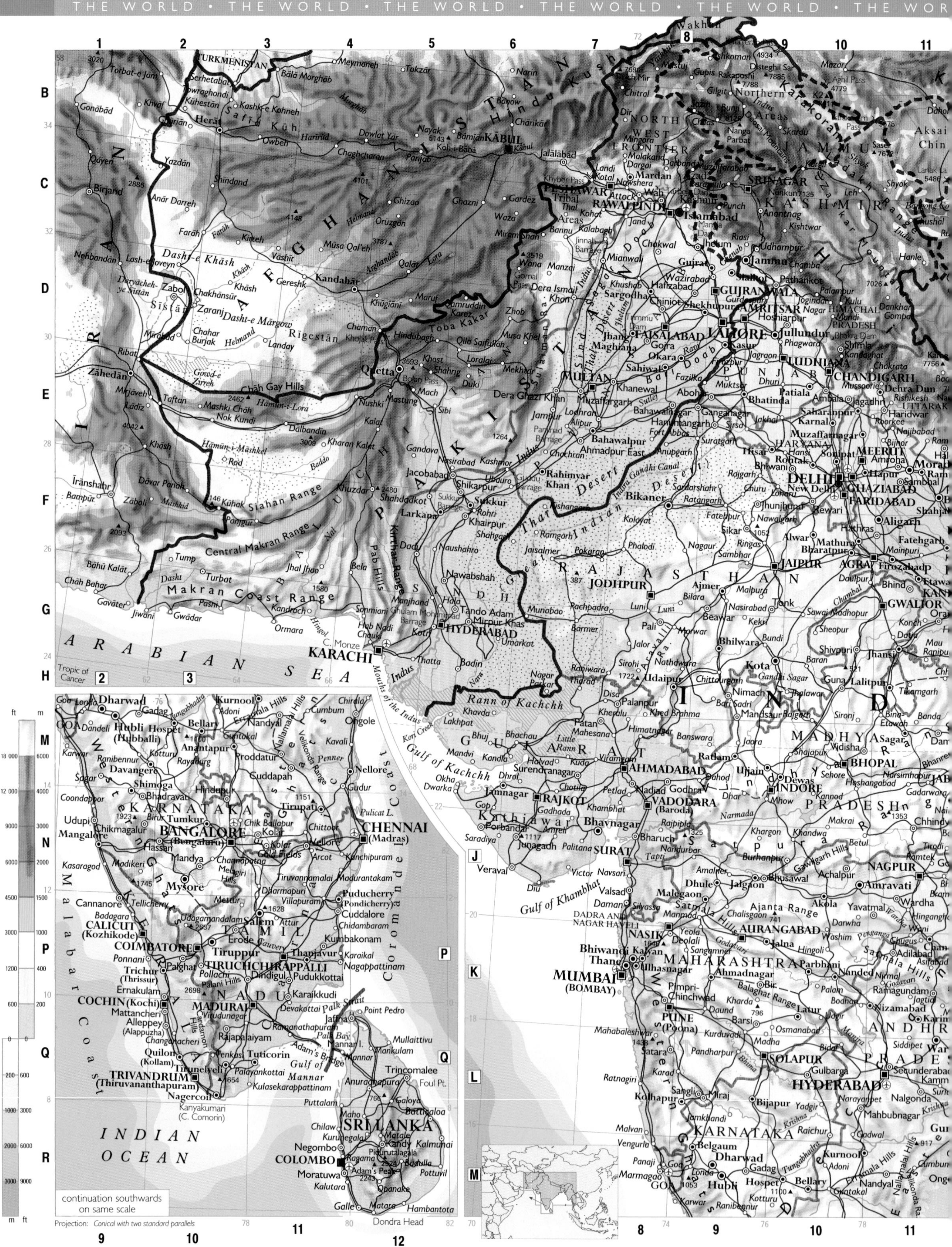

continuation southwards
on same scale

Projection: Conical with two standard parallels

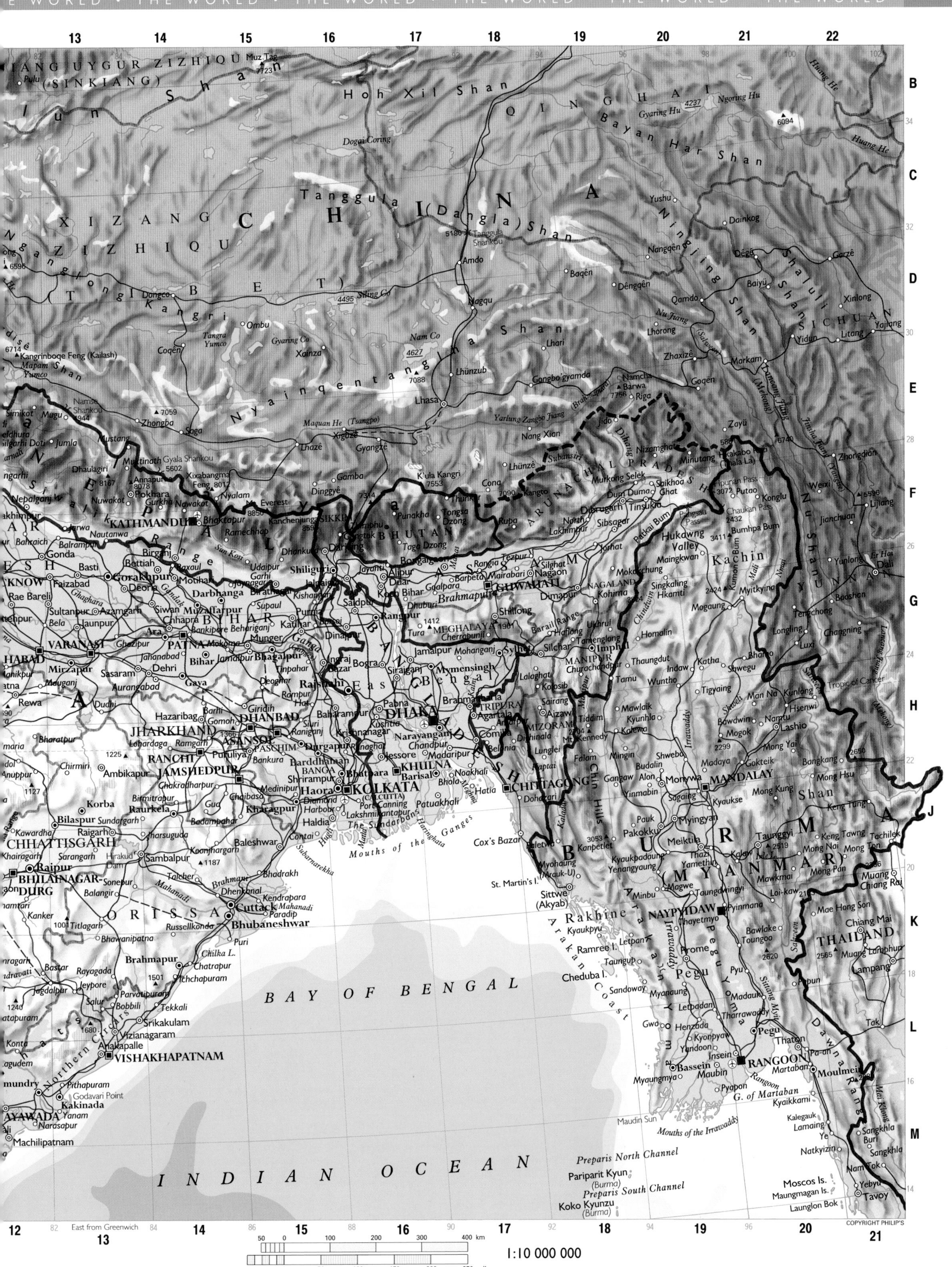
CHINA
XIZANG ZIZHIQU (TIBET)
XINJIANG UYGUR ZIZHIQU (SINKIANG)
QINGHAI
SICHUAN
YUNNAN
Hoh Xil Shan
Bayan Har Shan
Tanggula (Dangla) Shan
Nyainqentanglha Shan
Ningjing Shan
Shaluli Shan
Nu Shan
Gangdisê Shan
Kangri
Muz Tag 7723
Dogai Coring
Gyaring Hu
Ngoring Hu
Huang He
Yushu
Dainkog
Nangqên
Dêgê
Garzê
Baqên
Dêngqên
Qamdo
Baiyü
Xinlong
Yajiang
Yidun
Litang
Lhorong
Zhaxizê
Markam
Amdo
Nagqu
Siling Co
Nam Co
Lhari
Lhünzub
Lhasa
Gongbo'gyamda
Namcha Barwa 7756
Riga
Coqên
Dongco
Ombu
Tangra Yumco
Gyaring Co
Xainza
Kangrinboqe Feng (Kailash)
Mapam Yumco
Zhongba
Saga
Maquan He (Tsangpo)
Xigazê
Lhazê
Gyangzê
Yarlung Zangbo Jiang
Nang Xian
Lhünzê
Gamba
Dinggyê
K'ula Kangri 7553
Cona
Zayü
Zhongdian
Weixi
Lijiang
Jianchuan
Dali
Yunlong
Baoshan
Tengchong
Longling
Luxi
Changning
Tropic of Cancer
Mekong
Salween
Lancang Jiang
Jinsha Jiang
NEPAL
KATHMANDU
Bhaktapur
Pokhara
Dhaulagiri 8167
Annapurna 8078
Mustang
Jumla
Nepalganj
Everest 8850
Kanchenjunga 8598
Xixabangma Feng 8012
Nyalam
Siwalik Range
BHUTAN
Thimphu
Punakha
Tongsa Dzong
Taga Dzong
SIKKIM
Gangtok
Darjeeling
ARUNACHAL PRADESH
ASSAM
NAGALAND
MANIPUR
MIZORAM
TRIPURA
MEGHALAYA
Dibrugarh
Tinsukia
Sibsagar
North Lakhimpur
Jorhat
Tezpur
GUWAHATI
Shillong
Cherrapunji
Dimapur
Kohima
Imphal
Silchar
Aizawl
Agartala
Brahmaputra
BANGLADESH
DHAKA
CHITTAGONG
KHULNA
Rangpur
Dinajpur
Bogra
Rajshahi
Mymensingh
Sylhet
Comilla
Narayanganj
Jessore
Barisal
Cox's Bazar
Sundarbans
Mouths of the Ganges
INDIA
BIHAR
PATNA
Gaya
Bhagalpur
Muzaffarpur
Darbhanga
JHARKHAND
RANCHI
JAMSHEDPUR
DHANBAD
ASANSOL
PASCHIMBANGA
KOLKATA (CALCUTTA)
Haora
Haldia
Kharagpur
ORISSA
Cuttack
Bhubaneshwar
Puri
Baleshwar
Sambalpur
Raurkela
CHHATTISGARH
Raipur
BHILAINAGAR-DURG
Bilaspur
Korba
Brahmapur
Srikakulam
Vizianagaram
VISHAKHAPATNAM
Kakinada
VIJAYAWADA
Machilipatnam
Godavari Point
Northern Circars
VARANASI
Gorakhpur
Lucknow
Rae Bareli
Faizabad
Gonda
Jaunpur
Mirzapur
BURMA (MYANMAR)
MANDALAY
NAYPYIDAW
RANGOON
Kachin
Shan
Rakhine
Arakan Coast
Arakan Yoma
Pegu Yoma
Chin Hills
Hukawng Valley
Myitkyina
Bhamo
Lashio
Mogok
Monywa
Sagaing
Meiktila
Taunggyi
Magwe
Pakokku
Sittwe (Akyab)
Ramree I.
Cheduba I.
Sandoway
Prome
Pegu
Bassein
Moulmein
Martaban
Thaton
G. of Martaban
Mouths of the Irrawaddy
Irrawaddy
Chindwin
Sittang
Dawna Range
Tavoy
Moscos Is.
Preparis North Channel
Preparis South Channel
Pariparit Kyun (Burma)
Koko Kyunzu (Burma)
St. Martin's I.
THAILAND
Chiang Mai
Chiang Rai
Lampang
BAY OF BENGAL
INDIAN OCEAN
East from Greenwich
COPYRIGHT PHILIP'S

1:10 000 000

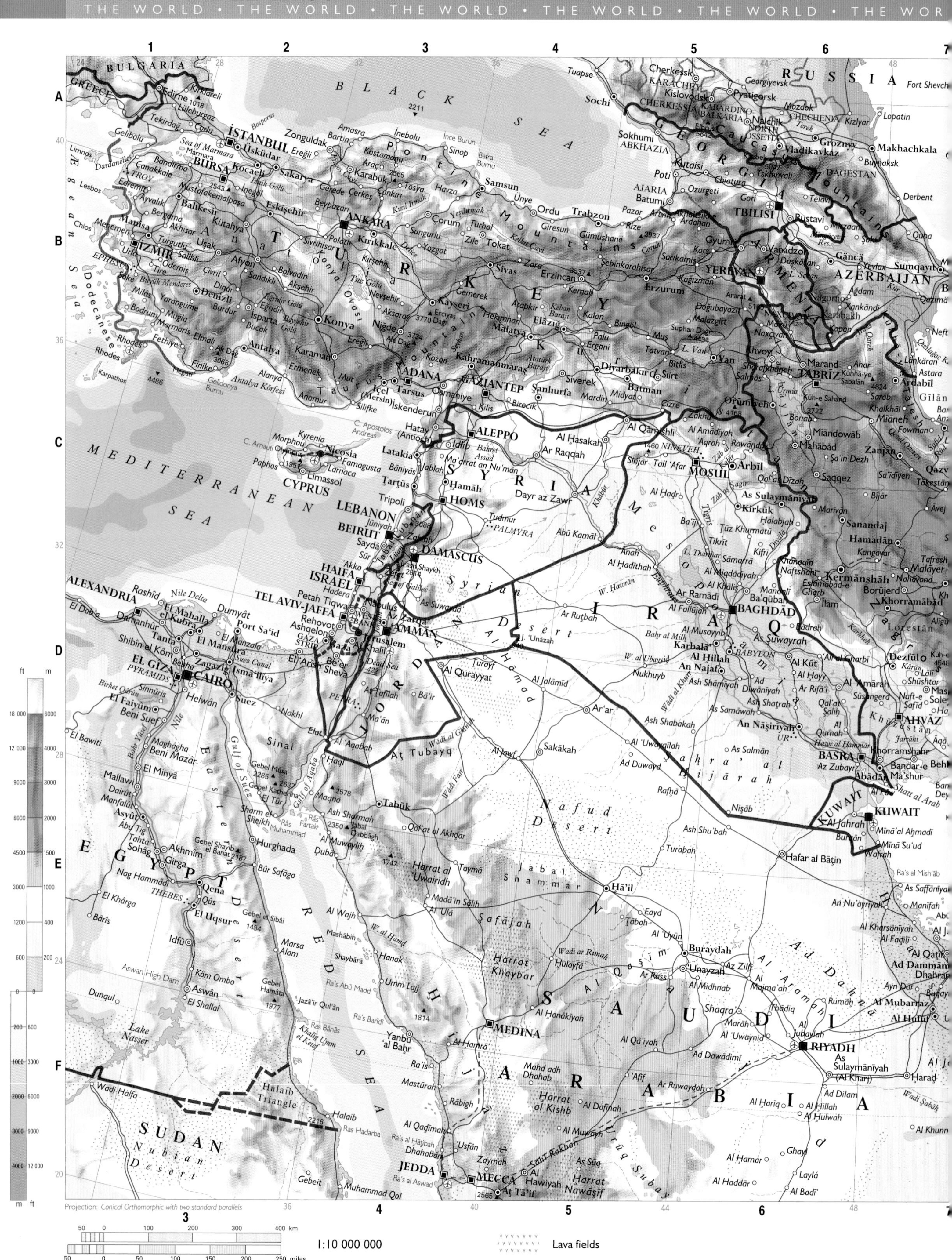

Projection: Conical Orthomorphic with two standard parallels

1:10 000 000

∨∨∨∨∨
∨∨∨∨∨∨ Lava fields
∨∨∨∨∨

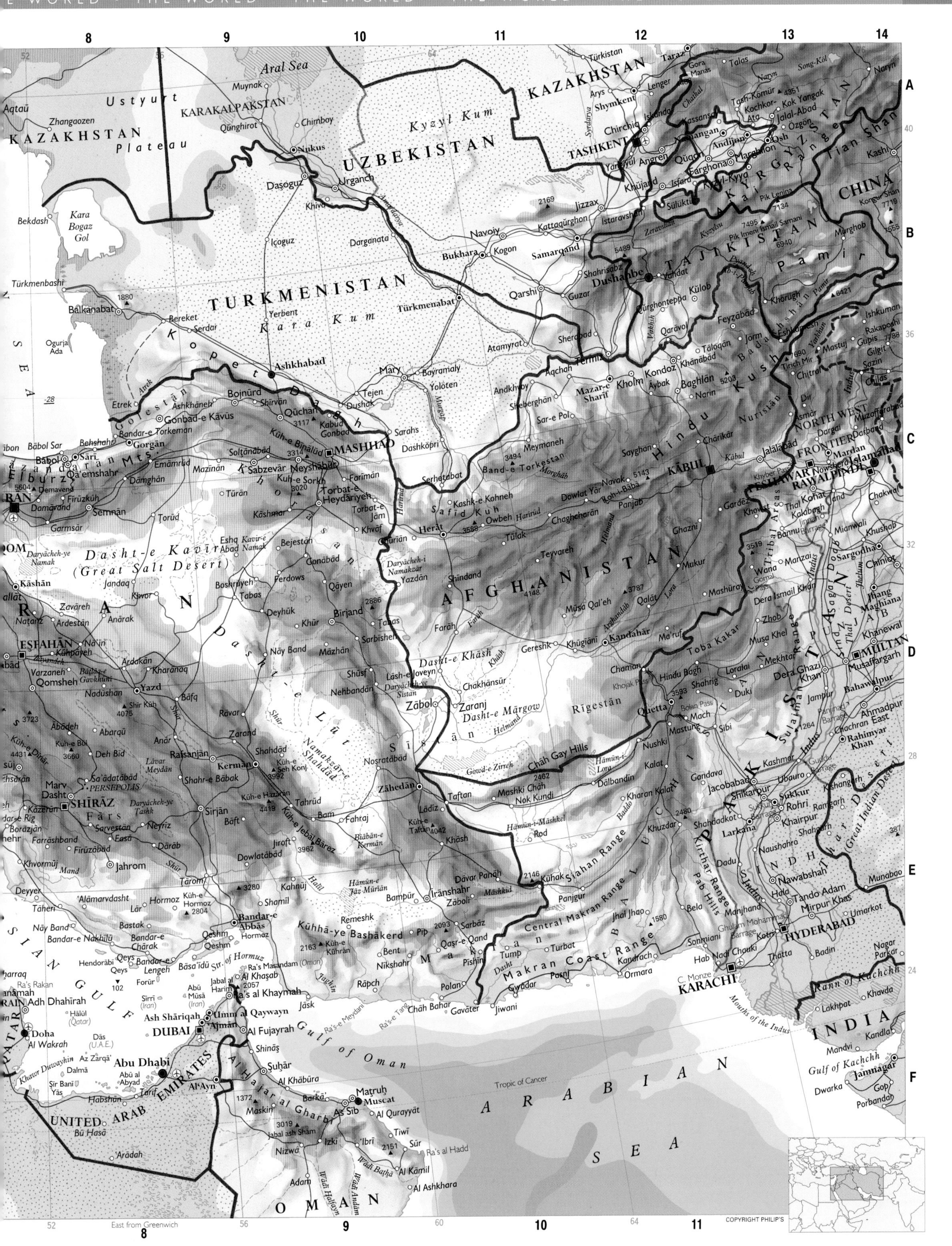
KAZAKHSTAN
UZBEKISTAN
TURKMENISTAN
KYRGYZSTAN
TAJIKISTAN
CHINA
AFGHANISTAN
PAKISTAN
IRAN
INDIA
OMAN
UNITED ARAB EMIRATES
Aral Sea
Kara Bogaz Gol
Ustyurt Plateau
KARAKALPAKSTAN
Kyzyl Kum
Kara Kum
Kopet Dagh
Elburz Mts
Dasht-e Kavir (Great Salt Desert)
Dasht-e Lūt
Dasht-e Khāsh
Dasht-e Mārgow
Rīgestān
Sīstān
Hindu Kush
Pamir
Tian Shan
Kyrgyz Range
Chah Gay Hills
Central Makran Range
Makran Coast Range
Kirthar Range
Sulaiman Range
Thar Desert
Great Indian Desert
Rann of Kachchh
Gulf of Kachchh
ARABIAN SEA
Gulf of Oman
PERSIAN GULF
Str. of Hormuz
Tropic of Cancer
TASHKENT
Dushanbe
KĀBUL
Islamabad
RAWALPINDI
PESHAWAR
MASHHAD
Herāt
Kandahār
Quetta
KARACHI
HYDERABAD
MULTAN
ESFAHĀN
SHĪRĀZ
Yazd
Kermān
Zāhedān
Bandar-e Abbās
DUBAI
Abu Dhabi
Muscat
Doha
Ashkhabad
Samarqand
Bukhara
Türkmenabat
Mary
Nukus
Urganch
Dashoguz
Türkmenbashi
Balkanabat
Mazar-e Sharif
Kunduz
Jalalabad
Osh
Andijon
Namangan
Farghona
Khujand
Shymkent
Taraz
Kashi
Zābol
Zaranj
Gwadar
Jiwani
Chāh Bahār
NORTH WEST FRONTIER
SIND
PUNJAB
BALUCHISTAN
East from Greenwich
COPYRIGHT PHILIP'S

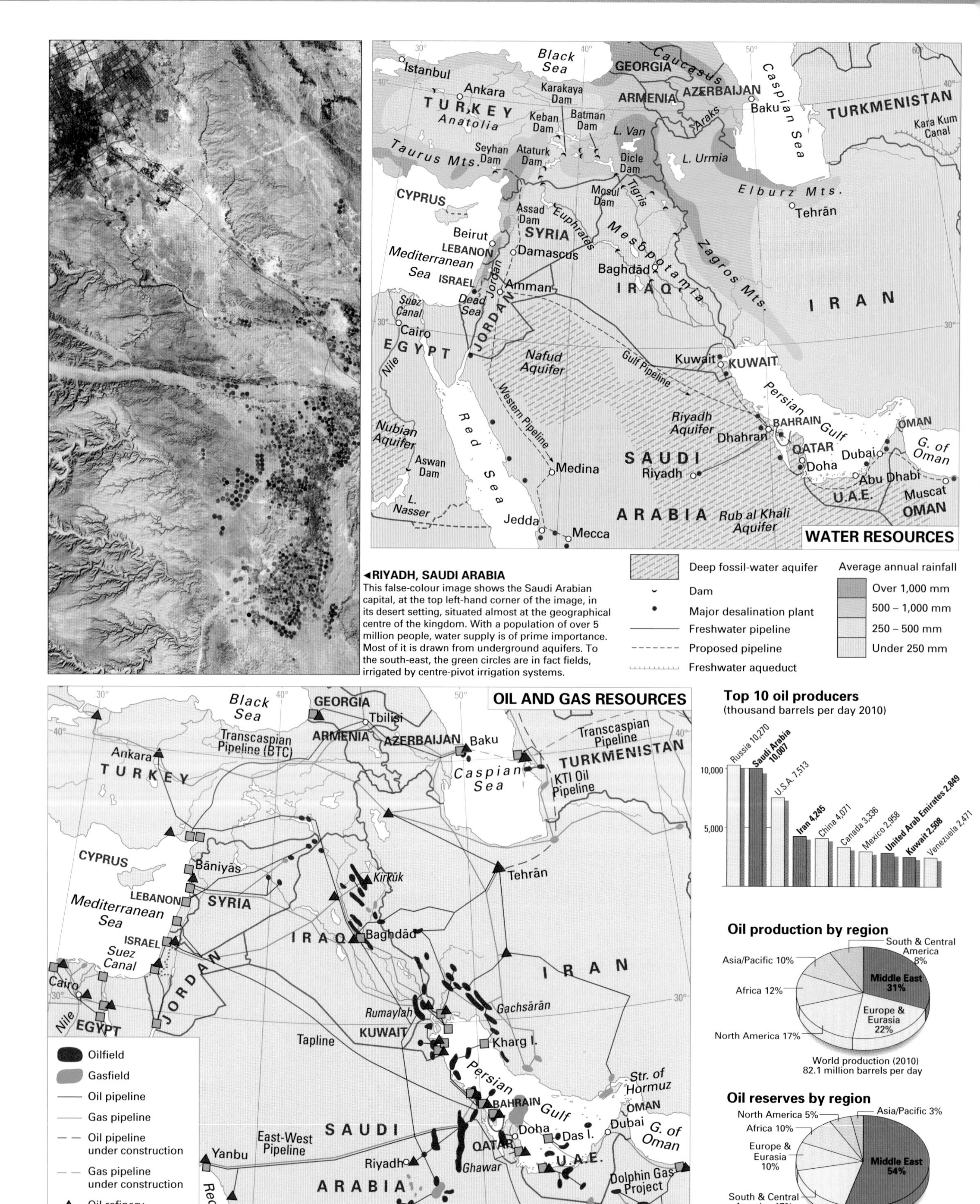

WATER RESOURCES

◄ RIYADH, SAUDI ARABIA
This false-colour image shows the Saudi Arabian capital, at the top left-hand corner of the image, in its desert setting, situated almost at the geographical centre of the kingdom. With a population of over 5 million people, water supply is of prime importance. Most of it is drawn from underground aquifers. To the south-east, the green circles are in fact fields, irrigated by centre-pivot irrigation systems.

Legend (Water Resources):
- Deep fossil-water aquifer
- Dam
- Major desalination plant
- Freshwater pipeline
- Proposed pipeline
- Freshwater aqueduct

Average annual rainfall
- Over 1,000 mm
- 500 – 1,000 mm
- 250 – 500 mm
- Under 250 mm

OIL AND GAS RESOURCES

Legend (Oil and Gas Resources):
- Oilfield
- Gasfield
- Oil pipeline
- Gas pipeline
- Oil pipeline under construction
- Gas pipeline under construction
- Oil refinery
- Tanker terminal

Top 10 oil producers
(thousand barrels per day 2010)

Russia 10,270
Saudi Arabia 10,007
U.S.A. 7,513
Iran 4,245
China 4,071
Canada 3,336
Mexico 2,958
United Arab Emirates 2,849
Kuwait 2,508
Venezuela 2,471

Oil production by region
- Asia/Pacific 10%
- Africa 12%
- North America 17%
- Europe & Eurasia 22%
- Middle East 31%
- South & Central America 8%

World production (2010)
82.1 million barrels per day

Oil reserves by region
- North America 5%
- Africa 10%
- Europe & Eurasia 10%
- South & Central America 17%
- Asia/Pacific 3%
- Middle East 54%

World proved reserves (2010)
1,383.2 billion barrels

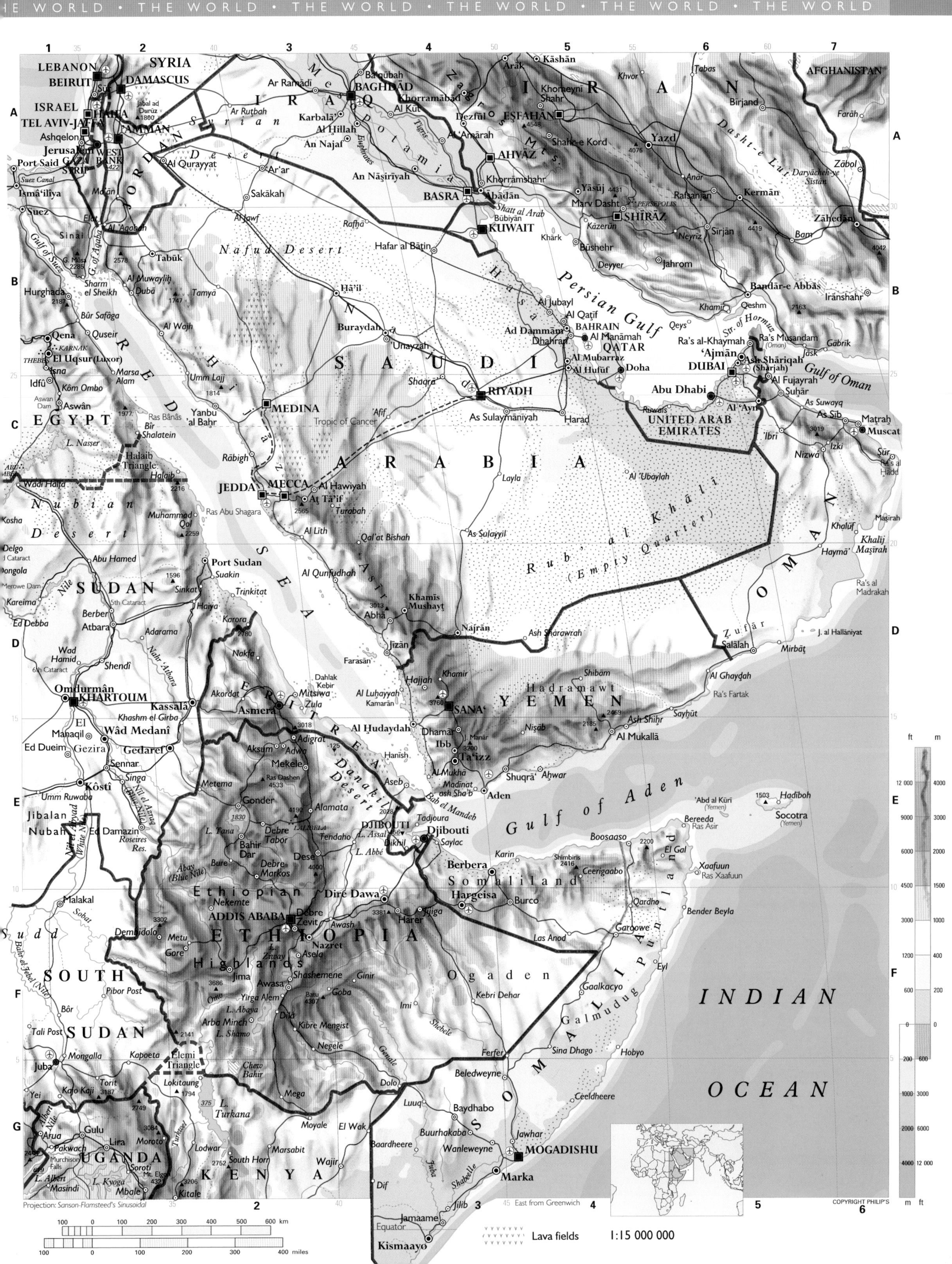

Projection: Sanson-Flamsteed's Sinusoidal

| 100 | 0 | 100 | 200 | 300 | 400 | 500 | 600 km |
| 100 | 0 | 100 | 200 | 300 | 400 miles |

∨∨∨∨ Lava fields   1:15 000 000

COPYRIGHT PHILIP'S

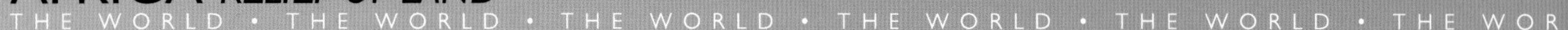

THE WORLD • THE WORLD • THE WORLD • THE WORLD • THE WORLD • THE WORL

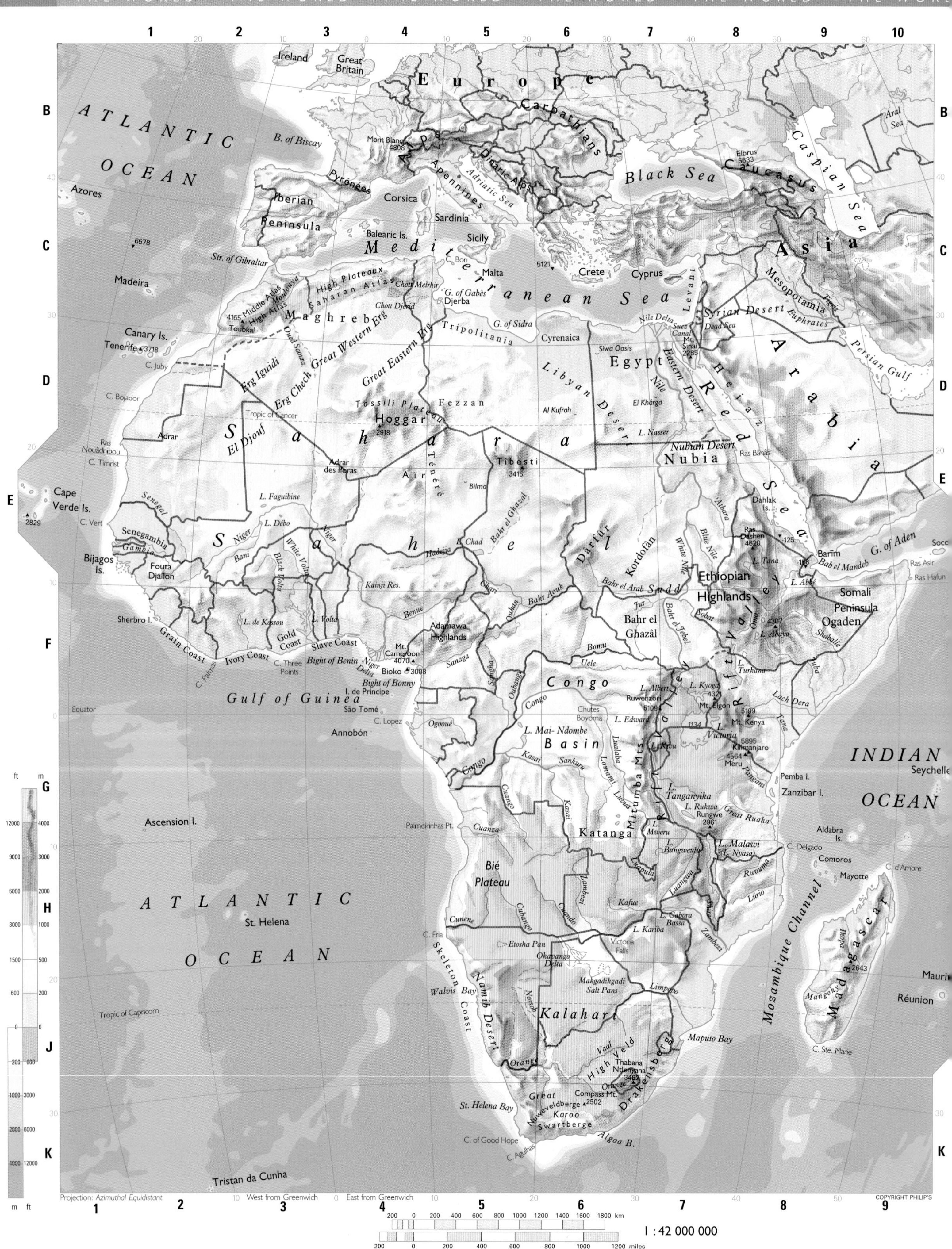

ATLANTIC OCEAN
Azores
Madeira
Canary Is.
Tenerife 3718
C. Juby
C. Bojador
Tropic of Cancer
Ras Nouâdhibou
C. Timris
Cape Verde Is.
2829
C. Vert
Senegambia
Gambia
Bijagos Is.
Fouta Djallon
Sherbro I.
Grain Coast
Ivory Coast
Gold Coast
Slave Coast
C. Palmas
C. Three Points
Bight of Benin
Niger Delta
Bight of Bonny
Mt. Cameroon 4070
Bioko 3008
I. de Principe
São Tomé
Gulf of Guinea
Equator
C. Lopez
Annobón
Ireland
Great Britain
Europe
B. of Biscay
Mont Blanc 4808
Alps
Pyrénées
Iberian Peninsula
Corsica
Sardinia
Balearic Is.
Sicily
Str. of Gibraltar
Apennines
Adriatic Sea
Dinaric Alps
Carpathians
Black Sea
Caucasus
Elbrus 5633
Caspian Sea
Aral Sea
Mediterranean Sea
C. Bon
Malta
5121
Crete
Cyprus
Levant
Asia
Mesopotamia
Tigris
Euphrates
Syrian Desert
Dead Sea
Persian Gulf
Arabia
Hejaz
Red Sea
Nile Delta
Suez Canal
Mt. Sinai 2285
Eastern Desert
Egypt
Siwa Oasis
Cyrenaica
Libyan Desert
Al Kufrah
El Khârga
Nile
L. Nasser
Nubian Desert
Nubia
Ras Banâs
Middle Atlas
High Atlas
4165
Toubkal
Moulouya
High Plateaux
Saharan Atlas
Chott Melrhir
Chott Djerid
G. of Gabès
Djerba
Maghreb
Great Western Erg
Great Eastern Erg
Oued Saoura
Erg Iguidi
Erg Chech
Tripolitania
G. of Sidra
Fezzan
Tassili Plateau
Hoggar
2918
Sahara
Adrar
El Djouf
Adrar des Iforas
Aïr
Ténéré
Tibesti
3415
Bilma
L. Faguibine
L. Débo
Senegal
Niger
Bani
White Volta
Black Volta
Sahel
L. Chad
Hadejia
Bahr el Ghazal
Dârfûr
Kordofân
Kainji Res.
Benue
L. de Kossou
L. Volta
Adamawa Highlands
Chari
Ouham
Bahr Aouk
Bahr el Arab
Sadd
Jur
Bahr el Ghazâl
Bahr el Jebel
Sobat
White Nile
Blue Nile
Atbara
Dahlak Is.
Ras Dashen 4620
L. Tana
-125
-155
Barīm
Bab el Mandeb
G. of Aden
Ras Asir
Ras Hafun
L. Abbé
Ethiopian Highlands
Somali Peninsula
Ogaden
Shabelle
Omo
4307
L. Abaya
Rift Valley
L. Turkana
Juba
Lach Dera
Tana
Sanaga
Sangha
Oubangui
Uele
Bomu
Congo
Ogooué
Chutes Boyoma
L. Albert
Ruwenzori 5109
L. Kyoga 4321
Mt. Elgon
5199
Mt. Kenya
L. Edward
1134
L. Victoria
L. Kivu
5895
Kilimanjaro
4564
Meru
Pangani
L. Mai-Ndombe
Basin
Kasai
Sankuru
Lomami
Lualaba
Lueua
Mitumba Mts.
L. Tanganyika
L. Rukwa
Rungwe 2961
Great Ruaha
Pemba I.
Zanzibar I.
INDIAN OCEAN
Seychelles
Aldabra Is.
C. Delgado
Comoros
Mayotte
C. d'Ambre
Cuango
Palmeirinhas Pt.
Cuanza
Katanga
L. Mweru
L. Bangweulu
Luapula
L. Malawi (L. Nyasa)
Ruvuma
Lúrio
Luangwa
Shire
Bié Plateau
Zambezi
Cubango
Cuando
Kafue
L. Cabora Bassa
L. Kariba
Victoria Falls
Mozambique Channel
Madagascar
Ilopa
2643
Mangoky
Mauritius
Réunion
C. Ste. Marie
Cunene
C. Fria
Skeleton Coast
Etosha Pan
Okavango Delta
Makgadikgadi Salt Pans
Limpopo
Walvis Bay
Namib Desert
Nossob
Kalahari
Maputo Bay
Vaal
High Veld
Thabana Ntlenyana 3482
Drakensberg
Orange
Great Nuweveldberge
Compass Mt. 2502
Karoo
Swartberge
St. Helena Bay
C. of Good Hope
C. Agulhas
Algoa B.
Ascension I.
ATLANTIC OCEAN
St. Helena
Tropic of Capricorn
Tristan da Cunha
Projection: Azimuthal Equidistant
West from Greenwich
East from Greenwich
COPYRIGHT PHILIP'S
1 : 42 000 000
200 0 200 400 600 800 1000 1200 1400 1600 1800 km
200 0 200 400 600 800 1000 1200 miles
ft m
12000 4000
9000 3000
6000 2000
3000 1000
1500 500
600 200
0 0
200 600
1000 3000
2000 6000
4000 12000
m ft

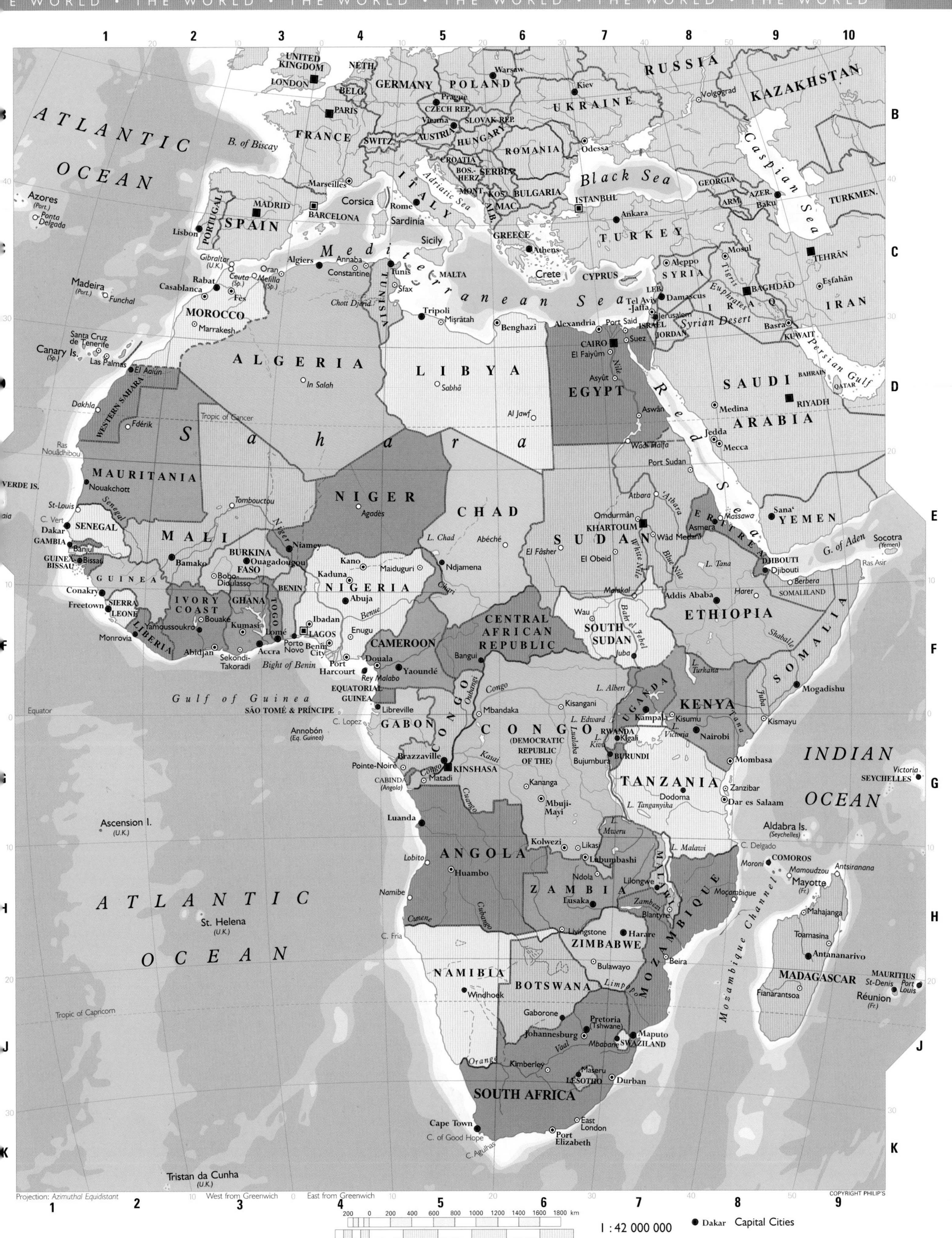

Projection: *Azimuthal Equidistant*

West from Greenwich   East from Greenwich

COPYRIGHT PHILIP'S

1 : 42 000 000   ● Dakar   Capital Cities

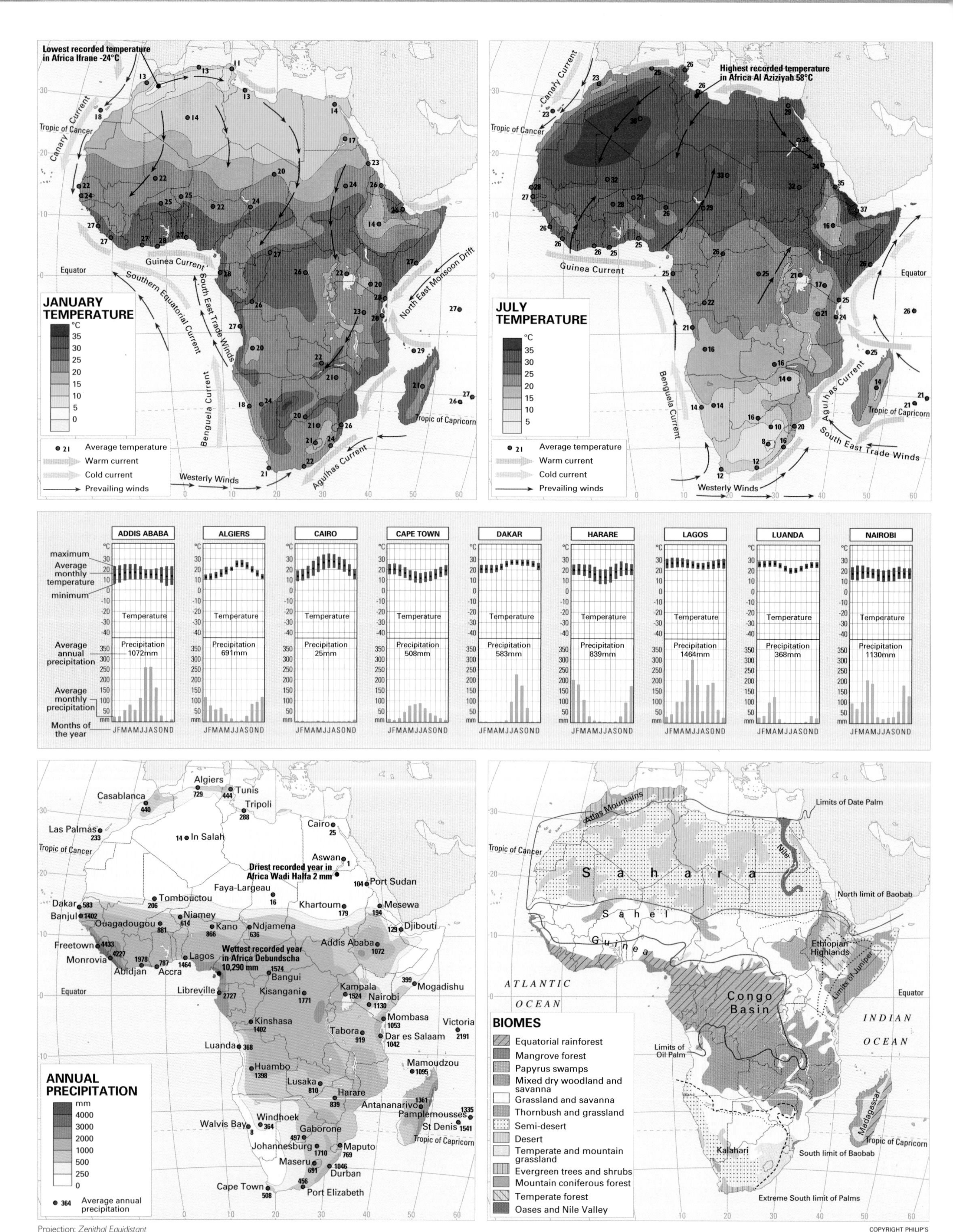

JANUARY TEMPERATURE

Lowest recorded temperature in Africa Ifrane -24°C

°C
35
30
25
20
15
10
5
0

• 21 Average temperature
Warm current
Cold current
Prevailing winds

JULY TEMPERATURE

Highest recorded temperature in Africa Al Aziziyah 58°C

°C
35
30
25
20
15
5

• 21 Average temperature
Warm current
Cold current
Prevailing winds

Climate graphs: ADDIS ABABA (Precipitation 1072mm), ALGIERS (691mm), CAIRO (25mm), CAPE TOWN (508mm), DAKAR (583mm), HARARE (839mm), LAGOS (1464mm), LUANDA (368mm), NAIROBI (1130mm)

ANNUAL PRECIPITATION

Driest recorded year in Africa Wadi Halfa 2 mm
Wettest recorded year in Africa Debundscha 10,290 mm

mm
4000
3000
2000
1000
500
250
0

• 364 Average annual precipitation

Algiers 729, Tunis 444, Tripoli 288, Casablanca 440, Las Palmas 233, In Salah 14, Cairo 25, Aswan 1, Port Sudan 104, Faya-Largeau 16, Tombouctou 206, Khartoum 179, Mesewa 194, Dakar 583, Niamey 614, Kano 866, Ndjamena 636, Djibouti 125, Banjul 1402, Ouagadougou 881, Freetown 4433, Monrovia 4227, Abidjan 1978, Accra 787, Lagos 1464, Bangui 1574, Addis Ababa 1072, Libreville 2727, Kisangani 1771, Kampala 1524, Nairobi 1130, Mogadishu 399, Kinshasa 1402, Mombasa 1053, Tabora 919, Dar es Salaam 1042, Victoria 2191, Luanda 368, Huambo 1398, Mamoudzou 1095, Lusaka 810, Harare 839, Antananarivo 1361, Pamplemousses 1305, Windhoek 364, Gaborone 497, St Denis 1541, Walvis Bay 8, Johannesburg 709, Maputo 769, Maseru 691, Durban 1046, Cape Town 508, Port Elizabeth 456

BIOMES

- Equatorial rainforest
- Mangrove forest
- Papyrus swamps
- Mixed dry woodland and savanna
- Grassland and savanna
- Thornbush and grassland
- Semi-desert
- Desert
- Temperate and mountain grassland
- Evergreen trees and shrubs
- Mountain coniferous forest
- Temperate forest
- Oases and Nile Valley

Limits of Date Palm, North limit of Baobab, South limit of Baobab, Extreme South limit of Palms, Limits of Oil Palm, Limits of Juniper

Projection: Zenithal Equidistant

COPYRIGHT PHILIP'S

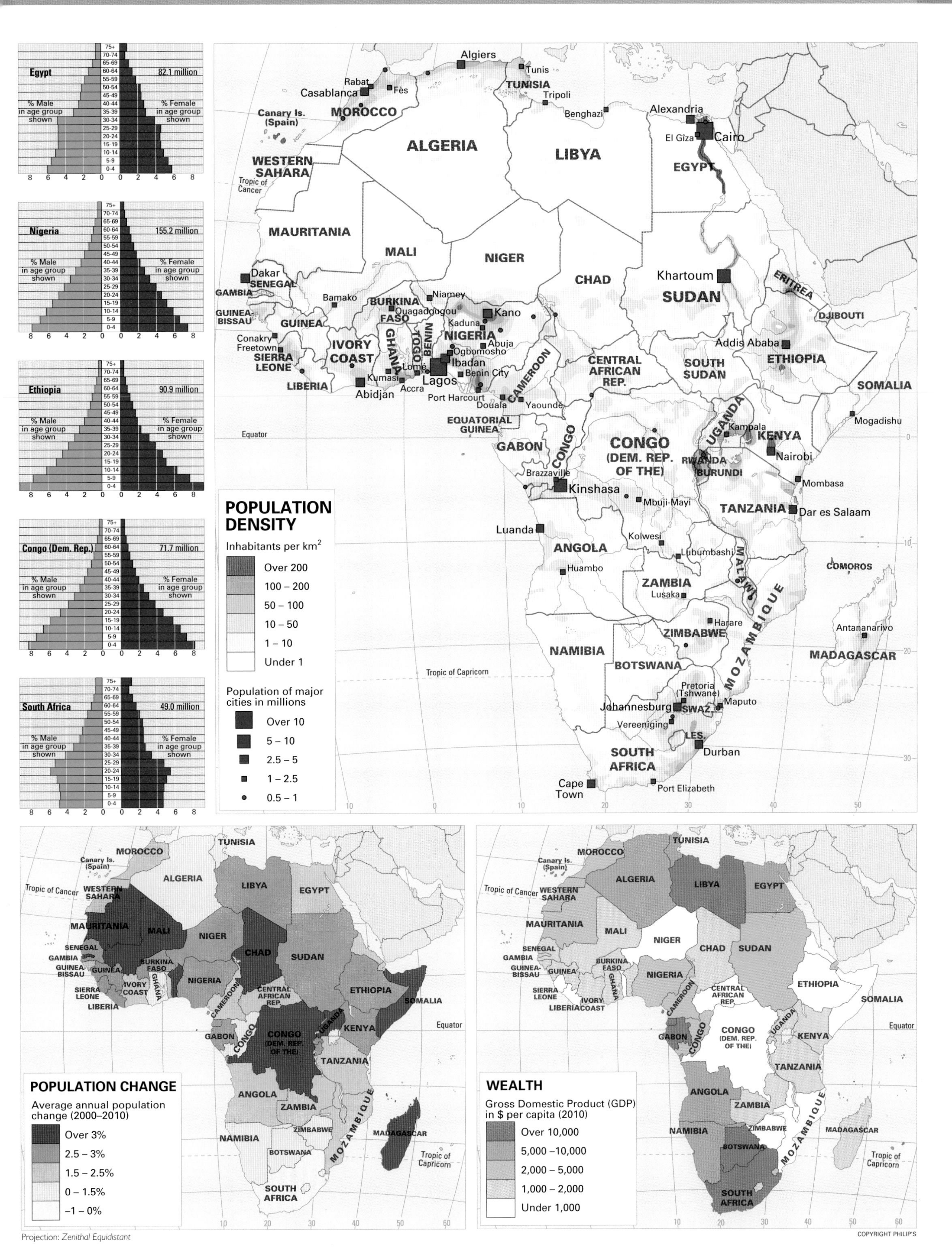

Egypt 82.1 million
75+
70–74
65–69
60–64
55–59
50–54
45–49
40–44
35–39
30–34
25–29
20–24
15–19
10–14
5–9
0–4
% Male in age group shown
% Female in age group shown
8 6 4 2 0 0 2 4 6 8

Nigeria 155.2 million
% Male in age group shown
% Female in age group shown
8 6 4 2 0 0 2 4 6 8

Ethiopia 90.9 million
% Male in age group shown
% Female in age group shown
8 6 4 2 0 0 2 4 6 8

Congo (Dem. Rep.) 71.7 million
% Male in age group shown
% Female in age group shown
8 6 4 2 0 0 2 4 6 8

South Africa 49.0 million
% Male in age group shown
% Female in age group shown
8 6 4 2 0 0 2 4 6 8

POPULATION DENSITY

Inhabitants per km²

Over 200
100 – 200
50 – 100
10 – 50
1 – 10
Under 1

Population of major cities in millions

Over 10
5 – 10
2.5 – 5
1 – 2.5
0.5 – 1

POPULATION CHANGE

Average annual population change (2000–2010)

Over 3%
2.5 – 3%
1.5 – 2.5%
0 – 1.5%
–1 – 0%

Projection: Zenithal Equidistant

WEALTH

Gross Domestic Product (GDP) in $ per capita (2010)

Over 10,000
5,000 – 10,000
2,000 – 5,000
1,000 – 2,000
Under 1,000

COPYRIGHT PHILIP'S

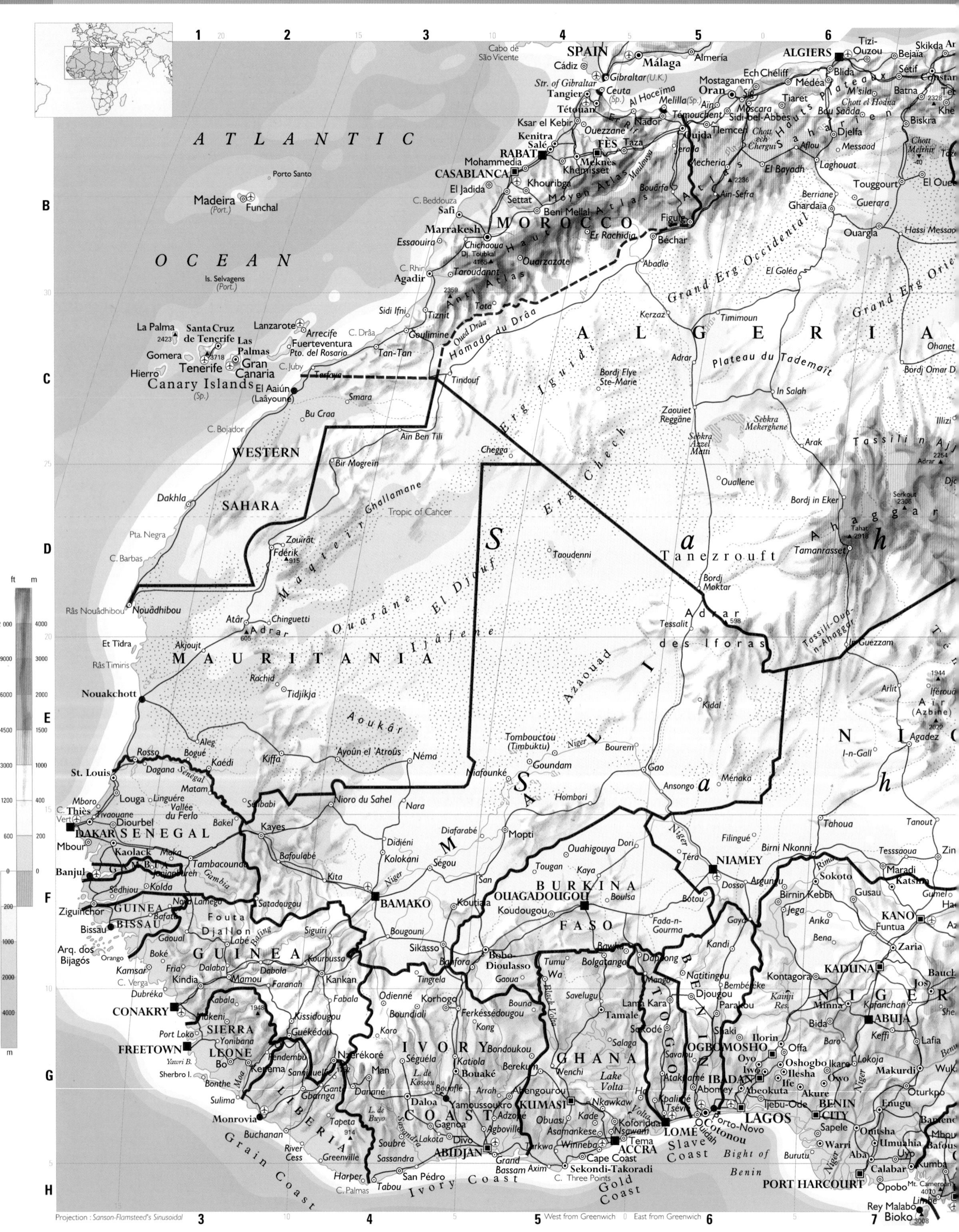
ATLANTIC
OCEAN
MOROCCO
ALGERIA
WESTERN
SAHARA
MAURITANIA
MALI
SENEGAL
GAMBIA
GUINEA-BISSAU
GUINEA
SIERRA LEONE
LIBERIA
IVORY COAST
BURKINA FASO
GHANA
TOGO
BENIN
NIGER
NIGERIA
SPAIN
ALGIERS
RABAT
CASABLANCA
Madeira (Port.)
Funchal
Porto Santo
Canary Islands (Sp.)
Is. Selvagens (Port.)
Tropic of Cancer
Nouakchott
Nouâdhibou
DAKAR
Banjul
Bissau
CONAKRY
FREETOWN
Monrovia
BAMAKO
OUAGADOUGOU
NIAMEY
ABIDJAN
ACCRA
LOME
Porto-Novo
LAGOS
ABUJA
KANO
KADUNA
IBADAN
OGBOMOSHO
BENIN CITY
PORT HARCOURT
KUMASI
Tombouctou (Timbuktu)
Tamanrasset
Ahaggar
Tanezrouft
Erg Chech
Erg Iguidi
Grand Erg Occidental
Grand Erg Oriental
Hamada du Drâa
Plateau du Tademaït
Adrar des Iforas
Azaouad
Aoukâr
Fouta Djallon
Grain Coast
Ivory Coast
Gold Coast
Slave Coast
Bight of Benin
Bioko
Projection : Sanson-Flamsteed's Sinusoidal
West from Greenwich
East from Greenwich

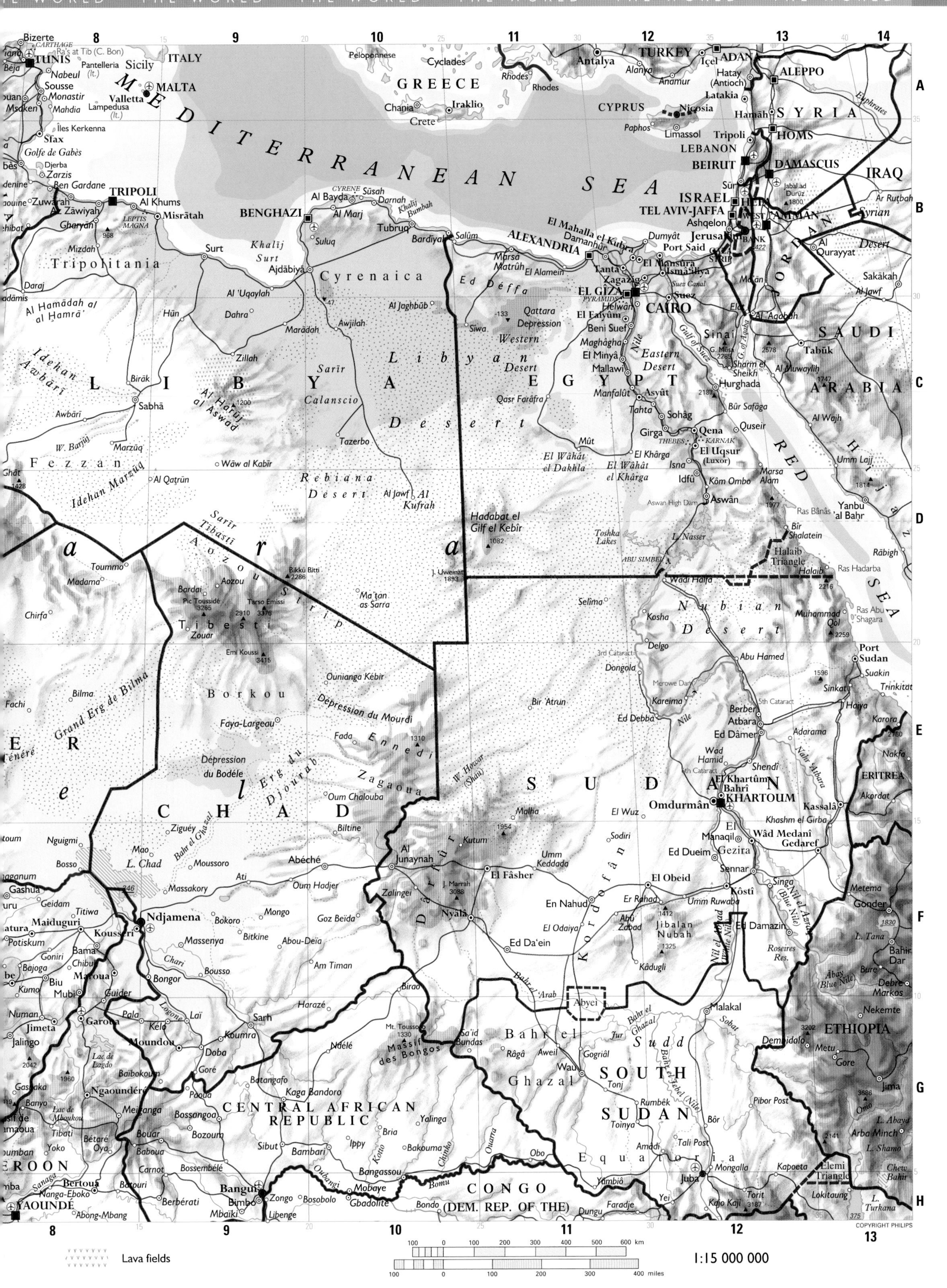
MEDITERRANEAN SEA
RED SEA
LIBYA
EGYPT
SUDAN
SOUTH SUDAN
CHAD
CENTRAL AFRICAN REPUBLIC
CONGO (DEM. REP. OF THE)
ETHIOPIA
ERITREA
SAUDI ARABIA
SYRIA
JORDAN
ISRAEL
LEBANON
IRAQ
TURKEY
CYPRUS
GREECE
ITALY
MALTA
TUNIS
Bizerte
Sfax
Sicily
Valletta
Crete
Iraklio
Chania
Rhodes
Antalya
ADANA
ALEPPO
HOMS
DAMASCUS
BEIRUT
TEL AVIV-JAFFA
AMMAN
Jerusalem
Nicosia
Limassol
TRIPOLI
Misrātah
BENGHAZI
Tubruq
ALEXANDRIA
CAIRO
EL GIZA
Port Said
Suez
Aswân
Luxor
Sinai
Tripolitania
Cyrenaica
Fezzan
Sabhā
Libyan Desert
Western Desert
Eastern Desert
Nubian Desert
Qattara Depression
Rebiana Desert
Al Kufrah
Tibesti
Aozou Strip
Emi Koussi 3415
Borkou
Ennedi
Faya-Largeau
Dépression du Bodélé
L. Chad
Ndjamena
Abéché
Sarh
Moundou
Maiduguri
Garoua
Ngaoundéré
YAOUNDÉ
Bangui
Bangassou
Wadi Halfa
L. Nasser
Halaib Triangle
Port Sudan
Atbara
Omdurmân
KHARTOUM
El Obeid
Kordofân
Dârfûr
El Fâsher
Nyala
Kassalâ
Gedaref
Abyei
Malakal
Wau
Juba
Bahr el Ghazal
Sudd
Equatoria
Elemi Triangle
L. Tana
L. Turkana
Lava fields
1:15 000 000
COPYRIGHT PHILIPS

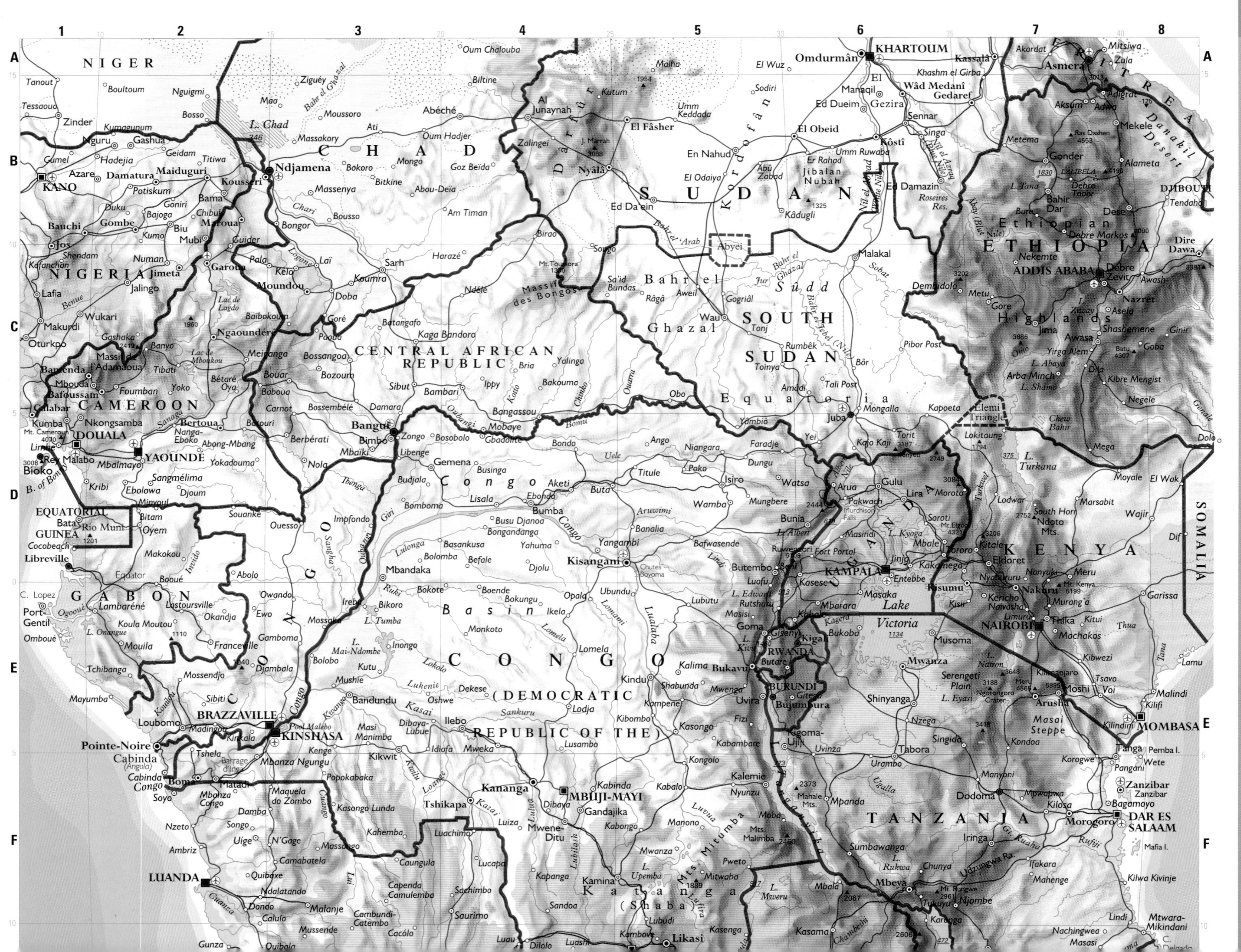
NIGER
CHAD
SUDAN
SOUTH SUDAN
ETHIOPIA
ERITREA
DJIBOUTI
SOMALIA
KENYA
UGANDA
RWANDA
BURUNDI
TANZANIA
NIGERIA
CAMEROON
CENTRAL AFRICAN REPUBLIC
CONGO
CONGO (DEMOCRATIC REPUBLIC OF THE)
GABON
EQUATORIAL GUINEA
KHARTOUM
Omdurmân
ADDIS ABABA
Asmera
NAIROBI
MOMBASA
DAR ES SALAAM
KAMPALA
Kigali
Bujumbura
KINSHASA
BRAZZAVILLE
LUANDA
YAOUNDÉ
DOUALA
Ndjamena
Bangui
Juba
Libreville
Kisangani
MBUJI-MAYI
KANO
Lake Victoria
L. Turkana
L. Chad
Congo Basin
Danakil Desert
Ethiopian Highlands
Masai Steppe
Serengeti Plain
Sudd
Bahr el Ghazal
Equatoria
Kordofân
Dârfûr
Jibalan Nubah
Massif des Bongos
Massif de l'Adamaoua
Mts. Mitumba
Katanga (Shaba)
Abyei
Elemi Triangle

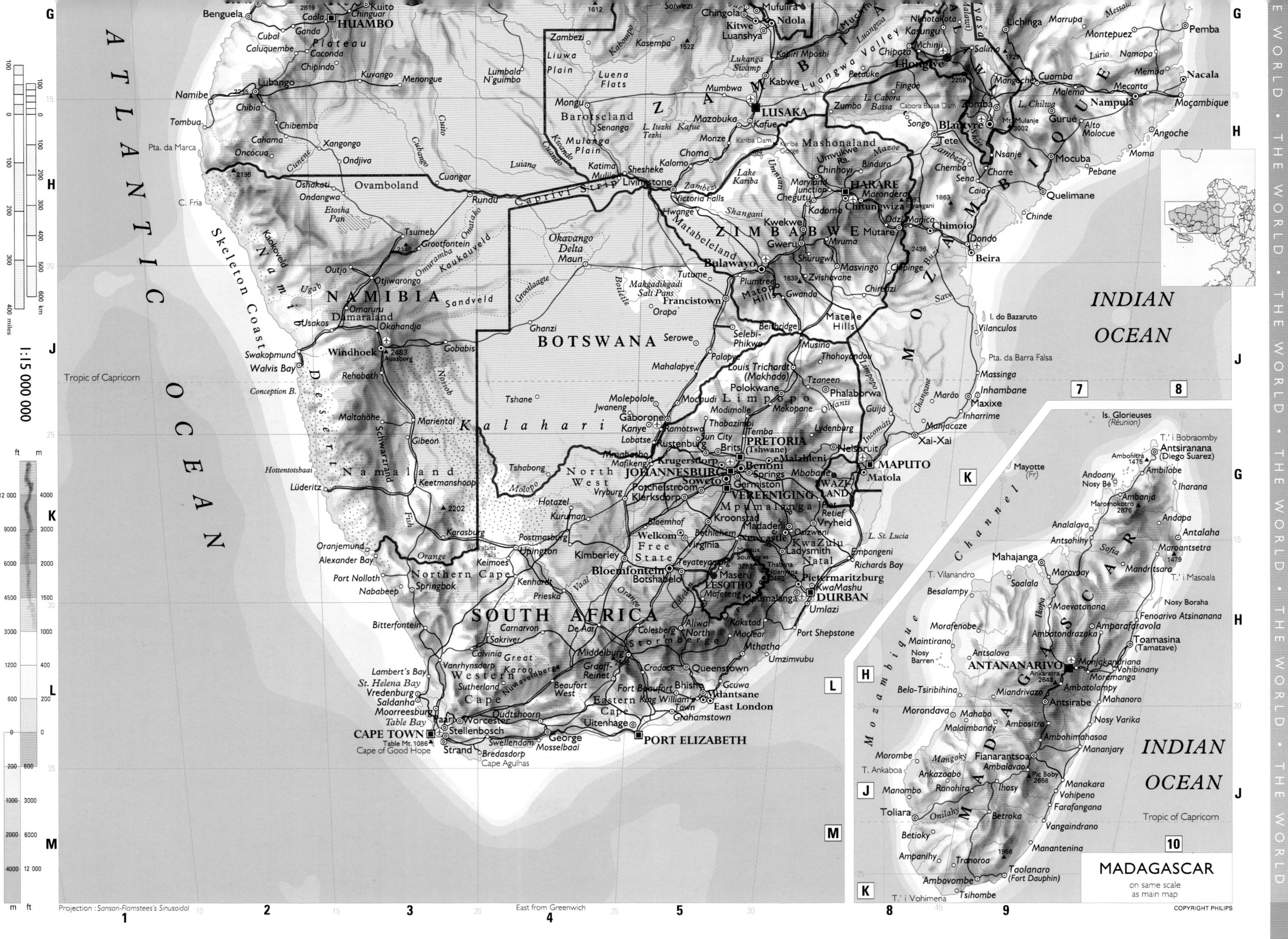
ATLANTIC OCEAN
INDIAN OCEAN
MADAGASCAR
on same scale as main map
COPYRIGHT PHILIPS
SOUTH AFRICA
NAMIBIA
BOTSWANA
ZIMBABWE
ZAMBIA
MOZAMBIQUE
LESOTHO
SWAZILAND
Kalahari
Namib Desert
Skeleton Coast
Mozambique Channel
Tropic of Capricorn
CAPE TOWN
PORT ELIZABETH
DURBAN
JOHANNESBURG
PRETORIA
MAPUTO
HARARE
LUSAKA
Bulawayo
Windhoek
Gaborone
Beira
Maseru
Bloemfontein
East London
Kimberley
Walvis Bay
Lüderitz
ANTANANARIVO
Toamasina
Mahajanga
Toliara
Fianarantsoa
Antsiranana
Cape of Good Hope
Cape Agulhas
Projection: Sanson-Flamstees's Sinusoidal
East from Greenwich
1:15 000 000
km
miles
m
ft

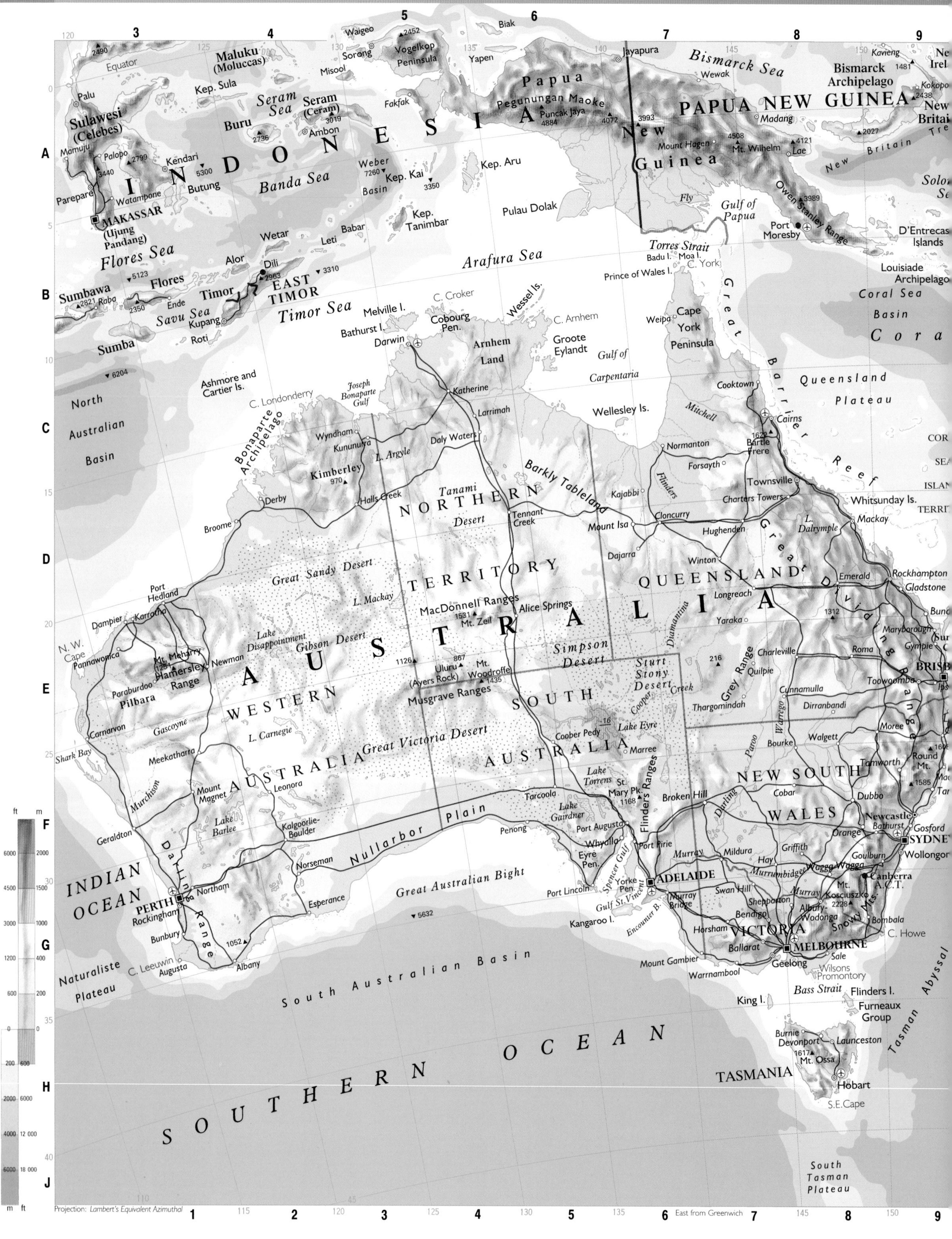
Equator
Maluku (Moluccas)
Waigeo
Sorong
Vogelkop Peninsula
Biak
Yapen
Jayapura
Bismarck Sea
Wewak
Kavieng
Bismarck Archipelago
Palu
Kep. Sula
Misool
Seram Sea
Seram (Ceram)
Fakfak
Papua
Pegunungan Maoke
Puncak Jaya 4884
PAPUA NEW GUINEA
Madang
Kokopo
New Britain
Sulawesi (Celebes)
Buru
Ambon
INDONESIA
New Guinea
Mount Hagen
Mt. Wilhelm
Lae
Mamuju
Palopo
Kendari
Weber Basin
Kep. Kai
Kep. Aru
Parepare
Watampone
Butung
Banda Sea
Pulau Dolak
Fly
Gulf of Papua
Owen Stanley Range
MAKASSAR (Ujung Pandang)
Kep. Tanimbar
Port Moresby
D'Entrecasteaux Islands
Wetar
Babar
Leti
Torres Strait
Badu I.
Moa I.
Flores Sea
Alor
Dili
Arafura Sea
Prince of Wales I.
C. York
Louisiade Archipelago
Sumbawa
Raba
Flores
Ende
Timor
EAST TIMOR
Coral Sea Basin
Savu Sea
Kupang
Timor Sea
Melville I.
C. Croker
Wessel Is.
C. Arnhem
Weipa
Cape York Peninsula
Great Barrier Reef
Bathurst I.
Cobourg Pen.
Sumba
Roti
Darwin
Arnhem Land
Groote Eylandt
Gulf of Carpentaria
Coral
Ashmore and Cartier Is.
Joseph Bonaparte Gulf
Katherine
Cooktown
Queensland Plateau
North Australian Basin
C. Londonderry
Larrimah
Wellesley Is.
Mitchell
Cairns
Bonaparte Archipelago
Wyndham
Kununurra
L. Argyle
Daly Waters
Normanton
Bartle Frere
Forsayth
Kimberley
Barkly Tableland
Tanami Desert
Townsville
Charters Towers
Whitsunday Is.
Mackay
Derby
Halls Creek
NORTHERN TERRITORY
Kajabbi
Flinders
Broome
Tennant Creek
Mount Isa
Cloncurry
Hughenden
L. Dalrymple
Great Dividing Range
Dajarra
Winton
Emerald
Rockhampton
Gladstone
Great Sandy Desert
QUEENSLAND
Port Hedland
L. Mackay
MacDonnell Ranges
Mt. Zeil
Alice Springs
Longreach
Dampier
Karratha
AUSTRALIA
Diamantina
Yaraka
Maryborough
Gympie
N. W. Cape
Pannawonica
Lake Disappointment
Gibson Desert
Simpson Desert
Mt. Meharry
Hamersley Range
Newman
Uluru (Ayers Rock)
Mt. Woodroffe
Sturt Stony Desert
Grey Range
Charleville
Roma
Quilpie
Paraburdoo
Pilbara
Musgrave Ranges
SOUTH AUSTRALIA
Cooper Creek
Cunnamulla
Toowoomba
WESTERN AUSTRALIA
Thargomindah
Dirranbandi
Carnarvon
Gascoyne
L. Carnegie
Great Victoria Desert
Coober Pedy
Lake Eyre
Warrego
Moree
Shark Bay
Meekatharra
Marree
Paroo
Bourke
Walgett
Tamworth
Round Mt.
Murchison
Mount Magnet
Leonora
Lake Torrens
Flinders Ranges
NEW SOUTH WALES
Tarcoola
St. Mary Pk.
Broken Hill
Darling
Cobar
Dubbo
Lake Barlee
Kalgoorlie-Boulder
Nullarbor Plain
Lake Gairdner
Port Augusta
Newcastle
Bathurst
Gosford
Geraldton
Penong
Whyalla
Port Pirie
Orange
SYDNEY
Wollongong
Eyre Pen.
Spencer Gulf
Mildura
Murray
Griffith
Hay
Goulburn
Norseman
Great Australian Bight
Murrumbidgee
Wagga Wagga
Canberra A.C.T.
INDIAN OCEAN
Darling Range
Northam
PERTH
Rockingham
Esperance
Port Lincoln
Yorke Pen.
ADELAIDE
Gulf St. Vincent
Murray Bridge
Swan Hill
Shepparton
Mt. Kosciuszko
Albury-Wodonga
Snowy Mts.
Bendigo
Kangaroo I.
Encounter B.
Horsham
VICTORIA
Bombala
C. Howe
Bunbury
Ballarat
MELBOURNE
Sale
Naturaliste Plateau
C. Leeuwin
Augusta
Albany
South Australian Basin
Mount Gambier
Geelong
Wilsons Promontory
Warrnambool
Bass Strait
Flinders I.
Furneaux Group
King I.
Tasman Abyssal
SOUTHERN OCEAN
Burnie
Devonport
Launceston
Mt. Ossa
TASMANIA
Hobart
S.E.Cape
South Tasman Plateau
Projection: Lambert's Equivalent Azimuthal
East from Greenwich

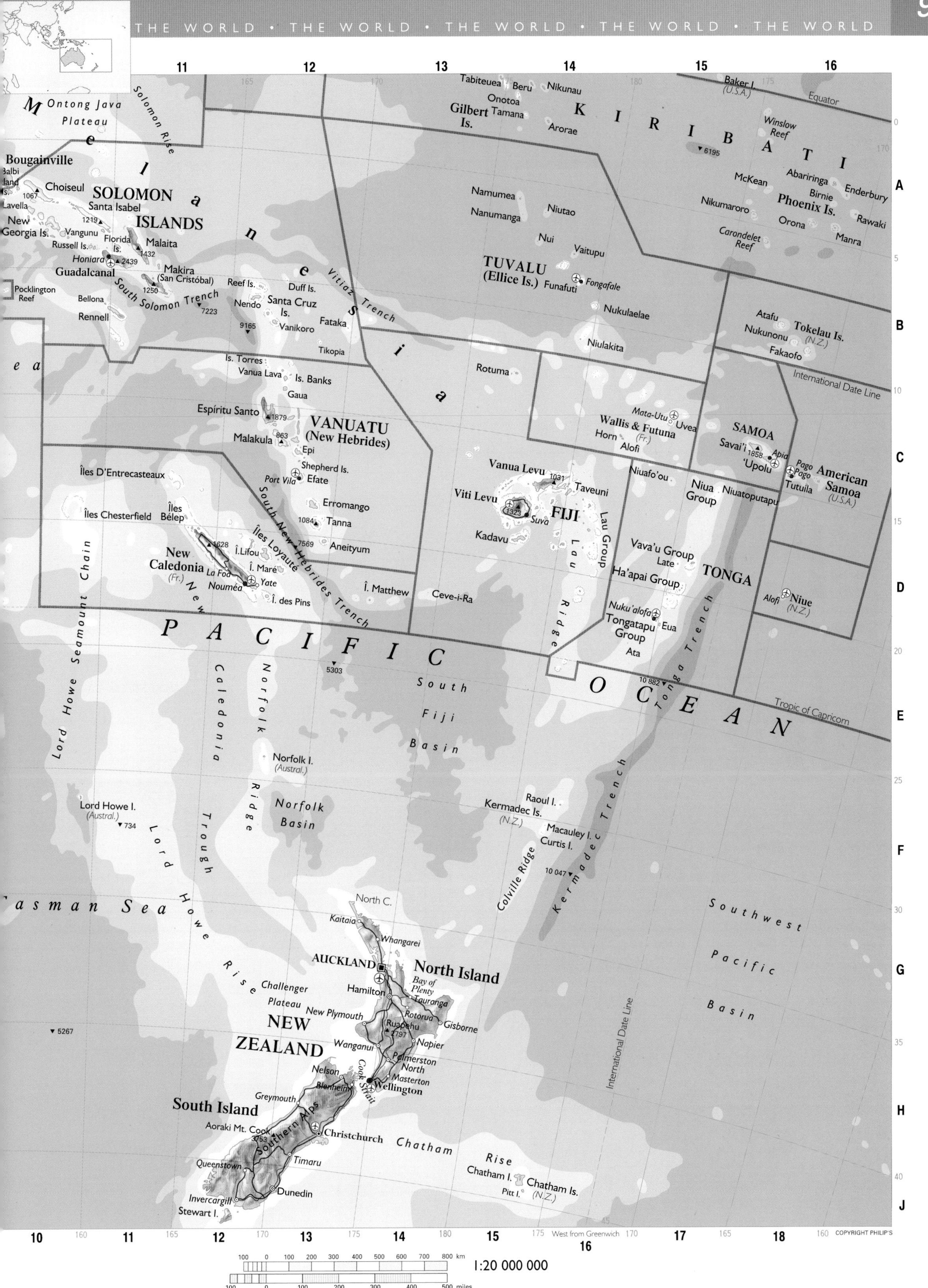
Melanesia
Ontong Java Plateau
Solomon Rise
Bougainville
Choiseul
SOLOMON ISLANDS
Santa Isabel
New Georgia Is.
Vangunu
Russell Is.
Florida Is.
Malaita
Honiara
Guadalcanal
Makira (San Cristóbal)
Pocklington Reef
Bellona
Rennell
South Solomon Trench
Reef Is.
Duff Is.
Nendo
Santa Cruz Is.
Vanikoro
Fataka
Tikopia
Vitiaz Trench
Tabiteuea
Beru
Nikunau
Onotoa
Gilbert Is.
Tamana
Arorae
KIRIBATI
Baker I. (U.S.A.)
Equator
Winslow Reef
McKean
Abariringa
Enderbury
Birnie
Phoenix Is.
Nikumaroro
Orona
Rawaki
Carondelet Reef
Manra
Namumea
Nanumanga
Niutao
Nui
Vaitupu
TUVALU (Ellice Is.)
Funafuti
Fongafale
Nukulaelae
Niulakita
Atafu
Nukunonu
Tokelau Is. (N.Z.)
Fakaofo
International Date Line
Rotuma
Is. Torres
Vanua Lava
Is. Banks
Gaua
Espíritu Santo
VANUATU (New Hebrides)
Malakula
Epi
Shepherd Is.
Port Vila
Efate
Erromango
Tanna
Aneityum
Mata-Utu
Uvea
Wallis & Futuna (Fr.)
Horn
Alofi
SAMOA
Savai'i
Apia
'Upolu
Pago Pago
American Samoa (U.S.A.)
Tutuila
Vanua Levu
Taveuni
Viti Levu
FIJI
Suva
Kadavu
Lau Group
Lau Ridge
Niuafo'ou
Niua Group
Niuatoputapu
Vava'u Group
Late
Ha'apai Group
TONGA
Alofi
Niue (N.Z.)
Nuku'alofa
Tongatapu Group
Eua
Ata
Îles D'Entrecasteaux
Îles Chesterfield
Îles Bélep
New Caledonia (Fr.)
La Foa
Nouméa
Yate
Î. Lifou
Î. Maré
Îles Loyauté
Î. des Pins
South New Hebrides Trench
Î. Matthew
Ceve-i-Ra
PACIFIC OCEAN
South Fiji Basin
Tonga Trench
Tropic of Capricorn
Lord Howe Seamount Chain
Caledonia Trough
Norfolk Ridge
New Caledonia
Norfolk I. (Austral.)
Norfolk Basin
Lord Howe I. (Austral.)
Lord Howe Rise
Raoul I.
Kermadec Is. (N.Z.)
Macauley I.
Curtis I.
Colville Ridge
Kermadec Trench
Tasman Sea
Southwest Pacific Basin
North C.
Kaitaia
Whangarei
AUCKLAND
North Island
Bay of Plenty
Hamilton
Tauranga
Challenger Plateau
New Plymouth
Rotorua
Gisborne
NEW ZEALAND
Ruapehu
Napier
Wanganui
Palmerston North
Nelson
Cook Strait
Masterton
Blenheim
Wellington
Greymouth
South Island
Southern Alps
Aoraki Mt. Cook
Christchurch
Chatham Rise
Queenstown
Timaru
Chatham I.
Chatham Is. (N.Z.)
Pitt I.
Dunedin
Invercargill
Stewart I.
International Date Line
West from Greenwich
1:20 000 000
km
miles
COPYRIGHT PHILIP'S

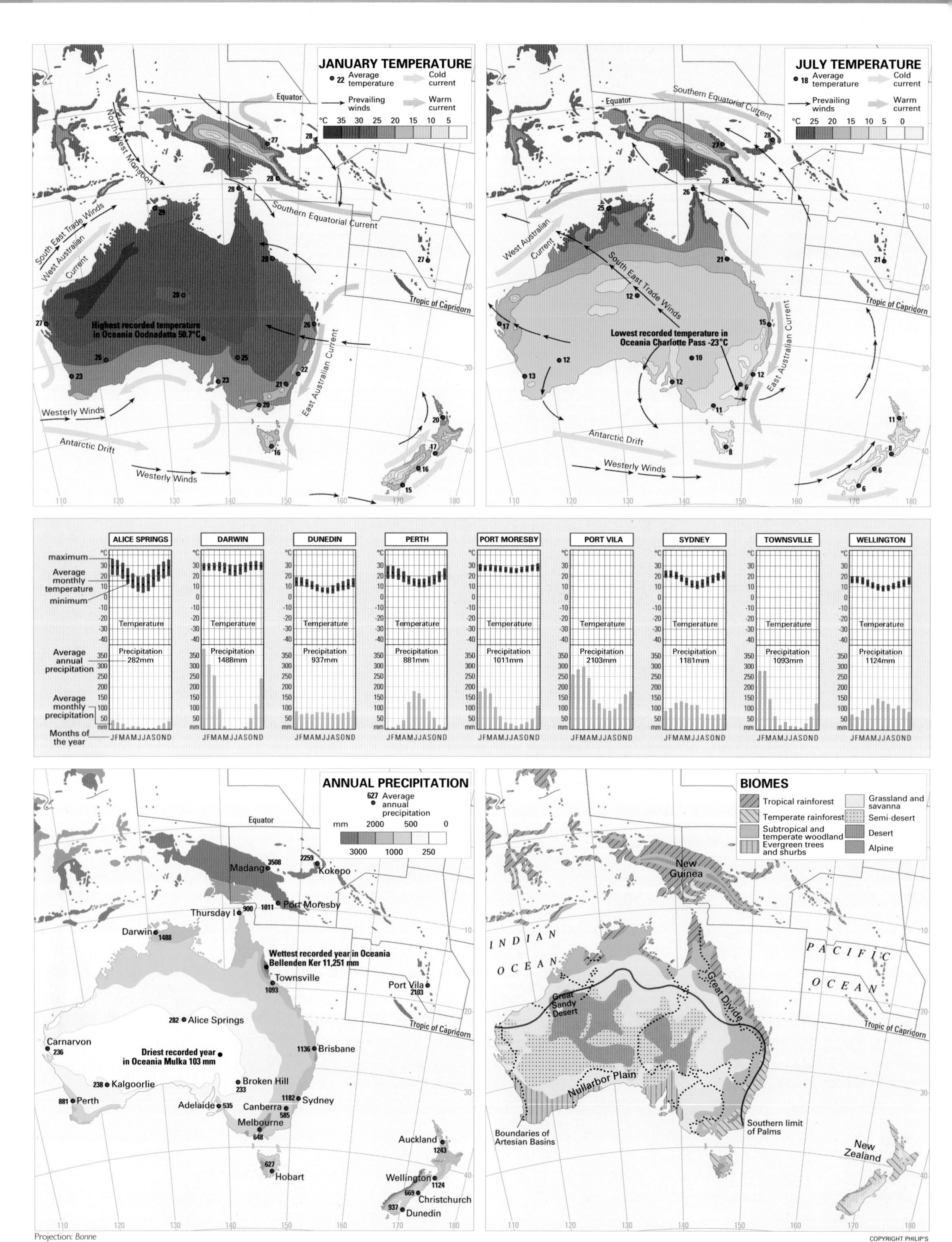

JANUARY TEMPERATURE
- 22 Average temperature
- Prevailing winds
- Cold current
- Warm current
- °C 35 30 25 20 15 10 5

Highest recorded temperature in Oceania Oodnadatta 50.7°C

JULY TEMPERATURE
- 18 Average temperature
- Prevailing winds
- Cold current
- Warm current
- °C 25 20 15 10 5 0

Lowest recorded temperature in Oceania Charlotte Pass -23°C

Climate graphs: ALICE SPRINGS (Precipitation 282mm), DARWIN (Precipitation 1488mm), DUNEDIN (Precipitation 937mm), PERTH (Precipitation 881mm), PORT MORESBY (Precipitation 1011mm), PORT VILA (Precipitation 2103mm), SYDNEY (Precipitation 1181mm), TOWNSVILLE (Precipitation 1093mm), WELLINGTON (Precipitation 1124mm)

ANNUAL PRECIPITATION
- 627 Average annual precipitation
- mm 2000 500 0
- 3000 1000 250

Wettest recorded year in Oceania Bellenden Ker 11,251 mm
Driest recorded year in Oceania Mulka 103 mm

Madang 3508, Kokopo 2259, Thursday I 900, Port Moresby 1011, Darwin 1488, Townsville 1093, Port Vila 2103, Alice Springs 282, Carnarvon 236, Brisbane 1136, Kalgoorlie 238, Broken Hill 233, Perth 881, Adelaide 535, Canberra 585, Sydney 1182, Melbourne 648, Hobart 627, Auckland 1243, Wellington 1124, Christchurch 669, Dunedin 937

BIOMES
- Tropical rainforest
- Temperate rainforest
- Subtropical and temperate woodland
- Evergreen trees and shrubs
- Grassland and savanna
- Semi-desert
- Desert
- Alpine
- Boundaries of Artesian Basins
- Southern limit of Palms

New Guinea, Great Sandy Desert, Great Divide, Nullarbor Plain, New Zealand

Projection: Bonne

COPYRIGHT PHILIP'S

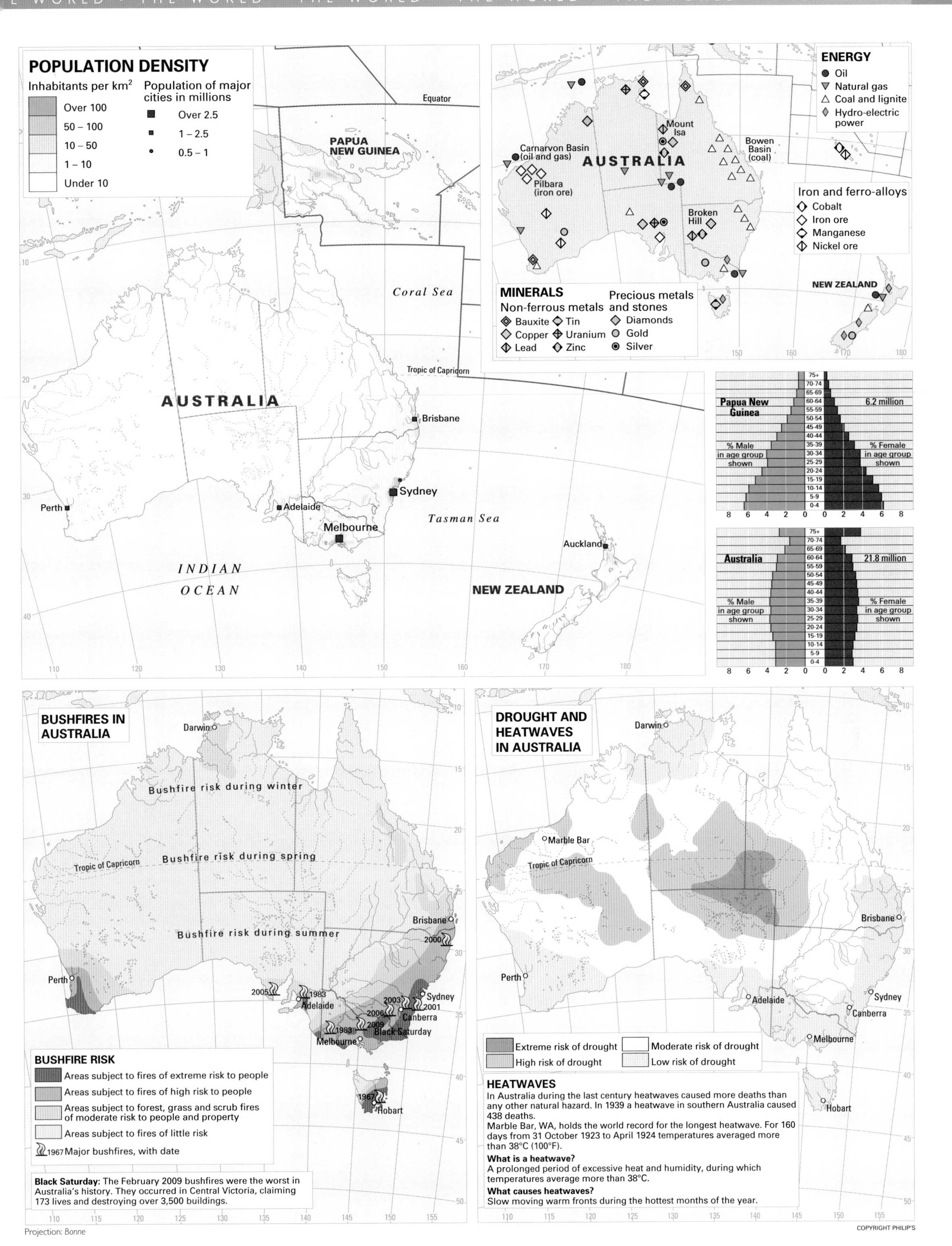

POPULATION DENSITY

Inhabitants per km²

- Over 100
- 50 – 100
- 10 – 50
- 1 – 10
- Under 10

Population of major cities in millions

- Over 2.5
- 1 – 2.5
- 0.5 – 1

PAPUA NEW GUINEA

Equator

AUSTRALIA

Coral Sea

Tropic of Capricorn

Brisbane

Sydney

Perth

Adelaide

Melbourne

Tasman Sea

Auckland

INDIAN OCEAN

NEW ZEALAND

ENERGY

- Oil
- Natural gas
- Coal and lignite
- Hydro-electric power

AUSTRALIA

Carnarvon Basin (oil and gas)

Pilbara (iron ore)

Mount Isa

Bowen Basin (coal)

Broken Hill

NEW ZEALAND

Iron and ferro-alloys

- Cobalt
- Iron ore
- Manganese
- Nickel ore

MINERALS

Non-ferrous metals

- Bauxite
- Copper
- Lead

- Tin
- Uranium
- Zinc

Precious metals and stones

- Diamonds
- Gold
- Silver

Papua New Guinea — 6.2 million

75+ / 70-74 / 65-69 / 60-64 / 55-59 / 50-54 / 45-49 / 40-44 / 35-39 / 30-34 / 25-29 / 20-24 / 15-19 / 10-14 / 5-9 / 0-4

% Male in age group shown — % Female in age group shown

8 6 4 2 0 0 2 4 6 8

Australia — 21.8 million

75+ / 70-74 / 65-69 / 60-64 / 55-59 / 50-54 / 45-49 / 40-44 / 35-39 / 30-34 / 25-29 / 20-24 / 15-19 / 10-14 / 5-9 / 0-4

% Male in age group shown — % Female in age group shown

8 6 4 2 0 0 2 4 6 8

BUSHFIRES IN AUSTRALIA

Darwin

Bushfire risk during winter

Tropic of Capricorn

Bushfire risk during spring

Bushfire risk during summer

Brisbane

Perth

2005

2000

1983

Adelaide

2003

2001

Sydney

2006

Canberra

2009

1983

Black Saturday

Melbourne

1967

Hobart

BUSHFIRE RISK

- Areas subject to fires of extreme risk to people
- Areas subject to fires of high risk to people
- Areas subject to forest, grass and scrub fires of moderate risk to people and property
- Areas subject to fires of little risk
- 1967 Major bushfires, with date

Black Saturday: The February 2009 bushfires were the worst in Australia's history. They occurred in Central Victoria, claiming 173 lives and destroying over 3,500 buildings.

DROUGHT AND HEATWAVES IN AUSTRALIA

Darwin

Marble Bar

Tropic of Capricorn

Brisbane

Perth

Adelaide

Sydney

Canberra

Melbourne

Hobart

- Extreme risk of drought
- High risk of drought
- Moderate risk of drought
- Low risk of drought

HEATWAVES

In Australia during the last century heatwaves caused more deaths than any other natural hazard. In 1939 a heatwave in southern Australia caused 438 deaths.

Marble Bar, WA, holds the world record for the longest heatwave. For 160 days from 31 October 1923 to April 1924 temperatures averaged more than 38°C (100°F).

What is a heatwave?
A prolonged period of excessive heat and humidity, during which temperatures average more than 38°C.

What causes heatwaves?
Slow moving warm fronts during the hottest months of the year.

Projection: Bonne

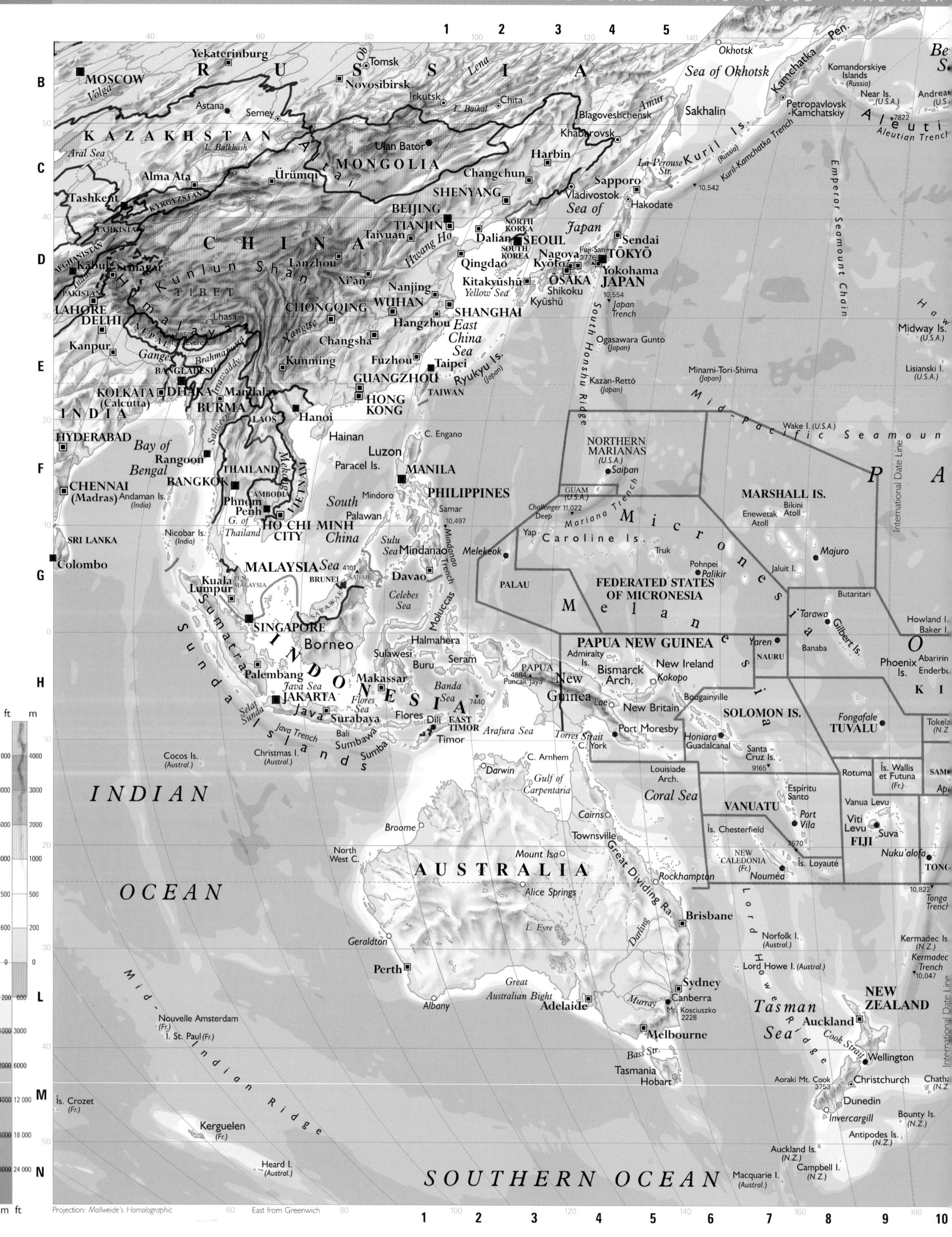
RUSSIA
MOSCOW
Volga
Yekaterinburg
Ob
Tomsk
Novosibirsk
Lena
Irkutsk
L. Baikal
Chita
Sea of Okhotsk
Okhotsk
Kamchatka Pen.
Komandorskiye Islands (Russia)
Near Is. (U.S.A.)
Petropavlovsk-Kamchatskiy
Aleutian Trench
Amur
Blagoveshchensk
Sakhalin
Khabarovsk
Astana
Semey
KAZAKHSTAN
L. Balkhash
Aral Sea
Altai
Ulan Bator
MONGOLIA
Harbin
Kuril Is. (Russia)
Kuril-Kamchatka Trench
La Perouse Str.
10,542
Alma Ata
Ürümqi
Changchun
Sapporo
Hakodate
Tashkent
KYRGYZSTAN
TAJIKISTAN
SHENYANG
Vladivostok
Sea of Japan
Emperor Seamount Chain
BEIJING
TIANJIN
NORTH KOREA
CHINA
Taiyuan
Dalian
SEOUL
SOUTH KOREA
Sendai
AFGHANISTAN
Kabul
Indus
Srinagar
Lanzhou
Hwang Ho
Qingdao
Nagoya
Fuji-San 3776
TŌKYŌ
Kyōto
Yokohama
Kunlun Shan
Xi'an
Kitakyūshū
ŌSAKA
JAPAN
PAKISTAN
TIBET
Nanjing
Yellow Sea
Shikoku
Kyūshū
10,554
Japan Trench
LAHORE
Himalaya
WUHAN
CHONGQING
SHANGHAI
DELHI
Lhasa
NEPAL
8850 Mt. Everest
Yangtse
Hangzhou
East China Sea
Midway Is. (U.S.A.)
Kanpur
Ganges
Brahmaputra
Changsha
Ogasawara Gunto (Japan)
South Honshu Ridge
BANGLADESH
Kunming
Fuzhou
Taipei
Ryukyu Is. (Japan)
Minami-Tori-Shima (Japan)
Lisianski I. (U.S.A.)
Irrawaddy
KOLKATA (Calcutta)
DHAKA
Mandalay
GUANGZHOU
HONG KONG
TAIWAN
Kazan-Rettō (Japan)
INDIA
BURMA
Hanoi
LAOS
Mid-Pacific Seamounts
HYDERABAD
Salween
Hainan
C. Engano
Wake I. (U.S.A.)
Bay of Bengal
Rangoon
Luzon
NORTHERN MARIANAS (U.S.A.)
Saipan
THAILAND
Mekong
VIETNAM
Paracel Is.
MANILA
International Date Line
CHENNAI (Madras)
BANGKOK
Andaman Is. (India)
CAMBODIA
Phnom Penh
Mindoro
PHILIPPINES
GUAM (U.S.A.)
Mariana Trench
MARSHALL IS.
Bikini Atoll
Enewetak Atoll
South China Sea
Palawan
Samar
Challenger Deep 11,022
G. of Thailand
HO CHI MINH CITY
10,497
Micronesia
Caroline Is.
SRI LANKA
Nicobar Is. (India)
Sulu Sea
Mindanao
Mindanao Trench
Melekeok
Yap
Truk
Majuro
Colombo
MALAYSIA
4101
Pohnpei
Palikir
Jaluit I.
BRUNEI
SABAH
Davao
PALAU
FEDERATED STATES OF MICRONESIA
Kuala Lumpur
PEN. MALAYSIA
SARAWAK
Celebes Sea
Butaritari
Sumatra
SINGAPORE
Moluccas
Melanesia
Tarawa
Howland I.
Baker I.
Borneo
Halmahera
PAPUA NEW GUINEA
Yaren
NAURU
Gilbert Is.
Banaba
Sulawesi
Seram
Admiralty Is.
Bismarck Arch.
New Ireland
Phoenix Is.
Abariringa
Enderbury
Sunda Islands
INDONESIA
Palembang
Buru
PAPUA
4884 Puncak Jaya
New Guinea
Kokopo
Makassar
Banda Sea
Java Sea
JAKARTA
Flores Sea
7440
Lae
Bougainville
New Britain
SOLOMON IS.
Fongafale
TUVALU
Tokelau (N.Z.)
Selat Sunda
Java
Surabaya
Flores
Dili
EAST TIMOR
Arafura Sea
Torres Strait
Port Moresby
Honiara
Guadalcanal
Java Trench
Bali
Sumbawa
Sumba
Timor
C. York
Santa Cruz Is.
9165
Cocos Is. (Austral.)
Christmas I. (Austral.)
C. Arnhem
Darwin
Louisiade Arch.
Rotuma
Îs. Wallis et Futuna (Fr.)
SAMOA
Apia
INDIAN OCEAN
Gulf of Carpentaria
Coral Sea
Espíritu Santo
VANUATU
Port Vila
Vanua Levu
Viti Levu
Suva
FIJI
Cairns
Broome
Townsville
Îs. Chesterfield
7570
North West C.
Mount Isa
Great Dividing Ra.
NEW CALEDONIA (Fr.)
Nouméa
Îs. Loyauté
Nuku'alofa
TONGA
AUSTRALIA
Rockhampton
Alice Springs
10,822
Tonga Trench
Lord Howe Rise
OCEAN
Brisbane
L. Eyre
Darling
Norfolk I. (Austral.)
Kermadec Is. (N.Z.)
Geraldton
Kermadec Trench
10,047
Lord Howe I. (Austral.)
Perth
Sydney
Great Australian Bight
Canberra
Mid-Indian Ridge
Albany
Adelaide
Murray
Mt. Kosciuszko 2228
Tasman Sea
NEW ZEALAND
Auckland
Nouvelle Amsterdam (Fr.)
I. St. Paul (Fr.)
Melbourne
Cook Strait
Bass Str.
Wellington
Tasmania
Hobart
Aoraki Mt. Cook 3753
Christchurch
Chatham Is. (N.Z.)
Îs. Crozet (Fr.)
Dunedin
Invercargill
Bounty Is. (N.Z.)
Kerguelen (Fr.)
Antipodes Is. (N.Z.)
Auckland Is. (N.Z.)
Campbell I. (N.Z.)
Heard I. (Austral.)
SOUTHERN OCEAN
Macquarie I. (Austral.)
Projection: Mollweide's Homolographic
East from Greenwich
ft
m
12 000
4000
9000
3000
6000
2000
3000
1000
1500
500
600
200
0
0
200
600
1000
3000
2000
6000
4000
12 000
6000
18 000
8000
24 000
m
ft

ALASKA
(U.S.A.)
Anchorage
5959

Bristol Bay

Gulf of Alaska

Prince of Wales I.
(U.S.A.) Prince Rupert
Queen Charlotte Is.
(Canada)

R O C K Y

C A N A D A

Edmonton

L. Winnipeg

Newfoundland

Vancouver I.
Vancouver
Victoria
Seattle
Portland
Boise

Calgary
Regina
Winnipeg
L. Superior

St. Lawrence

St. John's

Québec
Montréal
Ottawa

Minneapolis
Missouri
L. Michigan
TORONTO
L. Huron
L. Ontario
Detroit
L. Erie
Buffalo
Boston

NEW YORK
PHILADELPHIA
Baltimore
WASHINGTON D.C.

A T L A N T I C

C. Mendocino

Salt Lake
City

Denver
CHICAGO
Pittsburgh
Cincinnati

Sacramento
SAN FRANCISCO

4418

Kansas City
St. Louis

UNITED STATES

Oklahoma City
Memphis

ATLANTA

C. Hatteras

6741

LOS ANGELES
San Diego
Phoenix

Ciudad
Juárez

DALLAS

HOUSTON

Jacksonville

Bermuda
(U.K.)

Guadalupe
(Mex.)

San Antonio

New
Orleans

Sargasso Sea

O C E A N

Tropic of Cancer

C. San Lucas

Gulf of Mexico

Monterrey

MIAMI

Havana

Florida Str.

BAHAMAS

C U B A

West Indies

Honolulu
O'ahu
HAWAI'I
(U.S.A.)
Hawai'i
4205

Guadalajara

MEXICO
6610
Puebla

Acapulco

Yucatan Channel

Mérida

8605

7680

JAMAICA

HAITI

DOMINICAN REP.

Kingston

PUERTO
RICO
(U.S.A.)

Leeward
Is.

West Christmas Ridge

Is. de Revillagigedo
(Mex.)

Î. Clipperton
(Fr.)

BELIZE

GUATEMALA
Guatemala
San Salvador
EL SALVADOR

HONDURAS

NICARAGUA

Managua

Caribbean Sea

BARBADOS
Windward Is.

C I F I C

Palmyra Is.
(U.S.A.)

Teraina

Tabuaeran
Kiritimati

Equator

Barranquilla
San José
COSTA
RICA
Colón
PANAMA

Maracaibo

Caracas

Panamá

Orinoco

VENEZUELA

I. del Coco
(Costa Rica)

Medellín

BOGOTA

Jarvis I.
(U.S.A.)

Malden I.
Starbuck I.

Galápagos
(Ecuador)

I. de Malpelo
(Colombia)

Cali
COLOMBIA

Quito
ECUADOR

E A N

Guayaquil

Iquitos

Amazonas

Tongareva

Pukapuka
Manihiki

Suwarrow Is.

Cook Is.
(N.Z.)

Vostok I.

Flint I.

Caroline I.
(Millennium I.)

Îs. Marquises

C. Paliñas

BRAZIL

Îs. de la
Société

Papeete Tahiti

Îs. Tuamotu

Trujillo

6369

PERU

LIMA

Cusco

FRENCH POLYNESIA

Mururoa

Îs. Tubuaï

Tropic of Capricorn

Nevado Ancohuma
6550

Arequipa

L. Titicaca

6866

Peru-

Arica

Chile

La Paz
BOLIVIA

Rarotonga

Austral Seamount Chain

Henderson I.

Pitcairn I.
(U.K.)

Rapa

Sala-y-Gómez
(Chile)

I. de Pascua
(Chile)

San Félix
(Chile)

8050
Trench

San Ambrosio
(Chile)

Iquique

Antofagasta

PARAGUAY

Asunción

San Miguel
de Tucumán

Pôrto
Alegre

East Pacific Rise

Arch. de
Juan Fernández
(Chile)

Córdoba

Valparaíso

SANTIAGO

Aconcagua
6962

Rosario

URUGUAY

BUENOS
AIRES

Montevideo

Río de la Plata

Chile Rise

Concepción

ARGENTINA

Pacific-Antarctic Ridge

Patagonia

A T L A N T I C

O C E A N

6212

Punta Arenas

Magellan's Str.

Tierra del Fuego

Falkland Is.
(U.K.)

South Georgia
(U.K.)

C. Horn

West from Greenwich

COPYRIGHT PHILIP'S

Equatorial Scale 1:54 000 000

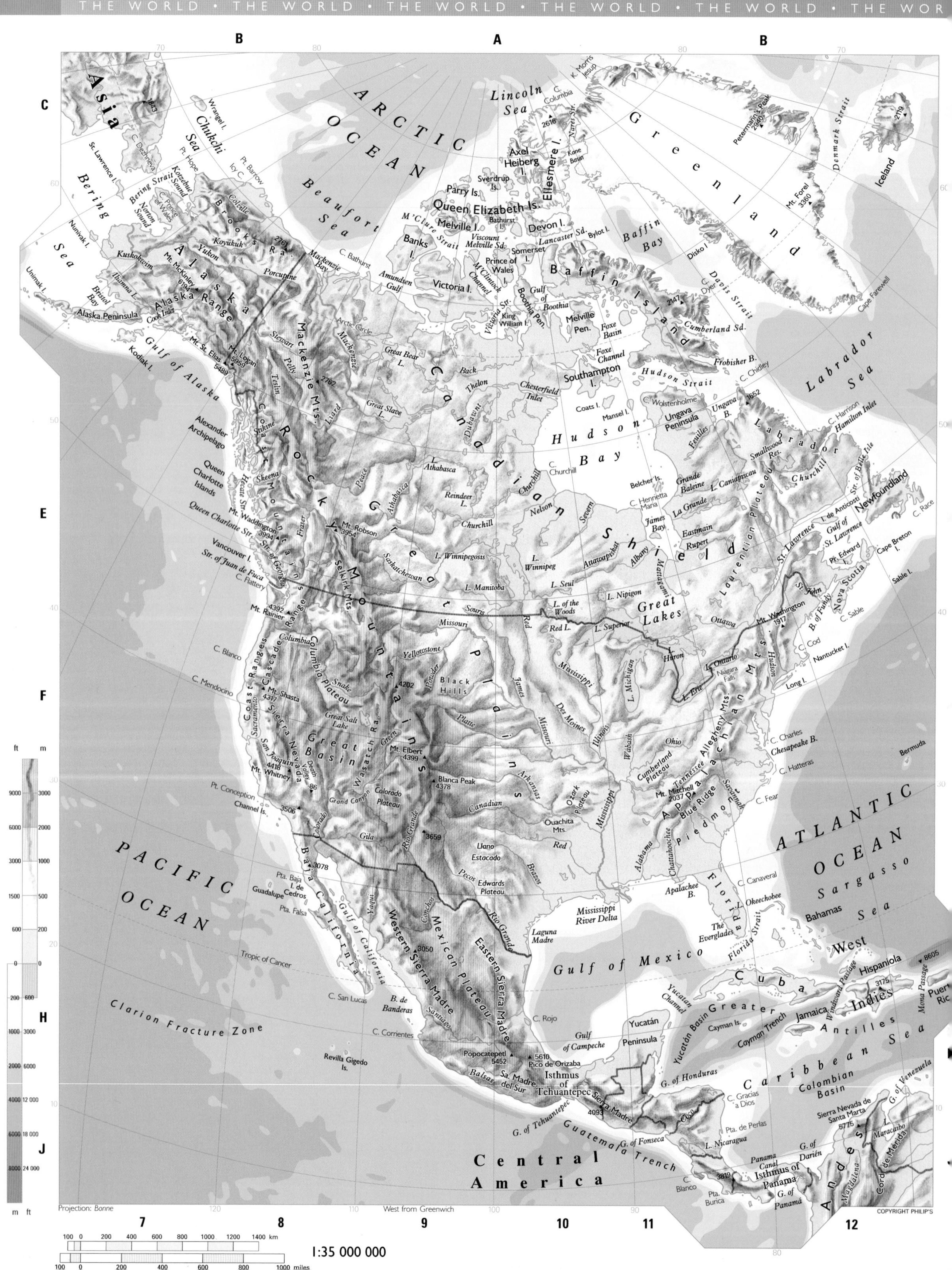
ARCTIC OCEAN
Lincoln Sea
Greenland
Asia
Chukchi Sea
Wrangel I.
Bering Sea
Bering Strait
St. Lawrence I.
Nunivak I.
Unimak I.
Beaufort Sea
Axel Heiberg I.
Ellesmere I.
Sverdrup Is.
Parry Is.
Queen Elizabeth Is.
Melville I.
Bathurst I.
Devon I.
Banks I.
Victoria I.
Prince of Wales I.
Somerset I.
Baffin Bay
Baffin Island
Lancaster Sd.
Bylot I.
Kane Basin
Disko I.
Davis Strait
Cumberland Sd.
Frobisher B.
Hudson Strait
C. Chidley
Labrador Sea
Denmark Strait
Iceland
Mt. Forel 3360
Petermann Peak 2940
Cape Farewell
Alaska
Alaska Range
Brooks Ra.
Mt. McKinley 6194
Alaska Peninsula
Cook Inlet
Kodiak I.
Gulf of Alaska
Mt. St. Elias 5489
Mt. Logan 5959
Yukon
Koyukuk
Kuskokwim
Porcupine
Kotzebue Sound
Norton Sound
Bristol Bay
Iliamna L.
Mackenzie Bay
Mackenzie
Mackenzie Mts.
Amundsen Gulf
Great Bear L.
Great Slave L.
Arctic Circle
Canadian Shield
Back
Thelon
Dubawnt
Chesterfield Inlet
Southampton I.
Foxe Channel
Foxe Basin
Melville Pen.
Boothia Pen.
Gulf of Boothia
King William I.
Victoria Str.
M'Clintock Channel
Viscount Melville Sd.
M'Clure Strait
C. Bathurst
Coats I.
Mansel I.
Hudson Bay
C. Churchill
Churchill
Nelson
Severn
Belcher Is.
James Bay
C. Henrietta Maria
Ungava Peninsula
Ungava B.
Wolstenholme
Labrador
Smallwood Res.
Hamilton Inlet
C. Harrison
Grande Baleine
La Grande
L. Caniapiscau
Eastmain
Rupert
Laurentian Plateau
Newfoundland
Str. of Belle Isle
Gulf of St. Lawrence
I. de Anticosti
C. Race
Cape Breton I.
Pr. Edward I.
Nova Scotia
Sable I.
B. of Fundy
St. John
St. Lawrence
Mt. Washington 1917
C. Sable
C. Cod
Nantucket I.
Long I.
Hudson
Ottawa
Great Lakes
L. Nipigon
L. Superior
L. Michigan
Huron
L. Ontario
L. Erie
Niagara Falls
L. of the Woods
Red L.
L. Seul
L. Winnipeg
L. Winnipegosis
L. Manitoba
L. Athabasca
Reindeer L.
Athabasca
Peace
Liard
Stikine
Skeena
Fraser
Rocky Mountains
Coast Mountains
Mt. Robson 3954
Mt. Waddington 3994
Selkirk Mts.
Saskatchewan
Great Plains
Souris
Missouri
Red
Attawapiskat
Albany
Mattagami
Alexander Archipelago
Queen Charlotte Islands
Hecate Str.
Queen Charlotte Str.
Vancouver I.
Str. of Georgia
Str. of Juan de Fuca
C. Flattery
Mt. Rainier 4392
Cascade Range
Columbia
Columbia Plateau
C. Blanco
C. Mendocino
Mt. Shasta 4317
Coast Ranges
Sacramento
San Joaquin
Sierra Nevada
Mt. Whitney 4418
Death Valley -86
Great Basin
Great Salt Lake
Wasatch Ra.
Snake
Yellowstone
Powder
Black Hills
Green
Mt. Elbert 4399
Blanca Peak 4378
Platte
James
Des Moines
Mississippi
Illinois
Wabash
Ohio
Cumberland Plateau
Tennessee
Allegheny Mts.
Appalachian Mts.
Mt. Mitchell 2037
Blue Ridge
Piedmont
Savannah
C. Charles
Chesapeake B.
C. Hatteras
C. Fear
Bermuda
Ozark Plateau
Arkansas
Ouachita Mts.
Canadian
Llano Estacado
Red
Brazos
Pecos
Edwards Plateau
Rio Grande
Gila
Colorado
Colorado Plateau
Grand Canyon
Pt. Conception
Channel Is.
Alabama
Chattahoochee
Apalachee B.
Florida
C. Canaveral
L. Okeechobee
The Everglades
Florida Strait
Mississippi River Delta
Laguna Madre
Gulf of Mexico
ATLANTIC OCEAN
Sargasso Sea
Bahamas
PACIFIC OCEAN
Baja California
Pta. Baja
I. de Cedros
Guadalupe
Pta. Falsa
Gulf of California
Yaqui
Conchos
Western Sierra Madre
Mexican Plateau
Eastern Sierra Madre
Santiago
Tropic of Cancer
C. San Lucas
B. de Banderas
C. Corrientes
Revilla Gigedo Is.
Clarion Fracture Zone
C. Rojo
Gulf of Campeche
Yucatán Peninsula
Yucatan Channel
Yucatán Basin
Popocatepetl 5452
Pico de Orizaba 5610
Balsas
Sa. Madre del Sur
Isthmus of Tehuantepec
Sierra Madre
G. of Tehuantepec
Guatemala Trench
G. of Honduras
G. of Fonseca
C. Gracias a Dios
Pta. de Perlas
L. Nicaragua
C. Blanco
Pta. Burica
Panama Canal
Isthmus of Panama
G. of Panamá
G. of Darién
Central America
Cuba
West Indies
Greater Antilles
Cayman Is.
Cayman Trench
Jamaica
Windward Passage
Hispaniola
Mona Passage
Caribbean Sea
Colombian Basin
Sierra Nevada de Santa Marta 5775
L. Maracaibo
G. of Venezuela
Andes
Magdalena
Cord. de Mérida
Projection: Bonne
West from Greenwich
COPYRIGHT PHILIP'S
1:35 000 000
km
miles

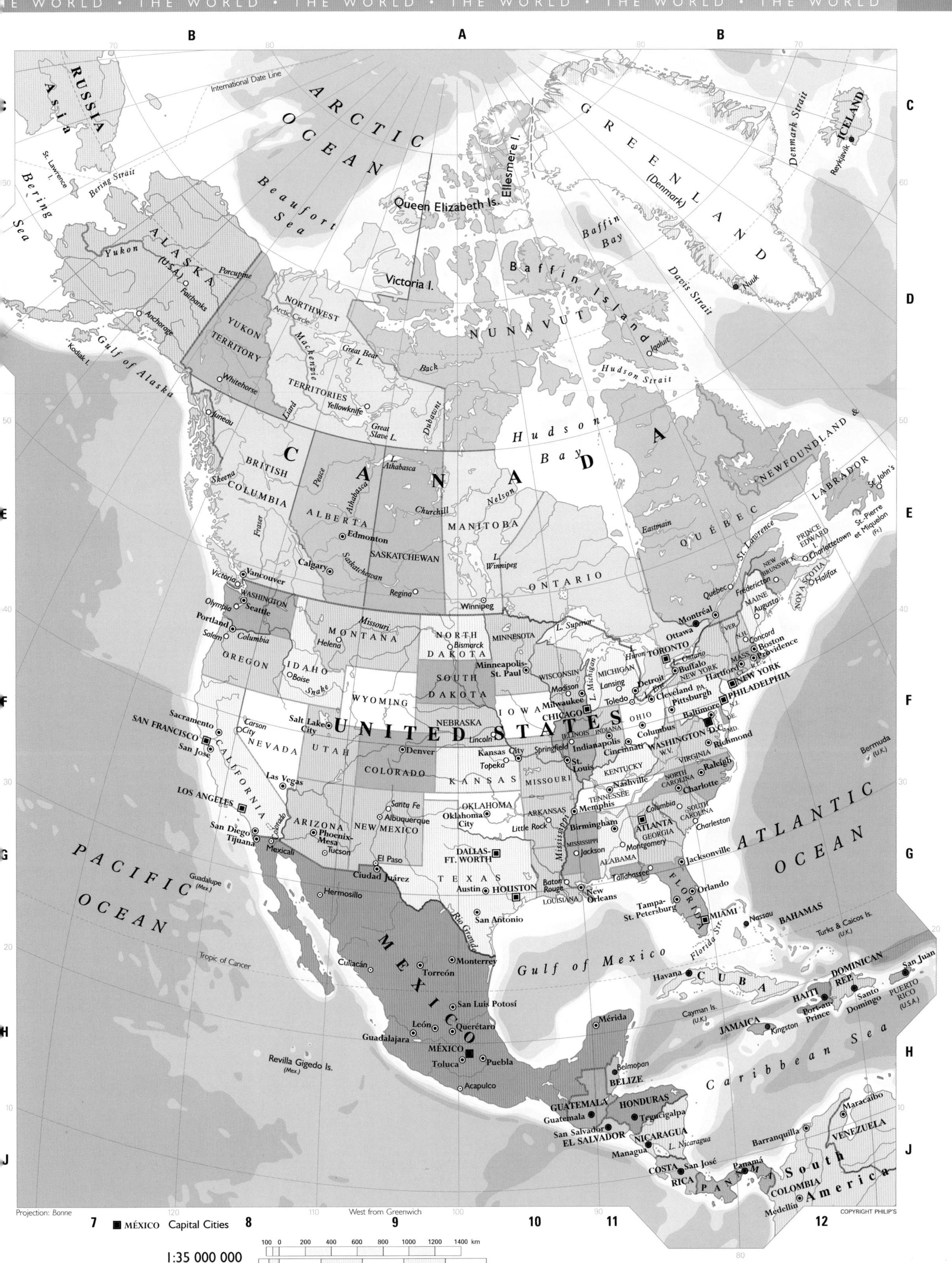

Projection: Bonne

West from Greenwich

7   ■ MÉXICO Capital Cities   8

1:35 000 000

100 0 200 400 600 800 1000 1200 1400 km

COPYRIGHT PHILIP'S

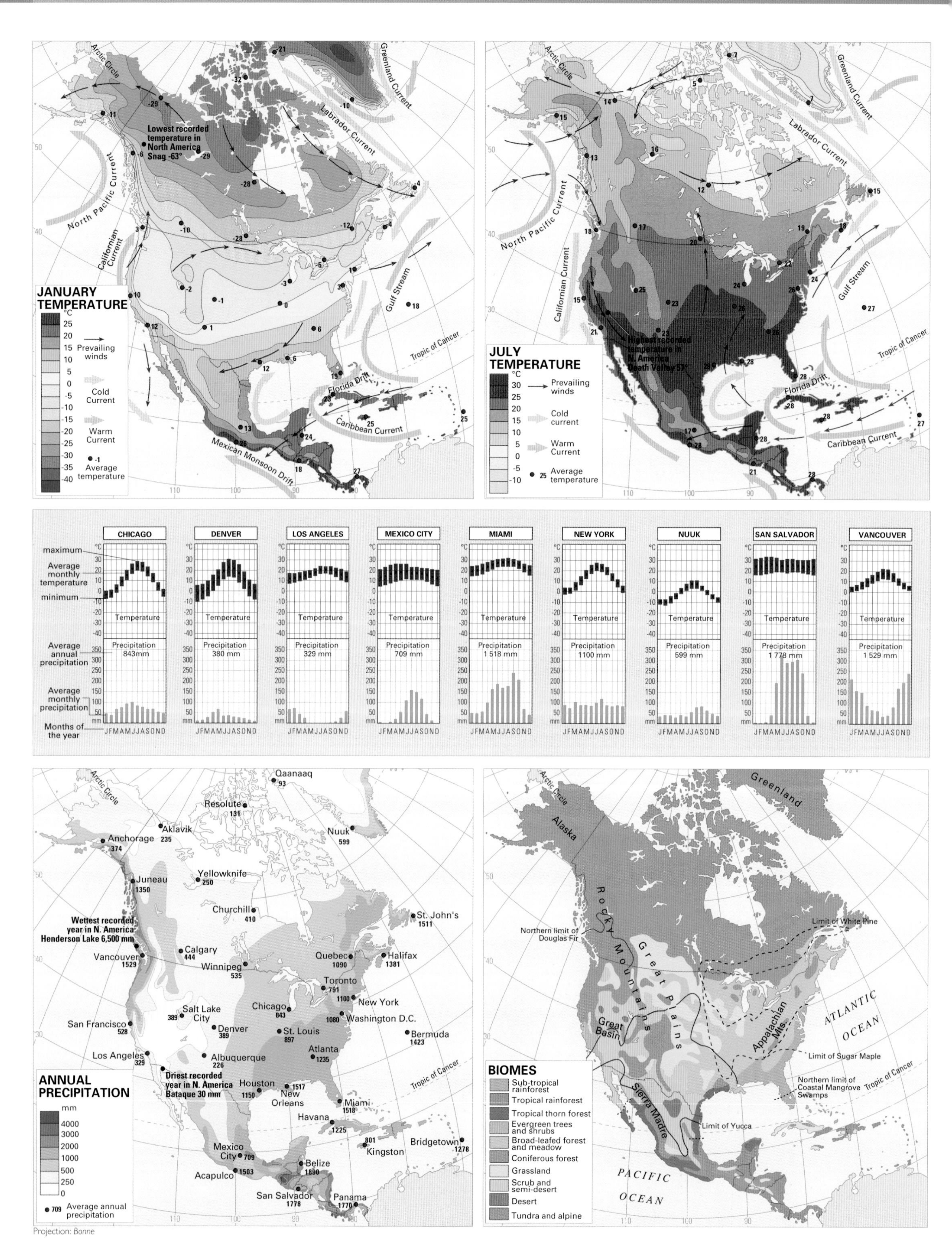

JANUARY TEMPERATURE
°C
25, 20, 15, 10, 5, 0, -5, -10, -15, -20, -25, -30, -35, -40
→ Prevailing winds
Cold Current
Warm Current
-1 Average temperature

Lowest recorded temperature in North America Snag -63°

JULY TEMPERATURE
°C
30, 25, 20, 15, 10, 5, 0, -5, -10
→ Prevailing winds
Cold current
Warm Current
25 Average temperature

Highest recorded temperature in N. America Death Valley 57°

Climate graphs: CHICAGO, DENVER, LOS ANGELES, MEXICO CITY, MIAMI, NEW YORK, NUUK, SAN SALVADOR, VANCOUVER

maximum / Average monthly temperature / minimum
Average annual precipitation / Average monthly precipitation / Months of the year

- Chicago — Precipitation 843mm
- Denver — Precipitation 380 mm
- Los Angeles — Precipitation 329 mm
- Mexico City — Precipitation 709 mm
- Miami — Precipitation 1 518 mm
- New York — Precipitation 1100 mm
- Nuuk — Precipitation 599 mm
- San Salvador — Precipitation 1 778 mm
- Vancouver — Precipitation 1 529 mm

ANNUAL PRECIPITATION
mm
4000, 3000, 2000, 1000, 500, 250, 0
709 Average annual precipitation

Wettest recorded year in N. America Henderson Lake 6,500 mm
Driest recorded year in N. America Bataque 30 mm

Qaanaaq 93, Resolute 131, Aklavik, Anchorage 374, Nuuk 599, Juneau 1350, Yellowknife 250, Churchill 410, St. John's 1511, Calgary 444, Vancouver 1529, Winnipeg 535, Quebec 1090, Halifax 1381, Toronto 791, New York 1100, Salt Lake City 389, Chicago 843, Washington D.C. 1080, San Francisco 528, Denver 389, St. Louis 897, Atlanta 1235, Bermuda 1423, Los Angeles 329, Albuquerque 226, Houston 1517, New Orleans 1150, Miami 1518, Havana 1225, Mexico City 709, Belize 1890, Bridgetown 1278, Kingston 801, Acapulco 1503, San Salvador 1778, Panama 1770

Projection: Bonne

BIOMES
- Sub-tropical rainforest
- Tropical rainforest
- Tropical thorn forest
- Evergreen trees and shrubs
- Broad-leafed forest and meadow
- Coniferous forest
- Grassland
- Scrub and semi-desert
- Desert
- Tundra and alpine

Northern limit of Douglas Fir
Limit of White Pine
Limit of Sugar Maple
Northern limit of Coastal Mangrove Swamps
Limit of Yucca

Rocky Mountains, Great Plains, Great Basin, Appalachian Mts., Sierra Madre
Greenland, Alaska
ATLANTIC OCEAN, PACIFIC OCEAN

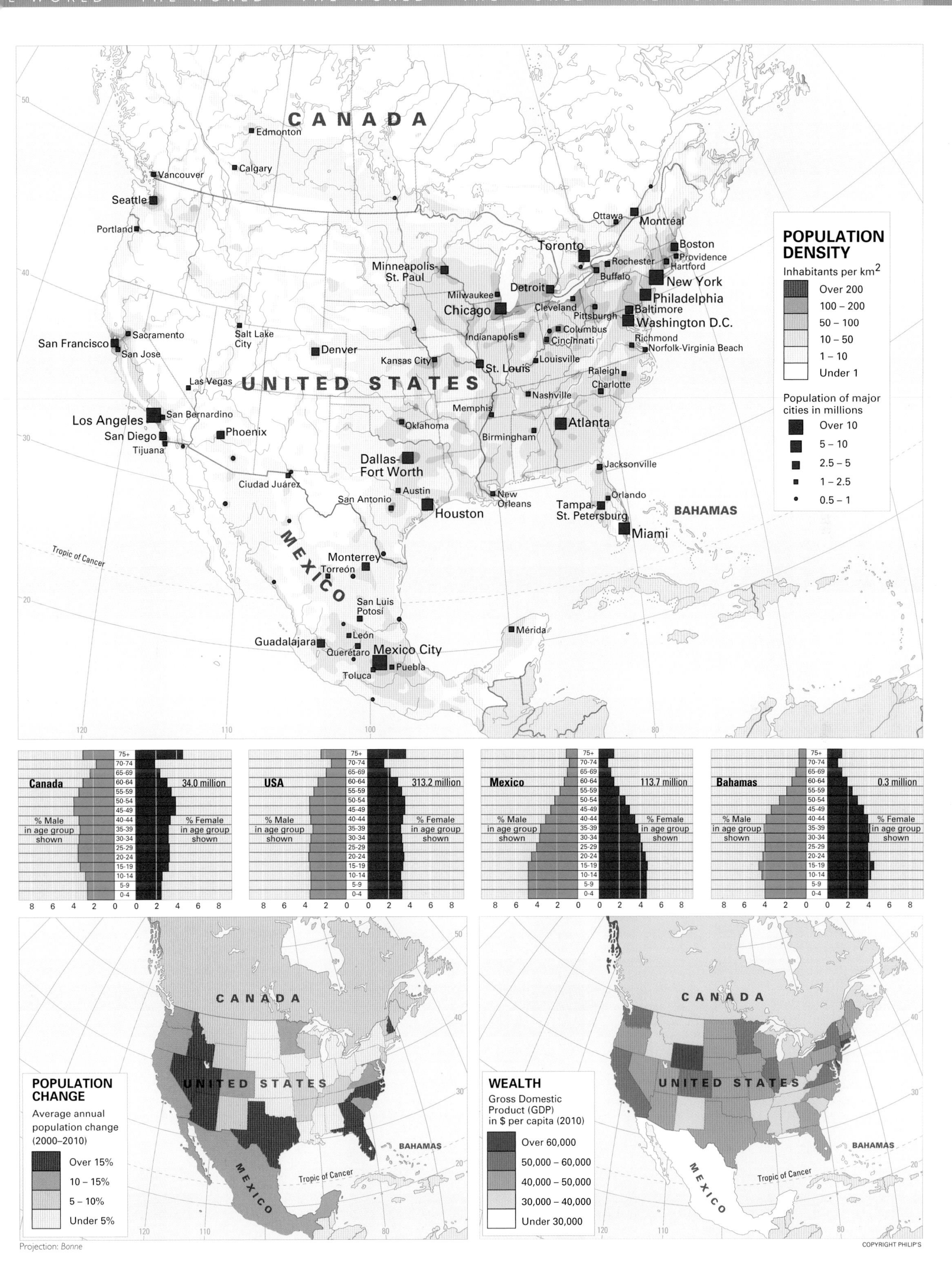

POPULATION
DENSITY

Inhabitants per km^2

Over 200
100 – 200
50 – 100
10 – 50
1 – 10
Under 1

Population of major
cities in millions

■ Over 10
■ 5 – 10
■ 2.5 – 5
■ 1 – 2.5
• 0.5 – 1

Canada 34.0 million
% Male in age group shown / % Female in age group shown

USA 313.2 million
% Male in age group shown / % Female in age group shown

Mexico 113.7 million
% Male in age group shown / % Female in age group shown

Bahamas 0.3 million
% Male in age group shown / % Female in age group shown

POPULATION
CHANGE

Average annual
population change
(2000–2010)

Over 15%
10 – 15%
5 – 10%
Under 5%

WEALTH

Gross Domestic
Product (GDP)
in $ per capita (2010)

Over 60,000
50,000 – 60,000
40,000 – 50,000
30,000 – 40,000
Under 30,000

Projection: Bonne

COPYRIGHT PHILIP'S

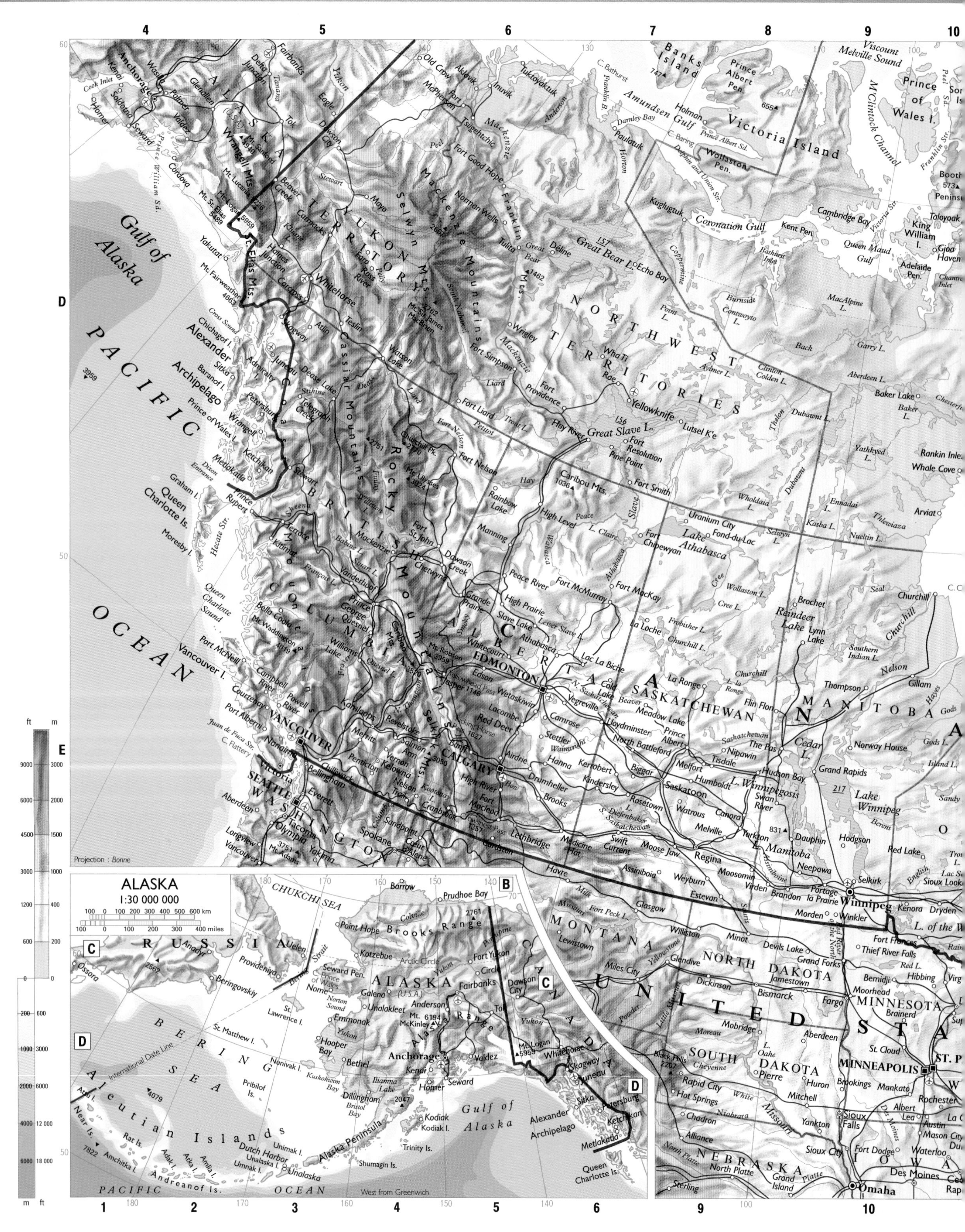
Gulf of Alaska
PACIFIC OCEAN
ALASKA
YUKON TERRITORY
NORTHWEST TERRITORIES
BRITISH COLUMBIA
ALBERTA
SASKATCHEWAN
MANITOBA
WASHINGTON
MONTANA
NORTH DAKOTA
SOUTH DAKOTA
MINNESOTA
NEBRASKA
IOWA
UNITED STATES
Victoria Island
Banks Island
Prince of Wales I.
Amundsen Gulf
Great Bear L.
Great Slave L.
Lake Athabasca
Lake Winnipeg
Rocky Mountains
Mackenzie Mountains
Selwyn Mts.
Cassiar Mountains
Coast Mountains
Queen Charlotte Is.
Vancouver I.
Alexander Archipelago
Anchorage
Fairbanks
Whitehorse
Dawson City
Inuvik
Yellowknife
Edmonton
Calgary
Vancouver
Victoria
Seattle
Saskatoon
Regina
Winnipeg
Churchill
Minneapolis
Omaha
Projection : Bonne
ALASKA
1:30 000 000
CHUKCHI SEA
BERING SEA
Aleutian Islands
RUSSIA
CANADA
Brooks Range
Alaska Range
Gulf of Alaska
International Date Line
West from Greenwich
PACIFIC OCEAN

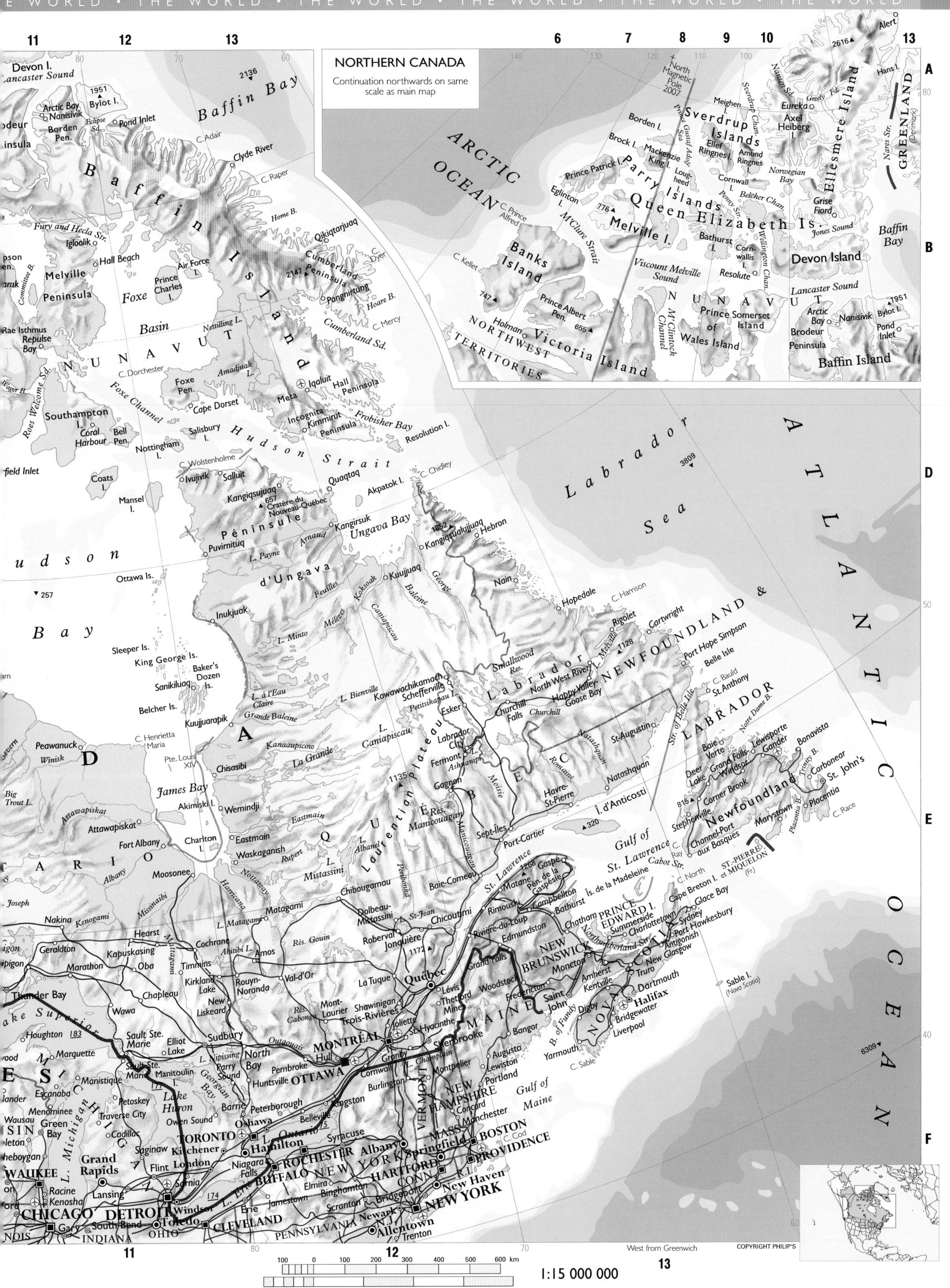

NORTHERN CANADA

Continuation northwards on same scale as main map

1:15 000 000

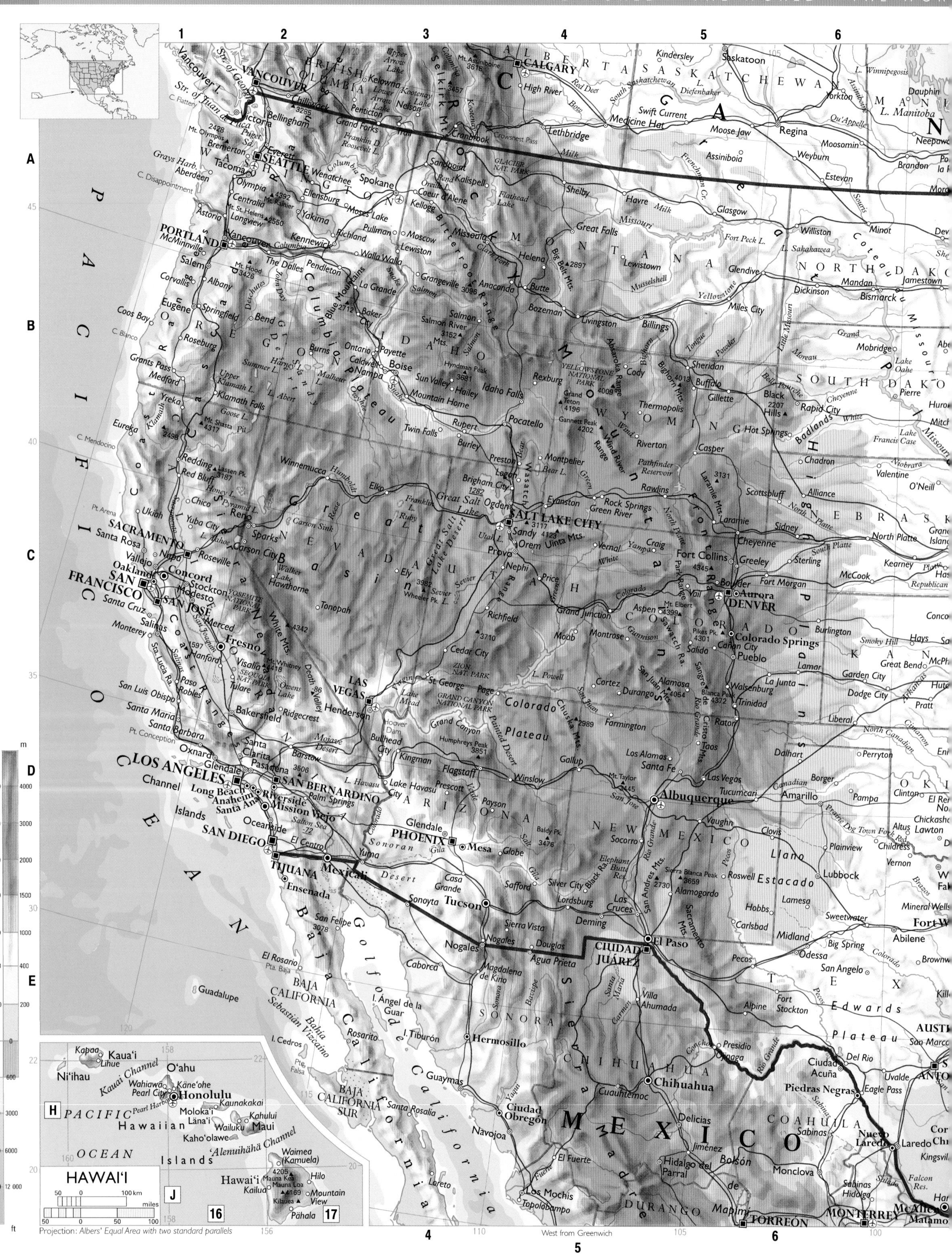

Projection: Albers' Equal Area with two standard parallels

West from Greenwich

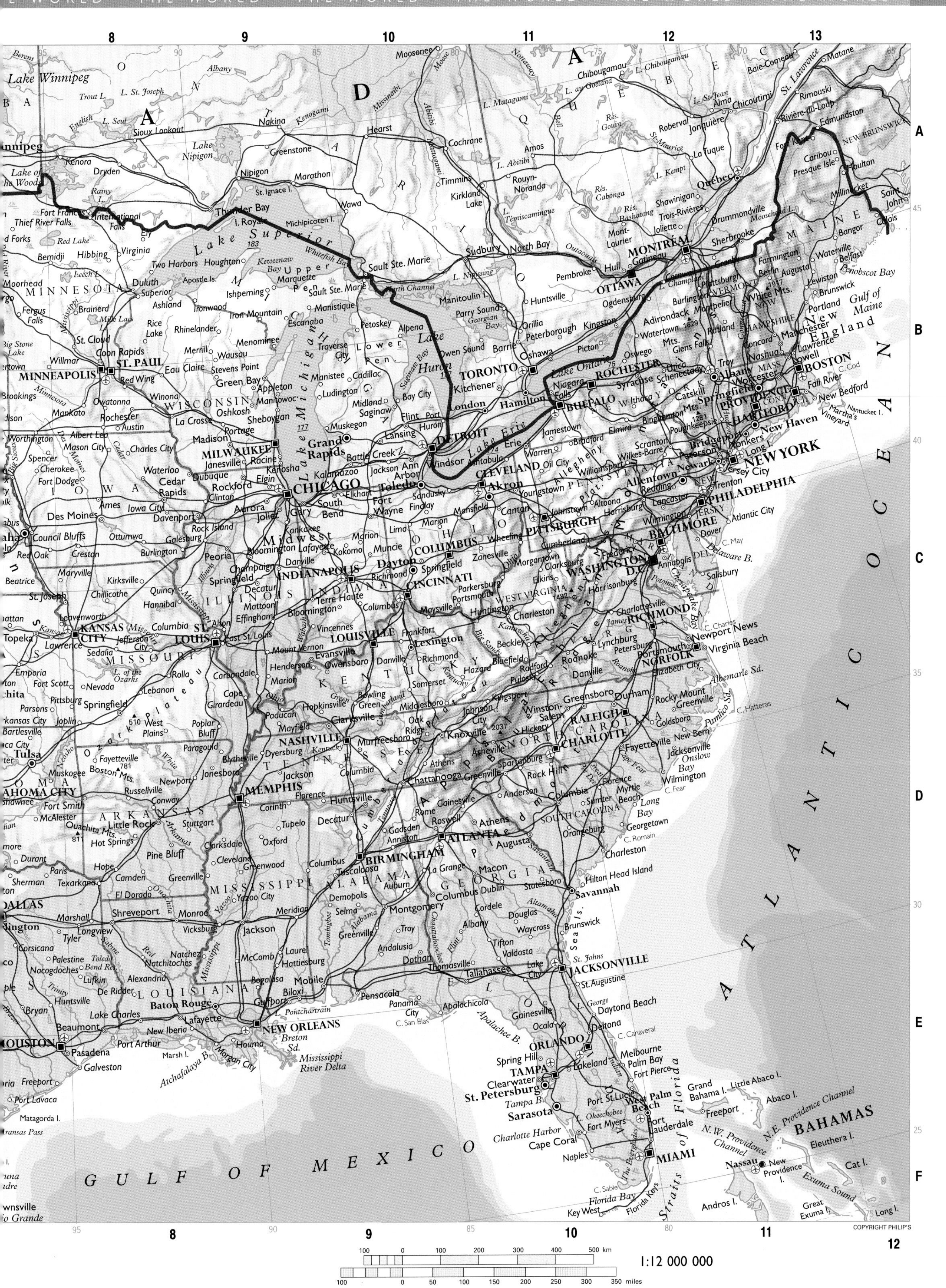

1:12 000 000

COPYRIGHT PHILIP'S

C A N A D A
Q U E B E C
O N T A R I O
Lake Winnipeg
Lake of the Woods
Lake Nipigon
Lake Superior
Lake Michigan
Lake Huron
Georgian Bay
Lake Erie
Lake Ontario
L. Nipissing
L. Abitibi
L. Témiscamingue
L. St. Joseph
L. Seul
L. Matagami
L. Chibougamau
L. St-Jean
L. Kempt
Rés. Gouin
Rés. Cabonga
Rés. Baskatong
Moosonee
Hearst
Cochrane
Timmins
Kirkland Lake
Rouyn-Noranda
Amos
Chibougamau
Roberval
Jonquière
Alma
Chicoutimi
Baie-Comeau
Matane
Rimouski
Rivière-du-Loup
Edmundston
La Tuque
Québec
Shawinigan
Trois-Rivières
Drummondville
Sherbrooke
Joliette
Mont-Laurier
MONTRÉAL
Gatineau
Hull
OTTAWA
Pembroke
North Bay
Sudbury
Sault Ste. Marie
Wawa
Marathon
Nipigon
Thunder Bay
Kenora
Dryden
Fort Frances
International Falls
Sioux Lookout
Nakina
Greenstone
Huntsville
Parry Sound
Orillia
Barrie
Peterborough
Kingston
Oshawa
TORONTO
Kitchener
London
Hamilton
Windsor
Owen Sound
Manitoulin I.
St. Lawrence
NEW BRUNSWICK
Saint John
Calais
Fort Kent
Caribou
Presque Isle
Houlton
Millinocket
Bangor
Waterville
Belfast
Penobscot Bay
Gulf of Maine
Augusta
Lewiston
Brunswick
Portland
Farmington
Berlin
White Mts.
Mt. Washington 1917
MAINE
NEW HAMPSHIRE
VERMONT
New England
Concord
Manchester
Nashua
Lowell
Lawrence
BOSTON
Worcester
Fall River
New Bedford
Martha's Vineyard
Nantucket I.
C. Cod
PROVIDENCE
HARTFORD
New Haven
Springfield
Albany
Troy
Rutland
Montpelier
Burlington
Plattsburgh
L. Champlain
Adirondack Mts.
Mt. Marcy 1629
Glens Falls
Watertown
Ogdensburg
Oswego
Syracuse
Utica
Schenectady
ROCHESTER
BUFFALO
Niagara Falls
Ithaca
Binghamton
Elmira
Catskill Mts.
Poughkeepsie
Bridgeport
Yonkers
Long I.
NEW YORK
Jersey City
Newark
Paterson
Trenton
Allentown
Reading
Scranton
Wilkes-Barre
Williamsport
PENNSYLVANIA
Lancaster
Harrisburg
PHILADELPHIA
Wilmington
Atlantic City
Dover
C. May
Delaware B.
BALTIMORE
WASHINGTON D.C.
Annapolis
Salisbury
Chesapeake Bay
Potomac
Frederick
Cumberland
Hagerstown
Altoona
Johnstown
PITTSBURGH
Allegheny Plat.
Erie
Jamestown
Bradford
Oil City
Warren
Youngstown
Akron
CLEVELAND
Ashtabula
Canton
Mansfield
Sandusky
Toledo
Findlay
Lima
Marion
COLUMBUS
Zanesville
Wheeling
Dayton
Springfield
CINCINNATI
Hamilton
Richmond
Muncie
Kokomo
Lafayette
INDIANAPOLIS
Fort Wayne
South Bend
Elkhart
Gary
CHICAGO
Joliet
Aurora
Elgin
Kankakee
Rockford
Kenosha
Racine
MILWAUKEE
Janesville
Madison
Sheboygan
Oshkosh
Appleton
Manitowoc
Green Bay
Stevens Point
Wausau
Eau Claire
La Crosse
WISCONSIN
Rhinelander
Merrill
Menominee
Escanaba
Marquette
Ishpeming
Iron Mountain
Ironwood
Ashland
Houghton
Keweenaw Bay
Upper Peninsula
Manistique
Petoskey
Alpena
Traverse City
Cadillac
Manistee
Ludington
Midland
Saginaw
Saginaw Bay
Bay City
Flint
Port Huron
Lansing
Grand Rapids
Muskegon
Kalamazoo
Battle Creek
Jackson
Ann Arbor
DETROIT
MICHIGAN
Lower Peninsula
Duluth
Superior
Two Harbors
Apostle Is.
I. Royale
Michipicoten I.
Whitefish Bay
MINNESOTA
Hibbing
Virginia
Ely
Bemidji
Thief River Falls
Grand Forks
Red Lake
Moorhead
Fergus Falls
Brainerd
Mille Lacs
St. Cloud
Coon Rapids
MINNEAPOLIS
ST. PAUL
Red Wing
Winona
Rochester
Austin
Owatonna
Mankato
Albert Lea
Mason City
Charles City
Waterloo
Cedar Rapids
Dubuque
Clinton
Davenport
Iowa City
Des Moines
Ames
Fort Dodge
Spencer
Cherokee
Council Bluffs
Ottumwa
Burlington
Creston
Red Oak
IOWA
Rock Island
Galesburg
Peoria
Bloomington
Champaign
Decatur
Springfield
Quincy
Hannibal
Mattoon
Effingham
ILLINOIS
INDIANA
Midwest
Terre Haute
Bloomington
Columbus
Danville
Vincennes
Evansville
Mount Vernon
Owensboro
Henderson
Carbondale
Marion
Paducah
Mayfield
LOUISVILLE
Frankfort
Lexington
Richmond
Danville
Somerset
Hazard
KENTUCKY
Maysville
Huntington
Portsmouth
Parkersburg
Charleston
Clarksburg
Morgantown
Elkins
WEST VIRGINIA
Beckley
Bluefield
Harrisonburg
Charlottesville
RICHMOND
Lynchburg
Roanoke
Petersburg
Danville
Radford
Pulaski
Portsmouth
NORFOLK
Newport News
Virginia Beach
Elizabeth City
C. Charles
Albemarle Sd.
Pamlico Sd.
C. Hatteras
Rocky Mount
Greenville
Goldsboro
New Bern
Jacksonville
Onslow Bay
Wilmington
C. Fear
Fayetteville
RALEIGH
Durham
Greensboro
Winston-Salem
Hickory
NORTH CAROLINA
CHARLOTTE
Asheville
Mt. Mitchell 2037
Kingsport
Johnson City
Knoxville
Oak Ridge
Middlesboro
Bowling Green
Hopkinsville
Clarksville
NASHVILLE
Murfreesboro
Columbia
Jackson
TENNESSEE
Dyersburg
MEMPHIS
Chattanooga
Athens
Cleveland
Spartanburg
Greenville
Anderson
Rock Hill
Columbia
Sumter
Florence
Myrtle Beach
Long Bay
Georgetown
C. Romain
Charleston
SOUTH CAROLINA
Orangeburg
Augusta
Hilton Head Island
Savannah
Statesboro
ATLANTA
Athens
Gainesville
Rome
Roswell
Anniston
Gadsden
BIRMINGHAM
Tuscaloosa
Huntsville
Florence
Decatur
ALABAMA
Auburn
La Grange
Macon
Columbus
Dublin
GEORGIA
Montgomery
Selma
Demopolis
Troy
Greenville
Dothan
Andalusia
Albany
Cordele
Tifton
Douglas
Waycross
Brunswick
Valdosta
Thomasville
Tallahassee
Lake City
JACKSONVILLE
St. Augustine
Gainesville
Ocala
Daytona Beach
Deltona
ORLANDO
C. Canaveral
Melbourne
Palm Bay
Fort Pierce
Lakeland
Spring Hill
Clearwater
TAMPA
St. Petersburg
Tampa B.
Sarasota
Charlotte Harbor
Cape Coral
Fort Myers
Naples
L. Okeechobee
Port St. Lucie
West Palm Beach
Fort Lauderdale
MIAMI
C. Sable
Florida Bay
Florida Keys
Key West
The Everglades
Straits of Florida
FLORIDA
Apalachicola
Panama City
C. San Blas
Apalachee B.
Pensacola
Mobile
Biloxi
Gulfport
Hattiesburg
Laurel
Meridian
Jackson
Vicksburg
McComb
Natchez
Bogalusa
Tupelo
Oxford
Corinth
Clarksdale
Greenwood
Cleveland
Greenville
Yazoo City
MISSISSIPPI
NEW ORLEANS
L. Pontchartrain
Breton Sd.
Mississippi River Delta
Houma
Morgan City
Atchafalaya B.
Marsh I.
Baton Rouge
Lafayette
New Iberia
Lake Charles
LOUISIANA
Alexandria
Natchitoches
De Ridder
Monroe
Shreveport
El Dorado
Camden
Texarkana
Hope
Pine Bluff
Stuttgart
Little Rock
Hot Springs
Ouachita Mts.
ARKANSAS
Conway
Russellville
Fort Smith
Fayetteville
Boston Mts.
Jonesboro
Newport
Blytheville
Paragould
Poplar Bluff
West Plains
Ozark Plateau
Springfield
Joplin
Rolla
Lebanon
Cape Girardeau
ST. LOUIS
East St. Louis
Alton
Columbia
Jefferson City
Sedalia
MISSOURI
L. of the Ozarks
KANSAS CITY
Lawrence
Topeka
Leavenworth
St. Joseph
Chillicothe
Kirksville
Maryville
Beatrice
Emporia
Fort Scott
Nevada
Pittsburg
Parsons
Bartlesville
Tulsa
Muskogee
McAlester
OKLAHOMA CITY
Shawnee
Durant
Paris
Sherman
DALLAS
Marshall
Longview
Tyler
Corsicana
Palestine
Nacogdoches
Lufkin
Huntsville
Bryan
Beaumont
Port Arthur
HOUSTON
Pasadena
Galveston
Freeport
Port Lavaca
Matagorda I.
Toledo Bend Res.
GULF OF MEXICO
ATLANTIC OCEAN
Grand Bahama I.
Freeport
Little Abaco I.
Abaco I.
N.E. Providence Channel
N.W. Providence Channel
BAHAMAS
Nassau
New Providence I.
Eleuthera I.
Exuma Sound
Cat I.
Great Exuma I.
Andros I.
Long I.
100 0 100 200 300 400 500 km
100 0 50 100 150 200 250 300 350 miles

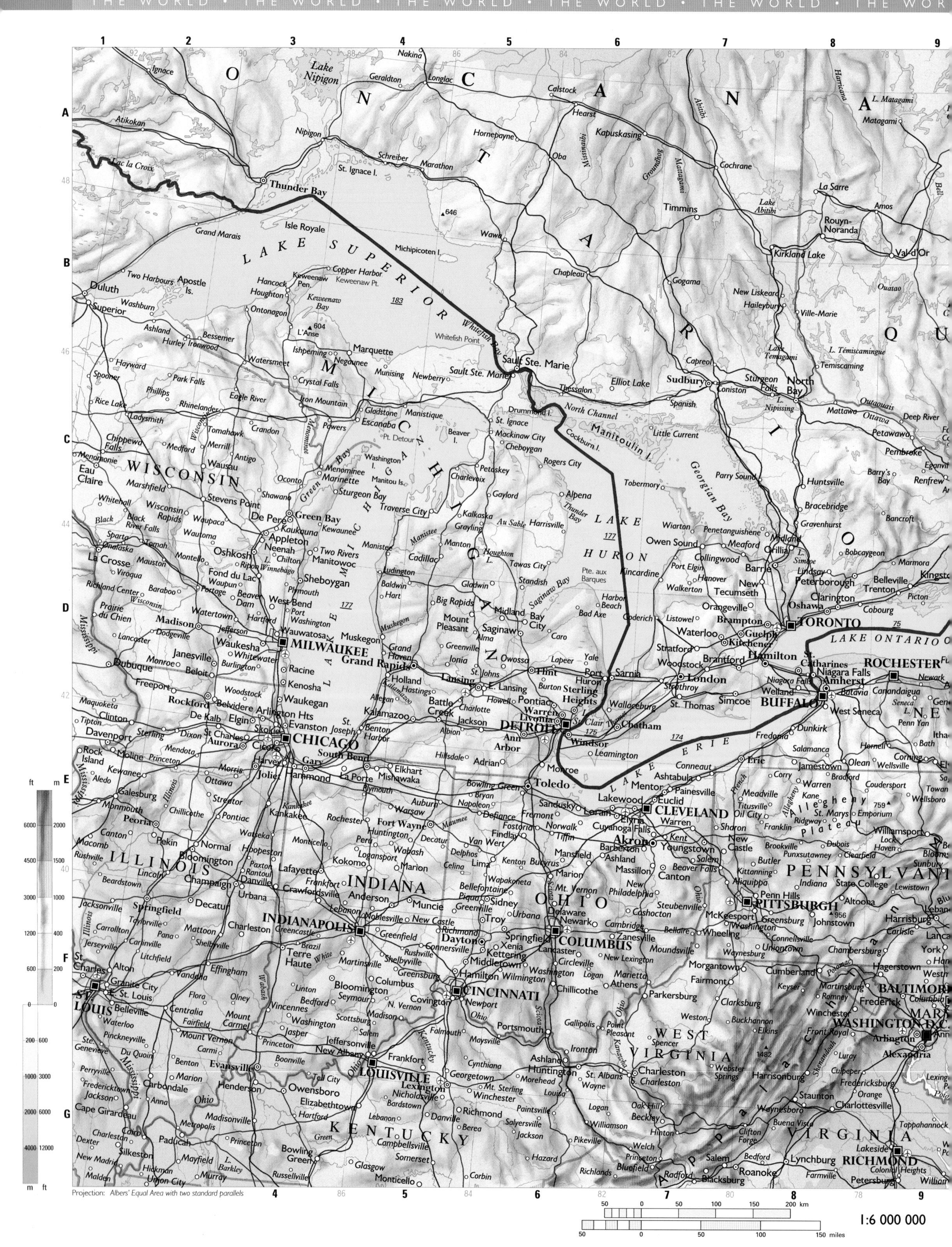
ONTARIO
CANADA
QU
LAKE SUPERIOR
LAKE MICHIGAN
LAKE HURON
LAKE ONTARIO
LAKE ERIE
Georgian Bay
North Channel
Manitoulin I.
Green Bay
Saginaw Bay
Lake Nipigon
Lake Abitibi
L. Nipissing
WISCONSIN
MICHIGAN
ILLINOIS
INDIANA
OHIO
KENTUCKY
WEST VIRGINIA
VIRGINIA
PENNSYLVANIA
Allegheny Plateau
Appalachian
Thunder Bay
Duluth
Superior
Sault Ste. Marie
Sudbury
Timmins
North Bay
TORONTO
Hamilton
London
Windsor
DETROIT
Flint
Lansing
Grand Rapids
Saginaw
Toledo
CLEVELAND
Akron
Youngstown
COLUMBUS
Dayton
CINCINNATI
Erie
BUFFALO
ROCHESTER
PITTSBURGH
MILWAUKEE
CHICAGO
Madison
Green Bay
Rockford
Peoria
Springfield
INDIANAPOLIS
Fort Wayne
South Bend
LOUISVILLE
Lexington
Evansville
ST. LOUIS
Charleston
Huntington
WASHINGTON D.C.
BALTIMORE
RICHMOND
Projection: Albers' Equal Area with two standard parallels
1:6 000 000
km
miles

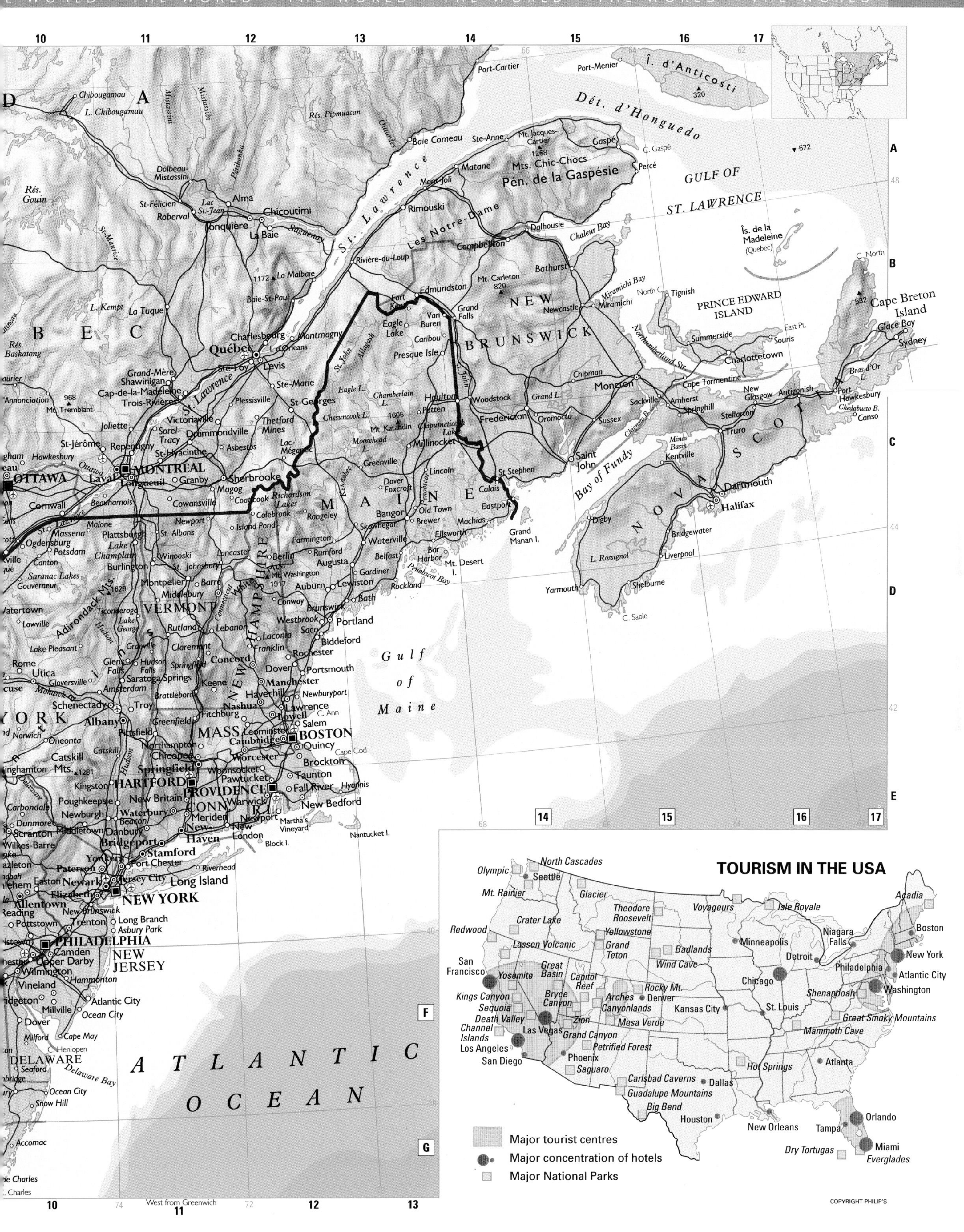
Î. d'Anticosti
Dét. d'Honguedo
GULF OF ST. LAWRENCE
Pén. de la Gaspésie
Mts. Chic-Chocs
St. Lawrence
Les Notre-Dame
Chaleur Bay
Îs. de la Madeleine (Quebec)
PRINCE EDWARD ISLAND
Cape Breton Island
NEW BRUNSWICK
NOVA SCOTIA
Bay of Fundy
Northumberland Str.
MAINE
VERMONT
NEW HAMPSHIRE
MASS.
CONN.
R.I.
NEW YORK
NEW JERSEY
DELAWARE
Delaware Bay
Gulf of Maine
ATLANTIC OCEAN
Adirondack Mts.
White Mts.
Catskill Mts.
Long Island
Cape Cod
Martha's Vineyard
Nantucket I.
Block I.
Grand Manan I.
Mt. Desert I.
Penobscot Bay
C. Sable
C. Gaspé
C. North
Québec
MONTREAL
OTTAWA
BOSTON
PROVIDENCE
HARTFORD
NEW YORK
PHILADELPHIA
Halifax
Saint John
Fredericton
Charlottetown
Sydney
Moncton
Portland
Bangor
Augusta
Concord
Springfield
Albany
Chicoutimi
Trois-Rivières
Sherbrooke
Rimouski
Gaspé
West from Greenwich
TOURISM IN THE USA
Major tourist centres
Major concentration of hotels
Major National Parks
COPYRIGHT PHILIP'S

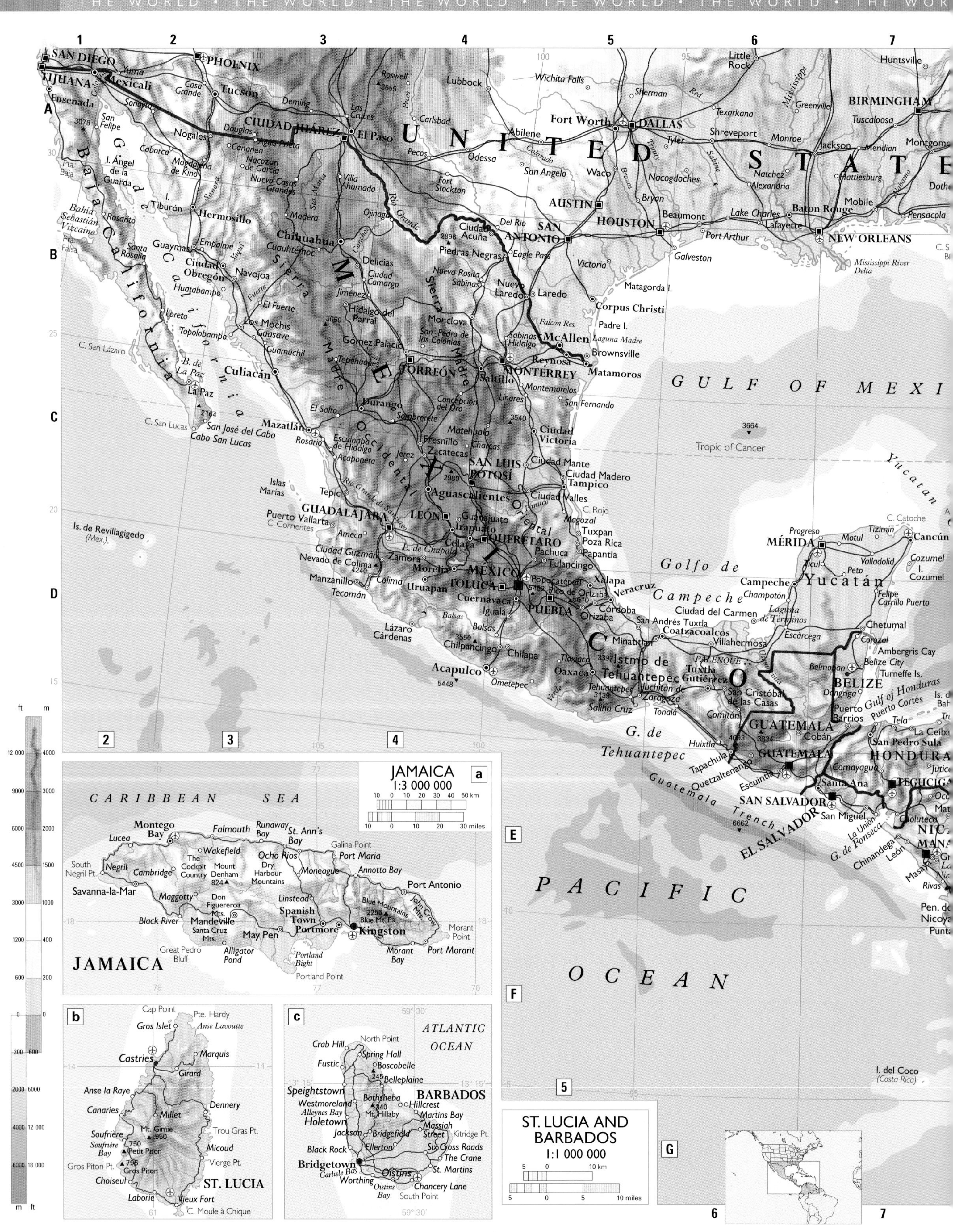
UNITED STATES
MEXICO
GULF OF MEXICO
PACIFIC OCEAN
Golfo de Campeche
Yucatán
Gulf of Honduras
G. de Tehuantepec
Guatemala Trench
Tropic of Cancer
Sierra Madre Occidental
Sierra Madre Oriental
Baja California
Golfo de California
Istmo de Tehuantepec
SAN DIEGO
TIJUANA
Mexicali
Yuma
Ensenada
PHOENIX
Tucson
Nogales
CIUDAD JUÁREZ
El Paso
Chihuahua
Hermosillo
Guaymas
Ciudad Obregón
Navojoa
Los Mochis
Culiacán
La Paz
Cabo San Lucas
San José del Cabo
Mazatlán
Durango
TORREÓN
MONTERREY
Saltillo
Nuevo Laredo
Laredo
Reynosa
McAllen
Matamoros
Brownsville
Corpus Christi
SAN ANTONIO
AUSTIN
HOUSTON
DALLAS
Fort Worth
NEW ORLEANS
BIRMINGHAM
Zacatecas
SAN LUIS POTOSÍ
Aguascalientes
GUADALAJARA
LEÓN
Guanajuato
QUERÉTARO
MEXICO
TOLUCA
PUEBLA
Cuernavaca
Acapulco
Veracruz
Xalapa
Tampico
Ciudad Victoria
Oaxaca
Coatzacoalcos
Villahermosa
Campeche
MÉRIDA
Cancún
Cozumel
Chetumal
BELIZE
Belmopan
Belize City
GUATEMALA
SAN SALVADOR
EL SALVADOR
TEGUCIGALPA
HONDURAS
San Pedro Sula
Tapachula
Quetzaltenango
Tuxtla Gutiérrez
San Cristóbal de las Casas
Popocatépetl 5452
Pico de Orizaba 5610
Is. de Revillagigedo (Mex.)
I. del Coco (Costa Rica)
JAMAICA
1:3 000 000
CARIBBEAN SEA
Montego Bay
Falmouth
Ocho Rios
Port Maria
Port Antonio
Kingston
Spanish Town
Portmore
May Pen
Mandeville
Savanna-la-Mar
Negril
Lucea
Blue Mountains
Blue Mt. Pk. 2256
John Crow Mts.
Morant Point
Port Morant
Black River
ST. LUCIA
Castries
Gros Islet
Cap Point
Soufrière
Vieux Fort
Mt. Gimie 950
Petit Piton
Gros Piton
BARBADOS
ATLANTIC OCEAN
Bridgetown
Speightstown
Holetown
Oistins
Bathsheba
Mt. Hillaby 340
North Point
South Point
ST. LUCIA AND BARBADOS
1:1 000 000

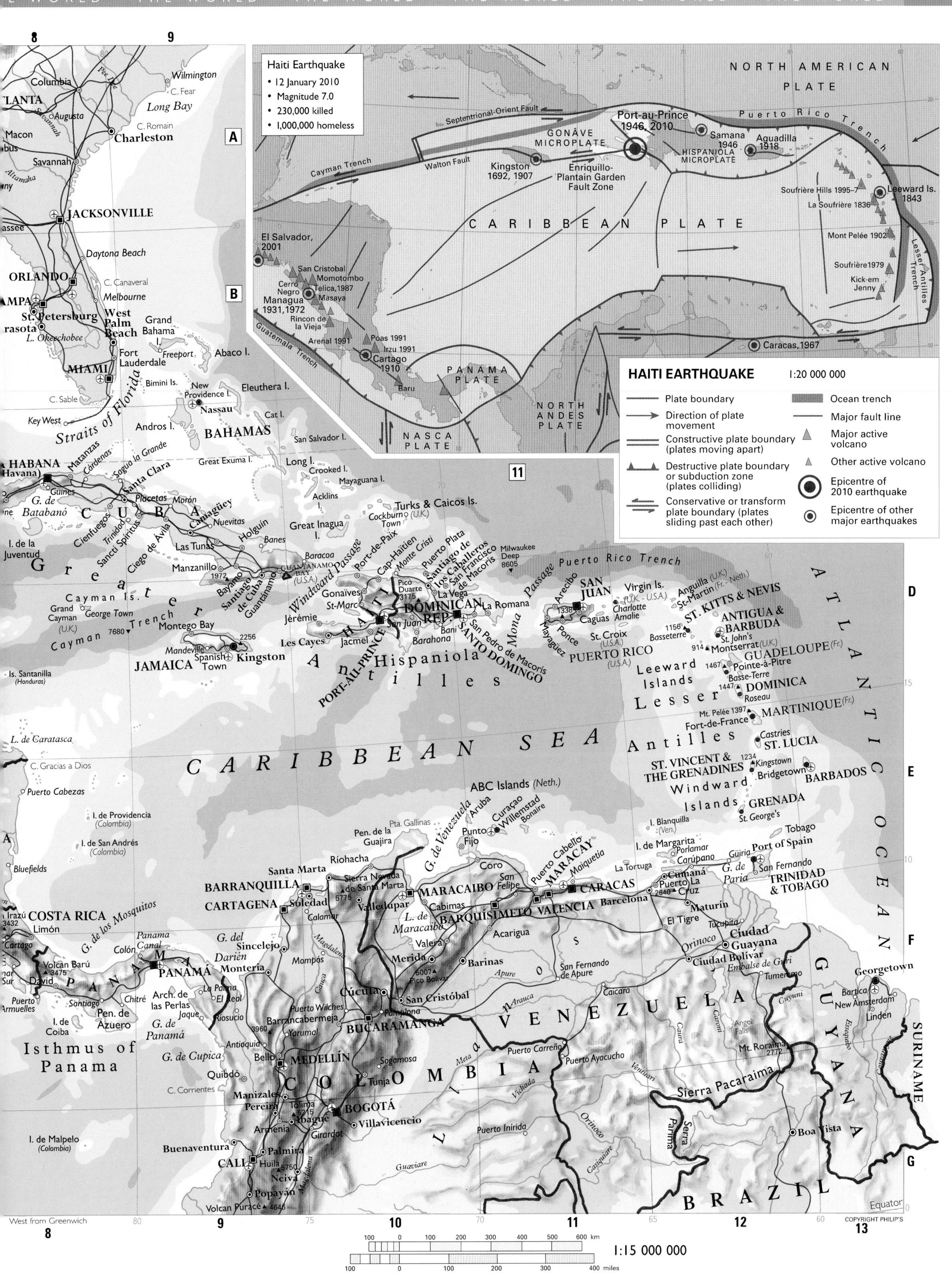
Haiti Earthquake
• 12 January 2010
• Magnitude 7.0
• 230,000 killed
• 1,000,000 homeless
NORTH AMERICAN PLATE
Septentrional-Orient Fault
Port-au-Prince 1946, 2010
Puerto Rico Trench
GONÂVE MICROPLATE
HISPANIOLA MICROPLATE
Samana 1946
Aguadilla 1918
Cayman Trench
Walton Fault
Kingston 1692, 1907
Enriquillo-Plantain Garden Fault Zone
Soufrière Hills 1995–7
La Soufrière 1836
Leeward Is. 1843
CARIBBEAN PLATE
El Salvador, 2001
Mont Pelée 1902
Lesser Antilles Trench
Soufrière1979
Kick-em Jenny
San Cristobal
Momotombo
Cerro Negro
Telica,1987
Masaya
Managua 1931,1972
Rincon de la Vieja
Guatemala Trench
Arenal 1991
Poas 1991
Irazu 1991
Cartago 1910
Baru
PANAMA PLATE
NASCA PLATE
NORTH ANDES PLATE
Caracas,1967
HAITI EARTHQUAKE 1:20 000 000
Plate boundary
Direction of plate movement
Constructive plate boundary (plates moving apart)
Destructive plate boundary or subduction zone (plates colliding)
Conservative or transform plate boundary (plates sliding past each other)
Ocean trench
Major fault line
Major active volcano
Other active volcano
Epicentre of 2010 earthquake
Epicentre of other major earthquakes
Wilmington
C. Fear
Long Bay
C. Romain
Charleston
Columbia
Augusta
Macon
Savannah
JACKSONVILLE
Daytona Beach
ORLANDO
C. Canaveral
Melbourne
St. Petersburg
West Palm Beach
L. Okeechobee
Fort Lauderdale
MIAMI
Grand Bahama I.
Freeport
Abaco I.
Bimini Is.
C. Sable
Key West
Straits of Florida
New Providence I.
Nassau
Eleuthera I.
Andros I.
Cat I.
BAHAMAS
San Salvador I.
Great Exuma I.
Long I.
Crooked I.
Mayaguana I.
Acklins I.
Turks & Caicos Is. (U.K.)
Cockburn Town
Great Inagua I.
HABANA (Havana)
G. de Batabanó
CUBA
Matanzas
Cárdenas
Sagua la Grande
Santa Clara
Placetas
Morón
Camagüey
Nuevitas
Holguín
Banes
Cienfuegos
Trinidad
Sancti Spíritus
Ciego de Ávila
Las Tunas
I. de la Juventud
Manzanillo
Bayamo
Santiago de Cuba
Guantánamo
GUANTANAMO BAY (U.S.A.)
Baracoa
Greater Antilles
Cayman Is. (U.K.)
Grand Cayman
George Town
Cayman Trench
Montego Bay
JAMAICA
Mandeville
Spanish Town
Kingston
Windward Passage
Port-de-Paix
Cap-Haïtien
Monte Cristi
Puerto Plata
Santiago de los Caballeros
San Francisco de Macorís
Gonaïves
St-Marc
Pico Duarte 3175
La Vega
DOMINICAN REP.
HAITI
Jérémie
Les Cayes
Jacmel
PORT-AU-PRINCE
Barahona
Baní
SANTO DOMINGO
San Pedro de Macorís
La Romana
Hispaniola
Milwaukee Deep 8605
Puerto Rico Trench
Mona Passage
Arecibo
SAN JUAN
Mayagüez
Ponce
Caguas
PUERTO RICO (U.S.A.)
Virgin Is. (U.K. - U.S.A.)
Charlotte Amalie
St. Croix (U.S.A.)
Anguilla (U.K.)
St-Martin (Fr. - Neth.)
ST. KITTS & NEVIS
Basseterre
ANTIGUA & BARBUDA
St. John's
Montserrat (U.K.)
GUADELOUPE (Fr.)
Pointe-à-Pitre
Basse-Terre
DOMINICA
Roseau
Leeward Islands
Lesser Antilles
MARTINIQUE (Fr.)
Mt. Pelée 1397
Fort-de-France
Castries
ST. LUCIA
ST. VINCENT & THE GRENADINES
Kingstown
Bridgetown
BARBADOS
Windward Islands
GRENADA
St. George's
ATLANTIC OCEAN
CARIBBEAN SEA
Is. Santanilla (Honduras)
L. de Caratasca
C. Gracias a Dios
Puerto Cabezas
I. de Providencia (Colombia)
I. de San Andrés (Colombia)
Bluefields
ABC Islands (Neth.)
Aruba
Curaçao
Willemstad
Bonaire
Pta. Gallinas
Pen. de la Guajira
G. de Venezuela
Punto Fijo
Ríohacha
Santa Marta
Sierra Nevada de Santa Marta 5775
BARRANQUILLA
CARTAGENA
Soledad
Valledupar
Calamar
MARACAIBO
L. de Maracaibo
Cabimas
Coro
San Felipe
Puerto Cabello
MARACAY
Maiquetía
CARACAS
VALENCIA
BARQUISIMETO
Barcelona
La Tortuga
I. Blanquilla (Ven.)
I. de Margarita
Porlamar
Carúpano
Cumaná
Puerto La Cruz
Güiria
G. de Paria
Port of Spain
San Fernando
Tobago
TRINIDAD & TOBAGO
Maturín
El Tigre
Tucupita
Orinoco
Ciudad Guayana
Ciudad Bolívar
Embalse de Guri
Tumeremo
Georgetown
Bartica
New Amsterdam
Linden
GUYANA
SURINAME
Irazú 3432
COSTA RICA
Limón
Cartago
G. de los Mosquitos
Panama Canal
Colón
PANAMÁ
PANAMA
Volcan Barú 3475
David
Puerto Armuelles
Santiago
Chitré
Pen. de Azuero
I. de Coiba
Arch. de las Perlas
G. de Panamá
Isthmus of Panama
G. del Darién
Sincelejo
Montería
Mompós
La Palma
El Real
Riosucio
Jaqué
G. de Cupica
Quibdó
C. Corrientes
Antioquia
Bello
MEDELLÍN
Puerto Wilches
Barrancabermeja
Yarumal
3960
BUCARAMANGA
Cúcuta
Pamplona
San Cristóbal
Mérida
5007 Pico Bolívar
Valera
Barinas
Acarigua
Apure
San Fernando de Apure
Caicara
Arauca
VENEZUELA
Puerto Carreño
Puerto Ayacucho
Meta
Vichada
Ventuari
Caura
Caroní
Angel Falls
Mt. Roraima 2772
Cuyuni
Essequibo
Sierra Pacaraima
Sierra Parima
Boa Vista
Sogamosa
Tunja
COLOMBIA
Manizales
Pereira
Tolima 5215
Ibagué
Armenia
BOGOTÁ
Villavicencio
Girardot
Llanos
Puerto Inírida
Orinoco
Casiquiare
Guaviare
Buenaventura
Palmira
CALI
Huila 5750
Neiva
Magdalena
Cauca
Popayán
Volcan Puracé 4646
I. de Malpelo (Colombia)
BRAZIL
Equator
West from Greenwich
1:15 000 000
100 0 100 200 300 400 500 600 km
100 0 100 200 300 400 miles

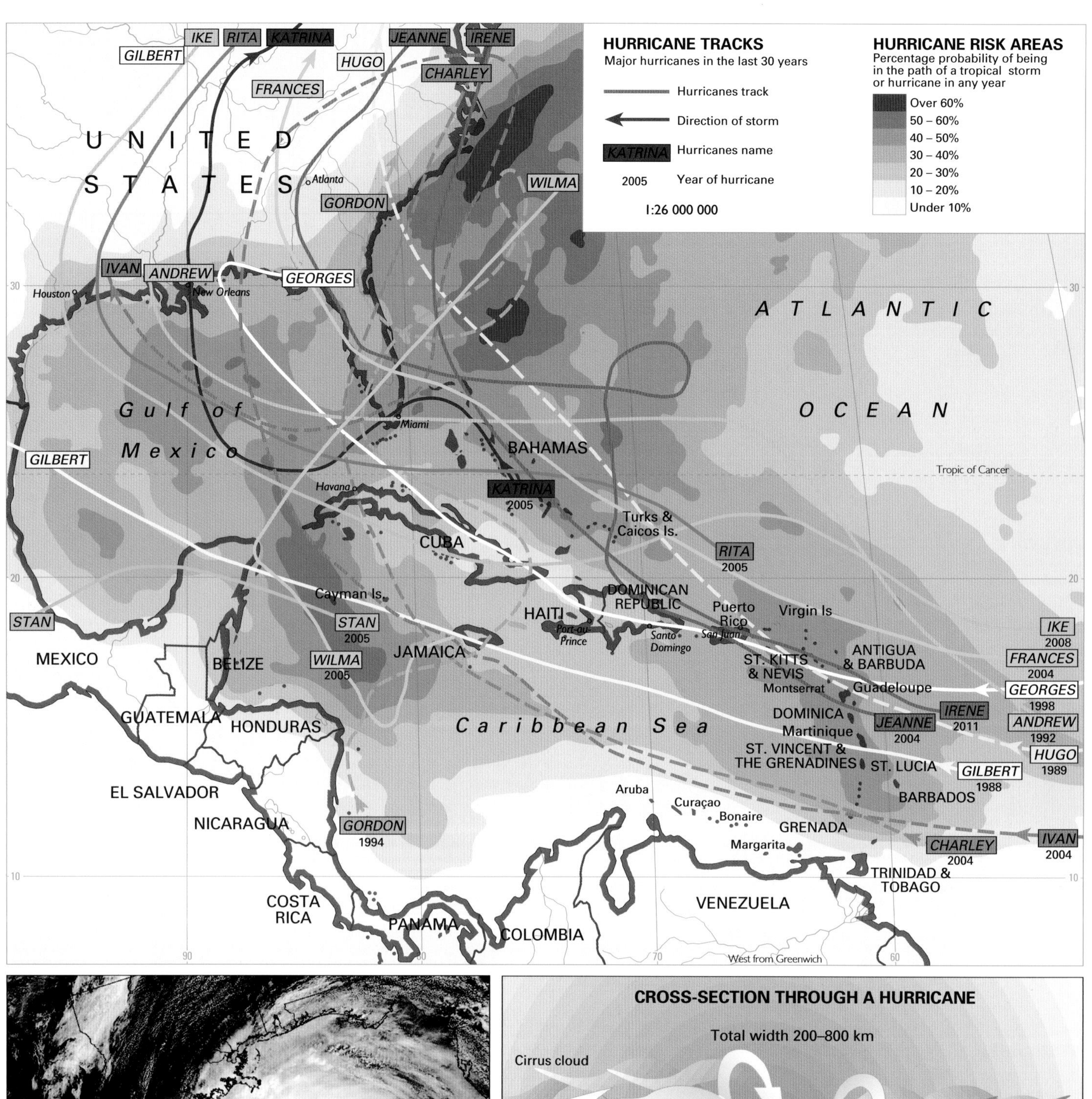

HURRICANE TRACKS
Major hurricanes in the last 30 years

- ~~~~~~~~ Hurricanes track
- ⟵ Direction of storm
- **KATRINA** Hurricanes name
- 2005 Year of hurricane

1:26 000 000

HURRICANE RISK AREAS
Percentage probability of being in the path of a tropical storm or hurricane in any year

- Over 60%
- 50 – 60%
- 40 – 50%
- 30 – 40%
- 20 – 30%
- 10 – 20%
- Under 10%

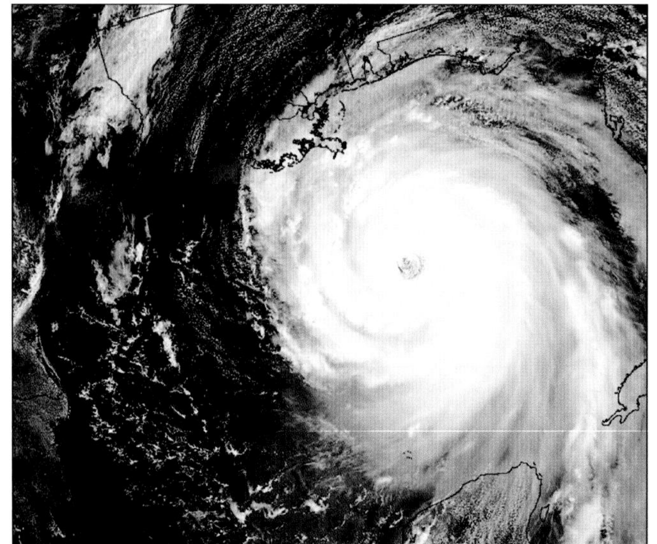

▲ Hurricane Katrina hit the USA's Gulf Coast on 29th August 2005. It was the costliest and one of the five deadliest hurricanes ever to strike the United States. This satellite image shows the storm approaching the US coastline.

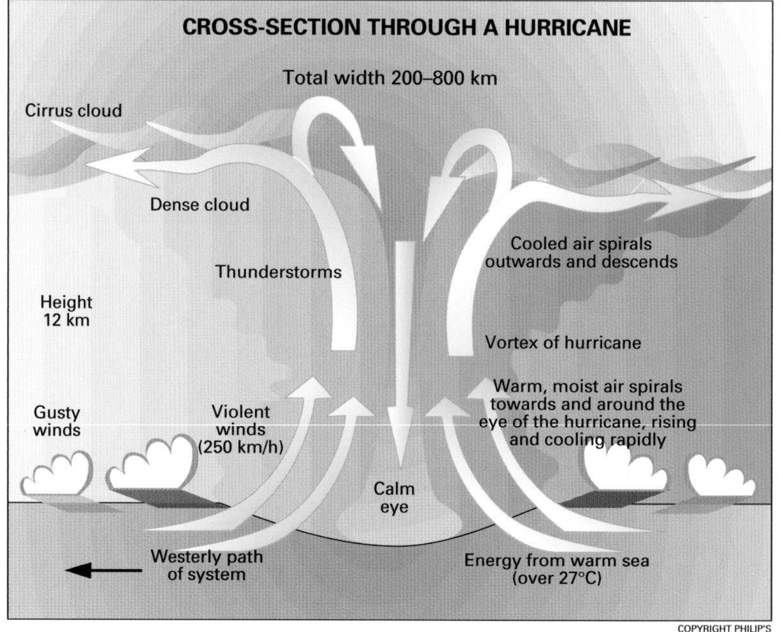

CROSS-SECTION THROUGH A HURRICANE

Total width 200–800 km

- Cirrus cloud
- Dense cloud
- Thunderstorms
- Cooled air spirals outwards and descends
- Vortex of hurricane
- Warm, moist air spirals towards and around the eye of the hurricane, rising and cooling rapidly
- Height 12 km
- Gusty winds
- Violent winds (250 km/h)
- Calm eye
- Westerly path of system
- Energy from warm sea (over 27°C)

COPYRIGHT PHILIP'S

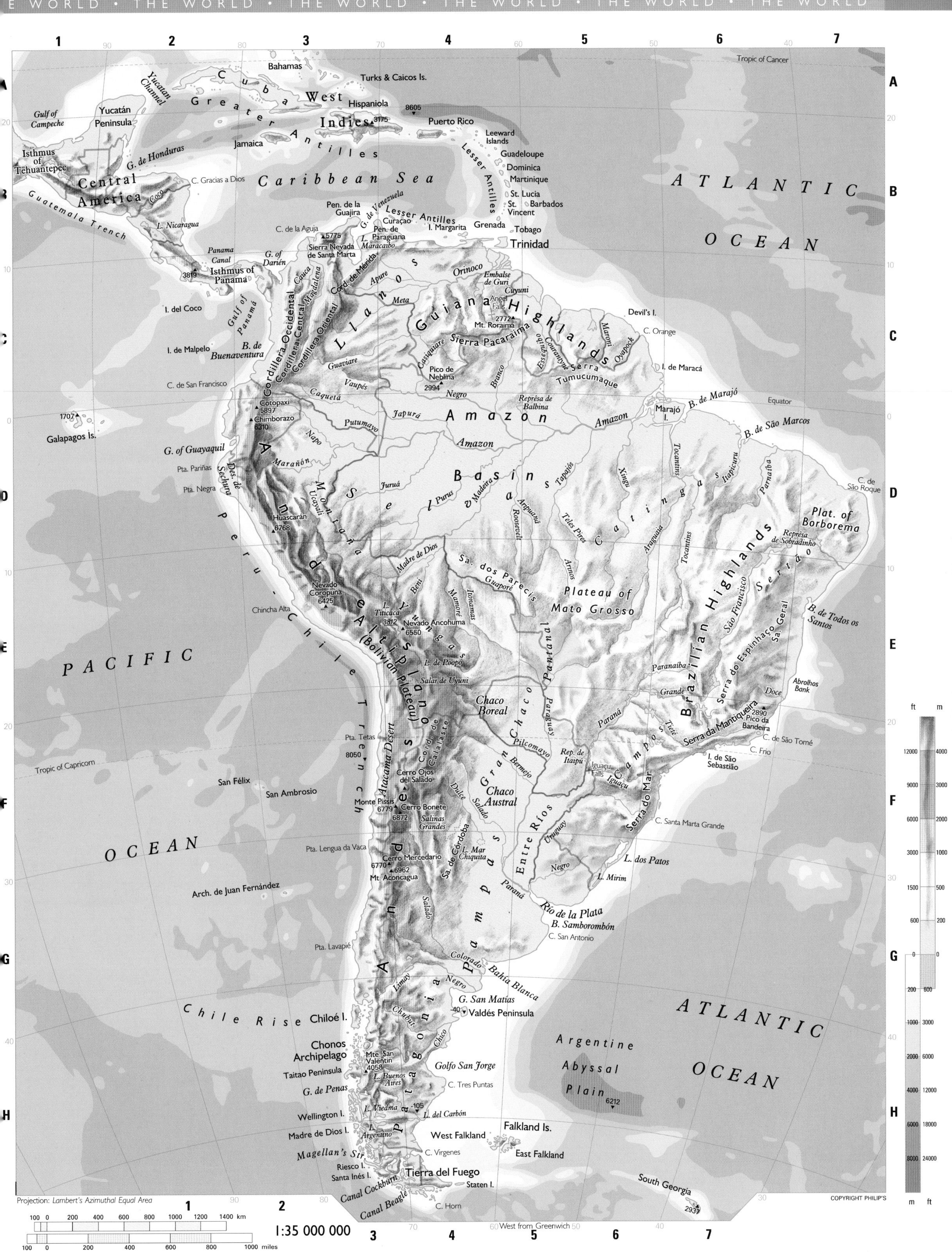

Projection: Lambert's Azimuthal Equal Area

1:35 000 000

COPYRIGHT PHILIP'S

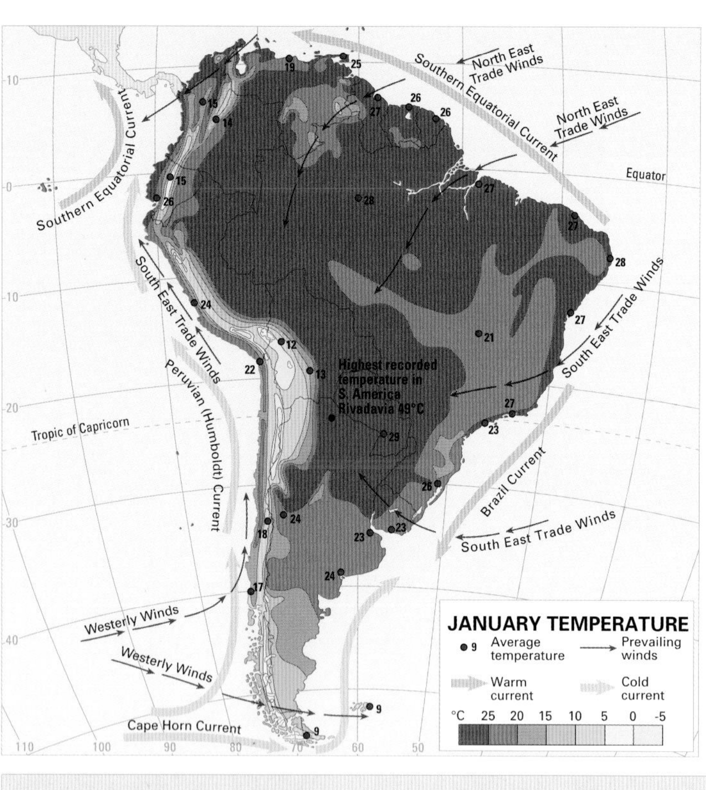

JANUARY TEMPERATURE

- **9** Average temperature
- → Prevailing winds
- Warm current
- Cold current

°C 25 20 15 10 5 0 -5

Highest recorded temperature in S. America Rivadavia 49°C

North East Trade Winds
Southern Trade Winds
North East Trade Winds
Southern Equatorial Current
North East Trade Winds
Equator
South East Trade Winds
South East Trade Winds
Brazil Current
South East Trade Winds
Southern Equatorial Current
Peruvian (Humboldt) Current
South East Trade Winds
Tropic of Capricorn
Westerly Winds
Westerly Winds
Cape Horn Current

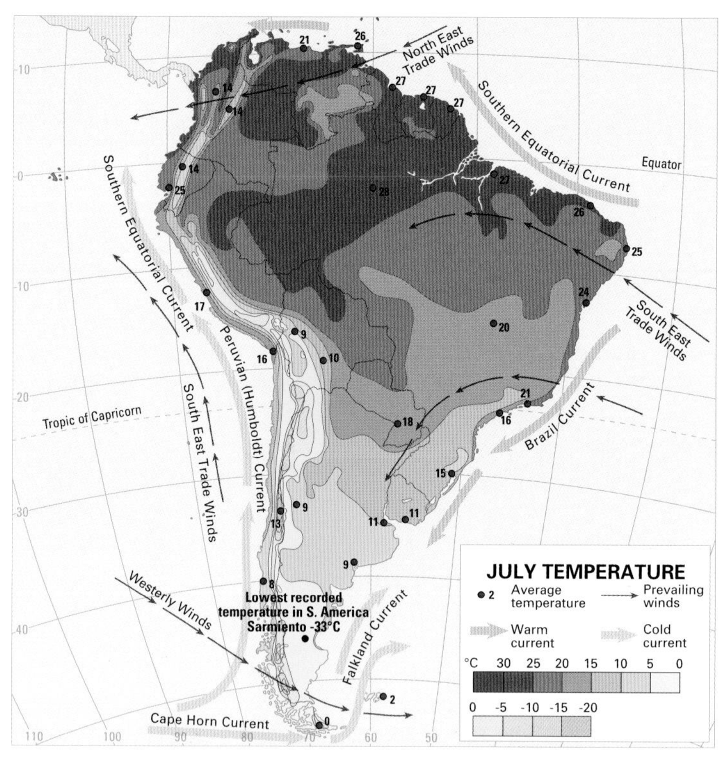

JULY TEMPERATURE

- **2** Average temperature
- → Prevailing winds
- Warm current
- Cold current

°C 30 25 20 15 10 5 0
0 -5 -10 -15 -20

Lowest recorded temperature in S. America Sarmiento -33°C

North East Trade Winds
Southern Equatorial Current
Equator
South East Trade Winds
Brazil Current
Southern Equatorial Current
Peruvian (Humboldt) Current
South East Trade Winds
Tropic of Capricorn
Westerly Winds
Falkland Current
Cape Horn Current

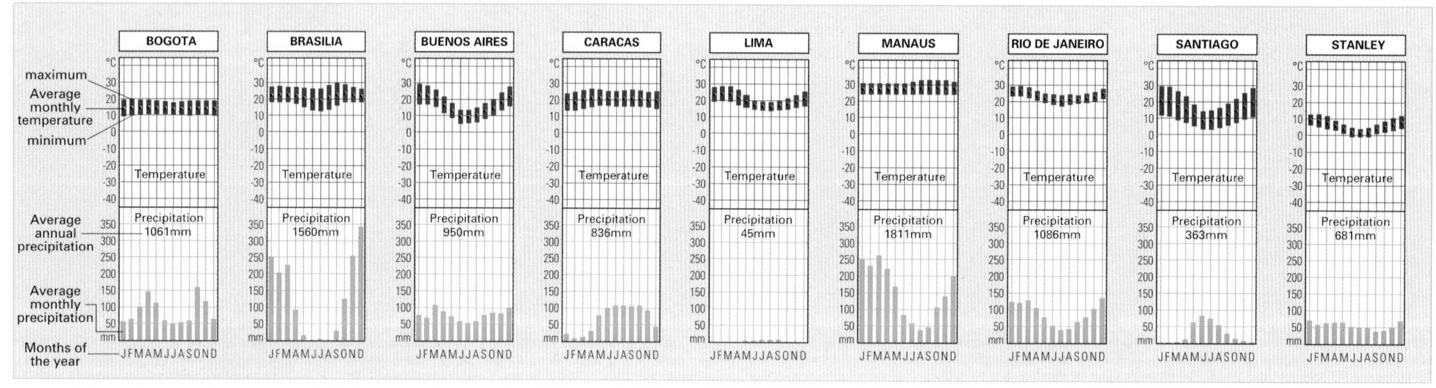

Climate graphs (left to right): BOGOTA, BRASILIA, BUENOS AIRES, CARACAS, LIMA, MANAUS, RIO DE JANEIRO, SANTIAGO, STANLEY

- maximum
- Average monthly temperature
- minimum
- Average annual precipitation
- Average monthly precipitation
- Months of the year

Station	Average annual precipitation
BOGOTA	1061mm
BRASILIA	1560mm
BUENOS AIRES	950mm
CARACAS	836mm
LIMA	45mm
MANAUS	1811mm
RIO DE JANEIRO	1086mm
SANTIAGO	363mm
STANLEY	681mm

Temperature / Precipitation
JFMAMJJASOND

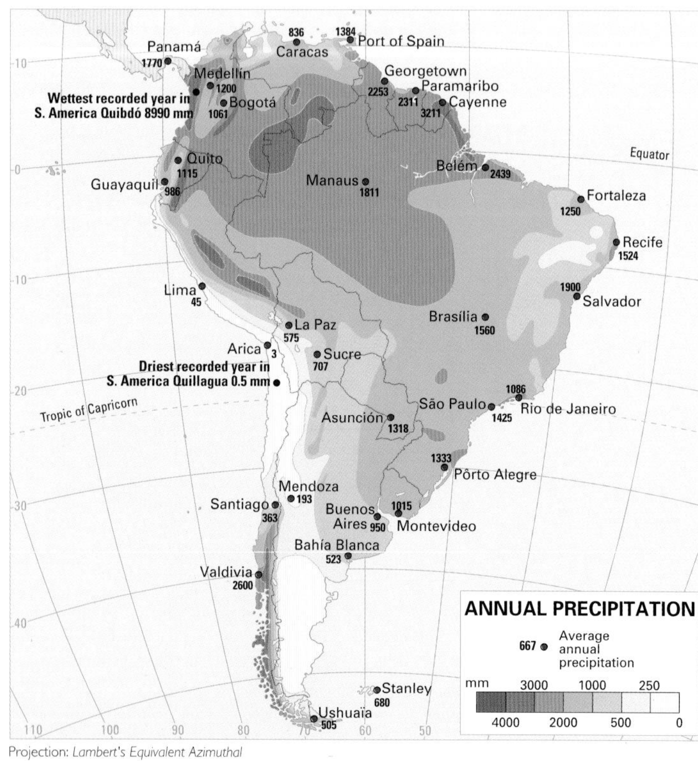

ANNUAL PRECIPITATION

- **667** Average annual precipitation

mm 4000 3000 2000 1000 500 250 0

- Panamá 1770
- Caracas 836
- Port of Spain 1384
- Medellín 1200
- Bogotá 1061
- Georgetown 2253
- Paramaribo 2311
- Cayenne 3211
- Wettest recorded year in S. America Quibdó 8990 mm
- Quito 1115
- Guayaquil 986
- Manaus 1811
- Belém 2439
- Fortaleza 1250
- Recife 1524
- Lima 45
- La Paz 575
- Brasília 1560
- Salvador 1900
- Arica 3
- Sucre 707
- Driest recorded year in S. America Quillagua 0.5 mm
- São Paulo 1086
- Rio de Janeiro 1425
- Asunción 1318
- Pôrto Alegre 1333
- Mendoza 193
- Santiago 363
- Buenos Aires 1015
- Montevideo 950
- Bahía Blanca 523
- Valdivia 2600
- Stanley 680
- Ushuaia 505

Equator
Tropic of Capricorn

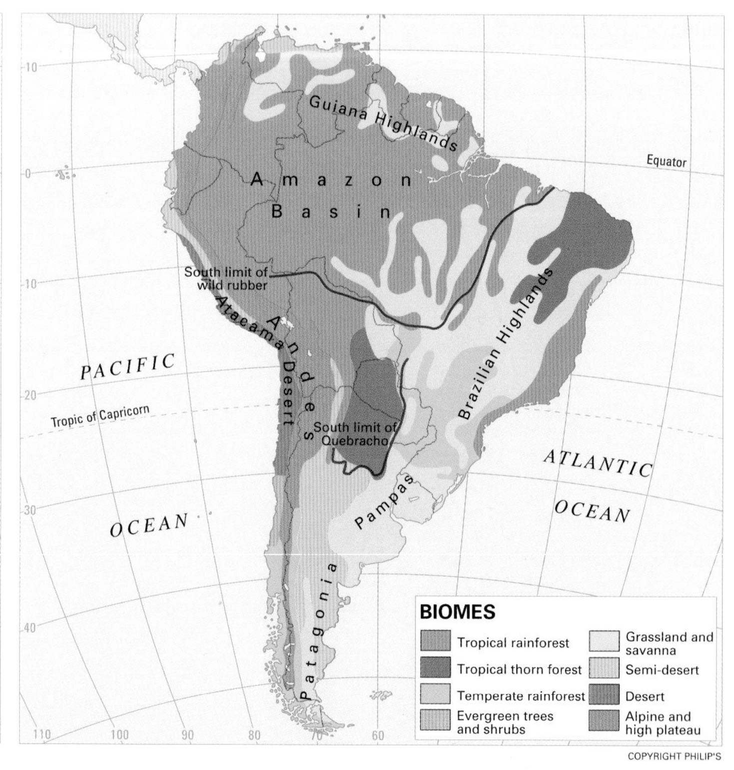

BIOMES

- Tropical rainforest
- Tropical thorn forest
- Temperate rainforest
- Evergreen trees and shrubs
- Grassland and savanna
- Semi-desert
- Desert
- Alpine and high plateau

Guiana Highlands
Amazon Basin
South limit of wild rubber
Andes
Atacama Desert
Brazilian Highlands
South limit of Quebracho
PACIFIC OCEAN
Pampas
Patagonia
ATLANTIC OCEAN
Equator
Tropic of Capricorn

Projection: Lambert's Equivalent Azimuthal

COPYRIGHT PHILIP'S

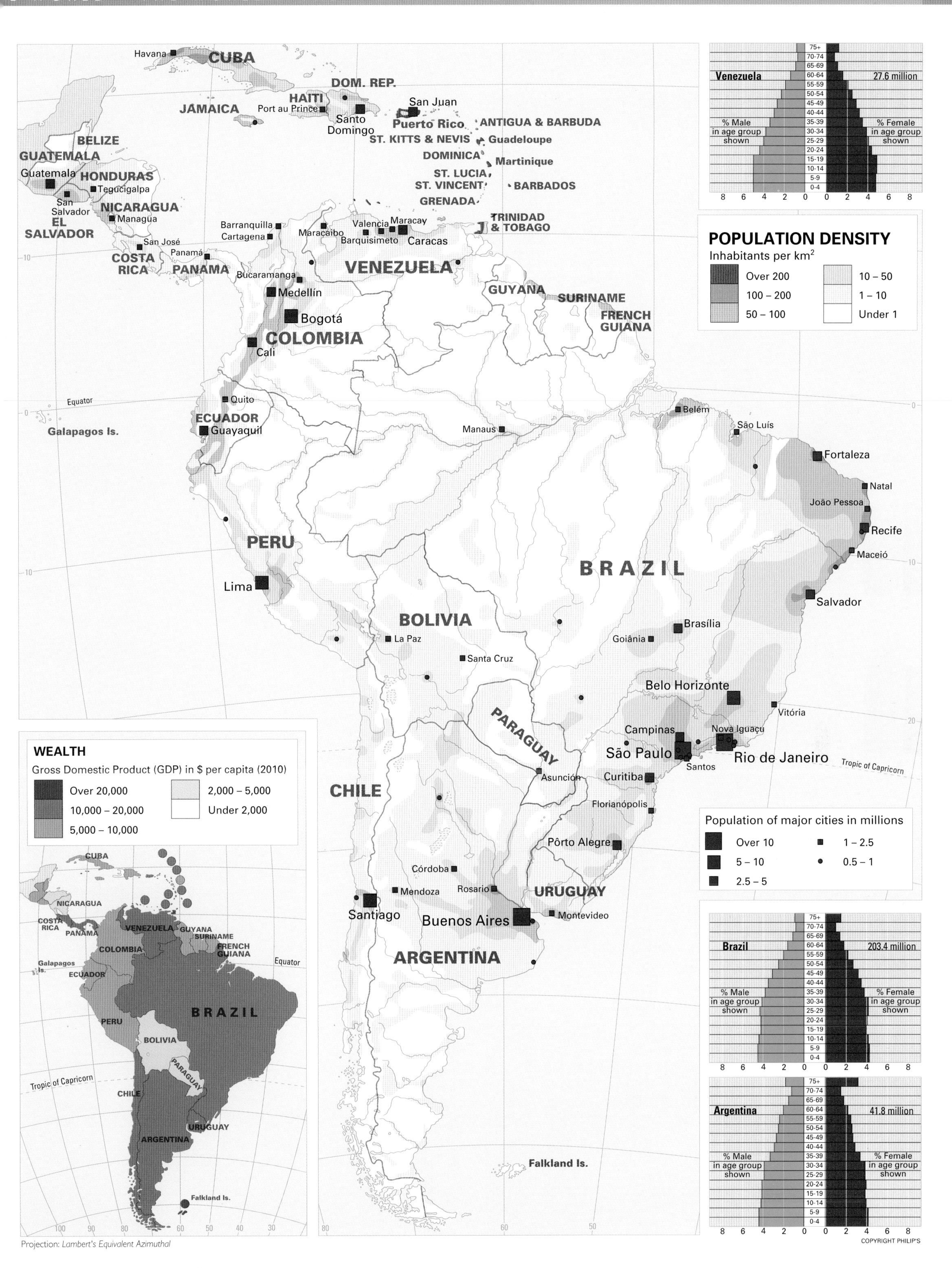
POPULATION DENSITY
Inhabitants per km²
Over 200
100 – 200
50 – 100
10 – 50
1 – 10
Under 1
WEALTH
Gross Domestic Product (GDP) in $ per capita (2010)
Over 20,000
10,000 – 20,000
5,000 – 10,000
2,000 – 5,000
Under 2,000
Population of major cities in millions
Over 10
5 – 10
2.5 – 5
1 – 2.5
0.5 – 1
Venezuela
27.6 million
Brazil
203.4 million
Argentina
41.8 million
% Male in age group shown
% Female in age group shown
75+
70-74
65-69
60-64
55-59
50-54
45-49
40-44
35-39
30-34
25-29
20-24
15-19
10-14
5-9
0-4
8 6 4 2 0 0 2 4 6 8
CUBA
Havana
DOM. REP.
HAITI
Port au Prince
Santo Domingo
JAMAICA
San Juan
Puerto Rico
ANTIGUA & BARBUDA
ST. KITTS & NEVIS
Guadeloupe
DOMINICA
Martinique
ST. LUCIA
ST. VINCENT
BARBADOS
GRENADA
TRINIDAD & TOBAGO
BELIZE
GUATEMALA
Guatemala
HONDURAS
Tegucigalpa
San Salvador
EL SALVADOR
NICARAGUA
Managua
San José
COSTA RICA
Panamá
PANAMA
Barranquilla
Cartagena
Maracaibo
Valencia
Maracay
Barquisimeto
Caracas
VENEZUELA
Bucaramanga
Medellín
Bogotá
COLOMBIA
Cali
GUYANA
SURINAME
FRENCH GUIANA
Equator
Quito
ECUADOR
Guayaquil
Galapagos Is.
Manaus
Belém
São Luís
Fortaleza
Natal
João Pessoa
Recife
Maceió
BRAZIL
Salvador
PERU
Lima
BOLIVIA
La Paz
Santa Cruz
Brasília
Goiânia
Belo Horizonte
Vitória
PARAGUAY
Campinas
Nova Iguaçu
São Paulo
Rio de Janeiro
Santos
Tropic of Capricorn
Asunción
Curitiba
CHILE
Florianópolis
Pôrto Alegre
Córdoba
Mendoza
Rosario
URUGUAY
Santiago
Buenos Aires
Montevideo
ARGENTINA
Falkland Is.
Projection: Lambert's Equivalent Azimuthal

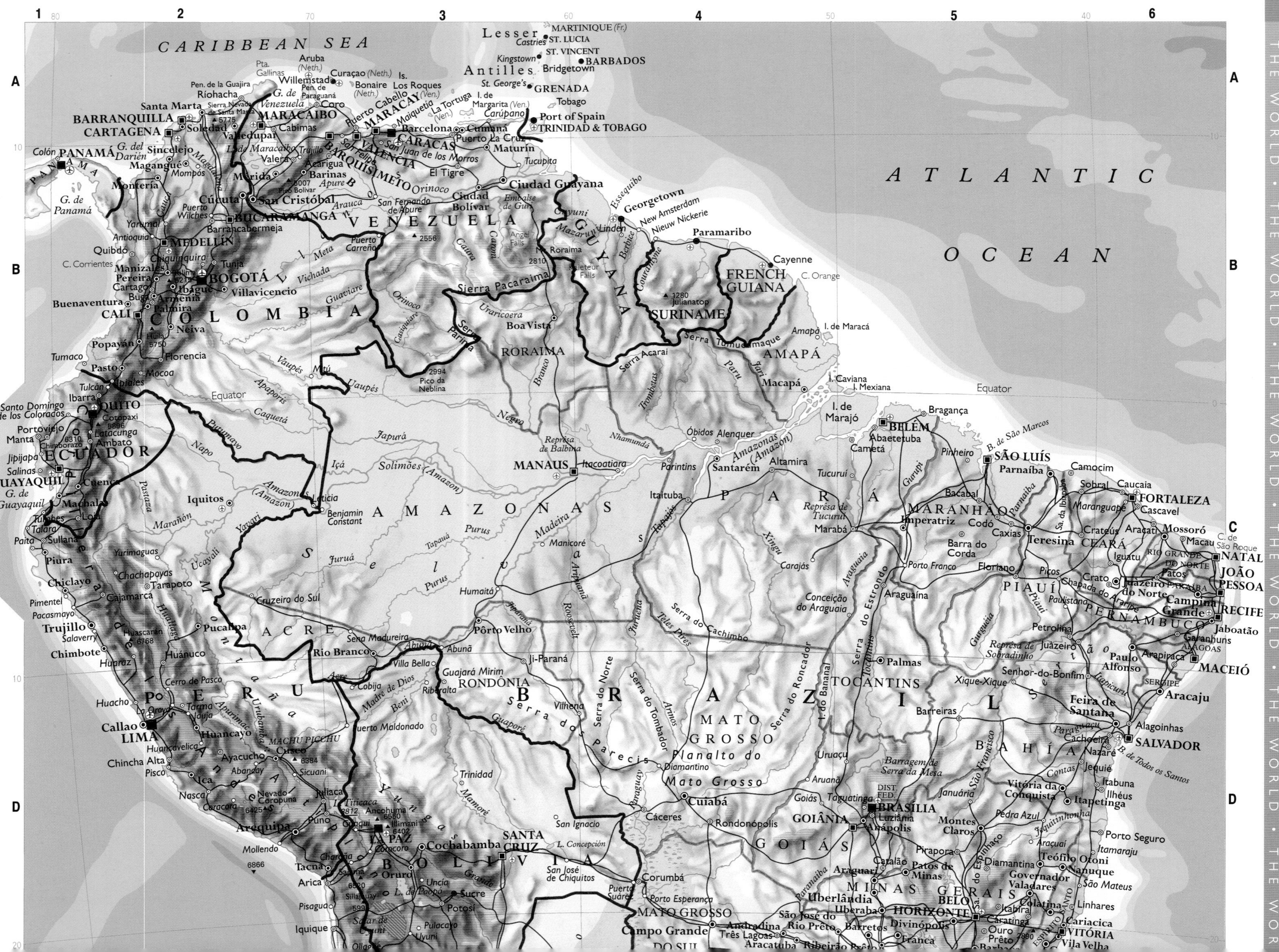
CARIBBEAN SEA
ATLANTIC
OCEAN
Lesser Antilles
MARTINIQUE (Fr.)
ST. LUCIA
ST. VINCENT
BARBADOS
GRENADA
TRINIDAD & TOBAGO
Port of Spain
VENEZUELA
CARACAS
MARACAIBO
GUYANA
Georgetown
SURINAME
Paramaribo
FRENCH GUIANA
Cayenne
COLOMBIA
BOGOTÁ
MEDELLÍN
CALI
BARRANQUILLA
CARTAGENA
ECUADOR
QUITO
GUAYAQUIL
PERU
LIMA
Callao
Arequipa
Cusco
BOLIVIA
LA PAZ
SANTA CRUZ
Cochabamba
BRAZIL
MANAUS
BELÉM
SÃO LUÍS
FORTALEZA
NATAL
JOÃO PESSOA
RECIFE
MACEIÓ
SALVADOR
BRASÍLIA
GOIÂNIA
BELO HORIZONTE
AMAZONAS
PARÁ
MATO GROSSO
TOCANTINS
BAHIA
MARANHÃO
PIAUÍ
CEARÁ
PERNAMBUCO
RONDÔNIA
ACRE
RORAIMA
AMAPÁ
GOIÁS
MINAS GERAIS
Equator
PANAMÁ

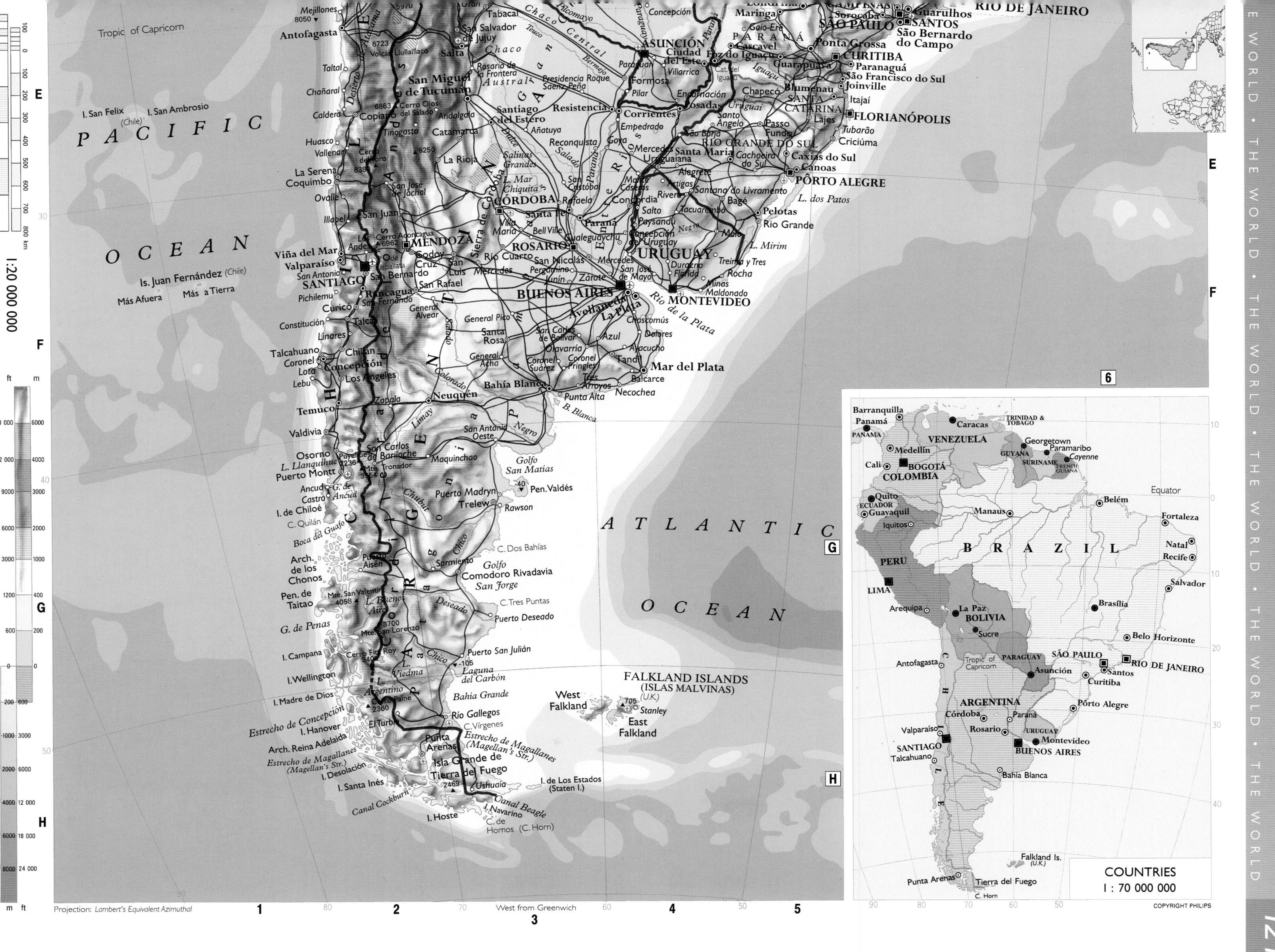

1:20 000 000
km
miles
ft
m
Tropic of Capricorn
PACIFIC
OCEAN
I. San Felix (Chile)
I. San Ambrosio
Is. Juan Fernández (Chile)
Más Afuera
Más a Tierra
ATLANTIC
OCEAN
FALKLAND ISLANDS (ISLAS MALVINAS) (U.K.)
West Falkland
East Falkland
Stanley
Antofagasta
Mejillones
Taltal
Chañaral
Caldera
Copiapó
Huasco
Vallenar
La Serena
Coquimbo
Ovalle
Illapel
Viña del Mar
Valparaíso
San Antonio
SANTIAGO
Pichilemu
Curicó
Constitución
Linares
Talcahuano
Coronel
Lota
Lebu
Concepción
Chillán
Los Angeles
Temuco
Valdivia
Osorno
L. Llanquihue
Puerto Montt
Ancud
Castro
I. de Chiloé
C. Quilán
Boca del Guafo
Arch. de los Chonos
Pen. de Taitao
G. de Penas
I. Campana
I. Wellington
I. Madre de Dios
Estrecho de Concepción
I. Hanover
Arch. Reina Adelaida
Estrecho de Magallanes (Magellan's Str.)
I. Desolación
I. Santa Inés
Canal Cockburn
I. Hoste
I. Navarino
C. de Hornos (C. Horn)
Canal Beagle
Ushuaia
Isla Grande de Tierra del Fuego
Punta Arenas
Río Gallegos
C. Vírgenes
Bahía Grande
Laguna del Carbón
Puerto San Julián
Puerto Deseado
C. Tres Puntas
Golfo San Jorge
Comodoro Rivadavia
Sarmiento
C. Dos Bahías
Rawson
Trelew
Puerto Madryn
Pen. Valdés
Golfo San Matías
San Antonio Oeste
Maquinchao
San Carlos de Bariloche
Neuquén
Bahía Blanca
B. Blanca
Punta Alta
Necochea
Mar del Plata
Balcarce
Tandil
Azul
Dolores
Chascomús
La Plata
Avellaneda
BUENOS AIRES
Río de la Plata
MONTEVIDEO
Maldonado
Minas
Rocha
URUGUAY
Paysandú
Salto
Concordia
Paraná
Santa Fe
ROSARIO
CÓRDOBA
Río Cuarto
San Luis
San Rafael
MENDOZA
San Juan
La Rioja
Catamarca
San Miguel de Tucumán
Santiago del Estero
Salta
San Salvador de Jujuy
Resistencia
Corrientes
Formosa
ASUNCIÓN
Ciudad del Este
Foz do Iguaçu
Cascavel
Maringá
SÃO PAULO
Sorocaba
Guarulhos
SANTOS
São Bernardo do Campo
RIO DE JANEIRO
Ponta Grossa
CURITIBA
Paranaguá
São Francisco do Sul
Joinville
Blumenau
Itajaí
FLORIANÓPOLIS
Tubarão
Criciúma
Lajes
Caxias do Sul
Canoas
PÔRTO ALEGRE
L. dos Patos
Pelotas
Rio Grande
L. Mirim
Bagé
Santana do Livramento
Uruguaiana
Santa Maria
Passo Fundo
RIO GRANDE DO SUL
SANTA CATARINA
PARANÁ
Projection: Lambert's Equivalent Azimuthal
West from Greenwich
COUNTRIES
1 : 70 000 000
COPYRIGHT PHILIPS
Equator
Barranquilla
Panamá
PANAMA
Caracas
TRINIDAD & TOBAGO
VENEZUELA
Medellín
Cali
BOGOTÁ
COLOMBIA
Georgetown
Paramaribo
Cayenne
GUYANA
SURINAME
FRENCH GUIANA
Quito
ECUADOR
Guayaquil
Iquitos
Manaus
Belém
Fortaleza
Natal
Recife
Salvador
BRAZIL
PERU
LIMA
Arequipa
La Paz
BOLIVIA
Sucre
Brasília
Belo Horizonte
PARAGUAY
Asunción
SÃO PAULO
Santos
Curitiba
Pôrto Alegre
Antofagasta
Tropic of Capricorn
ARGENTINA
Córdoba
Paraná
Rosario
URUGUAY
Montevideo
BUENOS AIRES
Valparaíso
SANTIAGO
Talcahuano
Bahía Blanca
Falkland Is. (U.K.)
Punta Arenas
Tierra del Fuego
C. Horn

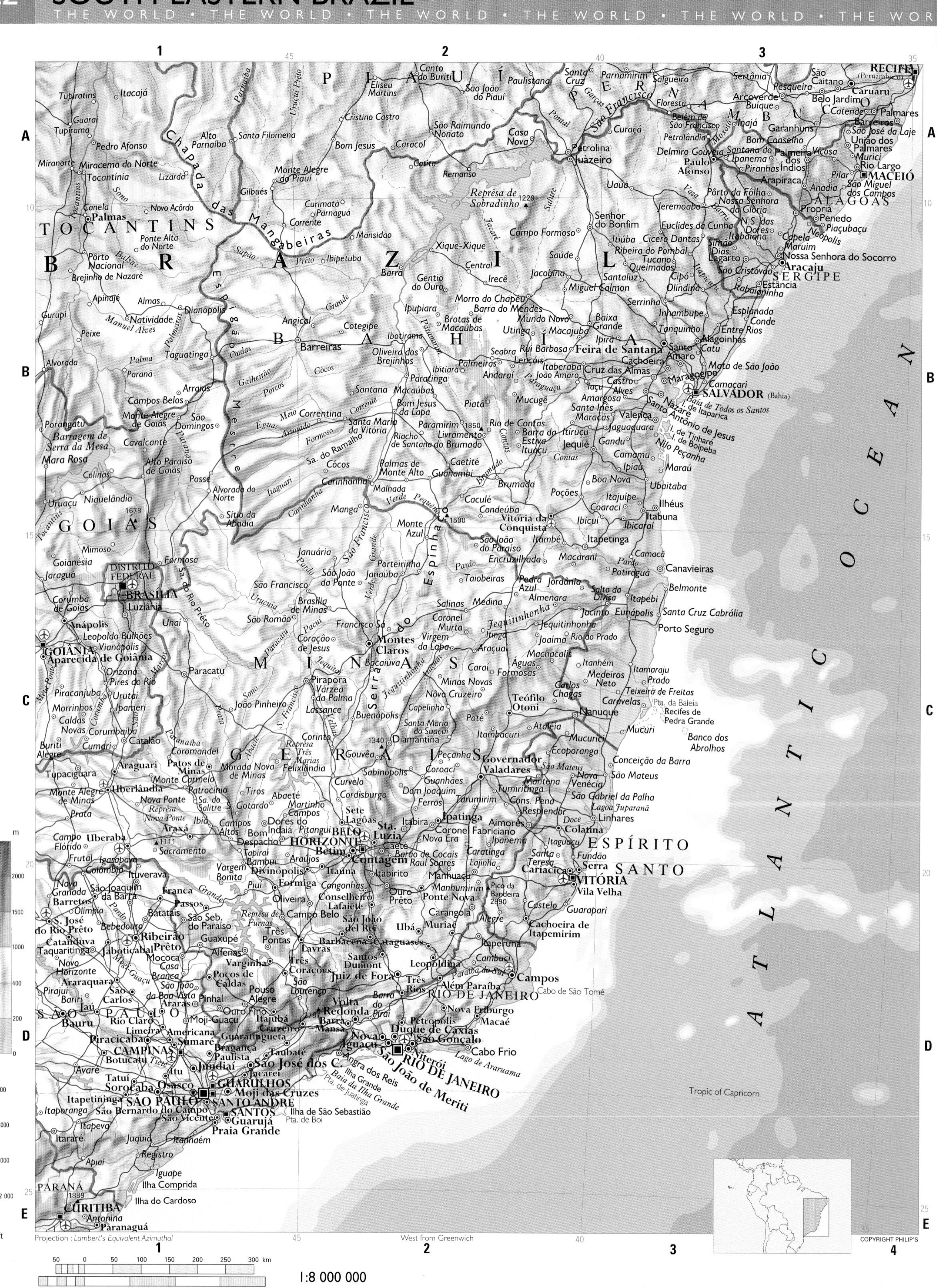

Projection : Lambert's Equivalent Azimuthal

West from Greenwich

1:8 000 000

COPYRIGHT PHILIP'S

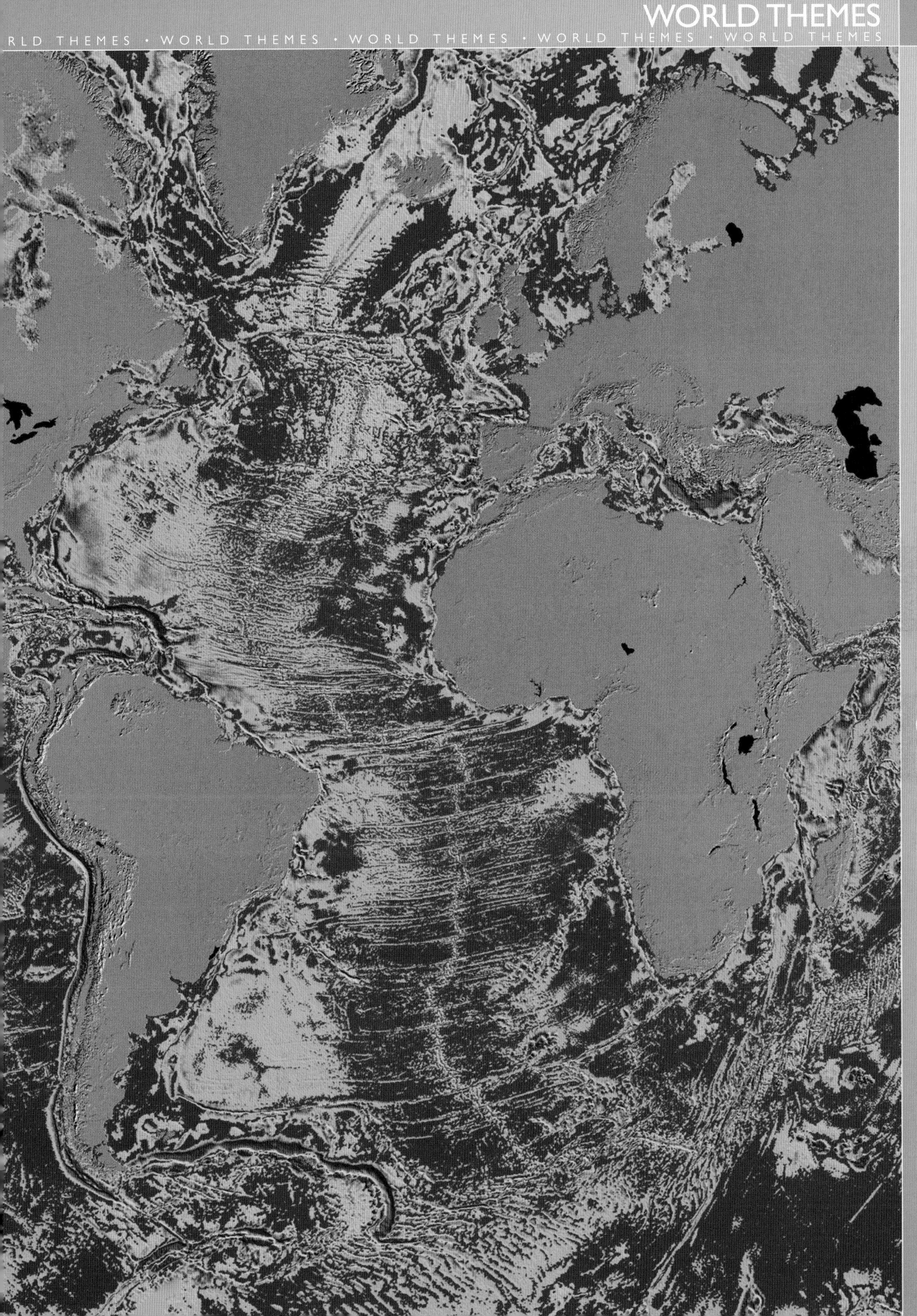

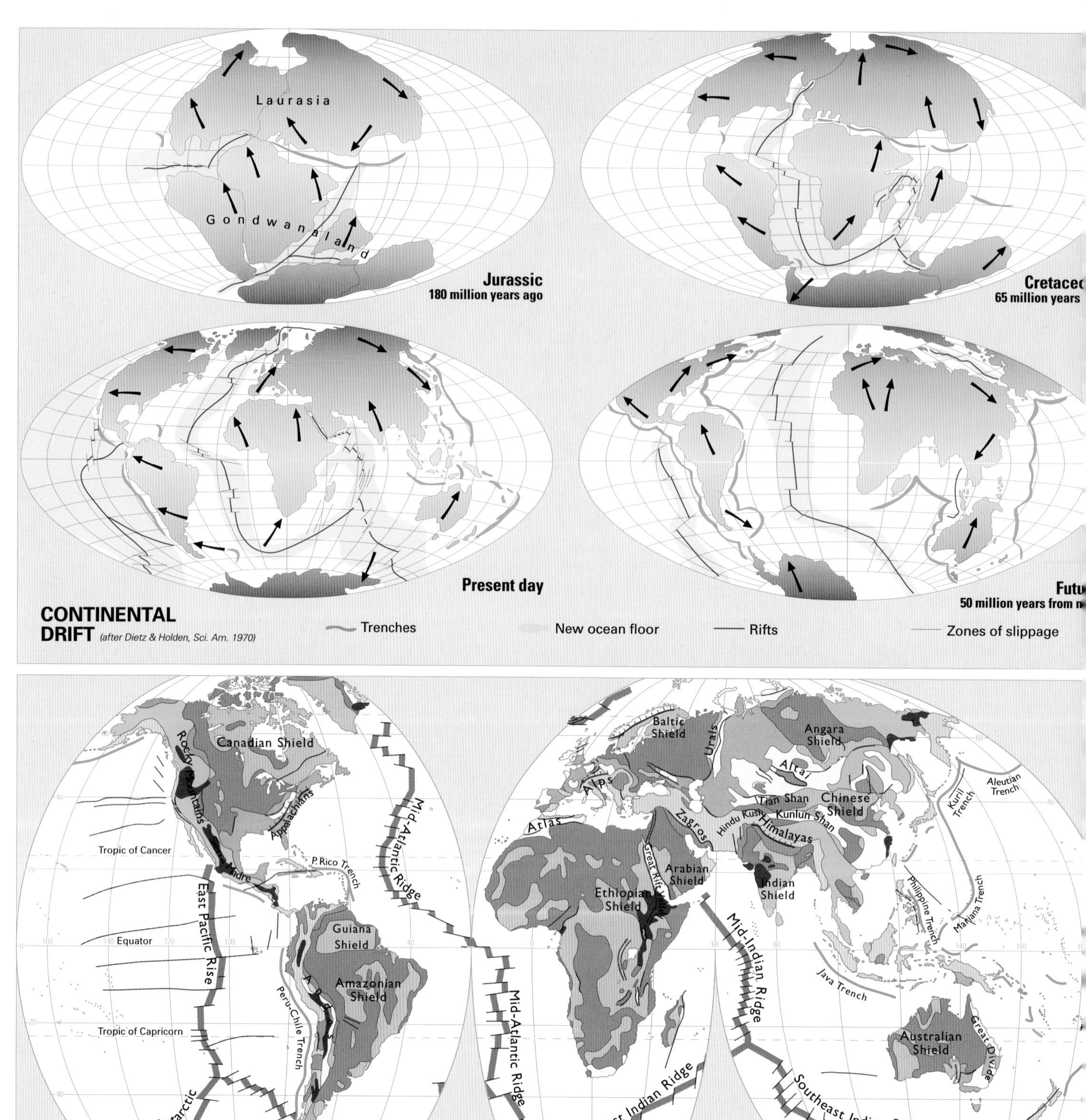

Jurassic
180 million years ago

Cretaceo
65 million years

Laurasia

Gondwanaland

Present day

Futu
50 million years from n

CONTINENTAL DRIFT *(after Dietz & Holden, Sci. Am. 1970)*

| Trenches | New ocean floor | Rifts | Zones of slippage |

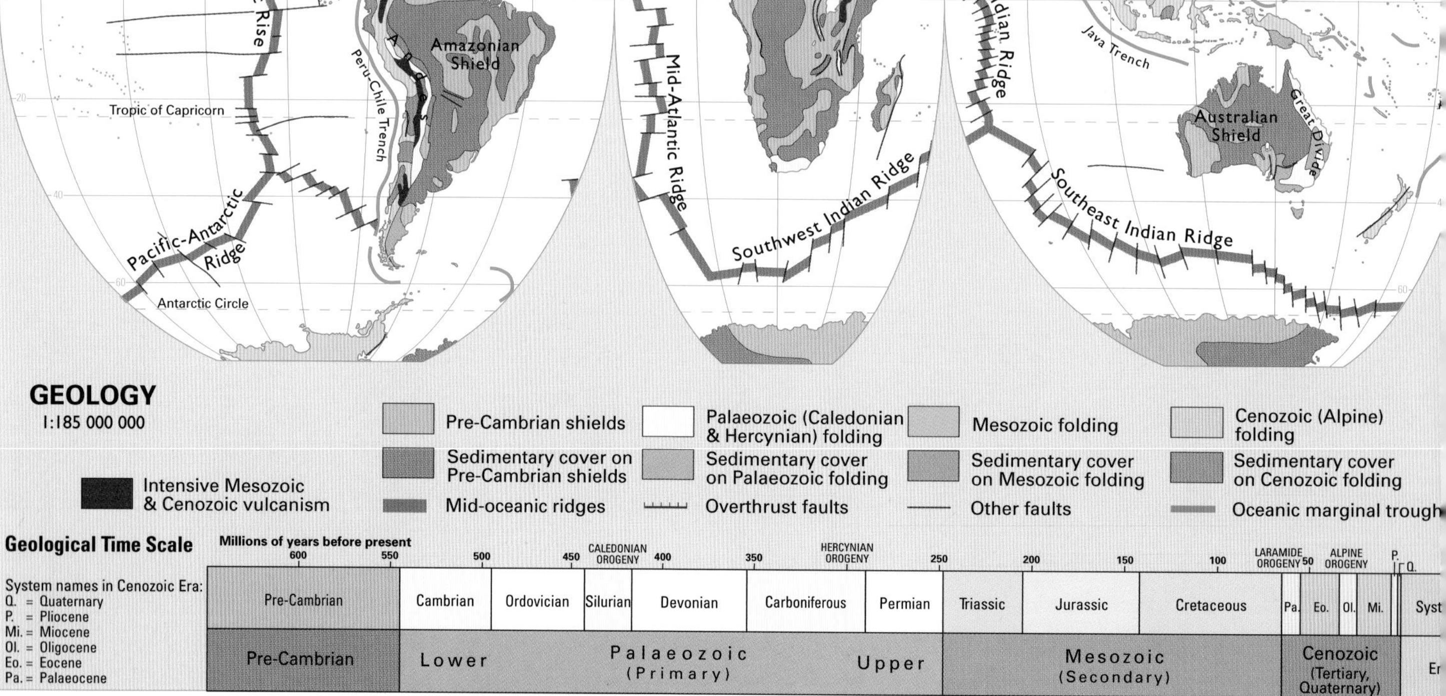

GEOLOGY
1:185 000 000

Intensive Mesozoic & Cenozoic vulcanism

Pre-Cambrian shields	Palaeozoic (Caledonian & Hercynian) folding
Sedimentary cover on Pre-Cambrian shields	Sedimentary cover on Palaeozoic folding
Mid-oceanic ridges	Overthrust faults
Mesozoic folding	Cenozoic (Alpine) folding
Sedimentary cover on Mesozoic folding	Sedimentary cover on Cenozoic folding
Other faults	Oceanic marginal trough

Geological Time Scale

System names in Cenozoic Era:
Q. = Quaternary
P. = Pliocene
Mi. = Miocene
Ol. = Oligocene
Eo. = Eocene
Pa. = Palaeocene

Millions of years before present																	
600	550	500	450	400	350	250	200	150	100	50			
			CALEDONIAN OROGENY		HERCYNIAN OROGENY					LARAMIDE OROGENY	ALPINE OROGENY	P. Q.	
Pre-Cambrian		Cambrian	Ordovician	Silurian	Devonian	Carboniferous	Permian	Triassic	Jurassic	Cretaceous	Pa.	Eo.	Ol.	Mi.		Syst
Pre-Cambrian		Lower			Palaeozoic (Primary)		Upper		Mesozoic (Secondary)			Cenozoic (Tertiary, Quaternary)			Er

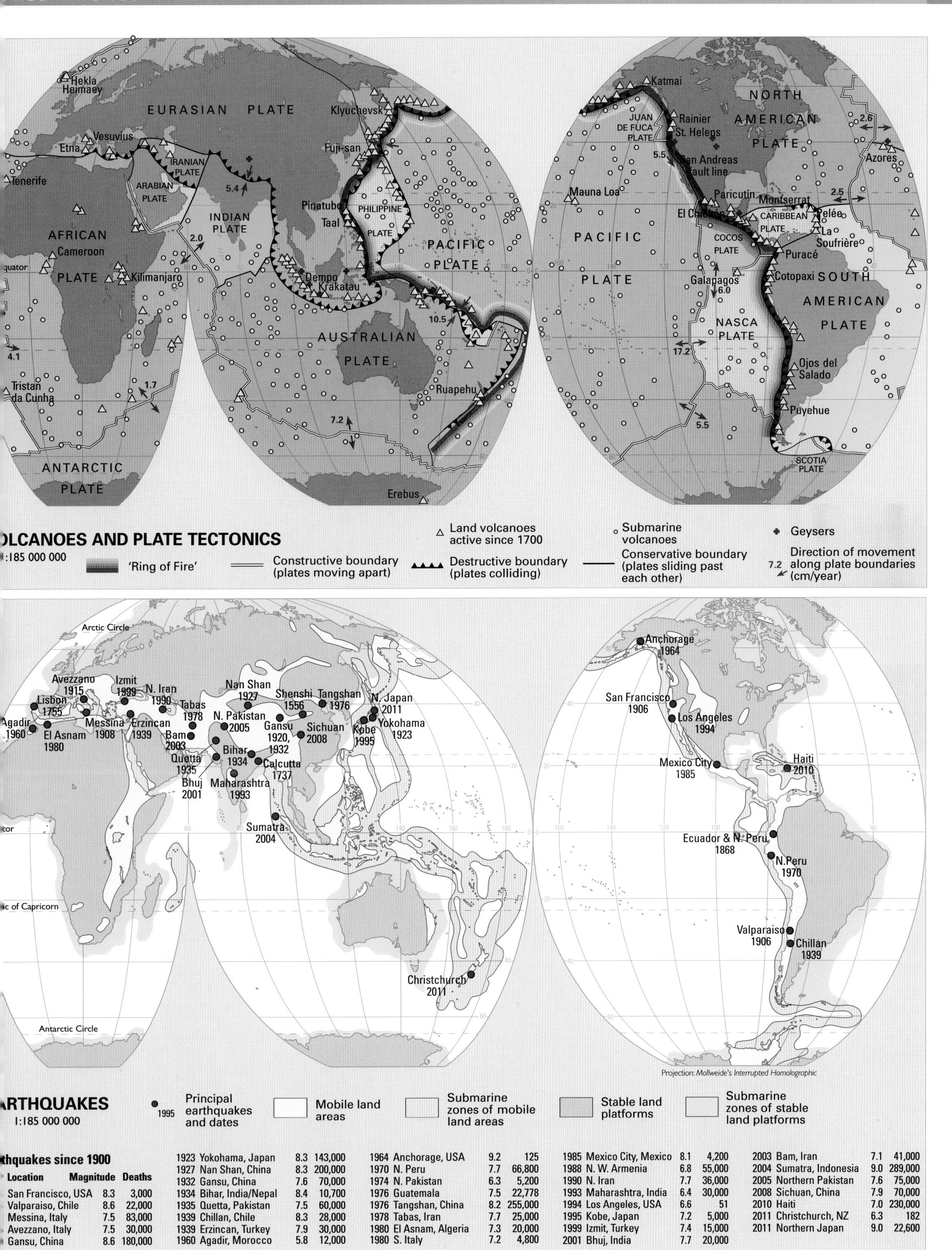

VOLCANOES AND PLATE TECTONICS

1:185 000 000

- 'Ring of Fire'
- △ Land volcanoes active since 1700
- ○ Submarine volcanoes
- ✦ Geysers
- —— Constructive boundary (plates moving apart)
- ▲▲▲ Destructive boundary (plates colliding)
- —— Conservative boundary (plates sliding past each other)
- 7.2 ← Direction of movement along plate boundaries (cm/year)

EARTHQUAKES

1:185 000 000

- ● 1995 Principal earthquakes and dates
- Mobile land areas
- Submarine zones of mobile land areas
- Stable land platforms
- Submarine zones of stable land platforms

Projection: Mollweide's Interrupted Homolographic

Earthquakes since 1900

Location	Magnitude	Deaths									
San Francisco, USA	8.3	3,000	1923 Yokohama, Japan	8.3	143,000	1964 Anchorage, USA	9.2	125	1985 Mexico City, Mexico	8.1	4,200
Valparaiso, Chile	8.6	22,000	1927 Nan Shan, China	8.3	200,000	1970 N. Peru	7.7	66,800	1988 N. W. Armenia	6.8	55,000
Messina, Italy	7.5	83,000	1932 Gansu, China	7.6	70,000	1974 N. Pakistan	6.3	5,200	1990 N. Iran	7.7	36,000
Avezzano, Italy	7.5	30,000	1934 Bihar, India/Nepal	8.4	10,700	1976 Guatemala	7.5	22,778	1993 Maharashtra, India	6.4	30,000
Gansu, China	8.6	180,000	1935 Quetta, Pakistan	7.5	60,000	1976 Tangshan, China	8.2	255,000	1994 Los Angeles, USA	6.6	51
			1939 Chillan, Chile	8.3	28,000	1978 Tabas, Iran	7.7	25,000	1995 Kobe, Japan	7.2	5,000
			1939 Erzincan, Turkey	7.9	30,000	1980 El Asnam, Algeria	7.3	20,000	1999 Izmit, Turkey	7.4	15,000
			1960 Agadir, Morocco	5.8	12,000	1980 S. Italy	7.2	4,800	2001 Bhuj, India	7.7	20,000

2003 Bam, Iran	7.1	41,000		
2004 Sumatra, Indonesia	9.0	289,000		
2005 Northern Pakistan	7.6	75,000		
2008 Sichuan, China	7.9	70,000		
2010 Haiti	7.0	230,000		
2011 Christchurch, NZ	6.3	182		
2011 Northern Japan	9.0	22,600		

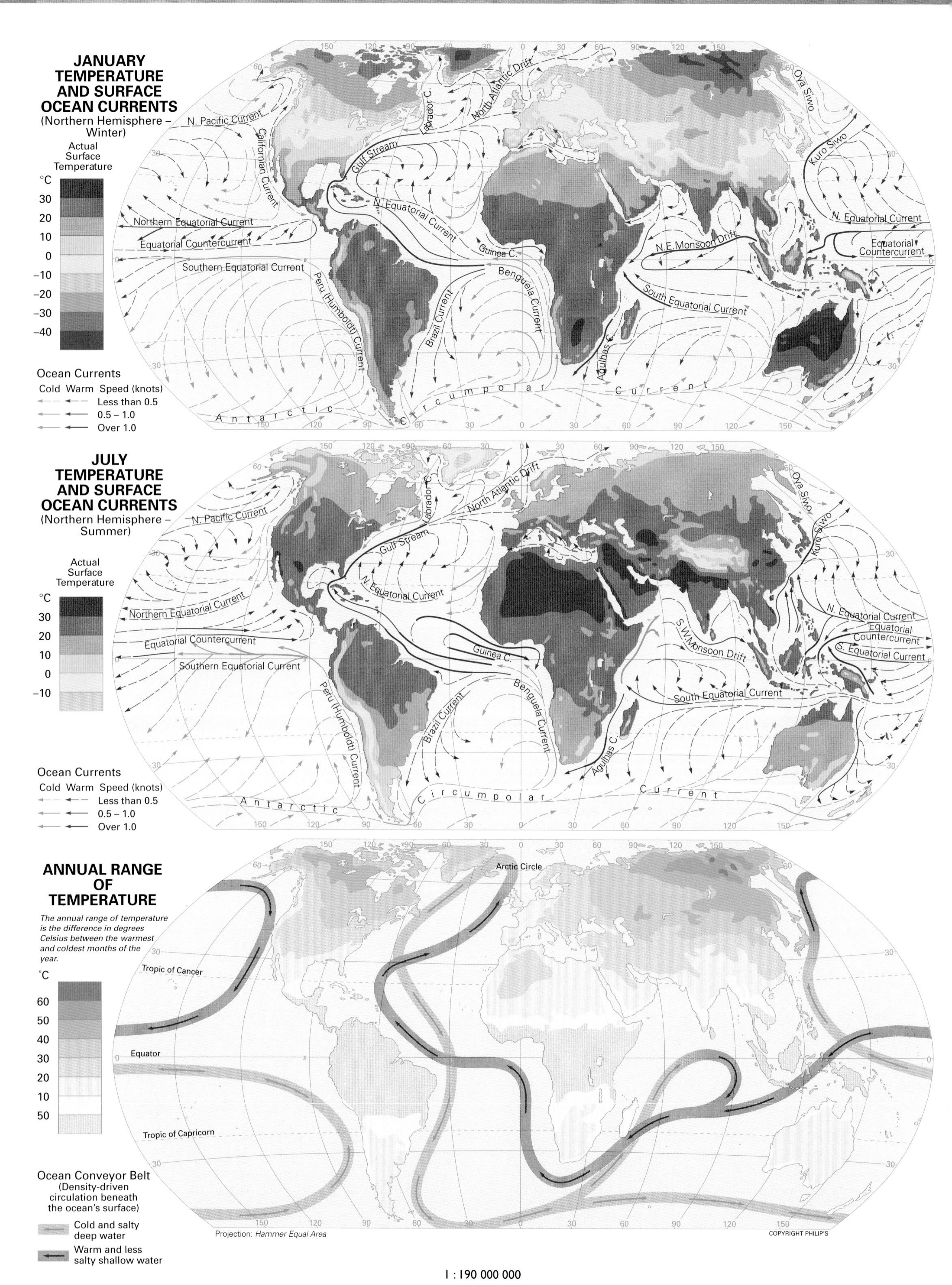

JANUARY TEMPERATURE AND SURFACE OCEAN CURRENTS
(Northern Hemisphere – Winter)

Actual Surface Temperature

°C
30
20
10
0
-10
-20
-30
-40

Ocean Currents

Cold Warm Speed (knots)
Less than 0.5
0.5 – 1.0
Over 1.0

JULY TEMPERATURE AND SURFACE OCEAN CURRENTS
(Northern Hemisphere – Summer)

Actual Surface Temperature

°C
30
20
10
0
-10

Ocean Currents

Cold Warm Speed (knots)
Less than 0.5
0.5 – 1.0
Over 1.0

ANNUAL RANGE OF TEMPERATURE

The annual range of temperature is the difference in degrees Celsius between the warmest and coldest months of the year.

°C
60
50
40
30
20
10
50

Ocean Conveyor Belt
(Density-driven circulation beneath the ocean's surface)

Cold and salty deep water

Warm and less salty shallow water

Projection: *Hammer Equal Area*

COPYRIGHT PHILIP'S

1 : 190 000 000

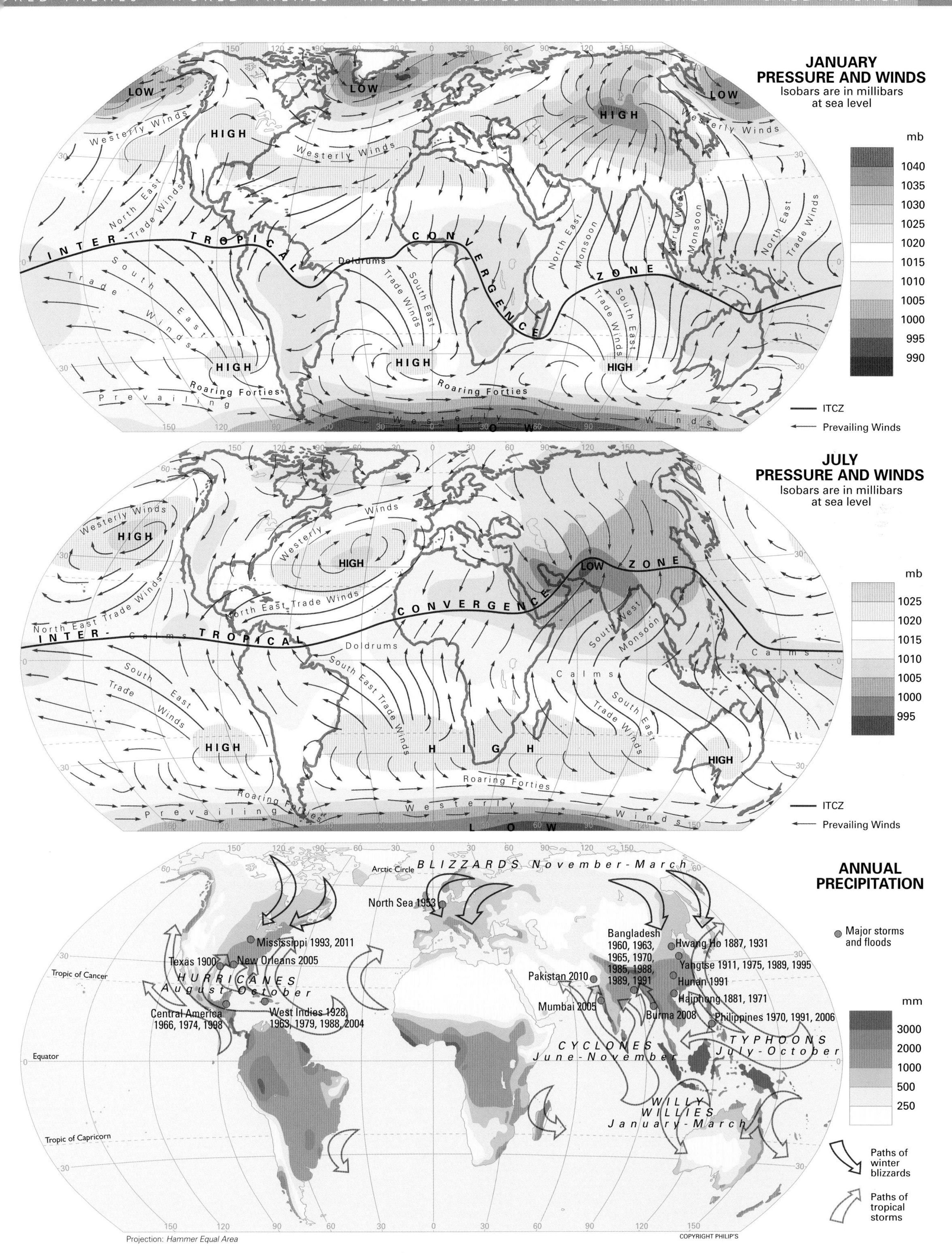

JANUARY PRESSURE AND WINDS
Isobars are in millibars at sea level

mb

1040
1035
1030
1025
1020
1015
1010
1005
1000
995
990

—— ITCZ
←— Prevailing Winds

JULY PRESSURE AND WINDS
Isobars are in millibars at sea level

mb

1025
1020
1015
1010
1005
1000
995

—— ITCZ
←— Prevailing Winds

ANNUAL PRECIPITATION

⬤ Major storms and floods

mm

3000
2000
1000
500
250

Paths of winter blizzards

Paths of tropical storms

Projection: Hammer Equal Area

COPYRIGHT PHILIP'S

KEY TO CLIMATE REGIONS MAP

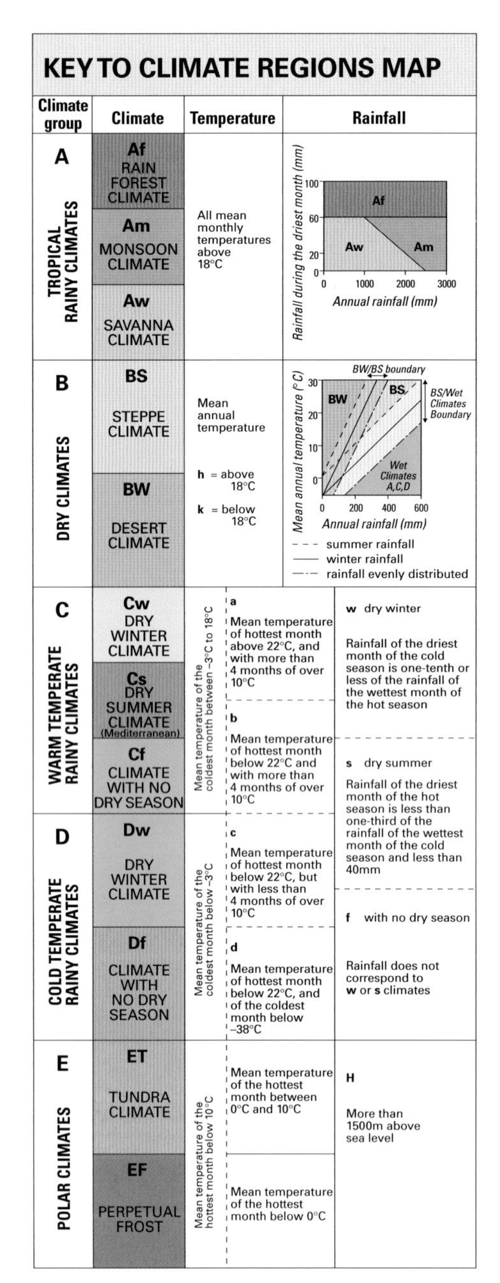

Climate group	Climate	Temperature	Rainfall
A TROPICAL RAINY CLIMATES	**Af** RAIN FOREST CLIMATE	All mean monthly temperatures above 18°C	*(graph: Rainfall during the driest month (mm) vs Annual rainfall (mm); Af, Aw, Am zones)*
	Am MONSOON CLIMATE		
	Aw SAVANNA CLIMATE		
B DRY CLIMATES	**BS** STEPPE CLIMATE	Mean annual temperature	*(graph: Mean annual temperature (°C) vs Annual rainfall (mm); BW, BS, BW/BS boundary, BS/Wet Climates Boundary, Wet Climates A,C,D)*
	BW DESERT CLIMATE	**h** = above 18°C **k** = below 18°C	— — — summer rainfall ——— winter rainfall —·—·— rainfall evenly distributed
C WARM TEMPERATE RAINY CLIMATES	**Cw** DRY WINTER CLIMATE	Mean temperature of the coldest month between −3°C to 18°C	**a** Mean temperature of hottest month above 22°C, and with more than 4 months of over 10°C; **w** dry winter – Rainfall of the driest month of the cold season is one-tenth or less of the rainfall of the wettest month of the hot season
	Cs DRY SUMMER CLIMATE (Mediterranean)		**b** Mean temperature of hottest month below 22°C and with more than 4 months of over 10°C; **s** dry summer – Rainfall of the driest month of the hot season is less than one-third of the rainfall of the wettest month of the cold season and less than 40mm
	Cf CLIMATE WITH NO DRY SEASON		
D COLD TEMPERATE RAINY CLIMATES	**Dw** DRY WINTER CLIMATE	Mean temperature of the coldest month below −3°C	**c** Mean temperature of hottest month below 22°C, but with less than 4 months of over 10°C
	Df CLIMATE WITH NO DRY SEASON	Mean temperature of hottest month below 22°C, and of the coldest month below −38°C	**d** Mean temperature of hottest month below 22°C, and of the coldest month below −38°C; **f** with no dry season – Rainfall does not correspond to **w** or **s** climates
E POLAR CLIMATES	**ET** TUNDRA CLIMATE	Mean temperature of the hottest month between 0°C and 10°C	**H** More than 1500m above sea level
	EF PERPETUAL FROST	Mean temperature of the hottest month below 0°C	

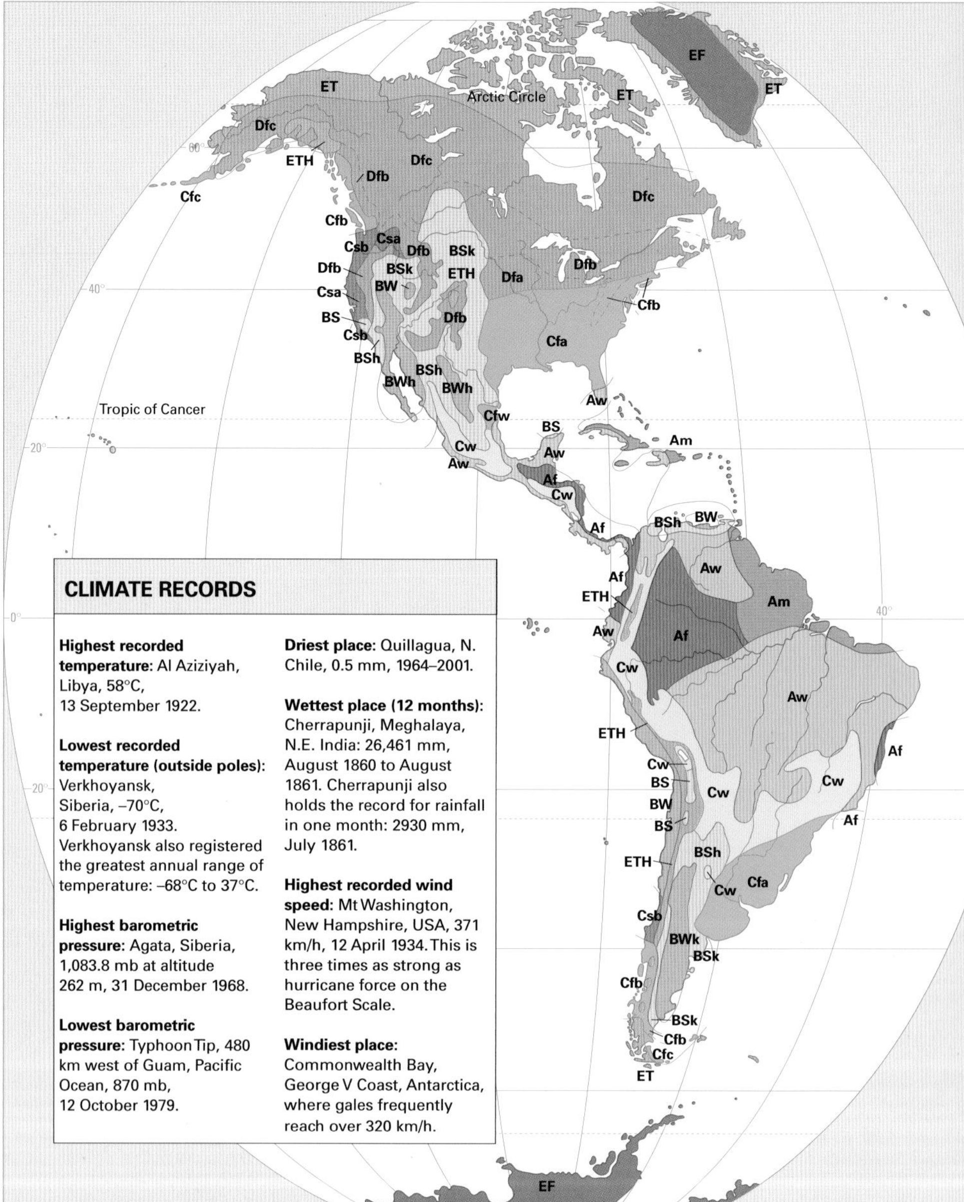

CLIMATE RECORDS

Highest recorded temperature: Al Aziziyah, Libya, 58°C, 13 September 1922.

Lowest recorded temperature (outside poles): Verkhoyansk, Siberia, −70°C, 6 February 1933. Verkhoyansk also registered the greatest annual range of temperature: −68°C to 37°C.

Highest barometric pressure: Agata, Siberia, 1,083.8 mb at altitude 262 m, 31 December 1968.

Lowest barometric pressure: Typhoon Tip, 480 km west of Guam, Pacific Ocean, 870 mb, 12 October 1979.

Driest place: Quillagua, N. Chile, 0.5 mm, 1964–2001.

Wettest place (12 months): Cherrapunji, Meghalaya, N.E. India: 26,461 mm, August 1860 to August 1861. Cherrapunji also holds the record for rainfall in one month: 2930 mm, July 1861.

Highest recorded wind speed: Mt Washington, New Hampshire, USA, 371 km/h, 12 April 1934. This is three times as strong as hurricane force on the Beaufort Scale.

Windiest place: Commonwealth Bay, George V Coast, Antarctica, where gales frequently reach over 320 km/h.

Projection: Interrupted Mollweide's Homolographic

THE MONSOON   1:90 000 000

Monthly rainfall

mm	
400	100
200	50
100	25
	0

→ wind direction

▓▓▓ ITCZ (intertropical convergence zone)

In early March, which normally marks the end of the subcontinent's cool season and the start of the hot season, winds blow outwards from the mainland. But as the overhead sun and the ITCZ move northwards, the land is intensely heated, and a low-pressure system develops. The south-east trade winds, which are drawn across the Equator, change direction and are sucked into the interior to become south-westerly winds, bringing heavy rain. By November, the overhead sun and the ITCZ have again moved southwards and the wind directions are again reversed. Cool winds blow from the Asian interior to the sea, losing any moisture on the Himalayas before descending to the coast.

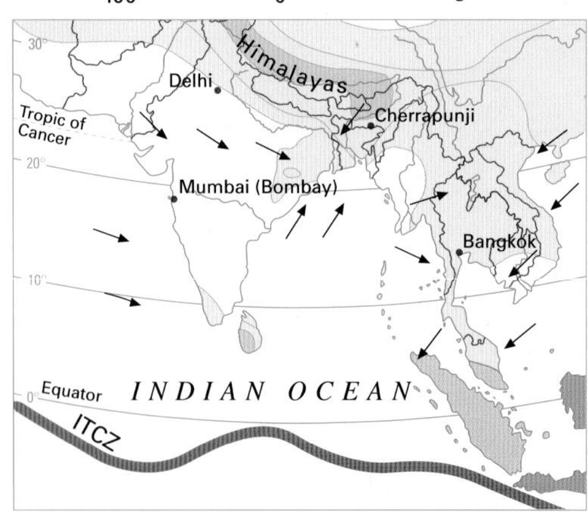

March – Start of the hot, dry season, the ITCZ is over the southern Indian Ocean.

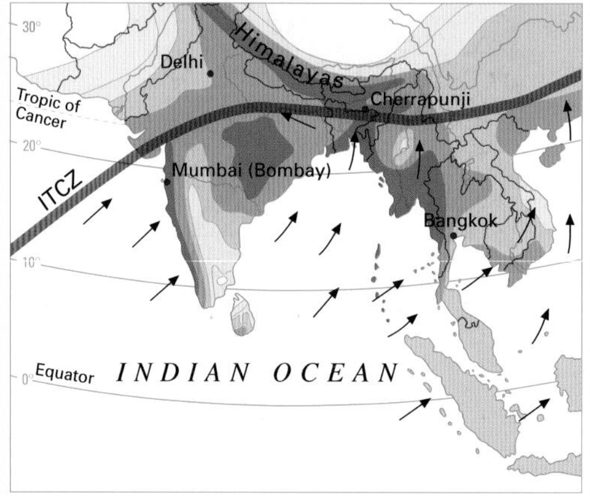

July – The rainy season, the ITCZ has migrated northwards; winds blow onshore.

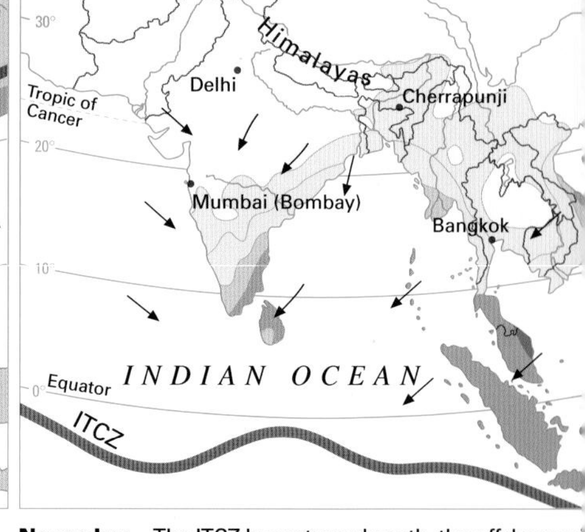

November – The ITCZ has returned south, the offshore winds are cool and dry.

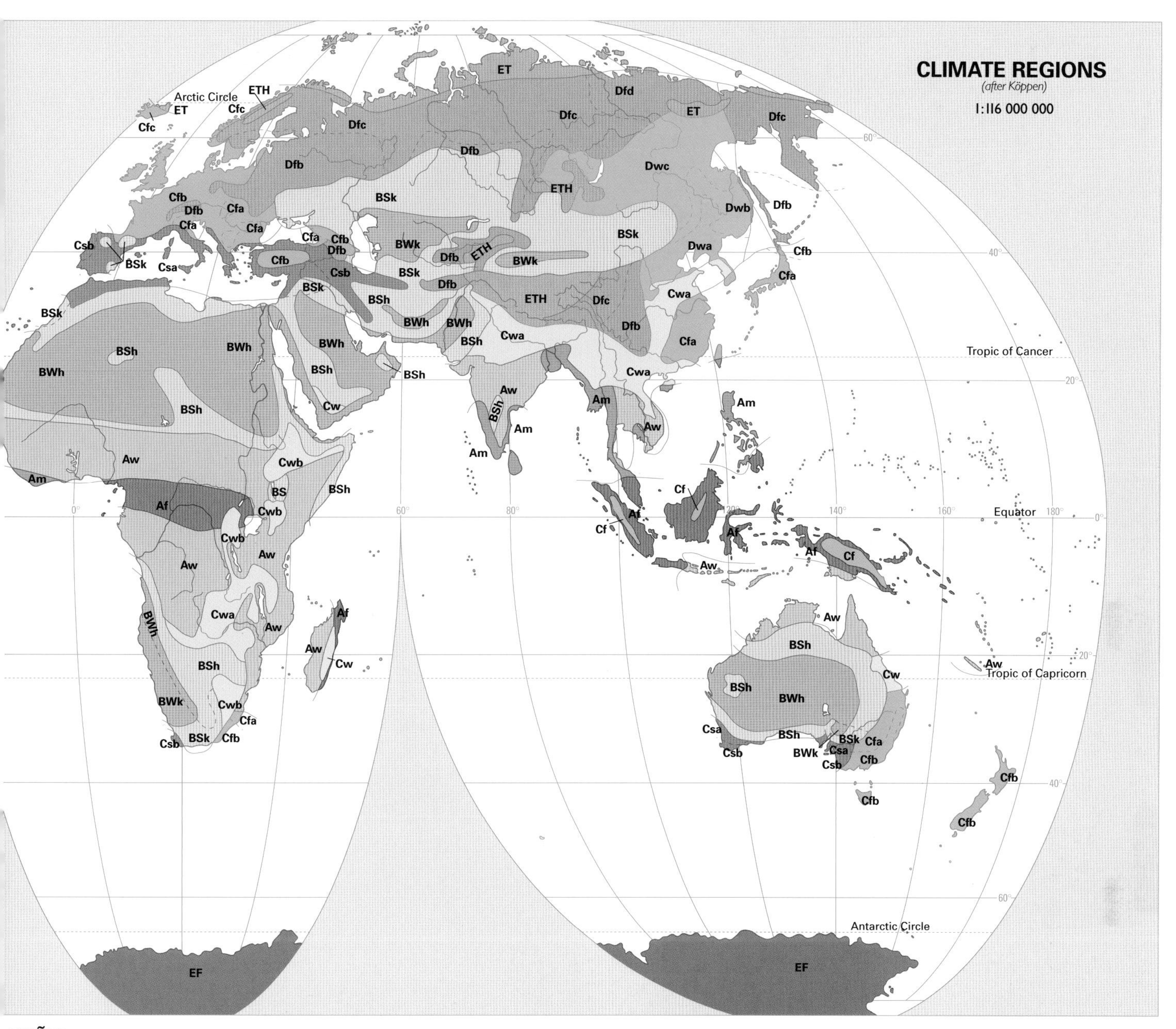

CLIMATE REGIONS
(after Köppen)

1:116 000 000

NIÑO

iño, 'The Little Boy' in Spanish, was originally the name given by local fishermen to the
m current that can appear off the Pacific coast of South America. In a normal year,
th-easterly trade winds drive surface waters westwards off the coast of South America,
wing cold, nutrient-rich water up from below. In an El Niño year, warm water from the
t Pacific suppresses upwelling in the east, depriving the region of nutrients and driving
fish away. The water is warmed by as much as 7°C, disturbing the tropical atmosphere
ulation. During an intense El Niño, the south-east trade winds change direction and
ome equatorial westerlies, resulting in climatic extremes in many regions of the world,
h as drought in parts of Australia and India, and heavy rainfall in south-eastern USA.

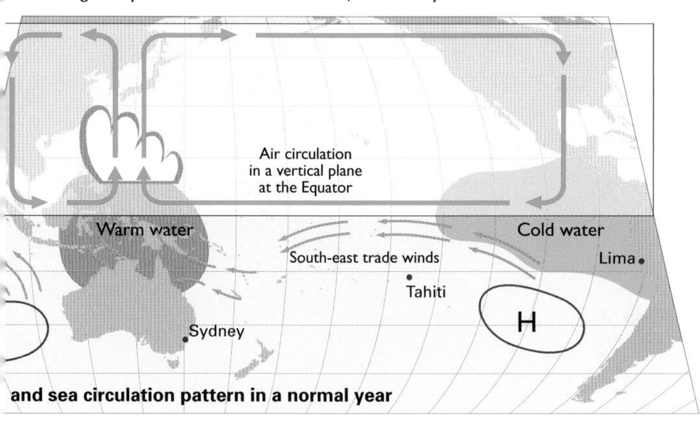

El Niño air and sea circulation pattern

El Niño events occur about every 4 to 7 years and typically last for around 12 to 18
months. El Niño usually results in reduced rainfall across northern and eastern Australia.
This can lead to widespread and severe drought, as well as increased temperatures and
bushfire risk. However, each El Niño event is unique in terms of its strength as well as its
impact. It is measured by the Southern Oscillation Index (SOI) and the changes in ocean
temperatures.

La Niña, or 'The Little Girl', is associated with cooler waters in the central and eastern
Pacific. A La Niña year can result in cooler land temperatures across the tropics and
subtropics and more storms in the North Atlantic.

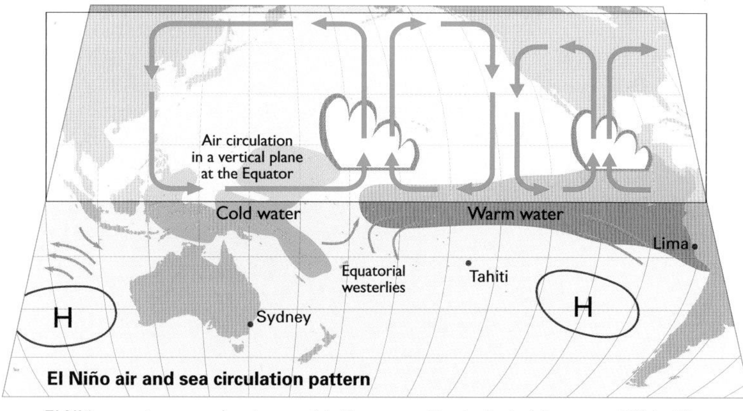

and sea circulation pattern in a normal year

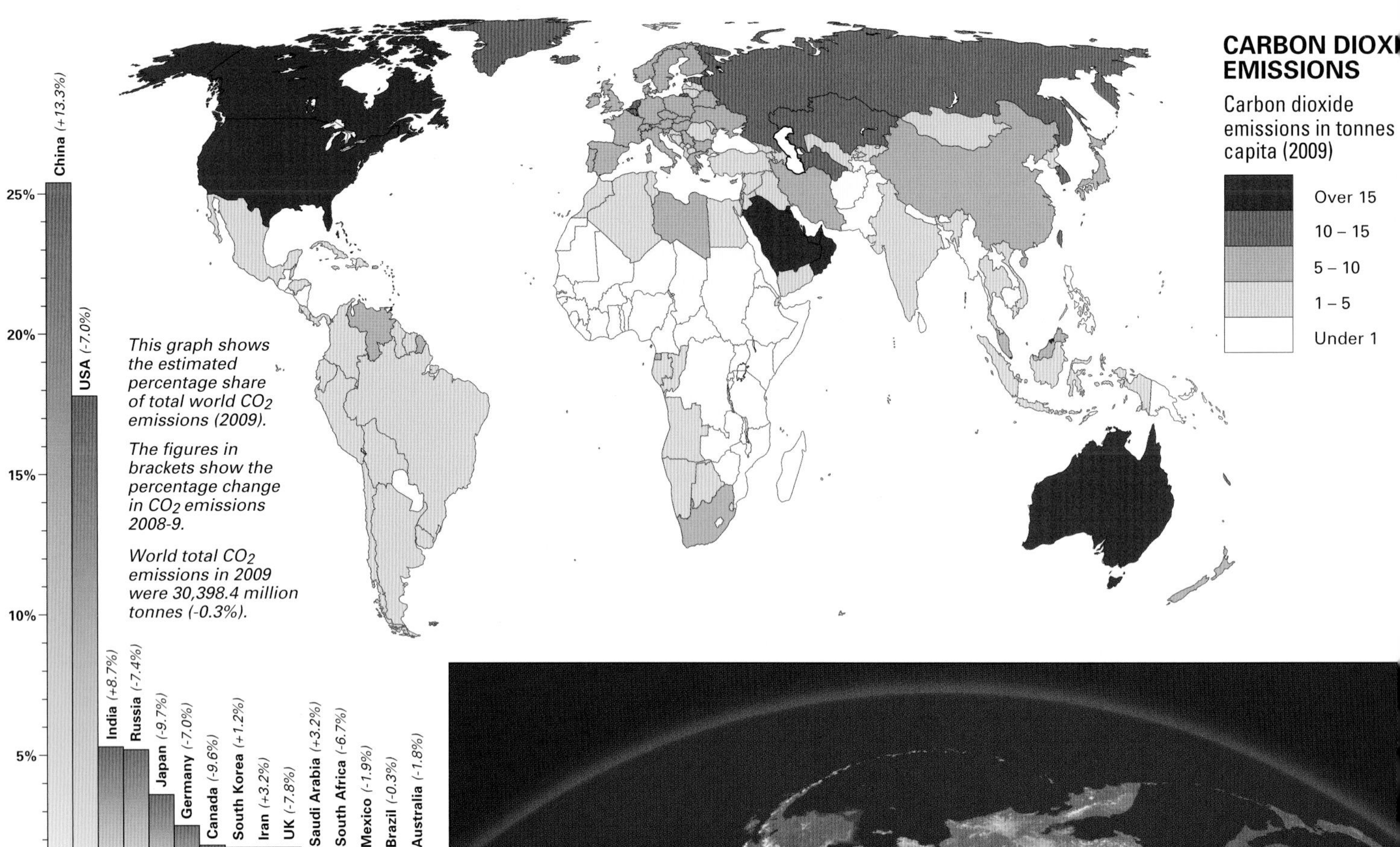

CARBON DIOXIDE EMISSIONS

Carbon dioxide emissions in tonnes capita (2009)

- Over 15
- 10 – 15
- 5 – 10
- 1 – 5
- Under 1

This graph shows the estimated percentage share of total world CO₂ emissions (2009).

The figures in brackets show the percentage change in CO₂ emissions 2008-9.

World total CO₂ emissions in 2009 were 30,398.4 million tonnes (-0.3%).

China (+13.3%)
USA (-7.0%)
India (+8.7%)
Russia (-7.4%)
Japan (-9.7%)
Germany (-7.0%)
Canada (-9.6%)
South Korea (+1.2%)
Iran (+3.2%)
UK (-7.8%)
Saudi Arabia (+3.2%)
South Africa (-6.7%)
Mexico (-1.9%)
Brazil (-0.3%)
Australia (-1.8%)

Arctic Ice Cap

This image shows the extent of sea-ice in the Arctic in September 2008. The sea-ice area expands and contracts seasonally and September, at the end of the northern hemisphere summer, represents its smallest extent. The year 2008 showed the biggest reduction in sea-ice since satellite surveillance began in 1979 and this is believed to be related to climate change and global warming. Although dramatic, the sea-ice itself is thought to be quite thin, on average about 3 m (10 ft) thick. Even large reductions would not in themselves involve any sea-level change since the ice is floating and displaces the sea water. One by-product of this is the opening-up of clear sea. This would enable shipping in the northern hemisphere to move between the Atlantic and Pacific Oceans using the much shorter routes around the north coasts of Canada and of Russia, rather than heading south to do this.

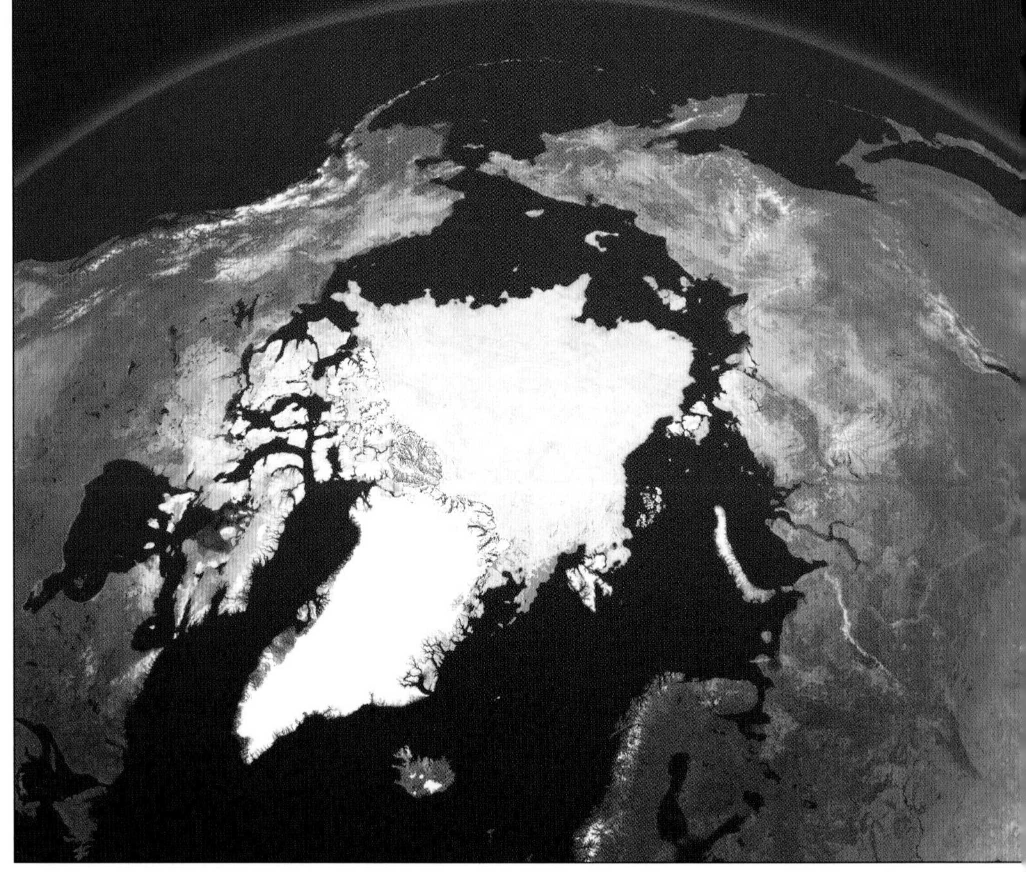

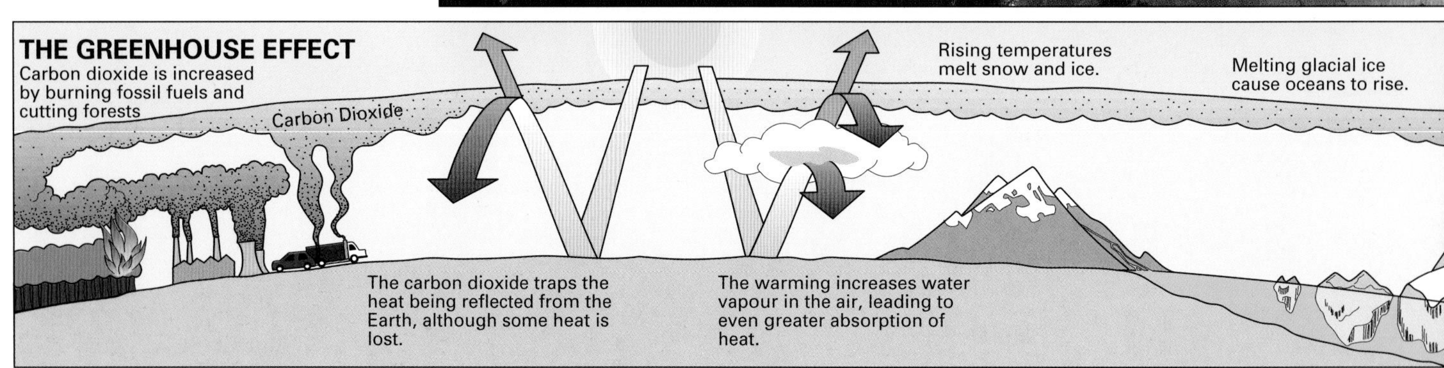

THE GREENHOUSE EFFECT

Carbon dioxide is increased by burning fossil fuels and cutting forests

Carbon Dioxide

Rising temperatures melt snow and ice.

Melting glacial ice cause oceans to rise.

The carbon dioxide traps the heat being reflected from the Earth, although some heat is lost.

The warming increases water vapour in the air, leading to even greater absorption of heat.

COPYRIGHT

PREDICTED CHANGE IN TEMPERATURE

The difference between actual annual average surface air temperature, 1960–90, and predicted annual average surface air temperature, 2070–2100. This map shows the predicted increase, assuming a 'medium growth' of the global economy and assuming that no measures to combat the emission of greenhouse gases are taken.

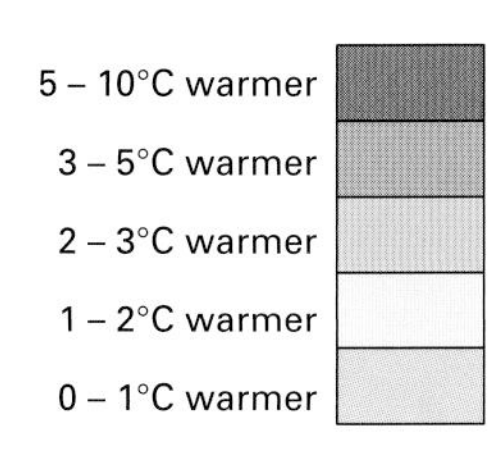

- 5 – 10°C warmer
- 3 – 5°C warmer
- 2 – 3°C warmer
- 1 – 2°C warmer
- 0 – 1°C warmer

Source: The Hadley Centre of Climate Prediction and Research, The Met. Office.

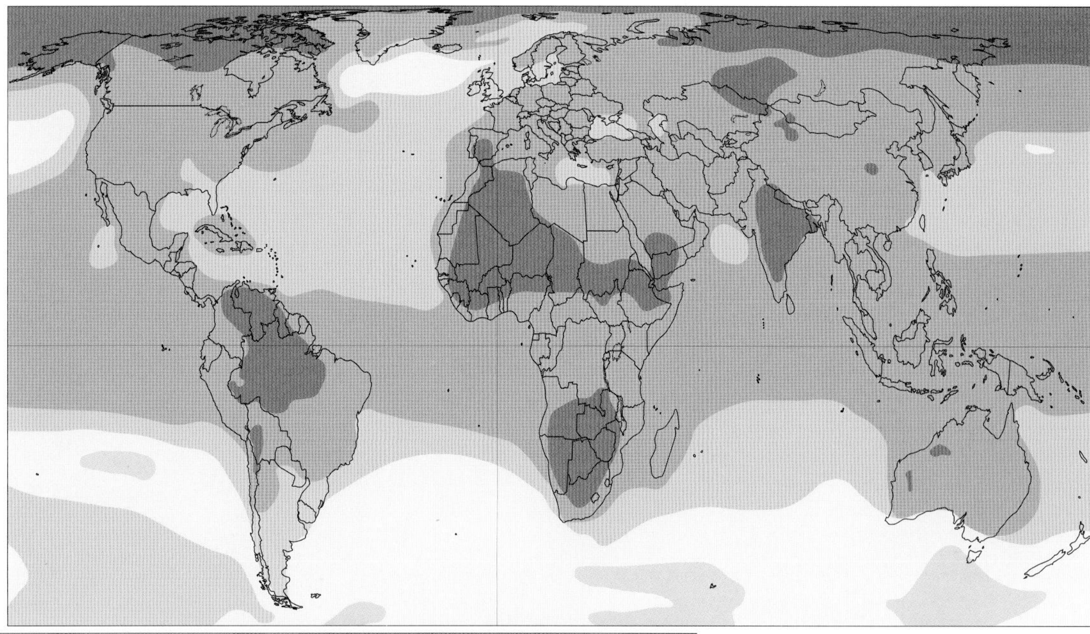

PREDICTED CHANGE IN PRECIPITATION

The difference between actual annual average precipitation, 1960–90, and predicted annual average precipitation, 2070–2100. It should be noted that these predicted annual mean changes mask quite significant seasonal detail.

- Over 2 mm more rain per day
- 1 – 2 mm more rain per day
- 0.5 – 1 mm more rain per day
- 0.2 – 0.5 mm more rain per day
- No change
- 0.2 – 0.5 mm less rain per day
- 0.5 – 1 mm less rain per day
- 1 – 2 mm less rain per day
- Over 2 mm less rain per day

DESERTIFICATION AND DEFORESTATION

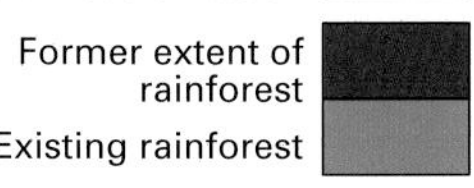

- Existing deserts and dry areas
- Areas with a high risk of desertification
- Areas with a moderate risk of desertification
- Former extent of rainforest
- Existing rainforest

Deforestation 1990–2010

	Total forest cover in million ha 1990	Total forest cover in million ha 2010	% change 1990-2010
alia	574.8	519.5	-9.6
esia	153.4	147.4	-3.9
	118.5	90.9	-23.3
	69.9	67.0	-4.1
a	62.8	57.2	-8.9
New Guinea	31.5	28.6	-9.2
roon	24.3	19.9	-18.1
	22.7	22.3	-1.8
ysia	20.4	18.6	-8.8
ia	17.0	8.7	-48.8
nd	16.9	15.0	-11.2
gascar	13.5	12.1	-10.4

COPYRIGHT PHILIP'S

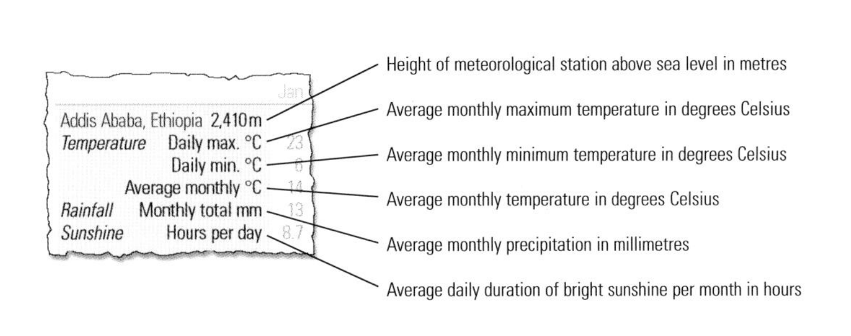
Addis Ababa, Ethiopia 2,410m
Jan
Temperature Daily max. °C 23
Daily min. °C 6
Average monthly °C 14
Rainfall Monthly total mm 13
Sunshine Hours per day 8.7
Height of meteorological station above sea level in metres
Average monthly maximum temperature in degrees Celsius
Average monthly minimum temperature in degrees Celsius
Average monthly temperature in degrees Celsius
Average monthly precipitation in millimetres
Average daily duration of bright sunshine per month in hours

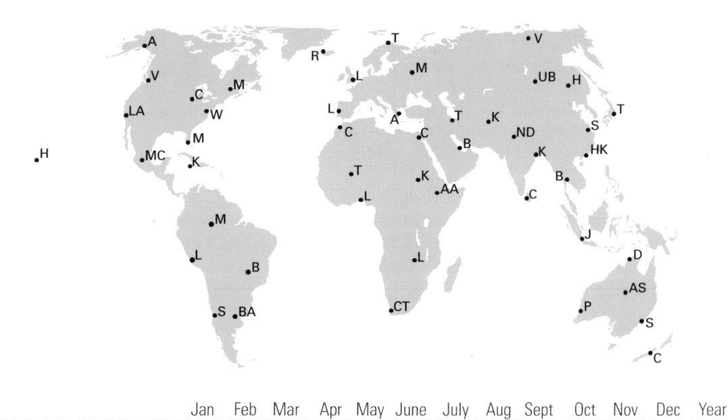

Addis Ababa, Ethiopia 2,410m	Jan	Feb	Mar	Apr	May	June	July	Aug	Sept	Oct	Nov	Dec	Year
Temperature Daily max. °C	23	24	25	24	25	23	20	20	21	22	23	22	23
Daily min. °C	6	7	9	10	9	10	11	11	10	7	5	5	8
Average monthly °C	14	15	17	17	17	16	16	15	15	15	14	14	15
Rainfall Monthly total mm	13	35	67	91	81	117	247	255	167	29	8	5	1,115
Sunshine Hours per day	8.7	8.2	7.6	8.1	6.5	4.8	2.8	3.2	5.2	7.6	6.7	7	6.4

Alice Springs, Australia 580m	Jan	Feb	Mar	Apr	May	June	July	Aug	Sept	Oct	Nov	Dec	Year
Temperature Daily max. °C	35	35	32	27	23	19	19	23	27	31	33	35	28
Daily min. °C	21	20	17	12	8	5	4	6	10	15	18	20	13
Average monthly °C	28	27	25	20	15	12	12	14	18	23	25	27	21
Rainfall Monthly total mm	44	33	27	10	15	13	7	8	7	18	29	38	249
Sunshine Hours per day	10.3	10.4	9.3	9.2	8	8	8.9	9.8	10	9.7	10.1	10	9.5

Anchorage, USA 183m	Jan	Feb	Mar	Apr	May	June	July	Aug	Sept	Oct	Nov	Dec	Year
Temperature Daily max. °C	–7	–3	0	7	13	18	19	17	13	6	–2	–6	–6
Daily min. °C	–15	–12	–9	–2	4	8	10	9	5	–2	–9	–14	–2
Average monthly °C	–11	–7	–4	3	9	13	15	13	9	2	–5	–10	–4
Rainfall Monthly total mm	20	18	13	11	13	25	47	64	64	47	28	24	374
Sunshine Hours per day	2.4	4.1	6.6	8.3	8.3	9.2	8.5	6	4.4	3.1	2.6	1.6	5.4

Athens, Greece 107m	Jan	Feb	Mar	Apr	May	June	July	Aug	Sept	Oct	Nov	Dec	Year
Temperature Daily max. °C	13	14	16	20	25	30	33	33	29	24	19	15	23
Daily min. °C	6	7	8	11	16	20	23	23	19	15	12	8	14
Average monthly °C	10	10	12	16	20	25	28	28	24	20	15	11	18
Rainfall Monthly total mm	62	37	37	23	23	14	6	7	15	51	56	71	402
Sunshine Hours per day	3.9	5.2	5.8	7.7	8.9	10.7	11.9	11.5	9.4	6.8	4.8	3.8	7.3

Bahrain City, Bahrain 2m	Jan	Feb	Mar	Apr	May	June	July	Aug	Sept	Oct	Nov	Dec	Year
Temperature Daily max. °C	20	21	25	29	33	36	37	38	36	32	27	22	30
Daily min. °C	14	15	18	22	25	29	31	32	29	25	22	16	23
Average monthly °C	17	18	21	25	29	32	34	35	32	29	25	19	26
Rainfall Monthly total mm	18	12	10	9	2	0	0	0	0	0.4	3	16	70
Sunshine Hours per day	5.9	6.9	7.9	8.8	10.6	13.2	12.1	12	12	10.3	7.7	6.4	9.5

Bangkok, Thailand 10m	Jan	Feb	Mar	Apr	May	June	July	Aug	Sept	Oct	Nov	Dec	Year
Temperature Daily max. °C	32	33	34	35	34	33	32	32	32	31	31	31	33
Daily min. °C	20	23	24	26	25	25	25	24	24	24	23	20	24
Average monthly °C	26	28	29	30	30	29	28	28	28	28	27	26	28
Rainfall Monthly total mm	9	30	36	82	165	153	168	183	310	239	55	8	1,438
Sunshine Hours per day	8.2	8	8	10	7.5	6.1	4.7	5.2	5.2	6.1	7.3	7.8	7

Brasilia, Brazil 910m	Jan	Feb	Mar	Apr	May	June	July	Aug	Sept	Oct	Nov	Dec	Year
Temperature Daily max. °C	28	28	28	28	27	27	27	29	30	29	28	27	28
Daily min. °C	18	18	18	17	15	13	13	14	16	18	18	18	16
Average monthly °C	23	23	23	22	21	20	20	21	23	24	23	22	22
Rainfall Monthly total mm	252	204	227	93	17	3	6	3	30	127	255	343	1,560
Sunshine Hours per day	5.8	5.7	6	7.4	8.7	9.3	9.6	9.8	7.9	6.5	4.8	4.4	7.2

Buenos Aires, Argentina 25m	Jan	Feb	Mar	Apr	May	June	July	Aug	Sept	Oct	Nov	Dec	Year
Temperature Daily max. °C	30	29	26	22	18	14	14	16	18	21	25	28	22
Daily min. °C	17	17	16	12	9	5	6	6	8	10	14	16	11
Average monthly °C	23	23	21	17	13	10	10	11	13	15	19	22	16
Rainfall Monthly total mm	79	71	109	89	76	61	56	61	79	86	84	99	950
Sunshine Hours per day	9.2	8.5	7.5	6.8	4.9	3.5	3.8	5.2	6	6.8	8.1	8.5	6.6

Cairo, Egypt 75m	Jan	Feb	Mar	Apr	May	June	July	Aug	Sept	Oct	Nov	Dec	Year
Temperature Daily max. °C	19	21	24	28	32	35	35	35	33	30	26	21	28
Daily min. °C	9	9	12	14	18	20	22	22	20	18	14	10	16
Average monthly °C	14	15	18	21	25	28	29	28	26	24	20	16	22
Rainfall Monthly total mm	4	4	3	1	2	1	0	0	1	1	3	7	27
Sunshine Hours per day	6.9	8.4	8.7	9.7	10.5	11.9	11.7	11.3	10.4	9.4	8.3	6.4	9.5

Cape Town, South Africa 44m	Jan	Feb	Mar	Apr	May	June	July	Aug	Sept	Oct	Nov	Dec	Year
Temperature Daily max. °C	26	26	25	23	20	18	17	18	19	21	24	25	22
Daily min. °C	15	15	14	11	9	7	7	7	8	10	13	15	11
Average monthly °C	21	20	20	17	14	13	12	12	14	16	18	20	16
Rainfall Monthly total mm	12	19	17	42	67	98	68	76	36	45	12	13	505
Sunshine Hours per day	11.4	10.2	9.4	7.7	6.1	5.7	6.4	6.6	7.6	8.6	10.2	10.9	8.4

Casablanca, Morocco 59m	Jan	Feb	Mar	Apr	May	June	July	Aug	Sept	Oct	Nov	Dec	Year
Temperature Daily max. °C	17	18	20	21	22	24	26	26	26	24	21	18	22
Daily min. °C	8	9	11	12	15	18	19	20	18	15	12	10	14
Average monthly °C	13	13	15	16	18	21	23	23	22	20	17	14	18
Rainfall Monthly total mm	78	61	54	37	20	3	0	1	6	28	58	94	440
Sunshine Hours per day	5.2	6.3	7.3	9	9.4	9.7	10.2	9.7	9.1	7.4	5.9	5.3	7.9

Chicago, USA 186m	Jan	Feb	Mar	Apr	May	June	July	Aug	Sept	Oct	Nov	Dec	Year
Temperature Daily max. °C	1	2	6	14	21	26	29	28	24	17	8	2	15
Daily min. °C	–7	–6	–2	5	11	16	20	19	14	8	0	–5	–6
Average monthly °C	–3	–2	2	9	16	21	24	23	19	13	4	–2	4
Rainfall Monthly total mm	47	41	70	77	96	103	86	80	69	71	56	48	844
Sunshine Hours per day	4	5	6.6	6.9	8.9	10.2	10	9.2	8.2	6.9	4.5	3.7	7

Christchurch, New Zealand 5m	Jan	Feb	Mar	Apr	May	June	July	Aug	Sept	Oct	Nov	Dec	Year
Temperature Daily max. °C	21	21	19	17	13	11	10	11	14	17	19	21	16
Daily min. °C	12	12	10	7	4	2	1	3	5	7	8	11	7
Average monthly °C	16	16	15	12	9	6	6	7	9	12	13	16	11
Rainfall Monthly total mm	56	46	43	46	76	69	61	58	51	51	51	61	669
Sunshine Hours per day	7	6.5	5.6	4.7	4.3	3.9	4.1	4.7	5.6	6.1	6.9	6.3	5.5

Colombo, Sri Lanka 10m	Jan	Feb	Mar	Apr	May	June	July	Aug	Sept	Oct	Nov	Dec	Year
Temperature Daily max. °C	30	31	31	31	30	30	29	29	30	29	29	30	30
Daily min. °C	22	22	23	24	25	25	25	25	25	24	23	22	24
Average monthly °C	26	26	27	28	28	27	27	27	27	27	26	26	27
Rainfall Monthly total mm	101	66	118	230	394	220	140	102	174	348	333	142	2,368
Sunshine Hours per day	7.9	9	8.1	7.2	6.4	5.4	6.1	6.3	6.2	6.5	6.4	7.8	6.9

Darwin, Australia 30m	Jan	Feb	Mar	Apr	May	June	July	Aug	Sept	Oct	Nov	Dec	Year
Temperature Daily max. °C	32	32	33	33	33	31	31	32	33	34	34	33	33
Daily min. °C	25	25	25	24	23	21	19	21	23	25	26	26	24
Average monthly °C	29	29	29	29	28	26	25	26	28	29	30	29	28
Rainfall Monthly total mm	405	309	279	77	8	2	0	1	15	48	108	214	1,466
Sunshine Hours per day	5.8	5.8	6.6	9.8	9.3	10	9.9	10.4	10.1	9.4	9.6	6.8	8.6

Harbin, China 175m	Jan	Feb	Mar	Apr	May	June	July	Aug	Sept	Oct	Nov	Dec	Year
Temperature Daily max. °C	–14	–9	0	12	21	26	29	27	20	12	–1	–11	9
Daily min. °C	–26	–23	–12	–1	7	14	18	16	8	0	–12	–22	–3
Average monthly °C	–20	–16	–6	6	14	20	23	22	14	6	–7	–17	3
Rainfall Monthly total mm	4	6	17	23	44	92	167	119	52	36	12	5	577
Sunshine Hours per day	6.4	7.8	8	7.8	8.3	8.6	8.6	8.2	7.2	6.9	6.1	5.7	7.5

Hong Kong, China 35m	Jan	Feb	Mar	Apr	May	June	July	Aug	Sept	Oct	Nov	Dec	Year
Temperature Daily max. °C	18	18	20	24	28	30	31	31	30	27	24	20	25
Daily min. °C	13	13	16	19	23	26	26	26	25	23	19	15	20
Average monthly °C	16	15	18	22	25	28	28	28	27	25	21	17	23
Rainfall Monthly total mm	30	60	70	133	332	479	286	415	364	33	46	17	2,265
Sunshine Hours per day	4.7	3.5	3.1	3.8	5	5.4	6.8	6.5	6.6	7	6.2	5.5	5.3

Honolulu, Hawaii 5m	Jan	Feb	Mar	Apr	May	June	July	Aug	Sept	Oct	Nov	Dec	Year
Temperature Daily max. °C	26	26	26	27	28	29	29	29	30	29	28	26	28
Daily min. °C	19	19	19	20	21	22	23	23	23	22	21	20	21
Average monthly °C	23	22	23	23	24	26	26	26	26	26	24	23	24
Rainfall Monthly total mm	96	84	73	33	25	8	11	23	25	47	55	76	556
Sunshine Hours per day	7.3	7.7	8.3	8.6	8.8	9.1	9.4	9.3	9.2	8.3	7.5	6.2	8.3

Jakarta, Indonesia 10m	Jan	Feb	Mar	Apr	May	June	July	Aug	Sept	Oct	Nov	Dec	Year
Temperature Daily max. °C	29	29	30	31	31	31	31	31	31	31	30	29	30
Daily min. °C	23	23	23	24	24	23	23	23	23	23	23	23	23
Average monthly °C	26	26	27	27	27	27	27	27	27	27	27	26	27
Rainfall Monthly total mm	300	300	211	147	114	97	64	43	66	112	142	203	1,799
Sunshine Hours per day	6.1	6.5	7.7	8.5	8.4	8.5	9.1	9.5	9.6	9	7.7	7.1	8.1

Kabul, Afghanistan 1,791m	Jan	Feb	Mar	Apr	May	June	July	Aug	Sept	Oct	Nov	Dec	Year
Temperature Daily max. °C	2	4	12	19	26	31	33	33	30	22	17	8	20
Daily min. °C	–8	–6	1	6	11	13	16	15	11	6	1	–3	5
Average monthly °C	–3	–1	6	13	18	22	25	24	20	14	9	3	12
Rainfall Monthly total mm	28	61	72	117	33	1	7	1	0	1	37	14	372
Sunshine Hours per day	5.9	6	5.7	6.8	10.1	11.5	11.4	11.2	9.8	9.4	7.8	6.1	8.5

Khartoum, Sudan 380m	Jan	Feb	Mar	Apr	May	June	July	Aug	Sept	Oct	Nov	Dec	Year
Temperature Daily max. °C	32	33	37	40	42	41	38	36	38	39	35	32	37
Daily min. °C	16	17	20	23	26	27	26	25	25	25	21	17	22
Average monthly °C	24	25	28	32	34	34	32	30	32	32	28	25	30
Rainfall Monthly total mm	0	0	0	1	7	5	56	80	28	2	0	0	179
Sunshine Hours per day	10.6	11.2	10.4	10.8	10.4	10.1	8.6	8.6	9.6	10.3	10.8	10.6	10.2

Kingston, Jamaica 35m	Jan	Feb	Mar	Apr	May	June	July	Aug	Sept	Oct	Nov	Dec	Year
Temperature Daily max. °C	30	30	30	31	31	32	32	32	32	31	31	31	31
Daily min. °C	20	20	20	21	22	24	23	23	23	23	22	21	22
Average monthly °C	25	25	25	26	26	28	28	28	27	27	26	26	26
Rainfall Monthly total mm	23	15	23	31	102	89	38	91	99	180	74	36	801
Sunshine Hours per day	8.3	8.8	8.7	8.7	8.3	7.8	8.5	8.5	7.6	7.3	8.3	7.7	8.2

		Jan	Feb	Mar	Apr	May	June	July	Aug	Sept	Oct	Nov	Dec	Year
Kolkata (Calcutta), India 5 m														
Temperature	Daily max. °C	27	29	34	36	35	34	32	32	32	32	29	26	31
	Daily min. °C	13	15	21	24	25	26	26	26	26	23	18	13	21
	Average monthly °C	20	22	27	30	30	30	29	29	29	28	23	20	26
Rainfall	Monthly total mm	10	30	34	44	140	297	325	332	253	114	20	5	1,604
Sunshine	Hours per day	8.6	8.7	8.9	9	8.7	5.4	4.1	4.1	5.1	6.5	8.3	8.4	7.1
Lagos, Nigeria 40 m														
Temperature	Daily max. °C	32	33	33	32	31	29	28	28	29	30	31	32	31
	Daily min. °C	22	23	23	23	23	22	22	21	22	22	23	22	22
	Average monthly °C	27	28	28	28	27	26	25	24	25	26	27	27	26
Rainfall	Monthly total mm	28	41	99	99	203	300	180	56	180	190	63	25	1,464
Sunshine	Hours per day	5.9	6.8	6.3	6.1	5.6	3.8	2.8	3.3	3	5.1	6.6	6.5	5.2
Lima, Peru 120 m														
Temperature	Daily max. °C	28	29	29	27	24	20	20	19	20	22	24	26	24
	Daily min. °C	19	20	19	17	16	15	14	14	14	15	16	17	16
	Average monthly °C	24	24	24	22	20	17	17	16	17	18	20	21	20
Rainfall	Monthly total mm	1	1	1	1	5	5	8	8	8	3	3	1	45
Sunshine	Hours per day	6.3	6.8	6.9	6.7	4	1.4	1.1	1	1.1	2.5	4.1	5	3.9
Lisbon, Portugal 77 m														
Temperature	Daily max. °C	14	15	17	20	21	25	27	28	26	22	17	15	21
	Daily min. °C	8	8	10	12	13	15	17	17	17	14	11	9	13
	Average monthly °C	11	12	14	16	17	20	22	23	21	18	14	12	17
Rainfall	Monthly total mm	111	76	109	54	44	16	3	4	33	62	93	103	708
Sunshine	Hours per day	4.7	5.9	6	8.3	9.1	10.6	11.4	10.7	8.4	6.7	5.2	4.6	7.7
London (Kew), UK 5 m														
Temperature	Daily max. °C	6	7	10	13	17	20	22	21	19	14	10	7	14
	Daily min. °C	2	2	3	6	8	12	14	13	11	8	5	4	7
	Average monthly °C	4	5	7	9	12	16	18	17	15	11	8	5	11
Rainfall	Monthly total mm	54	40	37	37	46	45	57	59	49	57	64	48	593
Sunshine	Hours per day	1.7	2.3	3.5	5.7	6.7	7	6.6	6	5	3.3	1.9	1.4	4.3
Los Angeles, USA 30 m														
Temperature	Daily max. °C	18	18	18	19	20	22	24	24	24	23	22	19	21
	Daily min. °C	7	8	9	11	13	15	17	17	16	14	11	9	12
	Average monthly °C	12	13	14	15	17	18	21	21	20	18	16	14	17
Rainfall	Monthly total mm	69	74	46	28	3	3	0	0	5	10	28	61	327
Sunshine	Hours per day	6.9	8.2	8.9	8.8	9.5	10.3	11.7	11	10.1	8.6	8.2	7.6	9.2
Lusaka, Zambia 1,154 m														
Temperature	Daily max. °C	26	26	26	27	25	23	23	26	29	31	29	27	27
	Daily min. °C	17	17	16	15	12	10	9	11	15	18	18	17	15
	Average monthly °C	22	22	21	21	18	17	16	19	22	25	23	22	21
Rainfall	Monthly total mm	224	173	90	19	3	1	0	1	1	17	85	196	810
Sunshine	Hours per day	5.1	5.4	6.9	8.9	9	9	9.1	9.6	9.5	9	7	5.5	7.8
Manaus, Brazil 45 m														
Temperature	Daily max. °C	31	31	31	31	31	31	32	33	34	34	33	32	32
	Daily min. °C	24	24	24	24	24	24	24	24	24	25	25	24	24
	Average monthly °C	28	28	28	27	28	28	28	28	29	29	29	28	28
Rainfall	Monthly total mm	278	278	300	287	193	99	61	41	62	112	165	220	2,096
Sunshine	Hours per day	3.9	4	3.6	3.9	5.4	6.9	7.9	8.2	7.5	6.6	5.9	4.9	5.7
Mexico City, Mexico 2,309 m														
Temperature	Daily max. °C	21	23	26	27	26	25	23	24	23	22	21	21	24
	Daily min. °C	5	6	7	9	10	11	11	11	11	9	6	5	8
	Average monthly °C	13	15	16	18	18	18	17	17	17	16	14	13	16
Rainfall	Monthly total mm	8	4	9	23	57	111	160	149	119	46	16	7	709
Sunshine	Hours per day	7.3	8.1	8.5	8.1	7.8	7	6.2	6.4	5.6	6.3	7	7.3	7.1
Miami, USA 2 m														
Temperature	Daily max. °C	24	25	27	28	30	31	32	32	31	29	27	25	28
	Daily min. °C	14	15	16	19	21	23	24	24	24	22	18	15	20
	Average monthly °C	19	20	21	23	25	27	28	28	27	25	22	20	24
Rainfall	Monthly total mm	51	48	58	99	163	188	170	178	241	208	71	43	1,518
Sunshine	Hours per day	7.7	8.3	8.7	9.4	8.9	8.5	8.7	8.4	7.1	6.5	7.5	7.1	8.1
Montreal, Canada 57 m														
Temperature	Daily max. °C	−6	−4	2	11	18	23	26	25	20	14	5	−3	11
	Daily min. °C	−13	−11	−5	2	9	14	17	16	11	6	0	−9	3
	Average monthly °C	−9	−8	−2	6	13	19	22	20	16	10	3	−6	7
Rainfall	Monthly total mm	87	76	86	83	81	91	98	87	96	84	89	89	1,047
Sunshine	Hours per day	2.8	3.4	4.5	5.2	6.7	7.7	8.2	7.7	5.6	4.3	2.4	2.2	5.1
Moscow, Russia 156 m														
Temperature	Daily max. °C	−6	−4	1	9	18	22	24	22	17	10	1	−5	9
	Daily min. °C	−14	−16	−11	−1	5	9	12	9	4	−2	−6	−12	−2
	Average monthly °C	−10	−10	−5	4	12	15	18	16	10	4	−2	−8	4
Rainfall	Monthly total mm	31	28	33	35	52	67	74	74	58	51	36	36	575
Sunshine	Hours per day	1	1.9	3.7	5.2	7.8	8.3	8.4	7.1	4.4	2.4	1	0.6	4.4
New Delhi, India 220 m														
Temperature	Daily max. °C	21	24	29	36	41	39	35	34	34	34	28	23	32
	Daily min. °C	6	10	14	20	26	28	27	26	24	17	11	7	18
	Average monthly °C	14	17	22	28	33	34	31	30	29	26	20	15	25
Rainfall	Monthly total mm	25	21	13	8	13	77	178	184	123	10	2	11	665
Sunshine	Hours per day	7.7	8.2	8.2	8.7	9.2	7.9	6	6.3	6.9	9.4	8.7	8.3	8

		Jan	Feb	Mar	Apr	May	June	July	Aug	Sept	Oct	Nov	Dec	Year
Perth, Australia 60 m														
Temperature	Daily max. °C	29	30	27	25	21	18	17	18	19	21	25	27	23
	Daily min. °C	17	18	16	14	12	10	9	9	10	11	14	16	13
	Average monthly °C	23	24	22	19	16	14	13	13	15	16	19	22	18
Rainfall	Monthly total mm	8	13	22	44	128	189	177	145	84	58	19	13	900
Sunshine	Hours per day	10.4	9.8	8.8	7.5	5.7	4.8	5.4	6	7.2	8.1	9.6	10.4	7.8
Reykjavik, Iceland 18 m														
Temperature	Daily max. °C	2	3	5	6	10	13	15	14	12	8	5	4	8
	Daily min. °C	−3	−3	−1	1	4	7	9	8	6	3	0	−2	3
	Average monthly °C	0	0	2	4	7	10	12	11	9	5	3	1	5
Rainfall	Monthly total mm	89	64	62	56	42	42	50	56	67	94	78	79	779
Sunshine	Hours per day	0.8	2	3.6	4.5	5.9	6.1	5.8	5.4	3.5	2.3	1.1	0.3	3.7
Santiago, Chile 520 m														
Temperature	Daily max. °C	30	29	27	24	19	15	15	17	19	22	26	29	23
	Daily min. °C	12	11	10	7	5	3	3	4	6	7	9	11	7
	Average monthly °C	21	20	18	15	12	9	9	10	12	15	17	20	15
Rainfall	Monthly total mm	3	3	5	13	64	84	76	56	31	15	8	5	363
Sunshine	Hours per day	10.8	8.9	8.5	5.5	3.6	3.3	3.3	3.6	4.8	6.1	8.7	10.1	6.4
Shanghai, China 5 m														
Temperature	Daily max. °C	8	8	13	19	24	28	32	32	27	23	17	10	20
	Daily min. °C	−1	0	4	9	14	19	23	23	19	13	7	2	11
	Average monthly °C	3	4	8	14	19	23	27	27	23	18	12	6	15
Rainfall	Monthly total mm	48	59	84	94	94	180	147	142	130	71	51	36	1,136
Sunshine	Hours per day	4	3.7	4.4	4.8	5.4	4.7	6.9	7.5	5.3	5.6	4.7	4.5	5.1
Sydney, Australia 40 m														
Temperature	Daily max. °C	26	26	25	22	19	17	17	18	20	22	24	25	22
	Daily min. °C	18	19	17	14	11	9	8	9	11	13	16	17	14
	Average monthly °C	22	22	21	18	15	13	12	13	16	18	20	21	18
Rainfall	Monthly total mm	89	101	127	135	127	117	117	76	74	71	74	74	1,182
Sunshine	Hours per day	7.5	7	6.4	6.1	5.7	5.3	6.1	7	7.3	7.5	7.5	7.5	6.8
Tehran, Iran 1,191 m														
Temperature	Daily max. °C	9	11	16	21	29	30	37	36	29	24	16	11	22
	Daily min. °C	−1	1	4	10	16	20	23	23	18	12	6	1	11
	Average monthly °C	4	6	10	15	22	25	30	29	23	18	11	6	17
Rainfall	Monthly total mm	37	23	36	31	14	2	1	1	1	5	29	27	207
Sunshine	Hours per day	5.9	6.7	7.5	7.4	8.6	11.6	11.2	11	10.1	7.6	6.9	6.3	8.4
Timbuktu, Mali 269 m														
Temperature	Daily max. °C	31	35	38	41	43	42	38	35	38	40	37	31	37
	Daily min. °C	13	16	18	22	26	27	25	24	24	23	18	14	21
	Average monthly °C	22	25	28	31	34	34	32	30	31	31	28	23	29
Rainfall	Monthly total mm	0	0	0	1	4	20	54	93	31	3	0	0	206
Sunshine	Hours per day	9.1	9.6	9.6	9.7	9.8	9.4	9.6	9	9.3	9.5	9.5	8.9	9.4
Tokyo, Japan 5 m														
Temperature	Daily max. °C	9	9	12	18	22	25	29	30	27	20	16	11	19
	Daily min. °C	−1	−1	3	4	13	17	22	23	19	13	7	1	10
	Average monthly °C	4	4	8	11	18	21	25	26	23	17	11	6	14
Rainfall	Monthly total mm	48	73	101	135	131	182	146	147	217	220	101	61	1,562
Sunshine	Hours per day	6	5.9	5.7	6	6.2	5	5.8	6.6	4.5	4.4	4.8	5.4	5.5
Tromsø, Norway 100 m														
Temperature	Daily max. °C	−2	−2	0	3	7	12	16	14	10	5	2	0	5
	Daily min. °C	−6	−6	−5	−2	1	6	9	8	5	1	−2	−4	0
	Average monthly °C	−4	−4	−3	0	4	9	13	11	7	3	0	−2	3
Rainfall	Monthly total mm	96	79	91	65	61	59	56	80	109	115	88	95	994
Sunshine	Hours per day	0.1	1.6	2.9	6.1	5.7	6.9	7.9	4.8	3.5	1.7	0.3	0	3.5
Ulan Bator, Mongolia 1,305 m														
Temperature	Daily max. °C	−19	−13	−4	7	13	21	22	21	14	6	−6	−16	4
	Daily min. °C	−32	−29	−22	−8	−2	7	11	8	2	−8	−20	−28	−11
	Average monthly °C	−26	−21	−13	−1	6	14	16	14	8	−1	−13	−22	−4
Rainfall	Monthly total mm	1	1	2	5	10	28	76	51	23	5	5	2	209
Sunshine	Hours per day	6.4	7.8	8	7.8	8.3	8.6	8.6	8.2	7.2	6.9	6.1	5.7	7.5
Vancouver, Canada 5 m														
Temperature	Daily max. °C	6	7	10	14	17	20	23	22	19	14	9	7	14
	Daily min. °C	0	1	3	5	8	11	13	12	10	7	3	2	6
	Average monthly °C	3	4	6	9	13	16	18	17	14	10	6	4	10
Rainfall	Monthly total mm	214	161	151	90	69	65	39	44	83	172	198	243	1,529
Sunshine	Hours per day	1.6	3	3.8	5.9	7.5	7.4	9.5	8.2	6	3.7	2	1.4	5
Verkhoyansk, Russia 137 m														
Temperature	Daily max. °C	−47	−40	−20	−1	11	21	24	21	12	−8	−33	−42	−8
	Daily min. °C	−51	−48	−40	−25	−7	4	6	1	−6	−20	−39	−50	−23
	Average monthly °C	−49	−44	−30	−13	2	12	15	11	3	−14	−36	−46	−16
Rainfall	Monthly total mm	7	5	5	4	5	25	33	30	13	11	10	7	155
Sunshine	Hours per day	0	2.6	6.9	9.6	9.7	10	9.7	7.5	4.1	2.4	0.6	0	5.4
Washington, D.C., USA 22 m														
Temperature	Daily max. °C	7	8	12	19	25	29	31	30	26	20	14	8	19
	Daily min. °C	−1	−1	2	8	13	18	21	20	16	10	4	−1	9
	Average monthly °C	3	3	7	13	19	24	26	25	21	15	9	4	14
Rainfall	Monthly total mm	84	68	96	85	103	88	108	120	100	78	75	75	1,080
Sunshine	Hours per day	4.4	5.7	6.7	7.4	8.2	8.8	8.6	8.2	7.5	6.5	5.3	4.5	6.8

Tropical Rain Forest

Tall broadleaved evergreen forest, trees 30–50m high with climbers and epiphytes forming continuous canopies. Associated with wet climate, 2–3000mm precipitation per year and high temperatures 24–28°C. High diversity of species, typically 100 per ha, including lianas, bamboo, palms, rubber, mahogany. Mangrove swamps form in coastal areas.

This diagram shows the highly stratified nature of the tropical rain forest. Crowns of trees form numerous layers at different heights and the dense shade limits undergrowth.

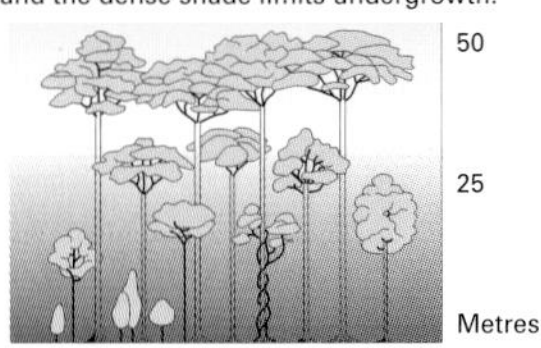

Temperate Deciduous and Coniferous Forest

A transition zone between broadleaves and conifers. Broadleaves are better suited to the warmer, damper and flatter locations.

Coniferous Forest (Taiga or Boreal)

Forming a large continuous belt across Northern America and Eurasia with a uniformity in tree species. Characteristically trees are tall, conical with short branches and wax-covered needle-shaped leaves to retain moisture. Cold climate with prolonged harsh winters and cool summers where average temperatures are under 0°C for more than six months of the year Undergrowth is sparse with mosses and lichens. Tree species include pine, fir, spruce, larch, tamarisk.

Mountainous Forest, mainly Coniferous

Mild winters, high humidity and high levels of rainfall throughout the year provide habitat for dense needle-leaf evergreen forests and the largest trees in the world, up to 100m, including the Douglas fir, redwood and giant sequoia.

High Plateau Steppe and Tundra

Similar to arctic tundra with frozen ground for the majority of the year. Very sparse ground coverage of low, shallow-rooted herbs, small shrubs, mosses, lichens and heather interspersed with bare soil.

Arctic Tundra

Average temperatures are 0°C, precipitation is mainly snowfall and the ground remains frozen for 10 months of the year. Vegetation flourishes when the shallow surface layer melts in the long summer days. Underlying permafrost remains frozen and surface water cannot drain away, making conditions marshy. Consists of sedges, snow lichen, arctic meadow grass, cotton grasses and dwarf willow.

Polar and Mountainous Ice Desert

Areas of bare rock and ice with patches of rock-strewn lithosols, low in organic matter and low water content. In sheltered patches only a few mosses, lichens and low shrubs can grow, including woolly moss and purple saxifrage.

Subtropical and Temperate Rain Forest

Precipitation, which is less than in the Tropical Rain Forest, falls in the long wet season interspersed with a season of reduced rainfall and lower temperatures. As a result there are fewer species, thinner canopies, fewer lianas and denser ground level foliage. Vegetation consists of evergreen oak, laurel, bamboo, magnolia and tree ferns.

Monsoon Woodland and Open Jungle

Mostly deciduous trees, because of the long dry season and lower temperat Trees can reach 30m but are sparser than in the rain forests. There is competition for light and thick jungle vegetation grows at lower levels. species diversity includes lianas, bamboo, teak, sandalwood, sal and ban

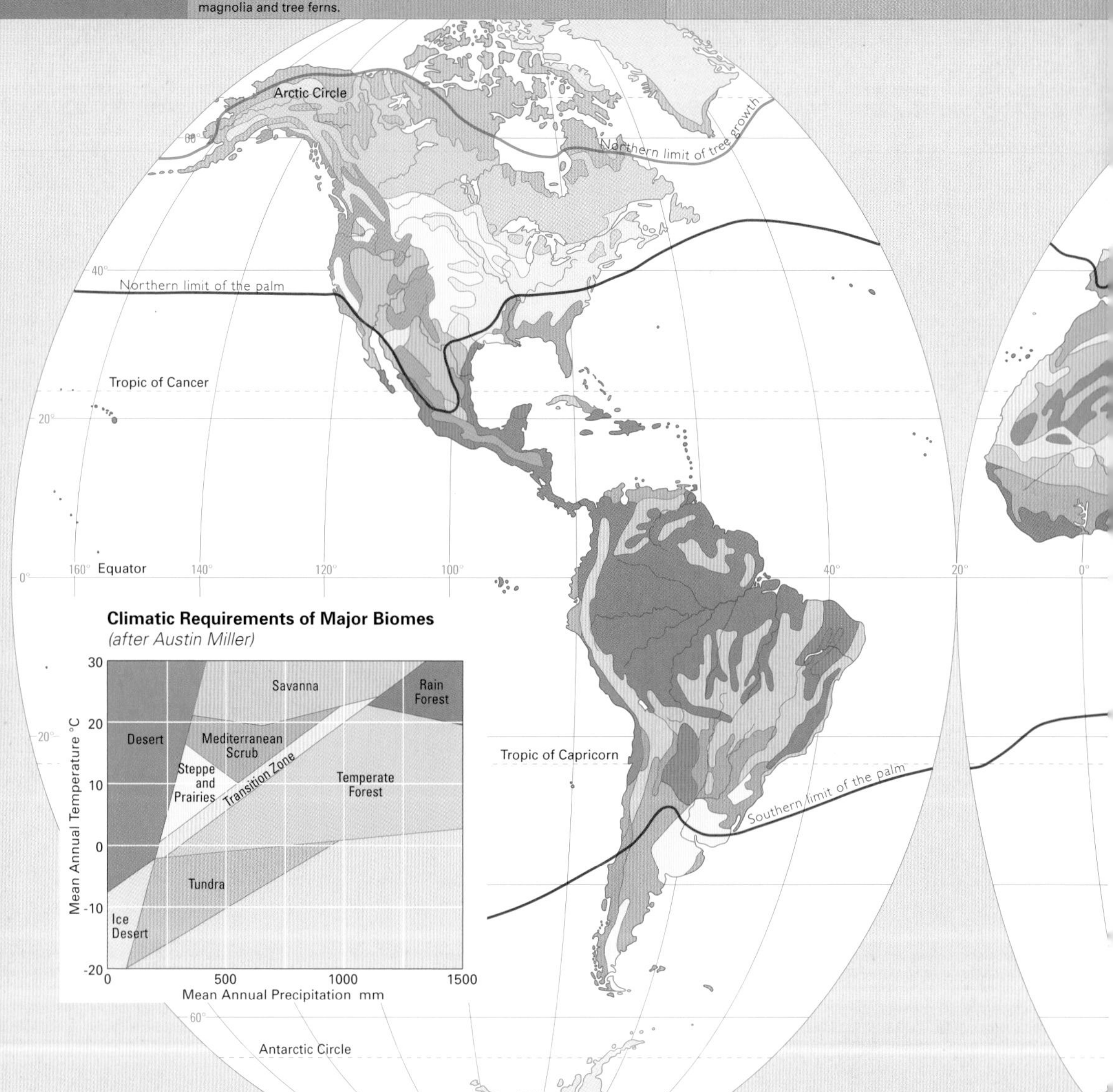

Climatic Requirements of Major Biomes
(after Austin Miller)

SOIL REGIONS
1:220 000 000

- Tundra soil
- Podzols
- Brown forest soil
- Lightly leached dry forest soil
- Red and yellow subtropical forest soil
- Reddish savanna soil and tropical red earths
- Laterites
- Chernozem
- Degraded chernozem
- Black savanna soil
- Chestnut steppe soil
- Desertic (arid) soil
- Alluvium
- Mountain and high plateau soils
- Oases soil
- Tropical and mangrove swamp

(after Glinka, Stremme, Marbut, and others)

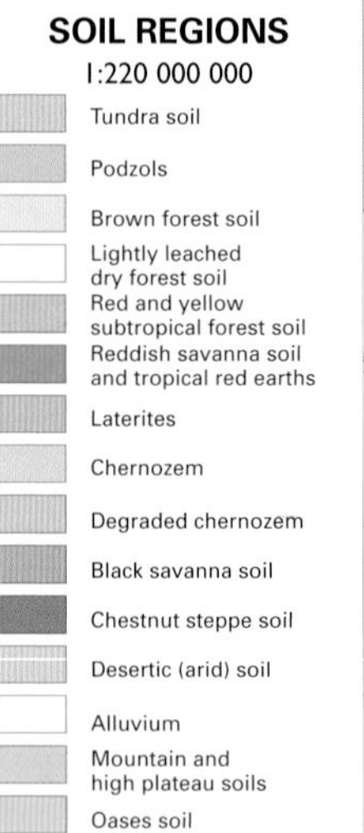

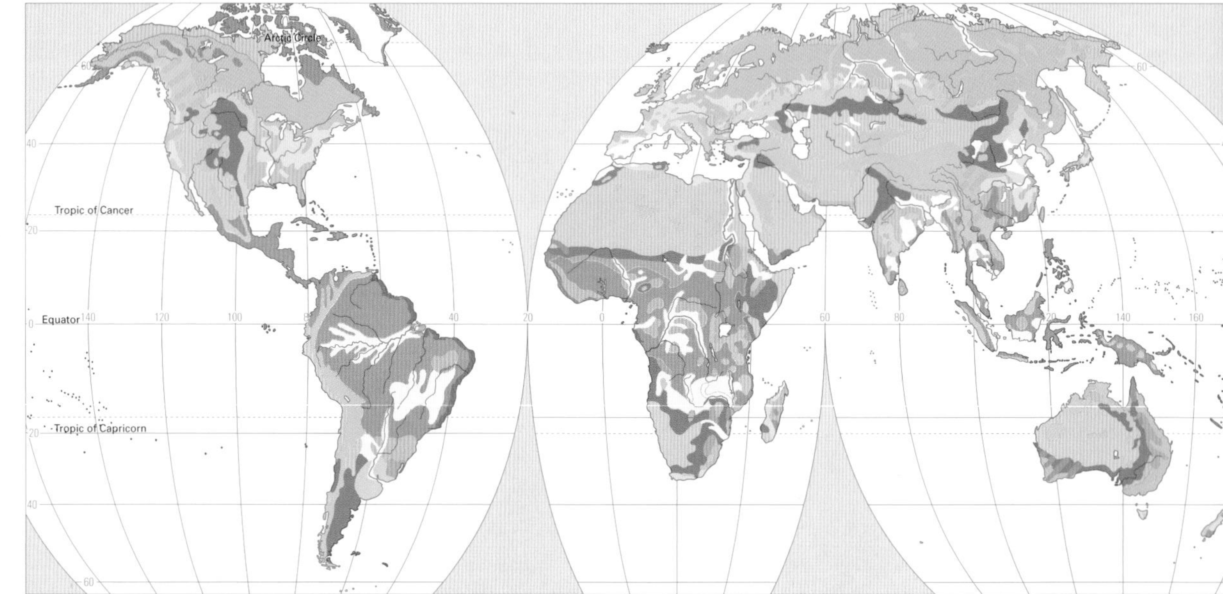

Projection: Interrupted Mollweide's Homolographic

Tropical and Temperate Woodland, Scrub and Bush
clearings with woody shrubs and tall grasses. Trees are fire-resistant and
deciduous or xerophytic because of long dry periods. Species include
yptus, acacia, mimosa and euphorbia.

Tropical Savanna with Low Trees and Bush
Tall, coarse grass with enough precipitation to support a scattering of short
deciduous trees and thorn scrub. Vegetation consists of elephant grass, acacia,
palms and baobob and is limited by aridity, grazing animals and periodic fires;
trees have developed thick, woody bark, small leaves or thorns.

Tropical Savanna and Grassland
Areas with a hot climate and long dry season. Extensive areas of tall grasses
often reach 3.5m with scattered fire and drought resistant bushes, low trees
and thickets of elephant grass. Shrubs include acacia, baobab and palms.

BIOMES
Classified by Climax Vegetation
1:116 000 000

Dry Semi-desert with Shrub and Grass
Xerophytic shrubs with thin grass cover and
few trees, limited by a long dry season and
short, hot, rainy period. Sagebrush, bunch
grass and acacia shrubs are common.

Desert Shrub
Scattered xerophytic plants able to withstand
daytime extremes in temperature and long
periods of drought. There is a large diversity
of desert flora such as cacti, yucca, tamarisk,
hard grass and artemisia.

Desert
Precipitation less than 250mm per year.
Vegetation is very sparse, mainly bare rock,
sand dunes and salt flats. Vegetation
comprises a few xerophytic shrubs and
ephemeral flowers.

Dry Steppe and Shrub
Semi-arid with cold, dry winters and hot
summers. Bare soil with sparsely distributed
short grasses and scattered shrubs and short
trees. Species include acacia, artemisia,
saksaul and tamarisk.

Temperate Grasslands, Prairie and Steppe
Continuous, tall, dense and deep-rooted
swards of ancient grasslands, considered to
be natural climax vegetation as determined
by soil and climate. Average precipitation
250–750mm, with a long dry season, limits
growth of trees and shrubs. Includes Stipa
grass, buffalo grass, blue stems and loco
weed.

Mediterranean Hardwood Forest and Scrub
Areas with hot and arid summers. Sparse
evergreen trees are short and twisted with
thick bark, interspersed with areas of scrub
land. Trees have waxy leaves or thorns and
deep root systems to resist drought. Many of
the hardwood forests have been cleared by
man, resulting in extensive scrub formation
– maquis and chaparral. Species found are
evergreen oak, stone pine, cork, olive and
myrtle.

Temperate Deciduous Forest and Meadow
Areas of relatively high, well-distributed
rainfall and temperature favourable for forest
growth. The Tall broadleaved trees form a
canopy in the summer, but shed their leaves
in the winter. The undergrowth is sparse and
poorly developed, but in the spring, herbs and
flowers develop quickly. Diverse species, with
up to 20 per ha, including oak, beech, birch,
maple, ash, elm, chestnut and hornbeam.
Many of these forests have been cleared for
urbanization and farming.

OIL DEGRADATION
1:220 000 000

reas of Concern

- Areas of serious concern
- Areas of some concern
- Stable terrain
- Non-vegetated land

**auses of soil
egradation
y region)**

- Grazing practices
- Other agricultural practices
- Industrialization
- Deforestation
- Fuelwood collection

(after Wageningen)

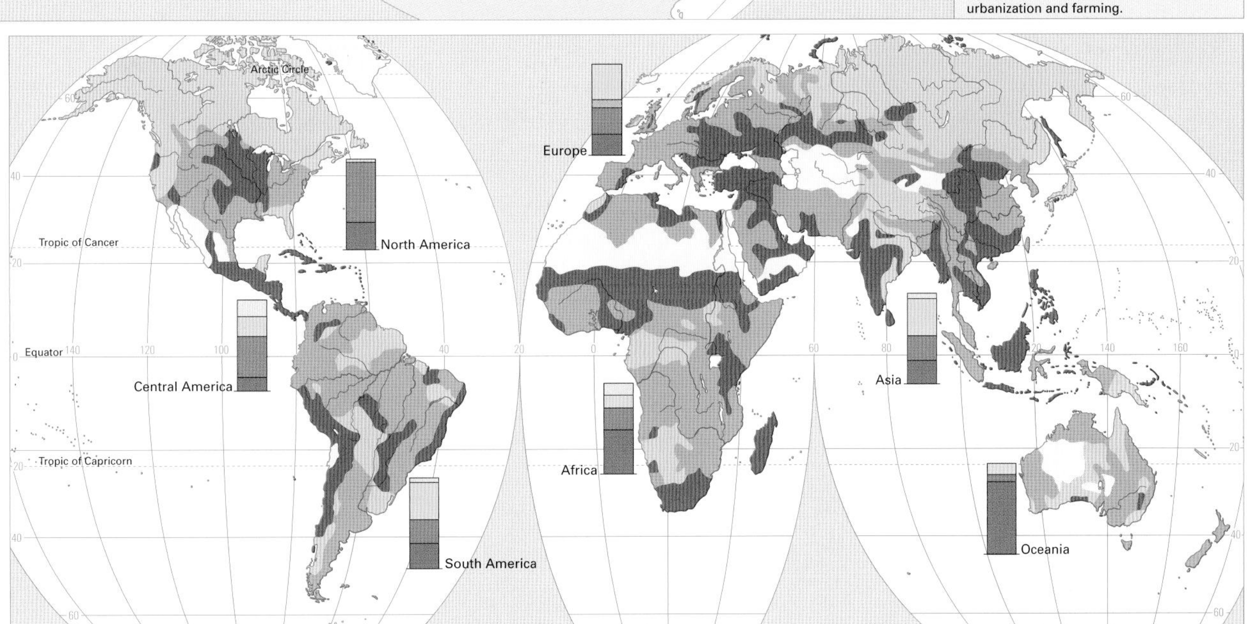

AGRICULTURAL PRODUCTION

Crops

Wheat

China 16.8% | India 11.8% | Russia 9.0% | USA 8.8% | France 5.6% | Canada 3.9% | Germany 3.7%

World total (2009): 685,614,000 tonnes

Rice

China 28.7% | India 19.5% | Indonesia 9.4% | Bangladesh 7.0% | Vietnam 5.7% | Burma 4.8% | Thailand 4.6%

World total (2009): 685,240,000 tonnes

Cassava

Nigeria 15.7% | Thailand 12.9% | Brazil 10.4% | Indonesia 9.4% | Congo (D.R.) 6.4% | Ghana 5.2%

World total (2009): 233,796,000 tonnes

Barley

Russia 11.8% | France 8.5% | Germany 8.1% | Ukraine 7.8% | Canada 6.3% | Australia 5.3%

World total (2009): 152,125,000 tonnes

Maize

USA 40.7% | China 20.0% | Brazil 6.3%

World total (2009): 818,823,000 tonnes

Potatoes

China 22.2% | Russia 10.4% | India 9.4% | Ukraine 6.0% | USA 5.9%

World total (2009): 329,581,000 tonnes

Soybeans

USA 41.0% | Brazil 25.7% | Argentina 13.9% | China 6.7%

World total (2009): 223,185,000 tonnes

Millet

India 33.0% | Nigeria 18.3% | Niger 10.0% | Mali 5.2% | China 4.6%

World total (2009): 26,702,000 tonnes

Sugar Cane

Brazil 40.4% | India 17.2% | China 7.0% | Thailand 4.0% | Pakistan 3.3% | Mexico 3.0%

World total (2009): 1,661,251,000 tonnes

Sugar Beet

France 15.4% | USA 11.8% | Germany 11.4% | Russia 11.0% | Turkey 7.6% | Poland 4.8% | UK 3.4%

World total (2009): 227,158,000 tonnes

Animal Products

Milk

India 16.0% | USA 12.2% | China 5.7% | Pakistan 4.9% | Russia 4.6% | Brazil 4.2%

World total (2009): 702,137,000 tonnes

Eggs

China 40.8% | USA 7.9% | India 4.7% | Japan 3.7%

World total (2009): 68,034,000 tonnes

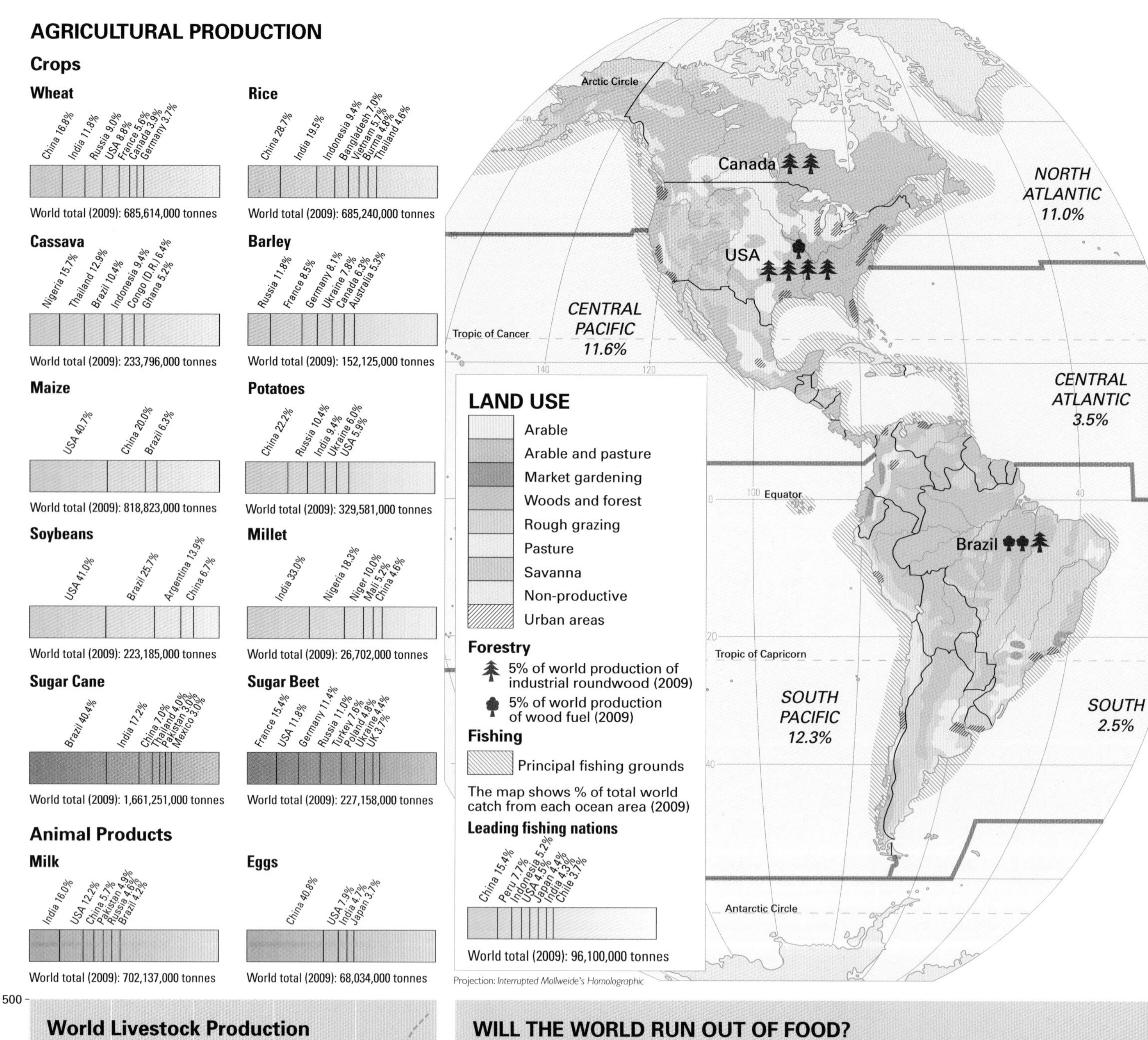

LAND USE

- Arable
- Arable and pasture
- Market gardening
- Woods and forest
- Rough grazing
- Pasture
- Savanna
- Non-productive
- Urban areas

Forestry

🌲 5% of world production of industrial roundwood (2009)

🌳 5% of world production of wood fuel (2009)

Fishing

▨ Principal fishing grounds

The map shows % of total world catch from each ocean area (2009)

Leading fishing nations

China 15.4% | Peru 7.7% | Indonesia 5.2% | USA 4.5% | Japan 4.3% | India 4.3% | Chile 3.7%

World total (2009): 96,100,000 tonnes

NORTH ATLANTIC 11.0%

CENTRAL PACIFIC 11.6%

CENTRAL ATLANTIC 3.5%

SOUTH PACIFIC 12.3%

SOUTH 2.5%

Canada / USA / Brazil

Arctic Circle • Tropic of Cancer • Equator • Tropic of Capricorn • Antarctic Circle

Projection: Interrupted Mollweide's Homolographic

World Livestock Production

- – – – Chickens
  World total (2009)
  18,631.4 million head
- —— Pigs
  World total (2009)
  941.8 million head
- —— Cattle
  World total (2009)
  1,380.2 million head
- – – – Sheep
  World total (2009)
  1,077.3 million head

1961 = 100

(y-axis: 150, 200, 250, 300, 350, 400, 450, 500)
(x-axis: 1961, 1971, 1981, 1991, 2001, 2011)

WILL THE WORLD RUN OUT OF FOOD?

At present-day rates, the world's population is predicted to reach at least 9 billion people by 2050. To sustain this population there will have to be a 70% increase in food production.

Currently, many people struggle to achieve the minimum food intake to sustain life. Globally, about 1 billion people are malnourished compared with 1 billion who are overweight.

Over 30% of the world's grain is fed to livestock because more and more people like to eat meat. But animals (and humans) are very inefficient in their utilization of nutrients; generally less than 20% of the nitrogen in their food is used; the rest is excreted, causing air and water pollution.

Meat is also very expensive in terms of water consumption: 0.5 kg of beef requires 8,442 litres of water to produce it. By 2030 there will be a 30% increase in water demand. Over 71% of the Earth's surface is covered in water but less than 3% of this is fresh water, of which over two-thirds is frozen in ice-caps and glaciers. Its over-exploitation in developed areas and availability in regions where it is scarce are major problems. For example, China currently has 23% of the world's population, but only 11% of its water.

How can we feed 9 billion people adequately and sustainably? The Royal Society has said that we need 'Sustainable Intensification', that is, to produce more using less and with less of an impact on the environment through good soil management, maintaining or enhancing crop genetic diversity, and introducing pest and disease resistance, as well as better fertiliser use.

Some, however, reject technological approaches and advocate extensive systems described as 'organic', 'bio-dynamic' or 'ecological', objecting to the reliance on chemical fertilisers and pesticides.

We need to reduce the 30% of the world's crop yield lost to pests, diseases and weeds; protect the fertile soil that irregularly covers only 11% of the global land surface and is a non-renewable asset; and cut back on food waste. In the UK it is estimated that 8.3 million tonnes of food worth £20 billion is sent to landfill each year. Some people now live on the food thrown away by shops – called 'skipping'.

If we adopt appropriate techniques and modify our behaviour, we stand a good chance of feeding the future, predominantly urban, population.

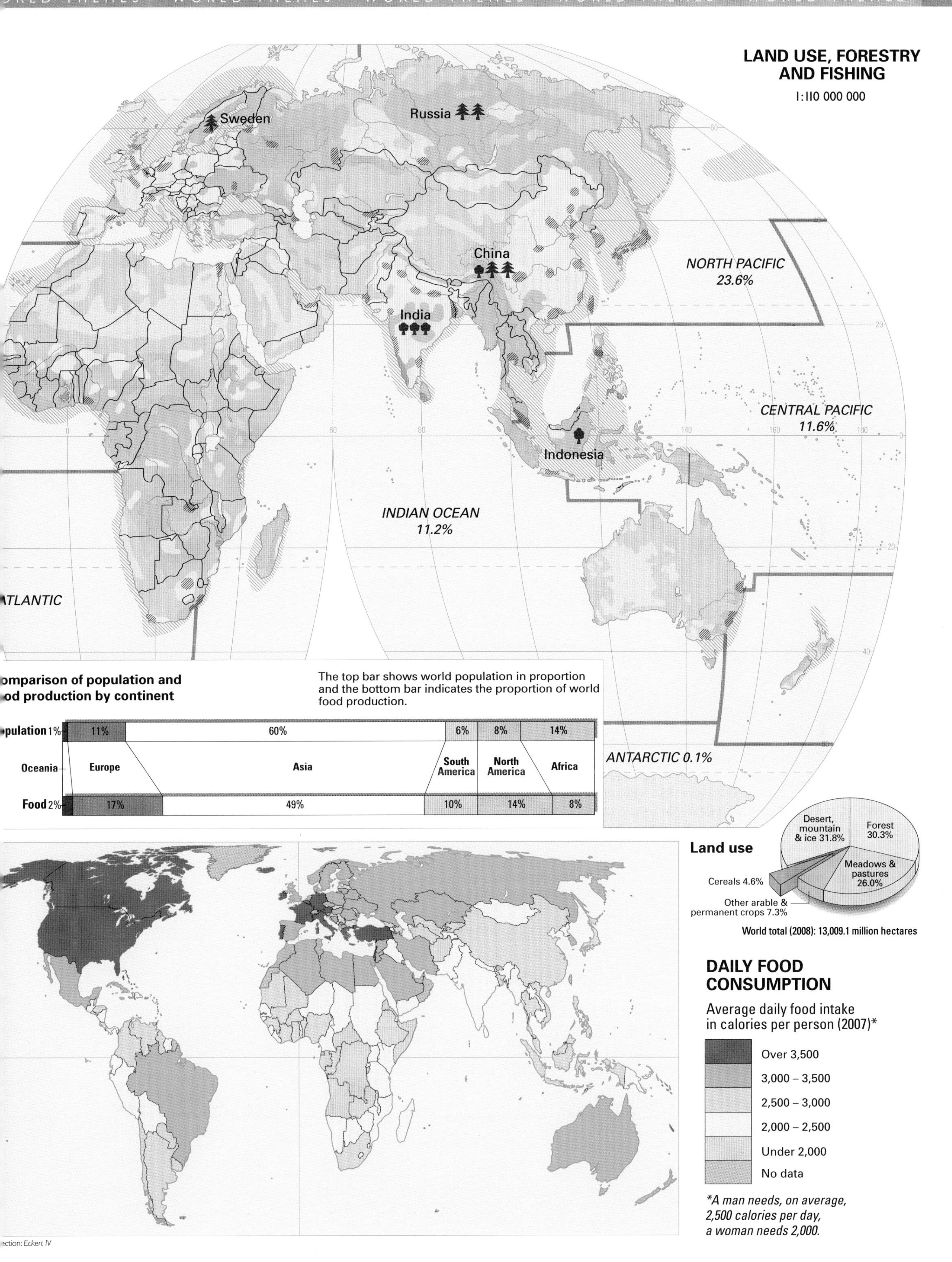

LAND USE, FORESTRY AND FISHING

1:110 000 000

Sweden

Russia

China

India

Indonesia

NORTH PACIFIC
23.6%

CENTRAL PACIFIC
11.6%

INDIAN OCEAN
11.2%

ATLANTIC

ANTARCTIC 0.1%

Comparison of population and food production by continent

The top bar shows world population in proportion and the bottom bar indicates the proportion of world food production.

Oceania	Europe	Asia	South America	North America	Africa
Population 1%	11%	60%	6%	8%	14%
Food 2%	17%	49%	10%	14%	8%

Land use

Desert, mountain & ice 31.8%

Forest 30.3%

Meadows & pastures 26.0%

Cereals 4.6%

Other arable & permanent crops 7.3%

World total (2008): 13,009.1 million hectares

DAILY FOOD CONSUMPTION

Average daily food intake in calories per person (2007)*

- Over 3,500
- 3,000 – 3,500
- 2,500 – 3,000
- 2,000 – 2,500
- Under 2,000
- No data

*A man needs, on average, 2,500 calories per day, a woman needs 2,000.

Projection: Eckert IV

ENERGY BALANCE

Difference between primary energy production and consumption in millions of tonnes of oil equivalent (MtOe) 2008

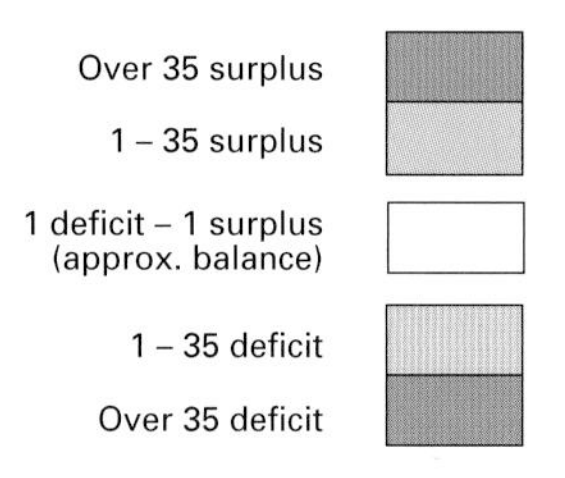

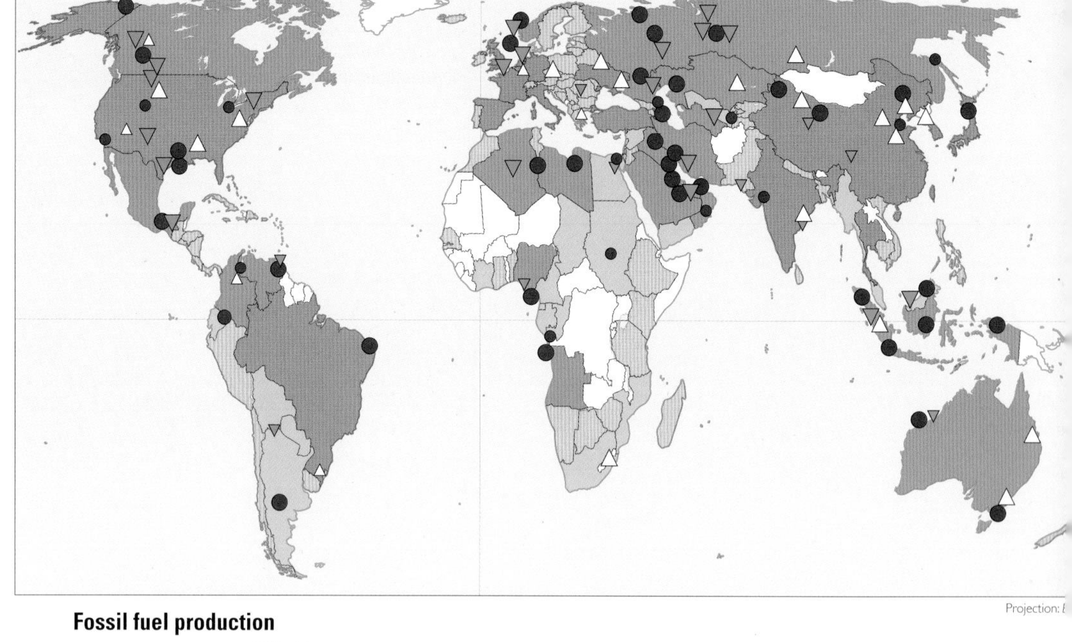

Over 35 surplus	
1 – 35 surplus	
1 deficit – 1 surplus (approx. balance)	
1 – 35 deficit	
Over 35 deficit	

Projection:

WORLD OIL RESERVES

World oil reserves by region and country, billion tonnes (2009)

World total 181.7 billion tonnes

Al:	Algeria	No:	Norway
Au:	Australia	Po:	Poland
Br:	Brazil	Ru:	Russia
Cn:	China	SA:	Saudi Arabia
In:	Indonesia	S Af:	South Africa
Iq:	Iraq	UAE:	United Arab Emirates
Ka:	Kazakhstan		
Li:	Libya	Uk:	Ukraine
Ni:	Nigeria	USA:	United States of America
		Ve:	Venezuela

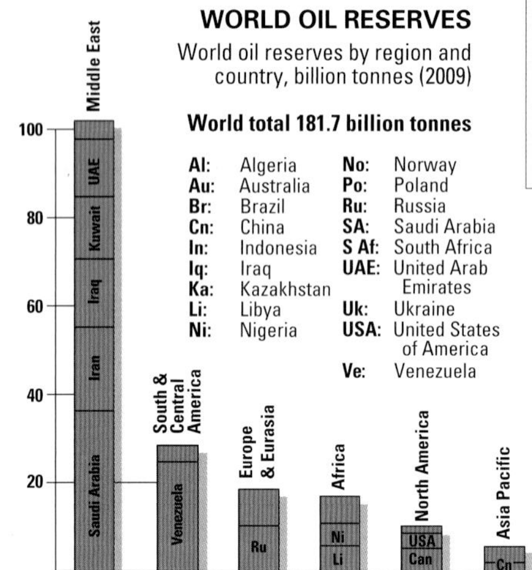

Fossil fuel production

Oilfields
Principal ● ● Secondary

Russia 12.9%
Saudi Arabia 12.0%
USA 8.7%
Iran 5.2%
China 5.2%
Canada 4.2%
Mexico 3.7%
UAE 3.3%
Venezuela 3.2%

Oil production

World total (2010): 3,913,700,000 tonnes

Gasfields
Principal ▽ ▽ Secondary

USA 19.3%
Russia 18.4%
Canada 5.0%
Iran 4.3%
Norway 3.3%
China 3.0%
Saudi Arabia 2.6%

Gas production

World total (2010): 2,880,900,000 tonnes of oil equivalent

Coalfields
Principal △ △ Secor

China 48.2%
USA 14.8%
Australia 6.3%
India 5.8%
Russia 4.0%
South

Coal production

World total (2010): 3,731,400,000 tonnes of equivalent

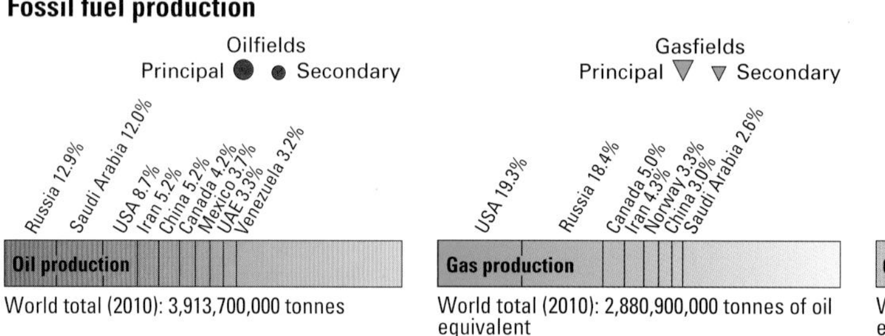

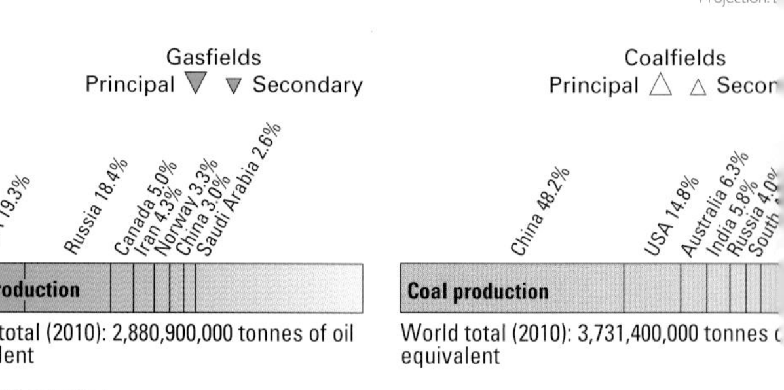

WORLD GAS RESERVES

World natural gas reserves by region and country, billion tonnes of oil equivalent (2009)

World total 172.1 billion tonnes of oil equivalent

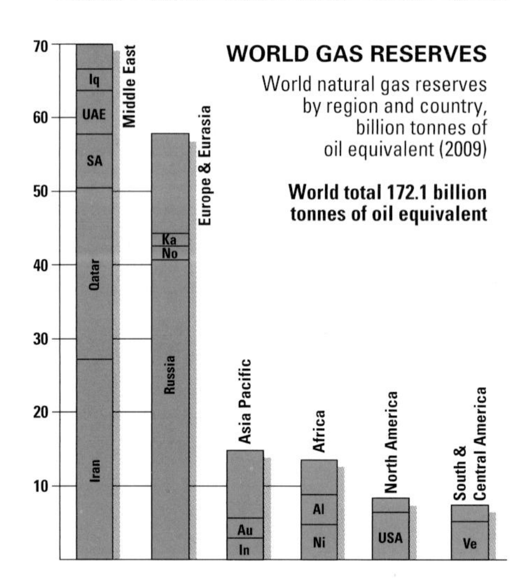

ENERGY PRODUCTION BY REGION

Each symbol represents 1% of world primary energy production (2008)

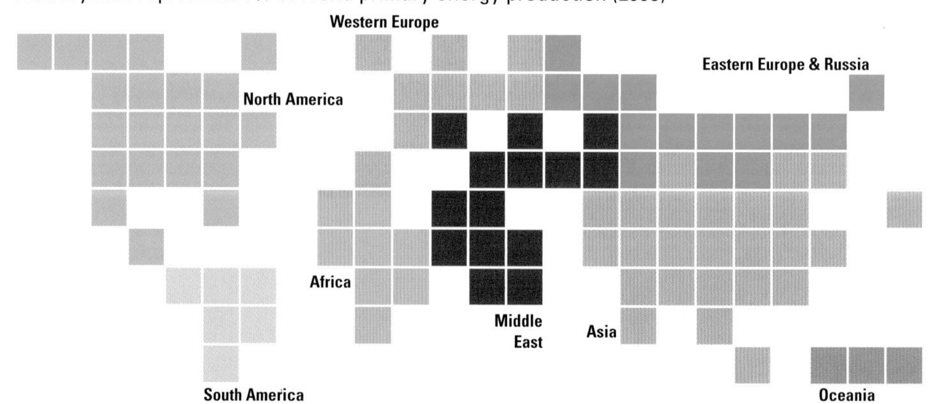

Western Europe
North America
Eastern Europe & Russia
Africa
Middle East
Asia
South America
Oceania

WORLD COAL RESERVES

World coal reserves (including lignite) by region and country, billion tonnes (2009)

World total 826.0 billion tonnes

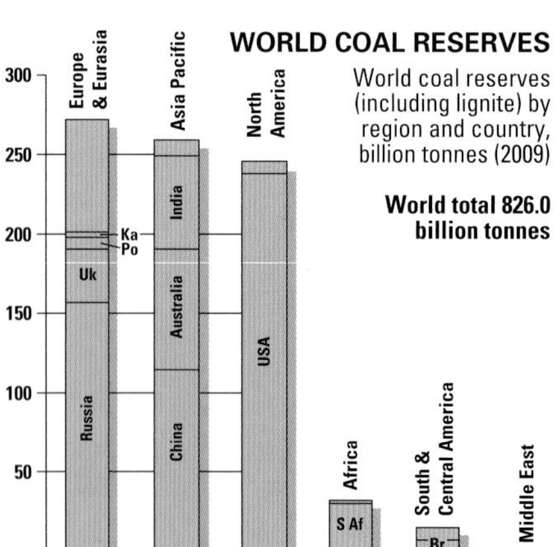

ENERGY CONSUMPTION BY REGION

Each symbol represents 1% of world primary energy consumption (2008)

Western Europe
North America
Eastern Europe & Russia
Africa
Middle East
Asia
South America
Oceania

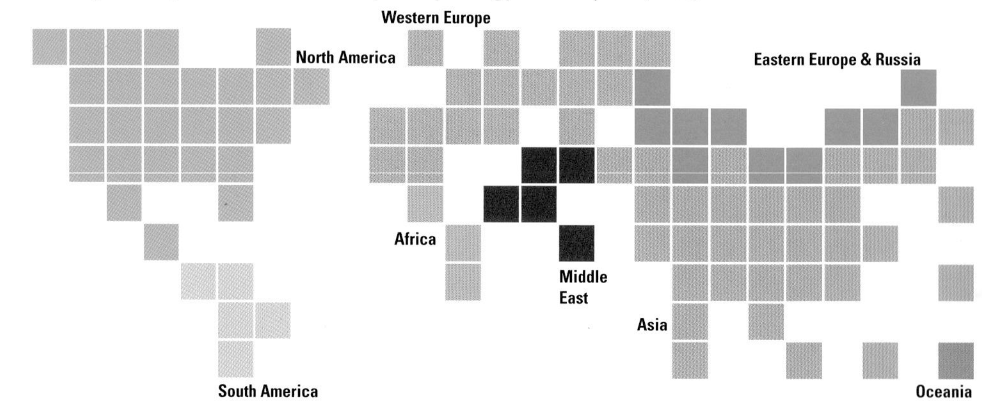

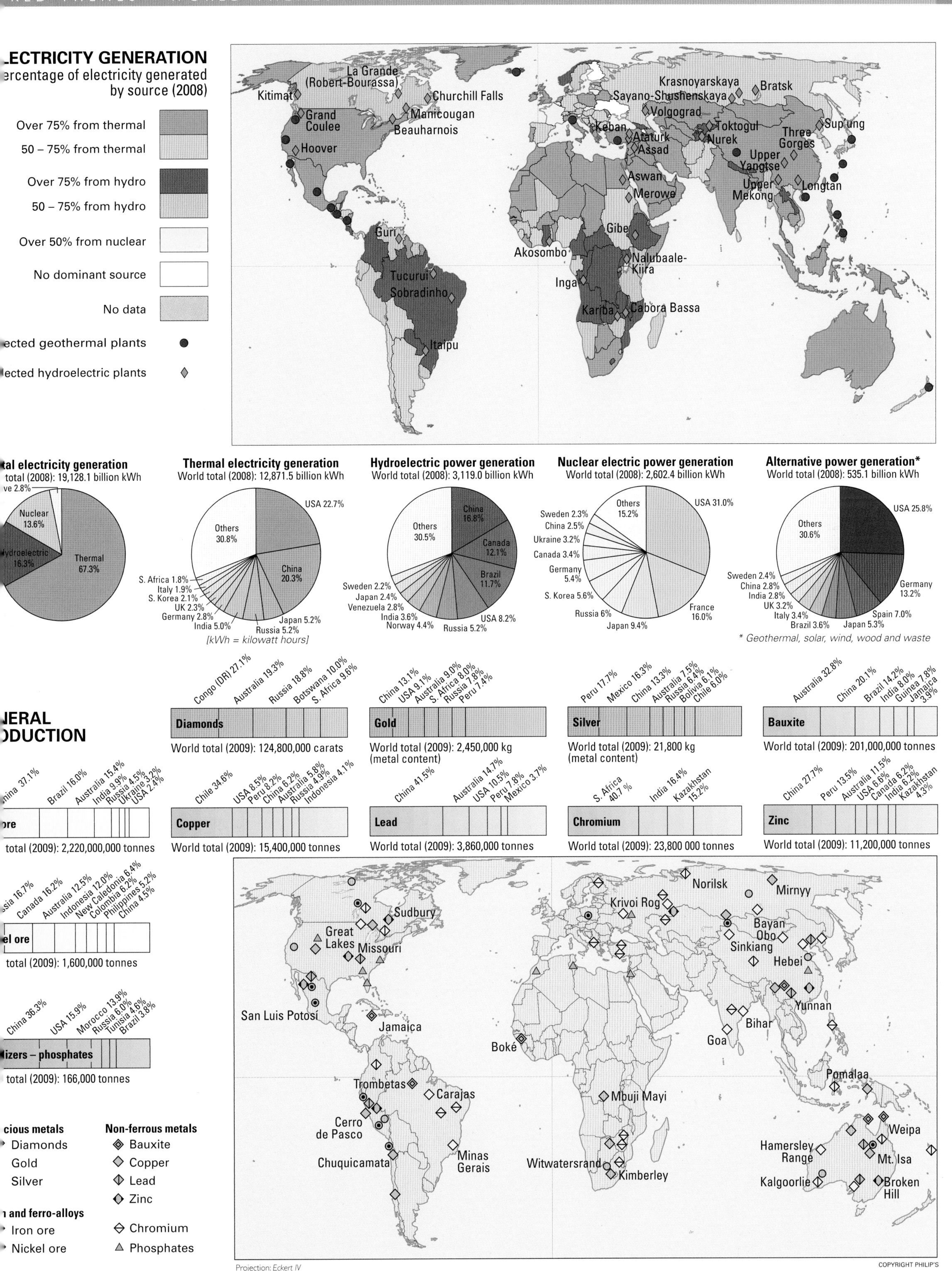

ELECTRICITY GENERATION

Percentage of electricity generated by source (2008)

- Over 75% from thermal
- 50 – 75% from thermal
- Over 75% from hydro
- 50 – 75% from hydro
- Over 50% from nuclear
- No dominant source
- No data
- Selected geothermal plants ●
- Selected hydroelectric plants ◆

Total electricity generation
World total (2008): 19,128.1 billion kWh
- Alternative 2.8%
- Nuclear 13.6%
- Hydroelectric 16.3%
- Thermal 67.3%

Thermal electricity generation
World total (2008): 12,871.5 billion kWh
- USA 22.7%
- China 20.3%
- Japan 5.2%
- Russia 5.2%
- India 5.0%
- Germany 2.8%
- UK 2.3%
- S. Korea 2.1%
- Italy 1.9%
- S. Africa 1.8%
- Others 30.8%

[kWh = kilowatt hours]

Hydroelectric power generation
World total (2008): 3,119.0 billion kWh
- China 16.8%
- Canada 12.1%
- Brazil 11.7%
- USA 8.2%
- Russia 5.2%
- Norway 4.4%
- India 3.6%
- Venezuela 2.8%
- Japan 2.4%
- Sweden 2.2%
- Others 30.5%

Nuclear electric power generation
World total (2008): 2,602.4 billion kWh
- USA 31.0%
- France 16.0%
- Japan 9.4%
- Russia 6%
- S. Korea 5.6%
- Germany 5.4%
- Canada 3.4%
- Ukraine 3.2%
- China 2.5%
- Sweden 2.3%
- Others 15.2%

Alternative power generation*
World total (2008): 535.1 billion kWh
- USA 25.8%
- Germany 13.2%
- Spain 7.0%
- Japan 5.3%
- Brazil 3.6%
- Italy 3.4%
- UK 3.2%
- India 2.8%
- China 2.8%
- Sweden 2.4%
- Others 30.6%

* Geothermal, solar, wind, wood and waste

MINERAL PRODUCTION

Iron ore
World total (2009): 2,220,000,000 tonnes
- China 37.1%
- Brazil 16.0%
- Australia 15.4%
- India 9.9%
- Russia 4.5%
- Ukraine 3.2%
- USA 2.4%

Nickel ore
World total (2009): 1,600,000 tonnes
- Russia 16.7%
- Canada 16.2%
- Australia 12.5%
- Indonesia 12.0%
- New Caledonia 6.2%
- Colombia 5.2%
- Philippines 4.5%
- China 6.4%

Fertilizers – phosphates
World total (2009): 166,000 tonnes
- China 36.3%
- USA 15.9%
- Morocco 13.9%
- Russia 6.0%
- Tunisia 4.6%
- Brazil 3.8%

Diamonds
World total (2009): 124,800,000 carats
- Congo (DR) 27.1%
- Australia 19.3%
- Russia 18.8%
- Botswana 10.0%
- S. Africa 9.6%

Copper
World total (2009): 15,400,000 tonnes
- Chile 34.6%
- USA 8.5%
- Peru 8.2%
- China 6.2%
- Australia 5.8%
- Russia 4.9%
- Indonesia 4.1%

Gold
World total (2009): 2,450,000 kg (metal content)
- China 13.1%
- USA 9.1%
- Australia 9.0%
- S. Africa 8.0%
- Russia 7.8%
- Peru 7.4%

Lead
World total (2009): 3,860,000 tonnes
- China 41.5%
- Australia 14.7%
- USA 10.5%
- Peru 7.8%
- Mexico 3.7%

Silver
World total (2009): 21,800 kg (metal content)
- Peru 17.7%
- Mexico 16.3%
- China 13.3%
- Australia 7.5%
- Russia 6.4%
- Bolivia 6.1%
- Chile 6.0%

Chromium
World total (2009): 23,800 000 tonnes
- S. Africa 40.7%
- India 16.4%
- Kazakhstan 15.2%

Bauxite
World total (2009): 201,000,000 tonnes
- Australia 32.8%
- China 20.1%
- Brazil 14.2%
- India 8.0%
- Guinea 7.8%
- Jamaica 3.3%

Zinc
World total (2009): 11,200,000 tonnes
- China 27.7%
- Peru 13.5%
- Australia 11.5%
- USA 6.6%
- Canada 6.2%
- India 6.2%
- Kazakhstan 4.3%

Precious metals
- ◆ Diamonds
- Gold
- Silver

Iron and ferro-alloys
- Iron ore
- Nickel ore

Non-ferrous metals
- ◆ Bauxite
- ◇ Copper
- ◈ Lead
- ◇ Zinc
- ◇ Chromium
- △ Phosphates

Projection: Eckert IV

COPYRIGHT PHILIP'S

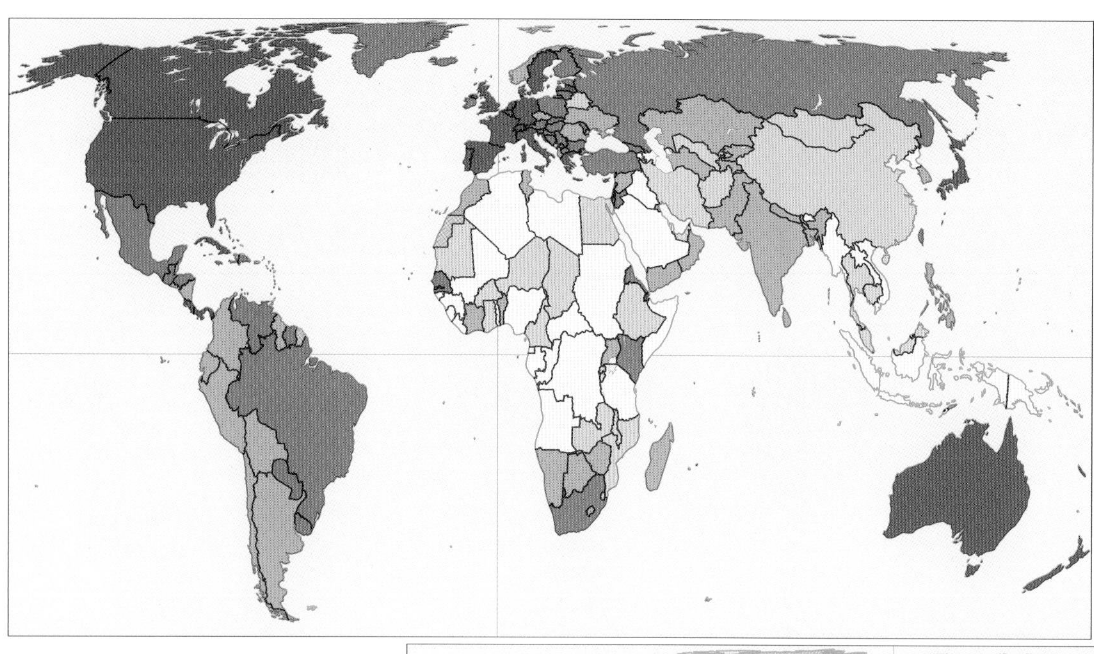

IMPORTANCE OF SERVICE SECTOR

Percentage of total GDP from service sector (2010)

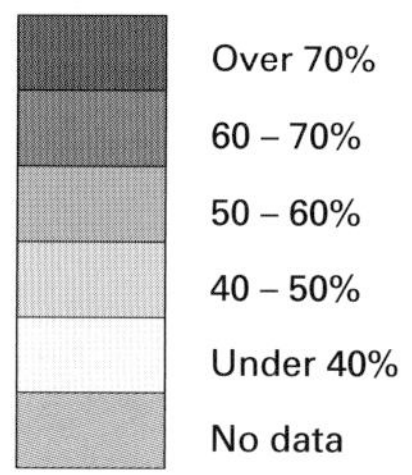

- Over 70%
- 60 – 70%
- 50 – 60%
- 40 – 50%
- Under 40%
- No data

Countries with the highest and lowest percentage of GDP from services

Highest		Lowest	
Monaco	95%	Eq. Guinea	4
Luxembourg	68%	Liberia	18
Bahamas	84%	Sierra Leone	20
Djibouti	82%	Qatar	21
Palau	82%	Angola	25

UK 77% from services

IMPORTANCE OF MANUFACTURING SECTOR

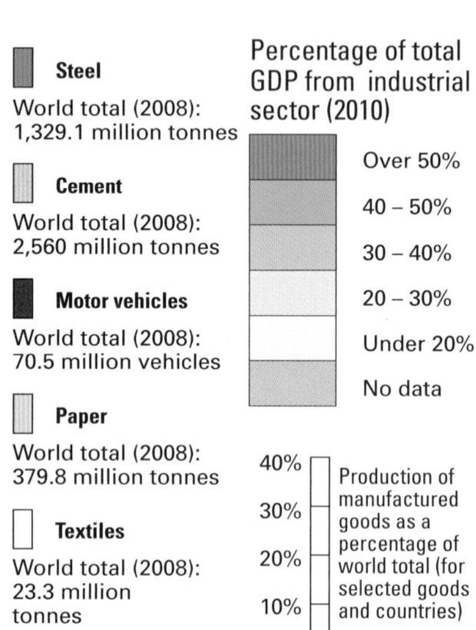

Steel
World total (2008): 1,329.1 million tonnes

Cement
World total (2008): 2,560 million tonnes

Motor vehicles
World total (2008): 70.5 million vehicles

Paper
World total (2008): 379.8 million tonnes

Textiles
World total (2008): 23.3 million tonnes

Percentage of total GDP from industrial sector (2010)

- Over 50%
- 40 – 50%
- 30 – 40%
- 20 – 30%
- Under 20%
- No data

40%
30%
20%
10%
Production of manufactured goods as a percentage of world total (for selected goods and countries)

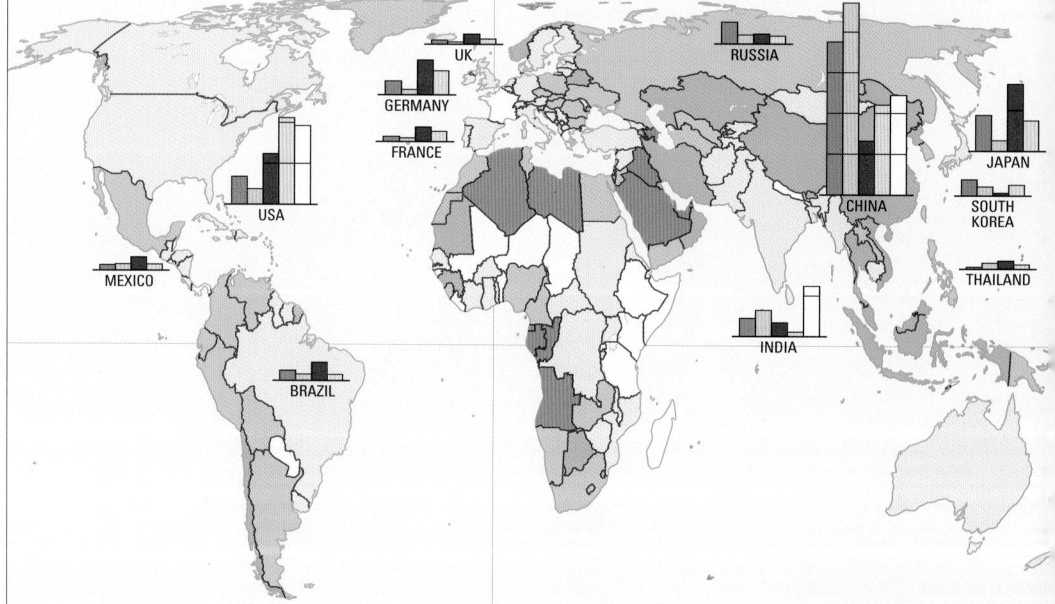

EMPLOYMENT BY ECONOMIC ACTIVITY Selected countries (2008)

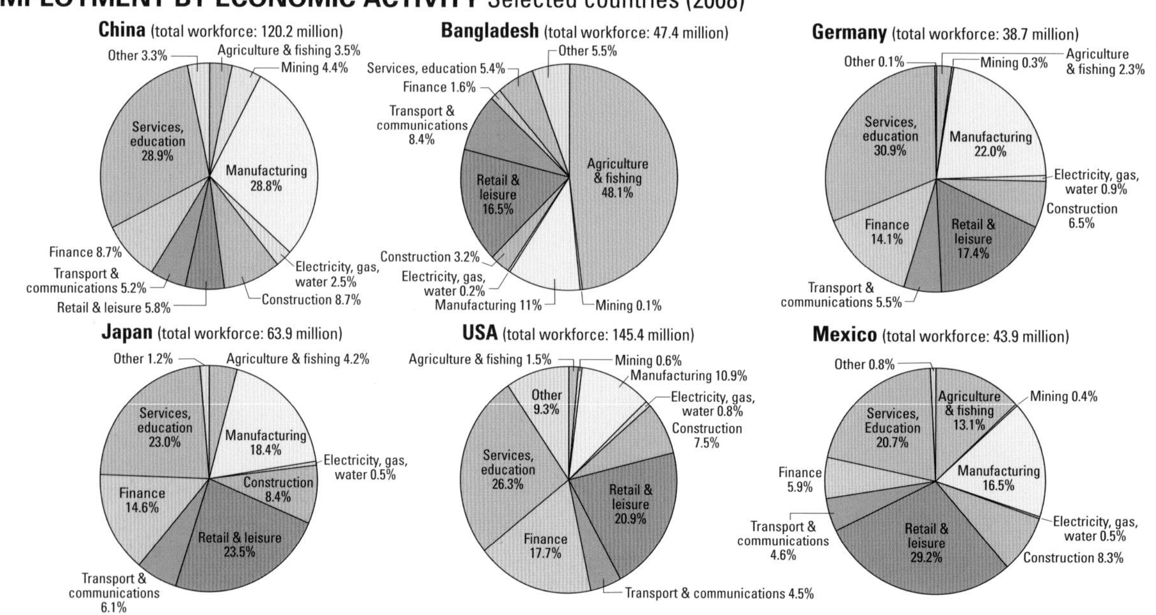

China (total workforce: 120.2 million)
- Other 3.3%
- Agriculture & fishing 3.5%
- Mining 4.4%
- Services, education 28.9%
- Manufacturing 28.8%
- Finance 8.7%
- Transport & communications 5.2%
- Retail & leisure 5.8%
- Electricity, gas, water 2.5%
- Construction 8.7%

Bangladesh (total workforce: 47.4 million)
- Other 5.5%
- Services, education 5.4%
- Finance 1.6%
- Transport & communications 8.4%
- Retail & leisure 16.5%
- Agriculture & fishing 48.1%
- Construction 3.2%
- Electricity, gas, water 0.2%
- Manufacturing 11%
- Mining 0.1%

Germany (total workforce: 38.7 million)
- Other 0.1%
- Mining 0.3%
- Agriculture & fishing 2.3%
- Services, education 30.9%
- Manufacturing 22.0%
- Electricity, gas, water 0.9%
- Construction 6.5%
- Finance 14.1%
- Retail & leisure 17.4%
- Transport & communications 5.5%

Japan (total workforce: 63.9 million)
- Other 1.2%
- Agriculture & fishing 4.2%
- Services, education 23.0%
- Manufacturing 18.4%
- Electricity, gas, water 0.5%
- Finance 14.6%
- Construction 8.4%
- Retail & leisure 23.5%
- Transport & communications 6.1%

USA (total workforce: 145.4 million)
- Agriculture & fishing 1.5%
- Mining 0.6%
- Manufacturing 10.9%
- Other 9.3%
- Electricity, gas, water 0.8%
- Construction 7.5%
- Services, education 26.3%
- Retail & leisure 20.9%
- Finance 17.7%
- Transport & communications 4.5%

Mexico (total workforce: 43.9 million)
- Other 0.8%
- Agriculture & fishing 13.1%
- Mining 0.4%
- Services, Education 20.7%
- Manufacturing 16.5%
- Finance 5.9%
- Electricity, gas, water 0.5%
- Transport & communications 4.6%
- Retail & leisure 29.2%
- Construction 8.3%

RESEARCH & DEVELOPME

Expenditure on R&D as a percentage of GDP (2008)

Country	Percentage
Israel	4.9
Sweden	3.8
Finland	3.5
Japan	3.4
South Korea	3.2
USA	2.8
Denmark	2.7
Iceland	2.7
Austria	2.7
Germany	2.5
France	2.0
Belgium	1.9
UK	1.9
Canada	1.8
Luxembourg	1.7
Slovenia	1.7
Netherlands	1.6
Norway	1.6
Portugal	1.5
Czech Republic	1.5
China	1.4
Ireland	1.4
Spain	1.3
Estonia	1.3
New Zealand	1.2

WORLD TRADE

Percentage share of total
world exports by value (2010)

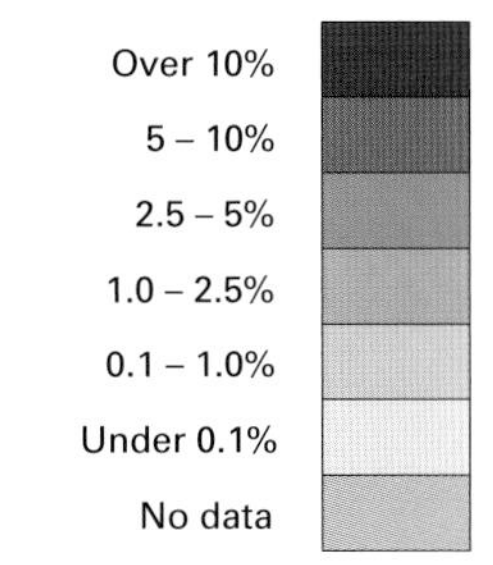

Over 10%	
5 – 10%	
2.5 – 5%	
1.0 – 2.5%	
0.1 – 1.0%	
Under 0.1%	
No data	

Top ten container ports ●

International trade is dominated by a
handful of powerful maritime nations;
the members of 'G8' (Canada, France,
Germany, Italy, Japan, Russia, UK and
USA) and the 'BRIC' nations (Brazil,
Russia, India and China).

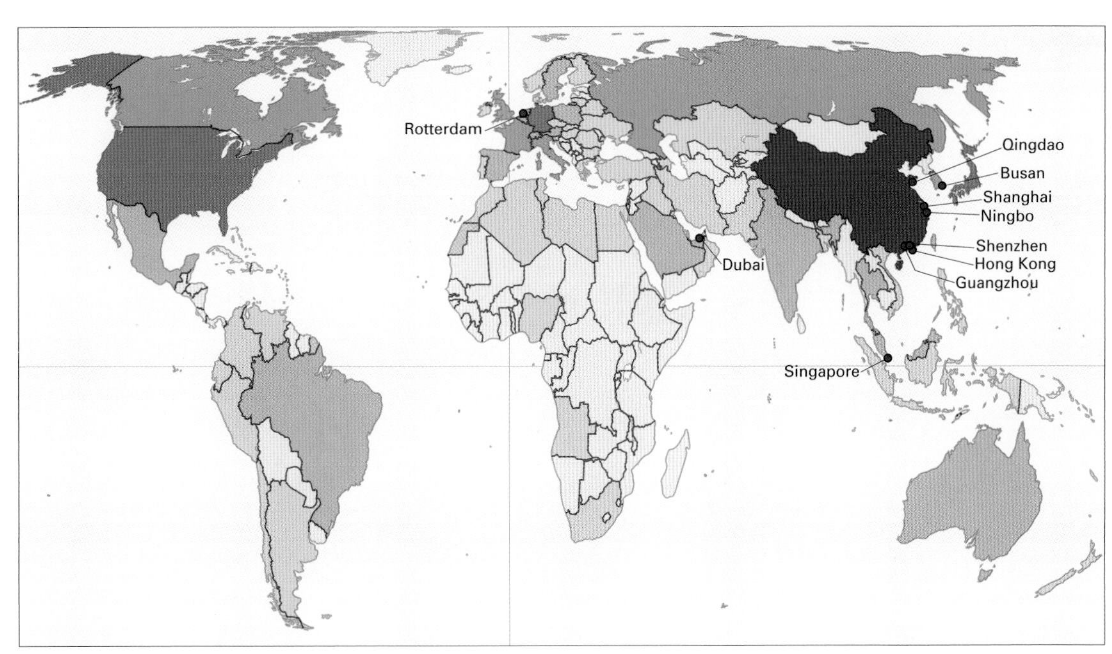

JOR EXPORTS Leading manufactured items and their exporters (2010)

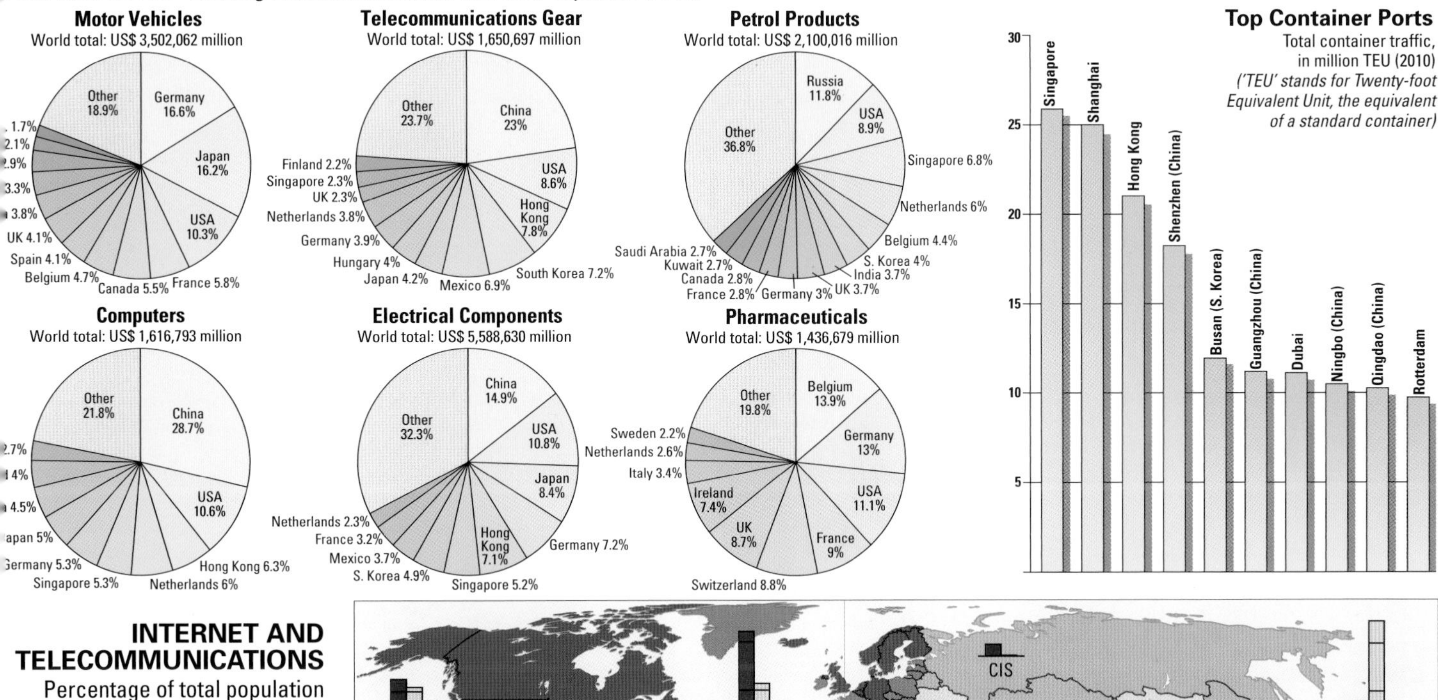

Motor Vehicles — World total: US$ 3,502,062 million
Telecommunications Gear — World total: US$ 1,650,697 million
Petrol Products — World total: US$ 2,100,016 million
Computers — World total: US$ 1,616,793 million
Electrical Components — World total: US$ 5,588,630 million
Pharmaceuticals — World total: US$ 1,436,679 million

Top Container Ports

Total container traffic,
in million TEU (2010)
('TEU' stands for Twenty-foot
Equivalent Unit, the equivalent
of a standard container)

INTERNET AND TELECOMMUNICATIONS

Percentage of total population
using the Internet (2009)

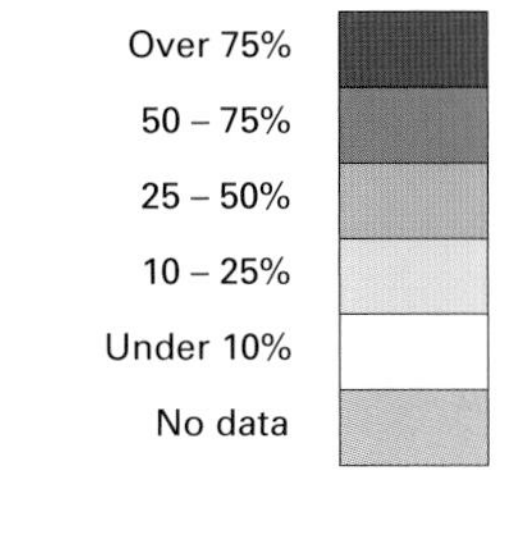

Over 75%	
50 – 75%	
25 – 50%	
10 – 25%	
Under 10%	
No data	

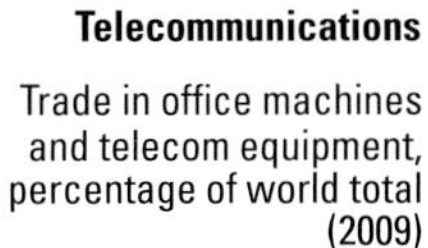

Telecommunications

Trade in office machines
and telecom equipment,
percentage of world total
(2009)

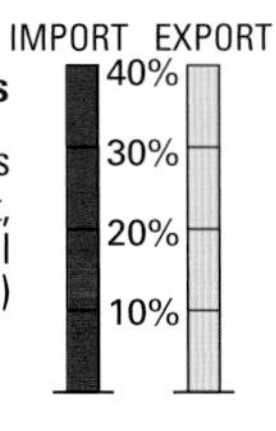

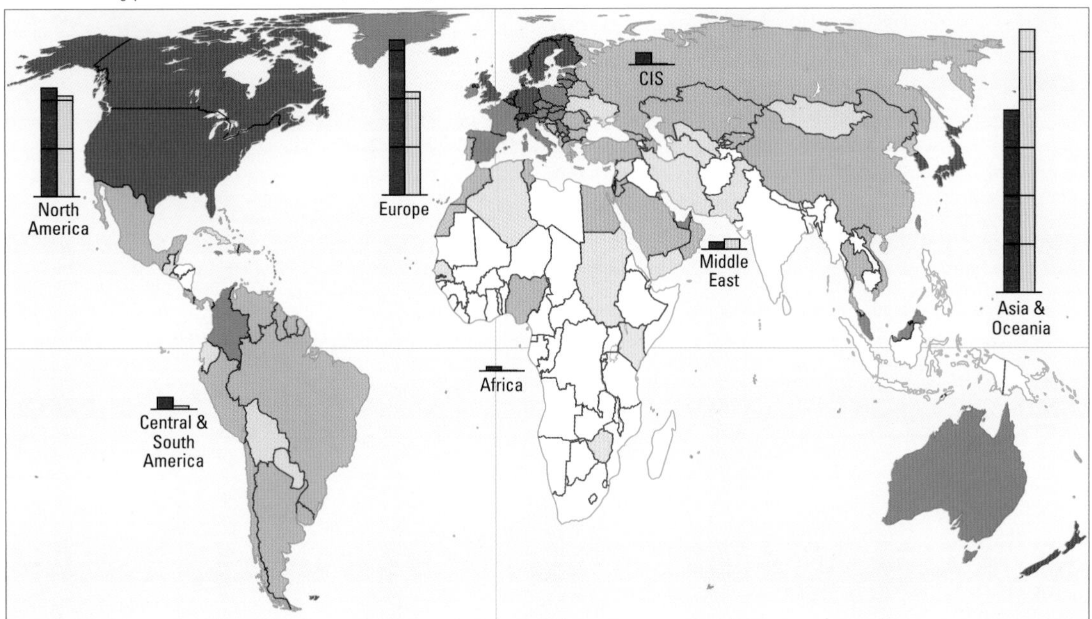

Projection: Eckert IV

COPYRIGHT PHILIP'S

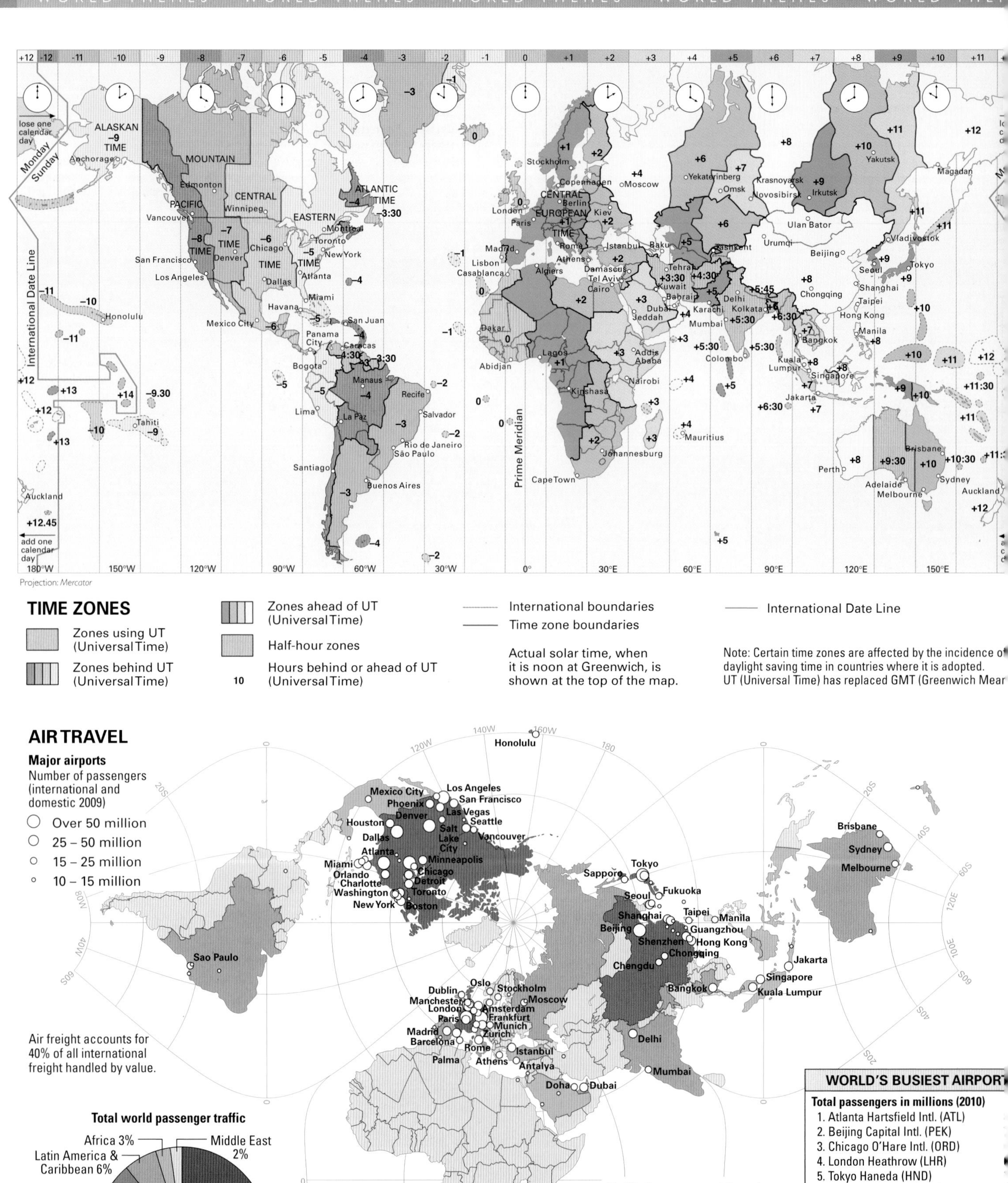

Projection: Mercator

TIME ZONES

Zones using UT (Universal Time)

Zones behind UT (Universal Time)

Zones ahead of UT (Universal Time)

Half-hour zones

10 Hours behind or ahead of UT (Universal Time)

International boundaries

Time zone boundaries

Actual solar time, when it is noon at Greenwich, is shown at the top of the map.

International Date Line

Note: Certain time zones are affected by the incidence of daylight saving time in countries where it is adopted. UT (Universal Time) has replaced GMT (Greenwich Mean

AIR TRAVEL

Major airports
Number of passengers (international and domestic 2009)

○ Over 50 million

○ 25 – 50 million

○ 15 – 25 million

○ 10 – 15 million

Air freight accounts for 40% of all international freight handled by value.

Total world passenger traffic

Africa 3%
Middle East 2%
Latin America & Caribbean 6%
Asia Pacific 21%
North America 37%
Europe 31%

Total world passenger traffic (2009)
4,796 million

Traffic in passenger kilometres
Passengers carried (international and domestic) multiplied by distance flown from airport of origin (2009)

over 100 billion

50 – 100 billion

20 – 50 million

Under 20 billion

Projection: Peirce

WORLD'S BUSIEST AIRPOR

Total passengers in millions (2010)
1. Atlanta Hartsfield Intl. (ATL)
2. Beijing Capital Intl. (PEK)
3. Chicago O'Hare Intl. (ORD)
4. London Heathrow (LHR)
5. Tokyo Haneda (HND)
6. Los Angeles Intl. (LAX)
7. Paris Charles de Gaulle (CDG)
8. Dallas/Fort Worth Intl. (DFW)
9. Frankfurt Intl. (FRA)
10. Denver Intl. (DEN)

London's Heathrow handles the most international passengers (61.3 million in 2009), followed by Paris Charles de Gau (55.8 million).

UNESCO WORLD HERITAGE SITES 2010

Total sites = 911 (704 cultural, 180 natural and 27 mixed)

Region	Cultural sites	Natural sites	Mixed sites
Africa	42	32	4
Arab States	61	4	1
Asia & Pacific	138	51	9
Europe & North America	377	58	10
Latin America & Caribbean	86	35	3

Some sites are trans-boundary, therefore the total figures may not add up

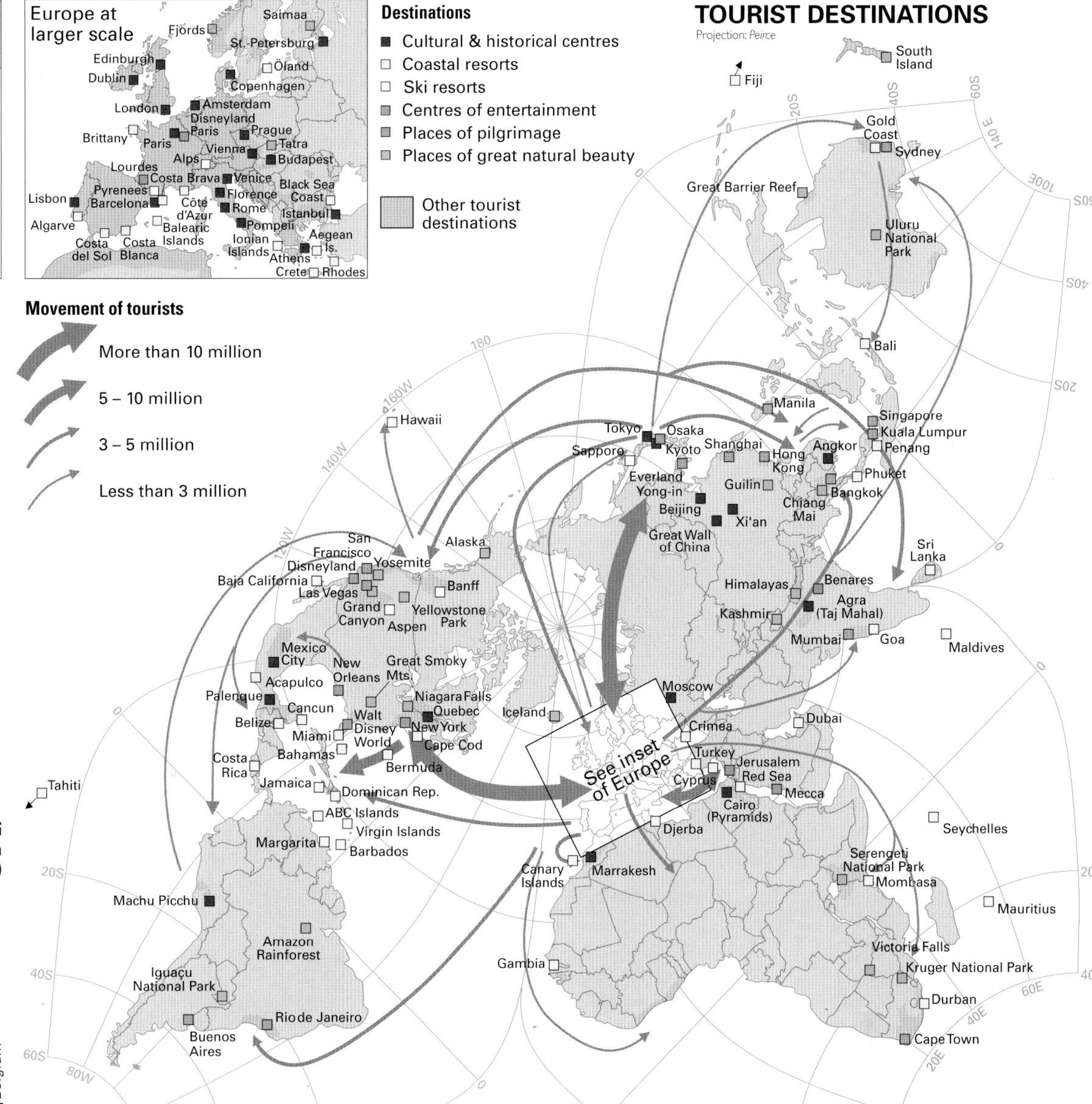

TOURIST EARNINGS

Countries receiving the most from overseas tourism, US$ million (2010)

USA, Spain, France, Italy, China, Germany, UK, Australia, Turkey, Austria, Thailand, Malaysia

TOURIST SPENDING

Countries spending the most on overseas tourism, US$ million (2010)

Germany, USA, UK, China, France, Italy, Japan, Canada, Russia, Netherlands, South Korea, Belgium

Europe at larger scale

Fjords, Saimaa, St. Petersburg, Öland, Edinburgh, Copenhagen, Dublin, London, Amsterdam, Prague, Brittany, Paris, Tatra, Vienna, Budapest, Lourdes, Alps, Costa Brava, Venice, Black Sea Coast, Pyrenees, Florence, Lisbon, Barcelona, Côte d'Azur, Rome, Istanbul, Algarve, Pompeii, Balearic Islands, Ionian Islands, Aegean Is., Costa del Sol, Costa Blanca, Athens, Crete, Rhodes

Destinations

- ■ Cultural & historical centres
- □ Coastal resorts
- □ Ski resorts
- Centres of entertainment
- Places of pilgrimage
- Places of great natural beauty
- Other tourist destinations

Movement of tourists

- More than 10 million
- 5 – 10 million
- 3 – 5 million
- Less than 3 million

TOURIST DESTINATIONS

Projection: Peirce

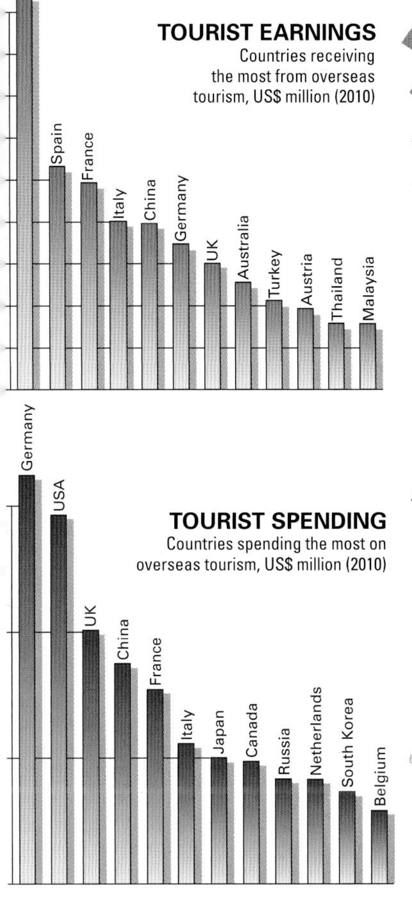

South Island, Fiji, Gold Coast, Sydney, Great Barrier Reef, Uluru National Park, Bali, Manila, Singapore, Kuala Lumpur, Penang, Phuket, Bangkok, Angkor, Chiang Mai, Tokyo, Osaka, Kyoto, Shanghai, Hong Kong, Sapporo, Everland Yong-in, Beijing, Guilin, Xi'an, Great Wall of China, Sri Lanka, Himalayas, Benares, Kashmir, Agra (Taj Mahal), Mumbai, Goa, Maldives, Moscow, Hawaii, Alaska, San Francisco, Disneyland, Yosemite, Banff, Baja California, Las Vegas, Grand Canyon, Yellowstone Park, Aspen, Mexico City, Acapulco, New Orleans, Great Smoky Mts., Niagara Falls, Iceland, Crimea, Dubai, Palenque, Cancun, Walt Disney World, Quebec, New York, Cape Cod, Turkey, Jerusalem, Red Sea, Belize, Miami, Cyprus, Mecca, Seychelles, Costa Rica, Bahamas, Bermuda, Cairo (Pyramids), Jamaica, Dominican Rep., Djerba, Serengeti National Park, Mombasa, Tahiti, ABC Islands, Virgin Islands, Margarita, Barbados, Canary Islands, Marrakesh, Mauritius, Machu Picchu, Gambia, Victoria Falls, Kruger National Park, Amazon Rainforest, Iguaçu National Park, Rio de Janeiro, Durban, Buenos Aires, Cape Town

See inset of Europe

IMPORTANCE OF TOURISM

Tourism receipts as a percentage of Gross National Income (2009)

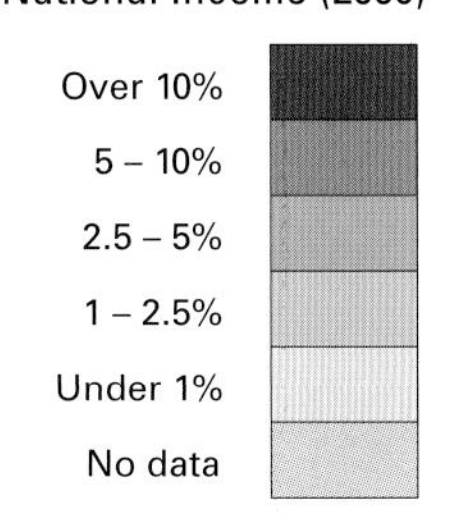

- Over 10%
- 5 – 10%
- 2.5 – 5%
- 1 – 2.5%
- Under 1%
- No data

Tourist arrivals in millions (2010)

Country	Millions
France	76.8
USA	59.7
China	55.7
Spain	52.7
Italy	43.6
UK	28.1

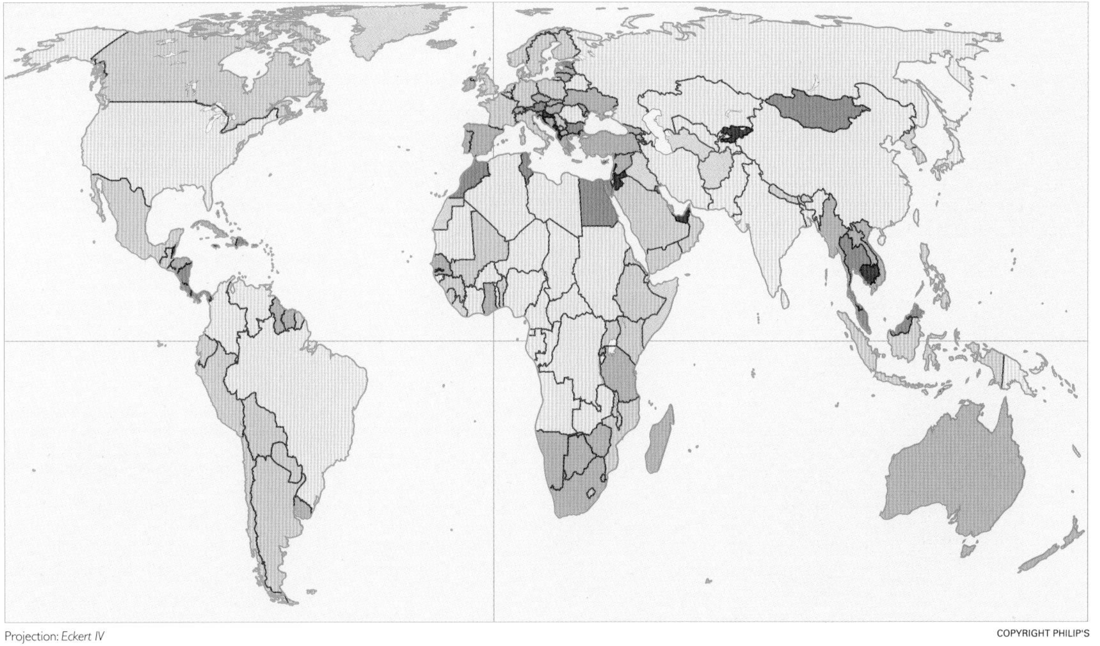

Projection: Eckert IV

COPYRIGHT PHILIP'S

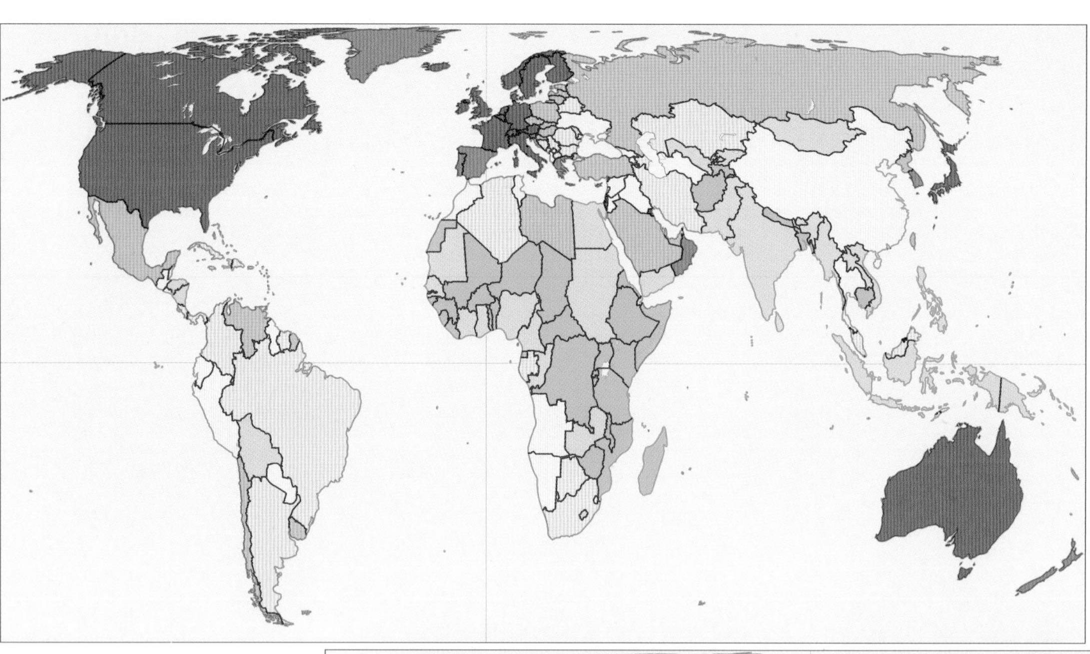

WEALTH

The value of total production divided by the population (the Gross National Income per capita, in 2009)

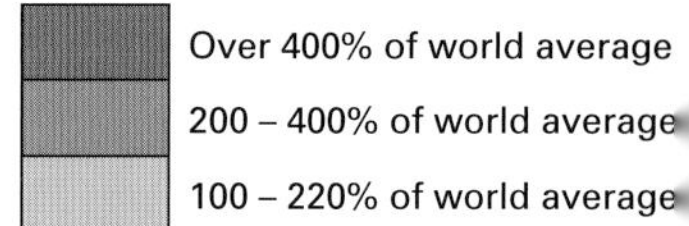

- Over 400% of world average
- 200 – 400% of world average
- 100 – 220% of world average

World average U$8,732

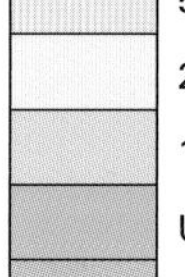

- 50 – 100% of world average
- 25 – 50% of world average
- 10 – 25% of world average
- Under 10% of world average
- No data

Top 5 countries		Bottom 5 countries	
Norway	$86,640	Burundi	$150
Luxbg.	$76,710	Liberia	$160
Switz.	$65,430	Congo (D. R.)	$160

UK $41,370

WATER SUPPLY

The percentage of total population with access to safe drinking water (2006)

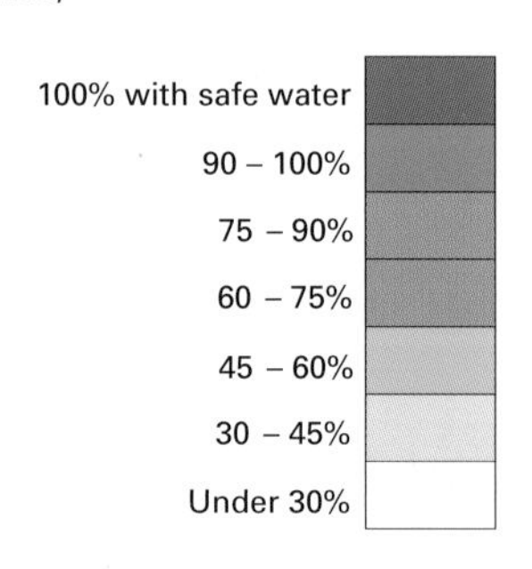

- 100% with safe water
- 90 – 100%
- 75 – 90%
- 60 – 75%
- 45 – 60%
- 30 – 45%
- Under 30%

Least well-provided countries

Western Sahara	26%
Somalia	29%
Papua New Guinea	40%

One person in eight in the world has no access to a safe water supply.

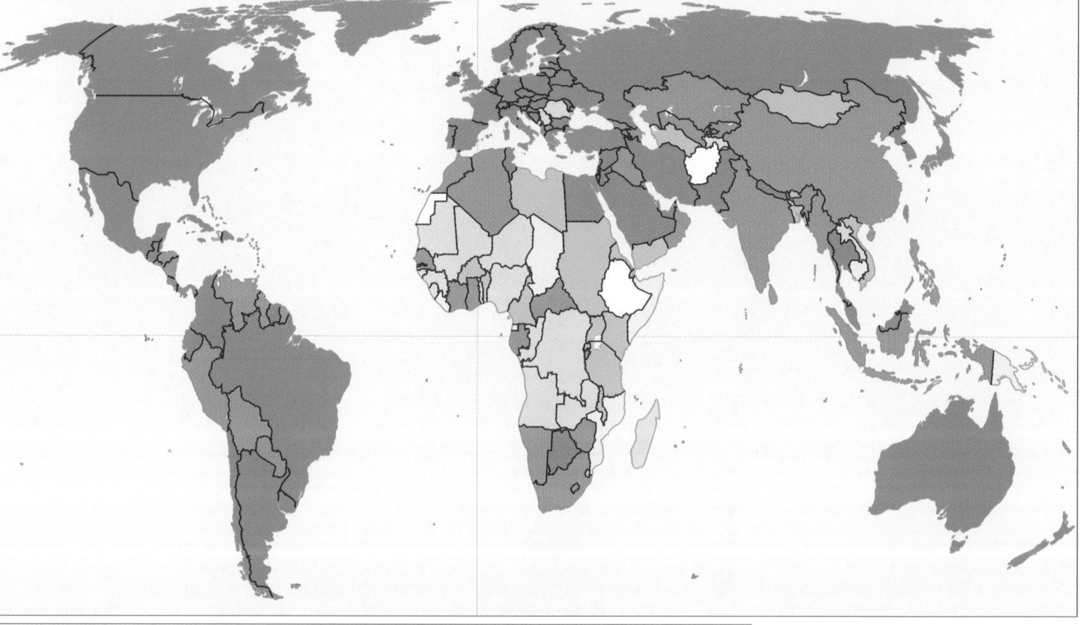

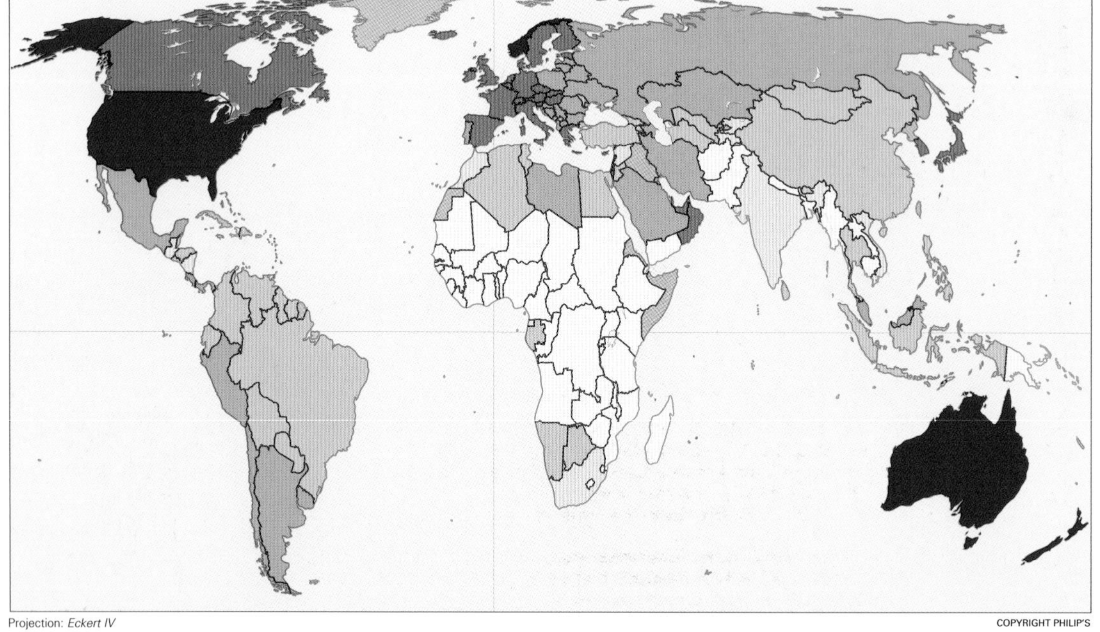

HUMAN DEVELOPMENT INDEX

The Human Development Index (HDI), calculated by the UN Development Programme (UNDP), gives a value to countries using indicators of life expectancy, education and standards of living in 2010 . Higher values show more developed countries.

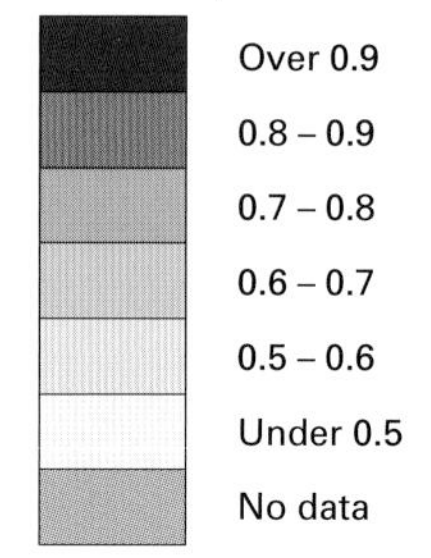

- Over 0.9
- 0.8 – 0.9
- 0.7 – 0.8
- 0.6 – 0.7
- 0.5 – 0.6
- Under 0.5
- No data

Highest values		Lowest values	
Norway	0.938	Zimbabwe	0.140
Australia	0.937	Congo (D. R.)	0.239
New Zealand	0.907	Niger	0.261

UK 0.849

Projection: *Eckert IV*

COPYRIGHT PHILIP'S

HEALTH CARE

Number of qualified doctors
per 100,000 people (2009)

	Over 400
	300 – 400
	200 – 300
	100 – 200
	Less than 100
	No data

Countries with the most and least
doctors per 100,000 people

Most doctors		Least doctors	
Cuba	640	Tanzania	2
Greece	540	Sierra Leone	3
St Lucia	500	Niger	3
Belarus	490	Liberia	3
Georgia	450	Burundi	3

UK 210 doctors

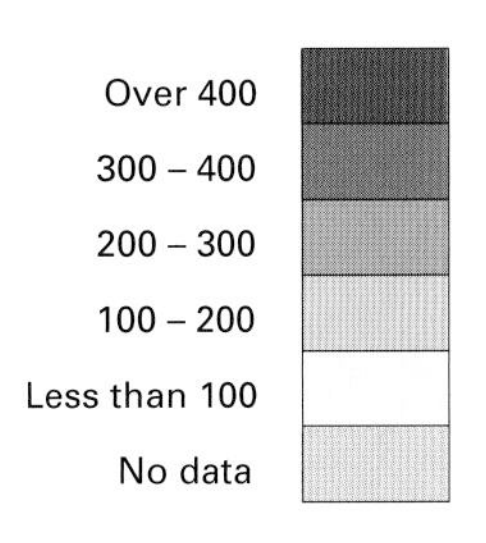

ILLITERACY

Percentage of adult total
population unable to read or
write (2009)

	Over 50%
	25 – 50%
	10 – 25%
	5 – 10%
	Under 5%
	No data

Countries with the highest
and lowest illiteracy rates

Highest (%)		Lowest (%)	
Mali	74	Australia	0
South Sudan	73	Denmark	0
Burkina Faso	71	Finland	0
Niger	71	Luxembourg	0
Chad	67	Norway	0

UK 1% adults

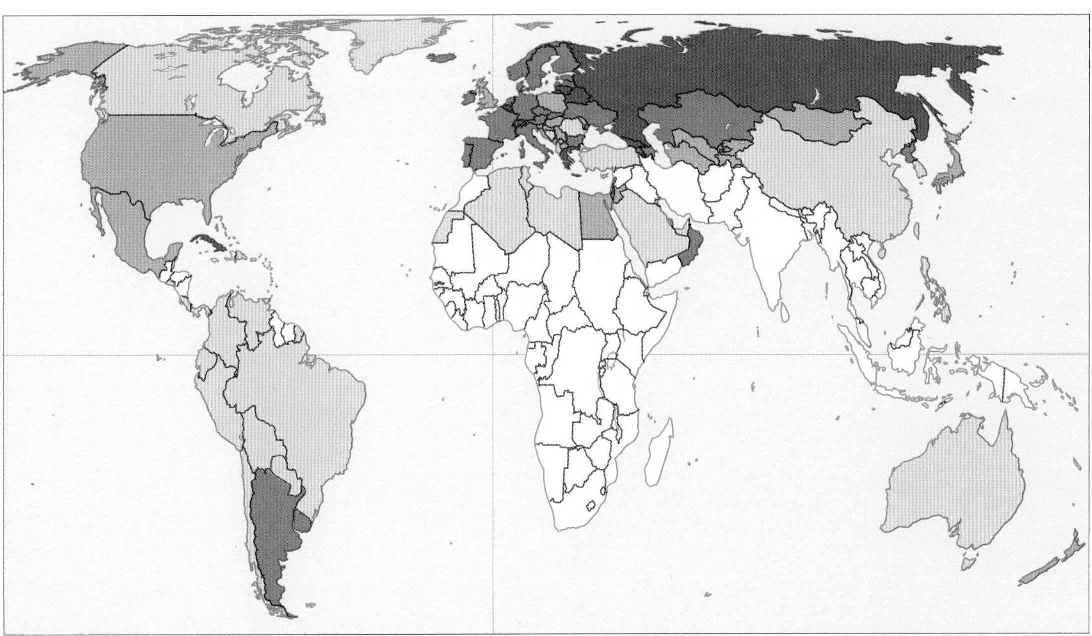

GENDER INEQUALITY INDEX

The Gender Inequality Index (GII) is a
composite measure reflecting inequality in
achievements between women and men in
three categories: reproductive health,
empowerment and the labour market.
It varies between 0, when women and men
fare equally, and 1, when women or men
fare poorly compared to the other in all
categories (2009).

	Over 0.75
	0.5 – 0.75
	0.25 – 0.5
	Under 0.25
	No data

Highest values		Lowest values	
Netherlands	0.174	Yemen	0.853
Denmark	0.209	Congo (DR)	0.814
Sweden	0.212	Niger	0.807

UK 0.355

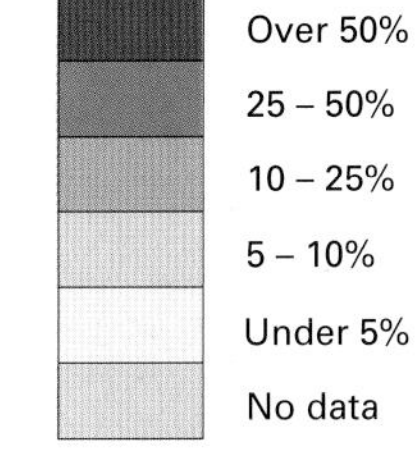
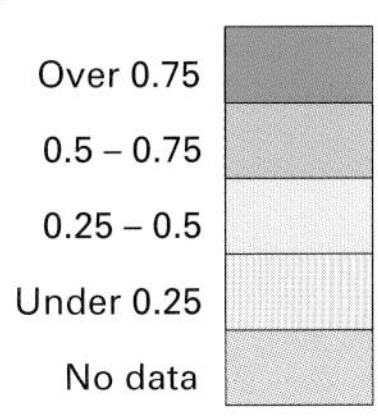
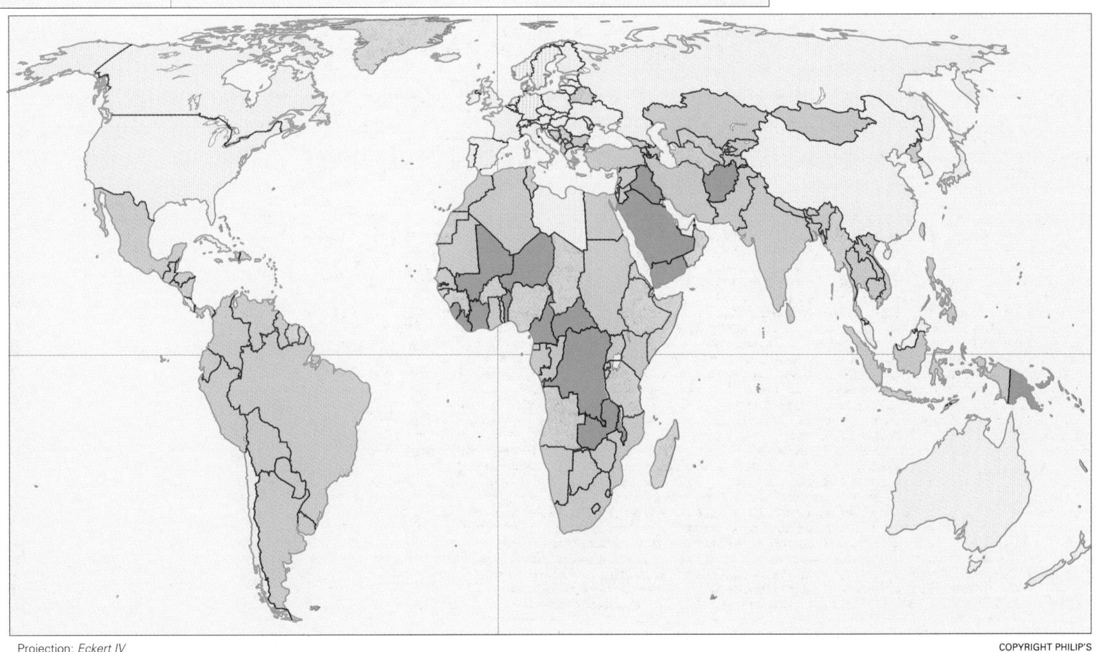

Projection: *Eckert IV*

AGE DISTRIBUTION PYRAMIDS

The bars represent the percentage of the total population (males plus females) in each age group. More Economically Developed Countries (MEDCs), such as New Zealand, have populations spread evenly across age groups and usually a growing percentage of elderly people. Less Economically Developed Countries (LEDCs), such as Kenya, have the great majority of their people in the younger age groups, about to enter their most fertile years.

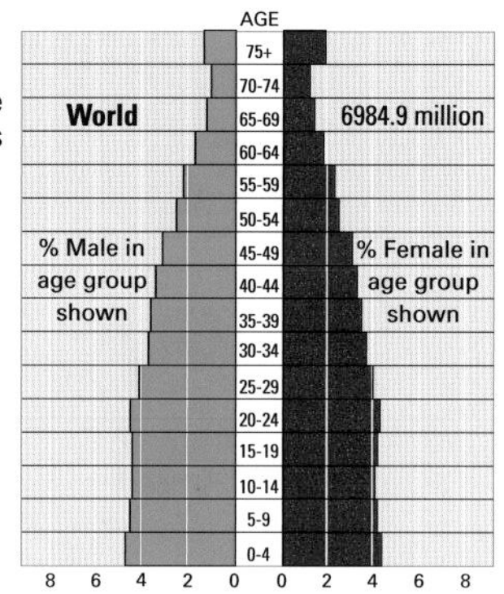

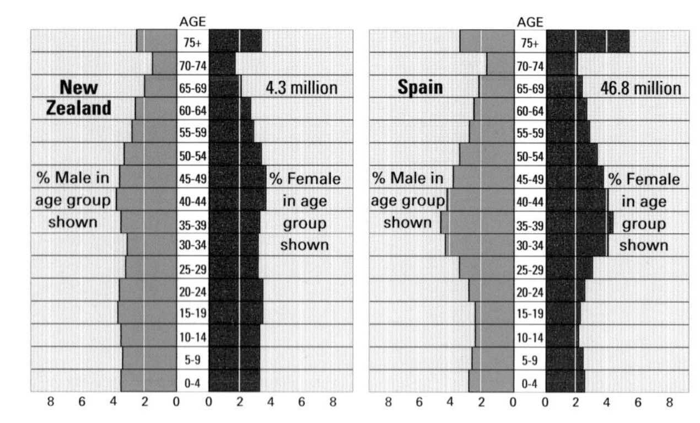

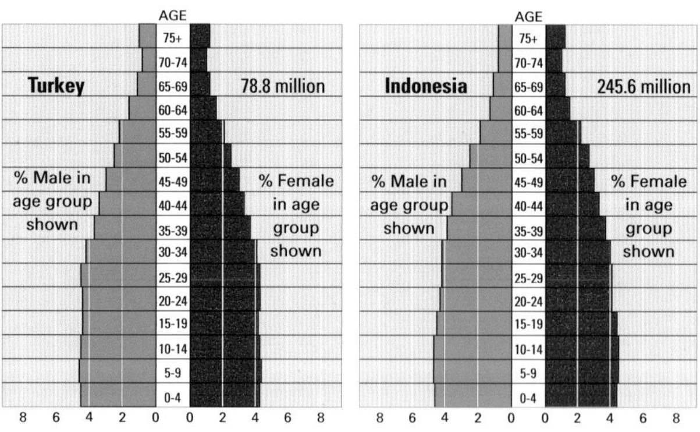

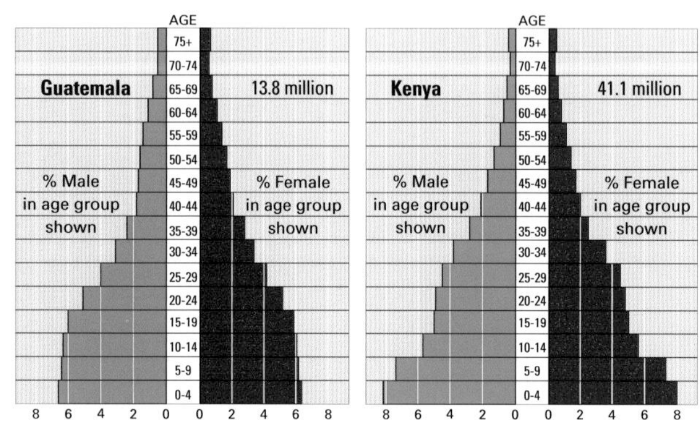

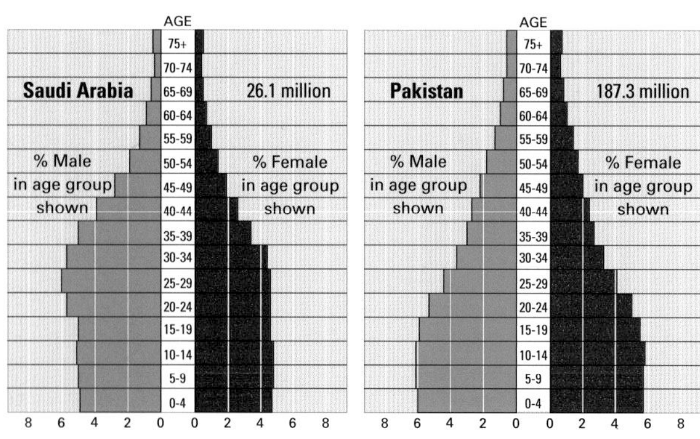

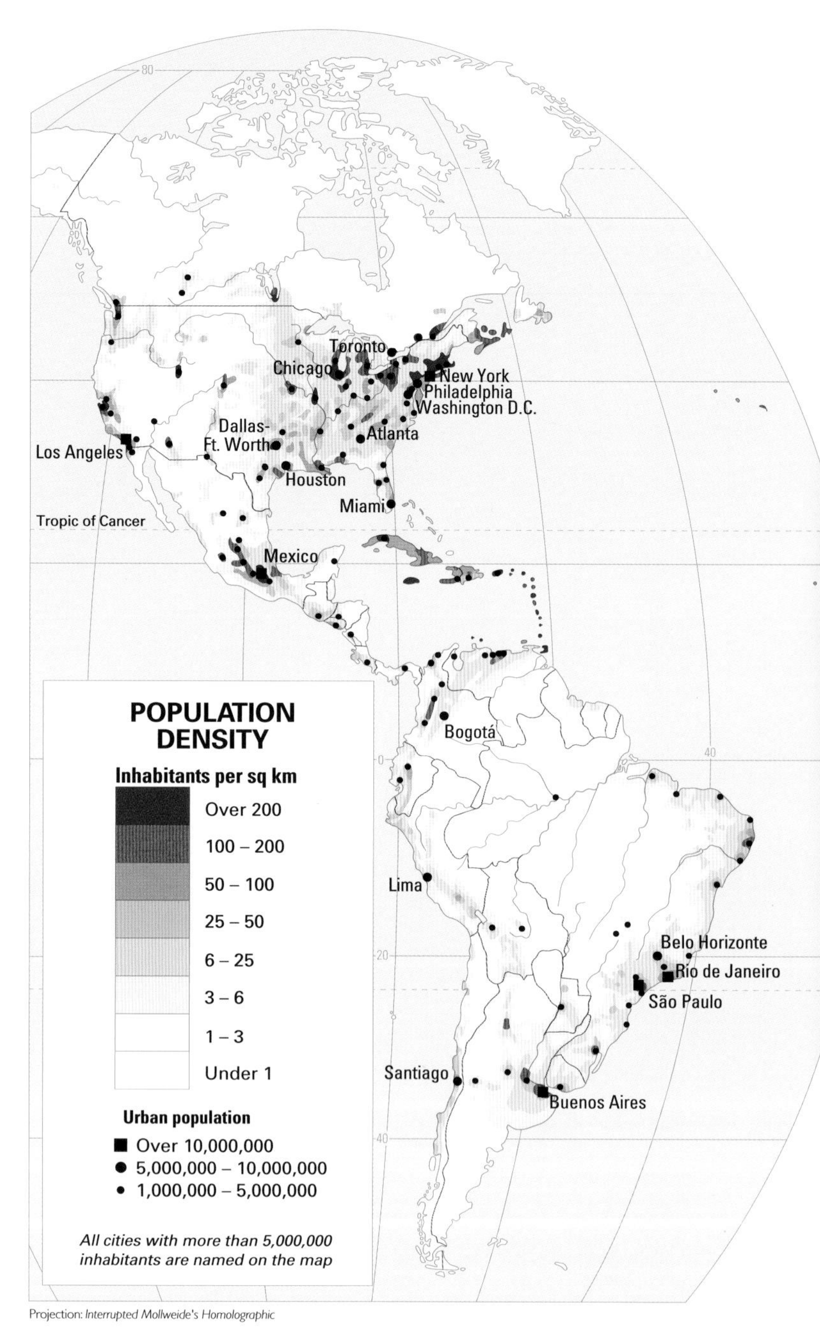

POPULATION DENSITY

Inhabitants per sq km

- Over 200
- 100 – 200
- 50 – 100
- 25 – 50
- 6 – 25
- 3 – 6
- 1 – 3
- Under 1

Urban population

- ■ Over 10,000,000
- ● 5,000,000 – 10,000,000
- • 1,000,000 – 5,000,000

All cities with more than 5,000,000 inhabitants are named on the map

Projection: *Interrupted Mollweide's Homolographic*

POPULATION CHANGE 1930–2020 · Population totals are in millions

Figures in italics represent the percentage average annual increase for the period shown

	1930	1930–1960	1960	1960–1990	1990	1990–2020	2020
World	2,013	*1.4%*	3,019	*1.9%*	5,292	*1.4%*	8,062
Africa	155	*2.0%*	281	*2.9%*	648	*2.7%*	1,441
North America	135	*1.3%*	199	*1.1%*	276	*0.6%*	327
Latin America*	129	*1.8%*	218	*2.4%*	448	*1.6%*	719
Asia	1,073	*1.5%*	1,669	*2.1%*	3,108	*1.4%*	4,680
Europe	355	*0.6%*	425	*0.6%*	498	*0.1%*	514
Oceania	10	*1.4%*	16	*1.8%*	27	*1.1%*	37
CIS†	176	*0.7%*	214	*1.0%*	288	*0.6%*	343

* South America plus Central America, Mexico and the West Indies
† Commonwealth of Independent States, formerly the USSR

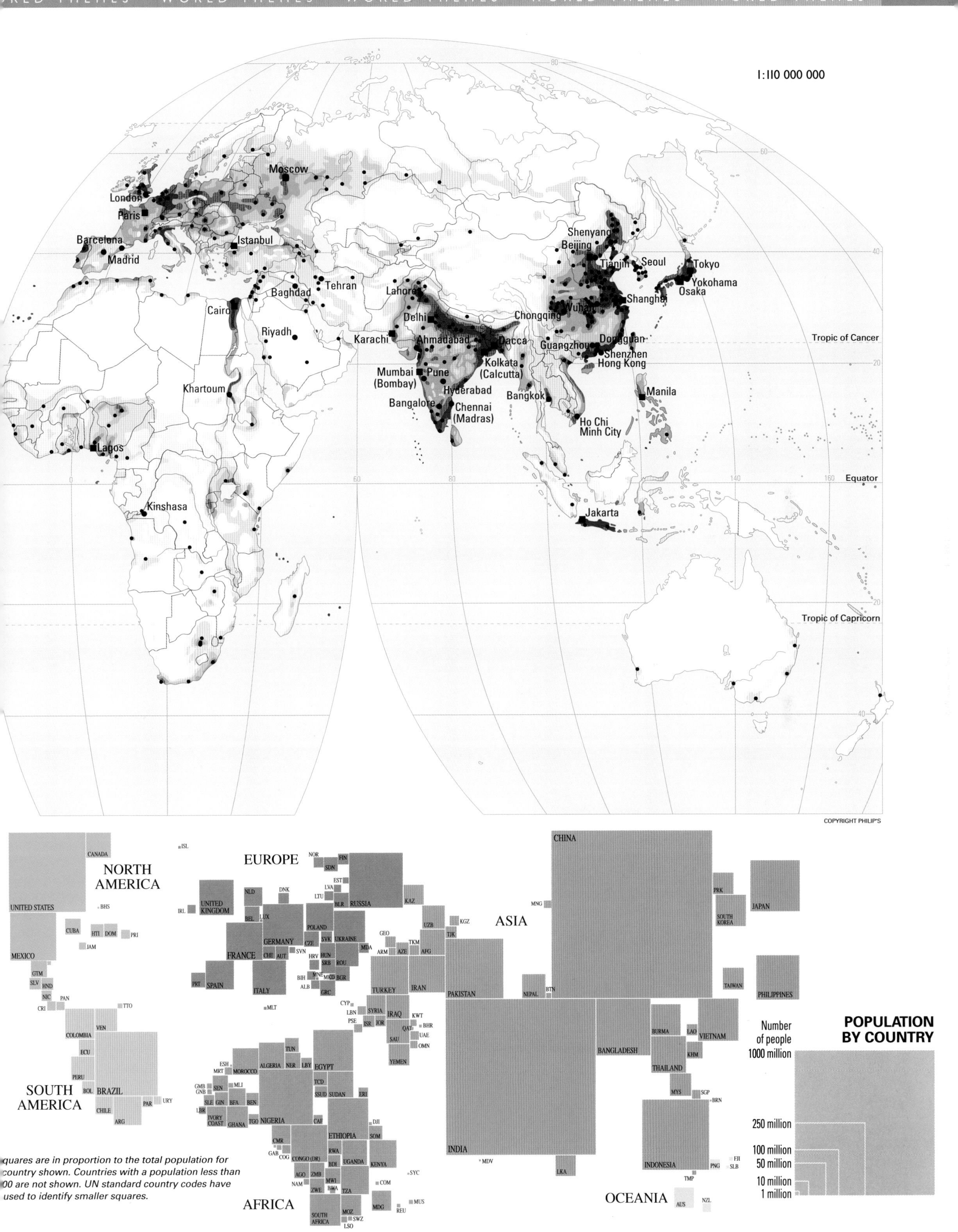

1:110 000 000

COPYRIGHT PHILIP'S

POPULATION BY COUNTRY

Number of people
1000 million
250 million
100 million
50 million
10 million
1 million

squares are in proportion to the total population for country shown. Countries with a population less than 00 are not shown. UN standard country codes have used to identify smaller squares.

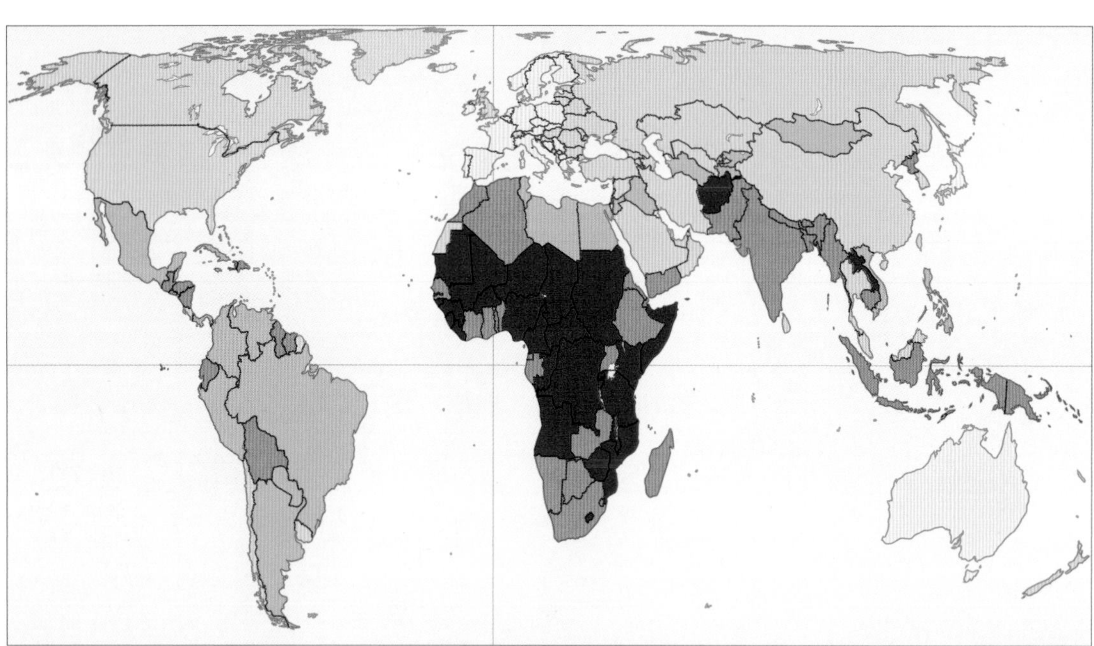

MATERNAL MORTALITY

The number of mothers who died per 100,000 live births (2008)

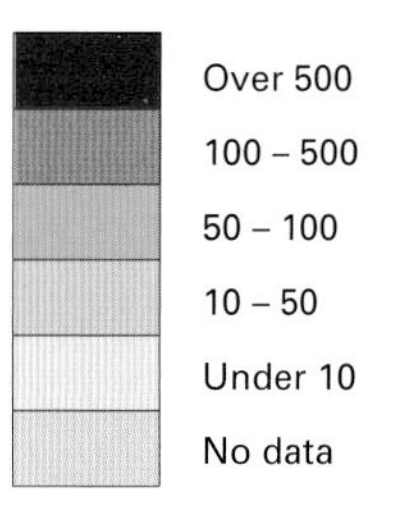

- Over 500
- 100 – 500
- 50 – 100
- 10 – 50
- Under 10
- No data

Countries with the highest and lowest maternal mortality

Highest		Lowest	
Afghanistan	1,400	Greece	2
Chad	1,200	Ireland	3
Somalia	1,200	Sweden	5
Guinea-Bissau	1,000	Italy	5
Liberia	990	Iceland	5

UK 12 mothers

POPULATION CHANGE

The projected population change for the years 2004–2050

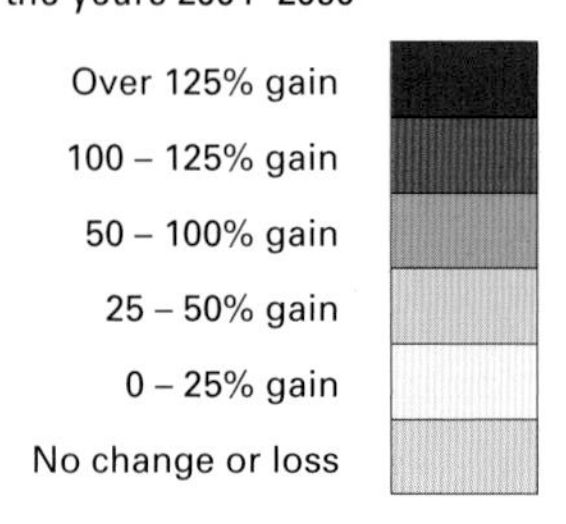

- Over 125% gain
- 100 – 125% gain
- 50 – 100% gain
- 25 – 50% gain
- 0 – 25% gain
- No change or loss

Based on estimates for the year 2050, the ten most populous nations in the world will be, in millions:

India	1,628	Pakistan	295
China	1,437	Bangladesh	280
USA	420	Brazil	221
Indonesia	308	Congo (DR)	181
Nigeria	307	Ethiopia	171

UK (2050) 77 million

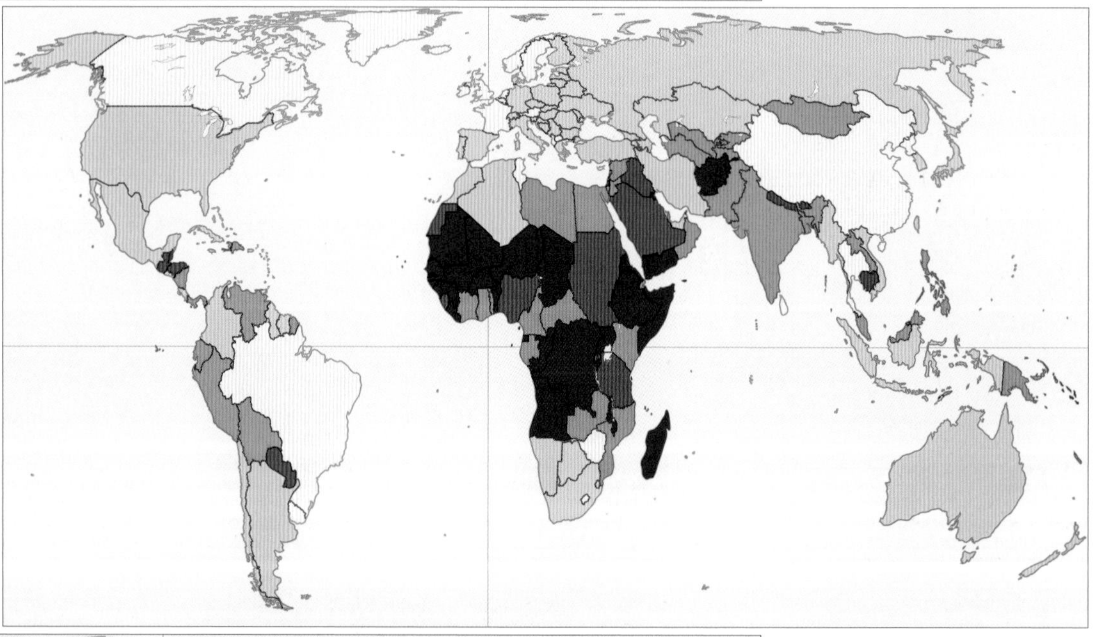

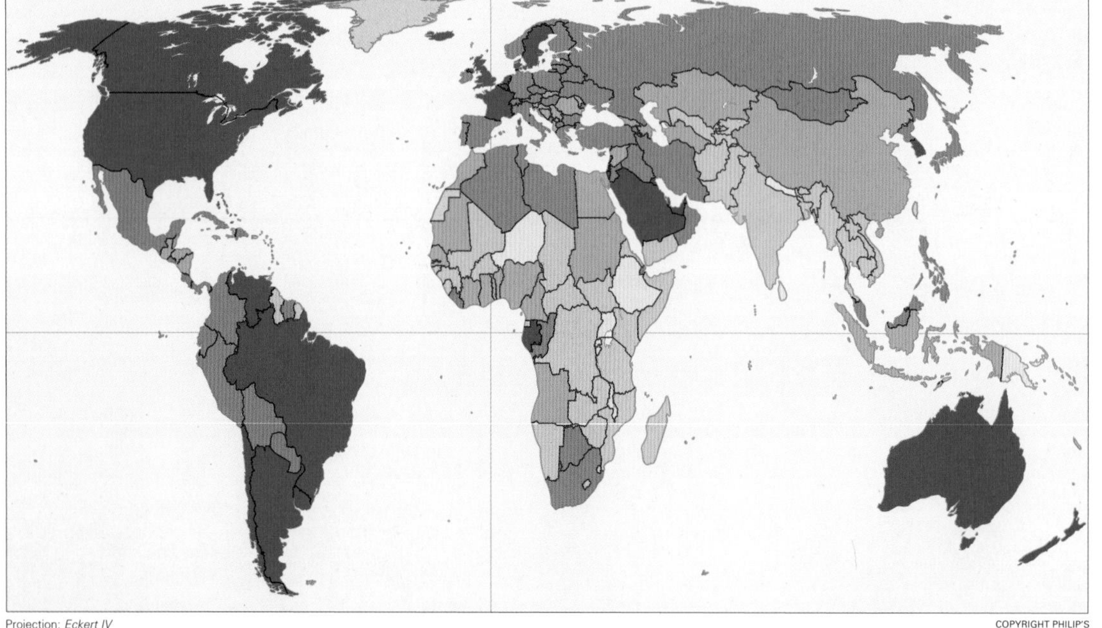

URBAN POPULATION

Percentage of total population living in towns and cities (2010)

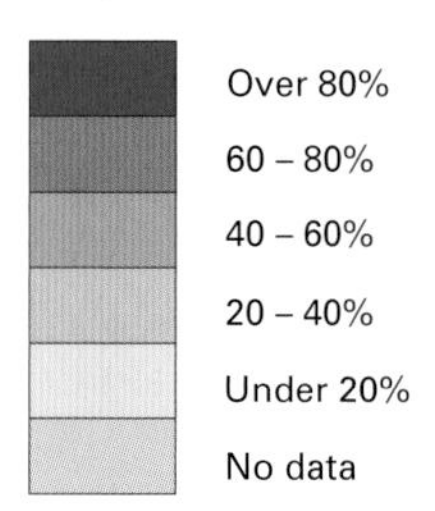

- Over 80%
- 60 – 80%
- 40 – 60%
- 20 – 40%
- Under 20%
- No data

Countries that are the most and least urbanized (%)

Most urbanized		Least urbanized	
Singapore	100	Burundi	11
Kuwait	98	Papua N. Guinea	13
Belgium	97	Uganda	13

UK 80% urban

In 2008, for the first time in history, more than half the world's population lived in urban areas.

Projection: *Eckert IV*

COPYRIGHT PHILIP'S

INFANT MORTALITY

Number of babies who died under
the age of one, per 1,000 live births
(2010)

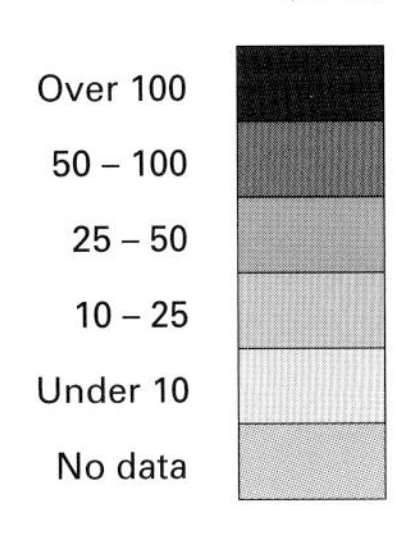

Over 100	
50 – 100	
25 – 50	
10 – 25	
Under 10	
No data	

Countries with the highest and
lowest child mortality

Highest		Lowest	
Angola	176	Monaco	2
Afghanistan	149	Singapore	2
Niger	112	Sweden	3

UK 5 babies

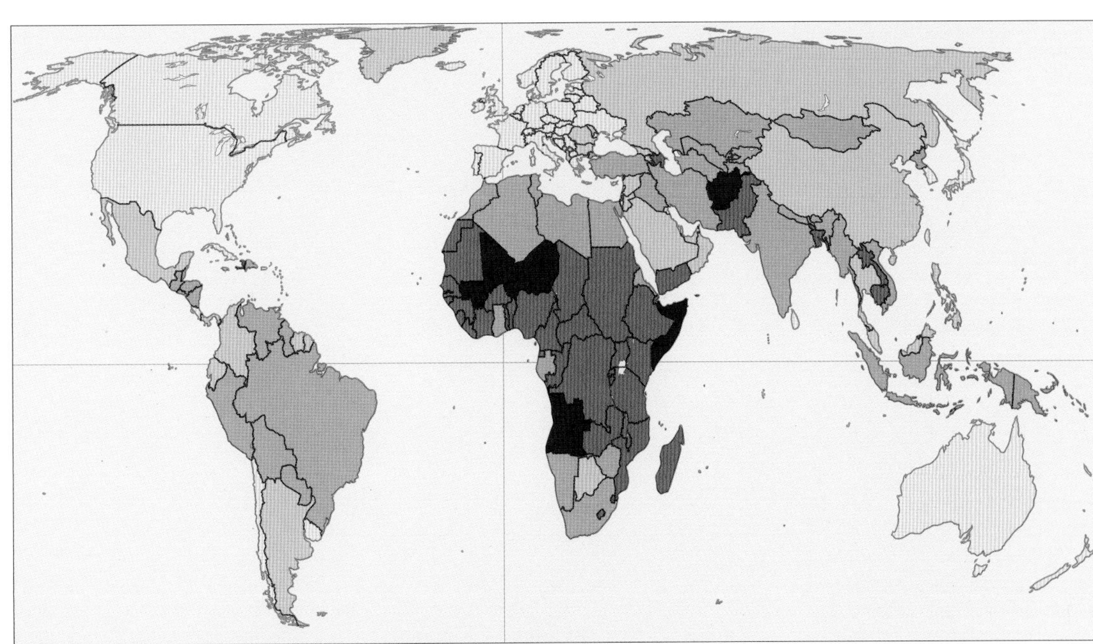

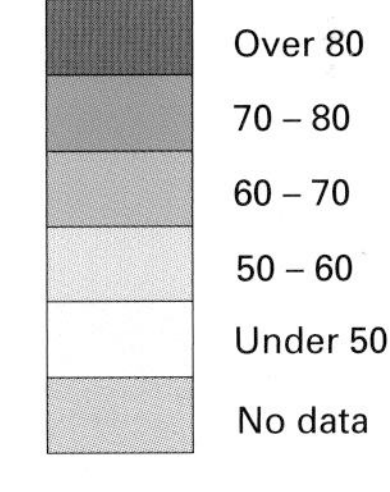

LIFE EXPECTANCY

The average expected lifespan
of babies born in 2010

Over 80	
70 – 80	
60 – 70	
50 – 60	
Under 50	
No data	

Countries with the highest and lowest
life expectancy at birth in years

Highest		Lowest	
Australia	82	Angola	39
Italy	82	Afghanistan	45
Japan	82	Nigeria	48
Singapore	82	Chad	48
Canada	81	South Africa	49

UK 80 years

FAMILY SIZE

Children born per woman (2010)

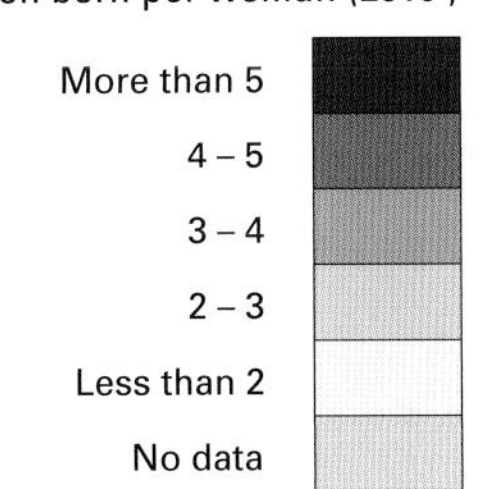

More than 5	
4 – 5	
3 – 4	
2 – 3	
Less than 2	
No data	

Countries with the largest and
smallest family size

Largest		Smallest	
Niger	7.6	Singapore	1.1
Uganda	6.7	Japan	1.2
Mali	6.4	Taiwan	1.2
Somalia	6.4	South Korea	1.2
Burundi	6.2	Lithuania	1.3

UK 1.9 children

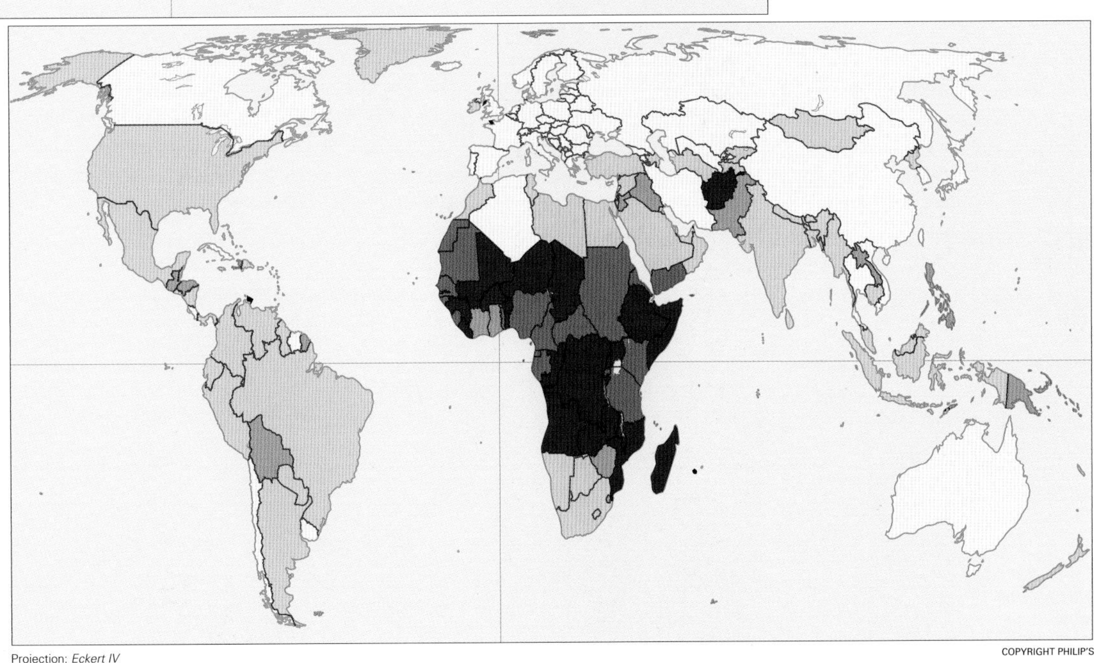

Projection: *Eckert IV*

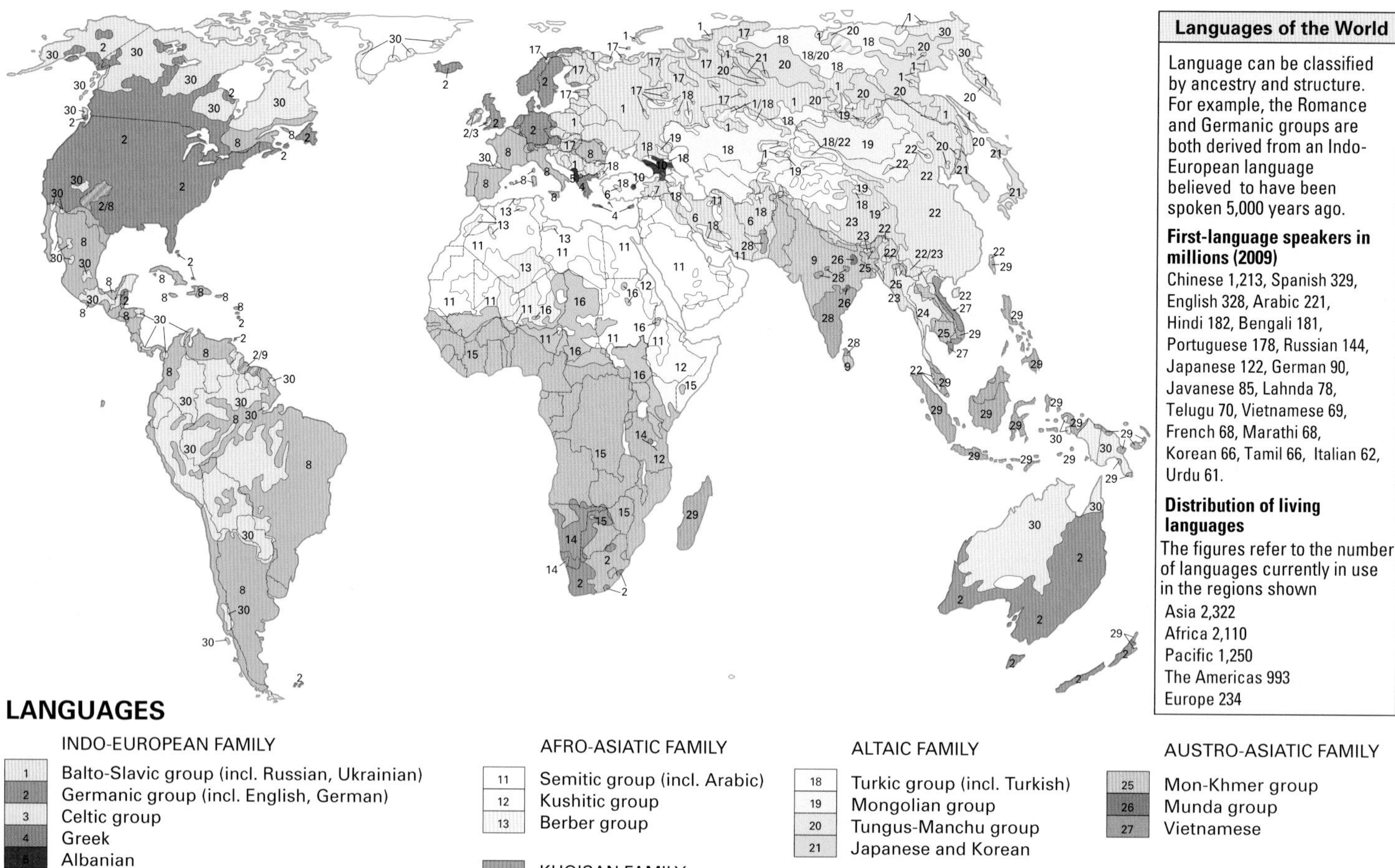

Languages of the World

Language can be classified by ancestry and structure. For example, the Romance and Germanic groups are both derived from an Indo-European language believed to have been spoken 5,000 years ago.

First-language speakers in millions (2009)

Chinese 1,213, Spanish 329, English 328, Arabic 221, Hindi 182, Bengali 181, Portuguese 178, Russian 144, Japanese 122, German 90, Javanese 85, Lahnda 78, Telugu 70, Vietnamese 69, French 68, Marathi 68, Korean 66, Tamil 66, Italian 62, Urdu 61.

Distribution of living languages

The figures refer to the number of languages currently in use in the regions shown
Asia 2,322
Africa 2,110
Pacific 1,250
The Americas 993
Europe 234

LANGUAGES

INDO-EUROPEAN FAMILY

1	Balto-Slavic group (incl. Russian, Ukrainian)
2	Germanic group (incl. English, German)
3	Celtic group
4	Greek
5	Albanian
6	Iranian group
7	Armenian
8	Romance group (incl. Spanish, Portuguese, French, Italian)
9	Indo-Aryan group (incl. Hindi, Bengali, Urdu, Punjabi, Marathi)
10	CAUCASIAN FAMILY

AFRO-ASIATIC FAMILY

11	Semitic group (incl. Arabic)
12	Kushitic group
13	Berber group
14	KHOISAN FAMILY
15	NIGER-CONGO FAMILY
16	NILO-SAHARAN FAMILY
17	URALIC FAMILY

ALTAIC FAMILY

18	Turkic group (incl. Turkish)
19	Mongolian group
20	Tungus-Manchu group
21	Japanese and Korean

SINO-TIBETAN FAMILY

22	Sinitic (Chinese) languages (incl. Mandarin, Wu, Yue)
23	Tibetic-Burmic languages
24	TAI FAMILY

AUSTRO-ASIATIC FAMILY

25	Mon-Khmer group
26	Munda group
27	Vietnamese
28	DRAVIDIAN FAMILY (incl. Telugu, Tamil)
29	AUSTRONESIAN FAMILY (incl. Malay-Indonesian, Javanese)
30	OTHER LANGUAGES

RELIGIONS

- ▲ Roman Catholicism
- Orthodox and other Eastern Churches
- ● Protestantism
- Sunni Islam
- Shiite Islam
- Buddhism
- Hinduism
- Confucianism
- ★ Judaism
- Shintoism
- Tribal Religions

Religious Adherents

Religious adherents in millions (2009)

Christianity	2,264	Buddhism	484
Roman Catholic	*1,143*	Chinese folk	455
Protestant	*413*	Ethnic religions	259
Orthodox	*273*	New religions	64
Anglican	*85*	Sikhism	24
Others	*350*	Spiritism	14
Islam	1,523	Judaism	15
Sunni	*1,279*	Taoism	9
Shi'ite	*213*	Baha'i	7
Others	*31*	Confucianism	6
Hindu	935	Jainism	6
Non-religious/ Agnostic/Atheist	779		

COPYRIGHT PHILIP'S

United Nations

Created in 1945 to promote peace and co-operation, and based in New York, the United Nations is the world's largest international organization, with 193 members and an annual budget of US $5.16 billion (2010). Each member of the General Assembly has one vote, while the five permanent members of the 15-nation Security Council – China, France, Russia, the UK and the USA – hold a veto. The Secretariat is the UN's principal administrative arm. The 54 members of the Economic and Social Council are responsible for economic, social, cultural, educational, health and related matters. The UN has 16 specialized agencies – based in Canada, France, Switzerland and Italy, as well as the USA – which help members in fields such as education (UNESCO), agriculture (FAO), medicine (WHO) and finance (IFC). By the end of 1994, all the original 11 trust territories of the Trusteeship Council had become independent.

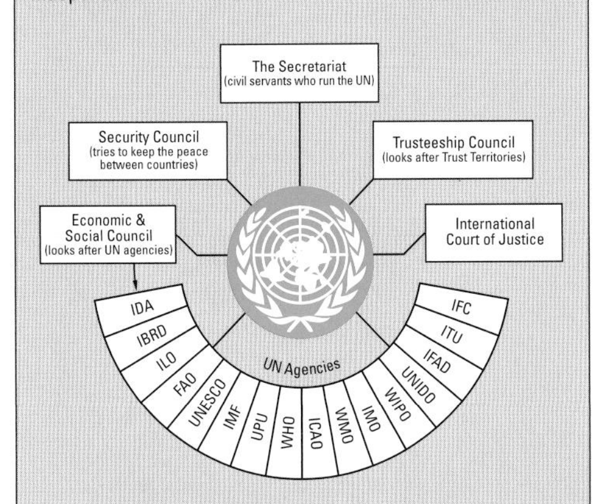

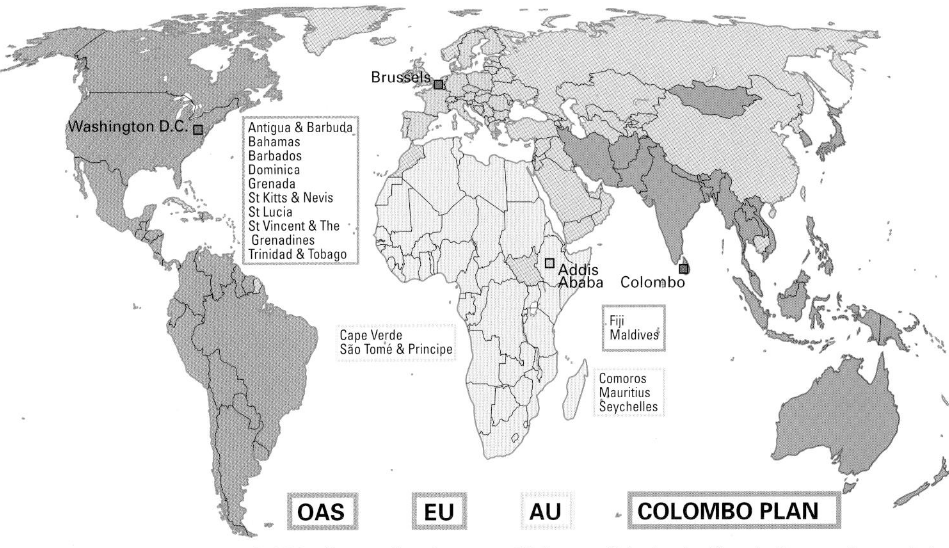

OAS   **EU**   **AU**   **COLOMBO PLAN**

AU The African Union was set up in 2002, taking over from the Organization of African Unity (1963). It has 54 members. Working languages are Arabic, English, French and Portuguese.

COLOMBO PLAN (formed in 1951) Its 25 members aim to promote economic and social development in Asia and the Pacific.

OAS Organization of American States (formed in 1948). It aims to promote social and economic co-operation between countries in the developed North America and developing Latin America.

EU European Union (evolved from the European Community in 1993). Cyprus, the Czech Republic, Estonia, Hungary, Latvia, Lithuania, Malta, Poland, the Slovak Republic and Slovenia joined the EU in May 2004, Bulgaria and Romania joined in 2007, Croatia joined in 2013. The other 15 members of the EU are Austria, Belgium, Denmark, Finland, France, Germany, Greece, Ireland, Italy, Luxembourg, Netherlands, Portugal, Spain, Sweden and the UK. Together, the 28 members aim to integrate economies, co-ordinate social developments and bring about political union. Its member states have set up common institutions to which they delegate some of their sovereignty so that decisions on specific matters of joint interest can be made democratically at European level.

ACP African-Caribbean-Pacific (formed in 1963). Members enjoy economic ties with the EU.

APEC Asia-Pacific Economic Co-operation (formed in 1989). It aims to enhance economic growth and prosperity for the region and to strengthen the Asia-Pacific community. APEC is the only intergovernmental grouping in the world operating on the basis of non-binding commitments, open dialogue, and equal respect for the views of all participants. There are 21 member economies.

G8 Group of eight leading industrialized nations, comprising Canada, France, Germany, Italy, Japan, Russia, the UK and the USA. Periodic meetings are held to discuss major world issues, such as world recessions.

OECD Organization for Economic Co-operation and Development (formed in 1961). It comprises 34 major free-market economies. The 'G8' is its 'inner group' of leading industrial nations, comprising Canada, France, Germany, Italy, Japan, Russia, the UK and the USA.

OPEC Organization of Petroleum Exporting Countries (formed in 1960). It controls about three-quarters of the world's oil supply. Gabon formally withdrew from OPEC in August 1996.

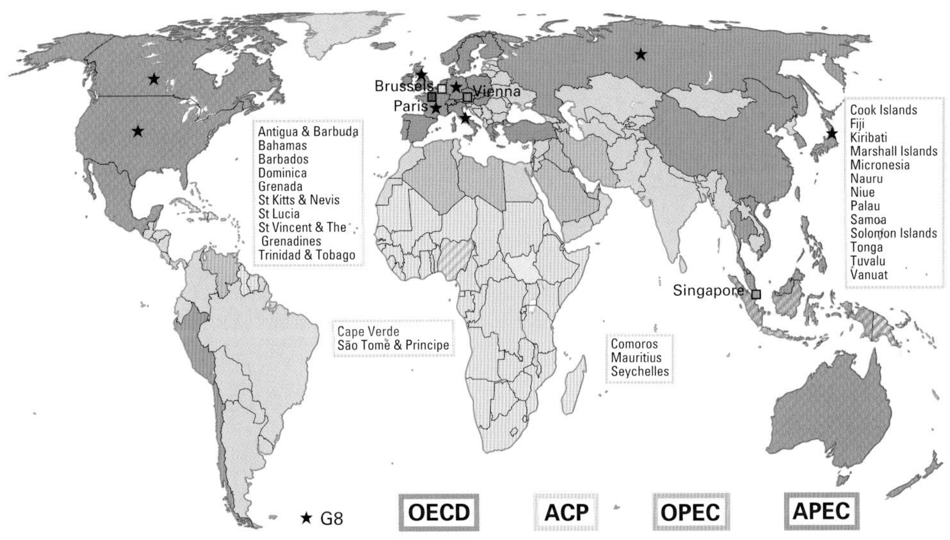

★ G8   **OECD**   **ACP**   **OPEC**   **APEC**

ARAB LEAGUE (1945) Aims to promote economic, social, political and military co-operation. There are 22 member nations.

ASEAN Association of South-east Asian Nations (formed in 1967). Cambodia joined in 1999.

BRIC This acronym refers to the four largest and fastest growing developing economies, Brazil, Russia, India and China.

COMMONWEALTH The Commonwealth of Nations evolved from the British Empire. Pakistan was suspended in 1999, but reinstated in 2004. Zimbabwe was suspended in 2002 and, in response to its continued suspension, left the Commonwealth in 2003. Fiji was suspended in 2006 following a military coup. Rwanda joined the Commonwealth in 2009, as the 54th member state, becoming only the second country which was not formerly a British colony to be admitted to the group.

LAIA The Latin American Integration Association (formed in 1980) superceded the Latin American Free Trade Association formed in 1961. Its aim is to promote freer regional trade.

NATO North Atlantic Treaty Organization (formed in 1949). It continues despite the winding-up of the Warsaw Pact in 1991. Bulgaria, Estonia, Latvia, Lithuania, Romania, the Slovak Republic and Slovenia became members in 2004 and Albania and Croatia in 2009.

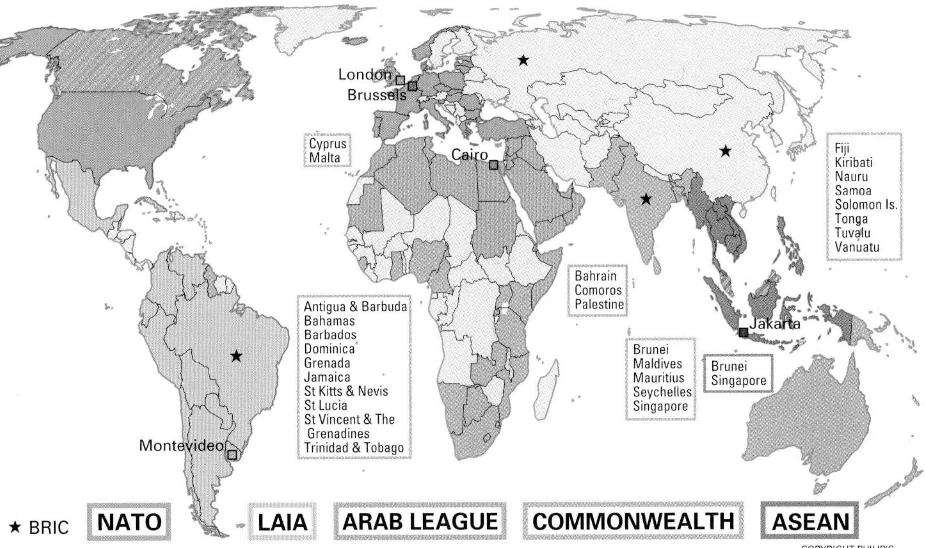

★ BRIC   **NATO**   **LAIA**   **ARAB LEAGUE**   **COMMONWEALTH**   **ASEAN**

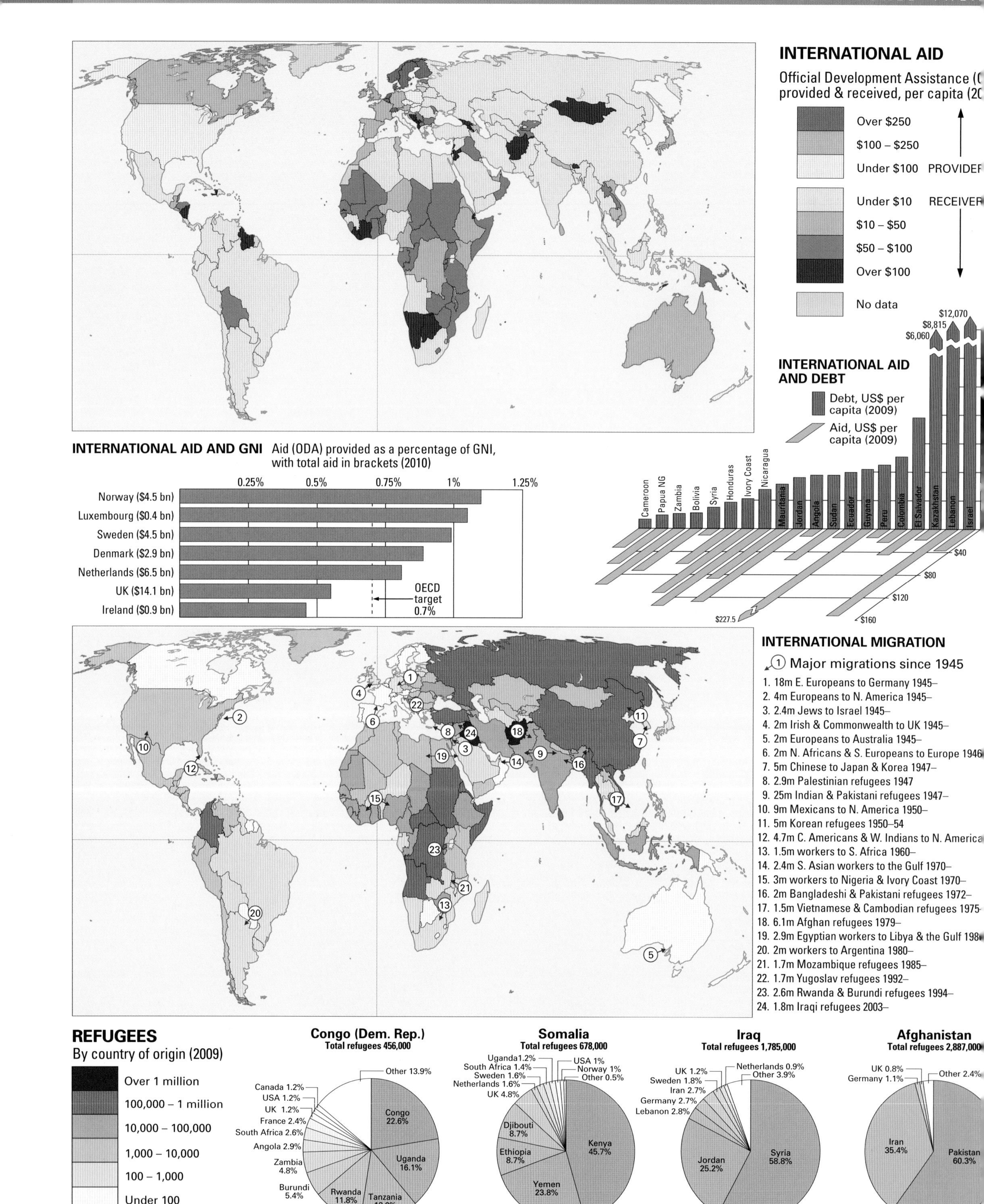

INTERNATIONAL AID

Official Development Assistance (C
provided & received, per capita (2C

Over $250	
$100 – $250	
Under $100	PROVIDEF
Under $10	RECEIVER
$10 – $50	
$50 – $100	
Over $100	
No data	

INTERNATIONAL AID AND DEBT

- Debt, US$ per capita (2009)
- Aid, US$ per capita (2009)

$12,070
$8,815
$6,060

Cameroon, Papua NG, Zambia, Bolivia, Syria, Honduras, Ivory Coast, Nicaragua, Mauritania, Jordan, Angola, Sudan, Ecuador, Guyana, Peru, Colombia, El Salvador, Kazakhstan, Lebanon, Israel

$40
$80
$120
$160
$227.5

INTERNATIONAL AID AND GNI

Aid (ODA) provided as a percentage of GNI, with total aid in brackets (2010)

0.25% 0.5% 0.75% 1% 1.25%

- Norway ($4.5 bn)
- Luxembourg ($0.4 bn)
- Sweden ($4.5 bn)
- Denmark ($2.9 bn)
- Netherlands ($6.5 bn)
- UK ($14.1 bn)
- Ireland ($0.9 bn)

OECD target 0.7%

INTERNATIONAL MIGRATION

① Major migrations since 1945

1. 18m E. Europeans to Germany 1945–
2. 4m Europeans to N. America 1945–
3. 2.4m Jews to Israel 1945–
4. 2m Irish & Commonwealth to UK 1945–
5. 2m Europeans to Australia 1945–
6. 2m N. Africans & S. Europeans to Europe 1946
7. 5m Chinese to Japan & Korea 1947–
8. 2.9m Palestinian refugees 1947
9. 25m Indian & Pakistani refugees 1947–
10. 9m Mexicans to N. America 1950–
11. 5m Korean refugees 1950–54
12. 4.7m C. Americans & W. Indians to N. America
13. 1.5m workers to S. Africa 1960–
14. 2.4m S. Asian workers to the Gulf 1970–
15. 3m workers to Nigeria & Ivory Coast 1970–
16. 2m Bangladeshi & Pakistani refugees 1972–
17. 1.5m Vietnamese & Cambodian refugees 1975–
18. 6.1m Afghan refugees 1979–
19. 2.9m Egyptian workers to Libya & the Gulf 198
20. 2m workers to Argentina 1980–
21. 1.7m Mozambique refugees 1985–
22. 1.7m Yugoslav refugees 1992–
23. 2.6m Rwanda & Burundi refugees 1994–
24. 1.8m Iraqi refugees 2003–

REFUGEES

By country of origin (2009)

Over 1 million	
100,000 – 1 million	
10,000 – 100,000	
1,000 – 10,000	
100 – 1,000	
Under 100	
No data	

Congo (Dem. Rep.)
Total refugees 456,000

- Other 13.9%
- Canada 1.2%
- USA 1.2%
- UK 1.2%
- France 2.4%
- South Africa 2.6%
- Angola 2.9%
- Zambia 4.8%
- Burundi 5.4%
- Rwanda 11.8%
- Tanzania 13.9%
- Uganda 16.1%
- Congo 22.6%

Somalia
Total refugees 678,000

- Uganda 1.2%
- South Africa 1.4%
- Sweden 1.6%
- Netherlands 1.6%
- UK 4.8%
- USA 1%
- Norway 1%
- Other 0.5%
- Djibouti 8.7%
- Ethiopia 8.7%
- Yemen 23.8%
- Kenya 45.7%

Iraq
Total refugees 1,785,000

- UK 1.2%
- Sweden 1.8%
- Iran 2.7%
- Germany 2.7%
- Lebanon 2.8%
- Netherlands 0.9%
- Other 3.9%
- Jordan 25.2%
- Syria 58.8%

Afghanistan
Total refugees 2,887,000

- UK 0.8%
- Germany 1.1%
- Other 2.4%
- Iran 35.4%
- Pakistan 60.3%

Projection: *Eckert IV*

COPYRIGHT P

ARMED CONFLICTS

Current military and civilian death
olls in countries with conflict (2010)

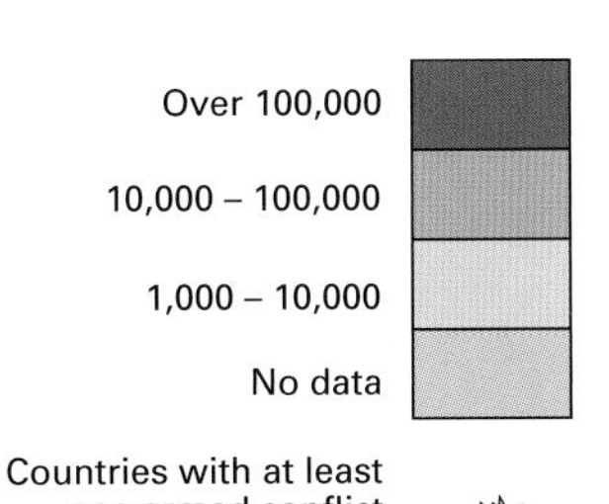

Over 100,000	
10,000 – 100,000	
1,000 – 10,000	
No data	

Countries with at least
one armed conflict
between 1994 and 2010

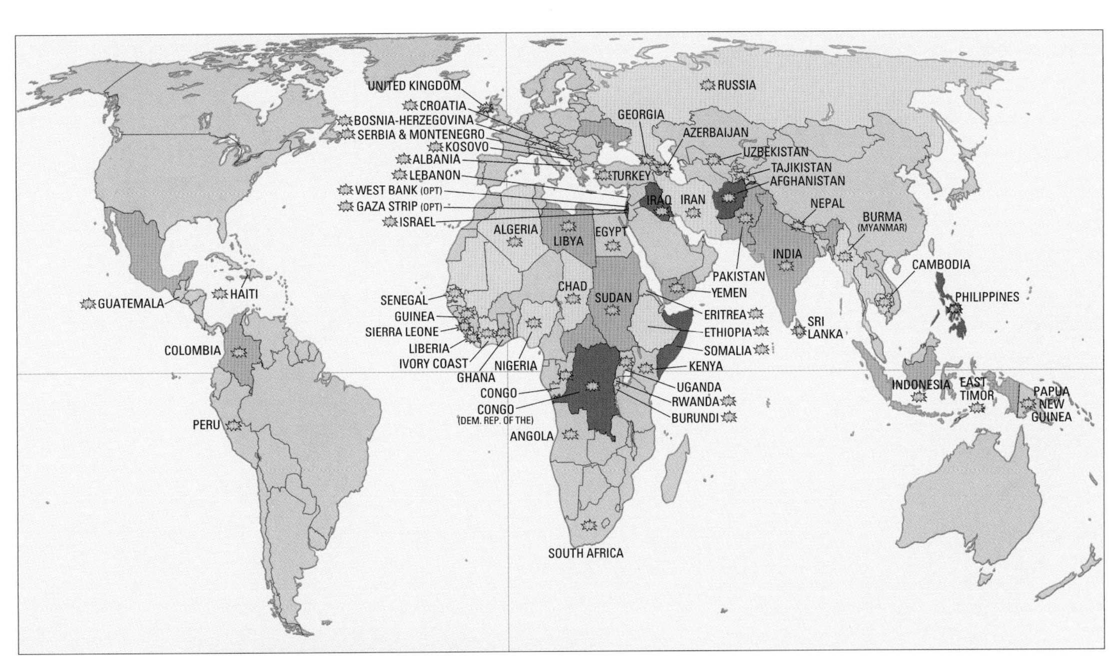

ading arms porting countries S $ million)		Leading recipients of arms deliveries (US $ million)	
SA	$14,000	Saudi Arabia	$4,100
ssia	$5,800	China	$2,900
K	$3,300	Israel	$1,500

SPREAD OF HIV/AIDS

Percentage of the population
living with HIV/AIDS (2009)

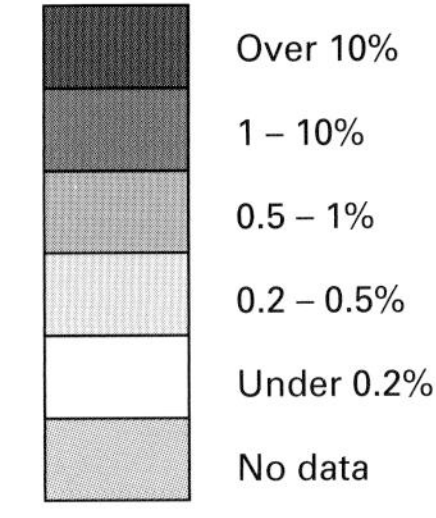

Over 10%	
1 – 10%	
0.5 – 1%	
0.2 – 0.5%	
Under 0.2%	
No data	

Caribbean 240,000 — Total number of adults and children living with HIV/AIDS by region (2009)

Human Immunodeficiency Virus (HIV) is passed
from one person to another and attacks the
body's defence against illness. It develops into
the Acquired Immunodeficiency Syndrome
(AIDS) when a particularly severe illness, such as
cancer, takes hold. The pandemic started just
over 20 years ago and by 2009 33 millon people
were living with HIV or AIDS.

TRAFFIC IN DRUGS

Countries producing illegal drugs

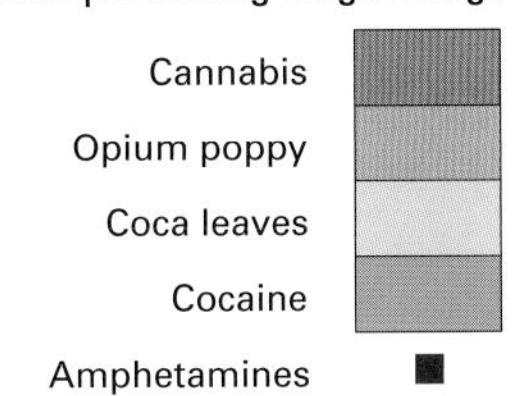

Cannabis
Opium poppy
Coca leaves
Cocaine
Amphetamines ■

Major routes of drug trafficking

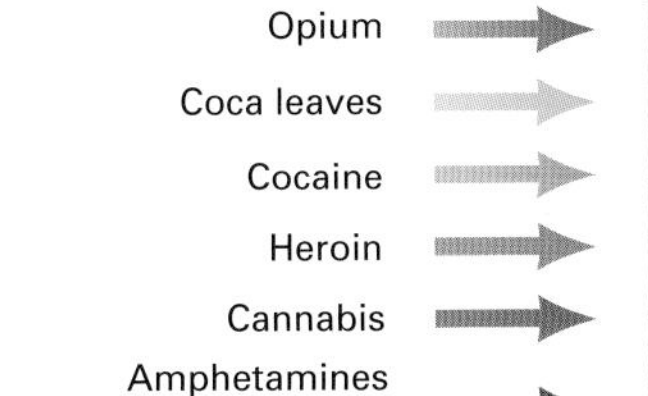

Opium
Coca leaves
Cocaine
Heroin
Cannabis
Amphetamines
(usually used within
producing countries)
Conflicts relating to
drug trafficking

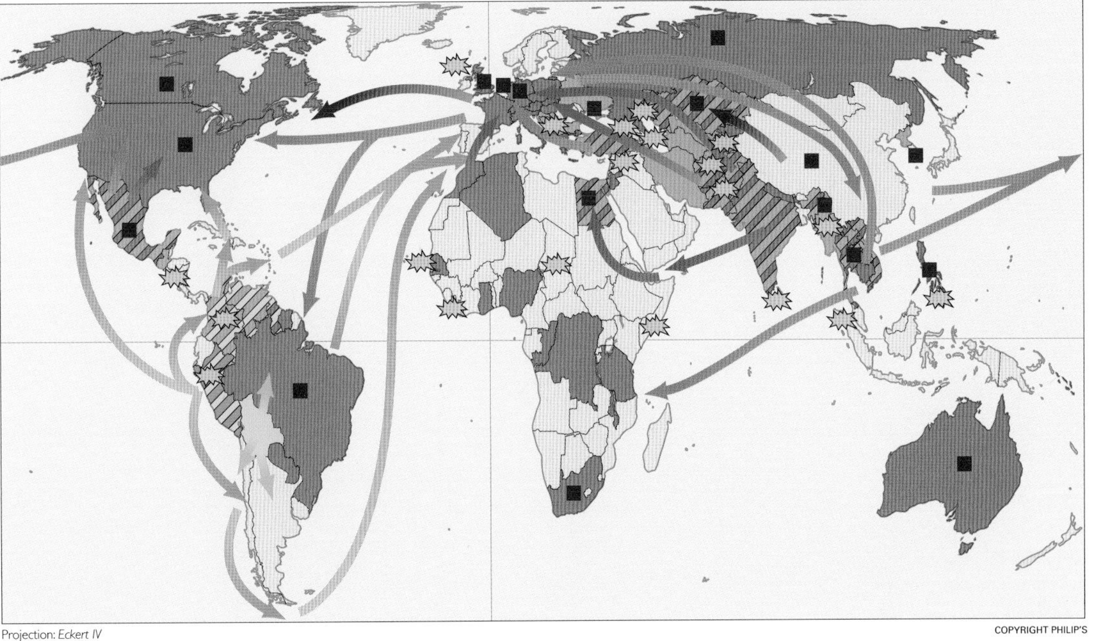

Projection: Eckert IV

COPYRIGHT PHILIP'S

	POPULATION						WEALTH						TRADE		
	Total population (millions 2010)	Population density (persons per km² 2010)	Population change (average annual percentage 2010)	Birth rate (births per thousand people 2010)	Death rate (deaths per thousand people 2010)	Urban population (percentage of total 2010)	Gross National Income (million US$ 2009)	Gross National Income per capita (PPP US$ 2009)	GDP growth rate (percentage 2010)	GDP from agriculture (percentage of GDP 2010)	GDP from industry (percentage of GDP 2010)	GDP from services (percentage of GDP 2010)	Imports (US$ per capita 2010)	Exports (US$ per capita 2010)	Tourism receipts (US$ per capita 2009)
Afghanistan	29.1	45	2.4	38	17	22	9,053	310	8.2	31.0	26.0	43.0	182	19	
Albania	3.0	104	0.3	12	6	52	12,634	4,000	3.5	18.9	23.5	57.6	1,537	519	
Algeria	34.6	15	1.2	17	5	67	154,202	4,420	3.3	8.3	61.5	30.2	1,072	1,523	
Angola	13.1	10	2.0	43	23	59	69,373	3,750	1.6	9.6	65.8	24.6	1,385	3,952	
Argentina	41.3	15	1.0	18	7	92	304,070	7,550	7.5	8.5	31.6	59.9	1,273	1,645	
Armenia	3.0	100	0.1	13	8	64	9,544	3,100	2.6	22.0	46.6	31.4	1,007	285	
Australia	21.5	3	1.1	12	7	89	957,519	43,770	2.7	4.0	24.8	71.2	9,314	9,793	1,
Austria	8.2	98	0.0	9	10	68	388,529	46,450	2.0	1.5	29.4	69.1	18,992	19,162	2,
Azerbaijan	8.3	96	0.8	18	8	52	42,529	4,840	5.0	5.5	61.4	33.1	847	3,380	
Bahamas	0.3	22	0.9	16	7	84	9,117	14,920	0.5	1.2	14.7	84.1	7,735	2,171	6,
Bahrain	0.7	1,110	2.8	15	3	89	19,712	25,420	4.1	0.5	56.6	42.9	16,450	20,501	2,
Bangladesh	156.1	1,084	1.6	23	6	28	93,470	580	6.0	18.4	28.7	52.9	137	104	
Barbados	0.3	663	0.4	12	8	44	3,551	16,140	-0.5	6.0	16.0	78.0	5,552	1,348	3,
Belarus	9.6	46	-0.4	10	14	75	53,707	5,560	7.6	9.0	42.9	48.1	3,099	2,548	
Belgium	10.4	341	0.1	10	11	97	488,429	45,270	2.0	0.7	22.1	77.2	27,025	26,786	
Belize	0.3	14	2.1	26	6	52	1,205	3,740	2.0	29.0	16.9	54.1	2,353	1,284	
Benin	9.1	80	2.9	38	9	42	6,715	750	2.5	33.2	14.5	52.3	200	124	
Bhutan	0.7	15	1.2	19	7	35	1,416	2,020	2.5	17.6	45.0	37.4	762	733	
Bolivia	9.9	9	1.7	25	7	67	16,061	1,630	4.2	11.0	38.0	51.0	539	699	
Bosnia-Herzegovina	4.6	90	0.0	9	9	49	17,704	4,700	0.8	6.5	28.4	65.1	1,995	1,039	
Botswana	2.0	3	1.7	22	11	61	12,211	6,260	8.6	2.3	45.8	51.9	2,226	2,178	
Brazil	201.1	24	1.1	18	6	87	1,557,007	8,070	7.5	6.1	26.4	67.5	933	993	
Brunei	0.4	68	1.7	18	3	76	10,211	49,900	4.1	0.7	74.1	25.2	6,607	27,011	
Bulgaria	7.1	64	-0.8	9	14	71	45,961	6,060	0.2	6.0	30.3	63.7	3,187	2,704	
Burkina Faso	16.2	59	3.1	44	13	26	8,036	510	5.8	30.1	20.7	49.2	91	61	
Burma (Myanmar)	53.4	79	1.1	19	8	34	17,766	150	5.3	43.2	20.0	36.8	85	147	
Burundi	9.9	354	3.5	41	10	11	1,232	1,290	3.9	31.6	21.4	47.0	34	7	
Cambodia	14.5	80	1.7	25	8	20	9,099	650	6.0	33.4	21.4	45.2	415	324	
Cameroon	19.3	41	2.1	33	12	58	23,189	1,190	3.0	20.0	30.9	49.1	252	227	
Canada	33.8	3	0.8	10	8	81	1,416,347	41,980	3.1	2.0	20.0	78.0	12,038	12,050	
Cape Verde Is.	0.5	126	1.4	21	6	61	1,520	3,010	5.4	9.0	16.2	74.8	1,687	224	
Central African Rep.	4.8	8	2.1	36	15	39	1,975	450	3.3	55.0	20.0	25.0	49	30	
Chad	10.5	8	2.0	39	15	28	5,845	600	5.1	50.5	7.0	42.5	250	288	
Chile	16.7	22	0.8	14	6	89	160,655	9,470	5.3	5.6	40.5	53.9	3,238	3,838	
China	1,330.1	139	0.5	14	7	47	4,856,148	3,650	10.3	9.6	46.8	43.6	983	1,132	
Colombia	44.2	39	1.2	17	5	75	227,814	4,990	4.3	9.3	38.0	52.7	820	910	
Comoros	0.8	356	2.7	34	7	28	571	810	2.1	40.0	4.0	56.0	185	41	
Congo	4.1	12	2.8	41	11	62	7,671	2,080	9.1	4.4	63.6	32.0	874	2,230	
Congo (Dem. Rep.)	70.9	30	2.6	38	11	35	10,609	160	7.2	37.4	26.0	36.6	73	54	
Costa Rica	4.5	88	1.3	17	4	64	28,664	6,260	4.2	6.3	22.9	70.8	2,949	2,216	1
Croatia	4.5	79	-0.1	17	12	58	60,797	13,770	-1.4	6.8	27.2	66.0	4,665	2,565	1,9
Cuba	11.5	104	-0.1	10	7	75	62,196	5,550	1.5	4.4	22.7	72.9	893	288	
Cyprus	1.1	119	1.6	11	6	70	21,366	30,480	1.0	2.1	18.6	79.3	7,221	2,024	2,0
Czech Republic	10.2	129	-0.1	8	11	74	181,547	17,310	2.3	2.2	38.3	59.5	10,704	11,420	6
Denmark	5.5	128	0.3	10	10	87	326,535	59,060	2.1	1.1	22.8	76.1	16,468	18,016	1,0
Djibouti	0.7	32	2.2	25	8	76	1,106	1,280	4.5	3.2	14.9	81.9	870	135	
Dominican Republic	9.8	202	1.3	20	4	69	45,937	4,550	7.8	11.5	21.0	67.5	1,479	627	4
East Timor	1.2	77	2.0	26	6	28	2,706	2,460	6.1	32.2	12.8	55.0	168	9	
Ecuador	14.8	52	1.4	20	5	67	54,130	3,970	3.2	6.4	35.9	57.7	1,193	1,174	
Egypt	80.5	80	2.0	25	5	43	172,048	2,070	5.1	13.5	37.9	48.6	578	315	
El Salvador	6.1	288	0.3	18	6	64	20,785	3,370	0.7	11.0	29.1	59.9	1,319	723	
Equatorial Guinea	0.7	23	2.6	35	9	40	8,398	12,420	-0.8	2.2	93.9	3.9	8,826	15,737	
Eritrea	5.8	48	2.5	33	8	22	1,351	320	2.2	11.8	20.4	67.8	127	4	
Estonia	1.3	29	-0.6	10	14	69	18,846	14,060	3.1	2.5	28.7	68.8	9,426	8,907	8
Ethiopia	88.0	78	3.2	43	11	17	27,149	330	8.0	42.9	13.7	43.4	85	20	
Fiji	0.9	48	0.8	21	6	52	3,259	3,840	0.1	8.9	13.5	77.6	3,562	1,372	4
Finland	5.3	16	0.1	10	10	85	245,256	45,940	3.1	2.6	29.1	68.3	13,151	13,992	5
France	64.8	118	0.5	12	9	85	2,750,916	42,620	1.5	1.8	19.2	79.0	8,919	7,854	7
Gabon	1.5	6	2.0	35	13	86	10,869	7,370	5.7	4.5	62.7	32.8	1,574	4,403	
Gambia, The	1.8	161	2.4	34	8	58	743	440	5.7	30.1	16.3	53.6	168	59	
Gaza Strip (OPT)*	1.6	4,456	3.2	35	3	74	2,843	2,968	7.0	5.0	14.0	81.0	2,351	330	
Georgia	4.6	66	-0.3	11	10	53	11,096	2,530	6.4	11.0	27.0	62.0	1,049	498	
Germany	82.3	230	-0.2	8	11	74	3,476,100	42,450	3.5	0.8	27.9	71.3	13,612	16,249	4
Ghana	24.3	102	1.8	28	9	51	28,383	1,190	5.7	33.7	24.7	41.6	418	301	
Greece	10.7	81	0.1	9	11	61	327,703	29,040	-4.5	4.0	17.6	78.4	4,177	1,967	1,3

ENERGY | LAND & AGRICULTURE | SOCIAL INDICATORS

	Energy produced (tonnes of oil equivalent per capita 2008)	Energy consumed (tonnes of oil equivalent per capita 2008)	CO_2 emissions (tonnes per capita 2009)	Land area (thousand km²)	Permanent crops and Arable (% of land area 2008)	Permanent pasture (% of land area 2008)	Forest (% of land area 2008)	Human Development Index (HDI) value 2009	Life expectancy (years 2010)	Food intake (calories per capita per day 2007)	Adults living with HIV/AIDS (percentage 2009)	Gender Inequality Index (GII value 2009)	Adult illiteracy rate (percentage 2008)	Motor vehicles (per thousand people 2009)	Internet usage (per thousand people 2009)
Afghanistan	0.01	0.01	0.03	652	12	46	2	0.349	45	–	–	0.797	72	27	3.5
Albania	0.36	0.77	1.52	28.7	25	18	28	0.719	77	2,880	0.1	0.545	1	114	35.7
Algeria	5.79	1.27	3.32	2,382	4	14	1	0.677	75	3,153	0.1	0.594	25	112	13.8
Angola	8.66	0.40	1.86	1,247	3	43	47	0.403	39	1,973	2.0	–	33	40	4.7
Argentina	2.21	2.03	4.06	2,780	12	36	11	0.775	77	2,941	0.5	0.534	2	314	33.5
Armenia	0.38	1.82	3.83	29.8	18	44	9	0.695	73	2,280	0.1	0.570	1	105	7.0
Australia	14.26	6.85	19.64	7,741	6	49	20	0.937	82	3,227	0.1	0.296	1	687	74.4
Austria	1.63	4.63	8.43	83.9	17	21	47	0.851	80	3,819	0.3	0.300	1	562	74.8
Azerbaijan	7.68	2.08	4.24	86.6	25	32	11	0.713	67	2,961	0.1	0.553	1	89	29.4
Bahamas	0.00	5.56	17.02	13.9	1	0	51	0.784	71	2,713	3.1	–	–	82	37.7
Bahrain	19.19	19.08	42.55	0.69	6	5	1	0.801	78	–	0.1	0.512	11	509	57.6
Bangladesh	0.11	0.14	0.36	144	67	5	11	0.469	70	2,281	0.1	0.734	47	2	0.4
Barbados	0.30	1.79	5.02	0.43	40	5	19	0.788	74	3,056	1.4	0.448	–	406	66.1
Belarus	0.21	2.99	6.28	208	27	16	45	0.732	71	3,146	0.3	–	1	282	27.4
Belgium	1.20	7.00	13.19	30.5	26	16	22	0.867	79	3,694	0.2	0.236	1	543	77.9
Belize	0.78	1.39	3.19	23	4	2	62	0.694	68	2,718	2.3	0.600	25	178	11.7
Benin	0.00	0.14	0.40	113	26	5	22	0.435	60	2,533	1.2	0.759	60	21	2.3
Bhutan	2.64	2.01	0.48	47	4	11	54	0.619	67	–	0.2	–	47	47	7.2
Bolivia	1.78	0.68	1.39	1,099	4	30	53	0.643	68	2,064	0.2	0.672	9	68	11.3
Bosnia-Herzegovina	1.27	1.62	3.98	51.2	21	20	43	0.710	79	3,078	0.1	–	3	135	30.8
Botswana	0.30	0.84	2.28	582	0	45	20	0.633	58	2,264	24.8	0.663	17	113	6.0
Brazil	1.09	1.35	2.14	8,514	8	23	62	0.699	73	3,113	0.6	0.631	10	198	38.2
Brunei	53.86	12.20	19.52	5.8	2	1	73	0.805	76	2,968	–	0.399	5	696	81.1
Bulgaria	1.36	2.87	6.18	111	30	18	35	0.743	74	2,766	0.1	0.627	2	353	47.1
Burkina Faso	0.00	0.03	0.09	274	23	22	21	0.305	54	2,677	1.2	–	71	11	1.1
Burma (Myanmar)	0.30	0.14	0.24	677	18	0	50	0.451	65	2,465	0.6	–	10	7	0.2
Burundi	0.01	0.02	0.04	27.8	50	35	7	0.282	59	1,685	3.3	–	41	6	1.7
Cambodia	0.00	0.12	0.28	181	37	9	51	0.494	63	2,268	0.5	0.672	24	1	0.5
Cameroon	0.30	0.13	0.40	475	15	4	51	0.460	54	2,269	5.3	0.763	32	4	4.0
Canada	14.39	10.56	16.15	9,971	6	2	34	0.888	81	3,532	0.4	0.289	1	605	80.5
Cape Verde Is.	0.00	0.27	0.68	4	17	6	21	0.534	71	2,572	–	–	16	94	34.9
Central African Rep.	0.01	0.03	0.06	623	3	5	36	0.315	50	1,986	4.7	0.768	51	1	0.5
Chad	0.72	0.01	0.03	1,284	3	36	9	0.295	48	2,056	3.4	–	68	6	1.6
Chile	0.55	1.85	3.77	757	2	19	22	0.783	78	2,920	0.4	0.505	4	172	42.2
China	1.49	1.60	5.82	9,597	13	43	22	0.663	75	2,981	0.1	0.405	7	37	29.1
Colombia	2.23	0.76	1.61	1,139	3	35	55	0.689	75	2,685	0.5	0.658	7	58	51.6
Comoros	0.00	0.06	0.20	2.2	73	8	2	0.428	64	1,884	0.1	–	25	33	3.2
Congo	3.34	0.24	1.57	342	2	29	66	0.489	55	2,512	3.4	0.744	19	26	6.1
Congo (Dem. Rep.)	0.04	0.04	0.04	2,345	3	7	68	0.239	55	1,605	3.2	0.814	33	5	0.4
Costa Rica	0.58	1.18	1.53	51.1	10	25	50	0.725	78	2,840	0.3	0.501	4	163	34.9
Croatia	0.90	2.27	4.74	56.5	17	6	34	0.767	76	2,990	0.1	0.345	1	388	49.8
Cuba	0.37	0.91	2.66	111	37	25	26	0.760	78	3,274	0.1	0.473	1	38	14.0
Cyprus	0.00	4.19	8.72	9.3	12	0	19	0.810	78	3,181	0.1	0.284	2	659	40.0
Czech Republic	2.54	3.95	9.33	78.9	42	13	34	0.841	77	3,260	0.1	0.330	1	513	65.4
Denmark	4.99	3.81	9.01	43.1	57	6	13	0.866	79	3,416	0.2	0.209	1	477	86.4
Djibouti	0.00	1.19	2.43	23.2	0	73	0	0.402	61	2,291	2.5	–	–	4	3.6
Dominican Republic	0.05	0.78	2.04	48.5	27	25	41	0.663	77	2,295	0.9	0.646	11	123	28.0
East Timor	4.40	0.11	0.34	14.9	15	10	51	0.502	68	2,066	–	–	50	–	0.2
Ecuador	2.22	0.89	1.89	284	10	20	41	0.695	76	2,301	0.4	0.645	9	63	23.0
Egypt	1.18	0.97	2.40	1,001	4	0	0	0.620	73	3,195	0.1	0.714	34	43	25.5
El Salvador	0.18	0.48	0.98	21	44	31	14	0.659	73	2,590	0.8	0.653	18	84	10.4
Equatorial Guinea	37.59	2.43	7.27	28.1	7	4	59	0.538	62	–	5.0	–	13	2	2.3
Eritrea	0.00	0.05	0.14	118	7	68	15	–	63	1,605	0.8	–	3	11	3.5
Estonia	2.60	4.67	13.51	45.1	14	5	53	0.812	73	3,154	1.2	0.409	1	477	74.8
Ethiopia	0.01	0.04	0.08	1,104	15	20	13	0.328	56	1,980	2.1	–	64	3	0.5
Fiji	0.17	1.07	2.56	18.3	14	10	55	0.669	71	3,041	0.1	–	–	175	12.1
Finland	2.35	6.16	9.93	338	7	0	73	0.871	79	3,221	0.1	0.248	1	534	83.7
France	2.00	4.40	6.30	552	35	18	29	0.872	81	3,532	0.4	0.260	1	598	0.1
Gabon	9.20	0.80	3.03	268	2	18	85	0.648	52	2,755	5.2	0.678	14	7	6.5
Gambia, The	0.00	0.08	0.25	11.3	40	26	48	0.390	64	2,385	2.0	0.742	–	7	7.3
Gaza Strip (OPT)*	0.00	0.94	0.78	0.4	36	25	2	–	74	2,020	–	–	8	39	88.9
Georgia	0.39	0.90	1.14	69.7	8	28	40	0.698	77	2,859	0.1	0.597	1	116	28.2
Germany	1.52	4.36	9.30	357	35	14	32	0.885	80	3,547	0.1	0.240	1	554	79.1
Ghana	0.08	0.18	0.34	239	32	37	23	0.467	61	2,907	1.8	0.729	35	33	5.4
Greece	0.90	3.43	9.35	132	25	11	30	0.855	80	3,725	0.1	0.317	3	560	46.3

	POPULATION						WEALTH						TRADE		
	Total population (millions 2010)	Population density (persons per km² 2010)	Population change (average annual percentage 2010)	Birth rate (births per thousand people 2010)	Death rate (deaths per thousand people 2010)	Urban population (percentage of total 2010)	Gross National Income (million US$ 2009)	Gross National Income per capita (PPP US$ 2009)	GDP growth rate (percentage 2010)	GDP from agriculture (percentage of GDP 2010)	GDP from industry (percentage of GDP 2010)	GDP from services (percentage of GDP 2010)	Imports (US$ per capita 2010)	Exports (US$ per capita 2010)	Tourism receipts (US$ per capita 2009)
Guatemala	13.6	124	2.0	27	5	49	37,189	2,650	2.6	13.3	24.4	62.3	934	625	
Guinea	10.3	42	2.6	37	10	35	3,771	370	1.9	25.8	45.7	28.5	150	142	
Guinea-Bissau	1.6	43	2.0	35	15	30	826	510	3.5	62.0	12.0	26.0	128	85	
Guyana	0.7	3	−0.4	17	7	29	1,109	2,660	3.6	24.3	24.7	51.0	1,825	1,088	
Haiti	9.6	348	0.8	24	8	52	10,000	1,180	−5.1	23.0	20.0	57.0	253	58	
Honduras	8.0	71	1.9	25	5	52	13,452	1,800	2.8	12.4	26.9	60.7	1,111	736	
Hungary	10.0	107	−0.2	10	13	68	130,114	12,980	1.2	3.3	30.8	65.9	8,751	9,381	
Iceland	0.3	3	0.7	13	7	93	13,858	43,430	−3.5	5.5	24.7	69.8	11,903	14,953	1
India	1,173.1	357	1.3	21	7	30	1,367,105	1,220	10.4	16.1	28.6	55.3	279	171	
Indonesia	243.0	127	1.1	18	6	44	470,980	2,050	6.1	16.5	46.4	37.1	457	602	
Iran	76.9	47	1.2	19	6	71	330,619	4,530	1.0	11.0	45.9	43.1	767	1,023	
Iraq	29.7	68	2.4	29	5	66	69,653	2,210	0.8	9.7	63.0	27.3	1,434	1,655	
Ireland	4.6	66	1.1	16	6	62	197,065	44,280	−1.0	2.0	29.0	69.0	15,220	25,027	10,
Israel	7.4	354	1.6	19	5	92	191,956	25,790	4.6	2.4	32.6	65.0	7,561	7,385	
Italy	58.1	193	0.4	9	10	68	2,114,481	35,110	1.3	1.8	24.9	73.3	7,913	7,891	
Ivory Coast	21.1	65	2.1	31	10	51	22,545	1,070	2.6	28.2	21.3	50.5	333	487	
Jamaica	2.8	259	0.7	19	7	52	12,402	4,590	−1.1	5.7	29.7	64.6	1,889	522	
Japan	126.8	336	−0.3	7	10	67	4,857,203	38,080	3.9	1.1	23.0	75.9	5,022	6,034	
Jordan	6.4	69	1.0	27	3	79	23,662	3,980	3.1	3.4	30.3	66.3	2,024	1,145	
Kazakhstan	15.5	6	0.4	17	9	59	109,977	6,920	7.0	5.4	42.8	51.8	1,948	3,832	
Kenya	40.0	69	2.5	34	9	22	30,269	760	5.0	22.0	16.0	62.0	260	128	
Korea, North	22.8	189	0.5	15	9	60	205,000	8,991	−0.9	21.0	46.9	32.1	136	88	
Korea, South	48.6	494	0.2	9	6	83	966,600	19,830	6.1	3.0	39.4	57.6	8,592	9,588	
Kosovo	1.8	220	–	–	–	–	5,855	3,240	4.0	12.9	22.6	64.5	1,432	290	
Kuwait	2.8	157	2.0	21	2	98	116,984	49,970	2.0	0.3	48.1	51.6	7,300	23,315	
Kyrgyzstan	5.5	28	1.4	24	7	35	4,613	870	−1.4	24.6	25.0	50.4	558	305	
Laos	6.4	27	1.6	26	8	33	5,550	880	7.7	29.8	31.7	38.5	236	306	
Latvia	2.2	34	−0.6	10	14	68	27,936	12,390	−0.3	4.2	20.6	75.2	4,127	3,556	3
Lebanon	4.1	397	0.2	15	7	87	34,052	8,060	7.5	5.1	15.9	79.0	4,356	1,257	1,
Lesotho	1.9	63	0.3	27	15	27	2,036	980	2.4	7.1	34.6	58.3	920	513	
Liberia	3.7	33	2.7	37	11	48	651	160	5.1	76.9	5.4	17.7	1,938	325	
Libya	6.5	4	2.1	24	3	78	77,185	12,020	4.2	2.6	63.8	33.6	3,787	6,947	
Lithuania	3.5	54	−0.3	9	11	67	38,095	11,410	1.3	4.3	27.6	68.1	5,737	5,441	
Luxembourg	0.5	192	1.1	12	8	85	38,188	76,710	3.4	0.4	13.6	86.0	47,574	35,816	8,
Macedonia (FYROM)	2.1	82	0.2	12	9	59	8,983	4,400	0.7	8.7	22.1	69.2	2,468	1,530	
Madagascar	21.3	36	3.0	38	8	30	7,932	430	−2.0	26.5	16.7	56.8	92	66	
Malawi	15.4	130	2.8	41	13	20	4,198	290	6.6	33.4	21.7	44.9	108	77	
Malaysia	28.3	86	1.6	21	5	72	201,839	7,350	7.2	9.1	41.6	49.3	6,165	7,438	5
Mali	13.8	11	2.6	46	14	36	8,862	680	4.5	45.0	17.0	38.0	171	21	
Malta	0.4	1,287	0.4	10	9	95	7,621	18,360	3.7	1.7	17.4	80.9	10,015	7,262	2,
Mauritania	3.2	3	2.3	33	9	41	3,159	990	4.7	12.5	46.7	40.8	460	435	
Mauritius	1.3	634	0.7	14	7	42	9,243	7,250	4.0	4.8	24.6	70.6	3,041	1,577	8
Mexico	112.5	57	1.1	19	5	78	962,076	8,960	5.5	4.2	33.3	62.5	2,721	2,694	
Micronesia, Fed. States	0.1	153	−0.3	22	4	23	277	2,500	0.3	28.9	15.2	55.9	1,238	131	
Moldova	4.3	128	−0.1	11	11	47	5,568	1,560	6.9	16.3	20.1	63.6	848	336	
Mongolia	3.1	2	1.5	21	6	62	4,361	1,630	6.1	21.2	29.5	49.3	690	616	
Montenegro	0.7	48	−0.7	11	9	61	4,149	6,650	1.1	10.0	20.0	70.0	902	257	9
Morocco	31.6	71	1.1	19	5	58	89,933	2,770	3.2	17.1	31.6	51.3	1,081	458	2
Mozambique	22.1	28	2.4	40	13	38	9,964	440	7.0	28.8	26.0	45.2	160	114	
Namibia	2.1	3	0.9	21	13	38	9,264	4,270	4.4	9.0	32.7	58.3	2,421	2,009	
Nepal	29.0	206	1.6	22	7	19	12,985	440	4.0	33.0	15.0	52.0	182	29	
Netherlands	16.8	404	0.4	10	9	83	801,120	48,460	1.7	2.6	24.9	72.5	24,334	26,890	
New Zealand	4.3	16	0.9	14	7	86	116,389	28,810	1.5	4.6	24.0	71.4	7,111	7,817	1,0
Nicaragua	6.0	46	1.1	19	5	57	5,726	1,000	4.5	17.6	26.4	56.0	784	531	
Niger	15.9	13	3.6	51	14	17	5,197	340	7.5	39.0	17.0	44.0	50	27	
Nigeria	152.2	165	1.9	36	16	50	184,656	1,190	8.4	31.9	32.9	35.2	225	501	
Norway	4.7	14	0.3	11	9	79	408,540	84,640	0.4	2.1	40.1	57.8	15,829	29,297	8
Oman	3.0	14	2.0	24	3	73	49,833	17,890	4.2	1.4	48.2	50.4	6,503	12,171	2
Pakistan	184.4	229	1.6	25	7	36	169,778	1,000	4.8	21.8	23.6	54.6	177	110	
Panama	3.4	44	1.4	19	5	75	22,683	6,570	7.5	5.8	16.6	77.6	4,706	3,671	4
Papua New Guinea	6.1	13	2.0	26	7	13	7,911	1,180	7.0	32.2	35.7	32.1	585	985	
Paraguay	6.4	16	1.3	17	5	62	14,279	2,250	15.3	21.7	18.2	60.1	1,501	1,250	
Peru	29.9	23	1.0	19	6	77	122,355	4,200	8.8	15.4	32.0	52.6	861	1,128	
Philippines	99.9	333	1.9	25	5	49	188,941	1,790	7.3	13.9	31.3	54.9	600	508	
Poland	38.5	123	−0.1	10	10	61	467,545	12,260	3.8	3.9	31.8	64.3	4,352	4,181	2

	ENERGY			LAND & AGRICULTURE				SOCIAL INDICATORS							
	Energy produced (tonnes of oil equivalent, per capita 2008)	Energy consumed (tonnes of oil equivalent, per capita 2008)	CO_2 emissions (tonnes per capita 2009)	Land area (thousand km²)	Arable and Permanent crops (% of land area 2008)	Permanent pasture (% of land area 2008)	Forest (% of land area 2008)	Human Development Index (HDI value 2009)	Life expectancy (years 2010)	Food intake (calories per capita per day 2007)	Adults living with HIV/AIDS (percentage 2009)	Gender Inequality Index (GII value 2009)	Adult illiteracy rate (percentage 2008)	Motor vehicles (per thousand people 2009)	Internet usage (per thousand people 2009)
emala	0.16	0.40	0.86	109	21	18	35	0.560	71	2,159	0.8	0.713	27	117	17.2
ea	0.01	0.06	0.13	246	13	44	27	0.340	58	2,568	1.3	–	71	1	0.9
ea-Bissau	0.00	0.10	0.30	36.1	19	39	78	0.289	49	2,306	2.5	–	35	33	2.4
ana	0.00	0.68	2.02	215	2	6	77	0.611	67	2,759	1.2	0.667	–	95	25.2
i	0.00	0.08	0.21	27.8	47	18	4	0.404	62	1,870	1.9	0.739	38	11	11.1
duras	0.08	0.44	1.02	112	13	16	49	0.604	71	2,623	0.8	0.680	16	97	9.3
gary	0.98	2.79	5.00	93	53	11	22	0.805	75	3,465	0.1	0.382	1	384	62.3
nd	16.58	20.52	11.12	103	0	23	0	0.869	81	3,362	0.3	0.279	1	767	98.3
	0.30	0.43	1.38	3,287	57	3	23	0.519	67	2,352	0.3	0.748	34	15	5.3
nesia	1.26	0.61	1.73	1,905	20	6	53	0.600	71	2,538	0.2	0.680	8	77	8.3
	5.07	3.08	6.96	1,648	12	18	7	0.702	70	3,044	0.2	0.674	18	128	12.4
	4.57	1.20	3.75	438	12	9	2	–	71	–	0.1	0.751	26	–	1.1
nd	0.30	4.15	8.79	70.3	16	45	10	0.895	80	3,612	0.2	0.344	1	534	72.4
l	0.19	3.02	9.69	20.6	18	6	7	0.872	81	3,527	0.2	0.332	3	313	62.6
	0.52	3.40	7.01	301	33	12	31	0.854	82	3,646	0.3	0.251	1	673	50.3
y Coast	0.26	0.15	0.32	322	22	42	33	0.397	57	2,528	3.4	0.765	51	20	4.7
ica	0.03	1.53	4.26	11	22	21	31	0.688	73	2,852	1.7	0.638	14	188	55.9
n	0.74	4.38	8.64	378	13	0	68	0.884	82	2,812	0.1	0.273	1	593	78.0
an	0.03	1.23	3.15	89.3	3	8	1	0.681	80	3,015	0.1	0.616	9	146	26.2
khstan	9.03	3.54	11.96	2,725	8	69	1	0.714	69	3,490	0.1	0.575	1	197	34.4
a	0.04	0.14	0.29	580	10	37	6	0.470	59	2,089	6.3	0.738	26	21	10.2
a, North	0.97	0.94	3.51	121	24	0	49	–	69	2,087	–	–	–	–	–
a, South	0.79	5.11	10.89	99.3	18	1	64	0.877	79	3,074	0.1	0.310	1	346	81.2
ovo	–	–	–	10.9	–	–	–	–	74	–	0.1	–	8	–	–
ait	60.68	11.48	31.08	17.8	1	8	0	0.771	77	3,064	0.1	0.451	6	507	40.9
yzstan	0.54	0.86	1.04	200	7	49	5	0.598	70	2,644	0.3	0.560	1	59	40.4
	0.17	0.16	0.20	237	6	4	69	0.497	62	2,240	0.2	0.650	27	21	4.4
ia	0.35	1.81	3.90	64.6	19	10	54	0.769	73	2,962	0.7	0.316	1	474	67.4
non	0.02	1.29	3.70	10.4	28	39	13	0.803	75	3,107	0.1	–	10	–	24.9
tho	0.02	0.07	0.13	30.4	12	66	1	0.427	52	2,476	23.6	0.685	18	–	3.6
ria	0.00	0.07	0.20	111	6	21	46	0.300	57	2,204	1.5	0.766	45	3	0.6
a	18.14	3.17	8.70	1,760	1	8	0	0.755	78	3,143	0.1	0.504	13	291	5.6
uania	0.73	2.76	4.48	65.2	30	12	34	0.783	75	3,436	0.1	0.359	1	546	55.2
mbourg	0.16	10.05	21.51	2.6	24	26	33	0.852	80	3,681	0.3	0.318	1	747	86.3
edonia (FYROM)	0.75	1.51	3.57	25.7	19	24	39	0.701	75	3,105	0.1	–	3	144	51.1
agascar	0.01	0.06	0.15	587	6	64	22	0.435	63	2,160	0.2	–	29	27	1.5
wi	0.03	0.06	0.09	118	38	20	35	0.385	52	2,172	11.0	0.758	28	9	4.8
ysia	3.75	2.43	5.38	330	23	1	63	0.744	74	2,923	0.5	0.493	8	334	59.7
	0.01	0.03	0.06	1,240	4	28	10	0.309	53	2,614	1.0	0.799	74	9	1.9
a	0.00	2.62	7.64	0.3	31	0	1	0.815	80	3,611	0.1	0.395	8	674	59.4
ritania	0.21	0.29	0.93	1,026	0	38	0	0.433	61	2,841	0.7	0.738	44	–	2.4
ritius	0.02	1.22	3.54	2	45	3	17	0.701	74	2,965	1.0	0.466	13	159	22.6
ico	2.09	1.66	3.99	1,958	14	39	33	0.750	76	3,266	0.3	0.576	7	264	27.9
onesia, Fed. States	–	–	–	0.7	28	4	0	0.614	72	–	–	–	–	36	15.8
dova	0.00	0.80	1.63	33.9	65	11	11	0.623	71	2,771	0.4	0.429	1	139	30.9
golia	0.76	0.74	2.43	1,567	1	74	7	0.622	68	2,285	0.1	0.523	3	72	10.9
tenegro	1.04	1.32	2.89	14	14	24	40	0.769	75	2,447	0.1	–	4	–	41.7
occo	0.01	0.41	1.16	447	20	47	11	0.567	76	3,236	0.1	0.693	44	71	42.2
ambique	0.32	0.20	0.11	802	6	56	39	0.284	52	2,067	11.5	0.718	56	13	2.8
ibia	0.18	0.89	1.93	824	1	46	9	0.606	52	2,383	13.1	0.615	12	109	6.0
al	0.03	0.06	0.12	147	17	12	25	0.428	66	2,360	0.4	0.716	44	5	2.0
herlands	4.33	6.50	14.89	41.5	33	25	11	0.890	80	3,278	0.2	0.174	1	515	89.0
Zealand	4.37	5.28	9.28	271	12	41	31	0.907	81	3,159	0.1	0.320	1	733	80.7
aragua	0.06	0.33	0.74	130	18	25	27	0.565	72	2,403	0.2	0.674	22	57	3.4
er	0.01	0.03	0.09	1,267	11	23	1	0.261	53	2,376	0.8	0.807	71	–	0.8
eria	1.01	0.19	0.52	924	44	42	11	0.423	48	2,741	3.6	–	28	31	29.5
way	54.51	10.46	8.49	324	3	1	32	0.938	80	3,464	0.1	0.234	1	575	95.1
an	19.06	5.38	16.80	310	0	5	0	0.846	74	–	0.1	–	16	225	42.9
stan	0.24	0.36	0.77	796	28	5	2	0.490	66	2,293	0.1	0.721	46	11	11.7
ama	0.29	1.80	4.54	75.5	9	21	44	0.755	78	2,484	0.9	0.634	7	120	42.9
a New Guinea	0.39	0.31	0.82	463	2	0	64	0.431	66	2,175	0.9	0.784	42	9	11.7
guay	1.98	1.60	0.63	407	11	41	45	0.640	76	2,634	0.3	0.643	5	82	15.8
	0.47	0.59	1.21	1,285	3	13	53	0.723	72	2,457	0.4	0.614	10	55	31.0
ppines	0.14	0.34	0.74	300	35	5	25	0.638	72	2,565	0.1	0.623	7	33	8.4
nd	1.72	2.52	7.43	323	43	10	31	0.795	76	3,421	0.1	0.325	1	495	59.3

	POPULATION						WEALTH						TRADE		
	Total Population (millions 2010)	Population density (persons per km² 2010)	Population change (percentage average annual 2010)	Birth rate (births per thousand people 2010)	Death rate (deaths per thousand people 2010)	Urban Population (percentage of total 2010)	Gross National Income (million US$ 2009)	Gross National Income per capita (PPP US$ 2009)	GDP growth rate (percentage 2010)	GDP from agriculture (percentage of GDP 2010)	GDP from industry (percentage of GDP 2010)	GDP from services (percentage of GDP 2010)	Imports (US$ per capita 2010)	Exports (US$ per capita 2010)	Tourism receipts (US$ per capita 2009)
Portugal	10.7	116	0.2	10	11	61	232,937	21,910	1.4	2.6	23.0	74.4	6,354	4,310	
Qatar	0.8	74	0.8	15	2	96	17,688	22,110	16.3	0.1	78.8	21.1	27,803	68,758	
Romania	22.0	92	−0.3	10	12	57	178,900	8,330	−1.3	12.8	36.0	51.2	2,725	2,364	
Russia	139.4	8	−0.5	11	16	73	1,324,416	9,340	4.0	4.2	33.8	62.0	1,702	2,702	
Rwanda	11.1	420	2.8	37	10	19	4,628	490	6.5	42.1	14.3	43.6	95	20	
Saudi Arabia	25.7	13	1.5	19	3	82	439,021	17,210	3.7	2.7	61.9	35.4	3,854	9,844	
Senegal	12.3	63	2.6	37	9	42	13,062	1,040	4.2	14.9	21.4	63.7	363	171	
Serbia†	7.3	83	−0.5	9	14	56	43,939	6,000	1.8	12.6	21.9	65.5	2,148	1,321	
Sierra Leone	5.2	73	2.3	38	12	38	1,938	340	5.0	49.0	31.0	20.0	107	41	
Singapore	4.7	6,784	0.8	9	5	100	185,655	37,220	14.5	0.0	27.2	72.8	66,028	74,706	
Slovak Republic	5.5	112	0.1	10	10	55	87,402	16,130	4.0	2.7	35.6	61.7	11,413	11,732	
Slovenia	2.0	99	−0.2	9	11	50	48,063	23,520	1.2	2.4	31.0	66.6	12,960	12,465	
Solomon Is.	0.6	20	2.2	28	4	19	477	910	5.6	42.0	11.0	47.0	458	424	
Somalia	10.1	16	1.6	43	15	37	959	130	2.6	65.0	10.0	25.0	79	30	
South Africa	49.1	40	−0.4	19	17	62	284,270	5,760	2.8	3.0	31.2	65.8	1,569	1,565	
South Sudan††	8.3	14	–	–	–	22.0	–	–	–	–	–	–	–	–	
Spain	46.5	92	0.6	11	9	77	1,476,169	32,120	−0.1	2.9	25.5	71.6	6,980	5,769	
Sri Lanka	21.5	328	0.9	17	6	14	40,385	1,990	9.1	12.6	29.8	57.6	539	368	
Sudan	35.7	19	2.5	36	11	40	51,524	1,220	5.1	32.1	29.0	38.9	193	223	
Suriname	0.5	3	1.1	16	6	69	2,454	4,760	4.4	10.8	24.4	64.8	2,665	2,859	
Swaziland	1.4	78	1.2	17	15	21	2,932	2,470	2.0	8.6	42.0	49.4	1,213	1,046	
Sweden	9.1	20	0.2	10	10	85	454,355	48,840	5.5	1.7	26.1	72.2	17,478	17,919	
Switzerland	7.6	185	0.2	10	9	74	505,827	65,430	2.6	1.3	27.5	71.2	29,685	30,511	
Syria	22.2	120	0.9	24	4	56	50,869	2,410	3.2	17.6	26.8	55.6	611	578	
Taiwan	23.0	640	0.2	9	7	78	1,016,390	44,190	10.8	1.4	31.1	67.5	10,919	11,926	
Tajikistan	7.5	52	1.8	26	7	26	4,841	700	6.5	19.2	22.6	58.2	441	176	
Tanzania	41.9	44	2.0	33	12	26	21,337	500	6.5	41.9	18.7	39.4	151	91	
Thailand	67.1	131	0.6	13	7	34	254,743	3,760	7.8	10.4	45.6	44.0	2,339	2,851	
Togo	6.6	116	2.8	36	8	43	2,883	440	3.4	47.4	25.4	27.2	203	130	
Trinidad & Tobago	1.2	240	−0.1	14	8	14	22,356	16,700	0.0	0.5	59.4	40.1	6,701	9,815	
Tunisia	10.6	65	1.0	17	6	67	38,845	3,720	3.7	10.6	34.6	54.8	1,891	1,521	
Turkey	77.8	100	1.2	18	6	70	652,358	8,720	8.2	8.8	25.7	65.5	2,137	1,509	
Turkmenistan	4.9	10	1.1	20	6	50	17,498	3,420	9.2	10.2	30.0	59.8	989	1,958	
Uganda	33.4	141	3.6	47	12	13	15,200	460	5.2	23.6	24.5	51.9	134	88	
Ukraine	45.4	75	−0.6	10	16	69	128,920	2,800	4.2	9.8	32.3	57.9	1,179	1,095	
United Arab Emirates	5.0	60	3.3	16	2	84	74,075	14,815	3.2	0.9	51.5	47.6	31,956	39,352	
United Kingdom	62.3	255	0.6	12	9	80	2,558,048	41,370	1.3	0.9	22.1	77.0	8,765	6,505	
USA	310.2	32	1.0	14	8	82	14,233,516	46,360	2.8	1.2	22.2	76.6	6,134	4,094	
Uruguay	3.5	20	0.2	14	10	92	30,154	9,010	8.5	9.3	22.8	67.9	2,364	1,909	
Uzbekistan	27.9	62	0.9	17	5	36	30,643	1,100	8.5	21.2	32.4	46.4	339	471	
Venezuela	27.2	30	1.5	20	5	93	286,354	10,090	−1.9	4.1	34.8	61.1	1,152	2,383	
Vietnam	89.6	272	1.1	17	6	30	81,591	1,000	6.8	20.6	41.1	38.3	941	804	
West Bank (OPT)*	2.5	429	2.1	25	4	74	2,843	1,855	7.0	5.0	14.0	81.0	1,500	210	
Western Sahara	0.5	2	3.1	32	9	94	–	–		30.0	30.0	40.0	–	–	
Yemen	23.5	45	2.6	33	7	32	25,026	1,060	8.0	8.2	38.8	53.0	355	318	
Zambia	13.5	18	3.1	44	13	36	12,560	960	7.6	19.7	33.7	46.6	368	480	
Zimbabwe	11.7	30	4.3	32	14	38	10,500	360	9.0	19.5	24.0	56.5	246	160	

NOTES

SERBIA†
Kosovo separated from Serbia in February 2008.

SOUTH SUDAN††
South Sudan separated from Sudan in May 2011.

OPT*
Occupied Palestinian Territory.

POPULATION TOTAL
These are estimates of the mid-year total in 2010.

POPULATION DENSITY
The total population divided by the land area (both are recorded in the table above).

BIRTH/DEATH RATES
These are 2010 estimates from the CIA World Factbook.

URBAN POPULATION
The urban population shows the percentage of the total population living in towns and cities (each country will differ with regard to the size or type of town that is defined as an urban area).

GNI
Gross National Income: this used to be referred to as GNP (Gross National Product) and is a good indication of a country's wealth. It is the income in US dollars from goods and services in a country for one year, including income from overseas.

GNI PER CAPITA
The GNI (see note) divided by the total population by using the PPP method (see note).

PER CAPITA
An amount divided by the total population of a country or the amount per person.

PPP
Purchasing Power Parity (PPP) is a method used to enable real comparisons to be made between countries when measuring wealth. The UN International Comparison Programme gives estimates of the PPP for each country, so it can be used as an indicator of real price levels for goods and services rather than using currency exchange rates (see GNI and GNI per capita).

AGRICULTURE, INDUSTRY AND SERVICES
The percentage contributions that each of these three sectors makes to a country's Gross Domestic Prod (GDP).

IMPORTS AND EXPORTS
The total value of goods imported into a country and exported to othe countries, given in US dollars ($) per capita.

TOURISM RECEIPTS
The amount of income generated fr tourism in US dollars per capita.

	ENERGY			LAND & AGRICULTURE				SOCIAL INDICATORS						
Energy produced (tonnes of oil equivalent per capita 2008)	Energy consumed (tonnes of oil equivalent per capita 2008)	CO₂ emissions (tonnes per capita 2009)	Land area (thousand km²)	Arable and Permanent crops (% of land area 2008)	Permanent pasture (% of land area 2008)	Forest (% of land area 2008)	Human Development Index (HDI) value 2009	Life expectancy (years 2010)	Food intake (calories per capita per day 2007)	Adults living with HIV/AIDS 2009	Gender Inequality Index (GII value 2009)	Adult illiteracy rate (percentage 2008)	Motor vehicles (per thousand people 2009)	Internet usage (per thousand people 2009)
ugal	0.34	2.48	5.28	88.8	18	20	38	0.795	79	3,584	0.6	0.310	5	509	48.3
r	156.24	30.38	76.38	11	1	4	0	0.803	76	–	0.1	0.671	7	724	67.7
ania	1.34	1.88	3.63	238	40	19	28	0.767	74	3,455	0.1	0.478	2	219	35.1
ia	9.61	5.41	11.12	17,075	8	6	49	0.719	66	3,376	1.0	0.442	1	245	29.2
nda	0.00	0.03	0.07	26.3	64	18	17	0.385	58	2,085	2.9	0.638	35	4	4.2
Arabia	22.42	5.98	17.30	2,150	2	79	0	0.752	74	3,144	0.1	0.760	17	340	34.1
gal	0.01	0.17	0.52	197	18	29	44	0.411	60	2,348	0.9	0.727	58	23	13.3
a†	1.13	1.79	5.45	77.5	41	16	30	0.735	74	2,710	0.1	–	4	227	55.7
a Leone	0.00	0.07	0.26	71.7	27	31	39	0.317	56	2,170	1.6	0.756	62	5	0.3
pore	0.00	12.89	33.57	0.7	1	0	3	0.846	82	–	0.1	0.255	6	150	69.5
k Republic	1.22	3.68	6.54	49	29	11	40	0.818	76	2,893	0.1	0.352	1	319	74.4
enia	1.92	4.08	8.67	20.3	10	15	62	0.828	77	3,223	0.1	0.293	1	565	64.7
mon Is.	0.00	0.14	0.53	28.9	3	0	79	0.494	74	2,422	–	–	23	–	1.7
alia	0.00	0.03	0.09	638	2	69	11	–	50	–	0.7	–	–	–	1.1
h Africa	3.16	2.93	9.20	1,221	13	69	8	0.597	49	2,999	17.8	0.635	12	159	9.0
h Sudan††	–	–	–	620	–	–	–	–	–	–	3.1	–	73	–	–
	0.84	4.02	7.13	498	37	21	29	0.863	81	3,272	0.4	0.280	2	606	69.4
anka	0.00	0.25	0.59	65.6	35	7	30	0.658	75	2,361	0.1	0.599	9	61	8.3
n	0.56	0.12	0.30	1,886	9	49	29	0.379	55	2,282	1.1	0.708	39	28	10.2
name	2.38	1.85	4.22	163	0	0	95	0.646	74	2,492	1.0	–	10	–	33.9
iland	0.22	0.43	1.03	17.4	11	60	32	0.498	49	2,292	25.9	0.668	20	89	6.7
den	3.90	6.13	5.58	450	6	1	69	0.885	81	3,110	0.1	0.212	1	521	92.7
zerland	2.13	4.35	6.00	41.3	11	28	31	0.874	81	3,465	0.4	0.228	1	89	80.9
	1.44	1.06	2.67	185	31	45	3	0.589	75	3,034	0.1	0.687	17	62	20.5
an	0.52	4.97	12.15	36	23	–	58	–	78	–	–	–	–	–	70.3
istan	0.55	0.89	0.84	143	6	28	3	0.580	66	2,118	0.2	0.568	1	38	9.5
ania	0.03	0.07	0.16	945	12	27	39	0.398	53	2,032	5.6	–	28	73	1.7
land	0.76	1.51	3.82	513	37	2	37	0.654	74	2,539	1.3	0.586	6	287	26.5
	0.00	0.17	0.45	56.8	48	18	6	0.428	63	2,161	3.2	0.731	47	2	5.9
dad & Tobago	35.79	18.01	38.60	5.1	14	1	44	0.736	71	2,725	1.5	0.473	1	351	48.2
sia	0.73	0.84	2.19	164	32	31	6	0.683	75	3,326	0.1	0.515	22	114	33.4
ey	0.42	1.50	3.29	775	32	19	14	0.679	73	3,517	0.1	0.621	11	138	35.5
menistan	14.48	4.80	11.60	488	4	65	9	0.669	69	2,731	0.1	–	1	106	16.5
da	0.01	0.00	0.06	241	40	26	16	0.422	53	2,211	6.5	0.715	26	7	9.9
ine	1.67	3.43	5.52	604	58	14	17	0.710	68	3,224	1.1	0.463	1	152	17.0
ed Arab Emirates	43.97	17.62	40.30	83.6	3	4	4	0.815	77	3,171	0.1	0.464	10	313	71.9
ed Kingdom	2.88	3.83	8.35	242	25	48	12	0.849	80	3,458	0.2	0.355	1	526	84.2
	6.04	8.19	17.67	9,629	19	26	33	0.902	78	3,748	0.6	0.400	1	809	79.7
guay	0.37	1.20	2.06	175	10	75	9	0.765	76	2,829	0.5	0.508	2	–	40.2
ekistan	2.51	2.15	4.17	447	11	52	8	0.617	73	2,581	0.1	–	3	–	17.0
zuela	7.27	3.02	5.93	912	4	20	53	0.696	74	2,632	0.7	0.561	5	147	33.3
nam	0.42	0.47	1.11	332	30	2	44	0.572	72	2,816	0.4	0.530	10	13	26.4
t Bank (OPT)*	0.00	0.58	0.78	5.9	36	25	2	–	75	2,020	–	–	–	39	57.1
tern Sahara	0.00	0.27	0.66	266	0	19	3	–	61	–	–	–	–	–	–
en	0.68	0.34	1.13	528	3	42	1	0.439	64	2,068	0.1	0.853	41	35	10.3
bia	0.20	0.27	0.20	753	3	27	57	0.395	52	1,873	13.5	0.752	29	18	6.9
abwe	0.27	0.36	0.93	391	10	31	42	0.140	50	2,238	14.3	0.705	9	106	12.5

DUCTION AND CONSUMPTION
NERGY
otal amount of commercial energy
ced or consumed in a country per
(see note). It is expressed in metric
s of oil equivalent (an energy unit
the heating value derived from one
of oil).

ON DIOXIDE EMISSIONS
mount of carbon dioxide that each
ry produces per capita.

AREA
s the total land area of a country,
e area of major lakes and rivers,
are kilometres.

LE AND PERMANENT CROPS
figures give a percentage of the

total land area that is used for crops and
fruit (including temporary fallow land or
meadows).

PERMANENT PASTURE
This is the percentage of land area that
has permanent forage crops for cattle or
horses, cultivated or wild. Some land may
be classified both as permanent pasture
or as forest.

FOREST
Natural/planted trees including cleared
land that will be reforested in the near
future as a percentage of the land area.

HUMAN DEVELOPMENT INDEX (HDI)
Produced by the UN Development
Programme using indicators of life
expectancy, knowledge and standards

of living to give a value between 0 and 1
for each country. A high value shows a
higher human development.

LIFE EXPECTANCY
The average age that a child born today
is expected to live to, if mortality levels
of today last throughout its lifetime.

FOOD INTAKE
The amount of food (measured in
calories) supplied, divided by the total
population to show the amount each
person consumes.

ADULTS LIVING WITH HIV/AIDS
The percentage of all adults (aged
15–49) who have the Human Immunodeficiency Virus or the Acquired
Immunodeficiency Syndrome.

The total number of adults and children
with HIV/AIDS in 2009 was 33 million.

GENDER INEQUALITY INDEX
Like the HDI (see note), the GII uses the
same UNDP indicators but gives a value
between 0 and 1 to measure the social and
economic differences between men and
women. The higher the value, the more
equality exists between men and women.

ILLITERACY
The percentage of all adult men and
women (over 15 years) who cannot
read or write simple sentences.

MOTOR VEHICLES AND
INTERNET USAGE
These are good indicators of a country's
development wealth.

Each topic list is divided into continents and within a continent the items are listed in order of size. The bottom part of many of the lists is selective in order to give examples from as many different countries as possible. The figures are rounded as appropriate.

World, Continents, Oceans

	km²	miles²	%
The World	509,450,000	196,672,000	–
Land	149,450,000	57,688,000	29.3
Water	360,000,000	138,984,000	70.7
Asia	44,500,000	17,177,000	29.8
Africa	30,302,000	11,697,000	20.3
North America	24,241,000	9,357,000	16.2
South America	17,793,000	6,868,000	11.9
Antarctica	14,100,000	5,443,000	9.4
Europe	9,957,000	3,843,000	6.7
Australia & Oceania	8,557,000	3,303,000	5.7
Pacific Ocean	155,557,000	60,061,000	46.4
Atlantic Ocean	76,762,000	29,638,000	22.9
Indian Ocean	68,556,000	26,470,000	20.4
Southern Ocean	20,327,000	7,848,000	6.1
Arctic Ocean	14,056,000	5,427,000	4.2

Ocean Depths

Atlantic Ocean	m	ft
Puerto Rico (Milwaukee) Deep	8,605	28,232
Cayman Trench	7,680	25,197
Gulf of Mexico	5,203	17,070
Mediterranean Sea	5,121	16,801
Black Sea	2,211	7,254
North Sea	660	2,165
Indian Ocean	**m**	**ft**
Java Trench	7,450	24,442
Red Sea	2,635	8,454
Pacific Ocean	**m**	**ft**
Mariana Trench	11,022	36,161
Tonga Trench	10,882	35,702
Japan Trench	10,554	34,626
Kuril Trench	10,542	34,587
Arctic Ocean	**m**	**ft**
Molloy Deep	5,608	18,399
Southern Ocean	**m**	**ft**
South Sandwich Trench	7,235	23,737

Mountains

Europe		m	ft
Elbrus	*Russia*	5,642	18,510
Dykh-Tau	*Russia*	5,205	17,076
Shkhara	*Russia/Georgia*	5,201	17,064
Koshtan-Tau	*Russia*	5,152	16,903
Kazbek	*Russia/Georgia*	5,047	16,558
Pushkin	*Russia/Georgia*	5,033	16,512
Katyn-Tau	*Russia/Georgia*	4,979	16,335
Shota Rustaveli	*Russia/Georgia*	4,860	15,945
Mont Blanc	*France/Italy*	4,808	15,774
Monte Rosa	*Italy/Switzerland*	4,634	15,203
Dom	*Switzerland*	4,545	14,911
Liskamm	*Switzerland*	4,527	14,852
Weisshorn	*Switzerland*	4,505	14,780
Taschorn	*Switzerland*	4,490	14,730
Matterhorn/Cervino	*Italy/Switzerland*	4,478	14,691
Grossglockner	*Austria*	3,797	12,457
Mulhacén	*Spain*	3,478	11,411
Zugspitze	*Germany*	2,962	9,718
Olympus	*Greece*	2,917	9,570
Galdhøpiggen	*Norway*	2,469	8,100
Kebnekaise	*Sweden*	2,117	6,946
Ben Nevis	*UK*	1,344	4,409
Asia		**m**	**ft**
Everest	*China/Nepal*	8,850	29,035
K2 (Godwin Austen)	*China/Kashmir*	8,611	28,251
Kanchenjunga	*India/Nepal*	8,598	28,208
Lhotse	*China/Nepal*	8,516	27,939
Makalu	*China/Nepal*	8,481	27,824
Cho Oyu	*China/Nepal*	8,201	26,906
Dhaulagiri	*Nepal*	8,167	26,795
Manaslu	*Nepal*	8,156	26,758
Nanga Parbat	*Kashmir*	8,126	26,660
Annapurna	*Nepal*	8,078	26,502
Gasherbrum	*China/Kashmir*	8,068	26,469
Broad Peak	*China/Kashmir*	8,051	26,414
Xixabangma	*China*	8,012	26,286
Kangbachen	*Nepal*	7,858	25,781
Trivor	*Pakistan*	7,720	25,328
Pik Imeni Ismail Samani	*Tajikistan*	7,495	24,590
Demavend	*Iran*	5,604	18,386
Ararat	*Turkey*	5,165	16,945
Gunong Kinabalu	*Malaysia (Borneo)*	4,101	13,455
Fuji-San	*Japan*	3,776	12,388
Africa		**m**	**ft**
Kilimanjaro	*Tanzania*	5,895	19,340
Mt Kenya	*Kenya*	5,199	17,057
Ruwenzori	*Uganda/Congo (D.R.)*	5,109	16,762
Meru	*Tanzania*	4,565	14,977
Ras Dashen	*Ethiopia*	4,553	14,937
Karisimbi	*Rwanda/Congo (D.R.)*	4,507	14,787
Mt Elgon	*Kenya/Uganda*	4,321	14,176
Batu	*Ethiopia*	4,307	14,130
Toubkal	*Morocco*	4,165	13,665
Mt Cameroun	*Cameroon*	4,070	13,353
Oceania		**m**	**ft**
Puncak Jaya	*Indonesia*	4,884	16,024
Puncak Trikora	*Indonesia*	4,730	15,518
Puncak Mandala	*Indonesia*	4,702	15,427
Mt Wilhelm	*Papua New Guinea*	4,508	14,790
Mauna Kea	*USA (Hawaii)*	4,205	13,796
Mauna Loa	*USA (Hawaii)*	4,169	13,678
Aoraki Mt Cook	*New Zealand*	3,753	12,313
Mt Kosciuszko	*Australia*	2,228	7,310
North America		**m**	**ft**
Mt McKinley (Denali)	*USA (Alaska)*	6,194	20,321
Mt Logan	*Canada*	5,959	19,551
Pico de Orizaba	*Mexico*	5,610	18,405
Mt St Elias	*USA/Canada*	5,489	18,008
Popocatépetl	*Mexico*	5,452	17,887
Mt Foraker	*USA (Alaska)*	5,304	17,401
Iztaccihuatl	*Mexico*	5,286	17,342
Lucania	*Canada*	5,226	17,146
Mt Steele	*Canada*	5,073	16,644
Mt Bona	*USA (Alaska)*	5,005	16,420
Mt Whitney	*USA*	4,418	14,495
Tajumulco	*Guatemala*	4,220	13,845
Chirripó Grande	*Costa Rica*	3,837	12,589
Pico Duarte	*Dominican Rep.*	3,175	10,417
South America		**m**	**ft**
Aconcagua	*Argentina*	6,962	22,841
Bonete	*Argentina*	6,872	22,546
Ojos del Salado	*Argentina/Chile*	6,863	22,516
Pissis	*Argentina*	6,779	22,241
Mercedario	*Argentina/Chile*	6,770	22,211
Huascarán	*Peru*	6,768	22,204
Llullaillaco	*Argentina/Chile*	6,723	22,057
Nevado de Cachi	*Argentina*	6,720	22,047
Yerupaja	*Peru*	6,632	21,758
Sajama	*Bolivia*	6,520	21,391
Chimborazo	*Ecuador*	6,267	20,561
Pico Cristóbal Colón	*Colombia*	5,800	19,029
Pico Bolivar	*Venezuela*	5,007	16,427
Antarctica		**m**	**ft**
Vinson Massif		4,897	16,066
Mt Kirkpatrick		4,528	14,855

Rivers

Europe		km	miles
Volga	*Caspian Sea*	3,700	2,300
Danube	*Black Sea*	2,850	1,770
Ural	*Caspian Sea*	2,535	1,575
Dnieper	*Black Sea*	2,285	1,420
Kama	*Volga*	2,030	1,260
Don	*Black Sea*	1,990	1,240
Petchora	*Arctic Ocean*	1,790	1,110
Oka	*Volga*	1,480	920
Dniester	*Black Sea*	1,400	870
Vyatka	*Kama*	1,370	850
Rhine	*North Sea*	1,320	820
North Dvina	*Arctic Ocean*	1,290	800
Elbe	*North Sea*	1,145	710
Asia		**km**	**miles**
Yangtse	*Pacific Ocean*	6,380	3,960
Yenisey–Angara	*Arctic Ocean*	5,550	3,445
Huang He	*Pacific Ocean*	5,464	3,395
Ob–Irtysh	*Arctic Ocean*	5,410	3,360
Mekong	*Pacific Ocean*	4,500	2,795
Amur	*Pacific Ocean*	4,442	2,760
Lena	*Arctic Ocean*	4,402	2,735
Irtysh	*Ob*	4,250	2,640
Yenisey	*Arctic Ocean*	4,090	2,540
Ob	*Arctic Ocean*	3,680	2,285
Indus	*Indian Ocean*	3,100	1,925
Brahmaputra	*Indian Ocean*	2,900	1,800
Syrdarya	*Aralkum Desert*	2,860	1,775
Salween	*Indian Ocean*	2,800	1,740
Euphrates	*Indian Ocean*	2,700	1,675
Amudarya	*Aralkum Desert*	2,540	1,575
Africa		**km**	**miles**
Nile	*Mediterranean*	6,695	4,160
Congo	*Atlantic Ocean*	4,670	2,900
Niger	*Atlantic Ocean*	4,180	2,595
Zambezi	*Indian Ocean*	3,540	2,200
Oubangi/Uele	*Congo (Dem. Rep.)*	2,250	1,400
Kasai	*Congo (Dem. Rep.)*	1,950	1,210
Shaballe	*Indian Ocean*	1,930	1,200
Orange	*Atlantic Ocean*	1,860	1,155
Cubango	*Okavango Delta*	1,800	1,120
Limpopo	*Indian Ocean*	1,770	1,100
Senegal	*Atlantic Ocean*	1,640	1,020
Australia		**km**	**miles**
Murray–Darling	*Southern Ocean*	3,750	2,330
Darling	*Murray*	3,070	1,905
Murray	*Southern Ocean*	2,575	1,600
Murrumbidgee	*Murray*	1,690	1,050
North America		**km**	**miles**
Mississippi–Missouri	*Gulf of Mexico*	5,971	3,710
Mackenzie	*Arctic Ocean*	4,240	2,630
Missouri	*Mississippi*	4,088	2,540
Mississippi	*Gulf of Mexico*	3,782	2,350
Yukon	*Pacific Ocean*	3,185	1,980
Rio Grande	*Gulf of Mexico*	3,030	1,880
Arkansas	*Mississippi*	2,340	1,450
Colorado	*Pacific Ocean*	2,330	1,445
Red	*Mississippi*	2,040	1,270
Columbia	*Pacific Ocean*	1,950	1,210
Saskatchewan	*Lake Winnipeg*	1,940	1,205
South America		**km**	**miles**
Amazon	*Atlantic Ocean*	6,450	4,010
Paraná–Plate	*Atlantic Ocean*	4,500	2,800
Purus	*Amazon*	3,350	2,080
Madeira	*Amazon*	3,200	1,990
São Francisco	*Atlantic Ocean*	2,900	1,800
Paraná	*Plate*	2,800	1,740
Tocantins	*Atlantic Ocean*	2,750	1,710
Orinoco	*Atlantic Ocean*	2,740	1,700
Paraguay	*Paraná*	2,550	1,580
Pilcomayo	*Paraná*	2,500	1,550
Araguaia	*Tocantins*	2,250	1,400

Lakes

Europe		km²	miles²
Lake Ladoga	*Russia*	17,700	6,800
Lake Onega	*Russia*	9,700	3,700
Saimaa system	*Finland*	8,000	3,100
Vänern	*Sweden*	5,500	2,100
Asia		**km²**	**miles²**
Caspian Sea	*Asia*	371,000	143,000
Lake Baikal	*Russia*	30,500	11,780
Tonlé Sap	*Cambodia*	20,000	7,700
Lake Balqash	*Kazakhstan*	18,500	7,100
Aral Sea	*Kazakhstan/Uzbekistan*	17,160	6,625
Africa		**km²**	**miles²**
Lake Victoria	*East Africa*	68,000	26,000
Lake Tanganyika	*Central Africa*	33,000	13,000
Lake Malawi/Nyasa	*East Africa*	29,600	11,430
Lake Chad	*Central Africa*	25,000	9,700
Lake Turkana	*Ethiopia/Kenya*	8,500	3,290
Lake Volta	*Ghana*	8,480	3,270
Australia		**km²**	**miles²**
Lake Eyre	*Australia*	8,900	3,400
Lake Torrens	*Australia*	5,800	2,200
Lake Gairdner	*Australia*	4,800	1,900
North America		**km²**	**miles²**
Lake Superior	*Canada/USA*	82,350	31,800
Lake Huron	*Canada/USA*	59,600	23,010
Lake Michigan	*USA*	58,000	22,400
Great Bear Lake	*Canada*	31,800	12,280
Great Slave Lake	*Canada*	28,500	11,000
Lake Erie	*Canada/USA*	25,700	9,900
Lake Winnipeg	*Canada*	24,400	9,400
Lake Ontario	*Canada/USA*	19,500	7,500
Lake Nicaragua	*Nicaragua*	8,200	3,200
South America		**km²**	**miles²**
Lake Titicaca	*Bolivia/Peru*	8,300	3,200
Lake Poopo	*Bolivia*	2,800	1,100

Islands

Europe		km²	miles²
Great Britain	*UK*	229,880	88,700
Iceland	*Atlantic Ocean*	103,000	39,800
Ireland	*Ireland/UK*	84,400	32,600
Novaya Zemlya (N.)	*Russia*	48,200	18,600
Sicily	*Italy*	25,500	9,800
Asia		**km²**	**miles²**
Borneo	*South-east Asia*	744,360	287,400
Sumatra	*Indonesia*	473,600	182,860
Honshu	*Japan*	230,500	88,980
Celebes	*Indonesia*	189,000	73,000
Java	*Indonesia*	126,700	48,900
Luzon	*Philippines*	104,700	40,400
Hokkaido	*Japan*	78,400	30,300
Africa		**km²**	**miles²**
Madagascar	*Indian Ocean*	587,040	226,660
Socotra	*Indian Ocean*	3,600	1,400
Réunion	*Indian Ocean*	2,500	965
Oceania		**km²**	**miles²**
New Guinea	*Indonesia/Papua NG*	821,030	317,000
New Zealand (S.)	*Pacific Ocean*	150,500	58,100
New Zealand (N.)	*Pacific Ocean*	114,700	44,300
Tasmania	*Australia*	67,800	26,200
New Caledonia	*Pacific Ocean*	16,650	6,470
North America		**km²**	**miles²**
Greenland	*Atlantic Ocean*	2,175,600	839,800
Baffin I.	*Canada*	508,000	196,100
Victoria I.	*Canada*	212,200	81,900
Ellesmere I.	*Canada*	212,000	81,800
Cuba	*Caribbean Sea*	110,860	42,800
Hispaniola	*Dominican Rep./Haiti*	76,200	29,400
Jamaica	*Caribbean Sea*	11,400	4,400
Puerto Rico	*Atlantic Ocean*	8,900	3,400
South America		**km²**	**miles²**
Tierra del Fuego	*Argentina/Chile*	47,000	18,100
Chiloé	*Chile*	8,480	3,275
Falkland I. (E.)	*Atlantic Ocean*	6,800	2,600

How to use the Index

The index contains the names of all the principal places and features shown on the maps. Each name is followed by an additional entry in italics giving the country or region within which it is located. The alphabetical order of names composed of two or more words is governed primarily by the first word and then by the second. This is an example of the rule:

Albert, L. *Africa* 1°30N 31°0E **96** D6
Albert Lea *U.S.A.* 43°39N 93°22W **111** B8
Albert Nile → *Uganda* 3°36N 32°2E **96** D6
Alberta ☐ *Canada* 54°40N 115°0W **108** D8
Albertville *France* 45°40N 6°22E **66** D7

Physical features composed of a proper name (Erie) and a description (Lake) are positioned alphabetically by the proper name. The description is positioned after the proper name and is usually abbreviated:

Erie, L. *N. Amer.* 42°15N 81°0W **112** D7

Where a description forms part of a settlement or administrative name, however, it is always written in full and put in its true alphabetical position:

Mount Isa *Australia* 20°42S 139°26E **98** E6

Names beginning with M' and Mc are indexed as if they were spelled Mac. Names beginning St. are alphabetized under Saint, but Santa and San are spelled in full and are alphabetized accordingly. If the same place name occurs two or more times in the index and all are in the same country, each is followed by the name of the administrative subdivision in which it is located.

The geographical co-ordinates that follow each name in the index give the latitude and longitude of each place. The first co-ordinate indicates latitude – the distance north or south of the Equator. The second co-ordinate indicates longitude – the distance east or west of the Greenwich Meridian. Both latitude and longitude are measured in degrees and minutes (there are 60 minutes in a degree).

The latitude is followed by N(orth) or S(outh) and the longitude by E(ast) or W(est).

The number in bold type that follows the geographical co-ordinates refers to the number of the map page where that feature or place will be found. This is usually the largest scale at which the place or feature appears.

The letter and figure that are immediately after the page number give the grid square on the map page, within which the feature is situated. The letter represents the latitude and the figure the longitude. A lower-case letter immediately after the page number refers to an inset map on that page.

In some cases the feature itself may fall within the specified square, while the name is outside. This is usually the case only with features that are larger than a grid square.

Rivers are indexed to their mouths or confluences, and carry the symbol → after their names. The following symbols are also used in the index: ■ country, ⊠ overseas territory or dependency, ☐ first-order administrative area, △ national park, ✈ (LHR) principal airport (and location identifier).

Abbreviations used in the Index

Afghan. – Afghanistan
Ala. – Alabama
Alta. – Alberta
Amer. – America(n)
Arch. – Archipelago
Ariz. – Arizona
Ark. – Arkansas
Atl. Oc. – Atlantic Ocean
B. – Baie, Bahía, Bay, Bucht, Bugt
B.C. – British Columbia
Bangla. – Bangladesh
C. – Cabo, Cap, Cape, Coast
C.A.R. – Central African Republic
Calif. – California
Cent. – Central
Chan. – Channel
Colo. – Colorado
Conn. – Connecticut
Cord. – Cordillera
Cr. – Creek
D.C. – District of Columbia
Del. – Delaware
Dom. Rep. – Dominican Republic
E. – East
El Salv. – El Salvador
Eq. Guin. – Equatorial Guinea
Fla. – Florida
Falk. Is. – Falkland Is.
G. – Golfe, Golfo, Gulf
Ga. – Georgia
Hd. – Head
Hts. – Heights
I.(s). – Île, Ilha, Insel, Isla, Island, Isle(s)
Ill. – Illinois
Ind. – Indiana
Ind. Oc. – Indian Ocean
Ivory C. – Ivory Coast
Kans. – Kansas
Ky. – Kentucky
L. – Lac, Lacul, Lago, Lagoa, Lake, Limni, Loch, Lough
La. – Louisiana
Lux. – Luxembourg
Madag. – Madagascar
Man. – Manitoba
Mass. – Massachusetts
Md. – Maryland
Me. – Maine
Mich. – Michigan
Minn. – Minnesota
Miss. – Mississippi
Mo. – Missouri
Mont. – Montana
Mozam. – Mozambique
Mt.(s) – Mont, Monte, Monti, Montaña, Mountain
N. – Nord, Norte, North, Northern,
N.B. – New Brunswick
N.C. – North Carolina
N. Cal. – New Caledonia
N. Dak. – North Dakota
N.H. – New Hampshire
N.J. – New Jersey
N. Mex. – New Mexico
N.S. – Nova Scotia
N.S.W. – New South Wales
N.W.T. – North West Territory
N.Y. – New York
N.Z. – New Zealand
Nat. Park – National Park
Nebr. – Nebraska
Neths. – Netherlands
Nev. – Nevada
Nfld. – Newfoundland and Labrador
Nic. – Nicaragua
Okla. – Oklahoma
Ont. – Ontario
Oreg. – Oregon
P.E.I. – Prince Edward Island
Pa. – Pennsylvania
Pac. Oc. – Pacific Ocean
Papua N.G. – Papua New Guinea
Pen. – Peninsula, Péninsule
Phil. – Philippines
Pk. – Peak
Plat. – Plateau
Prov. – Province, Provincial
Pt. – Point
Pta. – Ponta, Punta
Pte. – Pointe
Qué. – Québec
Queens. – Queensland
R. – Rio, River
R.I. – Rhode Island
Ra.(s) – Range(s)
Reg. – Region
Rep. – Republic
Res. – Reserve, Reservoir
S. – San, South
Si. Arabia – Saudi Arabia
S.C. – South Carolina
S. Dak. – South Dakota
Sa. – Serra, Sierra
Sask. – Saskatchewan
Scot. – Scotland
Sd. – Sound
Sib. – Siberia
St. – Saint, Sankt, Sint
Str. – Strait, Stretto
Switz. – Switzerland
Tas. – Tasmania
Tenn. – Tennessee
Tex. – Texas
Trin. & Tob.. – Trinidad & Tobago
U.A.E. – United Arab Emirates
U.K. – United Kingdom
U.S.A. – United States of America
Va. – Virginia
Vic. – Victoria
Vol. – Volcano
Vt. – Vermont
W. – West
W. Va. – West Virginia
Wash. – Washington
Wis. – Wisconsin

A

Aachen *Germany* 50°45N 6°6E **64** C4
Aalborg *Denmark* 57°2N 9°54E **63** F5
Aarau *Switz.* 47°23N 8°4E **64** E5
Aare → *Switz.* 47°33N 8°14E **64** E5
Aarhus *Denmark* 56°8N 10°11E **63** F6
Aba *Nigeria* 5°10N 7°19E **94** G7
Abaco I. *Bahamas* 26°25N 77°10W **115** B9
Ābādān *Iran* 30°22N 48°20E **86** D7
Abaetetuba *Brazil* 1°40S 48°50W **120** C5
Abakan *Russia* 53°40N 91°10E **77** D10
Abancay *Peru* 13°35S 72°55W **120** D2
Abariringa *Kiribati* 2°50S 171°40W **99** A16
Abaya, L. *Ethiopia* 6°30N 37°50E **89** F2
Abbé, L. *Ethiopia* 11°8N 41°47E **89** E3
Abbeville *France* 50°6N 1°49E **66** A4
Abbey Town *U.K.* 54°51N 3°17W **26** C2
Abbot Ice Shelf *Antarctica* 73°0S 92°0W **55** D16
Abbots Bromley *U.K.* 52°50N 1°52W **27** G5
Abbotsbury *U.K.* 50°40N 2°37W **30** E3
ABC Islands *W. Indies* 12°15N 69°0W **115** E11
Abéché *Chad* 13°50N 20°35E **95** F10
Abeokuta *Nigeria* 7°3N 3°19E **94** G6
Aberaeron *U.K.* 52°15N 4°15W **28** C5
Aberchirder *U.K.* 57°34N 2°37W **23** G12
Aberdare *U.K.* 51°43N 3°27W **28** D7
Aberdaugleddau = Milford Haven *U.K.* 51°42N 5°7W **28** D3
Aberdeen *China* 22°14N 114°8E **79** a
Aberdeen *U.K.* 57°9N 2°5W **23** H13
Aberdeen *S. Dak., U.S.A.* 45°28N 98°29W **110** A7
Aberdeen *Wash., U.S.A.* 46°59N 123°50W **110** A2
Aberdeenshire ☐ *U.K.* 57°17N 2°36W **23** H12
Aberdovey = Aberdyfi *U.K.* 52°33N 4°3W **28** B5
Aberdyfi *U.K.* 52°33N 4°3W **28** B5
Aberfeldy *U.K.* 56°37N 3°51W **25** A8
Aberfoyle *U.K.* 56°11N 4°23W **24** B7
Abergavenny *U.K.* 51°49N 3°1W **28** D7
Abergele *U.K.* 53°17N 3°35W **28** A6
Abergwaun = Fishguard *U.K.* 52°0N 4°58W **28** D4
Aberhonddu = Brecon *U.K.* 51°57N 3°23W **28** D7
Abermaw = Barmouth *U.K.* 52°44N 4°4W **28** B5
Aberpennar = Mountain Ash *U.K.* 51°40N 3°23W **28** D7
Aberporth *U.K.* 52°8N 4°33W **28** C4
Abersoch *U.K.* 52°49N 4°30W **28** B5
Abersychan *U.K.* 51°44N 3°3W **28** D7
Abert, L. *U.S.A.* 42°38N 120°14W **110** B2
Abertawe = Swansea *U.K.* 51°37N 3°57W **29** D6
Aberteifi = Cardigan *U.K.* 52°5N 4°40W **28** C4
Abertillery *U.K.* 51°44N 3°8W **28** D7
Aberystwyth *U.K.* 52°25N 4°5W **28** C5
Abhā *Si. Arabia* 18°0N 42°34E **89** D3
Abidjan *Ivory C.* 5°26N 3°58W **94** G5
Abilene *U.S.A.* 32°28N 99°43W **110** D7
Abingdon *U.K.* 51°40N 1°17W **30** C6
Abitibi, L. *Canada* 48°40N 79°40W **109** E12
Abkhazia ☐ *Georgia* 43°12N 41°5E **71** F7
Abomey *Benin* 7°10N 2°5E **94** G6
Aboyne *U.K.* 57°4N 2°47W **23** H12
Abrolhos, Banco dos *Brazil* 18°0S 38°0W **122** C3
Absaroka Range *U.S.A.* 44°45N 109°50W **110** B5
Abu Dhabi *U.A.E.* 24°28N 54°22E **87** E8
Abu Hamed *Sudan* 19°32N 33°13E **95** E12
Abuja *Nigeria* 9°5N 7°32E **94** G7
Abunã *Brazil* 9°40S 65°20W **120** C3
Abunã → *Brazil* 9°41S 65°20W **120** C3
Abyei ⊠ *Sudan* 9°30N 28°30E **95** G11
Acaponeta *Mexico* 22°30N 105°22W **114** C3
Acapulco *Mexico* 16°51N 99°55W **114** D5
Acaraí, Serra *Brazil* 1°50N 57°50W **120** B4
Acarigua *Venezuela* 9°33N 69°12W **120** B3
Accomac *U.S.A.* 37°43N 75°40W **113** G10
Accra *Ghana* 5°35N 0°6W **94** G5
Accrington *U.K.* 53°45N 2°22W **27** E4
Aceh ☐ *Indonesia* 4°15N 97°30E **82** D1
Acharnes *Greece* 38°5N 23°44E **69** E10
Acheloos → *Greece* 38°19N 21°7E **69** E9
Achill Hd. *Ireland* 53°58N 10°15W **18** D1
Achill I. *Ireland* 53°58N 10°1W **18** D1
Acklins I. *Bahamas* 22°30N 74°0W **115** C10
Acle *U.K.* 52°39N 1°33E **31** A12
Aconcagua, Cerro *Argentina* 32°39S 70°0W **121** F3
Acre ☐ *Brazil* 9°1S 71°0W **120** C2
Acre → *Brazil* 8°45S 67°22W **120** C3
Acton Burnell *U.K.* 52°37N 2°41W **27** G3
Ad Dammām *Si. Arabia* 26°20N 50°5E **86** E7
Ad Dīwānīyah *Iraq* 32°0N 45°0E **86** D6
Adair, C. *Canada* 71°30N 71°34W **109** B12
Adak I. *U.S.A.* 51°45N 176°45W **108** D2
Adamaoua, Massif de l' *Cameroon* 7°20N 12°20E **95** G8
Adam's Bridge *Sri Lanka* 9°15N 79°40E **84** Q11
Adana *Turkey* 37°0N 35°16E **71** G6
Adare, C. *Antarctica* 71°0S 171°0E **55** D11
Addis Ababa *Ethiopia* 9°2N 38°42E **89** F2
Adelaide *Australia* 34°52S 138°30E **98** G6
Adelaide I. *Antarctica* 67°15S 68°30W **55** C17
Adelaide Pen. *Canada* 68°15N 97°30W **108** C10
Adélie, Terre *Antarctica* 68°0S 140°0E **55** C10
Aden *Yemen* 12°45N 45°0E **89** E4
Aden, G. of *Ind. Oc.* 12°30N 47°30E **89** E4
Adige → *Italy* 45°9N 12°20E **68** B5
Adigrat *Ethiopia* 14°20N 39°26E **89** E2
Adirondack Mts. *U.S.A.* 44°0N 74°0W **113** D10
Admiralty Is. *Papua N. G.* 2°0S 147°0E **102** H6
Adour → *France* 43°32N 1°32W **66** E3
Adrar *Mauritania* 20°30N 7°30W **94** D3
Adrian *U.S.A.* 41°54N 84°2W **112** E5
Adriatic Sea *Medit. S.* 43°0N 16°0E **68** C6
Adwa *Ethiopia* 14°15N 38°52E **89** E2
Adwick le Street *U.K.* 53°34N 1°10W **27** E6
Adygea ☐ *Russia* 45°0N 40°0E **71** F7
Ægean Sea *Medit. S.* 38°30N 25°0E **69** E11
Afghanistan ■ *Asia* 33°0N 65°0E **87** C11
Africa 10°0N 20°0E **90** E6
Afyon *Turkey* 38°45N 30°33E **71** G5
Agadez *Niger* 16°58N 7°59E **94** E7
Agadir *Morocco* 30°28N 9°55W **94** B4
Agartala *India* 23°50N 91°23E **85** H17
Agen *France* 44°12N 0°38E **66** D4
Agra *India* 27°17N 77°58E **84** F10
Ağri *Turkey* 39°44N 43°3E **71** G7
Agrigento *Italy* 37°19N 13°34E **68** F5
Agua Prieta *Mexico* 31°18N 109°34W **114** A3
Aguascalientes *Mexico* 21°53N 102°18W **114** C4
Aguja, C. de la *Colombia* 11°18N 74°12W **117** B3
Agulhas, C. *S. Africa* 34°52S 20°0E **97** L4
Ahaggar *Algeria* 23°0N 6°30E **94** D7
Ahmadabad *India* 23°0N 72°40E **84** H8
Ahmadnagar *India* 19°7N 74°46E **84** K9
Ahmadpur East *Pakistan* 29°12N 71°10E **84** E7
Ahvāz *Iran* 31°20N 48°40E **86** D7
Ahvenanmaa *Finland* 60°15N 20°0E **63** E8
Aḩwar *Yemen* 13°30N 46°40E **89** E4
Ailsa Craig *U.K.* 55°15N 5°6W **24** D5
Aimorés *Brazil* 19°30S 41°4W **122** C2
Aïn Témouchent *Algeria* 35°16N 1°8W **94** A5
Ainsdale *U.K.* 53°37N 3°2W **27** E2
Aïr *Niger* 18°30N 8°0E **94** E7
Air Force I. *Canada* 67°58N 74°5W **109** C12
Aird, The *U.K.* 57°25N 4°33W **23** H8
Airdrie *Canada* 51°18N 114°2W **108** D8
Airdrie *U.K.* 55°52N 3°57W **25** C8
Aire → *U.K.* 53°43N 0°55W **27** E7
Aisgill *U.K.* 54°23N 2°21W **26** D4
Aisne → *France* 49°26N 2°50E **66** B5
Aix-en-Provence *France* 43°32N 5°27E **66** E6
Aix-les-Bains *France* 45°41N 5°53E **66** D6
Aizawl *India* 23°40N 92°44E **85** H18
Aizuwakamatsu *Japan* 37°30N 139°56E **81** E6
Ajaccio *France* 41°55N 8°40E **66** F8
Ajanta Ra. *India* 20°28N 75°50E **84** J9
Ajaria ☐ *Georgia* 41°30N 42°0E **71** F7
Ajdābiyā *Libya* 30°54N 20°4E **95** B10
'Ajmān *U.A.E.* 25°25N 55°30E **87** E8
Ajmer *India* 26°28N 74°37E **84** F9
Aketi *Dem. Rep. of the Congo* 2°38N 23°47E **96** D4
Akhisar *Turkey* 38°56N 27°48E **71** G4
Akimiski I. *Canada* 52°50N 81°30W **109** D11
Akita *Japan* 39°45N 140°7E **81** D7
'Akko *Israel* 32°55N 35°4E **86** C3
Aklavik *Canada* 68°12N 135°0W **108** C6
Akola *India* 20°42N 77°2E **84** J10
Akpatok I. *Canada* 60°25N 68°8W **109** C13
Akranes *Iceland* 64°19N 22°5W **63** B1
Akron *U.S.A.* 41°5N 81°31W **112** E7
Aksai Chin *China* 35°15N 79°55E **84** B11
Aksaray *Turkey* 38°25N 34°2E **71** G5
Akşehir Gölü *Turkey* 38°30N 31°25E **71** G5
Aksu *China* 41°5N 80°10E **78** C5
Aksum *Ethiopia* 14°5N 38°40E **89** E2
Akure *Nigeria* 7°15N 5°5E **94** G7
Akureyri *Iceland* 65°40N 18°6W **63** A2
Al 'Amārah *Iraq* 31°55N 47°15E **86** D6
Al 'Aqabah *Jordan* 29°31N 35°0E **86** D3
Al 'Aramah *Si. Arabia* 25°30N 46°0E **86** E6
Al 'Ayn *U.A.E.* 24°15N 55°45E **87** E8
Al Bayḑā *Libya* 32°50N 21°44E **95** B10
Al Fallūjah *Iraq* 33°20N 43°55E **86** C5
Al Fāw *Iraq* 30°0N 48°30E **86** D7
Al Ḩadīthah *Iraq* 34°0N 41°13E **86** C5
Al Ḩasakah *Syria* 36°35N 40°45E **86** B5
Al Ḩillah *Iraq* 32°30N 44°25E **86** C6
Al Hoceïma *Morocco* 35°8N 3°58W **94** A5
Al Ḩudaydah *Yemen* 14°50N 43°0E **89** E3
Al Hufūf *Si. Arabia* 25°25N 49°45E **86** E7
Al Jahrah *Kuwait* 29°25N 47°40E **86** D6
Al Jawf *Libya* 24°10N 23°24E **95** D10
Al Jawf *Si. Arabia* 29°55N 39°40E **86** D4
Al Jubayl *Si. Arabia* 27°0N 49°50E **86** E7
Al Khalīl *West Bank* 31°32N 35°6E **86** D3
Al Khums *Libya* 32°40N 14°17E **95** B8
Al Kufrah *Libya* 24°17N 23°15E **95** D10
Al Kūt *Iraq* 32°30N 46°0E **86** C6
Al Manāmah *Bahrain* 26°10N 50°30E **87** E7
Al Mubarraz *Si. Arabia* 25°30N 49°40E **86** E7
Al Mukallā *Yemen* 14°33N 49°2E **89** E4
Al Musayyib *Iraq* 32°49N 44°20E **86** C6
Al Qāmishlī *Syria* 37°2N 41°14E **86** B5
Al Qaţīf *Si. Arabia* 26°35N 50°0E **86** E7
Al Qunfudhah *Si. Arabia* 19°3N 41°4E **89** D3
Al Qurayyāt *Si. Arabia* 31°20N 37°20E **86** D4
Ala Tau *Asia* 45°30N 80°40E **78** B5
Alabama ☐ *U.S.A.* 33°0N 87°0W **111** D9
Alabama → *U.S.A.* 31°8N 87°57W **111** D9
Alagoas ☐ *Brazil* 9°0S 36°0W **122** A3
Alagoinhas *Brazil* 12°7S 38°20W **122** B3
Alai Range *Asia* 39°45N 72°0E **87** B13
Alamogordo *U.S.A.* 32°54N 105°57W **110** D5
Alamosa *U.S.A.* 37°28N 105°52W **110** C5
Åland = Ahvenanmaa *Finland* 60°15N 20°0E **63** E8
Alanya *Turkey* 36°38N 32°0E **71** G5
Alaşehir *Turkey* 38°23N 28°30E **71** G4
Alaska ☐ *U.S.A.* 64°0N 154°0W **108** C5
Alaska, G. of *Pac. Oc.* 58°0N 145°0W **108** D5
Alaska Peninsula *U.S.A.* 56°0N 159°0W **108** D4
Alaska Range *U.S.A.* 62°50N 151°0W **108** C4
Alba-Iulia *Romania* 46°8N 23°39E **65** E12
Albacete *Spain* 39°0N 1°50W **67** C5
Albanel, L. *Canada* 50°55N 73°12W **109** D12
Albania ■ *Europe* 41°0N 20°0E **69** D9
Albany *Australia* 35°1S 117°58E **98** H2
Albany *Ga., U.S.A.* 31°35N 84°10W **111** D10
Albany *N.Y., U.S.A.* 42°39N 73°45W **113** D11
Albany *Oreg., U.S.A.* 44°38N 123°6W **110** B2
Albany → *Canada* 52°17N 81°31W **109** D11
Albemarle Sd. *U.S.A.* 36°5N 76°0W **111** C11
Albert, L. *Africa* 1°30N 31°0E **96** D6
Albert Lea *U.S.A.* 43°39N 93°22W **111** B8
Albert Nile → *Uganda* 3°36N 32°2E **96** D6
Alberta ☐ *Canada* 54°40N 115°0W **108** D8
Albertville *France* 45°40N 6°22E **66** D7
Albi *France* 43°56N 2°9E **66** E5
Albion *U.S.A.* 42°15N 84°45W **112** D5
Albrighton *U.K.* 52°38N 2°16W **27** G4
Albuquerque *U.S.A.* 35°5N 106°39W **110** C5
Albury *Australia* 36°3S 146°56E **98** H8

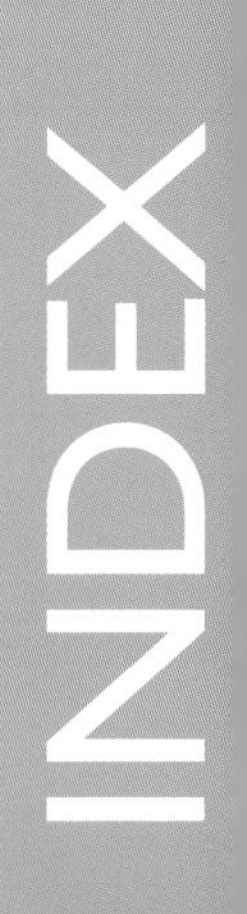

Alcalá de Henares Spain 40°28N 3°22W 67 B4
Alcester U.K. 52°14N 1°52W 30 B5
Alchevsk Ukraine 48°30N 38°45E 71 E6
Alcoy Spain 38°43N 0°30W 67 C5
Aldabra Is. Seychelles 9°22S 46°28E 91 G8
Aldan Russia 58°40N 125°30E 77 D13
Aldan → Russia 63°28N 129°35E 77 C13
Aldborough U.K. 54°5N 1°22W 26 D6
Aldbourne U.K. 51°29N 1°37W 30 D5
Aldbrough U.K. 53°49N 0°6W 27 E8
Aldeburgh U.K. 52°10N 1°37E 31 B12
Alderbury U.K. 51°3N 1°44W 30 D5
Alderley Edge U.K. 53°18N 2°13W 27 F4
Alderney U.K. 49°42N 2°11W 29 H9
Aldershot U.K. 51°15N 0°44W 31 D7
Aledo U.S.A. 41°12N 90°45W 112 E2
Alegrete Brazil 29°40S 56°0W 121 E4
Além Paraíba Brazil 21°52S 42°41W 122 D2
Alençon France 48°27N 0°4E 66 B4
Alenquer Brazil 1°56S 54°46W 120 C4
'Alenuihähä Channel U.S.A. 20°30N 156°0W 110 H17
Aleppo Syria 36°10N 37°15E 86 B4
Alert Canada 83°2N 60°0W 109 A13
Alès France 44°9N 4°5E 66 D6
Alessándria Italy 44°54N 8°37E 68 B3
Ålesund Norway 62°28N 6°12E 63 E5
Aleutian Is. Pac. Oc. 52°0N 175°0W 102 B10
Aleutian Trench Pac. Oc. 48°0N 180°0E 102 C10
Alexander Arch. U.S.A. 56°0N 136°0W 108 D6
Alexander I. Antarctica 69°0S 70°0W 55 C17
Alexandria Egypt 31°13N 29°58E 95 B11
Alexandria U.K. 55°59N 4°35W 24 C6
Alexandria La., U.S.A. 31°18N 92°27W 111 D8
Alexandria Va., U.S.A. 38°49N 77°5W 112 F9
Alford Aberds., U.K. 57°14N 2°41W 23 H12
Alford Lincs., U.K. 53°15N 0°10E 27 F9
Alfreton U.K. 53°6N 1°24W 27 F6
Alfriston U.K. 50°48N 0°10E 31 E9
Algarve Portugal 36°58N 8°20W 67 D1
Algeciras Spain 36°9N 5°28W 67 D3
Algeria ■ Africa 28°30N 2°0E 94 C6
Algiers Algeria 36°42N 3°8E 94 A6
Algoa B. S. Africa 33°50S 25°45E 90 K6
Alicante Spain 38°23N 0°30W 67 C5
Alice Springs Australia 23°40S 133°50E 98 E5
Aligarh India 27°55N 78°10E 84 F11
Alipur Duar India 26°30N 89°35E 85 F16
Aliquippa U.S.A. 40°37N 80°15W 112 E7
Aliwal North S. Africa 30°45S 26°45E 97 L5
Alkmaar Neths. 52°37N 4°45E 64 B3
Allahabad India 25°25N 81°58E 85 G12
Allegan U.S.A. 42°32N 85°51W 112 D5
Allegheny → U.S.A. 40°27N 80°1W 112 E8
Allegheny Mts. U.S.A. 38°15N 80°10W 111 C11
Allen → U.K. 54°58N 2°18W 26 C4
Allen, Bog of Ireland 53°15N 7°0W 21 B9
Allen, L. Ireland 54°8N 8°4W 18 C5
Allendale Town U.K. 54°53N 2°14W 26 C4
Allenheads U.K. 54°49N 2°12W 26 C4
Allentown U.S.A. 40°37N 75°29W 113 E10
Alleppey India 9°30N 76°28E 84 Q10
Alleynes B. Barbados 13°13N 59°39W 114 c
Alliance U.S.A. 42°6N 102°52W 110 B6
Allier → France 46°57N 3°4E 66 C5
Alligator Pond Jamaica 17°52N 77°34W 114 a
Alloa U.K. 56°7N 3°47W 25 B8
Allonby U.K. 54°46N 3°26W 26 C2
Alma U.S.A. 43°23N 84°39W 112 D5
Alma Ata Kazakhstan 43°15N 76°57E 76 E8
Almada Portugal 38°41N 9°8W 67 C1
Almelo Neths. 52°22N 6°42E 64 B4
Almería Spain 36°52N 2°27W 67 D4
Almondsbury U.K. 51°32N 2°34W 30 C3
Aln → U.K. 55°24N 1°37W 26 B5
Alness U.K. 57°41N 4°16W 23 G9
Alnmouth U.K. 55°24N 1°37W 26 B5
Alnwick U.K. 55°24N 1°42W 26 B5
Alor Indonesia 8°15S 124°30E 83 F6
Alor Setar Malaysia 6°7N 100°22E 82 C2
Alpena U.S.A. 45°4N 83°27W 112 C6
Alpes Maritimes Europe 44°10N 7°10E 66 D7
Alphington U.K. 50°42N 3°31W 29 F6
Alpine U.S.A. 30°22N 103°40W 110 D6
Alps Europe 46°30N 9°30E 64 E5
Alrewas U.K. 52°44N 1°44W 27 G5
Alsace □ France 48°15N 7°25E 66 B7
Alsager U.K. 53°6N 2°18W 27 F4
Alston U.K. 54°49N 2°25W 26 C4
Altai Mongolia 46°40N 92°45E 78 B7
Altamira Brazil 3°12S 52°10W 120 C4
Altamura Italy 40°49N 16°33E 68 D7
Altarnun U.K. 50°35N 4°32W 29 F4
Altay China 47°48N 88°10E 78 B6
Altay Mongolia 46°22N 96°15E 78 B8
Altiplano Bolivia 17°0S 68°0W 120 D3
Alton U.K. 51°9N 0°59W 31 D7
Alton U.S.A. 38°53N 90°11W 112 F2
Alton Towers U.K. 52°59N 1°52W 27 G5
Altoona U.S.A. 40°31N 78°24W 112 E8
Altrincham U.K. 53°24N 2°21W 27 F4
Altun Shan China 38°30N 88°0E 78 D6
Altus U.S.A. 34°38N 99°20W 110 D7
Alucra Turkey 40°22N 38°47E 71 F6
Alvechurch U.K. 52°21N 1°57W 30 B5
Alwar India 27°38N 76°34E 84 F10
Alwinton U.K. 55°21N 2°7W 26 B4
Alxa Zuoqi China 38°50N 105°40E 78 D10
Alyth U.K. 56°38N 3°13W 23 J11
Amadjuak L. Canada 65°0N 71°8W 109 C12
Amagasaki Japan 34°42N 135°23E 81 F4
Amapá Brazil 2°5N 50°50W 120 B4
Amapá □ Brazil 1°40N 52°0W 120 B4
Amarillo U.S.A. 35°13N 101°50W 110 C6
Amasya Turkey 40°40N 35°50E 71 F6
Amazon = Amazonas → S. Amer. 0°5S 50°0W 120 C4
Amazonas □ Brazil 5°0S 65°0W 120 C3
Amazonas → S. Amer. 0°5S 50°0W 120 C4
Ambala India 30°23N 76°56E 84 D10
Ambato Ecuador 1°5S 78°42W 120 C2
Ambergris Cay Belize 18°0N 87°55W 114 D7
Ambikapur India 23°15N 83°15E 85 H13
Ambilobé Madag. 13°10S 49°3E 97 G9
Amble U.K. 55°20N 1°36W 26 B5
Ambleside U.K. 54°26N 2°58W 26 D3
Ambon Indonesia 3°43S 128°12E 83 E7
Amchitka I. U.S.A. 51°32N 179°0E 108 D1
Amderma Russia 69°45N 61°30E 76 C7
Amdo China 32°20N 91°40E 78 E7
Ameca Mexico 20°33N 104°2W 114 C4
Ameland Neths. 53°27N 5°45E 64 B3
American Highland Antarctica 73°0S 75°0E 55 D6
American Samoa ☑ Pac. Oc. 14°20S 170°0W 99 C16
Americana Brazil 22°45S 47°20W 122 D1
Amersham U.K. 51°40N 0°36W 31 C7
Ames U.S.A. 42°2N 93°37W 111 B8
Amesbury U.K. 51°10N 1°46W 30 D5
Amherst Canada 45°48N 64°8W 109 E13
Amiens France 49°54N 2°16E 66 B5
Amirante Is. Seychelles 6°0S 53°0E 72 J7
Amlia I. U.S.A. 52°4N 173°30W 108 D2
Amlwch U.K. 53°24N 4°20W 28 A5
'Ammān Jordan 31°57N 35°52E 86 D3
Ammanford U.K. 51°48N 3°59W 28 D6
Amos Canada 48°35N 78°5W 109 E12
Ampleforth U.K. 54°13N 1°6W 26 D6
Ampthill U.K. 52°2N 0°30W 31 B8
Amravati India 20°55N 77°45E 84 J10
Amreli India 21°35N 71°17E 84 J7
Amritsar India 31°35N 74°57E 84 D9
Amroha India 28°53N 78°30E 84 E11
Amsterdam Neths. 52°23N 4°54E 64 B3
Amsterdam U.S.A. 42°56N 74°11W 113 D10
Amsterdam I. Ind. Oc. 38°30S 77°30E 53 F13
Amudarya → Uzbekistan 43°58N 59°34E 87 A9
Amund Ringnes I. Canada 78°20N 96°25W 109 B10
Amundsen Gulf Canada 71°0N 124°0W 108 B7
Amundsen Sea Antarctica 72°0S 115°0W 55 D15
Amuntai Indonesia 2°28S 115°25E 82 E5
Amur → Russia 52°56N 141°10E 77 D15
An Najaf Iraq 32°3N 44°15E 86 C6
Anaconda U.S.A. 46°8N 112°57W 110 A4
Anadyr Russia 64°35N 177°20E 77 C18
Anadyr, G. of Russia 64°0N 180°0E 77 C19
Anaheim U.S.A. 33°50N 117°55W 110 D3
Anambas, Kepulauan Indonesia 3°20N 106°30E 82 D3
Anamur Turkey 36°8N 32°58E 71 G5
Anantapur India 14°39N 77°42E 84 M10
Anápolis Brazil 16°15S 48°50W 122 C1
Anār Iran 30°55N 55°13E 87 D8
Anatolia Turkey 39°0N 30°0E 71 G5
Añatuya Argentina 28°20S 62°50W 121 E3
Ancaster U.K. 52°59N 0°32W 27 G7
Ancholme → U.K. 53°40N 0°32W 27 E7
Anchorage U.S.A. 61°13N 149°54W 108 C5
Anci China 39°20N 116°40E 79 D12
Ancohuma Bolivia 16°0S 68°50W 120 D3
Ancona Italy 43°38N 13°30E 68 C5
Ancrum U.K. 55°31N 2°35W 25 C10
Ancud Chile 42°0S 73°50W 121 G2
Ancud, G. de Chile 42°0S 73°0W 121 G2
Anda China 46°24N 125°19E 79 B14
Andalgalá Argentina 27°40S 66°30W 121 E3
Andalucía □ Spain 37°35N 5°0W 67 D3
Andalusia U.S.A. 31°18N 86°29W 111 D9
Andaman Is. Ind. Oc. 12°30N 92°45E 53 D14
Anderson Alaska, U.S.A. 64°25N 149°15W 108 C5
Anderson Ind., U.S.A. 40°10N 85°41W 112 E5
Anderson S.C., U.S.A. 34°31N 82°39W 111 D10
Anderson → Canada 69°42N 129°0W 108 C7
Andes, Cord. de los S. Amer. 20°0S 68°0W 121 E3
Andhra Pradesh □ India 18°0N 79°0E 84 L11
Andijon Uzbekistan 41°10N 72°15E 87 A13
Andorra ■ Europe 42°30N 1°30E 66 E4
Andorra La Vella Andorra 42°31N 1°32E 66 E4
Andover U.K. 51°12N 1°29W 30 D6
Andradina Brazil 20°54S 51°23W 120 E4
Andreanof Is. U.S.A. 51°30N 176°0W 108 D2
Ándria Italy 41°13N 16°17E 68 D7
Andros Greece 37°50N 24°57E 69 F11
Andros I. Bahamas 24°30N 78°0W 115 C9
Aneityum Vanuatu 20°12S 169°45E 99 E12
Angara → Russia 58°5N 94°20E 77 D10
Angarsk Russia 52°30N 104°0E 77 D11
Ånge Sweden 62°31N 15°35E 63 E7
Angel Falls Venezuela 5°57N 62°30W 120 B3
Angeles Phil. 15°9N 120°33E 83 A6
Ångermanälven → Sweden 64°0N 17°20E 63 E7
Angers France 47°30N 0°35W 66 C3
Anglesey □ U.K. 53°16N 4°18W 28 A5
Angoche Mozam. 16°8S 39°55E 97 H7
Angola ■ Africa 12°0S 18°0E 97 G3
Angoulême France 45°39N 0°10E 66 D4
Angoumois France 45°50N 0°25E 66 D3
Angra dos Reis Brazil 23°0S 44°10W 122 D2
Angren Uzbekistan 41°1N 70°12E 87 A12
Anguilla ☑ W. Indies 18°14N 63°5W 115 D12
Angus □ U.K. 56°46N 2°56W 23 J11
Angus, Braes of U.K. 56°51N 3°10W 23 J11
Anhui □ China 32°0N 117°0E 79 E12
Anjou France 47°20N 0°15W 66 C3
Ankang China 32°40N 109°1E 79 E10
Ankara Turkey 39°57N 32°54E 71 G5
Ann, C. U.S.A. 42°38N 70°35W 113 D12
Ann Arbor U.S.A. 42°17N 83°45W 112 D6
Annaba Algeria 36°50N 7°46E 94 A7
Annalee → Ireland 54°2N 7°24W 18 C7
Annan U.K. 54°59N 3°16W 25 E9
Annan → U.K. 54°58N 3°16W 25 E9
Annandale U.K. 55°10N 3°25W 25 D9
Annapolis U.S.A. 38°59N 76°30W 112 F9
Annapurna Nepal 28°34N 83°50E 85 E14
Annecy France 45°55N 6°8E 66 D7
Annfield Plain U.K. 54°52N 1°44W 26 C5
Anniston U.S.A. 33°39N 85°50W 111 D9
Annobón Atl. Oc. 1°25S 5°36E 90 G4
Annotto B. Jamaica 18°17N 76°45W 114 a
Anqing China 30°30N 117°3E 79 E12
Anse la Raye St. Lucia 13°55N 61°3W 114 b
Anshan China 41°5N 122°58E 79 C13
Anshun China 26°18N 105°57E 78 F10
Anstey U.K. 52°41N 1°12W 27 G6
Anstruther U.K. 56°14N 2°41W 25 B10
Antalaha Madag. 14°57S 50°20E 97 G10
Antalya Turkey 36°52N 30°45E 71 G5
Antalya Körfezi Turkey 36°15N 31°30E 71 G5
Antananarivo Madag. 18°55S 47°31E 97 H9
Antarctic Pen. Antarctica 67°0S 60°0W 55 C18
Antarctica 90°0S 0°0 55 E3
Anti Atlas Morocco 30°0N 8°30W 94 C4
Antibes France 43°34N 7°6E 66 E7
Anticosti, Î. d' Canada 49°30N 63°0W 109 E13
Antigo U.S.A. 45°9N 89°9W 112 C3
Antigonish Canada 45°38N 61°58W 109 E13
Antigua & Barbuda ■ W. Indies 17°20N 61°48W 115 D12
Antilles Cent. Amer. 15°0N 65°0W 115 E12
Antioch = Hatay Turkey 36°14N 36°10E 71 G6
Antioquia Colombia 6°40N 75°55W 120 B2
Antipodes Is. Pac. Oc. 49°45S 178°40E 102 M9
Antofagasta Chile 23°50S 70°30W 121 E2
Antrim U.K. 54°43N 6°14W 19 B9
Antrim □ U.K. 54°56N 6°25W 19 B9
Antrim, Mts. of U.K. 55°3N 6°14W 19 A9
Antsirabe Madag. 19°55S 47°2E 97 H9
Antsiranana Madag. 12°25S 49°20E 97 G9
Antwerp Belgium 51°13N 4°25E 64 C3
Anuradhapura Sri Lanka 8°22N 80°28E 84 Q12
Anxi China 40°30N 95°43E 78 C8
Anyang China 36°5N 114°21E 79 D11
Anzhero-Sudzhensk Russia 56°10N 86°0E 76 D9
Ánzio Italy 41°27N 12°37E 68 D5
Aomori Japan 40°45N 140°45E 81 C7
Aoraki Mount Cook N.Z. 43°36S 170°9E 99 J13
Aosta Italy 45°45N 7°20E 68 B2
Aozou Strip Chad 22°0N 19°0E 95 D9
Apalachee B. U.S.A. 30°0N 84°0W 111 E10
Apaporis → Colombia 1°23S 69°25W 120 C3
Aparecida de Goiânia Brazil 16°49S 49°14W 122 C1
Apatity Russia 67°34N 33°22E 70 A5
Apeldoorn Neths. 52°13N 5°57E 64 B3
Apia Samoa 13°50S 171°50W 99 C16
Apostle Is. U.S.A. 47°0N 90°40W 112 B2
Appalachian Mts. U.S.A. 38°0N 80°0W 112 G7
Appennini Italy 44°30N 10°0E 68 B4
Appleby-in-Westmorland U.K. 54°35N 2°29W 26 C4
Applecross Forest U.K. 57°27N 5°40W 22 H6
Appledore Devon, U.K. 51°3N 4°13W 29 E5
Appledore Kent, U.K. 51°1N 0°47E 31 D10
Appleton U.S.A. 44°16N 88°25W 112 C3
Apure → Venezuela 7°37N 66°25W 120 B3
Apurímac → Peru 12°17S 73°56W 120 D2
Aqaba, G. of Red Sea 29°0N 34°40E 86 D3
Aqtaū Kazakhstan 43°39N 51°12E 71 F9
Aqtöbe Kazakhstan 50°17N 57°10E 71 D10
Aquitain, Bassin France 44°0N 0°30W 66 D3
Ar Ramādī Iraq 33°25N 43°20E 86 C5
Ar Raqqah Syria 35°59N 39°8E 86 B4
Ara India 25°35N 84°32E 85 G14
'Arab, Bahr el → South Sudan 9°0N 29°30E 95 G11
Arab, Shatt al → Asia 29°57N 48°34E 86 D7
Arabia Asia 25°0N 45°0E 72 F6
Arabian Sea Ind. Oc. 16°0N 65°0E 72 G8
Aracaju Brazil 10°55S 37°4W 122 B3
Aracati Brazil 4°30S 37°44W 120 C6
Araçatuba Brazil 21°10S 50°30W 120 E4
Araçuai Brazil 16°52S 42°4W 122 C2
Arad Romania 46°10N 21°20E 65 E11
Arafura Sea E. Indies 9°0S 135°0E 98 B5
Aragón □ Spain 41°25N 0°40W 67 B5
Araguacema Brazil 8°50S 49°20W 120 C5
Araguaia → Brazil 5°21S 48°41W 120 C5
Araguari Brazil 18°38S 48°11W 122 C1
Arāk Iran 34°0N 49°40E 86 C7
Arakan Coast Burma 19°0N 94°0E 85 K19
Arakan Yoma Burma 20°0N 94°40E 85 K19
Aral Kazakhstan 46°41N 61°45E 76 E7
Aral Sea Asia 45°0N 58°20E 76 E6
Aran I. = Arranmore Ireland 55°0N 8°30W 18 B4
Aran Is. Ireland 53°6N 9°38W 20 B3
Aransas Pass U.S.A. 27°55N 97°9W 111 E7
Arapiraca Brazil 9°45S 36°39W 122 A3
Ar'ar Si. Arabia 30°59N 41°2E 86 D5
Araraquara Brazil 21°50S 48°0W 122 D1
Araras Brazil 22°22S 47°23W 122 D1
Ararat Turkey 39°50N 44°15E 71 G7
Araripe, Chapada do Brazil 7°20S 40°0W 120 C5
Aras, Rūd-e → Asia 40°5N 48°29E 86 A7
Arauca → Venezuela 7°24N 66°35W 120 B3
Araxá Brazil 19°35S 46°55W 122 C1
Arbil Iraq 36°15N 44°5E 86 B6
Arbroath U.K. 56°34N 2°35W 25 A10
Arcachon France 44°40N 1°10W 66 D3
Arctic Bay Canada 73°1N 85°7W 109 B11
Arctic Ocean Arctic 78°0N 160°0W 54 B18
Ardabīl Iran 38°15N 48°18E 86 B7
Ardee Ireland 53°52N 6°33W 19 D8
Ardennes Belgium 49°50N 5°5E 64 D3
Arderin Ireland 53°2N 7°39W 21 B7
Ardgour U.K. 56°45N 5°25W 22 J7
Ardingly U.K. 51°3N 0°4W 31 D8
Ardivachar Pt. U.K. 57°23N 7°26W 22 H3
Ardmore U.S.A. 34°10N 97°8W 111 D7
Ardnamurchan U.K. 56°43N 6°0W 22 J5
Ardnamurchan, Pt. of U.K. 56°43N 6°14W 22 J5
Ardnave Pt. U.K. 55°53N 6°20W 24 C3
Ardrossan U.K. 55°39N 4°49W 24 C6
Ards Pen. U.K. 54°33N 5°34W 19 B10
Arecibo Puerto Rico 18°29N 66°43W 115 D11
Arena, Pt. U.S.A. 38°57N 123°44W 110 C2
Arendal Norway 58°28N 8°46E 63 F5
Arequipa Peru 16°20S 71°30W 120 D2
Arezzo Italy 43°25N 11°53E 68 C4
Argentan France 48°45N 0°1W 66 B3
Argentina ■ S. Amer. 35°0S 66°0W 121 F3
Argentino, L. Argentina 50°10S 73°0W 121 H2
Argostoli Greece 38°11N 20°29E 69 E9
Argun → Russia 53°20N 121°28E 79 A13
Argyle, L. Australia 16°20S 128°40E 98 D4
Argyll U.K. 56°10N 5°20W 24 B5
Argyll & Bute □ U.K. 56°13N 5°28W 24 B4
Ariana Tunisia 36°52N 10°12E 95 A8
Arica Chile 18°32S 70°20W 120 D2
Arinos → Brazil 10°25S 58°20W 120 D4
Aripuanã → Brazil 5°7S 60°25W 120 C3
Arisaig U.K. 56°55N 5°51W 22 J6
Arizona □ U.S.A. 34°0N 112°0W 110 D4
Arkaig, L. U.K. 56°59N 5°10W 22 J7
Arkansas □ U.S.A. 35°0N 92°30W 111 D8
Arkansas → U.S.A. 33°47N 91°4W 111 D8
Arkansas City U.S.A. 37°4N 97°2W 111 C7
Arkhangelsk Russia 64°38N 40°36E 70 B7
Arkle → U.K. 54°24N 1°56W 26 D5
Arklow Ireland 52°48N 6°10W 21 C10
Arles France 43°41N 4°40E 66 E6
Arlington U.S.A. 38°53N 77°7W 112 F9
Arlon Belgium 49°42N 5°49E 64 D3
Armagh U.K. 54°21N 6°39W 19 C8
Armagh □ U.K. 54°18N 6°37W 19 C8
Armavir Russia 45°2N 41°7E 71 E7
Armenia Colombia 4°35N 75°45W 120 B2
Armenia ■ Asia 40°20N 45°0E 71 F7
Arnaud → Canada 59°59N 69°46W 109 D13
Arnhem Neths. 51°58N 5°55E 64 C3
Arnhem, C. Australia 12°20S 137°30E 98 C6
Arnhem Land Australia 13°10S 134°30E 98 C5
Arno → Italy 43°41N 10°17E 68 C4
Arnold U.K. 53°1N 1°7W 27 F6
Arnprior Canada 45°26N 76°21W 112 C9
Arnside U.K. 54°12N 2°49W 26 D3
Arra Mts. Ireland 52°50N 8°22W 20 C6
Arran U.K. 55°34N 5°12W 24 C5
Arranmore Ireland 55°0N 8°30W 18 B4
Arras France 50°17N 2°46E 66 A5
Arrecife Canary Is. 28°57N 13°37W 94 C3
Arrow, L. Ireland 54°3N 8°19W 18 C5
Artemovsk Ukraine 48°35N 38°0E 71 E6
Artigas Uruguay 30°20S 56°30W 121 F4
Artois France 50°20N 2°30E 66 A5
Artux China 39°40N 76°10E 78 D4
Artvin Turkey 41°14N 41°44E 71 F7
Aru, Kepulauan Indonesia 6°0S 134°30E 83 F8
Arua Uganda 3°1N 30°58E 96 D6
Aruanã Brazil 14°54S 51°10W 120 D4
Aruba ☑ W. Indies 12°30N 70°0W 115 E11
Arun → U.K. 50°49N 0°33W 31 E7
Arunachal Pradesh □ India 28°0N 95°0E 85 F19
Arundel U.K. 50°51N 0°33W 31 E7
Arusha Tanzania 3°20S 36°40E 96 E7
Aruwimi → Dem. Rep. of the Congo 1°13N 23°36E 96 D4
Arvayheer Mongolia 46°15N 102°48E 78 B9
Arviat Canada 61°6N 93°59W 108 C10
Arxan China 47°11N 119°57E 79 B12
Arzamas Russia 55°27N 43°55E 70 C7
As Sulaymānīyah Iraq 35°35N 45°29E 86 C6
As Sulaymānīyah Si. Arabia 24°9N 47°18E 86 E6
As Suwayq Oman 23°51N 57°26E 89 C6
Aş Şuwayrah Iraq 32°55N 45°0E 86 C6
Asahikawa Japan 43°46N 142°22E 81 B8
Asama-Yama Japan 36°24N 138°31E 81 E6
Asamankese Ghana 5°50N 0°40W 94 G5
Asansol India 23°40N 87°1E 85 H15
Asbestos Canada 45°47N 71°58W 113 C12
Asbury Park U.S.A. 40°13N 74°1W 113 E10
Ascension I. Atl. Oc. 7°57S 14°23W 52 E9
Áscoli Piceno Italy 42°51N 13°34E 68 C5
Ascot U.K. 51°25N 0°40W 31 D7
Aseb Eritrea 13°0N 42°40E 89 E3
Asenovgrad Bulgaria 42°1N 24°51E 69 C11
Asfordby U.K. 52°47N 0°57W 27 G7
Ash Kent, U.K. 51°16N 1°17E 31 D11
Ash Surrey, U.K. 51°15N 0°43W 31 D7
Ashbourne U.K. 53°2N 1°43W 27 F5
Ashburton U.K. 50°30N 3°46W 29 F6
Ashby de la Zouch U.K. 52°46N 1°29W 27 G6
Ashchurch U.K. 52°0N 2°5W 30 C4
Ashdown Forest U.K. 51°3N 0°5E 31 D9
Asheville U.S.A. 35°36N 82°33W 111 C10
Ashford Derby, U.K. 53°14N 1°42W 27 F5
Ashford Kent, U.K. 51°8N 0°53E 31 D10
Ashington U.K. 55°11N 1°33W 26 B5
Ashkhabad Turkmenistan 37°58N 58°24E 87 B9
Ashland Ky., U.S.A. 38°28N 82°38W 112 F6
Ashland Ohio, U.S.A. 40°52N 82°19W 112 E6
Ashland Wis., U.S.A. 46°35N 90°53W 111 A8
Ashqelon Israel 31°42N 34°35E 86 D3
Ashtabula U.S.A. 41°52N 80°47W 112 E7
Ashton-in-Makerfield U.K. 53°30N 2°40W 27 F3
Ashton under Lyne U.K. 53°29N 2°6W 27 F4
Ashuanipi, L. Canada 52°45N 66°15W 109 D13
Ashwater U.K. 50°43N 4°19W 29 F5
Ashwick U.K. 51°13N 2°31W 30 D3
Asia 45°0N 75°0E 72 E9
Asinara Italy 41°4N 8°16E 68 D3
'Asīr Si. Arabia 18°40N 42°30E 89 D3
Asir, Ras Somalia 11°55N 51°10E 89 E5
Askrigg U.K. 54°19N 2°6W 26 D4
Aslackby U.K. 52°53N 0°24W 27 G8
Asmera Eritrea 15°19N 38°55E 89 D2
Aspatria U.K. 54°47N 3°19W 26 C2
Aspen U.S.A. 39°11N 106°49W 110 C5
Assal, L. Djibouti 11°40N 42°26E 89 E3
Assam □ India 26°0N 93°0E 85 G18
Assen Neths. 53°0N 6°35E 64 B4
Assiniboia Canada 49°40N 105°59W 108 E9
Assiniboine → Canada 49°53N 97°8W 108 E10
Assisi Italy 43°4N 12°37E 68 C5
Assynt U.K. 58°12N 5°12W 22 F7
Assynt, L. U.K. 58°10N 5°3W 22 F7
Astana Kazakhstan 51°10N 71°30E 76 D8
Asti Italy 44°54N 8°12E 68 B3
Astipalea Greece 36°32N 26°22E 69 F12
Astoria U.S.A. 46°11N 123°50W 110 A2
Astrakhan Russia 46°25N 48°5E 71 E8
Asturias □ Spain 43°15N 6°0W 67 A3
Astwood Bank U.K. 52°15N 1°56W 30 B5
Asunción Paraguay 25°10S 57°30W 121 E4
Aswân Egypt 24°4N 32°57E 95 D12
Aswan High Dam Egypt 23°54N 32°54E 95 D12
Asyût Egypt 27°11N 31°4E 95 C12
Aţ Ţā'if Si. Arabia 21°5N 40°27E 89 C3
Atacama, Desierto de Chile 24°0S 69°20W 121 E3
Atatürk Barajı Turkey 37°28N 38°30E 71 G6
Atbara Sudan 17°42N 33°59E 95 E12
Atbara → Sudan 17°40N 33°56E 95 E12
Atchafalaya B. U.S.A. 29°25N 91°25W 111 E8
Athabasca Canada 54°45N 113°20W 108 D8
Athabasca → Canada 58°40N 110°50W 108 D8
Athabasca, L. Canada 59°15N 109°15W 108 D9
Athboy Ireland 53°36N 6°56W 19 D8
Athenry Ireland 53°18N 8°44W 20 B5
Athens Greece 37°58N 23°43E 69 F10
Athens Ga., U.S.A. 33°57N 83°23W 111 D10
Athens Ohio, U.S.A. 39°20N 82°6W 112 F6
Atherstone U.K. 52°35N 1°33W 27 G5
Atherton U.K. 53°32N 2°30W 27 E4
Athlone Ireland 53°25N 7°56W 20 B7
Atholl, Forest of U.K. 56°51N 3°50W 23 J10
Athos Greece 40°9N 24°22E 69 D11
Athy Ireland 53°0N 7°0W 21 B8
Atikokan Canada 48°45N 91°37W 112 A2
Atka I. U.S.A. 52°7N 174°30W 108 D2
Atlanta U.S.A. 33°45N 84°23W 111 D10
Atlantic City U.S.A. 39°21N 74°27W 113 F10
Atlantic Ocean 0°0 20°0W 50 D8
Atlas Saharien Algeria 33°30N 1°0E 94 B6
Atlin Canada 59°31N 133°41W 108 D6
Attawapiskat Canada 52°56N 82°24W 109 D11
Attawapiskat → Canada 52°57N 82°18W 109 D11
Attleborough U.K. 52°32N 1°1E 31 A11
Attu I. U.S.A. 52°55N 172°55E 108 D1
Atyraū Kazakhstan 47°5N 52°0E 71 E9
Au Sable → U.S.A. 44°25N 83°20W 112 C6
Aube → France 48°34N 3°43E 66 B5
Auburn Ind., U.S.A. 41°22N 85°4W 112 E5
Auburn N.Y., U.S.A. 42°56N 76°34W 112 D9
Aubusson France 45°57N 2°11E 66 D5
Auch France 43°39N 0°36E 66 E4
Auchterarder U.K. 56°18N 3°41W 25 B8
Auchtermuchty U.K. 56°18N 3°13W 25 B9
Auckland N.Z. 36°52S 174°46E 99 H13
Auckland Is. Pac. Oc. 50°40S 166°5E 102 N8
Aude → France 43°13N 3°14E 66 E5
Audlem U.K. 52°59N 2°30W 27 G4
Aughnacloy U.K. 54°25N 6°59W 19 C8
Augsburg Germany 48°25N 10°52E 64 D6
Augusta Australia 34°19S 115°9E 98 G2
Augusta U.S.A. 33°28N 81°58W 111 D10
Aunis France 46°5N 0°50W 66 C3
Aurangabad Bihar, India 24°45N 84°18E 85 G14
Aurangabad Maharashtra, India 19°50N 75°23E 84 K9
Aurillac France 44°55N 2°26E 66 D5
Aurora Colo., U.S.A. 39°43N 104°49W 110 C6
Aurora Ill., U.S.A. 41°45N 88°19W 112 E3
Austin U.S.A. 30°17N 97°45W 110 D7
Australia ■ Oceania 23°0S 135°0E 98 E3
Australian Capital Territory □ Australia 35°30S 149°0E 98 H8
Austria ■ Europe 47°0N 14°0E 64 E8
Autun France 46°58N 4°17E 66 C6
Auvergne □ France 45°20N 3°15E 66 D5
Auvergne, Mts. d' France 45°20N 2°55E 66 D5
Auxerre France 47°48N 3°32E 66 C5
Avallon France 47°30N 3°53E 66 C5
Avaré Brazil 23°4S 48°58W 122 D1
Avebury U.K. 51°26N 1°50W 30 D5
Avellaneda Argentina 34°40S 58°22W 121 F4
Avellino Italy 40°54N 14°47E 68 D6
Aversa Italy 40°58N 14°12E 68 D6
Aveton Gifford U.K. 50°18N 3°50W 29 G6
Aveyron → France 44°5N 1°16E 66 D4
Aviemore U.K. 57°12N 3°50W 23 H10
Avignon France 43°57N 4°50E 66 E6
Ávila Spain 40°39N 4°43W 67 B3
Avilés Spain 43°35N 5°57W 67 A3
Avoca → Ireland 52°48N 6°10W 21 C10
Avon → Bristol, U.K. 51°29N 2°41W 30 D3
Avon → Dorset, U.K. 50°44N 1°46W 30 E5
Avon → Warks., U.K. 52°0N 2°8W 30 B5
Avonmouth U.K. 51°30N 2°42W 30 C3
Avranches France 48°40N 1°20W 66 B3
Awasa Ethiopia 7°2N 38°28E 89 F2
Awash Ethiopia 9°1N 40°10E 89 F3
Awbārī, Idehan Libya 27°10N 11°30E 95 C8
Awe, L. U.K. 56°17N 5°16W 24 B5
Axbridge U.K. 51°17N 2°49W 30 D3
Axe → U.K. 50°42N 3°4W 29 E8
Axe Edge U.K. 53°14N 1°57W 27 F5
Axel Heiberg I. Canada 80°0N 90°0W 109 B11
Axholme, Isle of U.K. 53°32N 0°50W 27 E7
Axios → Greece 40°57N 22°35E 69 D10
Axminster U.K. 50°46N 3°0W 29 F8
Axmouth U.K. 50°42N 3°3W 29 F7
Ayacucho Argentina 37°5S 58°20W 121 F4
Ayacucho Peru 13°0S 74°0W 120 D2
Ayakkum Hu China 37°30N 89°20E 78 D6
Aydın Turkey 37°51N 27°51E 71 G4
Aydingkol Hu China 42°40N 89°15E 78 C6
Ayers Rock = Uluru Australia 25°23S 131°5E 98 F5
Aylesbury U.K. 51°49N 0°49W 31 C7
Aylesford U.K. 51°18N 0°30E 31 D10
Aylmer, L. Canada 64°5N 108°30W 108 C8
Aylsham U.K. 52°48N 1°15E 31 A11
Aynho U.K. 52°0N 1°15W 30 C6
Ayr U.K. 55°28N 4°38W 24 D6
Ayr → U.K. 55°28N 4°38W 24 D6
Aysgarth U.K. 54°18N 2°1W 26 D4
Ayton Borders, U.K. 55°51N 2°6W 25 C11
Ayton N. Yorks., U.K. 54°15N 0°28W 26 D8
Ayutthaya Thailand 14°25N 100°30E 82 B2
Ayvalık Turkey 39°20N 26°46E 71 G4
Az Zarqā Jordan 32°5N 36°4E 86 C4
Az Zāwiyah Libya 32°52N 12°56E 95 B8
Azad Kashmir □ Pakistan 33°50N 73°50E 84 B8
Azamgarh India 26°5N 83°13E 85 F13
Āzarbāyjān □ Iran 37°0N 44°30E 86 B6

INDEX 163

Azare — Białystok

Azare *Nigeria* 11°55N 10°10E **94 F8**
Azerbaijan ■ *Asia* 40°20N 48°0E **71 F8**
Azores *Atl. Oc.* 38°0N 27°0W **91 C1**
Azov *Russia* 47°3N 39°25E **71 E6**
Azov, Sea of *Europe* 46°0N 36°30E **71 E6**
Azuero, Pen. de *Panama* 7°30N 80°30W **115 F8**
Azul *Argentina* 36°42S 59°43W **121 F4**

B

Bab el Mandeb *Red Sea* 12°35N 43°25E **89 E3**
Bābā, Koh-i- *Afghan.* 34°30N 67°0E **84 B5**
Babine L. *Canada* 54°48N 126°0W **108 D7**
Bābol *Iran* 36°40N 52°50E **87 B8**
Babruysk *Belarus* 53°10N 29°15E **65 B15**
Babuyan Chan. *Phil.* 18°40N 121°30E **83 A6**
Babylon *Iraq* 32°34N 44°22E **86 C6**
Bac Lieu *Vietnam* 9°17N 105°43E **82 C3**
Bacabal *Brazil* 4°15S 44°45W **120 C5**
Bacău *Romania* 46°35N 26°55E **65 E14**
Back → *Canada* 65°10N 104°0W **108 C9**
Bacolod *Phil.* 10°40N 122°57E **83 B6**
Bacton *U.K.* 52°52N 1°27E **31 A11**
Bacup *U.K.* 53°42N 2°11W **27 E4**
Bad Axe *U.S.A.* 43°48N 83°0W **112 D6**
Badagara *India* 11°35N 75°40E **84 P9**
Badain Jaran Desert *China* 40°23N 102°0E **78 C9**
Badajoz *Spain* 38°50N 6°59W **67 C2**
Badakhshān □ *Afghan.* 36°30N 71°0E **87 B12**
Badalona *Spain* 41°26N 2°15E **67 B7**
Baden-Württemberg □ *Germany* 48°20N 8°40E **64 D5**
Badenoch *U.K.* 56°59N 4°15W **23 J9**
Badlands *U.S.A.* 43°55N 102°30W **110 B6**
Baffin B. *N. Amer.* 72°0N 64°0W **109 B13**
Baffin I. *Canada* 68°0N 75°0W **109 C12**
Bafoulabé *Mali* 13°50N 10°55W **94 F3**
Bafoussam *Cameroon* 5°28N 10°25E **96 C2**
Bafra *Turkey* 41°34N 35°54E **71 F6**
Bagamoyo *Tanzania* 6°28S 38°55E **96 F7**
Bagé *Brazil* 31°20S 54°15W **121 F4**
Bagenalstown *Ireland* 52°42N 6°58W **21 C9**
Baggy Pt. *U.K.* 51°8N 4°16W **29 E5**
Baghdād *Iraq* 33°20N 44°23E **86 C6**
Baghlān *Afghan.* 32°12N 68°46E **87 B12**
Bagshot *U.K.* 51°22N 0°41W **31 D7**
Baguio *Phil.* 16°26N 120°34E **83 A6**
Bahamas ■ *N. Amer.* 24°0N 75°0W **115 C10**
Baharampur *India* 24°2N 88°27E **85 G16**
Bahawalpur *Pakistan* 29°24N 71°40E **84 E7**
Bahía = Salvador *Brazil* 13°0S 38°30W **122 B3**
Bahía □ *Brazil* 12°0S 42°0W **122 B2**
Bahía, Is. de la *Honduras* 16°45N 86°15W **114 D7**
Bahía Blanca *Argentina* 38°35S 62°13W **121 F3**
Bahir Dar *Ethiopia* 11°37N 37°10E **89 E2**
Bahr el Ghazal □ *South Sudan* 7°30N 25°30E **95 G11**
Bahraich *India* 27°38N 81°37E **85 F12**
Bahrain ■ *Asia* 26°0N 50°35E **87 E7**
Baia Mare *Romania* 47°40N 23°35E **65 E12**
Baicheng *China* 45°38N 122°42E **79 B13**
Baie-Comeau *Canada* 49°12N 68°10W **109 E13**
Baie-St-Paul *Canada* 47°28N 70°32W **113 B12**
Baie Verte *Canada* 49°55N 56°12W **109 E14**
Ba'ījī *Iraq* 35°0N 43°30E **86 C5**
Baikal, L. *Russia* 53°0N 108°0E **77 D11**
Baildon *U.K.* 53°51N 1°46W **27 E5**
Baile Sear = Baleshare *U.K.* 57°31N 7°22W **22 G3**
Bain → *U.K.* 53°6N 0°12W **27 F8**
Bainbridge *U.K.* 54°18N 2°6W **26 D4**
Baja, Pta. *Mexico* 29°58N 115°49W **114 B1**
Baja California *Mexico* 31°10N 115°12W **114 A1**
Baker, L. *Canada* 64°0N 96°0W **108 C10**
Baker City *U.S.A.* 44°47N 117°50W **110 B3**
Baker I. *Pac. Oc.* 0°10N 176°35W **99 A15**
Baker Lake *Canada* 64°20N 96°3W **108 C10**
Bakers Dozen Is. *Canada* 56°45N 78°45W **109 D12**
Bakersfield *U.S.A.* 35°23N 119°1W **110 C3**
Bakewell *U.K.* 53°13N 1°40W **27 F5**
Baku *Azerbaijan* 40°29N 49°56E **71 F8**
Bala *U.K.* 52°54N 3°36W **28 B6**
Bala, L. *U.K.* 52°53N 3°37W **28 B6**
Balabac Str. *E. Indies* 7°53N 117°5E **82 C5**
Balaghat Ra. *India* 18°50N 76°30E **84 K10**
Balaklava *Ukraine* 44°30N 33°30E **71 F5**
Balakovo *Russia* 52°4N 47°55E **70 D8**
Balashov *Russia* 51°30N 43°10E **71 D7**
Balaton *Hungary* 46°50N 17°40E **65 E9**
Balbi, Mt. *Papua N. G.* 5°55S 154°58E **99 B10**
Balbina, Represa de *Brazil* 2°0S 59°30W **120 C4**
Balbriggan *Ireland* 53°37N 6°11W **19 D9**
Balcarce *Argentina* 38°0S 58°10W **121 F4**
Balderton *U.K.* 53°3N 0°47W **27 F7**
Baldock *U.K.* 52°0N 0°11W **31 C8**
Baldoyle *Ireland* 53°24N 6°8W **21 B10**
Baldwin *U.S.A.* 43°54N 85°51W **112 D5**
Baldy Peak *U.S.A.* 33°54N 109°34W **110 D5**
Balearic Is. *Spain* 39°30N 3°0E **67 C7**
Baleine → *Canada* 58°15N 67°40W **109 D13**
Baleshare *U.K.* 57°31N 7°22W **22 G3**
Baleshwar *India* 21°35N 87°3E **85 J15**
Bali *Indonesia* 8°20S 115°0E **82 F4**
Balıkeşir *Turkey* 39°39N 27°53E **71 G4**
Balikpapan *Indonesia* 1°10S 116°55E **82 E5**
Balkan Mts. *Bulgaria* 43°15N 23°0E **69 C10**
Balkanabat *Turkmenistan* 39°30N 54°22E **87 B8**
Balkhash, L. *Kazakhstan* 46°0N 74°50E **76 E8**
Ballachulish *U.K.* 56°41N 5°8W **22 J7**
Ballaghaderreen *Ireland* 53°55N 8°34W **18 D4**
Ballantrae *U.K.* 55°6N 4°59W **24 D6**
Ballarat *Australia* 37°33S 143°50E **98 H7**
Ballater *U.K.* 57°3N 3°3W **23 H11**
Ballenas, B. de *Mexico* 26°45N 113°26W **114 B2**
Balleny Is. *Antarctica* 66°30S 163°0E **55 C11**
Ballina *Ireland* 54°7N 9°9W **18 C3**
Ballinasloe *Ireland* 53°20N 8°13W **20 B6**
Ballinincollig *Ireland* 51°33N 8°35W **20 E5**
Ballinrobe *Ireland* 53°38N 9°13W **18 D3**
Ballinskelligs B. *Ireland* 51°48N 10°13W **20 E2**
Ballybunion *Ireland* 52°31N 9°40W **20 C3**
Ballycastle *U.K.* 55°12N 6°15W **19 A9**
Ballyclare *U.K.* 54°46N 6°0W **19 B10**
Ballycroy △ *Ireland* 54°5N 9°50W **18 C2**
Ballycummin *Ireland* 52°38N 8°38W **20 C5**
Ballyhaunis *Ireland* 53°46N 8°46W **18 D4**
Ballyhoura Mts. *Ireland* 52°18N 8°33W **20 D5**
Ballymena *U.K.* 54°52N 6°17W **19 B9**
Ballymoney *U.K.* 55°5N 6°31W **19 A8**
Ballymote *Ireland* 54°5N 8°31W **18 C4**
Ballynahinch *U.K.* 54°24N 5°54W **19 C10**
Ballyquintin Pt. *U.K.* 54°20N 5°30W **19 C11**
Ballyshannon *Ireland* 54°30N 8°11W **18 B5**
Balmoral Forest *U.K.* 57°0N 3°15W **23 J11**
Balrampur *India* 27°30N 82°20E **85 F13**
Balsas → *Mexico* 17°55N 102°10W **114 D4**
Baltic Sea *Europe* 57°0N 19°0E **63 F7**
Baltimore *Ireland* 51°29N 9°22W **20 F4**
Baltimore *U.S.A.* 39°17N 76°36W **112 F9**
Baluchistan □ *Pakistan* 27°30N 65°0E **84 F4**
Bam *Iran* 29°7N 58°14E **87 D9**
Bamako *Mali* 12°34N 7°55W **94 F4**
Bambari *C.A.R.* 5°40N 20°35E **96 C4**
Bamberg *Germany* 49°54N 10°54E **64 D6**
Bamburgh *U.K.* 55°37N 1°43W **26 A5**
Bamenda *Cameroon* 5°57N 10°11E **96 C2**
Bamford *U.K.* 53°22N 1°41W **27 F5**
Bampton *Devon, U.K.* 50°59N 3°29W **29 F7**
Bampton *Oxon., U.K.* 51°44N 1°32W **30 C5**
Banaba *Kiribati* 0°45S 169°50E **102 H8**
Bananal, I. do *Brazil* 11°30S 50°30W **120 D4**
Banbridge *U.K.* 54°22N 6°16W **19 C9**
Banbury *U.K.* 52°4N 1°20W **30 B6**
Banchory *U.K.* 57°3N 2°29W **23 H13**
Bancroft *Canada* 45°3N 77°51W **112 C9**
Banda *India* 25°30N 80°26E **84 G12**
Banda, Kepulauan *Indonesia* 4°37S 129°50E **83 E7**
Banda Aceh *Indonesia* 5°35N 95°20E **82 C1**
Banda Sea *Indonesia* 6°0S 130°0E **83 F7**
Bandar-e Abbās *Iran* 27°15N 56°15E **87 E9**
Bandar-e Anzalī *Iran* 37°30N 49°30E **86 B7**
Bandar-e Ma'shur *Iran* 30°35N 49°10E **86 D7**
Bandar-e Torkeman *Iran* 37°0N 54°10E **87 B8**
Bandar Lampung *Indonesia* 5°20S 105°10E **82 F3**
Bandar Seri Begawan *Brunei* 4°52N 115°0E **82 C4**
Bandeira, Pico da *Brazil* 20°26S 41°47W **122 D2**
Banderas, B. de *Mexico* 20°40N 105°25W **104 G9**
Bandırma *Turkey* 40°20N 28°0E **71 F4**
Bandon *Ireland* 51°44N 8°44W **20 E5**
Bandon → *Ireland* 51°43N 8°37W **20 E5**
Bandundu *Dem. Rep. of the Congo* 3°15S 17°22E **96 E3**
Bandung *Indonesia* 6°54S 107°36E **82 F3**
Banes *Cuba* 21°0N 75°42W **115 C9**
Banff *Canada* 51°10N 115°34W **108 D8**
Banff *U.K.* 57°40N 2°33W **23 G12**
Bangalore *India* 12°59N 77°40E **84 N10**
Bangassou *C.A.R.* 4°55N 23°7E **96 D4**
Banggai, Kepulauan *Indonesia* 1°40S 123°30E **83 E6**
Bangka *Indonesia* 2°0S 105°50E **82 E3**
Bangkok *Thailand* 13°45N 100°35E **82 B2**
Bangladesh ■ *Asia* 24°0N 90°0E **85 H17**
Bangor *Down, U.K.* 54°40N 5°40W **19 B10**
Bangor *Gwynedd, U.K.* 53°14N 4°8W **28 A5**
Bangui *C.A.R.* 4°23N 18°35E **96 D3**
Bangweulu, L. *Zambia* 11°0S 30°0E **96 G6**
Banham *U.K.* 52°27N 1°2E **31 B11**
Baní *Dom. Rep.* 18°16N 70°22W **115 D10**
Banja Luka *Bos.-H.* 44°49N 17°11E **68 B7**
Banjarmasin *Indonesia* 3°20S 114°35E **82 E4**
Banjul *Gambia* 13°28N 16°40W **94 F2**
Bankend *U.K.* 55°1N 3°33W **25 D8**
Banks I. *Canada* 73°15N 121°30W **108 B7**
Banks Is. *Vanuatu* 13°50S 167°30E **99 C12**
Bann → *U.K.* 55°8N 6°41W **19 A8**
Bannockburn *U.K.* 56°5N 3°55W **25 B8**
Bannu *Pakistan* 33°0N 70°18E **84 C7**
Banská Bystrica *Slovak Rep.* 48°46N 19°14E **65 D10**
Bantry *Ireland* 51°41N 9°27W **20 E4**
Bantry B. *Ireland* 51°37N 9°44W **20 E3**
Banwell *U.K.* 51°19N 2°52W **30 D3**
Banyak, Kepulauan *Indonesia* 2°10N 97°10E **82 D1**
Banyuwangi *Indonesia* 8°13S 114°21E **82 F4**
Bao'an *China* 22°34N 113°52E **79 a**
Baoding *China* 38°50N 115°28E **79 D12**
Baoji *China* 34°20N 107°5E **78 E10**
Baoshan *China* 25°10N 99°5E **78 F8**
Baotou *China* 40°32N 110°2E **79 C11**
Ba'qūbah *Iraq* 33°45N 44°50E **86 C6**
Bar Harbor *U.S.A.* 44°23N 68°13W **113 C13**
Bar-le-Duc *France* 48°47N 5°10E **66 B6**
Baraboo *U.S.A.* 43°28N 89°45W **112 D3**
Baracoa *Cuba* 20°20N 74°30W **115 C10**
Barahona *Dom. Rep.* 18°13N 71°7W **115 D10**
Barail Range *India* 25°15N 93°20E **85 G18**
Barakaldo *Spain* 43°18N 2°59W **67 A4**
Baranavichy *Belarus* 53°10N 26°0E **65 B14**
Baranof I. *U.S.A.* 57°0N 135°0W **108 D6**
Barbacena *Brazil* 21°15S 43°56W **122 D2**
Barbados ■ *W. Indies* 13°10N 59°30W **114 c**
Barberton *U.S.A.* 41°1N 81°39W **112 E7**
Barcelona *Spain* 41°22N 2°10E **67 B7**
Barcelona *Venezuela* 10°10N 64°40W **120 A3**
Barddhaman *India* 23°14N 87°39E **85 H15**
Bardīyah *Libya* 31°45N 25°5E **95 B10**
Bardney *U.K.* 53°13N 0°19W **27 F8**
Bardsey I. *U.K.* 52°45N 4°47W **28 B4**
Bardstown *U.S.A.* 37°49N 85°28W **112 G5**
Bareilly *India* 28°22N 79°27E **84 E11**
Barents Sea *Arctic* 73°0N 39°0E **54 B9**
Barford *U.K.* 52°16N 1°35W **30 B5**
Bargoed *U.K.* 51°42N 3°15W **28 D7**
Barham *U.K.* 51°12N 1°11E **31 D11**
Barhi *India* 24°15N 85°25E **85 G14**
Bari *Italy* 41°8N 16°51E **68 D7**
Bari Doab *Pakistan* 30°20N 73°0E **84 D8**
Barīm *Yemen* 12°39N 43°25E **90 E8**
Barinas *Venezuela* 8°36N 70°15W **120 B2**
Baring, C. *Canada* 70°0N 117°30W **108 C8**
Barisal *Bangla.* 22°45N 90°20E **85 H17**
Barking and Dagenham □ *U.K.* 51°32N 0°10E **31 C9**
Barkly Tableland *Australia* 17°50S 136°40E **98 D6**
Barlborough *U.K.* 53°17N 1°17W **27 F6**
Barlby *U.K.* 53°48N 1°2W **27 E6**
Barlee, L. *Australia* 29°15S 119°30E **98 F2**
Barletta *Italy* 41°19N 16°17E **68 D7**
Barmby Moor *U.K.* 53°56N 0°49W **27 E7**
Barmer *India* 25°45N 71°20E **84 G7**
Barmoor Castle *U.K.* 55°39N 1°59W **26 A5**
Barmouth *U.K.* 52°44N 4°4W **28 B5**
Barnard Castle *U.K.* 54°33N 1°55W **26 C5**
Barnaul *Russia* 53°20N 83°40E **76 D9**
Barnet □ *U.K.* 51°38N 0°9W **31 C8**
Barnetby le Wold *U.K.* 53°34N 0°24W **27 E8**
Barnoldswick *U.K.* 53°55N 2°11W **27 E4**
Barnsley *U.K.* 53°34N 1°27W **27 E6**
Barnstaple *U.K.* 51°5N 4°4W **29 E5**
Barnstaple Bay = Bideford Bay *U.K.* 51°5N 4°20W **29 E5**
Barotseland *Zambia* 15°0S 24°0E **97 H4**
Barques, Pt. Aux *U.S.A.* 44°4N 82°58W **112 C6**
Barquisimeto *Venezuela* 10°4N 69°19W **120 A3**
Barra *Brazil* 11°5S 43°10W **122 B2**
Barra *U.K.* 57°0N 7°29W **22 J2**
Barra, Sd. of *U.K.* 57°4N 7°25W **22 H3**
Barra do Corda *Brazil* 5°30S 45°10W **120 C5**
Barra do Piraí *Brazil* 22°30S 43°50W **122 D2**
Barra Hd. *U.K.* 56°47N 7°40W **22 J2**
Barra Mansa *Brazil* 22°35S 44°12W **122 D2**
Barrancabermeja *Colombia* 7°0N 73°50W **120 B2**
Barranquilla *Colombia* 11°0N 74°50W **120 A2**
Barre *U.S.A.* 44°12N 72°30W **113 C11**
Barreiras *Brazil* 12°8S 45°0W **122 B2**
Barreiro *Portugal* 38°39N 9°5W **67 C1**
Barreiros *Brazil* 8°49S 35°12W **122 A3**
Barretos *Brazil* 20°30S 48°35W **122 D1**
Barrhead *U.K.* 55°48N 4°23W **24 C7**
Barrie *Canada* 44°24N 79°40W **109 E12**
Barrow *U.S.A.* 71°18N 156°47W **108 B4**
Barrow → *Ireland* 52°25N 6°58W **21 D9**
Barrow, Pt. *U.S.A.* 71°23N 156°29W **104 B4**
Barrow-in-Furness *U.K.* 54°7N 3°14W **26 D2**
Barrow upon Humber *U.K.* 53°41N 0°23W **27 E8**
Barrowford *U.K.* 53°51N 2°14W **27 E4**
Barry *U.K.* 51°24N 3°16W **29 E7**
Barry I. *U.K.* 51°23N 3°16W **29 E7**
Barry's Bay *Canada* 45°29N 77°41W **112 C9**
Barstow *U.S.A.* 34°54N 117°1W **110 D3**
Bartlesville *U.S.A.* 36°45N 95°59W **111 C7**
Barton *U.K.* 54°29N 1°38W **26 D5**
Barton upon Humber *U.K.* 53°41N 0°25W **27 E8**
Barú, Volcan *Panama* 8°55N 82°35W **115 F8**
Baruun-Urt *Mongolia* 46°46N 113°15E **79 B11**
Barwell *U.K.* 52°35N 1°21W **27 G6**
Barysaw *Belarus* 54°17N 28°28E **65 A15**
Bashkortostan □ *Russia* 54°0N 57°0E **70 D10**
Basilan I. *Phil.* 6°35N 122°0E **83 C6**
Basildon *U.K.* 51°34N 0°28E **31 C9**
Basingstoke *U.K.* 51°15N 1°5W **30 D6**
Baskatong, Rés. *Canada* 46°46N 75°50W **113 B10**
Basle *Switz.* 47°35N 7°35E **64 E4**
Basque Provinces = País Vasco □ *Spain* 42°50N 2°45W **67 A4**
Basra *Iraq* 30°30N 47°50E **86 D6**
Bass Rock *U.K.* 56°5N 2°38W **25 B10**
Bass Str. *Australia* 39°15S 146°30E **98 H8**
Bassas da India *Ind. Oc.* 22°0S 39°0E **97 J7**
Basse-Terre *Guadeloupe* 16°0N 61°44W **115 D12**
Bassein *Burma* 16°45N 94°30E **85 L19**
Bassenthwaite L. *U.K.* 54°40N 3°14W **26 C2**
Basseterre *St. Kitts & Nevis* 17°17N 62°43W **115 D12**
Basti *India* 26°52N 82°55E **85 F13**
Bastia *France* 42°40N 9°30E **66 E8**
Baston *U.K.* 52°43N 0°21W **27 G8**
Bata *Eq. Guin.* 1°57N 9°50E **96 D1**
Batabanó, G. de *Cuba* 22°30N 82°30W **115 C8**
Batangas *Phil.* 13°35N 121°10E **83 B6**
Batatais *Brazil* 20°54S 47°37W **122 D1**
Batavia *U.S.A.* 43°0N 78°11W **112 D8**
Bataysk *Russia* 47°3N 39°45E **71 E6**
Batdambang *Cambodia* 13°7N 103°12E **82 B2**
Bath *U.K.* 51°23N 2°22W **30 D4**
Bath *Maine, U.S.A.* 43°55N 69°49W **113 D13**
Bath *N.Y., U.S.A.* 42°20N 77°19W **112 D9**
Bathford *U.K.* 51°24N 2°18W **30 D4**
Bathgate *U.K.* 55°54N 3°39W **25 C8**
Bathsheba *Barbados* 13°13N 59°32W **114 c**
Bathurst *Australia* 33°25S 149°31E **98 G8**
Bathurst *Canada* 47°37N 65°43W **109 E13**
Bathurst, C. *Canada* 70°34N 128°0W **108 B7**
Bathurst I. *Canada* 76°0N 100°30W **104 B9**
Bathurst Inlet *Canada* 66°50N 108°1W **108 C9**
Batley *U.K.* 53°43N 1°38W **27 E5**
Batman *Turkey* 37°55N 41°5E **71 G7**
Batna *Algeria* 35°34N 6°15E **94 A7**
Baton Rouge *U.S.A.* 30°27N 91°11W **111 D8**
Batticaloa *Sri Lanka* 7°43N 81°45E **84 R12**
Battle *U.K.* 50°55N 0°30E **31 E9**
Battle Creek *U.S.A.* 42°19N 85°11W **112 D5**
Batu, Kepulauan *Indonesia* 0°30S 98°25E **82 E1**
Batu Pahat *Malaysia* 1°50N 102°56E **82 D2**
Batumi *Georgia* 41°39N 41°44E **71 F7**
Bauld, C. *Canada* 51°38N 55°26W **109 D14**
Bauru *Brazil* 22°10S 49°0W **122 D1**
Bavaria = Bayern □ *Germany* 48°50N 12°0E **64 D6**
Bawdsey *U.K.* 52°1N 1°27E **31 B11**
Bawtry *U.K.* 53°26N 1°2W **27 F6**
Bay City *U.S.A.* 43°36N 83°54W **112 D6**
Bayamo *Cuba* 20°20N 76°40W **115 C9**
Bayan Har Shan *China* 34°0N 98°0E **78 E8**
Bayan Obo *China* 41°52N 109°59E **79 C10**
Baydhabo *Somalia* 3°8N 43°30E **89 G3**
Bayern □ *Germany* 48°50N 12°0E **64 D6**
Bayeux *France* 49°17N 0°42W **66 B3**
Bayonne *France* 43°30N 1°28W **66 E3**
Beachley *U.K.* 51°37N 2°39W **30 C3**
Beachy Hd. *U.K.* 50°44N 0°15E **31 E9**
Beacon *U.S.A.* 41°30N 73°58W **113 E11**
Beaconsfield *U.K.* 51°36N 0°38W **31 C7**
Beadnell *U.K.* 55°33N 1°38W **26 A5**
Beagle, Canal *S. Amer.* 55°0S 68°30W **121 H3**
Beaminster *U.K.* 50°48N 2°44W **30 E3**
Bear → *U.S.A.* 41°30N 112°8W **110 B4**
Bear I. *Arctic* 74°30N 19°0E **54 B8**
Bear I. *Ireland* 51°38N 9°50W **20 E3**
Bear L. *U.S.A.* 41°59N 111°21W **110 B4**
Beardmore Glacier *Antarctica* 84°30S 170°0E **55 E11**
Beardstown *U.S.A.* 40°1N 90°26W **112 E2**
Béarn *France* 43°20N 0°30W **66 E3**
Bearsden *U.K.* 55°55N 4°21W **24 C7**
Bearsted *U.K.* 51°16N 0°35E **31 D10**
Beatrice *U.S.A.* 40°16N 96°45W **111 B7**
Beattock *U.K.* 55°20N 3°28W **25 D9**
Beattock Summit *U.K.* 52°25N 3°32W **25 D8**
Beauce, Plaine de la *France* 48°10N 1°45E **66 B4**
Beaufort Sea *Arctic* 72°0N 140°0W **104 B5**
Beaufort West *S. Africa* 32°18S 22°36E **97 L4**
Beauharnois *Canada* 45°20N 73°52W **113 C11**
Beaulieu *U.K.* 50°48N 1°27W **30 E6**
Beauly *U.K.* 57°30N 4°28W **23 H9**
Beauly → *U.K.* 57°29N 4°27W **23 H9**
Beauly Firth *U.K.* 57°30N 4°20W **23 H9**
Beaumaris *U.K.* 53°16N 4°6W **28 A5**
Beaumont *U.S.A.* 30°5N 94°6W **111 D8**
Beaune *France* 47°2N 4°50E **66 C6**
Beauvais *France* 49°25N 2°8E **66 B5**
Beaver → *Canada* 55°26N 107°45W **108 D9**
Beaver Creek *Canada* 63°0N 141°0W **108 C5**
Beaver Dam *U.S.A.* 43°28N 88°50W **112 D3**
Beaver Falls *U.S.A.* 40°46N 80°20W **112 E7**
Beaver I. *U.S.A.* 45°40N 85°33W **112 C5**
Beawar *India* 26°3N 74°18E **84 F9**
Bebedouro *Brazil* 21°0S 48°25W **122 D1**
Bebington *U.K.* 53°22N 3°0W **27 F3**
Beccles *U.K.* 52°27N 1°35E **31 B12**
Béchar *Algeria* 31°38N 2°18W **94 B5**
Beckermet *U.K.* 54°27N 3°30W **26 D1**
Beckfoot *U.K.* 54°50N 3°24W **26 C2**
Beckingham *U.K.* 53°24N 0°50W **27 F7**
Beckley *U.S.A.* 37°47N 81°11W **112 G7**
Bedale *U.K.* 54°18N 1°36W **26 D5**
Beddgelert *U.K.* 53°1N 4°6W **28 A5**
Bedford *U.K.* 52°8N 0°28W **31 B8**
Bedford *Ind., U.S.A.* 38°52N 86°29W **112 F4**
Bedford *Va., U.S.A.* 37°20N 79°31W **112 G8**
Bedford □ *U.K.* 52°4N 0°28W **31 B8**
Bedford Level *U.K.* 52°32N 0°7W **31 A8**
Bedlington *U.K.* 55°8N 1°35W **26 B5**
Bedworth *U.K.* 52°29N 1°28W **30 B6**
Beeford *U.K.* 53°58N 0°17W **27 E8**
Beer *U.K.* 50°41N 3°6W **29 F7**
Be'er Sheva *Israel* 31°15N 34°48E **86 D3**
Beeston *U.K.* 52°56N 1°14W **27 G6**
Bei Jiang → *China* 23°2N 112°58E **79 G11**
Bei Shan *China* 41°30N 96°0E **78 C8**
Bei'an *China* 48°10N 126°20E **79 B14**
Beighton *U.K.* 53°21N 1°20W **27 F6**
Beihai *China* 21°28N 109°6E **79 G10**
Beijing *China* 39°53N 116°21E **79 D12**
Beinn na Faoghla = Benbecula *U.K.* 57°26N 7°21W **22 H3**
Beira *Mozam.* 19°50S 34°52E **97 H6**
Beirut *Lebanon* 33°53N 35°31E **86 C3**
Beitbridge *Zimbabwe* 22°12S 30°0E **97 J6**
Beith *U.K.* 55°45N 4°38W **24 C6**
Béja *Tunisia* 36°43N 9°12E **95 A7**
Bejaïa *Algeria* 36°42N 5°2E **94 A7**
Békéscsaba *Hungary* 46°40N 21°5E **65 E11**
Bela *Pakistan* 26°12N 66°20E **84 F5**
Belarus ■ *Europe* 53°30N 27°0E **70 D4**
Belau = Palau ■ *Palau* 7°30N 134°30E **102 G5**
Belbroughton *U.K.* 52°24N 2°7W **30 B4**
Belcher Chan. *Canada* 77°15N 95°0W **109 B10**
Belcher Is. *Canada* 56°15N 78°45W **109 D12**
Beledweyne *Somalia* 4°30N 45°5E **89 G4**
Belém *Brazil* 1°20S 48°30W **120 C5**
Belep, Îs. *N. Cal.* 19°45S 163°40E **99 D11**
Belfast *U.K.* 54°37N 5°56W **19 B10**
Belfast *U.S.A.* 44°26N 69°1W **113 C13**
Belfast L. *U.K.* 54°40N 5°50W **19 B10**
Belford *U.K.* 55°36N 1°49W **26 A5**
Belfort *France* 47°38N 6°50E **66 C7**
Belgaum *India* 15°55N 74°35E **84 M9**
Belgium ■ *Europe* 50°30N 5°0E **64 C3**
Belgorod *Russia* 50°35N 36°35E **71 D6**
Belgrade *Serbia* 44°50N 20°37E **69 B9**
Belitung *Indonesia* 3°10S 107°50E **82 E3**
Belize ■ *Cent. Amer.* 17°0N 88°30W **114 D7**
Belize City *Belize* 17°25N 88°10W **114 D7**
Bell Peninsula *Canada* 63°50N 82°0W **109 C11**
Bell Ville *Argentina* 32°40S 62°40W **121 F3**
Bella Coola *Canada* 52°25N 126°40W **108 D7**
Bellaire *U.S.A.* 40°1N 80°45W **112 E7**
Bellary *India* 15°10N 76°56E **84 M10**
Belle Fourche → *U.S.A.* 44°26N 102°18W **110 B6**
Belle-Île *France* 47°20N 3°10W **66 C2**
Belle Isle *Canada* 51°57N 55°25W **109 D14**
Belle Isle, Str. of *Canada* 51°30N 56°30W **109 D14**
Bellefontaine *U.S.A.* 40°22N 83°46W **112 E6**
Belleplaine *Barbados* 13°15N 59°34W **114 c**
Belleville *Canada* 44°10N 77°23W **109 E12**
Belleville *U.S.A.* 38°31N 89°59W **112 F3**
Bellingham *U.K.* 55°9N 2°16W **26 B4**
Bellingham *U.S.A.* 48°46N 122°29W **110 A2**
Bellingshausen Sea *Antarctica* 66°0S 80°0W **55 C17**
Bellinzona *Switz.* 46°11N 9°1E **64 E5**
Belmonte *Brazil* 16°0S 39°0W **122 C3**
Belmopan *Belize* 17°18N 88°30W **114 D7**
Belmullet *Ireland* 54°14N 9°58W **18 C2**
Belo Horizonte *Brazil* 19°55S 43°56W **122 C2**
Belo Jardim *Brazil* 8°20S 36°26W **122 A3**
Belogorsk *Russia* 51°0N 128°20E **77 D13**
Beloit *U.S.A.* 42°31N 89°2W **112 D3**
Belomorsk *Russia* 64°35N 34°54E **70 B5**
Beloretsk *Russia* 53°58N 58°24E **70 D10**
Beloye, L. *Russia* 60°10N 37°35E **70 B6**
Belper *U.K.* 53°2N 1°29W **27 F6**
Belsay *U.K.* 55°6N 1°51W **26 B5**
Belton *N. Lincs., U.K.* 53°33N 0°48W **27 E7**
Belton *Norfolk, U.K.* 52°35N 1°40E **31 A12**
Beltsy *Moldova* 47°48N 27°58E **65 E14**
Belturbet *Ireland* 54°6N 7°26W **18 C7**
Belvidere *U.S.A.* 42°15N 88°50W **112 D3**
Bembridge *U.K.* 50°41N 1°5W **30 E6**
Bemidji *U.S.A.* 47°28N 94°53W **111 A8**
Ben Cruachan *U.K.* 56°26N 5°8W **24 B5**
Ben Dearg *U.K.* 57°47N 4°56W **23 G8**
Ben Hope *U.K.* 58°25N 4°36W **23 F8**
Ben Lawers *U.K.* 56°32N 4°14W **24 A7**
Ben Lomond *U.K.* 56°11N 4°38W **24 B6**
Ben Macdhui *U.K.* 57°4N 3°40W **23 H10**
Ben Mhor *U.K.* 57°15N 7°18W **22 H3**
Ben More *Argyll & Bute, U.K.* 56°26N 6°1W **24 B3**
Ben More *Stirling, U.K.* 56°23N 4°32W **24 B6**
Ben More Assynt *U.K.* 58°8N 4°52W **23 F8**
Ben Nevis *U.K.* 56°48N 5°1W **22 J7**
Ben Vorlich *U.K.* 56°21N 4°14W **24 B7**
Ben Wyvis *U.K.* 57°40N 4°35W **23 G8**
Benares = Varanasi *India* 25°22N 83°0E **85 G13**
Benbecula *U.K.* 57°26N 7°21W **22 H3**
Bend *U.S.A.* 44°4N 121°19W **110 B2**
Benderloch *U.K.* 56°30N 5°22W **24 A5**
Bendigo *Australia* 36°40S 144°15E **98 H7**
Benevento *Italy* 41°8N 14°45E **68 D6**
Bengal, Bay of *Ind. Oc.* 15°0N 90°0E **85 M17**
Bengbu *China* 32°58N 117°20E **79 E12**
Benghazi *Libya* 32°11N 20°3E **95 B10**
Bengkulu *Indonesia* 3°50S 102°12E **82 E2**
Benguela *Angola* 12°37S 13°25E **97 G2**
Beni → *Bolivia* 10°23S 65°24W **120 D3**
Beni Mellal *Morocco* 32°21N 6°21W **94 B4**
Beni Suef *Egypt* 29°5N 31°6E **95 C12**
Benidorm *Spain* 38°33N 0°9W **67 C5**
Benin ■ *Africa* 10°0N 2°0E **94 G6**
Benin, Bight of *W. Afr.* 5°0N 3°0E **94 H6**
Benin City *Nigeria* 6°20N 5°31E **94 G7**
Benington *U.K.* 53°0N 0°5E **27 F9**
Benjamin Constant *Brazil* 4°40S 70°15W **120 C2**
Benoni *S. Africa* 26°11S 28°18E **97 K5**
Benson *U.K.* 51°37N 1°6W **30 C6**
Bentley *Hants., U.K.* 51°12N 0°52W **31 D7**
Bentley *S. Yorks., U.K.* 53°33N 1°8W **27 E6**
Bentley Subglacial Trench *Antarctica* 80°0S 115°0W **55 E14**
Benton *U.S.A.* 38°0N 88°55W **112 G3**
Benton Harbor *U.S.A.* 42°6N 86°27W **112 D4**
Benue → *Nigeria* 7°48N 6°46E **94 G7**
Benxi *China* 41°20N 123°48E **79 C13**
Beppu *Japan* 33°15N 131°30E **81 G2**
Berber *Sudan* 18°0N 34°0E **95 E12**
Berbera *Somalia* 10°30N 45°2E **89 E4**
Berbérati *C.A.R.* 4°15N 15°40E **96 D3**
Berbice → *Guyana* 6°20N 57°32W **120 B4**
Berdyansk *Ukraine* 46°45N 36°50E **71 E6**
Berdychiv *Ukraine* 49°57N 28°30E **71 E4**
Bere Alston *U.K.* 50°29N 4°13W **29 G5**
Bere Regis *U.K.* 50°45N 2°14W **30 E4**
Berea *U.S.A.* 37°34N 84°17W **112 G5**
Berens → *Canada* 52°25N 97°2W **108 D10**
Berezina → *Belarus* 52°33N 30°14E **70 D5**
Bereznik *Russia* 62°51N 42°40E **70 B7**
Berezniki *Russia* 59°24N 56°46E **70 C10**
Bérgamo *Italy* 45°41N 9°43E **68 B3**
Bergen *Norway* 60°20N 5°20E **63 E5**
Bergerac *France* 44°51N 0°30E **66 D4**
Bering Sea *Pac. Oc.* 58°0N 171°0W **104 D2**
Bering Strait *Pac. Oc.* 65°30N 169°0W **108 C3**
Berkeley *U.K.* 51°41N 2°27W **30 C4**
Berkhamsted *U.K.* 51°45N 0°33W **31 C7**
Berkner I. *Antarctica* 79°30S 50°0W **55 D18**
Berkshire Downs *U.K.* 51°33N 1°29W **30 C6**
Berlin *Germany* 52°31N 13°23E **64 B7**
Berlin *U.S.A.* 44°28N 71°11W **113 C12**
Bermejo → *Argentina* 26°51S 58°23W **121 E4**
Bermuda ☑ *Atl. Oc.* 32°18N 64°45W **52 C6**
Bern *Switz.* 46°57N 7°28E **64 E4**
Berneray *U.K.* 57°43N 7°11W **22 G3**
Berry *France* 46°50N 2°0E **66 C5**
Berry Hd. *U.K.* 50°24N 3°29W **29 G7**
Bertraghboy B. *Ireland* 53°22N 9°54W **20 B3**
Berwick *U.S.A.* 41°3N 76°14W **112 E9**
Berwick-upon-Tweed *U.K.* 55°46N 2°0W **26 A5**
Berwyn Mts. *U.K.* 52°54N 3°26W **28 B7**
Besançon *France* 47°15N 6°2E **66 C7**
Bessarabiya *Moldova* 47°0N 28°10E **65 E15**
Bessemer *U.S.A.* 46°29N 90°3W **112 B2**
Bethel *U.S.A.* 60°48N 161°45W **108 C3**
Bethesda *U.K.* 53°10N 4°3W **28 A5**
Bethlehem *S. Africa* 28°14S 28°18E **97 K5**
Bethlehem *U.S.A.* 40°37N 75°23W **113 E10**
Béthune *France* 50°30N 2°38E **66 A5**
Betim *Brazil* 19°58S 44°7W **122 C2**
Bettiah *India* 26°48N 84°33E **85 F14**
Betul *India* 21°58N 77°59E **84 J10**
Betws-y-Coed *U.K.* 53°5N 3°48W **28 A6**
Beverley *U.K.* 53°51N 0°26W **27 E8**
Bewdley *U.K.* 52°23N 2°19W **30 B4**
Bexhill *U.K.* 50°51N 0°29E **31 E9**
Bexley □ *U.K.* 51°27N 0°9E **31 D9**
Beyneu *Kazakhstan* 45°18N 55°9E **71 E10**
Beypazarı *Turkey* 40°10N 31°56E **71 F5**
Beyşehir Gölü *Turkey* 37°41N 31°33E **71 G5**
Béziers *France* 43°20N 3°12E **66 E5**
Bhagalpur *India* 25°10N 87°0E **85 G15**
Bhaktapur *Nepal* 27°38N 85°24E **85 F14**
Bhanrer Ra. *India* 23°40N 79°45E **84 H11**
Bharatpur *India* 27°15N 77°30E **84 F10**
Bharraig = Barra *U.K.* 57°0N 7°29W **22 J2**
Bharuch *India* 21°47N 73°0E **84 J8**
Bhatarsaigh = Vatersay *U.K.* 56°55N 7°32W **22 J2**
Bhatpara *India* 22°50N 88°25E **85 H16**
Bhavnagar *India* 21°45N 72°10E **84 J8**
Bhearnaraigh = Berneray *U.K.* 57°43N 7°11W **22 G3**
Bhilainagar-Durg *India* 21°13N 81°26E **85 J12**
Bhilwara *India* 25°25N 74°38E **84 G9**
Bhima → *India* 16°25N 77°17E **84 L10**
Bhiwandi *India* 19°20N 73°0E **84 K8**
Bhiwani *India* 28°50N 76°9E **84 E10**
Bhopal *India* 23°20N 77°30E **84 H10**
Bhubaneshwar *India* 20°15N 85°50E **85 J14**
Bhuj *India* 23°15N 69°49E **84 H6**
Bhusawal *India* 21°3N 75°46E **84 J9**
Bhutan ■ *Asia* 27°25N 90°30E **85 F17**
Biała Podlaska *Poland* 52°4N 23°6E **65 B12**
Białystok *Poland* 53°10N 23°10E **65 B12**

Biarritz
Burnie

Burnley   Cheshire East

Burnley *U.K.* 53°47N 2°14W **27** E4
Burnmouth *U.K.* 55°50N 2°4W **25** C11
Burns *U.S.A.* 43°35N 119°3W **110** B3
Burnside → *Canada* 66°51N 108°4W **108** C9
Burntisland *U.K.* 56°4N 3°13W **25** B9
Burqin *China* 47°43N 87°0E **78** B6
Burray *U.K.* 58°51N 2°54W **23** E12
Burren △ *Ireland* 53°1N 8°58W **20** B4
Burrow Hd. *U.K.* 54°41N 4°24W **24** E7
Burry Port *U.K.* 51°41N 4°15W **28** D5
Bursa *Turkey* 40°15N 29°5E **71** F4
Burstwick *U.K.* 53°44N 0°8W **27** E8
Burton *U.K.* 54°11N 2°43W **26** D3
Burton Agnes *U.K.* 54°4N 0°18W **26** D8
Burton Bradstock *U.K.* 50°42N 2°43W **30** E3
Burton Fleming *U.K.* 54°8N 0°20W **26** D8
Burton Latimer *U.K.* 52°22N 0°41W **31** B7
Burton upon Stather *U.K.* 53°39N 0°41W **27** E7
Burton upon Trent *U.K.* 52°48N 1°38W **27** G5
Buru *Indonesia* 3°30S 126°30E **83** E7
Burundi ■ *Africa* 3°15S 30°0E **96** E5
Burwash *U.K.* 50°59N 0°23E **31** D9
Burwell *U.K.* 52°17N 0°20E **31** B9
Burwick *U.K.* 58°45N 2°58W **23** E12
Bury *U.K.* 53°35N 2°17W **27** E4
Bury St. Edmunds *U.K.* 52°15N 0°43E **31** B10
Buryatia □ *Russia* 53°0N 110°0E **77** D11
Busan *S. Korea* 35°5N 129°0E **79** D14
Büshehr *Iran* 28°55N 50°55E **87** D7
Bushey *U.K.* 51°38N 0°22W **31** C8
Busto Arsízio *Italy* 45°37N 8°51E **68** B3
Buta *Dem. Rep. of the Congo* 2°50N 24°53E **96** D4
Butare *Rwanda* 2°31S 29°52E **96** E5
Butaritari *Kiribati* 3°30N 174°0E **102** G9
Bute □ *U.K.* 55°48N 5°2W **24** C5
Bute, Kyles of *U.K.* 55°55N 5°10W **24** C5
Butembo *Dem. Rep. of the Congo* 0°9N 29°18E **96** D5
Butler *U.S.A.* 40°52N 79°54W **112** E8
Buton *Indonesia* 5°0S 122°45E **83** E6
Butte *U.S.A.* 46°0N 112°32W **110** A4
Buttermere *U.K.* 54°32N 3°16W **26** C2
Butterworth *Malaysia* 5°24N 100°23E **82** C2
Buttevant *Ireland* 52°14N 8°40W **20** D5
Butuan *Phil.* 8°57N 125°33E **83** C7
Buurhakaba *Somalia* 3°12N 44°20E **89** G3
Buxton *U.K.* 53°16N 1°54W **27** F5
Buyant-Uhaa *Mongolia* 44°55N 110°11E **79** C11
Buzău *Romania* 45°10N 26°50E **65** F14
Buzuluk *Russia* 52°48N 52°12E **70** D9
Bydgoszcz *Poland* 53°10N 18°0E **65** B9
Byfield *U.K.* 52°10N 1°14W **30** B6
Bylot I. *Canada* 73°13N 78°34W **109** B12
Byrranga Ra. *Russia* 75°0N 100°0E **77** B11
Bytom *Poland* 50°25N 18°54E **65** C10

C

Ca Mau *Vietnam* 9°7N 105°8E **82** C3
Cabanatuan *Phil.* 15°30N 120°58E **83** A6
Cabedelo *Brazil* 7°0S 34°50W **120** C6
Cabimas *Venezuela* 10°23N 71°25W **120** A2
Cabinda *Angola* 5°33S 12°11E **96** F2
Cabinda □ *Angola* 5°0S 12°30E **96** F2
Cabo Frio *Brazil* 22°51S 42°3W **122** D2
Cabo San Lucas *Mexico* 22°53N 109°54W **114** C3
Cabonga, Réservoir *Canada* 47°20N 76°40W **109** E12
Cabora Bassa Dam *Mozam.* 15°20S 32°50E **97** H6
Cabot Str. *Canada* 47°15N 59°40W **109** E14
Čačak *Serbia* 43°54N 20°20E **69** C9
Cáceres *Brazil* 16°5S 57°40W **120** D4
Cáceres *Spain* 39°26N 6°23W **67** C2
Cachimbo, Serra do *Brazil* 9°30S 55°30W **120** C4
Cachoeira *Brazil* 12°30S 39°0W **122** B3
Cachoeira do Sul *Brazil* 30°3S 52°53W **121** F4
Cachoeiro de Itapemirim
  Brazil 20°51S 41°7W **122** D2
Cader Idris *U.K.* 52°42N 3°53W **28** B6
Cadillac *U.S.A.* 44°15N 85°24W **112** C5
Cádiz *Spain* 36°30N 6°20W **67** D2
Cádiz, G. de *Spain* 36°40N 7°0W **67** D2
Caen *France* 49°10N 0°22W **66** B3
Caenby Corner *U.K.* 53°24N 0°33W **27** F7
Caerdydd = Cardiff *U.K.* 51°29N 3°10W **29** E7
Caerfyrddin = Carmarthen
  U.K. 51°52N 4°19W **28** D5
Caergybi = Holyhead *U.K.* 53°18N 4°38W **28** A4
Caernarfon *U.K.* 53°8N 4°16W **28** A5
Caernarfon B. *U.K.* 53°4N 4°40W **28** A4
Caerphilly *U.K.* 51°35N 3°13W **29** D7
Caersws *U.K.* 52°31N 3°26W **28** B7
Caeté *Brazil* 19°55S 43°40W **122** C2
Caetité *Brazil* 13°50S 42°32W **122** B2
Cagayan de Oro *Phil.* 8°30N 124°40E **83** C6
Cágliari *Italy* 39°13N 9°7E **68** E3
Caguas *Puerto Rico* 18°14N 66°2W **115** D11
Caha Mts. *Ireland* 51°45N 9°40W **20** E3
Cahir *Ireland* 52°22N 7°56W **21** D7
Cahirciveen *Ireland* 51°56N 10°14W **20** E2
Cahore Pt. *Ireland* 52°33N 6°12W **21** C10
Cahors *France* 44°27N 1°27E **66** D4
Cairn Gorm *U.K.* 57°7N 3°39W **23** H10
Cairn Toul *U.K.* 57°3N 3°42W **23** H10
Cairngorm Mts. *U.K.* 57°6N 3°42W **23** H10
Cairngorms △ *U.K.* 57°10N 3°50W **23** H10
Cairnryan *U.K.* 54°59N 5°1W **24** E6
Cairns *Australia* 16°57S 145°45E **98** D8
Cairnsmore of Fleet *U.K.* 54°59N 4°20W **24** E7
Cairo *Egypt* 30°2N 31°13E **95** B12
Cairo *U.S.A.* 37°0N 89°11W **112** G3
Caister-on-Sea *U.K.* 52°40N 1°43E **31** A12
Caistor *U.K.* 53°30N 0°18W **27** F8
Caithness *U.K.* 58°25N 3°35W **23** F10
Caithness, Ord of *U.K.* 58°8N 3°36W **23** F10
Cajamarca *Peru* 7°5S 78°28W **120** C2
Calabar *Nigeria* 4°57N 8°20E **94** H7
Calábria □ *Italy* 39°0N 16°30E **68** E7
Calais *France* 50°57N 1°56E **66** A4
Calais *U.S.A.* 45°11N 67°17W **113** C14
Calama *Chile* 22°30S 68°55W **121** E3
Calamian Group *Phil.* 11°50N 119°55E **83** B5
Calanscio, Sarîr *Libya* 27°30N 22°30E **95** C10
Calapan *Phil.* 13°25N 121°7E **83** B6

Calbayog *Phil.* 12°4N 124°38E **83** B6
Calcutta = Kolkata *India* 22°34N 88°21E **85** H16
Caldbeck *U.K.* 54°45N 3°3W **26** C2
Calder → *U.K.* 53°44N 1°22W **27** E6
Calder Bridge *U.K.* 54°27N 3°29W **26** D2
Caldera *Chile* 27°5S 70°55W **121** E2
Caldew → *U.K.* 54°54N 2°56W **26** C3
Caldwell *U.S.A.* 43°40N 116°41W **110** B3
Caledonian Canal *U.K.* 57°29N 4°15W **23** H9
Calgary *Canada* 51°0N 114°10W **108** D8
Cali *Colombia* 3°25N 76°35W **120** B2
Calicut *India* 11°15N 75°43E **84** P9
California □ *U.S.A.* 37°30N 119°30W **110** C2
California, G. de *Mexico* 27°0N 111°0W **114** B2
Callan *Ireland* 52°32N 7°24W **21** C8
Callander *U.K.* 56°15N 4°13W **24** B7
Callao *Peru* 12°3S 77°8W **120** D2
Calne *U.K.* 51°26N 2°0W **30** D5
Calshot *U.K.* 50°48N 1°19W **30** E6
Calstock *U.K.* 50°30N 4°13W **29** F5
Caltanissetta *Italy* 37°29N 14°4E **68** F6
Calvi *France* 42°34N 8°45E **66** E8
Calvinia *S. Africa* 31°28S 19°45E **97** L3
Cam → *U.K.* 52°21N 0°16E **31** B9
Cam Ranh *Vietnam* 11°54N 109°12E **82** B3
Camagüey *Cuba* 21°20N 77°55W **115** C9
Camargue *France* 43°34N 4°34E **66** E6
Camberley *U.K.* 51°20N 0°44W **31** D7
Cambo *U.K.* 55°10N 1°57W **26** B5
Cambodia ■ *Asia* 12°15N 105°0E **82** B3
Camborne *U.K.* 50°12N 5°19W **29** G3
Cambrai *France* 50°11N 3°14E **66** A5
Cambrian Mts. *U.K.* 52°3N 3°57W **28** C6
Cambridge *Jamaica* 18°18N 77°54W **114** a
Cambridge *U.K.* 52°12N 0°8E **31** B9
Cambridge *Mass., U.S.A.* 42°23N 71°7W **113** D12
Cambridge *Md., U.S.A.* 38°34N 76°5W **113** F9
Cambridge *Ohio, U.S.A.* 40°2N 81°35W **112** E7
Cambridge Bay *Canada* 69°10N 105°0W **108** C9
Cambridgeshire □ *U.K.* 52°25N 0°7W **31** B8
Camden *Ark., U.S.A.* 33°35N 92°50W **111** D8
Camden *N.J., U.S.A.* 39°55N 75°7W **113** F10
Camden □ *U.K.* 51°32N 0°8W **31** C8
Camel → *U.K.* 50°31N 4°51W **29** F4
Camelford *U.K.* 50°37N 4°42W **29** F4
Cameroon ■ *Africa* 6°0N 12°30E **96** C2
Cameroun, Mt. *Cameroon* 4°13N 9°10E **96** D1
Cametá *Brazil* 2°12S 49°30W **120** C5
Camocim *Brazil* 2°55S 40°50W **120** C5
Campana, I. *Chile* 48°20S 75°20W **121** G2
Campánia □ *Italy* 41°0N 14°30E **68** D6
Campbell I. *Pac. Oc.* 52°30S 169°0E **102** N8
Campbell River *Canada* 50°5N 125°20W **108** D7
Campbellsville *U.S.A.* 37°21N 85°20W **112** G5
Campbellton *Canada* 47°57N 66°43W **109** E13
Campbeltown *U.K.* 55°26N 5°36W **24** D4
Campeche *Mexico* 19°51N 90°32W **114** D6
Campeche, Golfo de *Mexico* 19°30N 93°0W **114** D6
Campina Grande *Brazil* 7°20S 35°47W **120** C6
Campinas *Brazil* 22°50S 47°0W **122** D1
Campo Belo *Brazil* 20°52S 45°16W **122** D1
Campo Grande *Brazil* 20°25S 54°40W **120** E4
Campobasso *Italy* 41°34N 14°39E **68** D6
Campos *Brazil* 21°50S 41°20W **122** D2
Campos Belos *Brazil* 13°10S 47°3W **122** B1
Camrose *Canada* 53°0N 112°50W **108** D8
Can Tho *Vietnam* 10°2N 105°46E **82** B3
Canada ■ *N. Amer.* 60°0N 100°0W **108** D10
Canadian → *U.S.A.* 35°28N 95°3W **111** C7
Canadian Shield *Canada* 53°0N 75°0W **104** D12
Çanakkale *Turkey* 40°8N 26°24E **71** F4
Canandaigua *U.S.A.* 42°54N 77°17W **112** D9
Cananea *Mexico* 31°0N 110°18W **114** A2
Canaries *St. Lucia* 13°55N 61°4W **114** b
Canary Is. *Atl. Oc.* 28°30N 16°0W **94** C2
Canaveral, C. *U.S.A.* 28°27N 80°32W **111** E10
Canavieiras *Brazil* 15°39S 39°0W **122** C3
Canberra *Australia* 35°15S 149°8E **98** H8
Cancún *Mexico* 21°8N 86°44W **114** C7
Cangzhou *China* 38°19N 116°52E **79** D12
Caniapiscau → *Canada* 56°40N 69°30W **109** D13
Caniapiscau, L. *Canada* 54°10N 69°55W **109** D13
Çankırı *Turkey* 40°40N 33°37E **71** F5
Canna *U.K.* 57°3N 6°33W **22** H4
Canna, Sd. of *U.K.* 57°1N 6°30W **22** H5
Cannanore *India* 11°53N 75°27E **84** P9
Cannes *France* 43°32N 7°1E **66** E7
Cannington *U.K.* 51°9N 3°4W **30** D2
Cannock *U.K.* 52°41N 2°1W **27** G4
Cannock Chase *U.K.* 52°44N 2°4W **27** G4
Canoas *Brazil* 29°56S 51°11W **121** E4
Cañon City *U.S.A.* 38°27N 105°14W **110** C5
Canonbie *U.K.* 55°5N 2°58W **25** D10
Canora *Canada* 51°40N 102°30W **108** D9
Canso *Canada* 45°20N 61°0W **113** C17
Cantabria □ *Spain* 43°10N 4°0W **67** A4
Cantábrica, Cordillera *Spain* 43°0N 5°10W **67** A3
Canterbury *U.K.* 51°16N 1°6E **31** D11
Canton = Guangzhou *China* 23°6N 113°13E **79** G11
Canton *Ill., U.S.A.* 40°33N 90°2W **112** E2
Canton *N.Y., U.S.A.* 44°36N 75°10W **113** C10
Canton *Ohio, U.S.A.* 40°48N 81°23W **112** E7
Canvey *U.K.* 51°31N 0°37E **31** C10
Cap-de-la-Madeleine
  Canada 46°22N 72°31W **113** B11
Cap-Haïtien *Haiti* 19°40N 72°20W **115** D10
Cap Pt. *St. Lucia* 14°7N 60°57W **114** b
Cape Breton I. *Canada* 46°0N 60°30W **113** C17
Cape Charles *U.S.A.* 37°16N 76°1W **113** G10
Cape Coast *Ghana* 5°5N 1°15W **94** G5
Cape Coral *U.S.A.* 26°33N 81°57W **111** E10
Cape Fear → *U.S.A.* 33°53N 78°1W **111** D11
Cape Girardeau *U.S.A.* 37°19N 89°32W **112** G3
Cape May *U.S.A.* 38°56N 74°56W **113** F10
Cape Town *S. Africa* 33°55S 18°22E **97** L3
Cape Verde Is. ■ *Atl. Oc.* 16°0N 24°0W **91** E1
Cape York Peninsula
  Australia 12°0S 142°30E **98** C7
Capela *Brazil* 10°30S 37°0W **122** B3
Capreol *Canada* 46°43N 80°56W **112** B7
Capri *Italy* 40°33N 14°14E **68** D6

Caprivi Strip *Namibia* 18°0S 23°0E **97** H4
Caquetá → *Colombia* 1°15S 69°15W **120** C3
Caracas *Venezuela* 10°30N 66°55W **120** A3
Caracol *Brazil* 9°15S 43°22W **122** A2
Carangola *Brazil* 20°44S 42°5W **122** D2
Caratasca, L. de *Honduras* 15°20N 83°40W **115** D8
Caratinga *Brazil* 19°50S 42°10W **122** C2
Caravelas *Brazil* 17°45S 39°15W **122** C3
Carbón, L. del *Argentina* 49°35S 68°21W **121** G3
Carbondale *Ill., U.S.A.* 37°44N 89°13W **112** G3
Carbondale *Pa., U.S.A.* 41°35N 75°30W **113** E10
Carbonear *Canada* 47°42N 53°13W **109** E14
Carcassonne *France* 43°13N 2°20E **66** E5
Carcross *Canada* 60°13N 134°45W **108** C6
Cardamon Hills *India* 9°30N 77°15E **84** Q10
Cárdenas *Cuba* 23°0N 81°30W **115** C8
Cardiff *U.K.* 51°29N 3°10W **29** E7
Cardigan *U.K.* 52°5N 4°40W **28** C4
Cardigan B. *U.K.* 52°30N 4°30W **28** B4
Cardington *U.K.* 52°6N 0°25W **31** B8
Cardston *Canada* 49°15N 113°20W **108** E8
Cariacica *Brazil* 20°16S 40°25W **122** D2
Caribbean Sea *W. Indies* 15°0N 75°0W **115** E10
Cariboo Mts. *Canada* 53°0N 121°0W **108** D7
Caribou *U.S.A.* 46°52N 68°1W **113** B13
Caribou Mts. *Canada* 59°12N 115°40W **108** D8
Carinhanha *Brazil* 14°15S 44°46W **122** B2
Carinhanha → *Brazil* 14°20S 43°47W **122** B2
Carinthia = Kärnten □
  Austria 46°52N 13°30E **64** E8
Carisbrooke *U.K.* 50°41N 1°19W **30** E6
Cark *U.K.* 54°11N 2°58W **26** D3
Carleton Place *Canada* 45°8N 76°9W **113** C9
Carleton Rode *U.K.* 52°30N 1°7E **31** A11
Carlingford L. *U.K.* 54°3N 6°9W **19** C9
Carlinville *U.S.A.* 39°17N 89°53W **112** F3
Carlisle *U.K.* 54°54N 2°56W **26** C3
Carlisle *U.S.A.* 40°12N 77°12W **112** E9
Carlisle B. *Barbados* 13°5N 59°37W **114** c
Carlops *U.K.* 55°47N 3°20W **25** C9
Carlow *Ireland* 52°50N 6°56W **21** C9
Carlow □ *Ireland* 52°43N 6°50W **21** C9
Carlsbad *U.S.A.* 32°25N 104°14W **110** D6
Carlton *U.K.* 52°59N 1°7W **27** G6
Carlton Colville *U.K.* 52°27N 1°43E **31** B12
Carlton Miniott *U.K.* 54°12N 1°22W **26** D6
Carluke *U.K.* 55°45N 3°50W **25** C8
Carmacks *Canada* 62°5N 136°16W **108** C6
Carmarthen *U.K.* 51°52N 4°19W **28** D5
Carmarthen B. *U.K.* 51°40N 4°30W **28** D4
Carmarthenshire □ *U.K.* 51°55N 4°13W **28** D5
Carmaux *France* 44°3N 2°10E **66** D5
Carmi *U.S.A.* 38°5N 88°10W **112** F3
Carn Ban *U.K.* 57°7N 4°15W **23** H9
Carn Eige *U.K.* 57°17N 5°8W **22** H7
Carnarvon *Australia* 24°51S 113°42E **98** E1
Carnarvon *S. Africa* 30°56S 22°8E **97** L4
Carndonagh *Ireland* 55°16N 7°15W **19** A7
Carnegie, L. *Australia* 26°5S 122°30E **98** F3
Carnforth *U.K.* 54°7N 2°45W **26** D3
Carno *U.K.* 52°34N 3°30W **28** B6
Carnoustie *U.K.* 56°30N 2°42W **25** A10
Carnsore Pt. *Ireland* 52°10N 6°22W **21** D10
Caro *U.S.A.* 43°29N 83°24W **112** D6
Caroline I. *Kiribati* 9°58S 150°13W **103** H12
Caroline Is. *Micronesia* 8°0N 150°0E **102** G6
Carondelet Reef *Kiribati* 5°33S 173°50E **99** B16
Caroní → *Venezuela* 8°21N 62°43W **120** B3
Carpathians *Europe* 49°30N 21°0E **65** D11
Carpentaria, G. of *Australia* 14°0S 139°0E **98** C6
Carpentras *France* 44°3N 5°2E **66** D6
Carpi *Italy* 44°47N 10°53E **68** B4
Carrara *Italy* 44°5N 10°6E **68** B4
Carrauntoohill *Ireland* 52°0N 9°45W **20** E3
Carrick-on-Shannon *Ireland* 53°57N 8°7W **18** D6
Carrick-on-Suir *Ireland* 52°21N 7°24W **21** D8
Carrickfergus *U.K.* 54°43N 5°49W **19** B10
Carrickmacross *Ireland* 53°59N 6°43W **19** D8
Carrigaline *Ireland* 51°48N 8°23W **20** E6
Carrollton *U.S.A.* 39°18N 90°24W **112** F2
Carron → *U.K.* 57°53N 4°22W **23** H9
Carron, L. *U.K.* 57°22N 5°35W **22** H6
Carson City *U.S.A.* 39°10N 119°46W **110** C3
Carson Sink *U.S.A.* 39°50N 118°25W **110** C3
Cartagena *Colombia* 10°25N 75°33W **120** A2
Cartagena *Spain* 37°38N 0°59W **67** D5
Cartago *Colombia* 4°45N 75°55W **120** B2
Carthage *Tunisia* 36°52N 10°20E **95** A8
Cartmel *U.K.* 54°12N 2°57W **26** D3
Cartwright *Canada* 53°41N 56°58W **109** D14
Caruaru *Brazil* 8°15S 35°55W **122** A3
Carúpano *Venezuela* 10°39N 63°15W **120** A3
Cas-gwent = Chepstow *U.K.* 51°38N 2°41W **28** D8
Casa Grande *U.S.A.* 32°53N 111°45W **110** D4
Casa Nova *Brazil* 9°25S 41°5W **122** A2
Casablanca *Morocco* 33°36N 7°36W **94** B4
Cascade Ra. *U.S.A.* 47°0N 121°30W **110** A2
Cascavel *Ceará, Brazil* 4°7S 38°14W **120** C6
Cascavel *Paraná, Brazil* 24°57S 53°28W **121** E4
Caserta *Italy* 41°4N 14°20E **68** D6
Cashel *Ireland* 52°30N 7°53W **20** D7
Casiquiare → *Venezuela* 2°1N 67°7W **120** B3
Casnewydd = Newport *U.K.* 51°35N 3°0W **29** D8
Casper *U.S.A.* 42°51N 106°19W **110** B5
Caspian Depression *Eurasia* 47°0N 48°0E **71** E8
Caspian Sea *Eurasia* 43°0N 50°0E **71** F9
Cassiar Mts. *Canada* 59°30N 130°30W **108** D6
Castell-Nedd = Neath *U.K.* 51°39N 3°48W **28** D6
Castellammare di Stábia *Italy* 40°42N 14°29E **68** D6
Castelló de la Plana *Spain* 39°58N 0°3W **67** C5
Castelsarrasin *France* 44°2N 1°7E **66** E4
Castilla-La Mancha □ *Spain* 39°30N 3°30W **67** C4
Castilla y León □ *Spain* 42°0N 5°0W **67** B3
Castle Acre *U.K.* 52°42N 0°42E **31** A10
Castle Cary *U.K.* 51°6N 2°31W **30** D5
Castle Donington *U.K.* 52°51N 1°20W **27** G6
Castle Douglas *U.K.* 54°56N 3°56W **25** E8
Castlebar *Ireland* 53°52N 9°18W **18** D3
Castlebay *U.K.* 56°57N 7°31W **22** J2
Castleblayney *Ireland* 54°7N 6°44W **19** C8
Castlederg *U.K.* 54°42N 7°36W **18** B6

Castleford *U.K.* 53°43N 1°21W **27** E6
Castlemaine Harbour *Ireland* 52°8N 9°50W **20** D3
Castlepollard *Ireland* 53°41N 7°19W **18** D7
Castlerea *Ireland* 53°46N 8°29W **18** D5
Castleside *U.K.* 54°50N 1°52W **26** C5
Castleton *Derby., U.K.* 53°22N 1°46W **27** F5
Castleton *N. Yorks., U.K.* 54°28N 0°57W **26** D7
Castletown *I. of Man* 54°5N 4°38W **19** C12
Castletown Bearhaven *Ireland* 51°39N 9°55W **20** E3
Castres *France* 43°37N 2°13E **66** E5
Castries *St. Lucia* 14°2N 60°58W **114** b
Castro *Chile* 42°30S 73°50W **121** G2
Castro Alves *Brazil* 12°46S 39°33W **122** B3
Cat I. *Bahamas* 24°30N 75°30W **115** C9
Cataguases *Brazil* 21°23S 42°39W **122** D2
Catalão *Brazil* 18°10S 47°57W **122** C1
Cataluña □ *Spain* 41°40N 1°15E **67** B6
Catamarca *Argentina* 28°30S 65°50W **121** E3
Catanduanes *Phil.* 13°50N 124°20E **83** B6
Catanduva *Brazil* 21°5S 48°58W **122** D1
Catánia *Italy* 37°30N 15°6E **68** F6
Catanzaro *Italy* 38°54N 16°35E **68** E7
Catcleugh *U.K.* 55°20N 2°24W **26** B4
Caterham *U.K.* 51°15N 0°4W **31** D8
Catoche, C. *Mexico* 21°35N 87°5W **114** C7
Caton *U.K.* 54°5N 2°42W **26** D3
Catsfield *U.K.* 50°54N 0°28E **31** E9
Catskill *U.S.A.* 42°14N 73°52W **113** D11
Catskill Mts. *U.S.A.* 42°10N 74°25W **113** D10
Catterick *U.K.* 54°23N 1°37W **26** D5
Catterick Camp *U.K.* 54°22N 1°42W **26** D5
Catton *U.K.* 54°55N 2°15W **26** C4
Cauca → *Colombia* 8°54N 74°28W **120** B2
Caucaia *Brazil* 3°40S 38°35W **120** C6
Caucasus Mountains *Eurasia* 42°50N 44°0E **71** F7
Caulkerbush *U.K.* 54°54N 3°41W **25** E9
Caura → *Venezuela* 7°38N 64°53W **120** B3
Cauvery → *India* 11°9N 78°52E **84** P11
Cavan *Ireland* 54°0N 7°22W **18** D7
Cavan □ *Ireland* 54°1N 7°16W **19** C7
Caviana, I. *Brazil* 0°10N 50°10W **120** B4
Cawood *U.K.* 53°50N 1°8W **27** E6
Cawston *U.K.* 52°47N 1°9E **31** A11
Caxias *Brazil* 4°55S 43°20W **120** C5
Caxias do Sul *Brazil* 29°10S 51°10W **121** E4
Cayenne *Fr. Guiana* 5°5N 52°18W **120** B4
Cayman Is. ☑ *W. Indies* 19°40N 80°30W **115** D8
Cayman Trench *Caribbean* 17°0N 83°0W **115** D8
Cayuga L. *U.S.A.* 42°41N 76°41W **112** D9
Ceará = Fortaleza *Brazil* 3°45S 38°35W **120** C6
Ceará □ *Brazil* 5°0S 40°0W **120** C6
Cebu *Phil.* 10°18N 123°54E **83** B6
Cedar → *U.S.A.* 37°41N 113°4W **110** C4
Cedar L. *Canada* 53°10N 100°0W **108** D10
Cedar Rapids *U.S.A.* 41°59N 91°40W **111** B8
Cefalù *Italy* 38°2N 14°1E **68** E6
Cegléd *Hungary* 47°11N 19°47E **65** E10
Celaya *Mexico* 20°31N 100°37W **114** C4
Celebes Sea *Indonesia* 3°0N 123°0E **83** D6
Celina *U.S.A.* 40°33N 84°35W **112** E5
Cellar Hd. *U.K.* 58°25N 6°11W **22** F5
Celtic Sea *Atl. Oc.* 50°9N 9°34W **62** F2
Cemaes *U.K.* 53°24N 4°27W **28** A5
Central, Cordillera *Colombia* 5°0N 75°0W **117** C3
Central African Rep. ■ *Africa* 7°0N 20°0E **96** C4
Central America *America* 12°0N 85°0W **104** H11
Central Bedfordshire □ *U.K.* 52°5N 0°20W **31** B8
Central Makran Range
  Pakistan 26°30N 64°15E **84** F4
Central Russian Uplands
  Europe 54°0N 36°0E **56** E13
Central Siberian Plateau
  Russia 65°0N 105°0E **72** B12
Centralia *Ill., U.S.A.* 38°32N 89°8W **112** F3
Centralia *Wash., U.S.A.* 46°43N 122°58W **110** A2
Cephalonia = Kefalonia
  Greece 38°15N 20°30E **69** E9
Ceredigion □ *U.K.* 52°16N 4°15W **28** C5
Cerignola *Italy* 41°17N 15°53E **68** D6
Cerne Abbas *U.K.* 50°49N 2°29W **30** E4
Cerrigydrudion *U.K.* 53°1N 3°35W **28** A6
Cerro de Pasco *Peru* 10°45S 76°10W **120** D2
Cesena *Italy* 44°8N 12°15E **68** B5
České Budějovice *Czech Rep.* 48°55N 14°25E **64** D8
Çeşme *Turkey* 38°20N 26°23E **71** G4
Ceuta *N. Afr.* 35°52N 5°18W **67** E3
Ceve-i-Ra *Fiji* 21°46S 174°31E **99** E13
Cévennes *France* 44°10N 3°50E **66** D5
Chacewater *U.K.* 50°15N 5°11W **29** G3
Chachapoyas *Peru* 6°15S 77°50W **120** C2
Chaco Austral *S. Amer.* 27°0S 61°30W **121** E3
Chaco Boreal *S. Amer.* 22°0S 60°0W **121** E4
Chaco Central *S. Amer.* 24°0S 61°0W **121** E3
Chad ■ *Africa* 15°0N 17°15E **95** F8
Chad, L. *Chad* 13°30N 14°30E **95** F8
Chadron *U.S.A.* 42°50N 103°0W **110** B6
Chagford *U.K.* 50°40N 3°50W **29** F6
Chaghcharān *Afghan.* 34°31N 65°15E **87** C11
Chagos Arch. ☑ *Ind. Oc.* 6°0S 72°0E **53** E13
Chāh Gay Hills *Afghan.* 29°30N 64°0E **87** D10
Chakradharpur *India* 22°45N 85°40E **85** H14
Chaleur B. *Canada* 47°55N 65°30W **113** B15
Chalisgaon *India* 20°30N 75°10E **84** J9
Challenger Deep *Pac. Oc.* 11°30N 142°0E **102** F6
Chalon-sur-Saône *France* 46°48N 4°50E **66** C6
Châlons-en-Champagne
  France 48°58N 4°20E **66** B6
Chambal → *India* 26°29N 79°15E **84** F11
Chambersburg *U.S.A.* 39°56N 77°40W **112** F9
Chambéry *France* 45°34N 5°55E **66** D6
Chamonix-Mont Blanc *France* 45°55N 6°51E **66** D7
Champagne *France* 48°40N 4°20E **66** B6
Champaign *U.S.A.* 40°7N 88°15W **112** E3
Champlain, L. *U.S.A.* 44°40N 73°20W **113** C11
Chañaral *Chile* 26°23S 70°40W **121** E2
Chandigarh *India* 30°43N 76°47E **84** D10
Chandler's Ford *U.K.* 50°59N 1°22W **30** E6
Chandpur *Bangla.* 23°8N 90°45E **85** H17
Chandrapur *India* 19°57N 79°25E **84** K11
Changbai Shan *China* 42°20N 129°0E **79** C14
Changchun *China* 43°57N 125°17E **79** C14

Changde *China* 29°4N 111°35E **79** F11
Changhua *Taiwan* 24°2N 120°30E **79** G13
Changji *China* 44°1N 87°19E **78** C6
Changsha *China* 28°12N 113°0E **79** F11
Changzhi *China* 36°10N 113°6E **79** D11
Changzhou *China* 31°47N 119°58E **79** E12
Chania *Greece* 35°30N 24°4E **69** G11
Channel Is. *U.K.* 49°19N 2°24W **29** J9
Channel Is. *U.S.A.* 33°40N 119°15W **110** D2
Channel-Port aux Basques
  Canada 47°30N 59°9W **109** E14
Chantrey Inlet *Canada* 67°48N 96°20W **108** C10
Chaoyang *China* 41°35N 120°22W **79** C13
Chaozhou *China* 23°42N 116°32E **79** G12
Chapala, L. de *Mexico* 20°15N 103°0W **114** C4
Chapayevsk *Russia* 53°0N 49°40E **70** D8
Chapel en le Frith *U.K.* 53°20N 1°54W **27** F5
Chapel St. Leonards *U.K.* 53°13N 0°20E **27** F9
Chapleau *Canada* 47°50N 83°24W **109** E11
Charaña *Bolivia* 17°30S 69°25W **120** D3
Chard *U.K.* 50°52N 2°58W **30** E3
Chari → *Chad* 12°58N 14°31E **95** F8
Chärïkär *Afghan.* 35°0N 69°10E **87** C12
Charing *U.K.* 51°12N 0°49E **31** D10
Charlbury *U.K.* 51°53N 1°28W **30** C6
Charleroi *Belgium* 50°24N 4°27E **64** C3
Charles, C. *U.S.A.* 37°7N 75°58W **113** G10
Charles City *U.S.A.* 43°4N 92°41W **111** B8
Charleston *Ill., U.S.A.* 39°30N 88°10W **112** F3
Charleston *Mo., U.S.A.* 36°55N 89°21W **112** G3
Charleston *S.C., U.S.A.* 32°46N 79°56W **111** D11
Charleston *W. Va., U.S.A.* 38°21N 81°38W **112** F7
Charlestown *Ireland* 53°58N 8°48W **18** D4
Charlestown of Aberlour
  U.K. 57°28N 3°14W **23** H11
Charleville *Australia* 26°24S 146°15E **98** F8
Charleville *Ireland* 52°21N 8°40W **20** D5
Charleville-Mézières *France* 49°44N 4°40E **66** B6
Charlevoix *U.S.A.* 45°19N 85°16W **112** C5
Charlotte *Mich., U.S.A.* 42°34N 84°50W **112** D5
Charlotte *N.C., U.S.A.* 35°13N 80°50W **111** C10
Charlotte Amalie
  U.S. Virgin Is. 18°21N 64°56W **115** D12
Charlotte Harbor *U.S.A.* 26°57N 82°4W **111** E10
Charlottesville *U.S.A.* 38°2N 78°30W **112** F8
Charlottetown *Canada* 46°14N 63°8W **113** B16
Charlton I. *Canada* 52°0N 79°20W **109** D12
Charlton Kings *U.K.* 51°53N 2°3W **30** C4
Charlwood *U.K.* 51°9N 0°13W **31** D8
Charminster *U.K.* 50°44N 2°28W **30** E4
Charmouth *U.K.* 50°44N 2°54W **30** E3
Charnwood Forest *U.K.* 52°44N 1°17W **27** G6
Charolles *France* 46°27N 4°16E **66** C6
Charters Towers *Australia* 20°5S 146°13E **98** E8
Chartham *U.K.* 51°14N 1°1E **31** D11
Chartres *France* 48°29N 1°30E **66** B4
Chascomús *Argentina* 35°30S 58°0W **121** F4
Châteaubriant *France* 47°43N 1°23E **66** C3
Châteaulin *France* 48°11N 4°8W **66** B1
Châteauroux *France* 46°50N 1°40E **66** C4
Châtellerault *France* 46°50N 0°30E **66** C4
Chatham *N.B., Canada* 47°2N 65°28W **109** E13
Chatham *Ont., Canada* 42°24N 82°11W **112** D6
Chatham *U.K.* 51°22N 0°32E **31** D10
Chatham Is. *Pac. Oc.* 44°0S 176°40W **99** J15
Chatsworth *U.K.* 53°13N 1°36W **27** F6
Chattahoochee → *U.S.A.* 30°54N 84°57W **104** F11
Chattanooga *U.S.A.* 35°3N 85°19W **111** C9
Chatteris *U.K.* 52°28N 0°2E **31** B9
Chatton *U.K.* 55°35N 2°0W **26** A5
Chaumont *France* 48°7N 5°8E **66** B6
Chaykovskiy *Russia* 56°47N 54°9E **70** C9
Cheadle *Gt. Man., U.K.* 53°23N 2°12W **27** F4
Cheadle *Staffs., U.K.* 52°59N 1°59W **27** G5
Cheb *Czech Rep.* 50°9N 12°28E **64** C7
Cheboksary *Russia* 56°8N 47°12E **70** C8
Cheboygan *U.S.A.* 45°39N 84°29W **112** C5
Chech, Erg *Africa* 25°0N 2°15W **94** D5
Chechenia □ *Russia* 43°30N 45°29E **71** F8
Chedabucto B. *Canada* 45°25N 61°8W **113** C17
Cheddar *U.K.* 51°17N 2°46W **30** D3
Cheddleton *U.K.* 53°4N 2°2W **27** F4
Cheduba I. *Burma* 18°45N 93°40E **85** K18
Chegutu *Zimbabwe* 18°10S 30°14E **97** H6
Chek Lap Kok *China* 22°18N 113°56E **79** a
Chelm *Poland* 51°8N 23°30E **65** C12
Chelmer → *U.K.* 51°44N 0°30E **31** C10
Chelmsford *U.K.* 51°44N 0°29E **31** C9
Cheltenham *U.K.* 51°54N 2°4W **30** C4
Chelyabinsk *Russia* 55°10N 61°24E **76** D7
Chelyuskin, C. *Russia* 77°30N 103°0E **77** B11
Chemnitz *Germany* 50°51N 12°54E **64** C7
Chenab → *Pakistan* 30°23N 71°2E **84** D7
Chengde *China* 40°59N 117°58E **79** C12
Chengdu *China* 30°38N 104°2E **78** E9
Chennai *India* 13°8N 80°19E **84** N12
Cheo, Eilean a' = Skye *U.K.* 57°15N 6°10W **22** H5
Chepstow *U.K.* 51°38N 2°41W **28** D8
Cher → *France* 47°21N 0°29E **66** C4
Cherbourg *France* 49°39N 1°40W **66** B3
Cheremkhovo *Russia* 53°8N 103°1E **78** A9
Cherepovets *Russia* 59°5N 37°55E **70** C6
Chergui, Chott ech *Algeria* 34°21N 0°25E **94** B6
Cheriton *U.K.* 51°3N 1°8W **30** D6
Cheriton Fitzpaine *U.K.* 50°51N 3°35W **29** F6
Cherkasy *Ukraine* 49°27N 32°4E **71** E5
Cherkessk *Russia* 44°15N 42°5E **71** F7
Chernivtsi *Ukraine* 51°28N 31°20E **70** D5
Chernobyl *Ukraine* 51°20N 30°15E **65** C16
Cherokee *U.S.A.* 42°45N 95°33W **111** B7
Cherrapunji *India* 25°17N 91°47E **85** G17
Cherski Ra. *Russia* 65°0N 143°0E **77** C15
Chertsey *U.K.* 51°23N 0°28W **31** D8
Chervonohrad *Ukraine* 50°25N 24°10E **71** D3
Cherwell → *U.K.* 51°44N 1°14W **30** C6
Chesapeake B. *U.S.A.* 38°0N 76°10W **112** F9
Chesha B. *Russia* 67°20N 47°0E **70** A8
Chesham *U.K.* 51°43N 0°36W **31** C7
Cheshire East □ *U.K.* 53°15N 2°15W **27** F4

Cheshire West and Chester □ U.K. 53°15N 2°40W 27 F3
Cheshunt U.K. 51°43N 0°1W 31 C8
Chesil Beach U.K. 50°37N 2°33W 30 E3
Chester U.K. 53°12N 2°53W 27 F3
Chester U.S.A. 39°51N 75°22W 113 F10
Chester-le-Street U.K. 54°51N 1°34W 26 C5
Chesterfield U.K. 53°15N 1°25W 27 F6
Chesterfield, Îs. N. Cal. 19°52S 158°15E 99 D10
Chesterfield Inlet Canada 63°30N 90°45W 108 C10
Chesuncook L. U.S.A. 46°0N 69°21W 113 B13
Chetumal Mexico 18°30N 88°20W 114 D7
Chetwynd Canada 55°45N 121°36W 108 D7
Cheviot, The U.K. 55°29N 2°9W 26 B4
Cheviot Hills U.K. 55°20N 2°30W 26 B3
Chew Bahir Ethiopia 4°40N 36°50E 89 G2
Chew Magna U.K. 51°22N 2°37W 30 D3
Cheyenne U.S.A. 41°8N 104°49W 110 B6
Cheyenne → U.S.A. 44°41N 101°18W 110 B6
Chhapra India 25°48N 84°44E 85 G14
Chhattisgarh □ India 22°0N 82°0E 85 J12
Chi → Thailand 15°11N 104°43E 83 A3
Chiai Taiwan 23°29N 120°25E 79 G13
Chiávari Italy 44°19N 9°19E 68 B3
Chiba Japan 35°30N 140°7E 81 F7
Chibougamau Canada 49°56N 74°24W 109 E12
Chibougamau, L. Canada 49°50N 74°20W 113 A10
Chic-Chocs, Mts. Canada 48°55N 66°0W 113 A14
Chicago U.S.A. 41°52N 87°38W 112 E4
Chichagof I. U.S.A. 57°30N 135°30W 108 D6
Chichester U.K. 50°50N 0°47W 31 E7
Chickasha U.S.A. 35°3N 97°58W 110 C7
Chiclayo Peru 6°42S 79°50W 120 C2
Chico U.S.A. 39°44N 121°50W 110 C2
Chico → Chubut, Argentina 44°0S 67°0W 121 G3
Chico → Santa Cruz, Argentina 50°0S 68°30W 121 G3
Chicopee U.S.A. 42°9N 72°37W 113 D11
Chicoutimi Canada 48°28N 71°5W 113 A12
Chiddingfold U.K. 51°7N 0°37W 31 D7
Chidley, C. Canada 60°23N 64°26W 109 C13
Chieti Italy 42°21N 14°10E 68 C6
Chifeng China 42°18N 118°58E 79 C12
Chihuahua Mexico 28°38N 106°5W 114 B3
Chilapa Mexico 17°36N 99°10W 114 D5
Chilaw Sri Lanka 7°30N 79°50E 84 R11
Childress U.S.A. 34°25N 100°13W 110 D6
Chile ■ S. Amer. 35°0S 72°0W 121 F2
Chilham U.K. 51°15N 0°59E 31 D10
Chililabombwe Zambia 12°18S 27°43E 97 G5
Chilka L. India 19°40N 85°25E 85 K14
Chillán Chile 36°40S 72°10W 121 F2
Chillicothe Ill., U.S.A. 40°55N 89°29W 112 E3
Chillicothe Ohio, U.S.A. 39°20N 82°59W 112 F6
Chilliwack Canada 49°10N 121°54W 108 E7
Chiloé, I. de Chile 42°30S 73°50W 121 G2
Chilpancingo Mexico 17°33N 99°30W 114 D5
Chiltern Hills U.K. 51°40N 0°53W 31 C7
Chilton U.S.A. 44°2N 88°10W 112 C3
Chilung Taiwan 25°3N 121°45E 79 F13
Chilwa, L. Malawi 15°15S 35°40E 97 H7
Chimborazo Ecuador 1°29S 78°55W 120 C2
Chimbote Peru 9°0S 78°35W 120 C2
Chimoio Mozam. 19°4S 33°30E 97 H6
Chin □ Burma 22°0N 93°0E 85 J18
Chin Hills Burma 22°30N 93°30E 85 H18
China ■ Asia 30°0N 110°0E 79 E11
China, Great Plain of Asia 35°0N 115°0E 72 E13
Chinandega Nic. 12°35N 87°12W 114 E7
Chincha Alta Peru 13°25S 76°7W 120 D2
Chindwin → Burma 21°26N 95°15E 85 J19
Chingola Zambia 12°31S 27°53E 97 G5
Chinhoyi Zimbabwe 17°20S 30°8E 97 H6
Chiniot Pakistan 31°45N 73°0E 84 D8
Chinmen Tao Taiwan 24°26N 118°22E 79 G12
Chinon France 47°10N 0°15E 66 C4
Chióggia Italy 45°13N 12°17E 68 B5
Chipata Zambia 13°38S 32°28E 97 G6
Chipman Canada 46°6N 65°53W 113 B15
Chippenham U.K. 51°27N 2°6W 30 D4
Chippewa Falls U.S.A. 44°56N 91°24W 112 C2
Chipping Campden U.K. 52°3N 1°45W 30 B5
Chipping Norton U.K. 51°56N 1°32W 30 C5
Chipping Ongar U.K. 51°42N 0°15E 31 C9
Chipping Sodbury U.K. 51°33N 2°23W 30 C4
Chiquinquira Colombia 5°37N 73°50W 120 B2
Chirbury U.K. 52°35N 3°4W 27 G2
Chirchiq Uzbekistan 41°29N 69°35E 87 A12
Chiredzi Zimbabwe 21°0S 31°38E 97 J6
Chirnside U.K. 55°48N 2°12W 25 C11
Chisasibi Canada 53°50N 79°0W 109 D12
Chiseldon U.K. 51°31N 1°44W 30 C5
Chistopol Russia 55°25N 50°38E 70 C9
Chita Russia 52°0N 113°35E 77 D12
Chitral Pakistan 35°50N 71°56E 84 B7
Chittagong Bangla. 22°19N 91°48E 85 H17
Chitungwiza Zimbabwe 18°0S 31°6E 97 H6
Choiseul St. Lucia 13°47N 61°3W 114 b
Choiseul Solomon Is. 7°0S 156°40E 99 B10
Chōkai-San Japan 39°6N 140°3E 81 D7
Cholet France 47°4N 0°52W 66 C3
Chollerton U.K. 55°4N 2°7W 26 B4
Cholsey U.K. 51°35N 1°8W 30 C6
Choluteca Honduras 13°20N 87°14W 114 E7
Chon Buri Thailand 13°21N 101°1E 82 B2
Ch'ŏngjin N. Korea 41°47N 129°50E 79 C14
Chongqing China 29°35N 106°25E 78 F10
Chongqing Shi □ China 30°0N 108°0E 78 F10
Chonos, Arch. de los Chile 45°0S 75°0W 121 G2
Chorley U.K. 53°39N 2°38W 27 E3
Chorzów Poland 50°18N 18°57E 65 C10
Choybalsan Mongolia 48°4N 114°30E 79 B11
Choyr Mongolia 46°24N 108°30E 79 B10
Christchurch N.Z. 43°33S 172°47E 99 J13
Christchurch U.K. 50°44N 1°47W 30 E5
Christmas I. Ind. Oc. 10°30S 105°40E 102 J2
Chubut → Argentina 43°20S 65°5W 121 G3
Chudleigh U.K. 50°36N 3°36W 29 F6
Chudskoye, L. Russia 58°13N 27°30E 70 C4
Chukchi Sea Russia 68°0N 175°0W 77 C19
Chukot Ra. Russia 68°0N 175°0E 77 C18
Chulmleigh U.K. 50°54N 3°51W 29 F6
Chuncheon S. Korea 37°58N 127°44E 79 D14
Chuquicamata Chile 22°15S 69°0W 121 E3
Chur Switz. 46°52N 9°32E 64 E5
Church Stretton U.K. 52°32N 2°48W 27 G3
Churchdown U.K. 51°52N 2°10W 30 C4
Churchill Canada 58°47N 94°11W 108 D10
Churchill → Man., Canada 58°47N 94°12W 108 D10
Churchill → Nfld. & L., Canada 53°19N 60°10W 109 D13
Churchill, C. Canada 58°46N 93°12W 108 D10
Churchill Falls Canada 53°36N 64°19W 109 D13
Churchill L. Canada 55°55N 108°20W 108 D9
Churchill Pk. Canada 58°10N 125°10W 108 D7
Churu India 28°20N 74°50E 84 E9
Chuska Mts. U.S.A. 36°15N 108°50W 110 C5
Chusovoy Russia 58°22N 57°50E 70 C10
Chuvashia □ Russia 55°30N 47°0E 70 C8
Chuxiong China 25°2N 101°28E 78 F9
Cicero U.S.A. 41°51N 87°44W 112 E4
Ciechanów Poland 52°52N 20°38E 65 B11
Ciego de Ávila Cuba 21°50N 78°50W 115 C9
Cienfuegos Cuba 22°10N 80°30W 115 C8
Cilo Dağı Turkey 37°28N 43°55E 71 G7
Cimarron → U.S.A. 36°10N 96°16W 111 C7
Cincinnati U.S.A. 39°9N 84°27W 112 F5
Cinderford U.K. 51°49N 2°30W 30 C3
Cinto, Mte. France 42°24N 8°54E 66 E8
Circle U.S.A. 65°50N 144°4W 108 C5
Circleville U.S.A. 39°36N 82°57W 112 F6
Cirebon Indonesia 6°45S 108°32E 82 F3
Cirencester U.K. 51°43N 1°57W 30 C5
Ciudad Acuña Mexico 29°18N 100°55W 114 B4
Ciudad Bolívar Venezuela 8°5N 63°36W 120 B3
Ciudad del Carmen Mexico 18°38N 91°50W 114 D6
Ciudad del Este Paraguay 25°30S 54°50W 121 E4
Ciudad Guayana Venezuela 8°0N 62°30W 120 B3
Ciudad Guzmán Mexico 19°41N 103°29W 114 D4
Ciudad Juárez Mexico 31°44N 106°29W 114 A3
Ciudad Madero Mexico 22°19N 97°50W 114 C5
Ciudad Mante Mexico 22°44N 98°59W 114 C5
Ciudad Obregón Mexico 27°29N 109°56W 114 B3
Ciudad Real Spain 38°59N 3°55W 67 C4
Ciudad Valles Mexico 21°59N 99°1W 114 C5
Ciudad Victoria Mexico 23°44N 99°8W 114 C5
Civitavécchia Italy 42°6N 11°48E 68 C4
Cizre Turkey 37°19N 42°10E 71 G7
Clackmannan U.K. 56°7N 3°45W 25 B8
Clacton-on-Sea U.K. 51°47N 1°11E 31 C11
Claire, L. Canada 58°35N 112°5W 108 D8
Clara Ireland 53°21N 7°37W 18 E6
Clare U.K. 52°4N 0°34E 31 B10
Clare □ Ireland 52°45N 9°0W 20 C4
Clare → Ireland 53°20N 9°2W 18 E3
Clare I. Ireland 53°47N 10°0W 18 D1
Claremont U.S.A. 43°23N 72°20W 113 D11
Clarion Fracture Zone Pac. Oc. 20°0N 120°0W 104 H7
Clark Fork → U.S.A. 48°9N 116°15W 110 A3
Clarksburg U.S.A. 39°17N 80°30W 112 F7
Clarksdale U.S.A. 34°12N 90°35W 111 D8
Clarksville U.S.A. 36°32N 87°21W 111 C9
Claverley U.K. 52°32N 2°18W 27 G4
Clay Cross U.K. 53°10N 1°25W 27 F6
Claydon U.K. 52°7N 1°8E 31 B11
Clear, C. Ireland 51°25N 9°32W 20 F3
Clear I. Ireland 51°26N 9°30W 20 F4
Clearfield U.S.A. 41°2N 78°27W 112 E8
Clearwater U.S.A. 27°59N 82°48W 111 E10
Cleator Moor U.K. 54°32N 3°30W 26 C2
Clee Hills U.K. 52°26N 2°35W 27 H3
Cleethorpes U.K. 53°33N 0°3W 27 E8
Cleeve Cloud U.K. 51°56N 2°0W 30 C5
Clent Hills U.K. 52°25N 2°4W 30 B4
Cleobury Mortimer U.K. 52°22N 2°28W 27 H4
Clermont-Ferrand France 45°46N 3°4E 66 D5
Clevedon U.K. 51°26N 2°52W 30 D3
Cleveland Miss., U.S.A. 33°45N 90°43W 111 D8
Cleveland Ohio, U.S.A. 41°29N 81°41W 112 E7
Cleveland Hills U.K. 54°25N 1°11W 26 D6
Clew B. Ireland 53°50N 9°49W 18 D2
Cley U.K. 52°57N 1°2E 31 A11
Clifden Ireland 53°29N 10°1W 18 E1
Cliffe U.K. 51°28N 0°31E 31 D10
Clifford U.K. 52°7N 3°6W 30 B2
Clinton Iowa, U.S.A. 41°51N 90°12W 112 E2
Clinton Okla., U.S.A. 35°31N 98°58W 110 C7
Clinton Colden L. Canada 63°58N 107°27W 108 C9
Clipperton, Î. Pac. Oc. 10°18N 109°13W 103 F17
Clipston U.K. 52°27N 0°58W 31 B7
Clitheroe U.K. 53°53N 2°22W 27 E4
Cloghaneely Ireland 55°8N 8°5W 18 A5
Clogher Hd. Ireland 53°48N 6°14W 19 D9
Cloghran Ireland 53°27N 6°14W 21 B10
Clonakilty Ireland 51°37N 8°53W 20 E5
Clonakilty B. Ireland 51°35N 8°51W 20 E5
Cloncurry → Australia 18°37S 140°40E 98 E7
Clondalkin Ireland 53°19N 6°25W 21 B10
Clones Ireland 54°11N 7°15W 19 C7
Clonmel Ireland 52°21N 7°42W 21 D7
Clontarf Ireland 53°22N 6°11W 21 B10
Cloughton U.K. 54°20N 0°26W 26 D8
Clovelly U.K. 51°0N 4°25W 29 F5
Clovis U.S.A. 34°24N 103°12W 110 D6
Clowne U.K. 53°16N 1°17W 27 F6
Cluj-Napoca Romania 46°47N 23°38E 65 E12
Clun Forest U.K. 52°27N 3°7W 27 H2
Clunbury U.K. 52°25N 2°55W 27 H3
Clwyd → U.K. 53°19N 3°31W 28 A6
Clyde → U.K. 55°55N 4°30W 24 C6
Clyde, Firth of U.K. 55°22N 5°1W 24 D5
Clyde River Canada 70°30N 68°30W 109 B13
Clydebank U.K. 55°54N 4°23W 24 C7
Clydesdale U.K. 55°43N 3°51W 25 C8
Coalbrookdale U.K. 52°39N 2°30W 27 G3
Coalisland U.K. 54°33N 6°42W 19 B8
Coalville U.K. 52°44N 1°23W 27 G6
Coast Mts. Canada 55°0N 129°20W 108 D7
Coast Ranges U.S.A. 39°0N 123°0W 110 B2
Coatbridge U.K. 55°52N 4°6W 24 C7
Coaticook Canada 45°10N 71°46W 113 C12
Coats I. Canada 62°30N 83°0W 109 C11
Coats Land Antarctica 77°0S 25°0W 55 D1
Coatzacoalcos Mexico 18°7N 94°25W 114 D6
Cobán Guatemala 15°30N 90°21W 114 D6
Cobar Australia 31°27S 145°48E 98 G8
Cobh Ireland 51°51N 8°17W 20 E6
Cobija Bolivia 11°0S 68°50W 120 D3
Cobourg Canada 43°58N 78°10W 112 D8
Cochabamba Bolivia 17°26S 66°10W 120 D3
Cochin India 9°58N 76°20E 84 Q10
Cochrane Canada 49°0N 81°0W 109 E11
Cockburn, Canal Chile 54°30S 72°0W 121 H2
Cockburn I. Canada 45°55N 83°22W 112 C6
Cockburn Town Bahamas 24°2N 74°31W 115 C10
Cockerham U.K. 53°58N 2°49W 27 E3
Cockermouth U.K. 54°40N 3°22W 26 C2
Cockfield U.K. 52°10N 0°48E 31 B10
Cockpit Country, The Jamaica 18°15N 77°45W 114 a
Coco → Cent. Amer. 15°0N 83°8W 115 E8
Cocos I. Pac. Oc. 5°25N 87°55W 114 F7
Cocos Is. Ind. Oc. 12°10S 96°55E 102 J1
Cod, C. U.S.A. 42°5N 70°10W 113 D12
Coddenham U.K. 52°9N 1°8E 31 B11
Codó Brazil 4°30S 43°55W 120 C5
Cody U.S.A. 44°32N 109°3W 110 B5
Coeur d'Alene U.S.A. 47°41N 116°46W 110 A3
Coggeshall U.K. 51°52N 0°42E 31 C10
Cognac France 45°41N 0°20W 66 D3
Coigach U.K. 57°59N 5°14W 22 G7
Coigeach, Rubha U.K. 58°6N 5°26W 22 F7
Coimbatore India 11°2N 76°59E 84 P10
Coimbra Portugal 40°15N 8°27W 67 B1
Colatina Brazil 19°32S 40°37W 122 C2
Colchester U.K. 51°54N 0°55E 31 C10
Cold Fell U.K. 54°53N 2°36W 26 C3
Coldstream U.K. 55°39N 2°15W 25 C11
Colebrook U.S.A. 44°54N 71°30W 113 C12
Colebrooke U.K. 50°47N 3°44W 29 F6
Coleford U.K. 51°47N 2°36W 30 C3
Coleraine U.K. 55°8N 6°41W 19 A8
Coleshill U.K. 52°30N 1°41W 27 G5
Colgrave Sd. U.K. 60°36N 0°58W 22 A16
Colima Mexico 19°14N 103°43W 114 D4
Colima, Nevado de Mexico 19°33N 103°38W 114 D4
Coll U.K. 56°39N 6°34W 24 J4
Collier Law U.K. 54°47N 1°59W 26 C5
Collin U.K. 55°4N 3°31W 25 D8
Collingbourne Kingston U.K. 51°18N 1°40W 30 D5
Collingham U.K. 53°8N 0°46W 27 F7
Collingwood Canada 44°29N 80°13W 112 C7
Collooney Ireland 54°11N 8°29W 18 C5
Colmar France 48°5N 7°20E 66 B7
Colne U.K. 53°51N 2°9W 27 E4
Colne → Bucks., U.K. 51°27N 0°32W 31 D7
Colne → Essex, U.K. 51°51N 0°58E 31 C10
Cologne Germany 50°56N 6°57E 64 C4
Colombia ■ S. Amer. 3°45N 73°0W 120 B2
Colombian Basin Caribbean 14°0N 76°0W 104 H12
Colombo Sri Lanka 6°56N 79°58E 84 R11
Colonsay U.K. 56°5N 6°12W 24 B3
Colorado □ U.S.A. 39°30N 105°30W 110 C5
Colorado → Argentina 39°50S 62°8W 121 F3
Colorado → N. Amer. 31°45N 114°40W 110 D4
Colorado → U.S.A. 28°36N 95°59W 111 E7
Colorado Plateau U.S.A. 37°0N 111°0W 110 C4
Colorado Springs U.S.A. 38°50N 104°49W 110 C6
Colsterworth U.K. 52°49N 0°37W 27 G7
Coltishall U.K. 52°44N 1°21E 31 A11
Columbia Mo., U.S.A. 38°57N 92°20W 111 C8
Columbia S.C., U.S.A. 34°0N 81°2W 111 D10
Columbia Tenn., U.S.A. 35°37N 87°2W 111 C9
Columbia → N. Amer. 46°15N 124°5W 110 A2
Columbia, C. Canada 83°6N 69°57W 104 A13
Columbia, District of □ U.S.A. 38°55N 77°0W 112 F9
Columbia Plateau U.S.A. 44°0N 117°30W 110 B3
Columbus Ga., U.S.A. 32°28N 84°59W 111 D10
Columbus Ind., U.S.A. 39°13N 85°55W 112 F5
Columbus Miss., U.S.A. 33°30N 88°25W 111 D9
Columbus Nebr., U.S.A. 41°26N 97°22W 111 B7
Columbus Ohio, U.S.A. 39°58N 83°0W 112 F6
Colville → U.S.A. 70°25N 150°30W 108 B4
Colwell U.K. 55°5N 2°4W 26 B4
Colwich U.K. 52°48N 1°58W 27 G5
Colwyn Bay U.K. 53°18N 3°44W 28 A6
Colyton U.K. 50°44N 3°5W 29 F7
Comayagua Honduras 14°25N 87°37W 114 E7
Combe Martin U.K. 51°12N 4°3W 29 E5
Comber U.K. 54°33N 5°45W 19 B10
Comeragh Mts. Ireland 52°18N 7°34W 21 D7
Comilla Bangla. 23°28N 91°10E 85 H17
Comitán Mexico 16°15N 92°8W 114 D6
Committee B. Canada 68°30N 86°30W 109 C11
Como Italy 45°47N 9°5E 68 B3
Como, Lago di Italy 46°0N 9°11E 68 B3
Comodoro Rivadavia Argentina 45°50S 67°40W 121 G3
Comoros ■ Ind. Oc. 12°10S 44°15E 91 H8
Compass Mt. S. Africa 31°45S 24°32E 90 K6
Compiègne France 49°24N 2°50E 66 B5
Conakry Guinea 9°29N 13°49W 94 G3
Conceição da Barra Brazil 18°35S 39°45W 122 C3
Concepción Chile 36°50S 73°0W 121 F2
Concepción Paraguay 23°22S 57°26W 121 E4
Concepción, Est. de Chile 50°30S 74°55W 121 H2
Concepción del Oro Mexico 24°38N 101°25W 114 C4
Concepción del Uruguay Argentina 32°35S 58°20W 121 F4
Conception, Pt. U.S.A. 34°27N 120°28W 110 D2
Conchos → Mexico 29°35N 104°25W 114 B4
Concord Calif., U.S.A. 37°59N 122°2W 110 C2
Concord N.H., U.S.A. 43°12N 71°32W 113 D12
Concordia Argentina 31°20S 58°2W 121 F4
Concordia U.S.A. 39°34N 97°40W 110 C7
Condeúba Brazil 14°52S 42°0W 122 B2
Condover U.K. 52°39N 2°44W 27 G3
Congleton U.K. 53°10N 2°13W 27 F4
Congo ■ Africa 1°0S 16°0E 96 E3
Congo → Africa 6°4S 12°24E 96 F2
Congo, Dem. Rep. of the ■ Africa 3°0S 23°0E 96 E4
Congo Basin Africa 0°10S 24°30E 96 E4
Congresbury U.K. 51°22N 2°48W 30 D3
Coningsby U.K. 53°7N 0°10W 27 F8
Conisbrough U.K. 53°29N 1°14W 27 F6
Coniston Canada 46°29N 80°51W 112 B7
Coniston U.K. 54°22N 3°5W 26 D2
Coniston Water U.K. 54°20N 3°5W 26 D2
Conn, L. Ireland 54°3N 9°15W 18 C3
Connah's Quay U.K. 53°13N 3°4W 28 A7
Connaught □ Ireland 53°43N 9°12W 18 D3
Conneaut U.S.A. 41°57N 80°34W 112 E7
Connecticut □ U.S.A. 41°30N 72°45W 113 E11
Connecticut → U.S.A. 41°16N 72°20W 113 E11
Connellsville U.S.A. 40°1N 79°35W 112 E8
Connemara Ireland 53°29N 9°45W 18 E2
Connemara △ Ireland 53°32N 9°52W 18 D2
Connersville U.S.A. 39°39N 85°8W 112 F5
Conselheiro Lafaiete Brazil 20°40S 43°48W 122 D2
Consett U.K. 54°51N 1°50W 26 C5
Constance, L. Europe 47°35N 9°25E 64 E5
Constanța Romania 44°14N 28°38E 65 F15
Constantine Algeria 36°25N 6°42E 94 A7
Constitución Chile 35°20S 72°30W 121 F2
Contagem Brazil 19°56S 44°3W 122 C2
Contas → Brazil 14°17S 39°1W 122 B3
Contwoyto L. Canada 65°42N 110°50W 108 C8
Conway Ark., U.S.A. 35°5N 92°26W 111 C8
Conway N.H., U.S.A. 43°59N 71°7W 113 D12
Conwy U.K. 53°17N 3°50W 28 A6
Conwy □ U.K. 53°10N 3°44W 28 A6
Conwy → U.K. 53°17N 3°50W 28 A6
Coober Pedy Australia 29°1S 134°43E 98 F6
Cook Inlet U.S.A. 60°0N 152°0W 108 D4
Cook Is. ☒ Pac. Oc. 17°0S 160°0W 103 J12
Cook Strait N.Z. 41°15S 174°29E 99 J13
Cookstown U.K. 54°38N 6°45W 19 B8
Cooktown Australia 15°30S 145°16E 98 D8
Coondapoor India 13°42N 74°40E 84 N9
Coos Bay U.S.A. 43°22N 124°13W 110 B2
Cootehill Ireland 54°4N 7°5W 19 C7
Copenhagen Denmark 55°40N 12°26E 63 F6
Copiapó Chile 27°30S 70°20W 121 E2
Copper Harbor U.S.A. 47°28N 87°53W 112 B4
Coppermine → Canada 67°49N 116°4W 108 C8
Coquet → U.K. 55°20N 1°32W 26 B5
Coquet I. U.K. 55°20N 1°36W 26 B5
Coquimbo Chile 30°0S 71°20W 121 E2
Coracora Peru 15°5S 73°45W 120 D2
Coral Harbour Canada 64°8N 83°10W 109 C11
Coral Sea Pac. Oc. 15°0S 150°0E 98 C9
Corbin U.S.A. 36°57N 84°6W 112 G5
Corbridge U.K. 54°58N 2°0W 26 C5
Corby U.K. 52°30N 0°41W 31 A7
Corby Glen U.K. 52°49N 0°30W 27 G7
Cordele U.S.A. 31°58N 83°47W 111 D10
Córdoba Argentina 31°20S 64°10W 121 F3
Córdoba Mexico 18°53N 96°56W 114 D5
Córdoba Spain 37°50N 4°50W 67 D3
Córdoba, Sierra de Argentina 31°10S 64°25W 121 F3
Cordova U.S.A. 60°33N 145°45W 108 C5
Corfe Castle U.K. 50°38N 2°3W 30 E4
Corfe Mullen U.K. 50°46N 2°1W 30 E4
Corfu Greece 39°38N 19°50E 69 E8
Corinth Greece 37°56N 22°55E 69 F10
Corinth U.S.A. 34°56N 88°31W 111 D9
Corinto Brazil 18°20S 44°30W 122 C2
Cork Ireland 51°54N 8°29W 20 E6
Cork □ Ireland 51°57N 8°40W 20 E5
Cork Harbour Ireland 51°47N 8°16W 20 E6
Corner Brook Canada 48°57N 57°58W 109 E14
Corning U.S.A. 42°9N 77°3W 112 D9
Cornwall Canada 45°2N 74°44W 113 C10
Cornwall □ U.K. 50°26N 4°40W 29 G4
Cornwall, C. U.K. 50°8N 5°43W 29 G2
Cornwall I. Canada 77°37N 94°38W 109 B10
Cornwallis I. Canada 75°8N 95°0W 109 B10
Coro Venezuela 11°25N 69°41W 120 A3
Corocoro Bolivia 17°15S 68°28W 120 D3
Coromandel Coast India 12°30N 81°0E 84 N12
Coronation Gulf Canada 68°25N 110°0W 108 B8
Coronel Chile 37°0S 73°10W 121 F2
Coronel Fabriciano Brazil 19°31S 42°38W 122 C2
Coronel Pringles Argentina 38°0S 61°30W 121 F3
Coronel Suárez Argentina 37°30S 61°52W 121 F3
Coropuna, Nevado Peru 15°30S 72°41W 120 D2
Corpus Christi U.S.A. 27°47N 97°24W 110 E7
Corraun Pen. Ireland 53°54N 9°54W 18 D2
Corrib, L. Ireland 53°27N 9°16W 20 B4
Corrientes Argentina 27°30S 58°45W 121 E4
Corrientes, C. Colombia 5°30N 77°34W 120 B2
Corrientes, C. Mexico 20°25N 105°42W 114 C3
Corringham U.K. 53°25N 0°41W 27 F7
Corry U.S.A. 41°55N 79°39W 112 E8
Corse, C. France 43°1N 9°25E 66 E8
Corsham U.K. 51°27N 2°10W 30 D4
Corsica □ France 42°0N 9°0E 66 F8
Corsicana U.S.A. 32°6N 96°28W 111 D7
Corsley U.K. 51°13N 2°14W 30 D4
Corte France 42°19N 9°11E 66 E8
Cortez U.S.A. 37°21N 108°35W 110 C5
Cortland U.S.A. 42°36N 76°11W 113 D9
Corton U.K. 52°31N 1°45E 31 A12
Çorum Turkey 40°30N 34°57E 71 F5
Corumbá Brazil 19°0S 57°30W 120 D4
Corunna = La Coruña Spain 43°20N 8°25W 67 A1
Corvallis U.S.A. 44°34N 123°16W 110 B2
Corve → U.K. 52°22N 2°43W 27 H3
Coseley U.K. 52°33N 2°5W 27 G4
Cosenza Italy 39°18N 16°15E 68 E7
Cosham U.K. 50°51N 1°2W 30 E6
Coshocton U.S.A. 40°16N 81°51W 112 E7
Costa Blanca Spain 38°25N 0°10W 67 C5
Costa Brava Spain 41°30N 3°0E 67 B7
Costa Cálida Spain 37°30N 1°30W 67 D5
Costa Daurada Spain 41°12N 1°15E 67 B6
Costa de la Luz Spain 36°15N 5°58W 67 D2
Costa del Azahar Spain 39°39N 0°13W 67 B6
Costa del Sol Spain 36°30N 4°30W 67 D3
Costa Rica ■ Cent. Amer. 10°0N 84°0W 115 F8
Costa Verde Spain 43°22N 4°14W 67 A3
Costessey U.K. 52°40N 1°13E 31 A11
Cotabato Phil. 7°14N 124°15E 83 C6
Côte d'Azur France 43°25N 7°10E 66 E7
Côte-d'Ivoire = Ivory Coast ■ Africa 7°30N 5°0W 94 G4
Coteau du Missouri U.S.A. 47°0N 100°0W 110 A6
Cotentin France 49°15N 1°30W 66 B3
Cotherstone U.K. 54°35N 1°59W 26 C5
Cotonou Benin 6°20N 2°25E 94 G6
Cotopaxi Ecuador 0°40S 78°30W 120 C2
Cotswold Hills U.K. 51°42N 2°10W 30 C4
Cottbus Germany 51°45N 14°20E 64 C8
Cottenham U.K. 52°18N 0°9E 31 B9
Coudersport U.S.A. 41°46N 78°1W 112 E8
Council Bluffs U.S.A. 41°16N 95°52W 111 B7
Courantyne → S. Amer. 5°55N 57°5W 120 B4
Courtenay Canada 49°45N 125°0W 108 E7
Cove U.K. 56°0N 4°51W 24 B6
Coventry U.K. 52°25N 1°28W 30 B6
Cover → U.K. 54°17N 1°47W 26 D5
Coverack U.K. 50°1N 5°7W 29 G3
Covington U.S.A. 39°5N 84°30W 112 F5
Cowal U.K. 56°5N 5°8W 24 B5
Cowbridge U.K. 51°27N 3°27W 29 E7
Cowdenbeath U.K. 56°7N 3°21W 25 B9
Cowes U.K. 50°45N 1°18W 30 E6
Cowfold U.K. 50°59N 0°16W 31 E8
Cowpen U.K. 55°8N 1°32W 26 B5
Cox's Bazar Bangla. 21°26N 91°59E 85 J17
Cozumel, Isla Mexico 20°30N 86°40W 114 C7
Crab Hill Barbados 13°19N 59°38W 114 c
Cradock S. Africa 32°8S 25°36E 97 L5
Craig U.S.A. 40°31N 107°33W 110 B5
Craigavon U.K. 54°27N 6°23W 19 C9
Crail U.K. 56°16N 2°37W 25 B10
Craiova Romania 44°21N 23°48E 65 F12
Cramlington U.K. 55°6N 1°34W 26 B5
Cranborne U.K. 50°55N 1°54W 30 E5
Cranborne Chase U.K. 50°56N 2°6W 30 E4
Cranbrook Canada 49°30N 115°46W 108 E8
Cranbrook U.K. 51°6N 0°34E 31 D10
Crandon U.S.A. 45°34N 88°54W 112 C3
Crane, The Barbados 13°6N 59°27W 114 c
Cranleigh U.K. 51°8N 0°28W 31 D8
Cranwell U.K. 53°3N 0°27W 27 F8
Crateús Brazil 5°10S 40°39W 120 C5
Crato Brazil 7°10S 39°25W 120 C6
Craven Arms U.K. 52°26N 2°50W 27 H3
Crawfordsville U.S.A. 40°2N 86°54W 112 E4
Crawley U.K. 51°7N 0°11W 31 D8
Credenhill U.K. 52°5N 2°48W 30 B3
Crediton U.K. 50°47N 3°40W 29 F6
Cree → Canada 58°57N 105°47W 108 D9
Cree → U.K. 54°55N 4°25W 24 E7
Cree L. Canada 57°30N 106°30W 108 D9
Cremona Italy 45°7N 10°2E 68 B4
Cres Croatia 44°58N 14°25E 68 B6
Crete Greece 35°15N 25°0E 69 G11
Créteil France 48°47N 2°27E 66 B5
Creuse → France 47°0N 0°34E 66 C4
Crewe U.K. 53°6N 2°26W 27 F4
Crewkerne U.K. 50°53N 2°48W 30 E3
Crianlarich U.K. 56°24N 4°37W 24 B6
Criccieth U.K. 52°55N 4°13W 28 B5
Crick U.K. 52°22N 1°8W 30 B6
Crickhowell U.K. 51°52N 3°8W 28 D7
Cricklade U.K. 51°38N 1°50W 30 C5
Crieff U.K. 56°22N 3°50W 25 B8
Criffell U.K. 54°56N 3°39W 25 E9
Crimea □ Ukraine 45°30N 33°10E 71 E5
Crimean Pen. Ukraine 45°0N 34°0E 71 F5
Crişul Alb → Romania 46°42N 21°17E 65 E11
Crişul Negru → Romania 46°42N 21°16E 65 E11
Croagh Patrick Ireland 53°46N 9°40W 18 D2
Croaghan Ireland 53°59N 10°10W 18 D1
Croatia ■ Europe 45°20N 16°0E 68 B7
Croglin U.K. 54°50N 2°39W 26 C3
Crohy Hd. Ireland 54°55N 8°26W 18 B5
Croker, C. Australia 10°58S 132°35E 98 C5
Cromarty U.K. 57°40N 4°2W 23 G9
Cromarty Firth U.K. 57°40N 4°15W 23 G9
Cromdale, Hills of U.K. 57°20N 3°28W 23 H11
Cromer U.K. 52°56N 1°17E 31 A11
Crondall U.K. 51°14N 0°51W 31 D7
Crook U.K. 54°43N 1°45W 26 C5
Crooked I. Bahamas 22°50N 74°10W 115 C10
Crooklands U.K. 54°16N 2°42W 26 D3
Crosby Cumb., U.K. 54°45N 3°25W 26 C2
Crosby Mersey., U.K. 53°30N 3°3W 27 F2
Crosby Ravensworth U.K. 54°33N 2°35W 26 C3
Cross Fell U.K. 54°43N 2°28W 26 C4
Cross Sound U.S.A. 58°0N 135°0W 108 D6
Crosshaven Ireland 51°47N 8°17W 20 E6
Crossmaglen U.K. 54°5N 6°36W 19 C8
Crotone Italy 39°5N 17°8E 68 E7
Crouch → U.K. 51°37N 0°53E 31 C10
Crow Hd. Ireland 51°35N 10°9W 20 E2
Crow Sound U.K. 49°56N 6°16W 29 H1
Crowborough U.K. 51°3N 0°11E 31 D9
Crowland U.K. 52°41N 0°10W 27 G8
Crowle U.K. 53°36N 0°49W 27 E7
Crowsnest Pass Canada 49°40N 114°40W 108 E8
Croyde U.K. 51°7N 4°14W 29 E5
Croydon □ U.K. 51°22N 0°5W 31 D8
Crozet, Îs. Ind. Oc. 46°27S 52°0E 53 G12
Cruden Bay U.K. 57°25N 1°52W 23 H14
Crudgington U.K. 52°46N 2°32W 27 G3
Crummock Water U.K. 54°33N 3°18W 26 C2
Cruz das Almas Brazil 12°0S 39°6W 122 B3
Cruzeiro Brazil 22°33S 45°0W 122 D1
Cruzeiro do Sul Brazil 7°35S 72°35W 120 C2
Crystal Falls U.S.A. 46°5N 88°20W 112 B3
Cuando → Angola 17°30S 23°15E 97 H4
Cuango → Dem. Rep. of the Congo 3°14S 17°22E 96 E3
Cuanza → Angola 9°21S 13°9E 96 F2
Cuauhtémoc Mexico 28°25N 106°52W 114 B3
Cuba ■ W. Indies 22°0N 79°0W 115 C9
Cubango → Africa 18°50S 22°25E 97 H4
Cuckfield U.K. 51°1N 0°8W 31 D8
Cúcuta Colombia 7°54N 72°31W 120 B2
Cuddalore India 11°46N 79°45E 84 P11
Cuenca Ecuador 2°50S 79°0W 120 C2
Cuenca Spain 40°5N 2°10W 67 B4

Cuernavaca Mexico 18°55N 99°15W 114 D5
Cuiabá Brazil 15°30S 56°0W 120 D4
Cuihangcun China 22°27N 113°32E 79 a
Cuillin Hills U.K. 57°13N 6°15W 22 H5
Cuillin Sd. U.K. 57°4N 6°20W 22 H5
Cuito → Angola 18°1S 20°48E 97 H4
Culiacán Mexico 24°50N 107°23W 114 C3
Cullen U.K. 57°42N 2°49W 23 G12
Cullompton U.K. 50°51N 3°24W 29 F7
Culm → U.K. 50°46N 3°31W 29 F6
Culpeper U.S.A. 38°30N 78°0W 112 F9
Cumaná Venezuela 10°30N 64°5W 120 A3
Cumberland U.S.A. 39°39N 78°46W 112 F8
Cumberland → U.S.A. 37°9N 88°25W 111 C9
Cumberland Pen. Canada 67°0N 64°0W 109 C13
Cumberland Plateau U.S.A. 36°0N 85°0W 111 C10
Cumberland Sd. Canada 65°30N 66°0W 109 C13
Cumbernauld U.K. 55°57N 3°58W 25 C8
Cumbrae Is. U.K. 55°46N 4°54W 24 C6
Cumbria □ U.K. 54°42N 2°52W 26 C3
Cumbrian Mts. U.K. 54°30N 3°0W 26 D2
Cummertrees U.K. 54°59N 3°20W 25 E9
Cumnock U.K. 55°28N 4°17W 24 D7
Cumnor U.K. 51°44N 1°19W 30 C6
Cumwhinton U.K. 54°52N 2°50W 26 C3
Cunene → Angola 17°20S 11°50E 97 H2
Cúneo Italy 44°23N 7°32E 68 B2
Cunnamulla Australia 28°2S 145°38E 98 F8
Cunninghame U.K. 55°38N 4°35W 24 C6
Cupar U.K. 56°19N 3°1W 25 B9
Curaçao W. Indies 12°10N 69°0W 115 E11
Curicó Chile 34°55S 71°20W 121 F2
Curitiba Brazil 25°20S 49°10W 122 E1
Curlew Mts. Ireland 54°0N 8°20W 18 D5
Curry Rivel U.K. 51°1N 2°52W 30 D3
Curvelo Brazil 18°45S 44°27W 122 C2
Cusco Peru 13°32S 72°0W 120 D2
Cuttack India 20°25N 85°57E 85 J14
Cuxhaven Germany 53°51N 8°41E 64 B5
Cuyahoga Falls U.S.A. 41°8N 81°29W 112 E7
Cuyuni → Guyana 6°23N 58°41W 120 B4
Cwmbran U.K. 51°39N 3°2W 28 D7
Cyclades Greece 37°0N 24°30E 69 F11
Cynthiana U.S.A. 38°23N 84°18W 112 F5
Cyprus ■ Asia 35°0N 33°0E 86 C3
Cyrenaica Libya 27°0N 23°0E 95 C10
Czech Rep. ■ Europe 50°0N 15°0E 64 D8
Częstochowa Poland 50°49N 19°7E 65 C10

D

Da Lat Vietnam 11°56N 108°25E 82 B3
Da Nang Vietnam 16°4N 108°13E 82 A3
Da Yunhe → China 34°25N 120°5E 79 E13
Daba Shan China 32°0N 109°0E 79 E10
Dabie Shan China 31°20N 115°20E 79 E12
Dadra & Nagar Haveli □ India 20°5N 73°0E 84 J8
Dadu Pakistan 26°45N 67°45E 84 F5
Daegu S. Korea 35°50N 128°37E 79 D14
Daejeon S. Korea 36°20N 127°28E 79 D14
Dagestan □ Russia 42°30N 47°0E 71 F8
Dagupan Phil. 16°3N 120°20E 83 A6
Dahod India 22°50N 74°15E 84 H9
Dahongliutan China 35°45N 79°20E 78 D4
Daingean Ireland 53°18N 7°17W 21 B8
Dajarra Australia 21°42S 139°30E 98 E6
Dakar Senegal 14°34N 17°29W 94 F2
Dakhla W. Sahara 23°50N 15°53W 94 D2
Dakhla, El Wâhât el Egypt 25°30N 28°50E 95 C11
Dalandzadgad Mongolia 43°27N 104°30E 78 C9
Dalbeattie U.K. 54°56N 3°50W 25 E8
Dalhart U.S.A. 36°4N 102°31W 110 C6
Dalhousie Canada 48°5N 66°26W 113 A14
Dali China 25°40N 100°10E 78 F9
Dalian China 38°50N 121°40E 79 D13
Daliang Shan China 28°0N 102°45E 78 F9
Dalkeith U.K. 55°54N 3°4W 25 C9
Dalkey Ireland 53°16N 6°6W 21 B10
Dallas U.S.A. 32°47N 96°48W 111 D7
Dalles, The U.S.A. 45°36N 121°10W 110 A2
Dalmatia Croatia 43°20N 17°0E 68 C7
Dalmellington U.K. 55°19N 4°23W 24 D7
Daloa Ivory C. 7°0N 6°30W 94 G4
Dalry U.K. 55°42N 4°43W 24 C6
Dalrymple, L. Australia 20°40S 147°0E 98 E8
Dalton Dumf. & Gall., U.K. 55°4N 3°24W 25 D9
Dalton N. Yorks., U.K. 54°28N 1°32W 26 D5
Dalton-in-Furness U.K. 54°10N 3°11W 26 D2
Daly Waters Australia 16°15S 133°24E 98 D5
Daman India 20°25N 72°57E 84 J8
Damanhûr Egypt 31°0N 30°30E 95 B12
Damaraland Namibia 20°0S 15°0E 97 H2
Damascus Syria 33°30N 36°18E 86 C4
Damerham U.K. 50°56N 1°51W 30 E5
Dampier Australia 20°41S 116°42E 98 E2
Danakil Desert Ethiopia 12°45N 41°0E 89 E3
Danbury U.S.A. 41°24N 73°28W 113 E11
Dandong China 40°10N 124°20E 79 C13
Danube → Europe 45°20N 29°40E 65 F15
Danville Ill., U.S.A. 40°8N 87°37W 112 E4
Danville Ky., U.S.A. 37°39N 84°46W 112 G5
Danville Va., U.S.A. 36°36N 79°23W 111 C11
Daqing China 46°35N 125°0E 79 B13
Dar Banda Africa 8°0N 23°0E 90 F6
Dar es Salaam Tanzania 6°50S 39°12E 96 F7
Darbhanga India 26°15N 85°55E 85 F14
Dardanelles Turkey 40°17N 26°32E 69 D12
Darent → U.K. 51°28N 0°14E 31 D9
Dârfûr Sudan 13°40N 24°0E 95 F10
Darhan Mongolia 49°37N 106°21E 78 B10
Darién, G. del Colombia 9°0N 77°0W 120 B2
Darjiling India 27°3N 88°18E 85 F16
Darling → Australia 34°4S 141°54E 98 G7
Darling Ra. Australia 32°30S 116°20E 98 G2
Darlington U.K. 54°32N 1°33W 26 C5
Darmstadt Germany 49°51N 8°39E 64 D5
Darnah Libya 32°45N 22°45E 95 B10
Darnley, C. Antarctica 68°0S 69°0E 55 C6
Darnley B. Canada 69°30N 123°30W 108 C7
Dart → U.K. 50°24N 3°39W 29 G6
Dartford U.K. 51°26N 0°13E 31 D9
Dartington U.K. 50°27N 3°43W 29 G6
Dartmoor △ U.K. 50°37N 3°59W 29 F6
Dartmouth Canada 44°40N 63°30W 113 C16
Dartmouth U.K. 50°21N 3°36W 29 G6
Darton U.K. 53°35N 1°31W 27 E5
Darwen U.K. 53°42N 2°29W 27 E4
Darwin Australia 12°25S 130°51E 98 C5
Dashen, Ras Ethiopia 13°8N 38°26E 89 E2
Dasht → Pakistan 25°10N 61°40E 84 G2
Daşoguz Turkmenistan 41°49N 59°58E 87 A9
Datong China 40°6N 113°18E 79 C11
Daugava → Latvia 57°4N 24°3E 63 F9
Daugavpils Latvia 55°53N 26°32E 63 F9
Dauphin Canada 51°9N 100°5W 108 D9
Dauphiné France 45°15N 5°25E 66 D6
Davangere India 14°25N 75°55E 84 M9
Davao Phil. 7°0N 125°40E 83 C7
Davenport U.S.A. 41°32N 90°35W 112 E2
Daventry U.K. 52°16N 1°10W 30 B6
David Panama 8°30N 82°30W 115 F8
Davis Str. N. Amer. 65°0N 58°0W 104 C14
Dawlish U.K. 50°35N 3°28W 29 F7
Dawna Ra. Burma 16°30N 98°30E 85 L21
Dawros Hd. Ireland 54°50N 8°33W 18 B4
Dawson City Canada 64°10N 139°30W 108 C6
Dawson Creek Canada 55°45N 120°15W 108 D7
Dax France 43°44N 1°3W 66 E3
Daxian China 31°15N 107°23E 78 E10
Daxue Shan China 30°30N 101°30E 78 E9
Dayr az Zawr Syria 35°20N 40°5E 86 C5
Dayton U.S.A. 39°45N 84°12W 112 F5
Daytona Beach U.S.A. 29°13N 81°1W 111 E10
De Aar S. Africa 30°39S 24°0E 97 L4
De Pere U.S.A. 44°27N 88°4W 112 C3
Dead Sea Asia 31°30N 35°30E 86 D3
Deal U.K. 51°13N 1°25E 31 D11
Dean, Forest of U.K. 51°45N 2°33W 30 C3
Dearham U.K. 54°44N 3°25W 26 C2
Dease → Canada 59°56N 128°32W 108 D7
Dease Lake Canada 58°25N 130°6W 108 D6
Death Valley U.S.A. 36°15N 116°50W 110 C3
Deben → U.K. 52°0N 1°25E 31 B11
Debenham U.K. 52°14N 1°12E 31 B11
Debre Markos Ethiopia 10°20N 37°40E 89 E2
Debre Tabor Ethiopia 11°50N 38°26E 89 E2
Debrecen Hungary 47°33N 21°42E 65 E11
Decatur Ala., U.S.A. 34°36N 86°59W 111 D9
Decatur Ill., U.S.A. 39°51N 88°57W 112 F3
Decatur Ind., U.S.A. 40°50N 84°56W 112 E5
Deccan India 18°0N 79°0E 84 L11
Deddington U.K. 51°59N 1°18W 30 C6
Dee → Aberds., U.K. 57°9N 2°5W 23 H13
Dee → Dumf. & Gall., U.K. 54°51N 4°3W 24 E7
Dee → Wales, U.K. 53°22N 3°17W 28 A7
Deeping Fen U.K. 52°45N 0°15W 27 G8
Deeping St. Nicholas U.K. 52°44N 0°12W 27 G8
Deer Lake Canada 49°11N 57°27W 109 E14
Defiance U.S.A. 41°17N 84°22W 112 E5
Dehra Dun India 30°20N 78°4E 84 D11
DeKalb U.S.A. 41°56N 88°46W 112 E3
Del Rio U.S.A. 29°22N 100°54W 110 E6
Delabole U.K. 50°37N 4°46W 29 F4
Delaware U.S.A. 40°18N 83°4W 112 E6
Delaware □ U.S.A. 39°0N 75°20W 113 F10
Delaware → U.S.A. 39°15N 75°20W 113 F10
Delaware B. U.S.A. 39°0N 75°10W 111 C12
Delgado, C. Mozam. 10°45S 40°40E 96 G8
Delhi India 28°39N 77°13E 84 E10
Delice Turkey 39°54N 34°2E 71 G5
Delicias Mexico 28°13N 105°28W 114 B3
Déline Canada 65°11N 123°25W 108 C7
Delphos U.S.A. 40°51N 84°21W 112 E5
Delta Junction U.S.A. 64°2N 145°44W 108 C5
Demanda, Sierra de la Spain 42°15N 3°0W 67 A4
Demavend Iran 35°56N 52°10E 87 C8
Deming U.S.A. 32°16N 107°46W 110 D5
Demopolis U.S.A. 32°31N 87°50W 111 D9
Den Helder Neths. 52°57N 4°45E 64 B3
Denbigh U.K. 53°12N 3°25W 28 A7
Denbighshire □ U.K. 53°8N 3°22W 28 A7
Denby Dale U.K. 53°34N 1°40W 27 E5
Denham, Mt. Jamaica 18°13N 77°32W 114 a
Denia Spain 38°49N 0°8E 67 C6
Denizli Turkey 37°42N 29°2E 71 G4
Denmark ■ Europe 55°45N 10°0E 63 F6
Denmark Str. Atl. Oc. 66°0N 30°0W 104 C17
Dennery St. Lucia 13°55N 60°54W 114 b
Denny U.K. 56°1N 3°55W 25 B8
Denpasar Indonesia 8°39S 115°13E 82 F5
Dent U.K. 54°17N 2°27W 26 D4
Denton Gt. Man., U.K. 53°27N 2°9W 27 F4
Denton Lincs., U.K. 52°53N 0°43W 27 G7
Denton U.S.A. 33°13N 97°8W 111 D7
D'Entrecasteaux Is. Papua N. G. 9°0S 151°0E 98 B9
Denver U.S.A. 39°42N 104°59W 110 C5
Deoghar India 24°30N 86°42E 85 G15
Deolali India 19°58N 73°50E 84 K8
Deosai Mts. Pakistan 35°40N 75°0E 84 B9
Dera Ghazi Khan Pakistan 30°5N 70°43E 84 D7
Dera Ismail Khan Pakistan 31°50N 70°50E 84 D7
Derbent Russia 42°5N 48°15E 71 F8
Derby Australia 17°18S 123°38E 98 D3
Derby U.K. 52°56N 1°28W 27 G6
Derbyshire □ U.K. 53°11N 1°38W 27 F5
Dereham U.K. 52°41N 0°57E 31 A10
Derg → U.K. 54°44N 7°26W 18 B7
Derg, L. Ireland 53°0N 8°20W 20 C6
Deridder U.S.A. 30°51N 93°17W 111 D8
Derry = Londonderry U.K. 55°0N 7°20W 18 A7
Derrynasaggart Mts. Ireland 51°58N 9°15W 20 E4
Derryveagh Mts. Ireland 54°56N 8°11W 18 B5
Derwent → Derby, U.K. 52°57N 1°28W 27 G6
Derwent → N. Yorks., U.K. 53°45N 0°58W 27 E7
Derwent → Tyne & W., U.K. 54°58N 1°41W 26 C5
Derwent Water U.K. 54°35N 3°9W 26 C2
Des Moines U.S.A. 41°35N 93°37W 111 B8
Des Moines → U.S.A. 40°23N 91°25W 111 B8
Desborough U.K. 52°27N 0°49W 31 B7
Deschutes → U.S.A. 45°38N 120°55W 110 A2
Dese Ethiopia 11°5N 39°40E 89 E2
Deseado → Argentina 47°45S 65°54W 121 G3
Desford U.K. 52°37N 1°17W 27 G6
Desolación, I. Chile 53°0S 74°0W 121 H2
Dessau Germany 51°51N 12°14E 64 C7
Detour, Pt. U.S.A. 45°40N 86°40W 112 C4
Detroit U.S.A. 42°19N 83°12W 112 D6
Deutsche Bucht Germany 54°15N 8°0E 64 A5
Deventer Neths. 52°15N 6°10E 64 B4
Deveron → U.K. 57°41N 2°32W 23 G12
Devils Lake U.S.A. 48°7N 98°52W 110 A7
Devizes U.K. 51°22N 1°58W 30 D5
Devon □ U.K. 50°50N 3°40W 29 F6
Devon I. Canada 75°10N 85°0W 109 B11
Devonport U.K. 50°22N 4°11W 29 G5
Dewsbury U.K. 53°42N 1°37W 27 E5
Dexter U.S.A. 36°48N 89°57W 112 G3
Deyang China 31°3N 104°27E 78 E9
Dezfūl Iran 32°20N 48°30E 86 C7
Dezhneva, C. Russia 66°5N 169°40W 77 C20
Dezhou China 37°26N 116°18E 79 D12
Dhahran Si. Arabia 26°10N 50°7E 86 E7
Dhaka Bangla. 23°43N 90°26E 85 H17
Dhaka □ Bangla. 24°25N 90°25E 85 G17
Dhamār Yemen 14°30N 44°20E 89 E3
Dhamtari India 20°42N 81°35E 85 J12
Dhanbad India 23°50N 86°30E 85 H15
Dharwad India 15°30N 75°4E 84 M9
Dhaulagiri Nepal 28°39N 83°28E 85 E13
Dhenkanal India 20°45N 85°35E 85 J14
Dhuburi India 26°2N 89°59E 85 F16
Dhule India 20°58N 74°50E 84 J9
Diamantina Brazil 18°17S 43°40W 122 C2
Diamantina → Australia 26°45S 139°10E 98 F6
Diamantino Brazil 14°30S 56°30W 120 D4
Dibrugarh India 27°29N 94°55E 85 F19
Dickinson U.S.A. 46°53N 102°47W 110 A6
Didcot U.K. 51°36N 1°14W 30 C6
Diefenbaker, L. Canada 51°0N 106°55W 108 D9
Dieppe France 49°54N 1°4E 66 B4
Digby Canada 44°38N 65°50W 109 E13
Digne-les-Bains France 44°5N 6°12E 66 D7
Dijon France 47°20N 5°3E 66 C6
Dikson Russia 73°40N 80°5E 76 B9
Dili E. Timor 8°39S 125°34E 83 F7
Dillingham U.S.A. 59°3N 158°28W 108 D4
Dimitrovgrad Bulgaria 42°5N 25°35E 69 C11
Dimitrovgrad Russia 54°14N 49°39E 70 D8
Dinajpur Bangla. 25°33N 88°43E 85 G16
Dinan France 48°28N 2°2W 66 B2
Dinant Belgium 50°16N 4°55E 64 C3
Dinaric Alps Croatia 44°0N 16°30E 68 C7
Dinbych-y-Pysgod = Tenby U.K. 51°40N 4°42W 28 D4
Dingle Ireland 52°9N 10°17W 20 D2
Dingle B. Ireland 52°3N 10°20W 20 D2
Dingle Pen. Ireland 52°12N 10°5W 20 D2
Dingwall U.K. 57°36N 4°26W 23 G9
Dipolog Phil. 8°36N 123°20E 83 C6
Dire Dawa Ethiopia 9°35N 41°45E 89 F3
Dirranbandi Australia 28°33S 148°17E 98 F8
Disappointment, C. U.S.A. 46°18N 124°5W 110 A2
Disappointment, L. Australia 23°20S 122°40E 98 E3
Diss U.K. 52°23N 1°7E 31 B11
Distington U.K. 54°36N 3°32W 26 C1
Distrito Federal □ Brazil 15°45S 47°45W 122 C1
Ditchingham U.K. 52°28N 1°28E 31 B11
Ditchling Beacon U.K. 50°54N 0°6W 31 E8
Dittisham U.K. 50°22N 3°37W 29 G6
Ditton Priors U.K. 52°30N 2°34W 27 H3
Diu India 20°45N 70°58E 84 J7
Divinópolis Brazil 20°10S 44°54W 122 D2
Dixon U.S.A. 41°50N 89°29W 112 E3
Dixon Entrance U.S.A. 54°30N 132°0W 108 D6
Diyarbakır Turkey 37°55N 40°18E 71 G7
Dizzard Pt. U.K. 50°44N 4°40W 29 F4
Djerba, Î. de Tunisia 33°50N 10°48E 95 B8
Djerid, Chott Tunisia 33°42N 8°30E 94 B7
Djibouti Djibouti 11°30N 43°5E 89 E3
Djibouti ■ Africa 12°0N 43°0E 89 E3
Djourab, Erg du Chad 16°40N 18°50E 95 E9
Dmitri Laptev Str. Russia 73°0N 140°0E 77 B15
Dnepropetrovsk Ukraine 48°30N 35°0E 71 E6
Dnieper → Ukraine 46°30N 32°18E 71 E5
Dniester → Europe 46°18N 30°17E 65 E16
Dniprodzerzhynsk Ukraine 48°32N 34°37E 71 E5
Doba Chad 8°40N 16°50E 95 G9
Doberai, Jazirah Indonesia 1°25S 133°0E 83 E8
Dobrich Bulgaria 43°37N 27°49E 69 C12
Dobruja Europe 44°30N 28°15E 65 F15
Docking U.K. 52°54N 0°38E 31 A10
Doddington Cambs., U.K. 52°30N 0°3E 31 B9
Doddington Northumberland, U.K. 55°33N 1°54W 26 A5
Dodecanese Greece 36°35N 27°0E 69 F12
Dodge City U.S.A. 37°45N 100°1W 110 C6
Dodman Pt. U.K. 50°13N 4°48W 29 G4
Dodoma Tanzania 6°8S 35°45E 96 F7
Doha Qatar 25°15N 51°35E 87 E7
Dokdo Asia 37°15N 131°52E 81 E2
Dolbeau-Mistassini Canada 48°53N 72°14W 109 E12
Dole France 47°7N 5°31E 66 C6
Dolgarrog U.K. 53°11N 3°50W 28 A6
Dolgellau U.K. 52°45N 3°53W 28 B6
Dolo Ethiopia 4°11N 42°3E 89 G3
Dolomites Italy 46°23N 11°51E 68 A4
Dolores Argentina 36°20S 57°40W 121 F4
Dolphin and Union Str. Canada 69°5N 114°45W 108 C8
Dolphinton U.K. 55°42N 3°25W 25 C9
Dolton U.K. 50°53N 4°2W 29 F5
Dominica ■ W. Indies 15°20N 61°20W 115 D12
Dominican Rep. ■ W. Indies 19°0N 70°30W 115 D10
Don → Russia 47°4N 39°18E 71 E6
Don → Aberds., U.K. 57°11N 2°5W 23 H13
Don → S. Yorks., U.K. 53°41N 0°52W 27 E7
Don Figueterea Mts. Jamaica 18°5N 77°36W 114 a
Donaghadee U.K. 54°39N 5°33W 19 B10
Doncaster U.K. 53°32N 1°6W 27 E6
Dondra Head Sri Lanka 5°55N 80°40E 84 S12
Donegal Ireland 54°39N 8°5W 18 B5
Donegal □ Ireland 54°53N 8°0W 18 B5
Donegal B. Ireland 54°31N 8°49W 18 B4
Donets → Russia 47°33N 40°55E 71 E7
Donetsk Ukraine 48°0N 37°45E 71 E6
Dong Hoi Vietnam 17°29N 106°36E 82 A3
Dongchuan China 26°8N 103°1E 78 F9
Dongguan China 22°58N 113°44E 79 G11
Dongola Sudan 19°9N 30°22E 95 E12
Dongsha Dao S. China Sea 20°45N 116°43E 79 G12
Dongsheng China 39°50N 110°0E 79 D10
Dongting Hu China 29°18N 112°45E 79 F11
Donhead U.K. 51°1N 2°7W 30 D4
Donington U.K. 52°54N 0°12W 27 G8
Donna Nook U.K. 53°29N 0°8E 27 F9
Donostia-San Sebastián Spain 43°17N 1°58W 67 A5
Doon → U.K. 55°27N 4°39W 24 D6
Dorchester Dorset, U.K. 50°42N 2°27W 30 E4
Dorchester Oxon., U.K. 51°39N 1°10W 30 C6
Dorchester, C. Canada 65°27N 77°27W 109 C12
Dordogne → France 45°2N 0°36W 66 D3
Dordrecht Neths. 51°48N 4°39E 64 C3
Dores do Indaiá Brazil 19°27S 45°36W 122 C1
Dorking U.K. 51°14N 0°19W 31 D8
Dornie U.K. 57°17N 5°31W 22 H6
Dornoch U.K. 57°53N 4°2W 23 G9
Dornoch Firth U.K. 57°51N 4°4W 23 G9
Döröö Nuur Mongolia 48°0N 93°0E 78 B7
Dorset □ U.K. 50°45N 2°26W 30 E4
Dorstone U.K. 52°3N 2°59W 30 B3
Dortmund Germany 51°30N 7°28E 64 C4
Dos Bahías, C. Argentina 44°58S 65°32W 121 G3
Dos Hermanas Spain 37°16N 5°55W 67 D3
Dothan U.S.A. 31°13N 85°24W 111 D9
Douai France 50°21N 3°4E 66 A5
Douala Cameroon 4°0N 9°45E 96 D1
Doubs → France 46°53N 5°1E 66 C6
Douglas Ireland 51°52N 8°25W 20 E6
Douglas I. of Man 54°10N 4°28W 19 C13
Douglas U.S.A. 31°21N 109°33W 110 D5
Dounreay U.K. 58°35N 3°44W 23 E10
Dourados Brazil 22°9S 54°50W 120 E4
Douro → Europe 41°8N 8°40W 67 B1
Dove → Derby, U.K. 52°51N 1°36W 27 G5
Dove → N. Yorks., U.K. 54°15N 0°55W 26 D7
Dove Dale U.K. 53°7N 1°46W 27 F5
Dover U.K. 51°7N 1°19E 31 D11
Dover Del., U.S.A. 39°10N 75°32W 113 F10
Dover N.H., U.S.A. 43°12N 70°56W 113 D12
Dover, Str. of Europe 51°0N 1°30E 62 F7
Dover-Foxcroft U.S.A. 45°11N 69°13W 113 C13
Doveridge U.K. 52°54N 1°49W 27 G5
Dovey = Dyfi → U.K. 52°32N 4°3W 28 B5
Dovrefjell Norway 62°15N 9°33E 63 E5
Down □ U.K. 54°23N 6°2W 19 C9
Downham U.K. 52°26N 0°14E 31 B9
Downham Market U.K. 52°37N 0°23E 31 A9
Downpatrick U.K. 54°20N 5°43W 19 C10
Downpatrick Hd. Ireland 54°20N 9°21W 18 C3
Downton U.K. 50°59N 1°44W 30 E5
Drâa, Oued → Morocco 28°40N 11°10W 94 C3
Draguignan France 43°32N 6°27E 66 E7
Drake Passage S. Ocean 58°0S 68°0W 55 B17
Drakensberg S. Africa 31°0S 28°0E 97 L5
Drammen Norway 59°42N 10°12E 63 F6
Drava → Croatia 45°33N 18°55E 69 B8
Dresden Germany 51°3N 13°44E 64 C7
Dreux France 48°44N 1°23E 66 B4
Driffield U.K. 54°0N 0°26W 27 E8
Drina → Bos.-H. 44°53N 19°21E 69 B8
Drobeta-Turnu Severin Romania 44°39N 22°41E 65 F12
Drogheda Ireland 53°43N 6°22W 19 D9
Drohobych Ukraine 49°20N 23°30E 71 E3
Droitwich U.K. 52°16N 2°8W 30 B4
Dromore U.K. 54°31N 7°28W 18 B7
Dromore West Ireland 54°15N 8°52W 18 C4
Dronfield U.K. 53°19N 1°27W 27 F6
Dronning Maud Land Antarctica 72°30S 12°0E 55 D3
Drum Hills Ireland 52°1N 7°45W 20 D7
Drumheller Canada 51°25N 112°40W 108 D8
Drummond I. U.S.A. 46°1N 83°39W 112 B5
Drummondville Canada 45°55N 72°25W 113 C11
Drumochter, Pass of U.K. 56°50N 4°15W 23 J9
Druridge B. U.K. 55°17N 1°32W 26 B5
Dry Harbour Mts. Jamaica 18°19N 77°24W 114 a
Dryden Canada 49°47N 92°50W 108 E10
Drygalski I. Antarctica 66°0S 92°0E 55 C7
Du Quoin U.S.A. 38°1N 89°14W 112 F3
Duarte, Pico Dom. Rep. 19°2N 70°59W 115 D10
Dubai U.A.E. 25°18N 55°20E 87 E8
Dubawnt → Canada 64°33N 100°6W 108 C9
Dubawnt L. Canada 63°8N 101°28W 108 C9
Dubbo Australia 32°11S 148°35E 98 G8
Dublin Ireland 53°21N 6°15W 21 B10
Dublin U.S.A. 32°32N 82°54W 111 D10
Dublin □ Ireland 53°24N 6°20W 21 B10
Dublin ✕ (DUB) Ireland 53°26N 6°15W 21 B10
DuBois U.S.A. 41°7N 78°46W 112 E8
Dubrovnik Croatia 42°39N 18°6E 69 C8
Dubuque U.S.A. 42°30N 90°41W 112 D2
Duddington U.K. 52°36N 0°32W 31 A7
Duddon → U.K. 54°12N 3°15W 26 D2
Dudinka Russia 69°30N 86°13E 77 C9
Dudley U.K. 52°31N 2°5W 27 G4
Duffield U.K. 52°59N 1°29W 27 G6
Dufftown U.K. 57°27N 3°8W 23 H11
Dugi Otok Croatia 44°0N 15°3E 68 C6
Duisburg Germany 51°26N 6°45E 64 C4
Dukinfield U.K. 53°28N 2°6W 27 F4
Dulce → Argentina 30°32S 62°33W 121 F3
Duluth U.S.A. 46°47N 92°6W 112 B1
Dulverton U.K. 51°2N 3°33W 29 E6
Dumaguete Phil. 9°17N 123°15E 83 C6
Dumbarton U.K. 55°57N 4°33W 24 C6
Dumfries U.K. 55°4N 3°37W 25 D8
Dumfries & Galloway □ U.K. 55°9N 3°58W 25 D8
Dumyât Egypt 31°24N 31°48E 95 B12
Dún Laoghaire Ireland 53°17N 6°8W 21 B10
Dunbar U.K. 56°0N 2°31W 25 B10
Dunblane U.K. 56°11N 3°58W 25 B8
Duncan U.S.A. 34°30N 97°57W 110 D7
Duncansby Head U.K. 58°38N 3°1W 23 E11
Dunchurch U.K. 52°21N 1°17W 30 B6
Dund-Us Mongolia 48°1N 91°38E 78 B7
Dundalk Ireland 54°1N 6°24W 19 C9
Dundalk Bay Ireland 53°55N 6°15W 19 D9
Dundee U.K. 56°28N 2°59W 25 B10
Dundrum Ireland 53°18N 6°14W 21 B10
Dundrum U.K. 54°16N 5°52W 19 C10
Dundrum B. U.K. 54°13N 5°47W 19 C10
Dunedin N.Z. 45°50S 170°33E 99 K13
Dunfermline U.K. 56°5N 3°27W 25 B9
Dungannon U.K. 54°31N 6°46W 19 B8
Dungarvan Ireland 52°5N 7°37W 21 D7
Dungarvan Harbour Ireland 52°4N 7°35W 21 D7
Dungeness U.K. 50°54N 0°59E 31 E10
Dunhua China 43°20N 128°14E 79 C14
Dunhuang China 40°8N 94°36E 78 C7
Dunkeld U.K. 56°34N 3°35W 25 A8
Dunkerque France 51°2N 2°20E 66 A5
Dunkery Beacon U.K. 51°9N 3°36W 29 E6
Dunkirk U.S.A. 42°29N 79°20W 112 D8
Dunleer Ireland 53°50N 6°24W 19 D9
Dunmanway Ireland 51°43N 9°6W 20 E4
Dunmore U.S.A. 41°25N 75°38W 113 E10
Dunnet Hd. U.K. 58°40N 3°21W 23 E11
Dunoon U.K. 55°57N 4°56W 24 C6
Duns U.K. 55°47N 2°20W 25 C11
Dunsford U.K. 50°41N 3°42W 29 F6
Dunstable U.K. 51°53N 0°32W 31 C7
Dunster U.K. 51°11N 3°27W 30 D2
Dunston U.K. 52°46N 2°7W 27 G4
Dunvegan U.K. 57°27N 6°35W 22 H4
Duolun China 42°12N 116°28E 79 C12
Duque de Caxias Brazil 22°46S 43°18W 122 D2
Durance → France 43°55N 4°45E 66 E6
Durango Mexico 24°3N 104°39W 114 C4
Durango U.S.A. 37°16N 107°53W 110 C5
Durant U.S.A. 33°59N 96°25W 111 D7
Durazno Uruguay 33°25S 56°31W 121 F4
Durban S. Africa 29°49S 31°1E 97 K6
Düren Germany 50°48N 6°29E 64 C4
Durgapur India 23°30N 87°20E 85 H15
Durham U.K. 54°47N 1°34W 26 C5
Durham U.S.A. 35°59N 78°54W 111 C11
Durham □ U.K. 54°42N 1°45W 26 C5
Durlston Hd. U.K. 50°36N 1°57W 30 E5
Durness U.K. 58°34N 4°45W 23 E8
Durrës Albania 41°19N 19°28E 69 D8
Durrington U.K. 51°12N 1°47W 30 D5
Durrow Ireland 52°51N 7°24W 21 C8
Dursey I. Ireland 51°36N 10°12W 20 E2
Dursley U.K. 51°40N 2°21W 30 C4
Dushanbe Tajikistan 38°33N 68°48E 87 B12
Düsseldorf Germany 51°14N 6°47E 64 C4
Dutch Harbor U.S.A. 53°53N 166°32W 108 D3
Duyun China 26°18N 107°29E 78 F10
Dvina, N. → Russia 64°32N 40°30E 70 B7
Dvina B. Russia 65°0N 39°0E 70 B6
Dwarka India 22°18N 69°8E 84 H6
Dyce U.K. 57°13N 2°12W 23 H13
Dyer, C. Canada 66°37N 61°16W 109 C13
Dyersburg U.S.A. 36°3N 89°23W 111 C9
Dyfi → U.K. 52°32N 4°3W 28 B5
Dymchurch U.K. 51°1N 1°0E 31 D11
Dymock U.K. 51°59N 2°26W 30 C4
Dzavhan Gol → Mongolia 48°54N 93°23E 78 B7
Dzerzhinsk Russia 56°14N 43°30E 70 C7
Dzhankoy Ukraine 45°40N 34°20E 71 E5
Dzhugdzhur Ra. Russia 57°30N 138°0E 77 D14
Dzungarian Basin China 44°30N 86°0E 78 C6
Dzungarian Gate Asia 45°10N 82°0E 78 B5
Dzüünmod Mongolia 47°45N 106°58E 78 B10

E

Eagle U.S.A. 64°47N 141°12W 108 C5
Eagle L. U.S.A. 46°20N 69°22W 113 B13
Eagle Pass U.S.A. 28°43N 100°30W 110 E6
Eagle River U.S.A. 47°25N 88°18W 112 B3
Eaglesfield U.K. 55°4N 3°12W 25 D9
Eakring U.K. 53°9N 0°58W 27 F7
Ealing □ U.K. 51°31N 0°20W 31 C8
Earby U.K. 53°55N 2°7W 27 E4
Eardisley U.K. 52°8N 3°1W 30 B2
Earith U.K. 52°22N 0°2E 31 B9
Earl Shilton U.K. 52°35N 1°18W 27 G6
Earl Soham U.K. 52°14N 1°18E 31 B11
Earls Barton U.K. 52°16N 0°45W 31 B7
Earl's Colne U.K. 51°56N 0°43E 31 C10
Earlston U.K. 55°39N 2°40W 25 C10
Earn → U.K. 56°21N 3°18W 25 B9
Earn, L. U.K. 56°23N 4°13W 24 B7
Earsdon U.K. 55°3N 1°29W 26 B6
Easebourne U.K. 51°0N 0°43W 31 E7
Easington Durham, U.K. 54°47N 1°21W 26 C6
Easington E. Riding, U.K. 53°39N 0°6E 27 E9
Easington Colliery U.K. 54°48N 1°19W 26 C6
Easingwold U.K. 54°8N 1°11W 26 D6
East Ayrshire □ U.K. 55°26N 4°11W 24 C7
East Bengal Bangla. 24°0N 90°0E 85 H17
East Bergholt U.K. 51°59N 1°3E 31 C11
East Beskids Europe 49°20N 22°0E 65 D11
East Brent U.K. 51°15N 2°56W 30 D3
East C. = Dezhneva, C. Russia 66°5N 169°40W 77 C20
East China Sea Asia 30°0N 126°0E 79 F14
East Cowes U.K. 50°45N 1°16W 30 E6
East Falkland Falk. Is. 51°30S 58°30W 121 H4
East Fen U.K. 53°4N 0°5E 27 F9
East Grinstead U.K. 51°7N 0°0 31 D9
East Harling U.K. 52°26N 0°56E 31 B10
East Ilsley U.K. 51°31N 1°16W 30 C6
East Indies Asia 0°0 120°0E 72 J14
East Kilbride U.K. 55°47N 4°11W 24 C7
East Lansing U.S.A. 42°44N 84°29W 112 D5
East London S. Africa 33°0S 27°55E 97 L5
East Lothian □ U.K. 55°58N 2°44W 25 C10
East Markham U.K. 53°15N 0°53W 27 F7
East Moor U.K. 53°16N 1°34W 27 F5
East Pt. Canada 46°27N 61°58W 113 B17
East St. Louis U.S.A. 38°37N 90°9W 112 F2
East Sea = Japan, Sea of Asia 40°0N 135°0E 81 D4

East Siberian Sea   Frederick

Fredericksburg U.S.A. 38°18N 77°28W 112 F9
Fredericktown U.S.A. 37°34N 90°18W 112 G2
Fredericton Canada 45°57N 66°40W 113 C14
Frederikshavn Denmark 57°28N 10°31E 63 F6
Fredonia U.S.A. 42°26N 79°20W 112 D8
Fredrikstad Norway 59°13N 10°57E 63 F6
Free State □ S. Africa 28°30S 27°0E 97 K5
Freeport Bahamas 26°30N 78°47W 115 B9
Freeport Ill., U.S.A. 42°17N 89°36W 112 D3
Freeport Tex., U.S.A. 28°57N 95°21W 111 E7
Freetown S. Leone 8°30N 13°17W 94 G3
Freiburg Germany 47°59N 7°51E 64 E4
Fréjus France 43°25N 6°44E 66 E7
Fremont U.S.A. 41°21N 83°7W 112 E6
French Creek → U.S.A. 41°24N 79°50W 112 E8
French Guiana ⊘ S. Amer. 4°0N 53°0W 120 B4
French Polynesia ⊘ Pac. Oc. 20°0S 145°0W 103 J13
Frenchman Cr. → N. Amer. 48°31N 107°10W 110 A5
Freshwater U.K. 50°41N 1°31W 30 E5
Fresnillo Mexico 23°10N 102°53W 114 C4
Fresno U.S.A. 36°44N 119°47W 110 C3
Fria, C. Namibia 18°0S 12°0E 90 H5
Fridaythorpe U.K. 54°2N 0°39W 27 D7
Friedrichshafen Germany 47°39N 9°30E 64 E5
Frimley U.K. 51°19N 0°44W 31 D7
Frinton-on-Sea U.K. 51°49N 1°15E 31 C11
Frio, C. Brazil 22°50S 41°50W 117 F6
Frizington U.K. 54°33N 3°28W 26 C2
Frobisher B. Canada 62°30N 66°0W 109 C13
Frobisher L. Canada 56°20N 108°15W 108 D9
Frodsham U.K. 53°18N 2°43W 27 F3
Frome U.K. 51°14N 2°19W 30 D4
Frome → U.K. 50°41N 2°6W 30 E4
Front Range U.S.A. 40°25N 105°45W 110 B5
Front Royal U.S.A. 38°55N 78°12W 112 F8
Frutal Brazil 20°0S 49°0W 122 C1
Frýdek-Místek Czech Rep. 49°40N 18°20E 65 D10
Fuchū Japan 34°34N 133°14E 81 F3
Fuengirola Spain 36°32N 4°41W 67 D3
Fuerte → Mexico 25°54N 109°22W 114 B3
Fuerteventura Canary Is. 28°30N 14°0W 94 C3
Fuidhaigh = Wiay U.K. 57°24N 7°13W 22 H3
Fuji Japan 35°9N 138°39E 81 F6
Fuji-San Japan 35°22N 138°44E 81 F6
Fujian □ China 26°0N 118°0E 79 F12
Fujin China 47°16N 132°1E 79 B15
Fukui Japan 36°5N 136°10E 81 E5
Fukuoka Japan 33°39N 130°21E 81 G2
Fukushima Japan 37°44N 140°28E 81 E7
Fukuyama Japan 34°35N 133°20E 81 F3
Fulda Germany 50°32N 9°40E 64 C5
Fulda → Germany 51°25N 9°39E 64 C5
Fulton U.S.A. 43°19N 76°25W 112 D9
Fulwood U.K. 53°47N 2°40W 27 E3
Funabashi Japan 35°45N 140°0E 81 F7
Funchal Madeira 32°38N 16°54W 94 B2
Fundy, B. of Canada 45°0N 66°0W 113 C15
Furnas, Represa de Brazil 20°50S 45°30W 122 D1
Furneaux Group Australia 40°10S 147°50E 98 J8
Fürth Germany 49°28N 10°59E 64 D6
Fury and Hecla Str. Canada 69°56N 84°0W 109 C11
Fushun China 41°50N 123°56E 79 C13
Fustic Barbados 13°16N 59°38W 114 c
Fuxin China 42°5N 121°48E 79 C13
Fuyang China 33°0N 115°48E 79 E12
Fuyong China 22°40N 113°49E 79 a
Fuyu Heilongjiang, China 47°49N 124°27E 79 B13
Fuyu Jilin, China 45°12N 124°43E 79 B13
Fuyun China 47°0N 89°28E 78 B6
Fuzhou China 26°5N 119°16E 79 F12
Fylingdales Moor U.K. 54°25N 0°41W 26 D7
Fyn Denmark 55°20N 10°30E 63 F6
Fyne, L. U.K. 55°59N 5°23W 24 C5

G

Gaalkacyo Somalia 6°30N 47°30E 89 F4
Gabès Tunisia 33°53N 10°2E 95 B8
Gabès, G. de Tunisia 34°0N 10°30E 95 B8
Gabon ■ Africa 0°10S 10°0E 96 E2
Gaborone Botswana 24°45S 25°57E 97 J5
Gabrovo Bulgaria 42°52N 25°19E 69 C11
Gachsārān Iran 30°15N 50°45E 87 D7
Gadarwara India 22°50N 78°50E 84 H11
Gadsden U.S.A. 34°1N 86°1W 111 D9
Gafsa Tunisia 34°24N 8°43E 95 B7
Găgăuzia □ Moldova 46°10N 28°40E 65 E15
Gagnoa Ivory C. 6°56N 5°16W 94 G4
Gagnon Canada 51°50N 68°5W 109 D13
Gainesville Fla., U.S.A. 29°40N 82°20W 111 E10
Gainesville Ga., U.S.A. 34°18N 83°50W 111 D10
Gainford U.K. 54°34N 1°43W 26 C5
Gainsborough U.K. 53°24N 0°46W 27 F7
Gairdner, L. Australia 31°30S 136°0E 98 G6
Gairloch U.K. 57°43N 5°41W 22 G6
Gairloch, L. U.K. 57°43N 5°45W 22 G6
Galapagos Ecuador 0°0 91°0W 117 D1
Galashiels U.K. 55°37N 2°49W 25 C10
Galaţi Romania 45°27N 28°2E 65 F15
Galdhøpiggen Norway 61°38N 8°18E 63 E5
Galena U.S.A. 64°44N 156°56W 108 C4
Galesburg U.S.A. 40°57N 90°22W 112 E2
Galgate U.K. 53°59N 2°46W 27 E3
Galicia □ Spain 42°43N 7°45W 67 A2
Galilee, Sea of Israel 32°45N 35°35E 86 C3
Galina Pt. Jamaica 18°24N 76°58W 114 a
Gallan Hd. U.K. 58°15N 7°2W 22 F3
Galle Sri Lanka 6°5N 80°10E 84 R12
Galley Hd. Ireland 51°32N 8°55W 20 E5
Gallinas, Pta. Colombia 12°28N 71°40W 120 A2
Gallipolis U.S.A. 38°49N 82°12W 112 F6
Gällivare Sweden 67°9N 20°40E 63 D8
Galloway U.K. 55°1N 4°29W 24 D7
Galloway, Mull of U.K. 54°39N 4°52W 24 E6
Gallup U.S.A. 35°32N 108°45W 110 C5
Galmpton U.K. 50°23N 3°35W 29 G6
Galmudug Somalia 6°30N 48°0E 89 F4
Galston U.K. 55°36N 4°24W 24 C7
Galty Mts. Ireland 52°22N 8°10W 20 D6
Galtymore Ireland 52°21N 8°11W 20 D6
Galveston U.S.A. 29°18N 94°48W 111 E8
Galway Ireland 53°17N 9°3W 20 B4
Galway □ Ireland 53°22N 9°1W 20 B4
Galway B. Ireland 53°13N 9°10W 20 B4
Gambia ■ W. Afr. 13°25N 16°0W 94 F2
Gambia → W. Afr. 13°28N 16°34W 94 F2
Gamlingay U.K. 52°10N 0°11W 31 B8
Gan Jiang → China 29°15N 116°0E 79 F12
Gananoque Canada 44°20N 76°10W 113 C9
Gäncä Azerbaijan 40°45N 46°20E 71 F8
Gand = Gent Belgium 51°2N 3°42E 64 C2
Gandak → India 25°39N 85°13E 85 G14
Gander Canada 48°58N 54°35W 109 E14
Gandhi Sagar India 24°40N 75°40E 84 G9
Gandia Spain 38°58N 0°9W 67 C5
Ganganagar India 29°56N 73°56E 84 E8
Gangdisê Shan China 31°20N 81°0E 78 E5
Ganges → India 23°20N 90°30E 85 H17
Gangneung S. Korea 37°45N 128°54E 79 D14
Gangtok India 27°20N 88°37E 85 F16
Gannett Peak U.S.A. 43°11N 109°39W 110 B5
Gansu □ China 36°0N 104°0E 78 D9
Ganzhou China 25°51N 114°56E 79 F11
Gao Mali 16°15N 0°5W 94 E5
Gap France 44°33N 6°5E 66 D7
Gar China 32°10N 79°58E 78 E4
Garanhuns Brazil 8°50S 36°30W 122 A3
Garboldisham U.K. 52°23N 0°57E 31 B10
Garda, L. di Italy 45°40N 10°41E 68 B4
Garden City U.S.A. 37°58N 100°53W 110 C6
Gardēz Afghan. 33°37N 69°9E 87 C12
Gare L. U.K. 56°1N 4°50W 24 B6
Garforth U.K. 53°47N 1°24W 27 E6
Gargrave U.K. 53°59N 2°7W 27 E4
Garioch U.K. 57°18N 2°40W 23 H12
Garissa Kenya 0°25S 39°40E 96 E7
Garonne → France 45°2N 0°36W 66 D3
Garoowe Somalia 8°25N 48°33E 89 F4
Garoua Cameroon 9°19N 13°21E 95 G8
Garron Pt. U.K. 55°3N 5°59W 19 A10
Garry → U.K. 56°44N 3°47W 23 J10
Garry, L. Canada 65°58N 100°18W 108 C9
Garsdale Head U.K. 54°20N 2°20W 26 D4
Garstang U.K. 53°55N 2°46W 27 E3
Gary U.S.A. 41°36N 87°20W 112 E4
Garzê China 31°38N 100°1E 78 E9
Gascogne France 43°45N 0°20E 66 E4
Gascogne, G. de Europe 44°0N 2°0W 66 D2
Gashua Nigeria 12°54N 11°0E 95 F8
Gaspé Canada 48°52N 64°30W 109 E13
Gaspé, C. de Canada 48°48N 64°7W 113 A15
Gaspésie, Pén. de la Canada 48°45N 65°40W 113 A15
Gata, Sierra de Spain 40°20N 6°45W 67 B2
Gatehouse of Fleet U.K. 54°53N 4°12W 24 E7
Gateshead U.K. 54°57N 1°35W 26 C5
Gatineau Canada 45°29N 75°39W 113 C10
Gatineau → Canada 45°27N 75°42W 113 C10
Gatley U.K. 53°24N 2°15W 27 F4
Gävle Sweden 60°40N 17°9E 63 E7
Gawilgarh Hills India 21°15N 76°45E 84 J10
Gawthwaite U.K. 54°16N 3°8W 26 D2
Gaxun Nur China 42°22N 100°30E 78 C9
Gaya India 24°47N 85°4E 85 G14
Gaylord U.S.A. 45°2N 84°41W 112 C5
Gayton U.K. 52°45N 0°36E 31 A10
Gaywood U.K. 52°46N 0°26E 31 A9
Gaza Gaza Strip 31°30N 34°28E 86 D3
Gaza Strip ■ Asia 31°29N 34°25E 86 D3
Gaziantep Turkey 37°6N 37°23E 71 G6
Gdańsk Poland 54°22N 18°40E 65 A10
Gdynia Poland 54°35N 18°33E 65 A10
Gebze Turkey 40°47N 29°25E 71 F4
Gedaref Sudan 14°2N 35°28E 95 F13
Gedney U.K. 52°48N 0°4E 27 G9
Gedser Denmark 54°35N 11°55E 63 G6
Geelong Australia 38°10S 144°22E 98 H7
Gejiu China 23°20N 103°10E 78 G9
Gela Italy 37°4N 14°15E 68 F6
Gelibolu Turkey 40°28N 26°43E 71 F4
Gelsenkirchen Germany 51°32N 7°6E 64 C4
General Acha Argentina 37°20S 64°38W 121 F3
General Alvear Argentina 35°0S 67°40W 121 F3
General Carrera, L. S. Amer. 46°35S 72°0W 121 G2
General Pico Argentina 35°45S 63°50W 121 F3
General Santos Phil. 6°5N 125°14E 83 C7
Geneva Switz. 46°12N 6°9E 64 E4
Geneva U.S.A. 42°52N 76°59W 112 D9
Geneva, L. = Léman, L. Europe 46°26N 6°30E 64 E4
Gennargentu, Mti. del Italy 40°1N 9°19E 68 D3
Genoa Italy 44°25N 8°57E 68 B3
Génova, G. di Italy 44°0N 9°0E 68 C3
Gent Belgium 51°2N 3°42E 64 C2
George S. Africa 33°58S 22°29E 97 L4
George → Canada 58°49N 66°10W 109 D13
George, L. U.S.A. 29°17N 81°36W 111 E10
George Town Cayman Is. 19°20N 81°24W 115 D8
George Town Malaysia 5°25N 100°20E 82 C2
George V Land Antarctica 69°0S 148°0E 55 C10
Georgetown Guyana 6°50N 58°12W 120 B4
Georgetown Ky., U.S.A. 38°13N 84°33W 112 F5
Georgetown S.C., U.S.A. 33°23N 79°17W 111 D11
Georgia □ U.S.A. 32°50N 83°15W 111 D10
Georgia ■ Asia 42°0N 43°0E 71 F7
Georgia, Str. of N. Amer. 49°25N 124°0W 104 E7
Georgian B. Canada 45°15N 81°0W 112 C7
Georgiyevsk Russia 44°12N 43°28E 71 F7
Gera Germany 50°53N 12°4E 64 C7
Geraldton Australia 28°48S 114°32E 98 F1
Germany ■ Europe 51°0N 10°0E 64 C6
Germiston S. Africa 26°13S 28°10E 97 K5
Gerrans B. U.K. 50°12N 4°57W 29 G4
Gerrards Cross U.K. 51°35N 0°33W 31 C7
Getafe Spain 40°18N 3°43W 67 B4
Ghadāmis Libya 30°11N 9°29E 95 B7
Ghaghara → India 25°45N 84°40E 85 G14
Ghana ■ W. Afr. 8°0N 1°0W 94 G5
Ghardaïa Algeria 32°20N 3°37E 94 B6
Gharyān Libya 32°10N 13°0E 95 B8
Ghats, Eastern India 14°0N 78°50E 84 N11
Ghats, Western India 14°0N 75°0E 84 N9
Ghazal, Bahr el → Chad 13°0N 15°47E 95 F9
Ghazal, Bahr el → South Sudan 9°31N 30°25E 95 G12
Ghaziabad India 28°42N 77°26E 84 E10
Ghazipur India 25°38N 83°35E 85 G13
Ghaznī Afghan. 33°30N 68°28E 87 C12
Ghent = Gent Belgium 51°2N 3°42E 64 C2
Giants Causeway U.K. 55°16N 6°29W 19 A9
Gibraltar ⊘ Europe 36°7N 5°22W 67 D3
Gibraltar, Str. of Medit. S. 35°55N 5°40W 67 E3
Gibraltar Pt. U.K. 53°6N 0°19E 27 F9
Gibson Desert Australia 24°0S 126°0E 98 E4
Gifu Japan 35°30N 136°45E 81 F5
Giggleswick U.K. 54°5N 2°17W 26 D4
Gigha U.K. 55°42N 5°44W 24 C4
Gijón Spain 43°32N 5°42W 67 A3
Gila → U.S.A. 32°43N 114°33W 110 D4
Gīlān □ Iran 37°0N 50°0E 86 B7
Gilbert Is. Kiribati 1°0N 172°0E 102 G9
Gilgit India 35°50N 74°15E 84 B9
Gillam Canada 56°20N 94°40W 108 D10
Gillette U.S.A. 44°18N 105°30W 110 B5
Gillingham Dorset, U.K. 51°2N 2°18W 30 D4
Gillingham Medway, U.K. 51°23N 0°33E 31 D10
Gilsland U.K. 55°0N 2°34W 26 C3
Gimie, Mt. St. Lucia 13°54N 61°0W 114 b
Girdle Ness U.K. 57°9N 2°3W 23 H13
Giresun Turkey 40°55N 38°30E 71 F6
Girga Egypt 26°17N 31°55E 95 C12
Girona Spain 41°58N 2°46E 67 B7
Gironde → France 45°32N 1°7W 66 D3
Girvan U.K. 55°14N 4°51W 24 D6
Gisborne N.Z. 38°39S 178°5E 99 H14
Gisburn U.K. 53°56N 2°16W 27 E4
Gitega Burundi 3°26S 29°56E 96 E5
Gizhiga Russia 62°3N 160°30E 77 C17
Gjoa Haven Canada 68°38N 95°53W 108 C10
Glace Bay Canada 46°11N 59°58W 113 B18
Glacier Nat. Park △ U.S.A. 48°42N 113°48W 110 A4
Gladstone Australia 23°52S 151°16E 98 E9
Gladstone U.S.A. 45°51N 87°1W 112 C4
Gladwin U.S.A. 43°59N 84°29W 112 D5
Glamorgan, Vale of □ U.K. 51°28N 3°25W 29 E7
Glanaruddery Mts. Ireland 52°20N 9°27W 20 D4
Glanton U.K. 55°26N 1°54W 26 B5
Glasgow U.K. 55°51N 4°15W 24 C7
Glasgow Ky., U.S.A. 37°0N 85°55W 112 G5
Glasgow Mont., U.S.A. 48°12N 106°38W 110 A5
Glasgow Int. ✕ (GLA) U.K. 55°51N 4°21W 24 C7
Glasnevin Ireland 53°22N 6°15W 21 B10
Glastonbury U.K. 51°9N 2°43W 30 D3
Glazov Russia 58°9N 52°40E 70 C9
Glemsford U.K. 52°6N 0°40E 31 B10
Glen → U.K. 52°51N 0°7W 27 G8
Glen Affric U.K. 57°17N 5°1W 22 H7
Glen Almond U.K. 56°28N 3°50W 25 B8
Glen Coe U.K. 56°40N 5°0W 22 J7
Glen Etive U.K. 56°37N 5°0W 24 A5
Glen Garry Highl., U.K. 57°3N 5°7W 22 H7
Glen Garry Perth & Kinr., U.K. 56°47N 4°5W 23 J9
Glen Mor U.K. 57°9N 4°37W 23 H8
Glen Moriston U.K. 57°11N 4°52W 23 H8
Glen Orchy U.K. 56°27N 4°52W 24 B6
Glen Orrin U.K. 57°31N 4°45W 23 G8
Glen Oykel U.K. 58°5N 4°50W 23 F8
Glen Roy U.K. 56°56N 4°50W 23 J8
Glen Shee U.K. 56°50N 3°28W 23 J11
Glen Shiel U.K. 57°9N 5°18W 22 H7
Glen Spean U.K. 56°53N 4°40W 23 J8
Glendale Ariz., U.S.A. 33°32N 112°11W 110 D4
Glendale Calif., U.S.A. 34°9N 118°15W 110 D3
Glendive U.S.A. 47°7N 104°43W 110 A6
Gleneagles U.K. 56°17N 3°43W 25 B8
Glenfinnan U.K. 56°53N 5°27W 22 J7
Glengarriff Ireland 51°45N 9°34W 20 E3
Glenkens, The U.K. 55°12N 4°12W 24 D7
Glenluce U.K. 54°52N 4°48W 24 E6
Glennallen U.S.A. 62°7N 145°33W 108 C5
Glennamaddy Ireland 53°37N 8°33W 18 D4
Glenrothes U.K. 56°12N 3°10W 25 B9
Glens Falls U.S.A. 43°19N 73°39W 113 D11
Glenties Ireland 54°48N 8°17W 18 B5
Glenveagh △ Ireland 55°3N 8°1W 18 A5
Gliwice Poland 50°22N 18°41E 65 C10
Globe U.S.A. 33°24N 110°47W 110 D4
Głogów Poland 51°37N 16°5E 64 C9
Glomma → Norway 59°12N 10°57E 63 F6
Glossop U.K. 53°27N 1°56W 27 F5
Gloucester U.K. 51°53N 2°15W 30 C4
Gloucestershire □ U.K. 51°46N 2°15W 30 C4
Gloversville U.S.A. 43°3N 74°21W 113 D10
Glyn Ebwy = Ebbw Vale U.K. 51°46N 3°12W 28 D7
Gniezno Poland 52°30N 17°35E 65 B9
Gnosall U.K. 52°48N 2°14W 27 G4
Goa India 15°33N 73°59E 84 M8
Goa □ India 15°33N 73°59E 84 M8
Goat Fell U.K. 55°38N 5°11W 24 C5
Gobi Asia 44°0N 110°0E 79 C10
Godalming U.K. 51°11N 0°36W 31 D7
Godavari → India 16°25N 82°18E 85 L13
Goderich Canada 43°45N 81°41W 112 D7
Godhra India 22°49N 73°40E 84 H8
Godmanchester U.K. 52°20N 0°11W 31 B8
Godoy Cruz Argentina 32°56S 68°52W 121 F3
Gods → Canada 56°22N 92°51W 108 D10
Gods L. Canada 54°40N 94°15W 108 D10
Godshill U.K. 50°38N 1°15W 30 E6
Godstone U.K. 51°14N 0°3W 31 D8
Gogama Canada 47°35N 81°43W 112 B7
Goiânia Brazil 16°43S 49°20W 122 C1
Goiás Brazil 15°55S 50°10W 120 D4
Goiás □ Brazil 12°10S 48°0W 120 D5
Goio-Erê Brazil 24°12S 53°1W 121 E4
Gold Coast Australia 28°0S 153°25E 98 F9
Gold Coast W. Afr. 4°0N 1°40W 94 H5
Golden Vale Ireland 52°33N 8°17W 20 C6
Goldsboro U.S.A. 35°23N 77°59W 111 C11
Golestān □ Iran 37°20N 55°25E 87 B8
Golmud China 36°25N 94°53E 78 D7
Golspie U.K. 57°58N 3°59W 23 G10
Goma Dem. Rep. of the Congo 1°37S 29°10E 96 E5
Gomel Belarus 52°28N 31°0E 65 B16
Gomera Canary Is. 28°7N 17°14W 94 C2
Gómez Palacio Mexico 25°34N 103°30W 114 B4
Gonābād Iran 34°15N 58°45E 87 C9
Gonaïves Haiti 19°20N 72°42W 115 D10
Gonbad-e Kāvūs Iran 37°20N 55°25E 87 B8
Gonda India 27°9N 81°58E 85 F12
Gonder Ethiopia 12°39N 37°30E 89 E2
Gongbei China 22°12N 113°32E 79 a
Gongga Shan China 29°40N 101°55E 78 F9
Good Hope, C. of S. Africa 34°24S 18°30E 97 L3
Goodrich U.K. 51°52N 2°37W 30 C3
Goodwood U.K. 50°53N 0°44W 31 E7
Goole U.K. 53°42N 0°53W 27 E7
Goose L. U.S.A. 41°56N 120°26W 110 B2
Gorakhpur India 26°47N 83°23E 85 F13
Gordon U.K. 55°41N 2°34W 25 C10
Gore Ethiopia 8°12N 35°32E 89 F2
Gorebridge U.K. 55°50N 3°2W 25 C9
Gorey Ireland 52°41N 6°18W 21 C10
Gorgān Iran 36°55N 54°30E 87 B8
Goring U.K. 51°31N 1°7W 30 C6
Goring-by-Sea U.K. 50°49N 0°24W 31 E8
Gorleston U.K. 52°35N 1°44E 31 A12
Görlitz Germany 51°9N 14°58E 64 C8
Gorno-Altay □ Russia 51°0N 86°0E 76 D9
Gorontalo Indonesia 0°35N 123°5E 83 D6
Gort Ireland 53°3N 8°49W 20 B5
Gorzów Wielkopolski Poland 52°43N 15°15E 64 B8
Gosberton U.K. 52°53N 0°9W 27 G8
Gosforth U.K. 54°26N 3°27W 26 D2
Gosport U.K. 50°48N 1°9W 30 E6
Göta kanal Sweden 58°30N 15°58E 63 F7
Götaland Sweden 57°30N 14°30E 63 F6
Göteborg Sweden 57°43N 11°59E 63 F6
Gotha Germany 50°56N 10°42E 64 C6
Gothenburg = Göteborg Sweden 57°43N 11°59E 63 F6
Gotland Sweden 57°30N 18°33E 63 F7
Gotō-Rettō Japan 32°55N 129°5E 81 G1
Göttingen Germany 51°31N 9°55E 64 C5
Gouda Neths. 52°1N 4°42E 64 B3
Goudhurst U.K. 51°6N 0°29E 31 D9
Gouin, Rés. Canada 48°35N 74°40W 113 A10
Goulburn Australia 34°44S 149°44E 98 G8
Goulimine Morocco 28°56N 10°0W 94 C3
Goundam Mali 16°27N 3°40W 94 E5
Gourock U.K. 55°57N 4°49W 24 C6
Governador Valadares Brazil 18°15S 41°57W 122 C2
Gower U.K. 51°35N 4°10W 29 D5
Gowna, L. Ireland 53°51N 7°34W 18 D6
Goya Argentina 29°10S 59°10W 121 E4
Gozo Malta 36°3N 14°15E 68 a
Graaff-Reinet S. Africa 32°13S 24°32E 97 L4
Gracias a Dios, C. Honduras 15°0N 83°10W 115 E8
Grafham Water U.K. 52°19N 0°18W 31 B8
Grafton Australia 29°38S 152°58E 98 F9
Grafton U.S.A. 48°25N 97°25W 111 A7
Graham Land Antarctica 65°0S 64°0W 55 C17
Grahamstown S. Africa 33°19S 26°31E 97 L5
Grain Coast W. Afr. 4°20N 10°0W 94 H3
Grainthorpe U.K. 53°27N 0°5E 27 F9
Grampian Mts. U.K. 56°50N 4°0W 23 J9
Gran Canaria Canary Is. 27°55N 15°35W 94 C2
Gran Chaco S. Amer. 25°0S 61°0W 121 E3
Gran Sasso d'Itália Italy 42°27N 13°42E 68 C5
Granada Nic. 11°58N 86°0W 114 E7
Granada Spain 37°10N 3°35W 67 D4
Granard Ireland 53°47N 7°30W 18 D6
Granby Canada 45°25N 72°45W 109 E12
Grand → U.S.A. 45°40N 100°45W 110 A6
Grand Bahama I. Bahamas 26°40N 78°30W 115 B9
Grand Canal → China 39°10N 117°10E 79 D12
Grand Canyon U.S.A. 36°3N 112°9W 110 C4
Grand Canyon Nat. Park △ U.S.A. 36°15N 112°30W 110 C4
Grand Cayman Cayman Is. 19°20N 81°20W 115 D8
Grand Falls Canada 47°3N 67°44W 109 E13
Grand Falls-Windsor Canada 48°56N 55°40W 109 E14
Grand Forks U.S.A. 47°55N 97°3W 111 A7
Grand Haven U.S.A. 43°4N 86°13W 112 D4
Grand Island U.S.A. 40°55N 98°21W 110 B7
Grand Junction U.S.A. 39°4N 108°33W 110 C5
Grand L. Canada 45°57N 66°7W 113 C14
Grand Manan I. Canada 44°45N 66°52W 113 C14
Grand-Mère Canada 46°36N 72°40W 113 B11
Grand Rapids Canada 53°12N 99°19W 108 D10
Grand Rapids U.S.A. 42°58N 85°40W 112 D4
Grand St-Bernard, Col du Europe 45°50N 7°10E 64 F4
Grand Teton U.S.A. 43°54N 110°50W 110 B4
Grande → Bolivia 15°51S 64°39W 120 D3
Grande → Brazil 11°30S 44°30W 122 B2
Grande, B. Argentina 50°30S 68°20W 121 H3
Grande, Rio → N. Amer. 25°58N 97°9W 111 E7
Grande Baleine → Canada 55°16N 77°47W 109 D12
Grande Prairie Canada 55°10N 118°50W 108 D8
Grange-over-Sands U.K. 54°12N 2°54W 26 D3
Grangemouth U.K. 56°1N 3°42W 25 B8
Grangeville U.S.A. 45°56N 116°7W 110 A3
Grantham U.K. 52°55N 0°38W 27 G7
Grantown-on-Spey U.K. 57°20N 3°36W 23 H10
Grants Pass U.S.A. 42°26N 123°19W 110 B2
Granville U.S.A. 43°24N 73°16W 113 D11
Grasmere U.K. 54°28N 3°1W 26 D2
Grasse France 43°38N 6°56E 66 E7
Grassington U.K. 54°5N 1°59W 26 D5
Graulhet France 43°45N 1°59E 66 E4
Gravesend U.K. 51°26N 0°22E 31 D9
Grayling U.S.A. 44°40N 84°43W 112 C5
Grayrigg U.K. 54°23N 2°39W 26 D3
Grays U.K. 51°28N 0°21E 31 D9
Graz Austria 47°4N 15°27E 64 E8
Great Australian Bight Australia 33°30S 130°0E 98 G5
Great Ayton U.K. 54°30N 1°8W 26 D6
Great Baddow U.K. 51°43N 0°31E 31 C10
Great Barrier Reef Australia 18°0S 146°50E 98 D8
Great Basin U.S.A. 40°0N 117°0W 110 B3
Great Bear → Canada 65°0N 126°0W 108 C7
Great Bear L. Canada 65°30N 120°0W 108 B7
Great Bend U.S.A. 38°22N 98°46W 110 C7
Great Bentley U.K. 51°51N 1°4E 31 C11
Great Bernera U.K. 58°14N 6°50W 22 F4
Great Blasket I. Ireland 52°6N 10°32W 20 D1
Great Britain Europe 54°0N 2°15W 62 D5
Great Broughton U.K. 54°26N 1°9W 26 D6
Great Chesterford U.K. 52°4N 0°13E 31 B9
Great Clifton U.K. 54°39N 3°29W 26 C2
Great Dividing Ra. Australia 23°0S 146°0E 98 E8
Great Dunmow U.K. 51°52N 0°23E 31 C9
Great Exuma I. Bahamas 23°30N 75°50W 115 C9
Great Falls U.S.A. 47°30N 111°17W 110 A4
Great Glen = Glen Mor U.K. 57°9N 4°37W 23 H8
Great Harwood U.K. 53°47N 2°24W 27 E4
Great Inagua I. Bahamas 21°0N 73°20W 115 C10
Great Karoo S. Africa 31°55S 21°0E 97 L4
Great Khingan Mts. China 48°0N 121°0E 79 B13
Great Lakes N. Amer. 46°0N 84°0W 104 E11
Great Malvern U.K. 52°7N 2°18W 30 B4
Great Massingham U.K. 52°47N 0°40E 31 A10
Great Missenden U.K. 51°42N 0°41W 31 C7
Great Ormes Head U.K. 53°20N 3°52W 28 A6
Great Ouse → U.K. 52°48N 0°21E 31 A9
Great Pedro Bluff Jamaica 17°51N 77°44W 114 a
Great Plains N. Amer. 47°0N 105°0W 110 A6
Great Salt Desert Iran 34°30N 55°0E 87 C8
Great Salt L. U.S.A. 41°15N 112°40W 110 B4
Great Salt Lake Desert U.S.A. 40°50N 113°30W 110 B4
Great Sandy Desert Australia 21°0S 124°0E 98 E3
Great Sandy Desert U.S.A. 43°35N 120°15W 110 B2
Great Shefford U.K. 51°28N 1°28W 30 D6
Great Shelford U.K. 52°9N 0°8E 31 B9
Great Shunner Fell U.K. 54°22N 2°14W 26 D4
Great Skellig Ireland 51°47N 10°33W 20 E1
Great Slave L. Canada 61°23N 115°38W 108 C8
Great Snow Mt. Canada 57°26N 124°0W 108 D7
Great Torrington U.K. 50°57N 4°9W 29 F5
Great Victoria Desert Australia 29°30S 126°30E 98 F4
Great Wall of China China 38°30N 109°30E 79 D10
Great Waltham U.K. 51°47N 0°28E 31 C9
Great Whernside U.K. 54°10N 1°58W 26 D5
Great Yarmouth U.K. 52°37N 1°44E 31 A12
Greater Antilles W. Indies 17°40N 74°0W 115 D10
Greater London □ U.K. 51°31N 0°6W 31 C8
Greater Manchester □ U.K. 53°30N 2°15W 27 E4
Greater Sunda Is. Indonesia 7°0S 112°0E 82 F4
Greatham U.K. 54°39N 1°14W 26 C6
Greece ■ Europe 40°0N 23°0E 69 E9
Greeley U.S.A. 40°25N 104°42W 110 B6
Greely Fd. Canada 80°30N 85°0W 109 A11
Green → Ky., U.S.A. 37°54N 87°30W 112 G4
Green → Utah, U.S.A. 38°11N 109°53W 110 C5
Green B. U.S.A. 45°0N 87°30W 112 C4
Green Bay U.S.A. 44°31N 88°0W 112 C4
Green Hammerton U.K. 54°1N 1°18W 27 D6
Green River U.S.A. 41°32N 109°28W 110 B5
Greencastle U.S.A. 39°38N 86°52W 112 F4
Greenfield Ind., U.S.A. 39°47N 85°46W 112 F5
Greenfield Mass., U.S.A. 42°35N 72°36W 113 D11
Greenhead U.K. 54°59N 2°30W 26 C3
Greenland ⊘ N. Amer. 66°0N 45°0W 54 C5
Greenland Sea Arctic 73°0N 10°0W 54 B7
Greenlaw U.K. 55°43N 2°27W 25 C11
Greenock U.K. 55°57N 4°46W 24 C6
Greenodd U.K. 54°14N 3°4W 26 D2
Greenore Ireland 54°1N 6°9W 19 C9
Greenore Pt. Ireland 52°14N 6°19W 21 D10
Greensboro U.S.A. 36°4N 79°48W 111 C11
Greensburg Ind., U.S.A. 39°20N 85°29W 112 F5
Greensburg Pa., U.S.A. 40°18N 79°33W 112 E8
Greenstone Pt. U.K. 57°55N 5°37W 22 G6
Greenville Ala., U.S.A. 31°50N 86°38W 111 D9
Greenville Maine, U.S.A. 45°28N 69°35W 113 C13
Greenville Mich., U.S.A. 43°11N 85°15W 112 D5
Greenville Miss., U.S.A. 33°24N 91°4W 111 D8
Greenville Ohio, U.S.A. 40°6N 84°38W 112 E5
Greenville S.C., U.S.A. 34°51N 82°24W 111 D10
Greenwich □ U.K. 51°29N 0°1E 31 D9
Greenwood U.S.A. 33°31N 90°11W 111 D8
Gremikha Russia 67°59N 39°47E 70 A6
Grenada ■ W. Indies 12°10N 61°40W 115 E12
Grenoble France 45°12N 5°42E 66 D6
Greta → U.K. 54°9N 2°37W 26 D3
Gretna U.K. 55°0N 3°3W 25 E9
Gretna Green U.K. 55°1N 3°3W 25 D9
Gretton U.K. 52°33N 0°40W 31 A7
Grey Ra. Australia 27°0S 143°30E 98 F7
Greymouth N.Z. 42°29S 171°13E 99 J13
Greystoke U.K. 54°41N 2°51W 26 C3
Greystones Ireland 53°9N 6°5W 21 B10
Griffith Australia 34°18S 146°2E 98 G8
Grimsay U.K. 57°29N 7°14W 22 H3
Grimsby U.K. 53°34N 0°5W 27 E8
Griomasaigh = Grimsay U.K. 57°29N 7°14W 22 H3
Gris-Nez, C. France 50°52N 1°35E 66 A4
Grise Fiord Canada 76°25N 82°57W 109 B11
Grizebeck U.K. 54°16N 3°10W 26 D2
Groningen Neths. 53°15N 6°35E 64 B4
Groote Eylandt Australia 14°0S 136°40E 98 C6
Gros Islet St. Lucia 14°5N 60°58W 114 b
Gros Piton St. Lucia 13°49N 61°5W 114 b
Gros Piton Pt. St. Lucia 13°49N 61°5W 114 b
Grosseto Italy 42°46N 11°8E 68 C4
Grossglockner Austria 47°5N 12°40E 64 E7
Groundhog → Canada 48°45N 82°58W 112 A6
Groznyy Russia 43°20N 45°45E 71 F8
Grudziądz Poland 53°30N 18°47E 65 B10
Gruinard B. U.K. 57°56N 5°35W 22 G6
Guadalajara Mexico 20°40N 103°20W 114 C4
Guadalajara Spain 40°37N 3°12W 67 B4
Guadalcanal Solomon Is. 9°32S 160°12E 99 B11
Guadalete → Spain 36°35N 6°13W 67 D2
Guadalquivir → Spain 36°47N 6°22W 67 D2
Guadalupe I. Pac. Oc. 29°0N 118°50W 104 G8
Guadarrama, Sierra de Spain 41°0N 4°0W 67 B4
Guadeloupe ⊘ W. Indies 16°15N 61°40W 115 D12
Guadiana → Portugal 37°14N 7°22W 67 D2
Guadix Spain 37°18N 3°11W 67 D4

Guafo, Boca del *Chile* 43°35S 74°0W **121 G2**
Guajará-Mirim *Brazil* 10°50S 65°20W **120 D3**
Guajira, Pen. de la *Colombia* 12°0N 72°0W **120 A2**
Gualeguaychú *Argentina* 33°3S 59°31W **121 F4**
Guam ⊠ *Pac. Oc.* 13°27N 144°45E **102 F6**
Guamúchil *Mexico* 25°28N 108°6W **114 B3**
Guanajuato *Mexico* 21°1N 101°15W **114 C4**
Guane *Cuba* 22°10N 84°7W **115 C8**
Guangdong □ *China* 23°0N 113°0E **79 G11**
Guangxi Zhuang □ *China* 24°0N 109°0E **79 G10**
Guangyuan *China* 32°26N 105°51E **78 E10**
Guangzhou *China* 23°6N 113°13E **79 G11**
Guantánamo *Cuba* 20°10N 75°14W **115 C9**
Guantánamo B. *Cuba* 19°59N 75°10W **115 D9**
Guaporé ➔ *Brazil* 11°55S 65°4W **120 D3**
Guaqui *Bolivia* 16°41S 68°54W **120 D3**
Guarapuava *Brazil* 25°20S 51°30W **121 E4**
Guaratinguetá *Brazil* 22°49S 45°9W **122 D1**
Guarulhos *Brazil* 23°29S 46°33W **122 D1**
Guatemala *Guatemala* 14°40N 90°22W **114 E6**
Guatemala ■ *Cent. Amer.* 15°40N 90°30W **114 D6**
Guatemala Trench *Pac. Oc.* 14°0N 95°0W **104 H10**
Guaviare ➔ *Colombia* 4°3N 67°44W **120 B3**
Guaxupé *Brazil* 21°10S 47°5W **122 D1**
Guayaquil *Ecuador* 2°15S 79°52W **120 C2**
Guayaquil, G. de *Ecuador* 3°10S 81°0W **120 C1**
Guaymas *Mexico* 27°56N 110°54W **114 B2**
Gubkin *Russia* 51°17N 37°32E **71 D6**
Guelph *Canada* 43°35N 80°20W **112 D7**
Guéret *France* 46°11N 1°51E **66 C4**
Guernsey *U.K.* 49°26N 2°35W **29 J8**
Guestling Green *U.K.* 50°53N 0°39E **31 E10**
Guiana Highlands *S. Amer.* 5°10N 60°40W **117 C4**
Guidónia-Montecélio *Italy* 42°1N 12°45E **68 C5**
Guildford *U.K.* 51°14N 0°34W **31 D7**
Guilin *China* 25°18N 110°15E **79 F11**
Guinea ■ *W. Afr.* 10°20N 11°30W **94 F3**
Guinea, Gulf of *Atl. Oc.* 3°0N 2°30E **90 F4**
Guinea-Bissau ■ *Africa* 12°0N 15°0W **94 F3**
Güines *Cuba* 22°50N 82°0W **115 C8**
Guingamp *France* 48°34N 3°10W **66 B2**
Guisborough *U.K.* 54°33N 1°4W **26 C6**
Guiyang *China* 26°32N 106°40E **78 F10**
Guizhou □ *China* 27°0N 107°0E **78 F10**
Gujarat □ *India* 23°20N 71°0E **84 H7**
Gujranwala *Pakistan* 32°10N 74°12E **84 C9**
Gujrat *Pakistan* 32°40N 74°2E **84 C9**
Gulbarga *India* 17°20N 76°50E **84 L10**
Gulf, The = Persian Gulf *Asia* 27°0N 50°0E **87 E7**
Gulfport *U.S.A.* 30°22N 89°6W **111 D9**
Gulian *China* 52°56N 122°21E **79 A13**
Gulu *Uganda* 2°48N 32°17E **96 D6**
Guna *India* 24°40N 77°19E **84 G10**
Gunnison ➔ *U.S.A.* 39°4N 108°35W **110 C5**
Gunsan *S. Korea* 35°59N 126°45E **79 D14**
Guntur *India* 16°23N 80°30E **85 L12**
Gurbantünggüt Desert *China* 45°8N 87°20E **78 B6**
Gurgueia ➔ *Brazil* 6°50S 43°24W **120 C5**
Guri, Embalse de *Venezuela* 7°50N 62°52W **120 B3**
Gurkha *Nepal* 28°5N 84°40E **85 E14**
Gurnard's Hd. *U.K.* 50°11N 5°37W **29 G2**
Gürün *Turkey* 38°43N 37°15E **71 G6**
Gurupi *Brazil* 11°43S 49°4W **122 B1**
Gurupi ➔ *Brazil* 1°13S 46°6W **120 C5**
Gurvan Sayhan Uul *Mongolia* 43°50N 104°0E **78 C9**
Gusau *Nigeria* 12°12N 6°40E **94 F7**
Guwahati *India* 26°10N 91°45E **85 F17**
Guyana ■ *S. Amer.* 5°0N 59°0W **120 B4**
Guyenne *France* 44°30N 0°40E **66 D4**
Gwādar *Pakistan* 25°10N 62°18E **84 G3**
Gwalchmai *U.K.* 53°16N 4°25W **28 A5**
Gwalior *India* 26°12N 78°10E **84 F11**
Gwanda *Zimbabwe* 20°55S 29°0E **97 J5**
Gwangju *S. Korea* 35°9N 126°54E **79 D14**
Gweebarra B. *Ireland* 54°51N 8°23W **18 B5**
Gweedore *Ireland* 55°3N 8°14W **18 A5**
Gweek *U.K.* 50°5N 5°13W **29 G3**
Gwennap *U.K.* 50°12N 5°11W **29 G3**
Gweru *Zimbabwe* 19°28S 29°45E **97 H5**
Gwynedd □ *U.K.* 52°52N 4°10W **28 B6**
Gyaring Hu *China* 34°50N 97°40E **78 E8**
Gydan Peninsula *Russia* 70°0N 78°0E **76 B8**
Gympie *Australia* 26°11S 152°38E **98 F9**
Győr *Hungary* 47°41N 17°40E **65 E9**
Gyumri *Armenia* 40°47N 43°50E **71 F7**

H

Ha'apai Group *Tonga* 19°47S 174°27W **99 D16**
Haarlem *Neths.* 52°23N 4°39E **64 B3**
Hachinohe *Japan* 40°30N 141°29E **81 C7**
Hackney □ *U.K.* 51°33N 0°3W **31 C8**
Hackthorpe *U.K.* 54°34N 2°42W **26 C3**
Ḥadd, Ra's al *Oman* 22°35N 59°50E **87 F9**
Haddenham *U.K.* 51°46N 0°55W **31 C7**
Haddington *U.K.* 55°57N 2°47W **25 C10**
Hadejia *Nigeria* 12°30N 10°5E **94 F7**
Hadleigh *U.K.* 52°3N 0°58E **31 B10**
Hadlow *U.K.* 51°13N 0°22E **31 D9**
Ḥaḍramawt □ *Yemen* 15°30N 49°30E **89 D4**
Hadrian's Wall *U.K.* 55°0N 2°30W **26 B4**
Haeju *N. Korea* 38°3N 125°45E **79 D14**
Hafizabad *Pakistan* 32°5N 73°40E **84 C8**
Hagen *Germany* 51°21N 7°27E **64 C4**
Hagerstown *U.S.A.* 39°39N 77°43W **112 F9**
Hags Hd. *Ireland* 52°57N 9°28W **20 C4**
Hague, C. de la *France* 49°44N 1°56W **66 B3**
Hague, The *Neths.* 52°7N 4°17E **64 B3**
Haguenau *France* 48°49N 7°47E **66 B7**
Haifa *Israel* 32°46N 35°0E **86 C3**
Haikou *China* 20°1N 110°16E **79 G11**
Ḥā'il *Si. Arabia* 27°28N 41°45E **86 E5**
Hailar *China* 49°10N 119°38E **79 B12**
Hailey *U.S.A.* 43°31N 114°19W **110 B4**
Haileybury *Canada* 47°30N 79°38W **112 B8**
Hailsham *U.K.* 50°52N 0°16E **31 E9**
Hailun *China* 47°28N 126°50E **79 B14**
Hainan □ *China* 19°0N 109°30E **79 H10**
Hainan Dao *China* 19°0N 109°30E **79 H10**
Hainan Str. *China* 20°10N 110°15E **79 G11**
Haines Junction *Canada* 60°45N 137°30W **108 C6**
Hainton *U.K.* 53°21N 0°14W **27 F8**
Haiphong *Vietnam* 20°47N 106°41E **78 G10**
Haiti ■ *W. Indies* 19°0N 72°30W **115 D10**
Haji Ibrahim *Iraq* 36°40N 44°30E **86 B6**
Ḥajjah *Yemen* 15°42N 43°36E **89 D3**
Hakkoda-San *Japan* 40°39N 140°53E **81 C7**
Hakodate *Japan* 41°45N 140°44E **81 C7**
Haku-San *Japan* 36°9N 136°46E **81 E5**
Halaib Triangle *Africa* 22°30N 35°20E **95 D12**
Halberstadt *Germany* 51°54N 11°3E **64 C6**
Halberton *U.K.* 50°54N 3°25W **29 F7**
Halden *Norway* 59°9N 11°23E **63 F6**
Haldia *India* 22°5N 88°3E **85 H16**
Haldwani *India* 29°31N 79°30E **84 E11**
Halesowen *U.K.* 52°27N 2°3W **27 H4**
Halesworth *U.K.* 52°20N 1°31E **31 B12**
Halifax *Canada* 44°38N 63°35W **113 C16**
Halifax *U.K.* 53°43N 1°52W **27 E5**
Halkirk *U.K.* 58°30N 3°29W **23 E11**
Hall Beach *Canada* 68°46N 81°12W **109 C11**
Hall Pen. *Canada* 63°30N 66°0W **109 C13**
Halle *Germany* 51°30N 11°56E **64 C6**
Hallow *U.K.* 52°14N 2°15W **30 B4**
Halls Creek *Australia* 18°16S 127°38E **98 D4**
Hallworthy *U.K.* 50°39N 4°35W **29 F4**
Halmahera *Indonesia* 0°40N 128°0E **83 D7**
Halmstad *Sweden* 56°41N 12°52E **63 F6**
Halstead *U.K.* 51°57N 0°40E **31 C10**
Haltwhistle *U.K.* 54°58N 2°26W **26 C4**
Hamadān *Iran* 34°52N 48°32E **86 C7**
Ḥamāh *Syria* 35°5N 36°40E **86 C4**
Hamamatsu *Japan* 34°45N 137°45E **81 F5**
Hamar *Norway* 60°48N 11°7E **63 E6**
Hambantota *Sri Lanka* 6°10N 81°10E **84 R12**
Hambledon *U.K.* 50°55N 1°5W **30 E6**
Hambleton Hills *U.K.* 54°17N 1°12W **26 D6**
Hamburg *Germany* 53°33N 9°59E **64 B5**
Hämeenlinna *Finland* 61°0N 24°28E **63 E8**
Hameln *Germany* 52°6N 9°21E **64 B5**
Hamersley Ra. *Australia* 22°0S 117°45E **98 E2**
Hamhŭng *N. Korea* 39°54N 127°30E **79 D14**
Hami *China* 42°55N 93°25E **78 C7**
Hamilton *Canada* 43°15N 79°50W **111 B11**
Hamilton *N.Z.* 37°47S 175°19E **99 H14**
Hamilton *U.K.* 55°46N 4°2W **24 C7**
Hamilton *U.S.A.* 39°24N 84°34W **112 F5**
Hamilton Inlet *Canada* 54°0N 57°30W **104 D14**
Hamm *Germany* 51°40N 7°50E **64 C4**
Hammerfest *Norway* 70°39N 23°41E **63 C8**
Hammersmith and Fulham □ *U.K.* 51°30N 0°14W **31 D8**
Hammond *U.S.A.* 41°38N 87°30W **112 E4**
Hammonton *U.S.A.* 39°39N 74°48W **113 F10**
Hampshire □ *U.K.* 51°7N 1°23W **30 D6**
Hampshire Downs *U.K.* 51°15N 1°10W **30 D6**
Hampton in Arden *U.K.* 52°26N 1°41W **27 H5**
Han Shui ➔ *China* 30°34N 114°17E **79 E11**
Hancock *U.S.A.* 47°8N 88°35W **112 B3**
Handan *China* 36°35N 114°28E **79 D11**
Hanford *U.S.A.* 36°20N 119°39W **110 C3**
Hangayn Nuruu *Mongolia* 47°30N 99°0E **78 B8**
Hangzhou *China* 30°18N 120°11E **79 E13**
Hangzhou Wan *China* 30°15N 120°45E **79 E13**
Hankö *Finland* 59°50N 22°57E **63 F8**
Hanna *Canada* 51°40N 111°54W **108 D8**
Hannibal *U.S.A.* 39°42N 91°22W **111 C8**
Hanningfield Res. *U.K.* 51°40N 0°31E **31 C10**
Hannover *Germany* 52°22N 9°46E **64 B5**
Hanoi *Vietnam* 21°5N 105°55E **78 G10**
Hanover *U.S.A.* 39°48N 76°59W **112 F9**
Hanover, I. *Chile* 51°0S 74°50W **121 H2**
Hans I. *Arctic* 80°49N 66°38W **109 A13**
Hanzhong *China* 33°10N 107°1E **78 E10**
Haora *India* 22°34N 88°18E **85 H16**
Haparanda *Sweden* 65°52N 24°8E **63 D8**
Happy Valley-Goose Bay *Canada* 53°15N 60°20W **109 D13**
Har Hu *China* 38°20N 97°38E **78 D8**
Har Us Nuur *Mongolia* 48°0N 92°0E **78 B7**
Ḥaraḍ *Si. Arabia* 24°22N 49°0E **86 E7**
Harare *Zimbabwe* 17°43S 31°2E **97 H6**
Harbin *China* 45°48N 126°40E **79 B14**
Harbor Beach *U.S.A.* 43°51N 82°39W **112 D6**
Hardangerfjorden *Norway* 60°5N 6°0E **63 E5**
Hardy, Pte. *St. Lucia* 14°6N 60°56W **114 b**
Harer *Ethiopia* 9°20N 42°8E **89 F3**
Harewood *U.K.* 53°54N 1°30W **27 E6**
Hargeisa *Somalia* 9°30N 44°2E **89 F3**
Haridwar *India* 29°58N 78°9E **84 E11**
Haringey □ *U.K.* 51°34N 0°5W **31 C8**
Haringhata ➔ *Bangla.* 22°0N 89°58E **85 J16**
Harīrūd ➔ *Asia* 37°24N 60°38E **87 B10**
Harlech *U.K.* 52°52N 4°6W **28 B5**
Harleston *U.K.* 52°24N 1°18E **31 B11**
Harlingen *U.S.A.* 26°12N 97°42W **110 E7**
Harlow *U.K.* 51°46N 0°8E **31 C9**
Harney L. *U.S.A.* 43°14N 119°8W **110 B3**
Härnösand *Sweden* 62°38N 17°55E **63 E7**
Haroldswick *U.K.* 60°48N 0°50W **22 A16**
Harpenden *U.K.* 51°49N 0°21W **31 C8**
Harricana ➔ *Canada* 50°56N 79°32W **109 D12**
Harrietsham *U.K.* 51°14N 0°41E **31 D10**
Harrington *U.K.* 54°37N 3°33W **26 C1**
Harris *U.K.* 57°50N 6°55W **22 G4**
Harris, Sd. of *U.K.* 57°44N 7°6W **22 G3**
Harrisburg *U.S.A.* 40°16N 76°53W **112 E9**
Harrison, C. *Canada* 54°55N 57°55W **109 D14**
Harrisonburg *U.S.A.* 38°27N 78°52W **112 F8**
Harrisville *U.S.A.* 44°39N 83°17W **112 C6**
Harrogate *U.K.* 54°0N 1°33W **27 D5**
Harrow □ *U.K.* 51°35N 0°21W **31 C8**
Hart *U.S.A.* 43°42N 86°22W **112 D4**
Hartest *U.K.* 52°8N 0°40E **31 B10**
Hartford *Conn., U.S.A.* 41°46N 72°41W **113 E11**
Hartford *Ky., U.S.A.* 37°27N 86°55W **112 G4**
Hartford *Wis., U.S.A.* 43°19N 88°22W **112 D3**
Hartland *U.K.* 50°59N 4°29W **29 F5**
Hartland Pt. *U.K.* 51°1N 4°32W **29 E4**
Hartlebury *U.K.* 52°20N 2°14W **30 B4**
Hartlepool *U.K.* 54°42N 1°13W **26 C6**
Hartley *U.K.* 55°5N 1°28W **26 B6**
Hartpury *U.K.* 51°55N 2°17W **30 C4**
Harvey *U.S.A.* 41°36N 87°50W **112 E4**
Harwell *U.K.* 51°36N 1°17W **30 C6**
Harwich *U.K.* 51°56N 1°17E **31 C11**
Haryana □ *India* 29°0N 76°10E **84 E10**
Harz *Germany* 51°38N 10°44E **64 C6**
Hasa *Si. Arabia* 25°50N 49°0E **86 E7**
Haslemere *U.K.* 51°5N 0°43W **31 D7**
Haslingden *U.K.* 53°42N 2°19W **27 E4**
Hastings *U.K.* 50°51N 0°35E **31 E10**
Hastings *U.S.A.* 40°35N 98°23W **110 B7**
Hat Yai *Thailand* 7°1N 100°27E **82 C2**
Hatay *Turkey* 36°14N 36°10E **71 G6**
Hatfield *U.K.* 51°46N 0°13W **31 C8**
Hatgal *Mongolia* 50°26N 100°9E **78 A9**
Hatherleigh *U.K.* 50°49N 4°5W **29 F5**
Hathersage *U.K.* 53°20N 1°39W **27 F5**
Hathras *India* 27°36N 78°6E **84 F11**
Hatia *Bangla.* 22°30N 91°5E **85 H17**
Hatteras, C. *U.S.A.* 35°14N 75°32W **111 C11**
Hattiesburg *U.S.A.* 31°20N 89°17W **111 D9**
Haugesund *Norway* 59°23N 5°13E **63 F5**
Haughley *U.K.* 52°14N 0°57E **31 B10**
Haut Atlas *Morocco* 32°30N 5°0W **94 B4**
Hauts Plateaux *Algeria* 35°0N 1°0E **94 B6**
Havana = La Habana *Cuba* 23°8N 82°22W **115 C8**
Havant *U.K.* 50°51N 0°58W **31 E7**
Havasu, L. *U.S.A.* 34°18N 114°28W **110 D4**
Havel ➔ *Germany* 52°50N 12°3E **64 B7**
Haverfordwest *U.K.* 51°48N 4°58W **28 D4**
Haverhill *U.K.* 52°5N 0°28E **31 B9**
Haverhill *U.S.A.* 42°47N 71°5W **113 D12**
Haverigg *U.K.* 54°13N 3°17W **26 D2**
Havering □ *U.K.* 51°34N 0°13E **31 C9**
Havre *U.S.A.* 48°33N 109°41W **110 A5**
Havre-St.-Pierre *Canada* 50°18N 63°33W **109 D13**
Hawai'i *U.S.A.* 19°30N 155°30W **110 J17**
Hawai'i □ *U.S.A.* 19°30N 156°30W **110 H16**
Hawaiian Is. *Pac. Oc.* 20°30N 156°0W **103 E12**
Hawes *U.K.* 54°19N 2°12W **26 D4**
Haweswater *U.K.* 54°31N 2°47W **26 C3**
Hawick *U.K.* 55°26N 2°47W **25 D10**
Hawkchurch *U.K.* 50°48N 2°56W **30 E3**
Hawkesbury *Canada* 45°37N 74°37W **113 C10**
Hawkesbury Upton *U.K.* 51°35N 2°19W **30 C4**
Hawkhurst *U.K.* 51°2N 0°32E **31 D10**
Hawkshead *U.K.* 54°23N 2°59W **26 D3**
Haworth *U.K.* 53°50N 1°58W **27 E5**
Hawsker *U.K.* 54°27N 0°34W **26 D7**
Haxby *U.K.* 54°1N 1°4W **27 D6**
Hay *Australia* 34°30S 144°51E **98 G8**
Hay ➔ *Canada* 60°50N 116°26W **108 C8**
Hay-on-Wye *U.K.* 52°5N 3°8W **28 C7**
Hay River *Canada* 60°51N 115°44W **108 C8**
Haydon Bridge *U.K.* 54°58N 2°14W **26 C4**
Hayes ➔ *Canada* 57°3N 92°12W **108 D10**
Hayle *U.K.* 50°11N 5°26W **29 G3**
Hays *U.S.A.* 38°53N 99°20W **110 C7**
Hayton *U.K.* 54°55N 2°45W **26 C3**
Hayward *U.S.A.* 46°1N 91°29W **112 B2**
Haywards Heath *U.K.* 51°0N 0°5W **31 E8**
Hazar *Turkmenistan* 39°34N 53°16E **71 G9**
Hazard *U.S.A.* 37°15N 83°12W **112 G6**
Hazaribag *India* 23°58N 85°26E **85 H14**
Heacham *U.K.* 52°54N 0°29E **31 A9**
Headcorn *U.K.* 51°10N 0°38E **31 D10**
Heanor *U.K.* 53°1N 1°21W **27 F6**
Heard I. *Ind. Oc.* 53°6S 72°36E **53 G13**
Hearst *Canada* 49°40N 83°41W **109 E11**
Heathfield *U.K.* 50°58N 0°16E **31 E9**
Hebburn *U.K.* 54°59N 1°32W **26 C5**
Hebden Bridge *U.K.* 53°45N 2°0W **27 E5**
Hebei □ *China* 39°0N 116°0E **79 D12**
Hebrides *U.K.* 57°30N 7°0W **56 D4**
Hebrides, Sea of the *U.K.* 57°5N 7°0W **22 H4**
Hebron *Canada* 58°5N 62°30W **109 D13**
Hecate Str. *Canada* 53°10N 130°30W **108 D6**
Hechi *China* 24°40N 108°2E **78 G10**
Hechuan *China* 30°2N 106°12E **78 E10**
Heckington *U.K.* 52°59N 0°17W **27 G8**
Hednesford *U.K.* 52°43N 1°59W **27 G5**
Hedon *U.K.* 53°44N 0°12W **27 E8**
Heerlen *Neths.* 50°55N 5°58E **64 C3**
Hefei *China* 31°52N 117°18E **79 E12**
Hegang *China* 47°20N 130°19E **79 B15**
Heidelberg *Germany* 49°24N 8°42E **64 D5**
Heihe *China* 50°10N 127°30E **79 A14**
Heilbronn *Germany* 49°9N 9°13E **64 D5**
Heilongjiang □ *China* 48°0N 126°0E **79 B14**
Heimaey *Iceland* 63°26N 20°17W **63 B1**
Hekla *Iceland* 63°56N 19°35W **63 B2**
Helena *U.S.A.* 46°36N 112°2W **110 A4**
Helensburgh *U.K.* 56°1N 4°43W **24 B6**
Helgoland *Germany* 54°10N 7°53E **64 A4**
Hellifield *U.K.* 54°1N 2°12W **27 D4**
Helmand ➔ *Afghan.* 31°12N 61°34E **87 D10**
Helmsdale *U.K.* 58°7N 3°39W **23 F10**
Helmsley *U.K.* 54°15N 1°3W **26 D6**
Helperby *U.K.* 54°8N 1°19W **26 D6**
Helsby *U.K.* 53°17N 2°46W **27 F3**
Helsingborg *Sweden* 56°3N 12°42E **63 F6**
Helsinki *Finland* 60°10N 24°55E **63 E9**
Helston *U.K.* 50°6N 5°17W **29 G3**
Helvellyn *U.K.* 54°32N 3°1W **26 C2**
Helwân *Egypt* 29°50N 31°20E **95 C12**
Hemel Hempstead *U.K.* 51°44N 0°28W **31 C8**
Hempton *U.K.* 52°50N 0°50E **31 A10**
Hemsworth *U.K.* 53°37N 1°21W **27 E6**
Hemyock *U.K.* 50°54N 3°15W **29 F7**
Henan □ *China* 34°0N 114°0E **79 E11**
Henderson *Ky., U.S.A.* 37°50N 87°35W **112 G4**
Henderson *Nev., U.S.A.* 36°2N 114°58W **110 C3**
Henfield *U.K.* 50°56N 0°16W **31 E8**
Hengduan Shan *China* 28°30N 98°50E **78 F8**
Henggang *China* 22°39N 114°12E **79 a**
Hengyang *China* 26°59N 112°22E **79 F11**
Henley-in-Arden *U.K.* 52°18N 1°46W **30 B5**
Henley-on-Thames *U.K.* 51°32N 0°54W **31 C7**
Henlopen, C. *U.S.A.* 38°48N 75°6W **113 F10**
Henlow *U.K.* 52°2N 0°17W **31 B8**
Henrietta Maria, C. *Canada* 55°9N 82°20W **109 D11**
Henstridge *U.K.* 50°58N 2°24W **30 E4**
Hentiyn Nuruu *Mongolia* 48°30N 108°30E **79 B10**
Herāt *Afghan.* 34°20N 62°7E **87 C10**
Hereford *U.K.* 52°4N 2°43W **30 B3**
Herefordshire □ *U.K.* 52°8N 2°40W **30 B3**
Herford *Germany* 52°7N 8°39E **64 B5**
Herlen ➔ *Asia* 48°48N 117°0E **79 B12**
Herm *U.K.* 49°30N 2°28W **29 J9**
Herma Ness *U.K.* 60°50N 0°54W **22 A16**
Hermosillo *Mexico* 29°10N 111°0W **114 B2**
Hernád ➔ *Hungary* 47°56N 21°8E **65 D11**
Herne Bay *U.K.* 51°21N 1°8E **31 D11**
Herstmonceux *U.K.* 50°53N 0°20E **31 E9**
Hertford *U.K.* 51°48N 0°4W **31 C8**
Hertfordshire □ *U.K.* 51°51N 0°5W **31 C8**
's-Hertogenbosch *Neths.* 51°42N 5°17E **64 C3**
Hessen □ *Germany* 50°30N 9°0E **64 C5**
Hessle *U.K.* 53°44N 0°24W **27 E8**
Hethersett *U.K.* 52°36N 1°10E **31 A11**
Hetton-le-Hole *U.K.* 54°50N 1°26W **26 C6**
Hexham *U.K.* 54°58N 2°4W **26 C4**
Heybridge *U.K.* 51°45N 0°42E **31 C10**
Heysham *U.K.* 54°3N 2°53W **26 D3**
Heytesbury *U.K.* 51°11N 2°6W **30 D4**
Heywood *U.K.* 53°35N 2°12W **27 E4**
Heze *China* 35°14N 115°20E **79 D12**
Hibbing *U.S.A.* 47°25N 92°56W **111 A8**
Hickman *U.S.A.* 36°34N 89°11W **112 G3**
Hidalgo del Parral *Mexico* 26°56N 105°40W **114 B3**
Hierro *Canary Is.* 27°44N 18°0W **94 C2**
Higashiōsaka *Japan* 34°39N 135°37E **81 F4**
High Bentham *U.K.* 54°7N 2°28W **26 D4**
High Ercall *U.K.* 52°45N 2°35W **27 G3**
High Hesket *U.K.* 54°48N 2°49W **26 C3**
High Level *Canada* 58°31N 117°8W **108 D8**
High Pike *U.K.* 54°42N 3°4W **26 C2**
High Prairie *Canada* 55°30N 116°30W **108 D8**
High River *Canada* 50°30N 113°50W **108 D8**
High Veld *Africa* 27°0S 27°0E **90 J6**
High Willhays *U.K.* 50°40N 4°0W **29 F5**
High Wycombe *U.K.* 51°37N 0°45W **31 C7**
Higham Ferrers *U.K.* 52°19N 0°35W **31 B7**
Highbridge *U.K.* 51°13N 2°58W **30 D3**
Highclere *U.K.* 51°20N 1°21W **30 D6**
Highland □ *U.K.* 57°17N 4°21W **22 H7**
Highley *U.K.* 52°27N 2°23W **27 H4**
Hightae *U.K.* 55°6N 3°26W **25 D9**
Highworth *U.K.* 51°37N 1°43W **30 C5**
Hiiumaa *Estonia* 58°50N 22°45E **63 F8**
Ḥijāz *Si. Arabia* 24°0N 40°0E **86 E4**
Hildesheim *Germany* 52°9N 9°56E **64 B5**
Hilgay *U.K.* 52°34N 0°24E **31 A9**
Hillaby, Mt. *Barbados* 13°12N 59°35W **114 c**
Hillcrest *Barbados* 13°13N 59°31W **114 c**
Hillingdon □ *U.K.* 51°32N 0°27W **31 C8**
Hillsborough *U.K.* 54°28N 6°5W **19 C9**
Hillsdale *U.S.A.* 41°56N 84°38W **112 E5**
Hilo *U.S.A.* 19°44N 155°5W **110 J17**
Hilpsford Pt. *U.K.* 54°3N 3°12W **26 D2**
Hilversum *Neths.* 52°14N 5°10E **64 B3**
Himachal Pradesh □ *India* 31°30N 77°0E **84 D10**
Himalaya *Asia* 29°0N 84°0E **85 E14**
Himeji *Japan* 34°50N 134°40E **81 F4**
Hinckley *U.K.* 52°33N 1°22W **27 G6**
Hinderwell *U.K.* 54°32N 0°45W **26 C7**
Hindhead *U.K.* 51°7N 0°43W **31 D7**
Hindley *U.K.* 53°33N 2°35W **27 E3**
Hindu Kush *Asia* 36°0N 71°0E **87 C12**
Hingham *U.K.* 52°35N 1°0E **31 A10**
Hingoli *India* 19°41N 77°15E **84 K10**
Hinkley Pt. *U.K.* 51°12N 3°8W **30 D2**
Hinstock *U.K.* 52°50N 2°27W **27 G4**
Hinton *U.S.A.* 37°40N 80°54W **112 G7**
Hios *Greece* 38°27N 26°9E **69 E12**
Hirosaki *Japan* 40°34N 140°28E **81 C7**
Hiroshima *Japan* 34°24N 132°30E **81 F3**
Hisar *India* 29°12N 75°45E **84 E9**
Hispaniola *W. Indies* 19°0N 71°0W **115 D10**
Histon *U.K.* 52°16N 0°7E **31 B9**
Hitachi *Japan* 36°36N 140°39E **81 E7**
Hitchin *U.K.* 51°58N 0°16W **31 C8**
Hjälmaren *Sweden* 59°18N 15°40E **63 F7**
Hkakabo Razi *Burma* 28°25N 97°23E **85 E20**
Ho Chi Minh City *Vietnam* 10°58N 106°40E **82 B3**
Hoare B. *Canada* 65°17N 62°30W **109 C13**
Hobart *Australia* 42°50S 147°21E **98 J8**
Hobbs *U.S.A.* 32°42N 103°8W **110 D6**
Hodder ➔ *U.K.* 53°57N 2°27W **27 E4**
Hoddesdon *U.K.* 51°45N 0°1W **31 C8**
Hodge ➔ *U.K.* 54°16N 0°56W **26 D7**
Hodgson *Canada* 51°13N 97°36W **108 D10**
Hódmezővásárhely *Hungary* 46°28N 20°22E **65 E11**
Hodna, Chott el *Algeria* 35°26N 4°43E **94 A6**
Hoek van Holland *Neths.* 52°0N 4°7E **64 B3**
Hoff *U.K.* 54°34N 2°31W **26 C3**
Hōfu *Japan* 34°3N 131°34E **81 F2**
Hog's Back *U.K.* 51°13N 0°38W **31 D7**
Hoh Xil Shan *China* 36°30N 89°0E **78 D6**
Hoher Rhön *Germany* 50°24N 9°58E **64 C5**
Hohhot *China* 40°52N 111°40E **79 C11**
Hokkaidō □ *Japan* 43°30N 143°0E **81 B8**
Holbeach *U.K.* 52°48N 0°1E **27 G9**
Holbeach Marsh *U.K.* 52°52N 0°5E **27 G9**
Holderness *U.K.* 53°45N 0°5W **27 E8**
Holetown *Barbados* 13°11N 59°38W **114 c**
Holguín *Cuba* 20°50N 76°20W **115 C9**
Holkham *U.K.* 52°57N 0°48E **31 A10**
Holland *U.S.A.* 42°47N 86°7W **112 D4**
Holland Fen *U.K.* 53°0N 0°8W **27 G8**
Holland on Sea *U.K.* 51°48N 1°13E **31 C11**
Holman *Canada* 70°44N 117°44W **108 B8**
Holme *U.K.* 53°50N 0°46W **27 E7**
Holmes Chapel *U.K.* 53°12N 2°21W **27 F4**
Holmfirth *U.K.* 53°35N 1°46W **27 E5**
Holstebro *Denmark* 56°22N 8°37E **63 F5**
Holsworthy *U.K.* 50°48N 4°22W **29 F5**
Holt *U.K.* 52°55N 1°6E **31 A11**
Holy I. *Anglesey, U.K.* 53°17N 4°37W **28 A4**
Holy I. *Northumberland, U.K.* 55°40N 1°47W **26 A5**
Holyhead *U.K.* 53°18N 4°38W **28 A4**
Holywell *U.K.* 53°16N 3°14W **28 A7**
Home B. *Canada* 68°40N 67°10W **109 C13**
Homer *U.S.A.* 59°39N 151°33W **108 D4**
Homs *Syria* 34°40N 36°45E **86 C4**
Honduras ■ *Cent. Amer.* 14°40N 86°30W **114 E7**
Honduras, G. of *Caribbean* 16°50N 87°0W **114 D7**
Hønefoss *Norway* 60°10N 10°18E **63 E6**
Honey L. *U.S.A.* 40°15N 120°19W **110 B2**
Hong Kong □ *China* 22°11N 114°14E **79 a**
Hong Kong Int. ✕ (HKG) *China* 22°19N 113°57E **79 a**
Hongjiang *China* 27°7N 109°59E **79 F10**
Hongshui He ➔ *China* 23°48N 109°30E **79 G10**
Hongze Hu *China* 33°15N 118°35E **79 E12**
Honiara *Solomon Is.* 9°27S 159°57E **99 B10**
Honington *U.K.* 52°59N 0°35W **27 G7**
Honiton *U.K.* 50°47N 3°11W **29 F7**
Honolulu *U.S.A.* 21°19N 157°52W **103 E12**
Honshū *Japan* 36°0N 138°0E **81 F6**
Hoo *U.K.* 51°25N 0°35E **31 D10**
Hood, Mt. *U.S.A.* 45°23N 121°42W **110 A2**
Hook *U.K.* 51°17N 0°57W **31 D7**
Hook Hd. *Ireland* 52°7N 6°56W **21 D9**
Hooper Bay *U.S.A.* 61°32N 166°6W **108 C3**
Hoopeston *U.S.A.* 40°28N 87°40W **112 E4**
Hoorn *Neths.* 52°38N 5°4E **64 B3**
Hoover Dam *U.S.A.* 36°1N 114°44W **110 C4**
Hope *U.S.A.* 33°40N 93°36W **111 D8**
Hope, Pt. *U.S.A.* 68°21N 166°47W **104 C3**
Hopedale *Canada* 55°28N 60°13W **109 D13**
Horden *U.K.* 54°46N 1°19W **26 C6**
Horley *U.K.* 51°10N 0°10W **31 D8**
Horlivka *Ukraine* 48°19N 38°5E **71 E6**
Hormuz, Str. of *The Gulf* 26°30N 56°30E **87 E9**
Horn, C. = Hornos, C. de *Chile* 55°50S 67°30W **121 H3**
Horn, Is. *Wall. & F. Is.* 14°16S 178°6W **99 C15**
Horn Head *Ireland* 55°14N 8°0W **18 A6**
Hornavan *Sweden* 66°15N 17°30E **63 D7**
Horncastle *U.K.* 53°13N 0°7W **27 F8**
Horndean *U.K.* 50°55N 1°1W **30 E6**
Hornell *U.S.A.* 42°20N 77°40W **112 D9**
Hornepayne *Canada* 49°14N 84°48W **112 A5**
Horningsham *U.K.* 51°10N 2°15W **30 D4**
Hornos, C. de *Chile* 55°50S 67°30W **121 H3**
Hornsea *U.K.* 53°55N 0°11W **27 E8**
Horqin Youyi Qianqi *China* 46°5N 122°3E **79 B13**
Horsforth *U.K.* 53°50N 1°39W **27 E5**
Horsham *Australia* 36°44S 142°13E **98 H7**
Horsham *U.K.* 51°4N 0°20W **31 D8**
Horsham St. Faith *U.K.* 52°43N 1°14E **31 A11**
Horsted Keynes *U.K.* 51°2N 0°1W **31 D8**
Horton ➔ *Canada* 69°56N 126°52W **108 C7**
Horton in Ribblesdale *U.K.* 54°9N 2°17W **26 D4**
Horwich *U.K.* 53°36N 2°33W **27 E3**
Hoste, I. *Chile* 55°0S 69°0W **121 H3**
Hot Springs *Ark., U.S.A.* 34°31N 93°3W **111 D8**
Hot Springs *S. Dak., U.S.A.* 43°26N 103°29W **110 B6**
Hotan *China* 37°25N 79°55E **78 D4**
Hotan He ➔ *China* 40°22N 80°56E **78 C5**
Houghton *U.S.A.* 47°7N 88°34W **112 B3**
Houghton L. *U.S.A.* 44°21N 84°44W **112 C5**
Houghton-le-Spring *U.K.* 54°51N 1°28W **26 C6**
Houghton Regis *U.K.* 51°54N 0°32W **31 C7**
Houlton *U.S.A.* 46°8N 67°51W **113 B14**
Houma *U.S.A.* 29°36N 90°43W **111 E8**
Hounslow □ *U.K.* 51°28N 0°21W **31 D8**
Hourn, L. *U.K.* 57°7N 5°35W **22 H6**
Houston *U.S.A.* 29°45N 95°21W **111 E7**
Hove *U.K.* 50°50N 0°10W **31 E8**
Hoveton *U.K.* 52°43N 1°25E **31 A11**
Hovingham *U.K.* 54°11N 0°58W **26 D7**
Hövsgöl Nuur *Mongolia* 51°0N 100°30E **78 A9**
Howden *U.K.* 53°45N 0°52W **27 E7**
Howe, C. *Australia* 37°30S 150°0E **98 H9**
Howell *U.S.A.* 42°36N 83°56W **112 D6**
Howland I. *Pac. Oc.* 0°48N 176°38W **102 G10**
Howth *Ireland* 53°23N 6°7W **21 B10**
Howth Hd. *Ireland* 53°22N 6°4W **21 B10**
Hoxne *U.K.* 52°21N 1°12E **31 B11**
Hoy *U.K.* 58°50N 3°15W **23 E11**
Høyanger *Norway* 61°13N 6°4E **63 E5**
Hoylake *U.K.* 53°24N 3°10W **27 F2**
Hradec Králové *Czech Rep.* 50°15N 15°50E **64 C8**
Hrodna *Belarus* 53°42N 23°52E **65 B12**
Hron ➔ *Slovak Rep.* 47°49N 18°45E **65 E10**
Hsinchu *Taiwan* 24°48N 120°58E **79 G13**
Huacho *Peru* 11°10S 77°35W **120 D2**
Huai He ➔ *China* 33°0N 118°30E **79 E12**
Huaibei *China* 34°0N 116°48E **79 E12**
Huaihua *China* 27°32N 109°57E **79 F10**
Huainan *China* 32°38N 116°58E **79 E12**
Huallaga ➔ *Peru* 5°15S 75°30W **120 C2**
Huambo *Angola* 12°42S 15°54E **97 G3**
Huancavelica *Peru* 12°50S 75°5W **120 D2**
Huancayo *Peru* 12°5S 75°12W **120 D2**
Huang He ➔ *China* 37°55N 118°50E **79 D12**
Huangshan *China* 29°42N 118°25E **79 F12**
Huangshi *China* 30°10N 115°3E **79 E12**
Huánuco *Peru* 9°55S 76°15W **120 C2**
Huaraz *Peru* 9°30S 77°32W **120 C2**
Huascarán, Nevado *Peru* 9°7S 77°37W **120 C2**
Huasco *Chile* 28°30S 71°15W **121 E2**
Huatabampo *Mexico* 26°50N 109°38W **114 B3**
Hubei □ *China* 31°0N 112°0E **79 E11**
Hubli *India* 15°22N 75°15E **84 M9**
Hucknall *U.K.* 53°3N 1°13W **27 F6**
Huddersfield *U.K.* 53°39N 1°47W **27 E5**
Hudiksvall *Sweden* 61°43N 17°10E **63 E7**
Hudson ➔ *U.S.A.* 40°42N 74°2W **113 E10**
Hudson Bay *Canada* 60°0N 86°0W **109 D11**
Hudson Falls *U.S.A.* 43°18N 73°35W **113 D11**
Hudson Str. *Canada* 62°0N 70°0W **109 C13**
Hue *Vietnam* 16°30N 107°35E **82 A3**
Huelva *Spain* 37°18N 6°57W **67 D2**
Huesca *Spain* 42°8N 0°25W **67 A5**
Hugh Town *U.K.* 49°55N 6°19W **29 H1**
Hughenden *Australia* 20°52S 144°10E **98 E7**
Hugli ➔ *India* 21°56N 88°4E **85 J16**

Huila, Nevado del   **Karamay**

Karatax Shan · Lafayette

Meta Incognita Pen.   Nazret

Ndjamena

Orléans, Î. d'

Porlock   Robson, Mt.

Santos

Somerby

Somerset   Tebay

Uniontown

White Horse, Vale of   Zwolle

Published in Great Britain in 2012 by Philip's, a division of Octopus Publishing Group Limited (www.octopusbooks.co.uk)

Endeavour House, 189 Shaftesbury Avenue, London WC2H 8JY

An Hachette UK Company (www.hachette.co.uk)

Ninety-seventh edition

Copyright © 2012 Philip's

Reprinted 2012 and 2014

ISBN 978-1-84907-193-2 (HARDBACK EDITION)
ISBN 978-1-84907-194-9 (PAPERBACK EDITION)

Printed in Hong Kong

A CIP catalogue record for this book is available from the British Library.

All rights reserved. Apart from any fair dealing for the purpose of private study, research, criticism or review, as permitted under the Copyright, Designs and Patents Act, 1988, no part of this publication may be reproduced, stored in a retrieval system, or transmitted in any form or by any means, electronic, electrical, chemical, mechanical, optical, photocopying, recording, or otherwise, without prior written permission. All enquiries should be addressed to the Publisher.

Details of other Philip's titles and services can be found on our website at: www.philips-maps.co.uk

Philip's World Atlases are published in association with The Royal Geographical Society (with The Institute of British Geographers).

The Society was founded in 1830 and given a Royal Charter in 1859 for 'the advancement of geographical science'. Today it is a leading world centre for geographical learning – supporting education, teaching, research and expeditions, and promoting public understanding of the subject.

Further information about the Society and how to join may be found on its website at: www.rgs.org

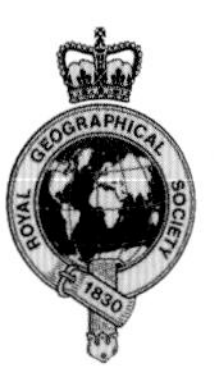

PHOTOGRAPHIC ACKNOWLEDGEMENTS

Satellite images in the atlas are courtesy of the following: China RSGS p. 14tl; DigitalGlobe p. 12t; EROS pp. 8, 9t, 9bc, 9b, 14bl, 14br; ESA p. 15b; Fugro NPA Ltd (www.satmaps.com) pp. 6, 11t, 14tr, 15t, 17, 49, 88, 123, 130; GeoEye pp. 12b, 16b; NASA pp. 9tc, 10, 11bl, 11br, 13, 116; Precision Terrain Surveys Ltd p. 16t.

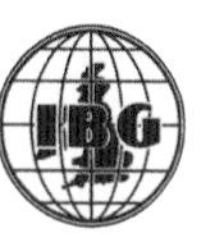